A BUDDHIST
BIBLE

A BUDDHIST BIBLE

Edited by Dwight Goddard
Introduction by Huston Smith

Beacon Press   Boston

CONTENTS

INTRODUCTION

Over thirty years have elapsed since *A Buddhist Bible* first appeared, and half that number since the publication of its present, enlarged edition. Meanwhile some twenty other anthologies of Buddhist texts in English translation have appeared to meet the growing Western interest in this Asian faith. In view of the merit of a number of these, some may wonder if Goddard's somewhat pioneering compilation warrants reissue.

It does. Historical reasons alone might suffice, for Goddard's was one of the books that stimulated the Western interest in Buddhism which in turn called forth the spate of books that followed. The real reason for restoring the book to print and for making it available to a wider audience through paperback is not historical, however, but contemporary. No other collection quite takes its place. Some of its companions have individual virtues which Goddard's collection cannot boast, but for the reader who is looking for scholarship *and* meaning, coverage *and* control — all four — I know no alternative that is its equal.

As Buddhist scholarship in the West has not been standing still, it is to be expected that some of Goddard's texts have received new translations that are in certain technical respects improvements — Yoshito S. Hakeda's rendering of Ashvaghosha's *The Awakening of Faith* (Columbia University Press, 1967) is a case in point. On the whole, however, the scholarship of these pages has stood up well. Further, the book's *prime* virtue is the way it puts the scholarship it does not claim yet appreciably possesses to the service of communication, specifically religious communication.

For the book is indeed a *Bible,* not only in the world's original meaning of book or library but also in its acquired connotation of writings with soteriological intent. Obviously the texts it assembles were written by convinced Buddhists — men who could write, for example, that "no teacher was so god-like

vii

as Lord Buddha . . . ; in his unbounded love for all beings Sakyamuni stands unparalleled . . . ; the Tathagata is the Light of
the World" (pp. 20, 21). What is not a matter of course is an
editor as turned on by his texts as were their authors by the
revelations that occasioned them. "The word Tao," writes
Goddard in noting its influence on Chinese Buddhism — I cite
this statement as illustrative of Goddard's feel for his material
— "is the name given to perhaps the grandest conception the
human mind has ever conceived" (p. 670). In selecting his
sources and helping to translate some of them Goddard used as
his guideline "the spiritual needs of his readers" (p. vii). Some
may fear that such a guideline compromises objectivity, but I
think that even in academia we have overcome that confusion.
What lies between these covers is religious material; without
the spiritual fervor that inspired them these writings would not
have come into being. To mirror that fervor in understanding
or participation is the supreme fidelity, the ultimate accuracy,
the final literalism. Those who open this book with historical,
comparative, or linguistic interest are of course welcome, but
one must protest any notion that Goddard's angle of interest
is any less appropriate or respectable. When he tells us (p. xv)
that his book "is not intended to be a source book for critical
literary and historical study; it is only intended to be a source
of spiritual inspiration designed to awaken faith and to develop
faith into aspiration and full realization," his "only" is speci-
fication, not apology.

One specific feature of this book deserves comment to obviate
possible misunderstanding. It would be unfortunate if anyone
glancing at its Contents were to dismiss it because it does not
include a section on "Selection from the Japanese Sources." In
view of the West's postwar fascination with Japan and with Zen
Buddhism in particular such dismissal would be understand-
able, but it would nevertheless be unwarranted. One tenth of
the entire book is given to as important a Zen text as was ever
written, "The Sutra Spoken by the Sixth Patriarch" (pp. 497–
558). And the one sutra that is chanted daily in every Zen monastery from Kyoto's Myoshinji to California's Zen Mountain
Center at Tassajara, "The Maha Prajna Parimita Hridya," is

produced in full on pages 85—86 — its *"Ga-te, ga-te, pa-ra-ga-te, pa-ra-sam-ga-te"* ("Gone, gone, gone to that other shore") rings in my ears with power at the very remembrance. Far from underrating Zen, Goddard gives it star billing: "Ch'an [pronounced Zen in Japanese] Buddhism seems to have discerned the essentials of Shakyamuni's teachings and spirit better than any other sect, and to have developed their deeper implications more faithfully" (p. 672).

The point, of course, is that Zen is not an independent Japanese entity. Dogen, who brought its Soto [Ts'ao-tung] branch from China, stressed Buddhism so much more than Zen that he never explicitly used the latter label. He would have agreed with another Japanese saint, Honen, who after summarizing the principal schools of Buddhism in his time concluded: "What they all say is exactly what the Sutras and Shastras say and corresponds to the golden words of Nyorai [Gautama] himself who, according to men's varying capacity, taught them at one time one thing and at another another, as circumstances required." Had Goddard been assembling his book today he might well have included selections by Eisai, Dogen, or perhaps Hakuin's *Zazen Wasan* in response to current Western interests. But for those who have eyes for the lesson, the very absence of Japanese texts can be instructive, helping to counter the romantic image of Zen as a self-sufficient blossom set *shibui* in a Japanese vase, an image that ignores the vital stem that joined it to Chinese Ch'an which in turn grew from the prolific roots of Indian Mahayana. Were this therefore a book dealing with history and geographical spread the absence of distinctively Japanese texts would be serious. As it is, it is a book on meaning, and the meaning of Zen is here. Indeed, the entire book is weighted in its favor, for Zen and Ch'an are Japanese and Chinese translations for the Sanskrit word *dhyana,* meaning meditation, and "the scriptures . . . selected are the generally accepted scriptures of the Dhyana Sects — Ch'an in China, Zen in Japan and Kargyupta in Tibet" (xv).

Finally, I wish to remark on the good sense of organizing a book on Buddhism around its *anatta* (no soul) doctrine. Goddard tells us that "the theme of this Buddhist Bible is designed

to show the unreality of all conceptions of a personal ego"
(xvi). I do not know whether this thesis is true; if I understood it better I might be in a better position to judge, but as
it is I find the claim too fundamental to be fully comprehensible. It haunts, intrigues, and beckons. At times I think I
have it and I then feel wonderfully exalted, but the vision fades.
Perhaps it must be lived to be known. What does abide is the
conviction that no issue — anthropological, psychological, philosophical, or theological — is more important than the way in
which the self is to be conceived: individually, as a skin-encap-
sulated ego; socially, in terms of interpersonal transactions, role
relations, situationism, or personality field theory; or cosmically,
as Atman, Oversoul, or Sunyata, Void in the sense of being
de-void of empirical determinability (see, e.g., the discussion on
pp. 514–15). Shortly before his death, Harvard's Gordon All-
port cited the problem of whether personality should be approached as integumented or situational as "the knottiest issue
in contemporary social science." I confess that I am unsure
where I myself come out on the anatta doctrine, but at the very
least I find it inviting a host of intriguing comparisons. For
example:

— Kant believed that the idea of a permanent, identical,
spiritual substance or soul involves "paralogisms" or logical
faculties. The "transcendental unity of apperception" or "I
think" must accompany all representations if objects of experience are to be known, but to say that such a logical subject is
a presupposition of the possibility of knowledge does not entail
the existence of a spiritual substance or soul.

— Freud traced both the self–other dichotomy and anxiety
back to our earliest, infant separation experiences, and he denied that the self-conscious "I" is a perception of one's total
person or even an identical fraction. Instead, he argued, it is
any consciousness — affect, idea, or action — that is colored by
intrapsychic conflict and anxiety. Neo-Freudians have gone on
to fill in the other side of the picture: where ego-functions are
anxiety-free we have that self-forgetfulness characteristic of
autonomous ego-functions using neutralized instinctual energy.

— Heidegger holds that man can never be understood as an apparatus primarily closed in on itself and transcending its limits only through a secondary movement toward its environment. He exists outside himself, in-the-world primarily and originally. He *is* his relationships with the things, creatures, and fellow human beings that come within the sphere of his existence. This sphere, in turn, is to be understood as man's openness to the world, his power of illuminating and bringing into its very being that which he encounters.

— Sartre argues in *Transcendence of the Ego* that "I" is deceptive, a fiction we construct in part to hide from ourselves the contingency of our perceptions. It is a major source of "bad faith" inasmuch as it induces us to identify ourselves mistakenly and needlessly with our past.

— Norman O. Brown argues in *Love's Body* that our real sickness is not repression but the idea of a repressing self, a separate self, the entire self–world dichotomy. To search for identity is to remain trapped in the notion of selfhood. "The solution to the problem of identity is, get lost."

A psychologist recently characterized the ego as "a convenient provisional delusion of considerable strategic utility." Whether it is more, this book will not determine. But I can think of no livelier point of contact between Buddhism and contemporary Western thought than its triple claim: that every error, including moral error, is ultimately traceable to the error of false attribution, specifically the reading of absoluteness into what. is relative; that the most typical expression of this error consists in treating the empirical "I" as "self"; and that only in proportion as we correct this error can we (to convert to Western idiom) perceive the face of God in all things and turn the world itself into a kind of beyond.

HUSTON SMITH
Professor of Philosophy
Massachusetts Institute
of Technology

Tokyo
12 October 1969

EDITOR'S PREFACE

The first edition of this Buddhist Bible was published in 1932. When the need of a new edition became evident, it was decided to enlarge it so as to include other Scriptures of like importance so as to make it more comprehensive. This involved making a number of new translations for which we are indebted to Bhikshu Wai-tao. We are also indebted and are very grateful to a number of other Buddhist Scholars for permission to use their translations, as noted in the Appendix.

The compiling of a Buddhist Bible is a very different matter from compiling the Christian Bible. In the first place, there is no Hierarchy or Ecclesiastic Council to pass upon the authenticity of different scriptures, and as to their canonicity. In the second place, Christian Scriptures are a closed system of doctrines and dogmas that have been inspired by the Holy Spirit and are to be accepted in faith. Buddhism, on the contrary, is looked upon as a growing organism whose scriptures are of many kinds as the organism has developed under different racial, temporal and cultural conditions. As disciples follow the Buddha's Noble Path and practice dhyana concentration and intuitive meditation they have an unfolding experience of spiritual insight and grace which any one of them may describe and elucidate. Some of these experiences are of highest value, some of less value. Some are concerned with the Dharma, some have to do with the rules of the Brotherhoods, some are philosophical, some psychological, some are commentaries and some are commentaries on commentaries. In the third place, there is the difference of quantity. In the Christian Bible there are sixty-six titles; Buddhist scriptures number over ten thousand, only a fraction of which have thus far been translated. In the Sung Dynasty about 972 AD a Chinese version of these scriptures was published consisting of 1521 works, in more than 5000 volumes, covering 130,000 pages.

The nearest approach to canonicity is the Pali Tripitika. That was the earliest collection and was supposed to be limited to the words of Buddha. Southern Buddhists are passionately devoted to these Pali Scriptures and are inclined to disparage and dispute the more philosophical scriptures of the Northern School that developed later after Buddhism had come in contact with other world religions in Persia, Palestine, Egypt and Greece. Under these conditions there developed in Northern India, and Kashgar, a succession of very able minds, Ashvaghosha, Nargajuna, Vasobandhu and his brother Asangha from whose writings and teachings there developed various important schools of philosophical thought that profoundly changed the understanding of Buddha's Dharma.

Later on as Buddhism spread into China and came under the influence of its immemorial culture and practical good sense, it took on forms of Taoist naturalism and kindly humanism, and there developed forms of "salvation by faith in Amitabha's mercy" and rebirth in his Pure Land. While in Tibet, coming in contact with its ancient Bon religion, and under the climatic conditions of its high altitudes, it took on forms of strenuousness and magic and tantric conceptions. Later on in Japan owing to political and social conditions incident to the presence of a limited but powerful noble class dominating a suppressed peasantry, which had developed extremes of loyalty and obedience and self-control, it took on forms of concentrative meditation known as Zen, and a still more widely divergent type of the True Pure Land Sect.

Naturally among these diverse conditions Buddhist scriptures vary widely, and the quantity of them being so enormous, they have become segregated into different groups as they are favored by different schools of thought and practice. The Tien-tai favor the more philosophical scriptures, the Shingon, the more esoteric, the Ch'an (Zen), the more intellectual, and the Pure Land, the more emotional. The present editor has been guided in his selection of scriptures for this Buddhist Bible by a sincere purpose to make the selection as comprehensive as possible within its limits and to represent as truly as possible the original teachings of the Blessed One both as understood by the Southern and more primitive school and by the Northern and more philosophical interpreters. He has also humbly tried to have the choice vouched for by his own spiritual experience in his practice of the Noble Path and especially during its Eighth Stage of intuitive Dhyana.

It follows, therefore, that the scriptures thus selected are the generally accepted scriptures of the Dhyana Sects—Ch'an in China, Zen in Japan and Kargyupta in Tibet. Of course among so enormous a collection of scriptures there are others that are favorites also, notably the *Saddharma-pundarika* (Lotus of the Perfect Law), and the *Avatamsaka,* said to be the grandest religious document ever written, but these are very large books in themselves. The late W. E. Soothil of London left a very careful translation of the Lotus that still waits a publisher. Dr. Suzuki of Kyoto has made a translation of the Gandhavyuha sections of the Avatamsaka that is now in process of being published. The inclusion of Laotzu's *Tao-teh-king* is open to question as it is not strictly a Buddhist text, but its teaching has such a close affinity to Buddhist teaching and nearly all early Chinese Masters of Buddhism were Taoist scholars who, upon becoming Buddhists, did not give up their Taoist conceptions and terms, and because the Lao-tzuan teaching in the *Tao-teh-king* has had such a wholesome influence on the development of Chinese Buddhism, and, in later years, wherever the *Tao-teh-king* is held in reverence, it has tended to restrain individual pride of egoism, religious ceremonial, ecclesiasticism, priestcraft and insincerity generally, we make no apology for including it. In fact, it is our earnest wish that the *Tao-teh-king* may become one of the foundation stones of American and European Buddhism.

Further introductory notes are reserved for the Appendix under the heads of the individual Scriptures, as are also grateful appreciation to those who have contributed to the preparation and publication of this Bible, especially to those Buddhist scholars who have courteously granted the Editor permission to use their translations for this purpose.

Just a closing word as to the rules that have guided the Editor in his choice and handling of textual material. He has always kept in mind the spiritual needs of his readers. This Buddhist Bible is not intended to be a source book for critical literary and historical study. It is only intended to be a source of spiritual inspiration designed to awaken faith and to develop faith into aspiration and full realization. The original texts having for centuries been carried in memory and transcribed by hand by scribes who were often more loyal to their Master than to historical exactness, are often overloaded with inter-

polations and extensions, and in places are confused and obscure. To carry out the design of the Editor, he has omitted
a great deal of matter not bearing directly upon the theme of
the particular Scripture, and has interpreted occasionally where
it seemed necessary and advisable, in order to provide an
easier and more inspiring reading. The need for this course
will become apparent to every earnest minded disciple.

In these days when Western civilization and culture is
buffeted as never before by foreboding waves of materialism
and selfish aggrandisement both individual and national,
Buddhism seems to hold out teachings of highest promise. For
two thousand years Dhyana Buddhism has powerfully conditioned the cultural, ethical and spiritual life of the great
Oriental nations. It well may be the salvation of Western
civilization. Its rationality, its discipline, its emphasis on simplicity and sincerity, its thoughtfulness, its cheerful industry
not for profit but for service, its love for all animate life, its
restraint of desire in all its subtle forms, its actual foretastes
of enlightenment and blissful peace, its patient acceptance of
karma and rebirth, all mark it out as being competent to meet
the problems of this excitement loving, materialistic, acquisitive
and thoughtless age.

Its basic principle of an eternal process based on unchanging law and operating in eternal recurrence, leading to mind-
control, to highest cognition, to purest conceptions of love and
compassion, to ever clearing insight, to highest perfect wisdom,
to the self-giving of Bodhisattvas, and Buddhas, to blissful
peace, is worthy of confidence; and its Noble Path worthy of
trial.

The theme of this Buddhist Bible is designed to show the
unreality of all conceptions of a personal ego. Its purpose is
to awaken faith in Buddhahood as being one's true self-nature;
to kindle aspiration to realize one's true Buddha-nature; to
energize effort to follow the Noble Path, to become Buddha.
The true response to the appeal of this Buddhist Bible is not
in outward activities, but in self-yielding, becoming a clear
channel for Buddhahood's indrawing compassion, that all sentient beings may become emancipated, enlightened and brought
to Buddhahood.

SELECTIONS
FROM PALI SOURCES

As one upon a rocky mountain standing,
Beholding all the people round about him
Plunged in their grief, by birth and age o'er powered,
E'en thus, O Thou with Wisdom filled, ascending
To th' Palace of the Dharma, all beholding,
Look down, Thou griefless One, upon the people!
Rise up, O Hero, victor in battle!
O Caravan-leader, free from debt, go through the world!
May the Lord deign to teach the Dharma,
There are those who'll understand.

THE HISTORIC BUDDHA

BUDDHISM, or, as it is known among its followers, the Dharma, is the religion preached by the Buddhas. A Buddha is one who has attained *Bodhi*. By Bodhi is meant an ideal state of intellectual and ethical perfection, which can be attained by man by purely human means. Of the many that have attained Bodhi the one best known to history is Gautama Sakyamuni.

Gautama Sakyamuni is generally spoken of as the founder of the Dharma. But Sakyamuni himself refers in his discourses to Buddhas who had preached the same doctrine befor him. Nor can we speak of the Buddha as the founder of Buddhism in the same sense as we speak of the founder of Christianity or Mahometanism. Their founder is essentially a supernatural being; he is the incarnation of the son of God, who is no other than God himself. No one can call himself a true Christian, who does not accept the divinity of Jesus, and who does not believe that Christ rose from the dead after dying on the cross to take upon himself the sins of all those who believe in him. Mahomet, the founder of the latter religion, though not an incarnation of God or any of his relations or servants, is yet a privileged human being, who was chosen as the special vehicle for the communication of a supernatural revelation to mankind, and no man can call himself a Mahometan who does not believe that Mahomet is the prophet of God. But the Buddha nowhere claims to be anything more than a human being. No doubt we find him a full and perfect man. All the same he is a man among men. He does not profess to bring a revelation from a supernatural source. He does not proclaim himself a saviour who will take upon himself the sins of those that follow him. He professes no more than to teach men the way by which they can liberate themselves as he has liberated himself. He distinctly tells us that every one must bear the burden of his own sins, that every man must be the fabricator of his own salvation, that not even a God can do for man what self-help in the form

3

of self-conquest and self-emancipation can accomplish. We read in the *Dharmapada*, a collection of verses attributed to the Blessed Sakyamuni:

Action?

All that we are is the result of what we have thought: it is founded on our thoughts, it is made up of our thoughts.

By oneself evil is done; by oneself one suffers; by oneself evil is left undone; by oneself one is purified. Purity and impurity belong to oneself; no one can purify another.

You yourself must make an effort; the Buddhas are only preachers. The thoughtful who enter the way are freed from the bondage of sin.

He who does not rouse himself when it is time to rise, who, though young and strong, is full of sloth, whose will and thoughts are weak, that lazy and idle man will never find the way to enlightenment.

Strenuousness is the path of immortality, sloth the path of death. Those who are strenuous do not die; those who are slothful are as if dead already.

Again in the *Mahaparanirvana Sutra* the Buddha gives the following admonition to Ananda, one of his beloved disciples:

O Ananda, be ye lamps unto yourselves. Be ye refuges to yourselves. Hold fast to the Dharma as a lamp. Hold fast to the Dharma as a refuge. Look not for refuge to any one beside yourselves.

And whosoever, Ananda, either now or after I am dead, shall be a lamp unto themselves and a refuge unto themselves . . . it is they, Ananda, among the seekers after Bodhi who shall reach the very topmost height.

Not only did the Buddha offer no support to favourable interference from supernatural agencies on behalf of man, not only did he offer no promise of exemption from suffering and sorrow as a reward of simple belief in him, but he went further in admonishing his disciples not to attach importance to his individual personality but to remember always the ideal. It is said in the *Vajracchedika:* He who looks for me, *i.e.,* the true Tathagata, through any material form, or seeks me through any audible sound, that man has entered on an erroneous course, and shall never behold Tathagata. Similarly in another place we read: Who say you see me and yet have transgressed the Dharma, are not seen by me, but as though you were distant by ten thousand miles, whereas the man who keeps the Dharma dwells ever in my sight. The same truth is much more impressively brought out in a conversation between the Blessed One and the Brahman Drona. Once upon a time the latter seeing the Blessed One sitting at the foot of a tree, asked him: Are you a *deva?* And the Exalted One answered: I am not. Are you a *gandharva?* —I am not. —Are you a *yaksha?* —I am not. Are you a man? —I am not a man. On the Brahman asking what he might be, the Blessed One replied: Those evil influences, those lusts, whose non-destruction would have individualised me as a deva, a gandharva, a yaksha, or a man, I have completely annihilated. Know, therefore, O Brahman, that I am a Buddha. Now the practical lesson of this anecdote is obvious. According to Hindu ideas a deva, a gandharva, a yaksha could assume a human form. It was therefore natural for the Brahman to ask if the being in human form before him was a deva, a gandharva, or a yaksha. But what perplexed the Brahman was that he received a negative answer to each one of his questions, and this led him to his general question. Buddha's answer to it was unequivocal. What was of importance in his eyes was not his form *(rupa)* but his character *(nama),* the embodiment in practical life of the ideas of compassion and wisdom summed up in the word Bodhi. He was not only Sakyamuni, but he was also Tathagata. The eternal truths he taught were nothing but what he himself was in the quintessence of his personality. He was *dharmadhatusvabhavatmaka,* representing in himself the ultimate reality embodied in the society of all human beings. No wonder therefore that the personality that dominates Buddhism is not Sakyamuni but the Buddha.

Though what is of primary importance is the life in accordance with the Dharma, yet the personality of the Great Teacher is not without value. In so far as that personality is the practical embodiment of his teachings, it serves as a model for the disciple to imitate and follow. As the *Amitayur-dhyana Sutra* says: Since they have meditated on Buddha's body, they will also see Buddha's mind. The Buddha's mind is his absolutely great compassion for all beings. But it must at the same time be remembered that the teaching of the Blessed One does not rest for its validity on any miracle or any special event in his life as is the case in many another religion.

Should the events in the life of Gautama Sakyamuni turn out to be unhistorical, that would not in the least detract from the merit of his teachings. As the Blessed One himself has said, the teaching carries with it its own demonstration.

Stripped of mythical embellishments, the principal events in the life of Gautama Buddha are easily told. He was born about the middle of the sixth century before the Christian era (563 B.C.) in Lumbini Park in the neighbourhood of Kapilavastu, now known as Padeira, in the north of the district of Gorakpur. To mark this spot as the birth of the greatest teacher of mankind and as a token of his reverence for him, Emperor Asoka erected in 239 B.C. a pillar bearing the inscription: Here was the Enlightened One born.

At Kapilavastu resided the chiefs of the Sakya clan, of whom little would have been remembered, had not Siddartha been born among them. Gautama's father, Suddhodana, and his mother, Maya, the daughter of Suprabuddha, belonged to this clan. The mother of Siddartha died seven days after his birth. Under the kind care of his maternal aunt, Prajapati Gautami, Siddartha spent his early years in ease, luxury and culture. No pains were spared to make the course of his life smooth. At the age of sixteen he was married to his cousin, Yasodhara, the daughter of the chief of Koli, and they had a son named Rahula. For twenty-five years Siddartha saw only the beautiful and pleasant. About this time the sorrows and sufferings of mankind affected him deeply, and made him reflect on the problem of life. Impelled by a strong desire to find the origin of suffering and sorrow and the means of extirpating them, he renounced at the age of twenty-nine all family ties and retired to the forest, as was the wont in his day.

> 'T was not through hatred of his children sweet,
> 'T was not through hatred of his lovely wife,
> Thraller of hearts—not that he loved them less—
> But Buddhahood more, that he renounced them all.

After this great renunciation (*abhinishkramana*) the Bodhisattva, the seeker after Bodhi, placed himself under the spiritual guidance of two renowned Brahman teachers, Arada Kalama and Udraka Ramaputra. The former lived at Vaisali and was the head of a large number of followers. He was evidently a follower of Kapila, the reputed founder of the Sankhya system of philosophy, and laid great stress on the belief in an *atman*. He regarded the disbelief in the existence of a soul as not tending towards religion. Without the belief in an eternal immaterial soul he could not see any way of salvation. Like the munga-grass when freed from its horny case, or like the wild bird when liberated from its trap, the soul, when freed from its material limitations (*upadhi*), would attain perfect release. When the ego discerned its immaterial nature, it would attain true deliverance. This teaching did not satisfy the Bodhisattva, and he quitted Arada Kalama, and placed himself under the tuition of Udraka Ramaputra. The latter, probably a follower of the Vaiseshika system, also expatiated on the question of I, but laid greater stress on the effects of Karma and the transmigration of souls. The Bodhisattva saw the truth in the doctrine of Karma, but he could not bring himself to believe in the existence of a soul or its transmigration. He therefore quitted Udraka also, and went to the priests officiating in temples to see if he could learn from them the way of escape from suffering and sorrow. But to the gentle nature of Gautama the unnecessarily cruel sacrifices performed on the altars of the gods were revolting, and he preached to the priests on the futility of atoning for evil deeds by the destruction of life and the impossibility of practising religion by the neglect of the moral life.

Wandering from Vaisali in search of a better system Siddartha came to a settlement of five pupils of Udraka, headed by Kaundinya, in the jungle of Uruvilva near Gaya in Magadha. There he saw these five keeping their senses in check, subduing their passions and practising austere penance. He admired their zeal and earnestness, and to give a trial to the means employed by them he applied himself to mortification. For six years he practised the most severe ascetic penances, till his body became shrunken like a withered branch. One day after bathing in the river Nairanjana (modern Phalgu) he strove to leave the water, but could not rise on account of his weakness. However with the aid of the stooping branch of a tree he raised himself and left the river. But while returning to his abode he again staggered and fell to the ground, and might perhaps have died, had not Sujata, the eldest daughter of a herdsman living near the jungle, who accidentally passed by the spot where the Bodhisattva had swooned, given him some rice-milk. Having thus refreshed himself he perceived that asceticism, instead of leading him to the goal he sought, brought about only an enfeeblement of both body and mind. Accordingly he gave up all ascetic practices, and paying due attention to the needs of the body he entered upon a course of reflection and self-examination, trusting to his own reason, the light which each one of us carries within himself, to attain the truth.

> "Truth is within ourselves; it takes no rise
> From outward things, whate'er you may believe.
> There is an inmost centre in us all,
> Where truth abides in fulness; and around,
> Wall upon wall, the gross flesh hems it in,
> This perfect clear perception which is truth.
> A baffling and perverting carnal mesh
> Binds it and makes all error: and to *know*
> Rather consists in opening out a way
> Whence the imprisoned splendour may escape,
> Than in effecting entry for a light
> Supposed to be without."

One night, while sitting in deep meditation under a fig tree (*ficus religiosa*), the consciousness of true insight possessed him. He saw the mistaken ways of the faiths that then obtained, he discerned the sources whence earthly suffering flowed, and the way that led to their annihilation. He saw that the cause of suffering lay in a selfish cleaving to life, and that the way of escape from suffering lay in the attainment of the ten perfections (*daca paramitas*). With the discernment of these grand truths and their realization in life the Bodhisattva became enlightened; he thus attained *Sambodhi* and became a Buddha. Rightly has *Sambodhi* been called *Svabodhanam* to emphasise the fact that it can be accomplished only by self-help without the extraneous aid of a teacher or an *Isvara*. As the poet says,

> "Save his own soul's light overhead,
> None leads man, none ever led."

Now arrived the most critical moment in the life of the Blessed One. After many struggles he had found the most profound truths, truths teeming with meaning but comprehensible only by the wise, truths fraught with blessings but difficult to discern by ordinary minds (*prtagjana*). Mankind were

worldly and hankering for pleasure. Though they possessed
the capacity for knowledge and virtue and could perceive the
true nature of things, they remained in ignorance, entangled
by deceptive thoughts. Could they comprehend the law of
Karma, the law of concatenation of cause and effect in the
moral world? Could they rid themselves of the animistic idea
of a soul and grasp the true nature of man? Could they overcome the propensity to seek salvation through a mediatorial
caste of priests? Could they understand the final state of
peace, that quenching of all worldly cravings which leads to
the blissful haven of Nirvana? Would it be advisable for him
in these circumstances to preach to all mankind the truths he
had discovered? Might not failure result in anguish and pain?
Such were the doubts and questions which arose in his mind,
but only to be smothered and quenched by thoughts of universal compassion. He who had abandoned all selfishness could
not but live for others. What could be a better way of living
for others than to show them the path of attaining perfect
bliss? What could be greater service to mankind than to rescue
the struggling creatures engulfed in the mournful sea of *samsara*? Is not the gift of Dharma the greatest of all gifts?
When the Perfect One considered how sorrow and suffering
oppressed all beings, he became very compassionate, and made
up his mind to preach to all mankind the eternal truths he
had discovered.

> Amongst the nations I shall go
> And ope the door that to the deathless leads.
> Let those that have ears to hear
> Master the noble path of salvation.

With this firm resolve he started for Benares which has been
famous for centuries as the centre of religious life and thought.
On his way the Blessed One met one of his former acquaintances, Upaka, a naked Jain monk, who, struck by his majestic
and joyful appearance, asked: Who is the teacher under whose
guidance you have renounced the world? The Enlightened One
replied: I have no master. To me there is no equal. I am the
Perfect One, the Buddha. I have attained peace. I have obtained Nirvana. To found the kingdom of righteousness I am
going to Benares. There I shall light the lamp of life for the
benefit of those who are enshrouded in the darkness of sin and
death. Upaka then asked: Do you profess to be the Jina, the

conqueror of the world? The Buddha replied: Jinas are those
who have conquered self and the passions of self, those alone
are victors who control their passions and abstain from sin.
I have conquered self and overcome all sin. Therefore am I
the Jina.

> He whose life is pure, whose thought is good,
> Whose subject senses own him sovereign lord,
> Whose heart and mind no attachment hampers,
> Whose head and heart love and gladness fill,
> Who remorseless ignorance has killed,
> Who pride of egoism has slain,
> Who, from all defilements purged and free,
> Combines truth and valour and resource
> With foresight, kindness and fixed resolve:
> He has all Fetters utterly destroyed
> And made the Conquest glorious and true.

At Benares he met Kaundinya and his four companions in
the Deer Park, Isipatana. When these five (the *pancha-vag-
giya*) saw the Tathagata coming towards them, they agreed
among themselves not to rise in salutation, nor greet him, nor
offer him the customary refreshments, when he came, for he
had broken his first vow by giving up ascetic practices. However, when the Tathagata approached them, they involuntarily
rose from their seats, and in spite of their resolution greeted
him and offered to wash his feet and do all that he might require. But they addressed him as Gautama after his family.
Then the Lord said to them: Call me not after my private
name, for it is a rude and careless way of addressing one who
has become an *Arhat*. My mind is undisturbed, whether people
treat me with respect or disrespect. But it is not courteous for
others to call one who looks equally with a kind heart upon
all living beings by his familiar name. Buddhas bring salvation
to the world, and therefore they ought to be treated with respect as children treat their fathers. Then he preached to them
his first great sermon, the *Dharmachakrapravartana Sutra*, in
which he explained the Four Great Truths and the Noble
Eightfold Path, and made converts of them. They received the
ordination and formed the first nucleus of the holy brotherhood
of disciples known as the *Sangha*. Soon after, one night the
Blessed One met Yacas, the youthful son of a rich merchant
(*Sreshti*) of Benares, who was wandering like a madman much

distressed by the sorrows of this world. The Tathagata consoled him by pointing out the way to the blessedness of Nirvana, and made him his disciple. Seeing that Yacas had become a bhikshu, his former fifty-four jovial companions also joined the Sangha. The Blessed One sent out these sixty as missionaries in different directions to preach his universal religion. Shortly afterwards the Buddha had an accession of a thousand new disciples by the conversion of three leading fire-worshipping ascetics, Uruvilva Kasyapa, Nadi Kasyapa and Gaya Kasyapa, all brothers, with all their followers. To these he preached on a hill near Gaya a sermon on the fire sacrifice. In this discourse he explained how ignorance produced the three fires of lust, hatred and delusion, which burnt all living beings, and how these three fires might be quenched by the giving up of sin and the pursuit of right conduct.

From Gaya followed by his numerous disciples the Blessed One proceeded to Rajagriha, the capital of Magadha. After his great renunciation Siddartha passed through Rajagriha, and Bimbisara, the king of Magadha, failing to dissuade him from his resolve to attain bodhi, requested the Bodhisattva to come back to Rajagriha after the accomplishment of his purpose and receive him as his disciple. In compliance with this request the Blessed One now visited Rajagriha. King Bimbisara, hearing of the arrival of the World-Honoured, went with his counsellors, generals and myriads of Magadha Brahmans and Sreshtis to the place where the Blessed One was. When the king and his followers saw Uruvilva Kasyapa with the Blessed One, they began to question if the latter had placed himself under the spiritual guidance of the former. But Kasyapa removed their doubt by prostrating himself at the feet of the Blessed One, and explained how, after seeing the peace of Nirvana, he could no longer find delight in sacrifices and offerings, which promised no better rewards than pleasures and women. The Blessed One, perceiving the state of mind of his audience, preached to them on the inconstancy of the self, the so-called lord of knowledge, which, originating from sensation and recollection, must necessarily be subject to the condition of cessation. On hearing this discourse the king and many of those that accompanied him took refuge in the Buddha, the Dharma and the Sangha, and became lay followers. The king then invited the Blessed One to the royal palace, entertained him and his bhikshus and presented to the Sangha his pleasure garden, the bamboo grove *Venuvana,* as a dwelling-place for the homeless disciples of the Great Teacher.

A much more important event connected with the Blessed One's stay at Rajagriha was the conversion of Sariputra and Maudgalyayana, both pupils of the wandering monk Sanjaya. One day as Asvajit, one of the first five that were ordained by the Buddha, was going on his alms-seeking round, Sariputra saw the noble and dignified mien of Asvajit, and asked him who his teacher was and what doctrine he professed. Asvajit replied that his teacher was the Blessed One and summed up the Tathagata's teaching in the well-known lines:

"Whatever things proceed from a cause,
Of them the Buddha has stated the cause
And what their dissolution is.
This is what the Great Sramana teaches."

On hearing this Sariputra went to Maudgalyayana and told him what he had heard. Then both of them went with all their followers to the Tathagata and took their refuge in the Buddha, the Dharma and the Sangha. The Buddha held both of them in high estimation for their intelligence and learning. Some of the books of the Abhidharma, the philosophical part of the Tripitaka, are ascribed to these two learned bhikshus. Another worthy acquisition to the faith during the Master's stay in the Bamboo Grove was the Brahman sage, Maha Kasyapa, who had renounced his handsome virtuous wife, his immense wealth and all his possessions to find out the way of salvation. It was he, who, after the *parinirvana* of the Lord, held a council at Rajagriha under the patronage of King Ajatasatru, and collected the Tripitaka, the Buddhist canon, with the help of a large number of bhikshus. He was in fact the first patriarch of the Buddhist Church.

During his active life as a teacher, the Blessed One made many converts. High and low, rich and poor, educated and illiterate, Brahamans and Chandalas, Jains and Ajivakas, householders and ascetics, robbers and cannibals, nobles and peasants, men and women—all classes and conditions of men furnished him with many disciples, both ordained and lay. Among his converts were King Prasenajit of Kosala, Panchasikha the follower of Kapila, Maha-Katyayana of Benares, King Udayana of Kausambi, Kutadanta, the head of the Brahman community of the village of Danamati, Krishi Bharadvaja of the Brahman village of Ekanala, Angulimala the bandit and assassin who was the terror of the kingdom of Kosaia, Alavaka the cannibal of Atavi, Ugrasena the acrobat, Upali the barber who had the honour of reciting the *Vinaya* collection of the Tripitaka in Kasyapa's Council, and Sunita the scavenger who was despised of men. Some of the members of the Sakya clan who were the close kith and kin of Siddartha also became the followers of Sakyamuni. Suddhodana, the father of Siddartha, became a lay disciple, and Rahula, his son, joined the Sangha. Yasodhara, the wife of Siddartha, and Prajapathi Gautami, his aunt, both joined the order of bhikshunis, which was established with some reluctance by the Master owing to the importunities of Prajapati Gautami and the intercession of Ananda. Ananda, who was the Buddha's constant companion and personal attendant, was one of his cousins.

Another of his cousins was Devadatta who became notorious in later days by attempting to found a new sect of his own with severer and stricter rules than those prescribed by the Buddha. When he did not succeed in getting many followers, even though he had a special Vihara built for him by King Ajatasutru, the son of King Bimbisara, he plotted many schemes to take the life of Sakyamuni. Murderers were set up to kill the Lord, but they were converted as soon as they saw him and listened to his preaching. The rock hurled down from the Gridhrakuta hill to hit the Master split in twain, and haply both pieces passed by without doing him much harm. The drunken elephant that was let loose on the royal highway just at the time when the Blessed One was coming along that path became docile in his presence. After these failures Ajatasatru, suffering greatly from the pangs of conscience, sought peace in his distress by going to the Blessed One and learning the way of salvation.

Twelve of Buddha's disciples became famous as preachers. These were Ajnata Kaundinya, Asvajit, Sariputra, Maudgalyayana, Maha Kasyapa, Maha Katayana, Anuruddha, Upale, Pindola Bharadvaja, Kausthila, Rahula and Purna Maitrayaniputra. In the conversation with Subhadra just before his death, the Blessed One said: Save in my religion the twelve great disciples, who, being good themselves, rouse up the world and deliver it from indifference, are not to be found.

Among the many patrons and benefactors of the Buddha no names are more famous than those of Anathapindika, the supporter of the orphans; Jivaka the physician; Visakha, the mother of Migara; and Ambapali, the courtezan of Vaisali. Sudatta, called Anathapindika on account of his charities to the orphans and the poor, was a merchant of Sravashti of immense wealth. He bought at an enormous price a magnificent park at Aravashti from Prince Jeta, and built the splendid Jetavana Vihara for the Buddha and his ordained disciples. Jivaka was the renowned physician-in-ordinary to Bimbisara, and was appointed by the king to undertake medical attendance on Buddha and his followers. It was at his instance that the bhikshus, who were previously wearing only cast-off rags, were permitted to accept robes from the laity. Visakha was the daughter-in-law of Migara, a rich Jain merchant of Sravashti, but she was generally known as the mother of Migara, as she was the cause of Migara's conversion to the Buddhist faith. She was the first to become a matron of the lay sisters, and obtained permission from the Lord to provide the chief necessaries of life on a large scale to the bhikshus and bhikshunis. Another service of hers was the erection of the Vihara of Purvarama near Sravashti, which in splendour was inferior only to the Vihara built by Anathapindika. Ambapali, who was beautiful, graceful, pleasant, gifted with the highest beauty of complexion, well-versed in dancing, singing and lute playing, and through whom Vaisali became more and more flourishing, presented to the Master her stately mansion and mango grove and became a bhikshuni.

The great popularity of the Master and the gifts which the pious laics bestowed on his followers created a jealousy in the hearts of the leaders of heretical sects. These conspired to sully the reputation of Sakyamuni and ruin him in the eyes of the people. They induced a heretical nun, Chincha, to accuse the Master of adultery before the assemblage. Her calumny was exposed and she was made to suffer terribly for her misdeed. Not baffled by this failure the heresiarchs made a second attempt to slander the Master. This time they induced one Sundari, a member of one of the heretical sects, to spread a rumour that she passed one night in the bed-chamber of the Teacher. After this slander had been made sufficiently public, the heretics bribed a gang of drunkards to assassinate Sundari.

These scoundrels killed her, and threw her corpse in the bushes close to the Jetavana Vihara. The heresiarchs then loudly clamoured for the institution of legal proceedings against the Lord. Luckily their plan failed owing to the imprudence of the assassins, who, reuniting after the murder in a tavern and excited by strong drink, quarrelled among themselves and reproached one another of having committed the crime. They were immediately arrested by the police and brought before the royal tribunal. When they were questioned as to the murder of Sundari, the scoundrels openly confessed their guilt, and declared also the names of those who had employed them to commit the crime. The king ordered the assassins as well as the instigators of the crime to be put to death. On another occasion the heretics instigated Srigupta to take the life of the Master by poisoning his food and misleading him into a pit of fire, but by pity and calm forgiveness the Holy One

> Saved Srigupta from spite and crime
> And showed how mercy conquers e'en a foe,
> And thus he taught forgiveness' rule sublime,
> To free his followers from the world and woe.

The manner in which the Enlightened One ordinarily spent each day was very simple. He used to rise up early, wash and dress himself without assistance. He would then meditate in solitude till it was time to go on his round for a meal. When the time arrived, he would, dressing himself suitably, with his bowl in hand, alone or attended by some disciples, visit the neighbouring town or village. After finishing his meal in some house, he would discourse on the Dharma to the host and his family with due regard to their capacity for spiritual enlightenment, return to his lodgings and wait in the open verandah till all his followers had finished their meal. He would then retire to his private apartment and, after suggesting subjects for thought to some of his disciples, take a short rest during the heat of the day. In the afternoon he would meet the folk from the neighbouring villages or town assembled in the lecture-hall, and discourse to them on the Dharma in a manner appropriate to the occasion and suited to their capacities. Then, at the close of the day, after refreshing himself with a bath when necessary, he would explain difficulties or expound the doctrine to some of his disciples thus spending the first watch of the night. Part of the remainder he spent in meditation walking up and down outside his chamber, and the other part sleeping in his bed-chamber. During the nine months of fair weather, the Lord was wont to go from place to place walking from fifteen to twenty miles a day. During the rainy season he generally stayed in the Jetavana Vihara or in the Purvarama.

The Blessed One's method of exposition differed entirely from those of the Brahmans. Far from presenting his thoughts under the concise form so characteristic of the Brahmans, he imparted his teaching in the form of sermons. Instead of mysterious teachings confided almost in secret to a small number, he spoke to large audiences composed of all those who desired to hear him. He spoke in a manner intelligible to all, and tried by frequent repetitions to impress his meaning on the least attentive minds and the most rebellious memories. He adapted himself to the capacities of his hearers. He first talked about the merits obtained in alms-giving, about the duties of morality, about future happiness, about the danger, the vanity and the defilement of lusts, and about the blessings of the abandonment of lusts. When he saw that the mind of his hearer was prepared, unprejudiced, impressionable, free from hindrances to the comprehension of the Truth, elated and believing, then he preached the special doctrine of the Buddha, namely, suffering, the cause of suffering, the cessation of suffering, and the Path. This profound difference between the Buddha's method and that of the Brahmans, whose most marked trait is proselytism penetrates to the very essence of Buddhism.

While his discussions with the learned were more or less formal and often coldly logical, in his conversation with ordinary men the Master generally resorted to similes and parables, fables and folklore, historical anecdotes and episodes, proverbs and popular sayings. The parable of the mustard-seed, described in the next chapter, illustrates how the Holy One brought home plain truths to the minds of simple folk. In the conversion of the wealthy Brahman, Krishi Bharadvaja, the Buddha worked out the process of agriculture into an elaborate allegory. One day while staying in the southern district of Magadha (*Dakshinagiri*) the Buddha visited the Brahman village of Ekanala. Bharadvaja was then superintending the laborers in his field. With alms-bowl in hand the Blessed One approached the Brahman. Some went up and paid reverence to the Lord, but the Brahman reproached the Master saying: "O

Sramana, I plough and sow, and having ploughed and sown, I eat; it would be better if you were in like manner to plough and sow, and then you would also have food to eat." "O Brahman, replied the Buddha, I too plough and sow, and having ploughed and sown, I eat." But, said the Brahman, "if you are a husbandman, where are the signs of it? Where are your bullocks, the seed, and the plough?" Then the Teacher answered: "Faith is the seed I sow; devotion is the rain that fertilizes it; modesty is the plough-shaft; the mind is the tie of the yoke; mindfulness is my ploughshare and goad. Truthfulness is the means to bind; tenderness, to untie. Energy is my team and bullock. Thus this ploughing is effected, destroying the weeds of delusion. The harvest that it yields is the ambrosia fruit of Nirvana, and by this ploughing all sorrow is brought to an end." Then the Brahman poured milk-rice into a golden bowl and handed it to the Lord saying: "Eat, O Gautama, the milk-rice. Indeed, thou art a husbandman; for thou, Gautama, accomplishest a ploughing, which yields the fruit of immortality." When the Holy One desired to point a moral or convey a reproof, he related an anecdote or a fable treating its characters as representing the previous existences of himself and the other persons concerned. Such anecdotes are known as *Jatakas* or birth-stories.

More potent than his method and his word was the Blessed One's wonderful personality. When he talked with men, his serene look inspired them with awe and reverence, and his lovely voice struck them with rapture and amazement. Could mere words have converted the robber Angulimala or the cannibal of Atavi? To have come under his spell is to be his for ever. He was a winner of hearts. It is not so much because he preached the truth that his hearers believed; it is because he had won their hearts that his words appeared to them true and salutary. A single word from him was enough to reconcile King Prasenajit to his Queen Mallika. His heart always overflowed with kindness. Was it not the effuence of the Master's love that made Roja the Mallian follow him as a calf does the cow? To meet him is to be penetrated by his love (*maitri*) and to know him is to love him for ever.

In his last preaching tour the Master came to the town of Pava, and there in the house of Chunda, a worker in metals, he had his last repast. After this he became ill and moved to

Kusinagara in the eastern part of the Nepalese Terai, where he died at the ripe age of eighty about 483 B.C. Even in his last moments he received a monk Subhadra, explained to him the Noble Eightfold Path, and converted him to the true faith. His last words to his disciples were: Decay is inherent in all compound things. Seek wisdom and work out your salvation with diligence.

The immediate cause of his death was some poisonous element in the food which Chunda, the blacksmith, offered to him. In the record of it, the word used is *sukara-maddava,* which can be translated either the flesh of a wild boar when used for food, or, pig-food, a kind of bulbous vegetable, *sukara-kanda,* in which there might have been some variety of poisonous mushroom unwittingly concealed. Buddha warned his disciples not to partake of it, but out of kindness to Chunda he ate of it.

The remains of the Blessed One were burnt by the Mallas of Kusinagara with all the honours and pomp worthy of a king of kings. After cremation the relics were carried to the town-hall, and guarded there for a week covered by a cupola of lances in an enclosure of bows and honoured with garlands, perfumes, music and dances. When Ajatasatru, the king of Magada, heard of the death of the Lord at Kusinagara, he sent an ambassador to the Mallas of that place to demand of them a portion of the relics, as he desired to erect a tumulus (stupa) in honour of these relics. The same demand was also made by the Licchavis of Vaisali, the Sakyas of Kapilavastu, the Bulis of Alahappa, the Koliyas of Ramagrama and the Mallas of Pava. A Brahman of Vethadvipa also demanded a share on the plea of his being a Brahman. At first the Mallas of Kusinagara were not willing to satisfy these demands, as the Lord attained *parinirvana* in their territory. But on the advice of the Brahman Drona, who pointed out to the Mallas the indecency of quarrelling over the relics of one who had preached universal brotherhood, the Mallas of Kusinagara changed their mind. Drona was then entrusted with the distribution, and he took for himself the urn, over which he desired to erect a stupa. After the division the Mauryas of Pippalavana sent an envoy demanding some relics, but they had to content themselves with the charcoal from the funeral pyre. Those that received a share of the relics (*dhatu*) preserved them in dagobas (*dhathugarbhas*) erected in their respective countries. It is said that Emperor Asoka opened these ancient dagobas and distributed the relics contained in them all over his wide empire, and built more than eighty thousand stupas and dagobas for their preservation.

Such is, freed from the fanciful additions of a pious posterity, the life of the historic Buddha. How much of it is real history, is rather difficult to say. But as to the historicity of Gautama Sakyamuni himself there can be no doubt.

Whatever may be the verdict of historic criticism on the details of the life of Gautama Sakyamuni, there can be no doubt that among the founders of religions he occupies a marked place. His dignified bearing, his high intellectual endowments, his penetrating glance, his oratorical power, the firmness of his convictions, his gentleness, kindness, and liberality, and the attractiveness of his character—all testify to his greatness. . . . But the impartial philosophic critic finds that Gautama Sakyamuni towers above the founders of all other religions by his life, by his personal character, by the methods of propagandism he employed, and by his final success. In him were united the truest princely qualities with the intelligence of a sage and the passionate devotion of a martyr. Though born of an aristocratic and ruling class, Gautama Buddha lived the life of an ordinary man, discarding the narrow distinctions of caste, rank and wealth. He knew the world. He was son, husband, father, and devoted friend. He was not only a man, but never professed to be anything more than a man. He gave a trial to the creeds of his ancestors, but ultimately made for himself a nobler faith. His teaching was perfect, but never pretended to be a supernatural revelation. He did not doubt the capacity of man to understand the truth, and never had recourse to the arts of exorcism. He based all his reasoning on the fact of man's existence, and developed his practical philosophy by the observation and minute study of human nature. In an age innocent of science he found for the problems of the Whence, the Whither and the Why, solutions worthy of a scientific age. His aim was to rescue mankind from the fetters of passion and avarice and to convince them of an ideal higher than mere worldly good. He preached the gospel of renunciation attainable by meditation, a renunciation which did not lead one to the dreamy quietism of pantheistic or nihilistic philosophy but to the purification of one's activity by intellectual and ethical enlightenment so as to bring one to the love of all beings by faith in an eternal Dharmakaya.

Among the world's religious teachers Gautama Sakyamuni alone has the glory of having rightly judged the intrinsic greatness of man's capacity to work out his salvation without extraneous aid. If the worth of a truly great man consists in his raising the worth of all mankind, who is better entitled to be called truly great than the Blessed One, who, instead of degrading man by placing another being over him, has exalted him to the highest pinnacle of wisdom and love? His figure is the noblest, the most perfect that man can ever attain. It was genius unequalled among the sons of men that inspired the Buddha's teaching. It was genius commanding in its dictatorial strength that held together his order. It was genius, the first and last that India saw, that in its lofty aims and universality, foreshadowed the possibility of uniting the people into one great nationality, if such had ever been possible. Indeed the Tathagata is the Light of the World. No wonder that even those who first rejected his teaching had at last to include him in their pantheon by making him an avatar of one of the very gods whom he had himself discarded!

Those only are godlike who shrink from sin
The white-souled tranquil votaries of good.

No teacher was so godless as Lord Buddha yet none so godlike. Though the master of all, he was the universal brother of each. While despising the follies of the world, he lived and moved among men serenely and lovingly. When surrounded by all his retinue of followers, and glorified by the whole world, he never once thought that these privileges were his; but went on doing good, just as the shower brings gladness yet reflects not on its work. Though exalted and adored, he never arrogated to himself divinity. The Burmese relate that, hearing all people singing his praises, the Blessed One called Ananda and said: All this is unworthy of me. No such vain homage can accomplish the words of the Dharma. They who do righteously pay me most honour, and please me most. To the unbiassed thinker even the legends which enshroud the life of Sakyasimha are not without significance. They set before him a truly admirable figure: a man of quiet majesty, of wisdom and pleasant humour, consistent in thought, word and deed, of perfect equanimity and moral fervour, exempt from every prejudice, overcoming evil with good, and full of tenderness for all beings. In some of the legends, the so-called birth-stories, the Buddha is represented as having voluntarily endured infinite trials through numberless ages and births, that he might deliver mankind, foregoing the right to enter Nirvana and casting himself again and again into the stream of human life and destiny for the sole purpose of teaching the way of liberation from sorrow and suffering. The ideal of persistent energy thus held up before the disciple is intensely human. And even if the virtues of the Tathagata are infinitely superior to those of ordinary men, still the ideal can serve as a pattern and guide. The disciple can always take the Buddha as his model so that the recollection of his heroic and saintly life may assist him to be a hero and a saint as well. In his unbounded love for all beings Sakyamuni stands unparalleled. And it is not a poetic fancy but a profound philosophic truth that makes him the best

"............who loveth best
All things both great and small."

THE WORD OF THE BUDDHA

The following selections are taken from the different Pali Scriptures as indicated by the letters placed in brackets just preceding each selection: (D) Digha-Nikaya. (M) Majjhima-Nikaya. (A) Anguttara-Nikaya. (S) Samyutta-Nikaya. (Dhp.) Dhammapada. (Ud.) Udana. (It.) Itivuttaka. (Snp.) Sutta-Nipata.

(M.141) The Perfect One, Brothers, the holy One, the Fully Enlightened One, at Isipatana in the deer-park at Benares, has established the Supreme Kingdom of Truth, which none can overthrow—neither ascetic nor priest, nor heavenly being, nor evil spirit, nor god, nor any one whosoever in all the world,—by proclaiming, pointing out, making known, establishing, unveiling, explaining and making evident the Four Noble Truths.

What are these Four Noble Truths? They are the Noble Truth of Suffering, the Noble Truth of the Origin of Suffering, the Noble Truth of the Extinction of Suffering, and the Noble Truth of the Path that leads to the Extinction of Suffering.

(S.54 (2)) And the Blessed One said: As long, Disciples, as the absolutely true knowledge and insight as regards these Four Noble Truths was not quite clear in me, so long was I not sure whether I had won to that supreme Enlightenment which is unsurpassed in all the world with its heavenly beings, evil spirits and gods, amongst all the hosts of ascetics and priests, heavenly beings and men. But as soon as the absolutely true knowledge and insight as regards these Four Noble Truths had become perfectly clear in me, there arose in me the assurance, that I had won to that supreme Enlightenment unsurpassed.

(M.26) And I discovered that profound truth, so difficult to perceive, difficult to understand, tranquillising and sublime, which is not to be gained by mere reasoning, and is visible only to the wise.

The world however is given to pleasure, delighted with pleasure, enchanted with pleasure. Verily such beings will hardly understand the law of conditionality, the Dependent Origination (*paticca-samuppada*) of everything; incomprehensible to them will also be the end of all formations, the forsaking of every substratum of rebirth, the fading away of craving, detachment, extinction, Nibbana.

Yet there are beings whose eyes are only a little covered with dust: they will understand the truth.

THE FIRST TRUTH
The Noble Truth of Suffering

(D.22) <u>What now is the Noble Truth of Suffering?</u>

<u>Birth is suffering; Decay is suffering; Death is suffering; Sorrow, Lamentation, Pain, Grief and Despair are suffering; not to get what one desires is suffering; in short: the Five Aggregates of Existence are suffering.</u>

What now is Birth? The birth of beings belonging to this or that order of beings, their being born, their conception and springing into existence, the manifestation of the aggregates of existence, the arising of sense activity: this is called birth.

And what is Decay? The decay of beings belonging to this or that order of beings; their getting aged, frail, grey and wrinkled; the failing of their vital force, the wearing out of the senses:—this is called decay.

And what is Death? The parting and vanishing of beings out of this or that order of beings, their destruction, disappearance, death, the completion of their life-period, dissolution of the aggregates of existence, the discarding of the body:—this is called death.

And what is Sorrow? The sorrow arising through this or that loss or misfortune which one encounters, the worrying oneself, the state of being alarmed, inward sorrow, inward woe:—this is called sorrow.

And what is Lamentation? Whatsoever, through this or that loss or misfortune, which befalls one, is wail and lament, wailing and lamenting, a state of woe and lamentation:—this is called lamentation.

And what is Pain? The bodily pain and unpleasantness, the painful and unpleasant feeling produced by bodily contact:—this is called pain.

And what is Grief? The mental pain and unpleasantness, the painful and unpleasant feeling produced by mental contact:—this is called grief.

And what is Despair? Distress and despair arising through

this or that loss or misfortune which one encounters, distress-edness and desperateness:—this is called despair.

And what is the Suffering of not getting what one desires? To beings, subject to birth, there comes the desire: O, that we were not subject to birth! O, that no new birth was before us! Subject to decay, disease, death, sorrow, lamentation, pain, grief and despair, the desire comes to them: O, that we were not subject to these things! O, that these things were not before us! But this cannot be got by mere desiring; and not to get what one desires is suffering.

And what, in brief, are the Five Aggregates connected with cleaving? They are bodily form, feeling, perception, (mental) formations and consciousness.

(S.21 (8)) Any material form, whether one's own or external, gross or subtle, lofty or low, far or near, belongs to the Aggregate of Bodily Form connected with cleaving; any feeling belongs to the Aggregate of Feeling; any perception belongs to the Aggregate of Perception; any formation belongs to the Aggregate of Formations; all consciousness belongs to the Aggregate of Consciousness.

(M.28) What now is the Aggregate of Bodily Form? It is the four primary elements and the bodily form derived from them.

And what are the four primary elements? They are the Solid Element, the Fluid Element, the Heating Element, the Vibrating Element.

1. What now is the Solid Element? The solid element may be subjective, or it may be objective. And what is the subjective solid element? The dependent properties which on one's own person and body are hard and solid, as the hairs of head and body, nails, teeth, skin, flesh, sinews, bones, marrow, kidneys, heart, liver, diaphragm, spleen, lungs, stomach, bowels, dysentery, excrement, or whatever other dependent properties which on one's own person and body are hard and solid—this is called the subjective solid element. Now, whether it be the subjective solid element, or whether it be the objective solid element: they are both only the solid element. One should understand according to reality and true wisdom:—This does not belong to me; this am I not; this is not my Ego.

2. What now is the Fluid Element? The fluid element may be subjective, or it may be objective. And what is the subjective fluid element? The dependent properties which on one's

own person and body are watery or cohesive, as bile, phlegm, pus, blood, sweat, lymph, tears, serum, spit, nasal mucus, oil of the joints, urine, or whatever other dependent properties which on one's own person and body are watery or cohesive—this is called the subjective fluid element. Now, whether it be the subjective fluid element, or whether it be the objective fluid element: they are both only the fluid element. One should understand according to reality and true wisdom:—This does not belong to me; this am I not; this is not my Ego.

3. What now is the Heating Element? The heating element may be subjective, or it may be objective. And what is the subjective heating element? The dependent properties which on one's own person and body are heating and radiating, as that whereby one is heated, consumed, scorched, whereby that which has been eaten, drunk, chewed or tasted, is fully digested, or whatever other dependent properties which on one's own person and body are heating and radiating—this is called the subjective heating element. Now, whether it be the subjective heating element, or whether it be the objective heating element; they are both only the heating element. One should understand according to reality and true wisdom—This does not belong to me; this am I not; this is not my Ego.

4. What now is the Vibrating Element? The vibrating element may be subjective, or it may be objective. And what is the subjective vibrating element? The dependent properties which on one's own person and body are mobile and gaseous, as the upward-going and downward-going winds, the winds of stomach and intestines, in-breathing and out-breathing, or whatever other dependent properties which on one's own person and body are mobile and gaseous—this is called the subjective vibrating element. Now, whether it be the subjective vibrating element, or whether it be the objective vibrating element: they are both only the vibrating element. One should understand according to reality and true wisdom: This does not belong to me; this am I not; this is not my Ego.

Just as one calls hut the circumscribed space which comes to be by means of wood and rushes, reeds and clay, even so we call body the circumscribed space that comes to be by means of bones and sinews, flesh and skin.

Now, though one's eye be intact, yet if the external forms do not fall within the field of vision, and no corresponding conjunction takes place, in that case there occurs no formation of the correspondent aspect of consciousness. Or, though one's eye be intact and the external forms fall within the field of vision, yet if no corresponding conjunction takes place, in that case also there occurs no formation of the corresponding aspect of consciousness. If, however, one's eye is intact, and the external forms fall within the field of vision, and the corresponding conjunction takes place, in that case there arises the corresponding aspect of consciousness.

(M.38) Hence I say: the arising of consciousness is dependent upon conditions, and without these conditions no consciousness arises. And upon whatsoever conditions the arising of consciousness is dependent, after these it is called.

Consciousness, whose arising depends on the eye and forms, is called eye-consciousness.

Consciousness, whose arising depends on the ear and sounds, is called ear-consciousness.

Consciousness, whose arising depends on the olfactory organ and odours, is called olfactory-consciousness.

Consciousness, whose arising depends on the tongue and taste, is called tongue-consciousness.

Consciousness, whose arising depends on the body and bodily contacts, is called body-consciousness.

Consciousness, whose arising depends on the mind and ideas, is called mind-consciousness.

(M.28) Whatsoever there is of form in the consciousness thus arisen, that belongs to the aggregate of bodily form connected with clinging to existence. Whatsoever there is of feeling therein, that belongs to the aggregate of feeling connected with clinging to existence. Whatsoever there is of perception therein, that belongs to the aggregate of perception connected with clinging to existence. Whatsoever there are of mental formations therein, that belongs to the aggregate of mental formations connected with clinging to existence. Whatsoever there is of consciousness therein, that belongs to the aggregate of consciousness connected with clinging to existence.

And it is impossible that any one can explain the passing out of one existence and the entering into a new existence, or the growth, increase and development of consciousness, independent of bodily form, feeling, perception and mental formations.

(S.21 (2)) All formations are transient (anicca); all formations are subject to suffering (dukkha); all things are without an Ego-entity (anatta). Form is transient, feeling is transient, perception is transient, mental formations are transient, consciousness is transient.

And that which is transient is subject to suffering; and of that which is transient and subject to suffering and change, one cannot rightly say:—This belongs to me; this am I; this is my Ego.

(S.21 (5)) Therefore, whatever there be of bodily form, of feeling, perception, mental formations or consciousness, whether one's own or external, whether gross or subtle, lofty or low, far or near, one should understand according to reality and true wisdom:—This does not belong to me; this am I not; this is not my Ego.

(S.21 (6)) Suppose, a man, who can see, were to behold the many bubbles on the Ganges as they are driving along. And he should watch them and carefully examine them. After carefully examining them, they will appear to him as empty, unreal, and unsubstantial. In exactly the same way does the monk behold all the bodily forms, feelings, perceptions, mental formations and states of consciousness—whether they be of the past, or the present, or the future, far or near. And he watches them and examines them carefully, and, after carefully examining them, they appear to him as empty, void and without an Ego.

(S.21 (3)) Whoso delights in bodily form, or feeling, or perception, or mental formations, or consciousness, he delights in suffering; and whoso delights in suffering will not be freed from suffering. Thus I say.

(Dhp. 146-48)
> How can you find delight and mirth
> Where there is burning without end?
> In deepest darkness you are wrapped!
> Why do you not seek for the light?

> Look at this puppet here, well rigged,
> A heap of many sores, piled up,
> Diseased and full of greediness,
> Unstable and impermanent!

Devoured by old age is this frame,
A prey of sickness, weak and frail;
To pieces breaks this putrid body,
All life must truly end in death.

(A III.35) Did you ever see in the world a man or a woman, eighty, ninety, or a hundred years old, frail, crooked as a gable-roof, bent down, supported on a staff, with tottering steps, infirm, youth long since fled, with broken teeth, grey and scanty hair, or bald-headed, wrinkled, with blotched limbs? And did the thought never come to you, that you also are subject to decay, that you cannot escape it?

Did you never see in the world a man or a woman, who, being sick, afflicted and grievously ill, and wallowing in one's own filth, was lifted up by some people and put to bed by others? And did the thought never come to you, that you also are subject to disease, that you cannot escape it?

Did you never see in the world the corpse of a man or a woman, one or two or three days after death, swollen up, blue-black in colour, and full of corruption? And did the thought never come to you, that you also are subject to death, that you cannot escape it?

(S.14 (1)) Inconceivable is the beginning of this Samsara, not to be discovered a first beginning of beings, who, obstructed by ignorance and ensnared by craving, are hurrying and hastening through this round of rebirths.

(S.14 (2)) Which do you think is more: the flood of tears, which weeping and wailing you have shed upon this long way —hurrying and hastening through this round of rebirths, united to the undesired, separated from the desired—this or the waters of the four oceans?

Long time have you suffered the death of father and mother, of sons, daughters, brothers and sisters. And whilst you were thus suffering, you have verily shed more tears upon this long way, than there is water in the four oceans.

Which do you think is more: the streams of blood that, through your being beheaded, have flowed upon this long way, or the waters in the four oceans?

Long time have you been caught as dacoits or highway men or adulterers; and, through your being beheaded verily more blood has flowed upon this long way, than there is water in the four oceans.

But how is this possible?

Inconceivable is the beginning of this Samsara, not to be discovered a first beginning of beings, who, obstructed by ignorance and ensnared by craving, are hurrying and hastening through this round of rebirths.

And thus have you long time undergone suffering, undergone torment, undergone misfortune and filled the graveyards full, verily long enough to be dissatisfied with every form of existence, long enough to turn away and free yourselves from them all.

THE SECOND TRUTH

The Noble Truth of
The Origin of Suffering

(D.22) What now is the Noble Truth of the Origin of Suffering? It is that craving which gives rise to fresh rebirth, and, bound up with pleasure and lust, now here, now there, finds ever fresh delight.

There is the Sensual Craving, the Craving for Eternal Existence, the Craving for Temporal Happiness.

But where does this craving arise and take root? Wherever in the world there is the delightful and pleasurable, there this craving arises and takes root. Eye, ear, nose, tongue, body and mind are delightful and pleasurable; there this craving arises and takes root.

Forms, sounds, smells, tastes, bodily touches and ideas are delightful and pleasurable: there this craving arises and takes root.

Consciousness, sense contact, the feeling born of sense contact, perception, will, craving, thinking and reflecting are delightful and pleasurable: there this craving arises and takes root.

(M.38) If namely, when perceiving a visible form, a sound, odour, taste, bodily contact or an idea in the mind, the object is pleasant, one is attracted, and if unpleasant, one is repelled.

Thus, whatever kind of Feeling one experiences,—pleasant, unpleasant or indifferent—one approves of and cherishes the feeling and clings to it; and while doing so, lust springs up; but lust for feelings means clinging to existence (*upadana*); and on clinging to existence depends the (action-) Process of

Becoming (*bhava,* here *kamma-bhava*); on the process of becoming depends (future) Birth (*jati*); and dependent on birth are Decay and Death, sorrow, lamentation, pain, grief and despair. Thus arises this whole mass of suffering.

This is called the Noble Truth of the Origin of Suffering.

(M.13) Verily, due to sensuous craving, conditioned through sensuous craving, impelled by sensuous craving, entirely moved by sensuous craving, kings fight with kings, princes with princes, priests with priests, citizens with citizens; the mother quarrels with the son, the son with the mother, the father with the son, the son with the father; brother quarrels with brother, brother with sister, sister with brother, friend with friend. Thus given to dissension, quarrelling and fighting, they fall upon one another with fists, sticks or weapons. And thereby they suffer death or deadly pain.

And further, due to sensuous craving, conditioned through sensuous craving, impelled by sensuous craving, entirely moved by sensuous craving, people break into houses, rob and plunder, pillage whole houses, commit highway robbery, seduce the wives of others. Then the rulers have such people caught and inflict on them various forms of punishment. And thereby they incur death or deadly pain. Now, this is the misery of sensuous craving, the heaping up of suffering in this present life, due to sensuous craving, conditioned through sensuous craving, caused by sensuous craving, entirely dependent on sensuous craving.

And further, people take the evil way in deeds, the evil way in words, the evil way in thoughts; and by taking the evil way in deeds, words and thoughts, at the dissolution of the body, after death, they fall into a downward state of existence, a state of suffering, into perdition and the abyss of hell. But this is the misery of sensuous craving, the heaping up of suffering in the future life, due to sensuous craving, conditioned through sensuous craving, caused by sensuous craving, entirely dependent on sensuous craving.

(Dhp.182)

> Not in the air, nor ocean-midst,
> Nor hiding in the mountain clefts,
> Not wilt thou find a place on earth,
> Where thou art freed from evil deeds.

(S.35) For: owners of their deeds are the beings, heirs of their deeds, their deeds are the womb from which they sprang, with their deeds they are bound up, their deeds are their refuge. Whatever deeds they do—good or evil—of such they will be the heirs.

(A.III.33) And wherever the beings spring into existence, there their deeds will ripen; and wherever their deeds ripen, there they will earn the fruits of those deeds, be it in this life, or be it in the next life, or be it in any other future life.

(S.21 (10)) There will come a time, when the mighty ocean will dry up, vanish, and be no more. There will come a time, when the mighty earth will be devoured by fire, perish, and be no more. But yet there will be no end to the suffering of beings, who, obstructed by ignorance and ensnared by craving, are hurrying and hastening through this round of rebirths.

THE THIRD TRUTH

The Noble Truth of
The Extinction of Suffering

(D.22) What now is the Noble Truth of the Extinction of Suffering? It is the complete fading away and extinction of this craving, its forsaking and giving up, the liberation and detachment from it.

But where may this craving vanish, where may it be extinguished? Wherever in the world there are delightful and pleasurable things, there this craving may vanish, there it may be extinguished.

(S. 12 (66)) Be it in the past, present or future: whosoever of the monks or priests regards the delightful and pleasurable things in the world as impermanent (*anicca*), miserable (*dukkha*) and without an Ego (*an-atta*), as a disease and sorrow, it is he who overcomes the craving.

(It.96) And released from Sensual Craving, released from the Craving for Existence, he does not return, does not enter again into existence.

(S.12) For, through the total fading away and extinction of Craving (*tanha*) Clinging to Existence (*upadana*) is extinguished; through the extinction of the clinging to existence the (action-) Process of Becoming (*Bhava*) is extinguished; through the extinction of the process of becoming Rebirth (*jati*) is extinguished; and through the extinction of rebirth

Decay and Death, sorrow, lamentation, suffering, grief and despair are extinguished. Thus comes about the extinction of this whole mass of suffering.

Hence, the annihilation, cessation and overcoming of bodily form, feeling, perception, mental formations and consciousness, this is the extinction of suffering, the end of disease, the overcoming of old age and death.

(A.III 32) This, truly, is the Peace, this is the Highest, namely the end of all formations, the forsaking of every substratum of rebirth, the fading away of craving, detachment, extinction, Nibbana.

Enraptured with lust, enraged with anger, blinded by delusion, overwhelmed, with mind ensnared, man aims at his own ruin, at the others' ruin, at the ruin of both parties, and he experiences mental pain and grief. But if lust, anger and delusion are given up, man aims neither at his own ruin, nor at the others' ruin, nor at the ruin of both parties, and he experiences no mental pain and grief. Thus is Nibbana immediate, visible in this life, inviting, attractive and comprehensible to the wise.

(A.III.53) The extinction of greed, the extinction of anger, the extinction of delusion: this indeed is called Nibbana.

(A.VI.55) And for a disciple thus freed, in whose heart dwells peace, there is nothing to be added to what has been done, and naught more remains for him to do. Just as a rock of one solid mass remains unshaken by the wind, even so, neither forms, nor sounds, nor odours, nor tastes, nor contacts of any kind, neither the desired nor the undesired, can cause such an one to waver. Steadfast is his mind, gained is deliverance.

(A.III.32) And he who has considered all the contrasts on this earth and is no more disturbed by anything whatever in the world, the peaceful-One, freed from rage, from sorrow and from longing, he has passed beyond birth and decay.

(Ud.VIII.1.) Verily, there is a realm, where there is neither the solid, nor the fluid, neither heat nor motion, neither this world nor any other world, neither sun nor moon.

This I call neither arising nor passing away, neither standing still, nor being born, nor dying. There is neither foothold, nor development, nor any basis. This is the end of suffering.

(Ud.VIII.3) There is an Unborn, Unoriginated, Uncreated, Unformed. If these were not this Unborn, this Unoriginated, this

Uncreated, this Unformed, escape from the world of the born, the originated, the created, the formed, would not be possible.

But since there is an Unborn, Unoriginated, Uncreated, Unformed, therefore is escape possible from the world of the born, the originated, the created, the formed.

THE FOURTH TRUTH

The Noble Truth of the Path that Leads to the Extinction of Suffering

(S.56) To give oneself up to indulgence in *Sensual Pleasure*, the base, common, vulgar, unholy, unprofitable, and also to give oneself up to *Self-mortification*, the painful, unholy, unprofitable; both these two extremes the Perfect One has avoided and found out the *Middle Path* which makes one both to see and to know, which leads to peace, to discernment, to enlightenment, to Nibbana.

It is the Noble Eightfold Path, the way that leads to the extinction of suffering, namely:

1. Right Understanding, *Samma-ditthi*
2. Right Mindedness, *Samma-sankappa*
3. Right Speech, *Samma-vaca*
4. Right Action, *Samma-kammanta*
5. Right Living, *Samma-ajiva*
6. Right Effort, *Samma-vayama*
7. Right Attentiveness, *Samma-sati*
8. Right Concentration, *Samma-samadhi*

This is the Middle Path which the Perfect One has found out, which makes one both to see and to know, which leads to peace, to discernment, to enlightenment, to Nibbana.

Free from pain and torture is this path, free from groaning and suffering, it is the perfect path.

(Dhp. 274-75) Truly, like this path there is no other path to the purity of insight. If you follow this path, you will put an end to suffering.

(Dhp. 276) But each one has to struggle for himself, the Perfect Ones have only pointed out the way.

(M. 26) Give ear then, for the Immortal is found. I reveal, I set forth the Truth. As I reveal it to you, so act! And that supreme goal of the holy life, for the sake of which sons of good families go forth from home to the homeless state: this you will, in no long time, in this very life, make known to yourself, realise and attain to it.

FIRST STEP

Right Understanding

(D. 22) What now is Right Understanding?

1. To understand suffering; 2. to understand the origin of suffering; 3. to understand the extinction of suffering; 4. to understand the path that leads to the extinction of suffering. This is called Right Understanding.

(M.9) Or, when the noble disciple understands, what demerit is and the root of demerit, what merit is and the root of merit, then he has Right Understanding.

What now is demerit?

1. Destruction of living beings is demerit.
2. Stealing is demerit.
3. Unlawful sexual intercourse is demerit.
4. Lying is demerit.
5. Tale-bearing is demerit.
6. Harsh language is demerit.
7. Frivolous talk is demerit.
8. Covetousness is demerit.
9. Ill-will is demerit.
10. Wrong views are demerit.

[handwritten marginal note: Buddah, More definition is needed]

And what is the root of demerit? Greed is a root of demerit; Anger is a root of demerit; Delusion is a root of demerit.

(A.X.174) Therefore, I say, these demeritorious actions are of three kinds: either due to greed, or due to anger, or due to delusion.

(M.9) What now is merit (*kusala*)?

1. To abstain from killing is merit.
2. To abstain from stealing is merit.
3. To abstain from unlawful sexual intercourse is merit.
4. To abstain from lying is merit.
5. To abstain from tale-bearing is merit.
6. To abstain from harsh language is merit.
7. To abstain from frivolous talk is merit.
8. Absence of covetousness is merit.
9. Absence of ill-will is merit.
10. Right understanding is merit.

And what is the Root of Merit? Absence of greed is a root of merit; absence of anger is a root of merit; absence of delusion is a root of merit.

(S.21 (5)) Or, when one understands that form, feeling, perception, mental formations and consciousness are transient, (subject to suffering and without an Ego) also in that case one possesses Right Understanding.

(M.63) Should anyone say that he does not wish to lead the holy life under the Blessed One, unless the Blessed One first tells him, whether the world is eternal or temporal, finite or infinite; whether the life principle is identical with the body, or something different; whether the Perfect One continues after death etc.—Such an one would die, ere the Perfect One could tell him all this.

It is as if a man were pierced by a poisoned arrow, and his friends, companions, or near relations called in a surgeon, but that man should say: I will not have this arrow pulled out until I know, who the man is, that has wounded me: whether he is a noble, a prince, a citizen, or a servant; or: whether he is tall, or short, or of medium height. Verily, such a man would die, ere he could adequately learn all this.

(Snp. 592) Therefore, the man, who seeks his own welfare, should pull out this arrow—this arrow of lamentation, pain and sorrow.

(M.63) For, whether the theory exists, or whether it does not exist, that the world is eternal, or temporal, or finite, or infinite—certainly, there is birth, there is decay, there is death, sorrow, lamentation, pain, grief, and despair, the extinction of which, attainable even in this present life, I make known unto you.

(M.2) There is, for instance, an unlearned worldling, void of regard for holy men, ignorant of the teaching of holy men, untrained in the noble doctrine. (M.64) And his heart is possessed and overcome by Self-Illusion, by Scepticism, by Attachment to Rule and Ritual, by Sensual Lust and by Ill-will, and how to free himself from these things, he does not really know.

(M.2) Not knowing what is worthy of consideration and what is unworthy of consideration, he considers the unworthy and not the worthy.

And unwisely he considers thus: Have I been in the past? Or, have I not been in the past? What have I been in the past? How have I been in the past? From what state and into what state did I change in the past?—Shall I be in the future? Or, shall I not be in the future? What shall I be in the future? How shall I be in the future? From what state and into what state shall I change in the future?—And the present also fills him with doubt: Am I? Or, am I not? What am I? How am I? This being, whence has it come? Whither will it go?

And with such unwise considerations, he falls into one or other of the six views, and it becomes his conviction and firm belief; I have an Ego; or: I have no Ego; or: With the Ego I perceive the Ego; or: With that which is no Ego I perceive the Ego; or: With the Ego I perceive that which is no Ego. Or, he falls into the following view: This my Ego, which can think and feel, and which, now here, now there, experiences the fruit of good and evil deeds:—this my Ego is permanent, stable, eternal, not subject to change and will thus eternally remain the same.

(M.22) If there really existed the Ego, there would be also something which belonged to the Ego. As, however, in truth and reality, neither an Ego nor anything belonging to an Ego can be found, is it therefore not really an utter fool's doctrine to say: This is the world, this am *I;* after death *I* shall be permanent, persisting and eternal?

These are called mere views, a thicket of views, a puppet-show of views, a snare of views; and ensnared in the fetter of views, the ignorant worldling will not be freed from rebirth, from decay and from death, from sorrow, pain, grief and despair; he will not be freed, I say, from suffering.

(M.2) The learned and noble disciple, however, who has regard for holy men, knows the teaching of holy men, is well trained in the noble doctrine, he understands what is worthy of consideration and what is unworthy. And knowing this, he considers the worthy and not the unworthy. What suffering is, he wisely considers. What the origin of suffering is, he wisely considers; what the extinction of suffering is, he wisely considers; what the path is that leads to the extinction of suffering, he wisely considers.

And by thus considering, three fetters vanish, namely: *Self-illusion, Scepticism* and *Attachment to Rule and Ritual.*

(M.22) But those disciples, in whom these three fetters have vanished, they have all entered the Stream (*sotapanna*), have for ever escaped the states of woe, and are assured of final enlightenment.

(Dhp. 178)

> More than any earthly power,
> More than all the joys of heaven,
> More than rule o'er all the world,
> Is the Entrance to the Stream.

(A.X.63) And verily those, who are filled with unshaken faith towards me, all those have entered the stream.

(M.117) Therefore, I say, Right Understanding is of two kinds:

1. The view that alms and offerings are not useless; that there is fruit and result both of good and bad actions; that there are such things as this life and the next life; that father and mother, as also spontaneously born beings (in the heavenly worlds) are no mere words; that there are in the world monks and priests, who are spotless and perfect, who can explain this life and the next life, which they themselves have understood: —this is called the Mundane Right Understanding, which yields worldly fruits and brings good results.

2. But whatsoever there is of wisdom, of penetration, of right understanding, conjoined with the Path (of the Sotapanna, Sakadagamin, Anagamin or Arahat)—the mind being turned away from the world and conjoined with the path, the holy path being pursued:—this is called the Ultramundane Right Understanding, which is not of the world, but is ultramundane and conjoined with the paths.

(M.117) Now, in understanding wrong understanding as wrong, and right understanding as right, one practices Right Understanding; and in making efforts to overcome wrong understanding, and to arouse right understanding, one practices Right effort; and in overcoming wrong understanding with attentive mind, and dwelling with attentive mind in possession of right understanding, one practises Right Attentiveness. Hence, there are three things that accompany and follow upon right understanding, namely: right understanding, right effort, and right attentiveness.

Now, if any one should put the question, whether I admit any view at all, he should be answered thus:—

(M.72) The Perfect One is free from any theory, for the Perfect One has understood what the body is, and how it arises, and passes away. He has understood what feeling is, and how it arises, and passes away. He has understood what perception is, and how it arises, and passes away. He has understood what the mental formations are, and how they arise, and pass away. He has understood what consciousness is, and how it arises, and passes away. Therefore, I say, the Perfect One has won complete deliverance through the extinction, fading away, disappearance, rejection, and getting rid of all opinions and conjectures, of all inclination to the vainglory of I and mine.

(A.III.134) Whether Perfect Ones (Buddhas) appear in the world, or whether Perfect Ones do not appear in the world, it still remains a firm condition, an immutable fact and fixed law: that all formations are impermanent; that all formations are subject to suffering; that everything is without an Ego.

(S.16 (10)) A bodily form, a feeling, a perception, a mental formation, a consciousness, that is permanent and persistent, eternal and not subject to change, such a thing the wise men in this world do not recognise; and I also say, there is no such thing.

(A.I. 15) And it is impossible that a being possessed of Right Understanding should regard anything as an Ego.

(D.15) Now, if someone should say that feeling is his Ego, he should be answered thus: There are three kinds of feeling: pleasurable, painful, and indifferent feeling. Which of these three feelings now do you consider as your Ego? At the moment namely of experiencing one of these feelings, one does not experience the other two. These three kinds of feeling are impermanent, of dependent origin, are subject to decay and dissolution, to fading away and extinction. Whosoever, in experiencing one of these feelings, thinks that this is his Ego, will, after the extinction of that feeling, admit that his Ego has become dissolved. And thus he will consider his Ego already in his present life as impermanent, mixed up with pleasure and pain, subject to rising and passing away.

If any one should say that feeling is not his Ego, and that his Ego is inaccessible to feeling, he should be asked thus: Now, where there is no feeling, is it there possible to say: This am I?

Or, someone might say: Feeling indeed is not my Ego, but also it is untrue that my Ego is inaccessible to feeling; for it is my Ego that feels, for my Ego has the faculty of feeling. Such a one should be answered thus: Suppose, feeling should become altogether totally extinguished; now, if there, after the extinction of feeling, no feeling whatever exists, is it then possible to say: This am I?

To say that the mind, or the mind-objects, or the mind-consciousness constitute the Ego: such an assertion is unfounded. For an arising and a passing away is seen there; and seeing the arising and passing away of these things, one should come to the conclusion that one's Ego arises and passes away.

(S.21 (7)) It would be better for the unlearned worldling to regard this body, built up of the four elements, as his Ego, rather than the mind. For it is evident that this body may last for a year, for two years, for three, four, five, or ten years, or even for a hundred years and more; but that which is called thought, or mind, or mind-consciousness, is continuously, during day and night, arising as one thing and passing away as another thing.

(S.21 (5)) Therefore, whatsoever there is of bodily form, of feeling, of perception, of mental formations, of consciousness, whether one's own or external, gross or subtle, lofty or low, far or near: there one should understand according to reality and true wisdom: This does not belong to me; this am I not; this is not my Ego.

(D.9) If now any one should ask: Have you been in the past, and is it untrue that you have not been? Will you be in the future, and is it untrue that you will not be? Are you, and is it untrue that you are not?—you ought to say that you have been in the past, and that it is untrue that you have not been; that you will be in the future, and that it is untrue that you will not be; that you are, and that it is untrue that you are not.

In the past only the past existence was real, but unreal the future and present existence. In the future only the future existence will be real, but unreal the past and present existence. Now only the present existence is real, but unreal the past and future existence.

Verily, he who perceives the Dependent Origination (patic-ca-samuppada) perceives the truth; and he who perceives the truth perceives the dependent origination. For, just as from the cow comes the milk, from milk curds, from curds butter, from butter ghee, from ghee the scum (of ghee); and when it is milk, it is not counted as curds or butter or ghee or scum of ghee, but only as milk; and when it is curds, it is only counted as curds:—even so was my past existence at that time real, but unreal the future and present existence; and my future existence will be at one time real, but unreal the past and present existence; and my present existence is now real, but unreal the past and future existence. All these are merely popular designations and expressions, mere conventional terms of speaking, mere popular notions. The Perfect One, indeed, makes use of these, without, however, clinging to them.

(S.42) Thus, he who does not understand bodily form, feeling, perception, mental formations and consciousness according to reality (*i.e.* as void of a personality or Ego), and not their arising, their extinction, and the way to their extinction, he is liable to believe, either that the Perfect One continues after death, or that he does not continue after death, and so forth.

(A.III.61) Verily, if one holds the view that the vital principle (Ego) is identical with this body, in that case a holy life is not possible; or, if one holds the view that the vital principle is something quite different from the body, in that case also a holy life is not possible. Both these two Extremes the Perfect One has avoided and shown the Middle Doctrine, which says:

On Delusion (*avijja*) depend the (life-affirming) Activities (*sankhara*).—On the Activities depends Consciousness (*vinnana*: here, rebirth-consciousness in the womb of the mother). —On consciousness depends the Psycho-physical Combination (*nama-rupa*).—On the psycho-physical combination depends the Sixfold Sense-activity (*chal-ayatana*).—On the sixfold sense-activity depends the Sensorial Impression (*phassa*).—On the sensorial impression depends Feeling (*vedana*).—On feeling depends Craving (*tanha*).—On craving depends Clinging to Existence (*upadana*).—On clinging to existence depends the Process of Becoming (*bhava;* here: *kamma-bhava,* or action process).— On the process of becoming depends Rebirth (*jati*).—On rebirth depends Decay and Death (*jara-marana*), sorrow, lamentation, pain, grief and despair. Thus arises this whole mass of suffering. This is called the noble truth of the origin of suffering.

(S.12 (6)) In whom, however, Delusion has disappeared and

wisdom arisen, such a disciple heaps up neither meritorious, nor demeritorious activities, nor activities leading to immovability.

(A.III.61) Thus, through the entire fading away and extinction of this Delusion, the (life-affirming) Activities are extinguished. Through the extinction of the activities Consciousness (rebirth) is extinguished. Through the extinction of consciousness, the Psycho-physical combination is extinguished. Through the extinction of the psycho-physical combination, the sixfold Sense-activity is extinguished. Through the extinction of the sixfold sense-activity, the Sensorial Impression is extinguished. Through the extinction of the sensorial impression, Feeling is extinguished. Through the extinction of feeling, Craving is extinguished. Through the extinction of craving, Clinging to Existence is extinguished. Through the extinction of clinging to existence, the Process of Becoming is extinguished. Through the extinction of the process of becoming, Rebirth is extinguished. Through the extinction of rebirth, decay and death, sorrow, lamentation, pain, grief and despair are extinguished. Thus takes place the extinction of this whole mass of suffering. This is called the noble truth of the extinction of suffering.

(M.43) Verily, because beings, obstructed by delusion and ensnared by craving, now here, now there, seek ever fresh delight, therefore it comes to ever fresh rebirth.

(A.III.33) And the action (*kamma*) that is done out of greed, anger and delusion (*lobha, dosa, moha*), that springs from them, has its source and origin there:—this action ripens wherever one is reborn; and wherever this action ripens, there one experiences the fruits of this action, be it in this life, or the next life, or in some future life.

(M.43) However, through the fading away of delusion, through the arising of wisdom, through the extinction of craving, no future rebirth takes place again.

(A.III.33) For the actions, which are not done out of greed, anger and delusion, which have not sprung from them, which have not their source and origin there:—such actions are, through the absence of greed, anger and delusion, abandoned, rooted out, like a palm tree torn out of the soil, destroyed, and not liable to spring up again.

(A.VIII.12) In this respect one may rightly say of me, that I teach annihilation, that I propound my doctrine for the purpose of annihilation, and that I herein train my disciples. For, certainly, I teach annihilation,—the annihilation namely of greed, anger and delusion, as well as of the manifold evil and demeritorious things.

SECOND STEP
Right Mindedness

(D.22) What now is Right Mindedness?
1. The thought free from lust.
2. The thought free from ill-will.
3. The thought free from cruelty.
This is called right mindedness.

(M.117) Now, right mindedness, let me tell you, is of two kinds:
1. The thoughts free from lust, from ill-will, and from cruelty:—this is called the Mundane Right Mindedness, which yields worldly fruits and brings good results.
2. But, whatsoever there is of thinking, considering, reasoning, thought, ratiocination, application—the mind being holy, being turned away from the world and conjoined with the path, the holy path being pursued:—these Verbal Operations of the mind are called the Ultramundane Right Mindedness, which is not of the world, but is ultramundane and conjoined with the paths.

Now, in understanding wrong-mindedness as wrong and right-mindedness as right, one practises Right Understanding; and in making efforts to overcome evil mindedness, and to arouse right mindedness, one practises Right Effort; and in overcoming evil-mindedness with attentive mind, and dwelling with attentive mind in possession of right mindedness, one practises Right Attentiveness. Hence, there are three things that accompany and follow upon right mindedness, namely: right understanding, right effort, and right attentiveness.

THIRD STEP
Right Speech

(A.X. 176) What now is Right Speech?
1. There, someone avoids lying, and abstains from it. He speaks the truth, is devoted to the truth, reliable, worthy of confidence, is not a deceiver of men. Being at a meeting, or

amongst people, or in the midst of his relatives, or in a society, or in the king's court, and called upon and asked as witness, to tell what he knows, he answers, if he knows nothing: I know nothing, and if he knows, he answers: I know; if he has seen nothing, he answers: I have seen nothing, and if he has seen, he answers: I have seen. Thus, he never knowingly speaks a lie, neither for the sake of his own advantage, nor for the sake of another person's advantage, nor for the sake of any advantage whatsoever.

2. He avoids tale-bearing, and abstains from it. What he has heard here, he does not repeat there, so as to cause dissension there; and what he has heard there, he does not repeat here, so as to cause dissension here. Thus he unites those that are divided, and those that are united he encourages. Concord gladdens him, he delights and rejoices in concord; and it is concord that he spreads by his words.

3. He avoids harsh language, and abstains from it. He speaks such words as are gentle, soothing to the ear, loving, going to the heart, courteous and dear, and agreeable to many.

4. He avoids vain talk, and abstains from it. He speaks at the right time, in accordance with facts, speaks what is useful, speaks about the law and the discipline; his speech is like a treasure, at the right moment accompanied by arguments, moderate and full of sense.

This is called right speech.

(M.117) Now right speech, let me tell you, is of two kinds:

1. Abstaining from lying, from tale-bearing, from harsh language, and from vain talk; this is called the Mundane Right Speech which yields worldly fruits and brings good results.

2. But the abhorrence of the practice of this fourfold wrong speech, the abstaining, withholding, refraining therefrom, the mind being holy, being turned away from the world and conjoined with the path, the holy path being pursued;—this is called the Ultramundane Right Speech, which is not of the world, but is ultramundane and conjoined with the paths.

Now, in understanding wrong speech as wrong, and right speech as right, one practises Right Understanding; and in making efforts to overcome evil speech, and to arouse right speech, one practises Right Effort; and in overcoming wrong speech with attentive mind, and dwelling with attentive mind in possession of right speech, one practises Right Attentiveness.

Hence, there are three things that accompany and follow upon right speech, namely: right understanding, right effort, and right attentiveness.

FOURTH STEP

Right Action

What now is Right Action?

(A.X. 176) 1. There someone avoids the killing of living beings, and abstains from it. Without stick or sword, conscientious, full of sympathy, he is anxious for the welfare of all living beings.

2. He avoids stealing, and abstains from it; what another person possesses of goods and chattels in the village or in the wood, that he does not take away with thievish intent.

3. He avoids unlawful sexual intercourse, and abstains from it. He has no intercourse with such persons as are still under the protection of father, mother, brother, sister or relatives, nor with married women, nor female convicts, nor even with flower-decked (engaged) girls.

This is called right action.

(M. 117) Now right action, let me tell you, is of two kinds:

1. Abstaining from killing, from stealing, and from unlawful sexual intercourse:—this is called the Mundane Right Action, which yields worldly fruits and brings good results.

2. But the abhorrence of the practice of this three-fold wrong action, the abstaining, withholding, refraining therefrom —the mind being holy, being turned away from the world and conjoined with the path, the holy path being pursued:—this is called the Ultramundane Right Action, which is not of the world, but is ultramundane and conjoined with the paths.

Now, in understanding wrong action as wrong, and right action as right, one practises Right Understanding; and in making efforts to overcome wrong action, and to arouse right action, one practises Right Effort; and in overcoming wrong action with attentive mind, and dwelling with attentive mind in possession of right action, one practises Right Attentiveness. Hence, there are three things that accompany and follow upon right action, namely: right understanding, right effort, and right attentiveness.

Fifth Step

Right Living

(D. 22) What now is Right Living?

When the noble disciple, avoiding a wrong living, gets his livelihood by a right way of living, this is called right living.

(M. 117) Now, right living, let me tell you, is of two kinds:

1. When the noble disciple, avoiding wrong living, gets his livelihood by a right way of living:—this is called the Mundane Right Living, which yields worldly fruits and brings good results.

2. But the abhorrence of wrong living, the abstaining, withholding, refraining therefrom—the mind being holy, being turned away from the world and conjoined with the path, the holy path being pursued:—this is called the Ultramundane Right Living (*lokuttara-samma-ajiva*), which is not of the world, but is ultramundane and conjoined with the paths.

Now, in understanding wrong living as wrong, and right living as right, one practises Right Understanding; and in making efforts to overcome wrong living, to arouse right living, one practises Right Effort; and in overcoming wrong living with attentive mind, and dwelling with attentive mind in possession of right living, one practises Right Attentiveness. Hence, there are three things that accompany and follow upon right living, namely: right understanding, right effort, and right attentiveness.

Sixth Step

Right Effort

What now is Right Effort?

(A.IV.13,14) There are Four Great Efforts: the effort to avoid, the effort to overcome, the effort to develop, and the effort to maintain.

1. What now is the effort to avoid? There the disciple incites his mind to avoid the arising of evil, demeritorious things, that have not yet arisen; and he strives, puts forth his energy, strains his mind and struggles.

Thus, when he perceives a form with the eye, a sound with the ear, an odour with the nose, a taste with the tongue, a contact with the body, or an object with the mind, he neither adheres to the whole, nor to its parts. And he strives to ward off that, through which evil and demeritorious things, greed and sorrow, would arise, if he remained with unguarded senses; and he watches over his senses, restrains his senses.

Possessed of this noble Control over the Senses, he experiences inwardly a feeling of joy, into which no evil thing can enter.

This is called the effort to avoid.

2. What now is the effort to overcome? There the disciple incites his mind to overcome the evil and demeritorious things, that have already arisen; and he strives, puts forth his energy, strains his mind and struggles.

He does not retain any thought of sensual lust, ill-will or grief, or any other evil and demeritorious states, that may have arisen; he abandons them, dispels them, destroys them, causes them to disappear.

(M. 20) If, whilst regarding a certain object, there arise, on account of it, in the disciple evil and demeritorious thoughts connected with greed, anger and delusion, then the disciple (1) should, by means of this object, gain another and wholesome object. (2) Or, he should reflect on the misery of these thoughts: Unwholesome truly are these thoughts! Blamable are these thoughts! Of painful result are these thoughts! (3) Or, he should pay no attention to these thoughts. (4) Or, he should consider the compounded nature of these thoughts. (5) Or, with teeth clenched and tongue pressed against the gums, he should with his mind restrain, suppress and root out these thoughts; and in doing so, these evil and demeritorious thoughts of greed, anger and delusion will dissolve and disappear, and the mind will inwardly become settled and calm, composed and concentrated.

This is called the effort to overcome.

(A.IV.13,14) 3. What now is the effort to develop? There the disciple incites his will to arouse meritorious conditions, that have not yet arisen; and he strives, puts forth his energy, strains his mind and struggles.

Thus he develops the Elements of Enlightenment (*bojjhanga*), bent on solitude, on detachment, on extinction, and ending in deliverance, namely: Attentiveness, Investigation of the Law, Energy, Rapture, Tranquillity, Concentration, and Equanimity.

This is called the effort to develop.

4. What now is the effort to maintain? There the disciple incites his will to maintain the meritorious conditions that have already arisen, and not to let them disappear, but to bring them to growth, to maturity and to the full perfection of development (*bhavana*); and he strives, puts forth his energy, strains his mind and struggles.

Thus, for example, he keeps firmly in his mind a favourable object of concentration that has arisen, as the mental image of a skeleton, of a corpse infested by worms, of a corpse riddled with holes, of a corpse swollen up.

This is called the effort to maintain.

(M. 70) Truly the disciple, who is possessed of faith and has penetrated the Teaching of the Master, is filled with the thought; May rather skin, sinews and bones wither away, may the flesh and blood of my body dry up; I shall not give up my efforts so long as I have not attained whatever is attainable by manly perseverance, energy and endeavour!

This is called right effort.

(A.IV. 14)

> The effort of avoiding, overcoming,
> Of developing and maintaining:
> Such four great efforts have been shown
> By him, the scion of the sun.
> And he who firmly clings to them
> May put an end to all the pain.

SEVENTH STEP

Right Attentiveness

What now is Right Attentiveness?

(D. 22) The only way that leads to the attainment of purity, to the overcoming of sorrow and lamentation, to the end of pain and grief, to the entering upon the right path and the realisation of Nibbana, is the Four Fundamentals of Attentiveness. And which are these four?

There the disciple lives in contemplation of the Body, in contemplation of Feeling, in contemplation of the Mind, in contemplation of Phenomena, ardent, clearly conscious and attentive, after putting away worldly greed and grief.

1. Contemplation of the Body.

But how does the disciple dwell in the contemplation of the body? There the disciple retires to the forest, to the foot of a tree, or to a solitary place, sits himself down, with legs crossed, body erect, and with attentiveness fixed before him.

With attentive mind he breathes in, with attentive mind he breathes out. When making a long inhalation, he knows: I make a long inhalation; when making a long exhalation, he knows: I make a long exhalation. When making a short inhalation, he knows: I make a short inhalation; when making a short exhalation, he knows: I make a short exhalation. Clearly perceiving the entire (breath-) body, I will breathe out: thus he trains himself. Calming this bodily function, (*kaya-sankhara*), I will breathe in: thus he trains himself; calming this bodily function, I will breathe out: thus he trains himself.

Thus he dwells in contemplation of the body, either with regard to his own person, or to other persons, or to both. He beholds, how the body arises; beholds how it passes away; beholds the arising and passing away of the body. A body is there—this clear consciousness is present in him, because of his knowledge and mindfulness, and he lives independent, unattached to anything in the world. Thus does the disciple dwell in contemplation of the body.

(D. 22) And further, whilst going, standing, sitting or lying down, the disciple understands (according to reality the expressions): I go; I stand; I sit; I lie down; he understands any position of the body.

And further, the disciple is clearly conscious in his going and coming; clearly conscious in looking forward and backward; clearly conscious in bending and stretching (any part of his body); clearly conscious in eating, drinking, chewing and tasting: clearly conscious in discharging excrement and urine; clearly conscious in walking, standing, sitting, falling asleep and awakening; clearly conscious in speaking and in keeping silent.

And further, the disciple contemplates this body from the sole of the foot upward, and from the top of the hair downward, with a skin stretched over it, and filled with manifold impurities: This body consists of hairs, nails, teeth, skin, flesh, sinews, bones, marrow, kidneys, heart, liver, diaphragm, spleen, lungs, intestines, bowels, stomach, and excrement; of bile, phlegm, pus, blood, sweat, lymph, tears, serum, spittle, nasal mucus, oil of the joints, and urine.

Just as if there were a sack, with openings at both ends, filled with all kinds of grain,—with paddy, beans, sesamum and husked rice—and a man not blind opened it and examined its contents, thus: That is paddy, these are beans, this is sesamum, this is husked rice; even so does the disciple investigate this body.

And further, the disciple contemplates this body with regard to the elements: This body consists of the solid element, the liquid element, the heating element, and the vibrating element. Just as a skilled butcher or butcher's apprentice, who has slaughtered a cow and divided it into separate portions, should sit down at the junction of four highroads; just so does the disciple contemplate this body with regard to the elements.

Thus he dwells in contemplation of the body, either with regard to his own person, or to other persons, or to both. He beholds, how the body arises; beholds how it passes away; beholds the arising and passing away of the body. A body is there: this clear consciousness is present in him, because of his knowledge and mindfulness, and he lives independent, unattached to anything in the world. Thus does the disciple dwell in contemplation of the body.

(M. 119) Once the contemplation of the body is practised, developed, often repeated, has become one's habit, one's foundation, is firmly established, strengthened and well perfected, one may expect ten blessings:

Over Delight and Discontent one has mastery; one does not allow one's self to be overcome by discontent; one subdues it as soon as it arises.

One conquers Fear and Anxiety; one does not allow one's self to be overcome by fear and anxiety; one subdues them as soon as they arise.

One endures cold and heat, hunger and thirst, wind and sun, attacks by gadflies, mosquitoes and reptiles; patiently one endures wicked and malicious speech, as well as bodily pains, that befall one, though they be piercing, sharp, bitter, unpleasant, disagreeable and dangerous to life.

The four Trances (*jhana*), the mind-purifying, bestowing-happiness even here: these one may enjoy at will, without difficulty, without effort.

(1) One may enjoy the different Magical Powers (*iddhi-vidha*).

(2) With the Heavenly Ear (*dibba-sota*), the purified, the super-human, one may hear both kinds of sounds, the heavenly and the earthly, the distant and the near.

(3) With the mind one may obtain Insight into the Hearts of Other Beings (*parassa cetoparinna-nana*), of other persons.

(4) One may obtain Remembrance of many Previous Births (*pubbenivas' anussati-nana*).

(5) With the Heavenly Eye (*dibba-cakkhu*), the purified, the super-human, one may see beings vanish and reappear, the base and the noble, the beautiful and the ugly, the happy and the unfortunate; one may perceive how beings are reborn according to their deeds.

(6) One may, through the Cessation of Passions (*asavak-khaya*), come to know for oneself, even in this life, the stainless deliverance of mind, the deliverance through wisdom.

(D. 22)   2. Contemplation of the Feelings.

But how does the disciple dwell in the contemplation of the feelings?

In experiencing feelings, the disciple knows: I have an agreeable feeling, or: I have a disagreeable feeling, or: I have an indifferent feeling; or: I have a worldly agreeable feeling, or: I have an unworldly agreeable feeling; or: I have a worldly disagreeable feeling, or: I have an unworldly disagreeable feeling; or: I have a worldly indifferent feeling, or: I have an unworldly indifferent feeling.

Thus he dwells in contemplation of the feelings, either with regard to his own person, or to other persons, or to both. He beholds how the feelings arise; beholds how they pass away; beholds the arising and passing away of the feelings. Feelings are there: this clear consciousness is present in him, because of his knowledge and mindfulness, and he lives independent, unattached to anything in the world. Thus does the disciple dwell in contemplation of the feelings.

3. Contemplation of the Mind.

(D. 22) But how does the disciple dwell in contemplation of the mind?

There the disciple knows the greedy mind as greedy, and the not-greedy mind as not-greedy; knows the angry mind as angry, and the not-angry mind as not-angry; knows the deluded mind as deluded, and the undeluded mind as undeluded. He knows the composed mind as composed, and the scattered mind as scattered; knows the developed mind as developed, and the undeveloped mind as undeveloped; knows the surpassable mind as surpassable, and the unsurpassable mind as unsurpassable; knows the concentrated mind as concentrated, and the unconcentrated mind as unconcentrated; knows the freed mind as freed, and the unfreed mind as unfreed.

Thus he dwells in contemplation of the mind, either with regard to his own person, or to other persons, or to both. He beholds how the mind arises; beholds how it passes away; beholds the arising and passing away of the mind. Mind is there: this clear consciousness is present in him, because of his knowledge and mindfulness, and he lives independent, unattached to anything in the world. Thus does the disciple dwell in contemplation of the mind.

4. Contemplation of the Phenomena.

But how does the disciple dwell in contemplation of the phenomena?

There the disciple dwells in contemplation of the phenomena, namely of the Five Hindrances.

He knows when there is Lust in him: In me is lust; knows when there is Anger in him: In me is anger; knows when there is Torpor and Drowsiness in him: In me is torpor and drowsiness; knows when there is Restlessness and Mental Worry in him: In me is restlessness and mental worry; knows when there are Doubts in him: In me are doubts. He knows when these hindrances are not in him: In me these hindrances are not. He knows how they come to arise; knows how, once arisen, they are overcome; knows how, once overcome, they do not rise again in the future.

And further: the disciple dwells in contemplation of the phenomena, namely of the five Aggregates of Existence. He knows, what Bodily Form (*rupa*) is, how it arises, how it passes away; knows what Feeling (*vedana*) is, how it arises, how it passes away; knows what Perception (*sanna*) is, how it arises, how it passes away; knows what the Mental Formations (*sankhara*) are, how they arise, how they pass away; knows what Consciousness (*vinnana*) is, how it arises, how it passes away.

And further: the disciple dwells in contemplation of the phenomena, namely of the six Subjective-Objective Sense-Factors. He knows eye and forms, ear and sounds, nose and odours, tongue and tastes, body and touches, mind and ideas; and the fetter that arises in dependence on them, he also knows. He knows how the fetter comes to arise, knows how the fetter is overcome, and how the abandoned fetter does not rise again in future.

And further: the disciple dwells in contemplation of the phenomena, namely of the seven Elements of Enlightenment. The disciple knows when there is Attentiveness in him; when there is Investigation of the Law in him; when there is Enthusiasm in him; when there is Tranquillity in him; when there is Concentration in him; when there is Equanimity in him. He knows when it is not in him; knows how it comes to arise, and how it is fully developed.

And further: the disciple dwells in contemplation of the phenomena, namely of the Four Noble Truths. He knows according to reality, what Suffering is; knows according to reality, what the Origin of suffering is; knows according to reality, what the Extinction of suffering is; knows according to reality, what the Path is, that leads to the extinction of suffering.

Thus he dwells in contemplation of the phenomena, either with regard to his own person, or to other persons, or to both. He beholds how the phenomena arise; beholds how they pass away; beholds the arising and passing away of the phenomena. Phenomena are there: this clear consciousness is present in him, because of his knowledge and mindfulness, and he lives independent, unattached to anything in the world. Thus does the disciple dwell in contemplation of the phenomena.

The only way that leads to the attainment of purity, to the overcoming of sorrow and lamentation, to the end of pain and grief, to the entering upon the right path and the realisation of Nibbana, is these four fundamentals of attentiveness.

(M. 118) Watching over In- and Out-breathing, practised and developed, brings the Four Fundamentals of Attentiveness to perfection; the four fundamentals of attentiveness, practised and developed, bring the seven Elements of Enlightenment to perfection; the seven elements of enlightenment, practised and developed, bring Wisdom and Deliverance to perfection.

But how does Watching over In- and Out-breathing, practised and developed, bring the four Fundamentals of Attentiveness to perfection?

1. Whenever the disciple (a) is conscious in making a long inhalation or exhalation, or (b) in making a short inhalation or exhalation, or (c) is training himself to inhale or exhale whilst feeling the whole (breath-) body, or (d) whilst calming down this bodily function (*i.e.* the breath)—at such a time the disciple is dwelling in contemplation of the body, full of energy, clearly conscious, attentive, after subduing worldly greed and grief. For, inhalation and exhalation I call one amongst the bodily things.

2. Whenever the disciple is training himself to inhale or exhale (a) whilst feeling, rapture, or (b) joy, or (c) the mental functions, or (d) whilst calming down the mental functions—at such a time he is dwelling in contemplation of the feelings, full of energy, clearly conscious, attentive after subduing worldly greed and grief. For, the full awareness of in- and out-breathing I call one amongst the feelings.

3. Whenever the disciple is training himself to inhale or exhale (a) whilst feeling the mind, or (b) whilst gladdening the mind, or (c) whilst concentrating the mind, or (d) whilst setting the mind free—at such a time he is dwelling in contemplation of the mind, full of energy, clearly conscious, attentive, after subduing worldly greed and grief. For, without attentiveness and clear consciousness, I say, there is no Watching over In- and Out-breathing.

4. Whenever the disciple is training himself to inhale or exhale, whilst contemplating (a) impermanency, or (b) the fading away of passion, or (c) extinction, or (d) detachment—at such a time he is dwelling in contemplation of the phenomena, full of energy, clearly conscious, attentive, after subduing worldly greed and grief.

Watching over in- and out-breathing, thus practised and developed, brings the four fundamentals of attentiveness to perfection.

But how do the four fundamentals of attentiveness, practised and developed, bring the seven Elements of Enlightenment to full perfection?

1. Whenever the disciple is dwelling in contemplation on the body, feelings, mind and phenomena, strenuous, clearly conscious, attentive, after subduing worldly greed and grief—at such a time his attentiveness is undisturbed; and whenever his attentiveness is present and undisturbed, at such a time he has gained and is developing the Element of Enlightenment Attentiveness; and thus this element of enlightenment reaches fullest perfection.

2. And whenever, whilst dwelling with attentive mind, he wisely investigates, examines and thinks over the Law (*dhamma*)—at such a time he has gained and is developing the Element of Enlightenment Investigation of the Law; and thus this element of enlightenment reaches fullest perfection.

3. And whenever, whilst wisely investigating, examining and thinking over the law, his energy is firm and unshaken—at such a time he has gained and is developing the Element of Enlightenment Energy; and thus the element of enlightenment reaches fullest perfection.

4. And whenever in him, whilst firm in energy, arises supersensuous rapture at such a time he has gained and is developing the Element of Enlightenment Rapture; and thus this element of enlightenment reaches fullest perfection.

5. And whenever, whilst enraptured in mind, his body and mind becomes tranquil at such a time he has gained and is developing the Element of Enlightenment Tranquillity; and thus this element of enlightenment reaches fullest perfection.

6. And whenever, whilst tranquillised in body and happy, his mind becomes concentrated—at such a time he has gained and is developing the Element of Enlightenment Concentration; and thus this element of enlightenment reaches fullest perfection.

7. And whenever he thoroughly looks with indifference to his mind thus concentrated—at such a time he has gained and is developing the Element of Enlightenment Equanimity.

The four fundamentals of attentiveness, thus practised and developed, bring the seven elements of enlightenment to full perfection.

But how do the seven elements of enlightenment, practised and developed, bring Wisdom and Deliverance to full perfection?

There the disciple is developing the elements of enlightenment: Attentiveness, Investigation of the Law, Energy, Rapture, Tranquillity, Concentration and Equanimity, bent on detachment, absence of desire, extinction and renunciation.

Thus practised and developed do the seven elements of enlightenment bring wisdom and deliverance to full perfection.

(M. 125) Just as the elephant hunter drives a huge stake into the ground and chains the wild elephant to it by the neck, in order to drive out of him his wonted forest ways and wishes, his forest unruliness, obstinacy and violence, and to accustom him to the environment of the village, and to teach him such good behaviour as is required amongst men:—in like manner also has the noble disciple to fix his mind firmly to these four fundamentals of attentiveness, so that he may drive out of himself his wonted worldly ways and wishes, his wonted worldly unruliness, obstinacy and violence, and win to the True and realise Nibbana.

EIGHTH STEP

Right Concentration

(M. 44) What now is Right Concentration?

Fixation of the mind to a single object, (lit. One-pointedness of mind);—this is concentration.

The four Fundamentals of Attentiveness;—these are the objects of concentration.

The four Great Efforts:—these are the requisites for concentration.

The practising, developing and cultivating of these things:—this is the Development of concentration.

(M. 141) Detached from sensual objects, detached from demeritorious things, the disciple enters into the first trance, which is accompanied by Verbal Thought and Rumination, is born of Detachment, and filled with Rapture and Happiness.

(M. 43) This first trance is free from five things, and five things are present: when the disciple enters the first trance, there have vanished (the 5 Hindrances): Lust, Ill-will, Torpor and Dullness, Restlessness and Mental Worry, Doubts; and there are present: Verbal Thought, Rumination, Rapture, Happiness, and Concentration.

(M. 27) And further: after the subsiding of verbal thought and rumination, and by the gaining of inward tranquillisation and oneness of mind, he enters into a state free from verbal thought and rumination, the second trance, which is born of Concentration and filled with Rapture and Happiness.

And further: after the fading away of rapture, he dwells in equanimity, attentive, clearly conscious, and he experiences in his person that feeling, of which the noble Ones say: Happy lives the man of equanimity and attentive mind—thus he enters the third trance.

And further: after the giving up of pleasure and pain, and through the disappearance of previous joy and grief, he enters into a state beyond pleasure and pain, into the fourth trance, which is purified by equanimity and attentiveness.

(S. 21 (1)) Develop your concentration; for he who has concentration understands things according to their reality. And what are these things? The arising and passing away of bodily form, of feeling, perception, mental formations and consciousness.

(M. 149) Thus these five Aggregates of existence must be wisely penetrated; delusion and craving must be wisely abandoned; Tranquillity and Insight must be wisely developed.

(S. 56) This is the Middle Path which the Perfect One has discovered, which makes one both to see and to know, and which leads to peace, to discernment, to enlightenment, to Nibbana.

(Dhp. 627) And following upon this path you will put an end to suffering.

GRADUAL REALISATION OF THE EIGHTFOLD PATH IN THE PROGRESS OF THE DISCIPLE

(A. IV. 198) Suppose, a householder, or his son, or someone reborn in any family hears the law, and after hearing the law he is filled with confidence in the Perfect One. And filled with this confidence, he thinks: Full of hindrances is household life, a refuse heap; but pilgrim life is like the open air. Not easy is it, when one lives at home, to fulfill point by point the rules of the holy life. How, if now I were to cut off hair and beard, put on the yellow robe and go forth from home to the homeless life? And in a short time, having given up his more or less extensive possessions, having forsaken a smaller or larger circle of relations, he cuts off hair and beard, puts on the yellow robe, and goes forth from home to the homeless life.

Having thus left the world, he fulfills the rules of the monks. He avoids the killing of living beings and abstains from it. Without stick or sword, conscientious, full of sympathy, he is anxious for the welfare of all living beings.—He avoids stealing and abstains from taking what is not given to him. Only what is given to him he takes, waiting till it is given; and he lives with a heart honest and pure.—He avoids unchastity, living chaste, resigned, and keeping aloof from sexual intercourse and the vulgar.—He avoids lying and abstains from it. He speaks the truth, is devoted to the truth, reliable, worthy of confidence, is not a deceiver of men.—He avoids tale-bearing and abstains from it. What he has heard here, he does not repeat there, so as to cause dissension there; and what he has heard there, he does not repeat here, so as to cause dissension here. Thus he unites those that are divided, and those that are united he encourages; concord gladdens him, he delights and rejoices in concord; and it is concord that he spreads by his words.—He avoids harsh language and abstains from it. He speaks such words as are gentle, soothing to the ear, loving, going to the heart, courteous and dear, and agreeable to many. —He avoids vain talk and abstains from it. He speaks at the right time, in accordance with facts, speaks what is useful, speaks about the law and the discipline; his speech is like a treasure, at the right moment accompanied by arguments, moderate, and full of sense.

He keeps aloof from dance, song, music and the visiting of shows; rejects flowers, perfumes, ointment, as well as every kind of adornment and embellishment. High and gorgeous beds he does not use. Raw corn and meat he does not accept. Women and girls he does not accept. He owns no male and female slaves, owns no goats, sheep, fowls, pigs, elephants, cows or horses, no land and goods. He does not go on errands and do the duties of a messenger. He keeps aloof from buying and selling things. He has nothing to do with false measures, metals and weights. He avoids crooked ways of bribery, deception and fraud. He keeps aloof from stabbing, beating, chaining, attacking, plundering and oppressing.

He contents himself with the robe that protects his body, and with the alms with which he keeps himself alive. Wherever he goes he is provided with these two things, just as a winged bird, in flying, carries his wings along with him. By fulfilling this noble Domain of Morality he feels in his heart an irreproachable happiness.

Now, in perceiving a form with the eye—a sound with the ear—an odour with the nose—a taste with the tongue—a touch with the body—an object with his mind, he sticks neither to the whole, nor to its details. And he tries to ward off that, which, by being unguarded in his senses, might give rise to evil and demeritorious states, to greed and sorrow; he watches over his senses, keeps his senses under control. By practising this noble Control of the Senses he feels in his heart an unblemished happiness.

Clearly conscious is he in his going and coming; clearly conscious in looking forward and backward; clearly conscious in bending and stretching his body; clearly conscious in eating, drinking, chewing and tasting; clearly conscious in discharging excrement and urine; clearly conscious in walking, standing, sitting, falling asleep and awakening; clearly conscious in speaking and keeping silent.

Now, being equipped with this lofty Morality (sila), equipped with this noble Control of the Senses (indriya-samvara), and filled with this noble Attentiveness and Clear Consciousness, he chooses a secluded dwelling in the forest, at the foot of a tree, on a mountain, in a cleft, in a rock cave, on a burial ground, on a woody table-land, in the open air, or on a heap of straw. Having returned from his alms-round, he, after the meal, sits himself down with legs crossed, body erect, with attentiveness fixed before him.

He has cast away Lust; he dwells with a heart free from lust; from lust he cleanses his heart.

He has cast away Ill-will; he dwells with a heart free from ill-will; cherishing love and compassion toward all living beings, he cleanses his heart from ill-will.

He has cast away Torpor and Dulness; he dwells free from torpor and dulness; loving the light, with watchful mind, with clear consciousness, he cleanses his mind from torpor and dulness.

He has cast away Restlessness and Mental Worry; dwelling with mind undisturbed, with heart full of peace, he cleanses his mind from restlessness and mental worry.

He has cast away Doubt; dwelling free from doubt, full of confidence in the good, he cleanses his heart from doubt.

He has put aside these five Hindrances and learnt to know the paralysing corruptions of the mind. And far from sensual impressions, far from demeritorious things, he enters into the Four Trances.

(A. IX. 36) But whatsoever there is of feeling, perception, mental formations, or consciousness—: all these phenomena he regards as impermanent, subject to pain, as infirm, as an ulcer, a thorn, a misery, a burden, an enemy, a disturbance, as empty and void of an Ego; and turning away from these things, he directs his mind towards the abiding, thus: This, verily, is the Peace, this is the Highest, namely the end of all formations, the forsaking of every substratum of rebirth, the fading away of craving, detachment, extinction, Nibbana. And in this state he reaches the cessation of passions.

(A. IV. 198) And his heart becomes free from sensual passion, free from the passion for existence, free from the passion of ignorance. Freed am I!: this knowledge arises in the liberated one; and he knows: Exhausted is rebirth, fulfilled the Holy Life; what was to be done, has been done; naught remains more for this world to do.

(M. 26)

> For ever am I liberated,
> This is the last time that I'm born,
> No new existence waits for me.

This, verily, is the highest, holiest wisdom: to know that all suffering has passed away.

(M. 140) This, verily, is the highest, holiest peace: appeasement of greed, hatred and delusion.

I am is a vain thought; I am not is a vain thought; I shall be is a vain thought; I shall not be is a vain thought. Vain thoughts are a sickness, an ulcer, a thorn. But after overcoming all vain thoughts one is called a silent thinker. And the thinker, the silent One, does no more arise, no more pass away, no more tremble, no more desire. For there is nothing in him that he should arise again. And as he arises no more, how should he grow old again? And as he grows no more old, how should he die again? And as he dies no more, how should he tremble? And as he trembles no more, how should he have desire?

(M. 29) Hence, the purpose of the Holy Life does not consist in acquiring alms, honour, or fame, nor in gaining morality, concentration, or the eye of knowledge. That unshakable deliverance of the heart: that, verily, is the object of the Holy Life, that is the essence, that is its goal.

(M. 51) And those, who formerly, in the past, were Holy and Enlightened Ones, also those Blessed Ones have pointed out to their disciples this self-same goal, as has been pointed out by me to my disciples. And those, who afterwards, in the future, will be Holy and Enlightened Ones, those Blessed Ones also will point out to their disciples this self-same goal, as has been pointed out by me to my disciples.

(D. 22) However, disciples, it may be that (after my passing away) you might think: Gone is the doctrine of our Master. We have no Master more. But thus you should not think; for the Law and the Discipline, which I have taught you, will, after my death, be your master.

> The Law be your light,
> The Law be your refuge!
> Do not look for any other refuge!

Therefore, disciples, the doctrines, which I advised you to penetrate, you should well preserve, well guard, so that this Holy Life may take its course and continue for ages, for the weal and welfare of the many, as a consolation to the world, for the happiness, weal and welfare of heavenly beings and men.

TEVIGGA SUTTA

THUS have I heard. At one time when the Blessed One was journeying through Kosala with a great company of Brethren about five hundred, he came to the Brahman village of Manasakata. And there the Blessed One staid in the mango grove on the bank of the river Akiravati to the south of Manasakata.

At that time many distinguished and wealthy Brahmans were living at Manasakata. Among them were two young men, Vasettha and Bharadvaga. One day when they were taking exercise after their bath, walking up and down in thoughtful mood, they discussed which was the true path to union with Brahma and which the false. The young Brahman Vasettha spake thus: I think that the path that has been announced by the Brahman Pokkarasati is the straight path, the direct way which leads him who acts according to it into a state of union with Brahma.

The young Brahman Bharadvaga said: I think the path announced by the Brahman Tarukkha is the straight path, the direct way which leads him who acts according to it into a state of union with Brahman. But neither was able to convince the other. Then the young Brahman Vasettha said to the young Brahman Bharadvaga: There is a Samana named Gotami of the Sakya clan who left them to adopt a religious life. He is now staying in the Mango grove near by. This venerable Gotama is of high reputation, he is even said to be "a fully enlightened One," blessed and worthy, abounding in wisdom and goodness, happy, with knowledge of the world, unsurpassed as a guide to erring mortals, a teacher of gods and men, a blessed Buddha. Come, Bharadvaga, let us go to the place where this Samana Gotama is staying, let us ask him and what he declares let us bear in mind. Very well, assented Bharadvaga.

Then the young Brahman Vasettha and the young Brahman Bharadvaga went on to the place where the Blessed One was staying. When they had come there they exchanged with the

Blessed One greetings and compliments of friendship and civility and sat down beside him. When they were thus seated the young Brahman said to the Blessed One:

As we were taking exercise, walking up and down, there sprang up a conversation between us as to which was the true path to union with Brahma. I said it was the one announced by the Brahman Pokkarasati; Bharadvaga said that it was the way announced by the Brahman Tarukka. Not being able to agree, we decided to refer the dispute to you.

Then the Blessed One said to the two young Brahmans: Vasettha, you said that it was the path taught by the Brahman Pokkarasati; Bharadvaga, you said that it was the way taught by the Brahman Tarukka. Where-in, then, Vasettha, is there a strife, a dispute, a difference of opinion between you?

Vasettha replied: Various Brahmans, Gotama, teach various paths to union with Brahma: Is one true and another false, or are all saving paths? Are they all paths which will lead one who acts according to them into a state of Union with Brahma? Is it like the different roads that come into a village and that all meet in the center? Is it in that sense that all the various teachings of the Brahmans are to be accepted? Are they all saving paths? Are they all paths which will lead one who acts according to them into a state of union with Brahma?

The Blessed One replied: Vasettha, do you think that all these various paths lead aright?

I think so, Gotama.

Would you be willing to assert that they all lead aright, Vasettha?

So I say, Gotama.

But then, Vasettha, is there a single one of the Brahmans versed in the Three Vedas who has ever seen Brahma face to face?

No, indeed, Gotama.

But is there then, Vasettha, a single one of the teachers of the Brahmans versed in the Three Vedas who has ever seen Brahma face to face?

No, indeed, Gotama.

But is there then, Vasettha, a single one of the pupils of the teachers of the Brahmans versed in the Three Vedas who has seen Brahma face to face?

No, indeed, Gotama.

But, Vasettha, is there a single one of the ancestors of all these Brahmans, back to the seventh generation, who has seen Brahma face to face?

No, indeed, Gotama.

Well, then, Vasettha, There are the ancient *Rishis* of the Brahmans versed in the Three Vedas, the authors of the verses, the utterers of the verses, whose ancient form of words are still chanted, uttered, or composed by the Brahmans of today, intoning and reciting them as has been done for ages, did they ever speak thus, saying: We know it, we have seen it, where Brahma is, whence Brahma came, whither Brahma goes?

Not so, Gotama.

Then you assert, Vasettha, that not one of the Brahmans, nor their teachers, nor their teacher's pupils, nor their ancestors back for seven generations, has ever seen Brahma face to face. And that even the *Rishis* of old, the authors and utterers of the ancient form of words which the Brahmans of today so carefully intone and recite precisely as they have been handed down, that even they did not pretend to know or to have seen where or whence or whither Brahma is. And yet, Vasettha, these Brahmans pretend that they can show the path to union with that which they have not seen and which they know not, saying: This is the straight path, this is the direct way, which leads him, who acts according to it, into a state of union with Brahma. Now what think you, Vasettha, does it not follow that this being so, that the talk of these Brahmans versed though they be in the Three Vedas, is foolish talk.

Yes, Gotama, this being so, it follows that the talk of these Brahmans versed in the Three Vedas is foolish talk.

Vasettha, it is like a string of blind men clinging to one another, the foremost can not see the way, neither can the middle one, nor the hindmost. Even so, methinks, Vasettha, that the talk of the Brahmans versed in the Three Vedas, is but blind talk. The first sees not, the middle one sees not, the hindmost sees not. The talk, then, of these Brahmans turns out to be ridiculous, mere words, vain and empty.

Just, Vasettha, as if a man should say, How I long for, how I love the most beautiful woman in this land! And people should ask him, Well, good friend! this most beautiful woman in the land whom you thus love and long for, do you know whether she is a noble lady or a Brahman woman, or of the trader caste, or a sudra? But when so asked he should answer, No, I do not know. And when people should ask him, Well, good friend! this most beautiful woman in all the land whom you so love and long for, do you know her name, or her family name, whether she is tall or short, dark or of medium complexion, black or fair, or in what village or town or city she dwells? But when so asked, he should answer, I do not know. And when people should say to him, So then, good friend, whom you know not, neither have seen, how do you love and long for her? And then when so asked, he should answer, Nevertheless, I love her. Now what think you, Vasettha? Would it not turn out, that being so, that the talk of that man was foolish talk?

In sooth, Gotama, it would turn out, that being so, that the talk of that man was foolish talk.

And just even so, Vasettha, though you say that the Brahmans and all connected with them, have never seen Brahma, Now what think you, Vasettha, does it not follow that this being so, the talk of the Brahmans versed though they be in the three Vedas, is foolish talk?

In sooth, Gotama, that being so, it follows that the talk of the Brahmans versed in the Vedas, is foolish talk.

Very good, Vasettha. Verily then, Vasettha, that Brahmans versed in the Three Vedas should be able to show the way to a state of union with that which they do not know, neither have seen—such a condition of things has no existence.

Just as if a man should make a stairway in a place where four roads met, Vasettha, and people should say to him, Well, good friend, where are you going to build your mansion for which you are building this stairway? Will it face the east, or the south, or the west, or the north? How large will it be? Large or small or of medium size? And when so asked he should answer, I do not know. And people should say to him, But then, good friend, are you making a stairway and do not have any idea in your mind as to what the mansion is to be like? And when so asked, he should answer, Yes. Now what think you, Vasettha? Would it not turn out, that being so, that the thing which the man was doing was a foolish thing to do?

In sooth, Gotama, that being so, it would be a foolish thing he was doing.

And just even so, Vasettha, The way to union with Brahma which the Brahmans are proclaiming without having seen Brahma or knowing anything about him, is just as foolish. Is it not so?

In sooth, Gotama, that being so, it follows that the talk of the Brahmans is foolish.

Very good, Vasettha, for these Brahmans to proclaim a way to union with Brahma which they do not know, neither have seen—such a condition of things has no existence.

Again, Vasettha. If this river Akiravati were full of water even to the brim and overflowing, and a man should come up and want to cross over because he had business on the other side, and he standing on this bank should say, Come hither, O further bank! come over to this side! Now what think you, Vasettha, would the further bank of the river, because of the man's invoking and praying and hoping and praising, come over to this side?

Certainly not, Gotama.

In just the same way, Vasettha, do the Brahmans versed in the Three Vedas,—omitting the practice of those qualities which really make a man a Brahman and adopting the practice of those qualities which really make men not Brahmans—say thus, Indra we call upon thee, Soma we call upon thee, Varuna we call upon thee, Isana we call upon thee, Pragapati we call upon thee, Brahma we call upon thee, Mahiddhi we call upon thee, Yama we call upon thee! Verily, Vasettha, that those Brahmans versed in the Three Vedas, but omitting the practice of those qualities which really make a man a Brahman, and adopting the practice of those qualities which really make men not Brahmans—that they, by reason of their invoking and praying and hoping and praising, should, after death and when the body is dissolved, become united with Brahma—verily such a condition of things has no existence.

Just, Vasettha, as if this river Akiravati were full, even to the brim and overflowing, and a man with business on the other side should come up and want to cross over. Now, suppose this man was bound with a heavy chain his arms behind his back, what think you, Vasettha, would that man be able to get over the river Akiravati to the further bank?

Certainly not, Gotama.

In the same way, Vasettha, there are five things leading to

desire and lust which are called in the discipline of the Noble Path a "chain" and a "bond." What are the five? Forms perceptible to the eye—desirable, agreeable, pleasant, attractive forms—that cause delight and are accompanied by desire and lust. Sounds of the same kind perceptible to the ear; odours of the same kind perceptible to the nose; tastes of the same kind that are perceptible to the tongue; substances of the same kind perceptible to the body by touch. These five things predisposing to passion are called in the discipline of the Noble One, a "chain" and a "bond." And these five things predisposing to lust, Vasettha, do the Brahmans versed in the Three Vedas cling to; they are infatuated by them, guilty of them, see not the danger of them, know not how unreliable they are, and so enjoy them.

And verily, Vasettha, that Brahmans versed in the Three Vedas but omitting the practice of those qualities which really make a man a Brahman, and adopting the practice of those qualities which make men non-Brahmans—clinging to those five things that predispose to passion, infatuated by them, guilty of them, seeing not their danger, knowing not their unreliability, and so enjoying them—that these Brahmans after death on the dissolution of the body, become united with Brahma—such a condition of things has no existence.

Again Vasettha, if this river Akiravati were full of water even to the brim and overflowing, and a man with business on the other side should come up and want to cross over, and suppose he should lie down and cover himself up even to his head, and go to sleep. What think you, Vasettha? Would that man be able to get over from this bank of the river to the further bank?

Certainly not, Gotama.

Vasettha, in the discipline of the Noble Path, there are these five hindrances, which are called, "veils," "hindrances," "obstacles," and "entanglements." What are the five? The hindrance of lustful desire, the hindrance of malice, the hindrance of sloth and idleness, the hindrance of pride and self-righteousness, the hindrance of doubt. These are the five hindrances that in the discipline of the Noble Path are called veils and hindrances and obstacles and entanglements. Now with these five hindrances, Vasettha, the Brahmans versed in the Three Vedas are veiled, hindered, obstructed, entangled. And verily,

Vasettha, the Brahmans versed in the Three Vedas but omitting the practice of those qualities which really make a man a Brahman and adopting the practice of those qualities which make men non-Brahmans—veiled, hindered, obstructed, entangled—that these Brahmans after death on the dissolution of the body become united to Brahma—such a condition of things has no existence.

Now, Vasettha, when you have been among Brahmans, listening as they talked among themselves, learners and teachers and those aged and well stricken in years, what have you learned from them and of them? Is Brahma in possession of wives and wealth, or is he not?

He is not, Gotama.

Is his mind full of anger, or is it free from anger?

Free from anger, Gotama.

Is his mind full of malice or free from malice?

Free from malice, Gotama.

Is his mind depraved, or pure?

It is pure, Gotama.

Has he self-mastery, or has he not?

He has, Gotama.

Now what think you, Vasettha? Are the Brahmans versed in the Three Vedas, are they in possession of wives and wealth, or are they not?

They are, Gotama.

Have they anger in their hearts?

They have, Gotama.

Do they bear malice, or do they not?

They do, Gotama.

Are they pure in heart or are they not?

They are not, Gotama.

Then you say, Vasettha, that the Brahmans are in possession of wives and wealth, and that Brahma is not. Can there be agreement and likeness between the Brahmans with their wives and property and Brahma who has none of these things?

Certainly not, Gotama.

Very good, Vasettha. But verily, that these Brahmans versed in the Three Vedas, who live married and wealthy should, after death when the body is dissolved, become united with Brahma who has none of these things—such a condition of things has no existence.

You say, Vasettha, that the Brahmans bear anger and malice in their hearts, and are sinful and uncontrolled, while Brahma is free from anger and malice, and is sinless, and has self-mastery. How can there be concord and likeness between Brahmans and Brahma?

There can not be, Gotama.

Very good, Vasettha. That these Brahmans versed in the Vedas and yet bearing anger and malice in their hearts, sinful and uncontrolled, should after death, when the body is dissolved, become united with Brahma who is free from anger and malice, sinless and has self-mastery—such a condition of things has no existence.

So, Vasettha, the Brahmans, versed though they be in the Three Vedas, while they rest in confidence are really sinking. They think they are crossing over into some happier land, but so sinking they can only arrive at despair. Therefore, the three-fold knowledge of the Brahmans in the Vedas is a waterless desert, their knowledge a pathless waste, their knowledge their destruction.

When he had finished speaking, the young Brahman Vasettha said to the Blessed One: It has been told me, Gotama, that the Samana Gotama knows the way to a state of Union with Brahma. Can you teach us?

What do you think, Vasettha, is the village of Manasakata near from this place or far from it?

Manasakata is not far from here, it is quite near.

Vasettha, supposing there was a man born in this village of Manasakata and who never to this time had left it, and people should ask him the way to Manasakata. Would that man born and brought up there be in any doubt or uncertainty about the way?

Certainly not, Gotama. He would be perfectly familiar with every road leading to his native village.

That man, Vasettha, born and brought up in Manasakata might, if he were asked the way to Manasakata, fall into doubt and difficulty, but with the Tathagata, when asked about the path which leads to the world of Brahma, there can be neither doubt nor difficulty. For Brahma, the world of Brahma, the path which leadeth to the world of Brahma, I fully know. Yea, I know it even as one who was born there and lives there.

When he had thus spoken, Vasettha the young Brahman said to the Blessed One: So it has been told me, Gotama, even that the Samana Gotama knows the way to a state of union with Brahma. It is well! Let the venerable Gotama be pleased to show us the way to a state of union with Brahma; let the venerable Gotama save the Brahman race.

Listen then, Vasettha, and I will speak.

So be it, Lord.

Then the Blessed One spake and said:—Know, Vasettha, that from time to time a Tathagata is born into the world, a fully Enlightened One, blessed and worthy, abounding in wisdom and goodness, happy with knowledge of the worlds, unsurpassed as a guide to erring mortals, a teacher of gods and men, a Blessed Buddha. He thoroughly understands this universe, as though he saw it face to face,—the world below with all its people, the worlds above, of Mara and of Brahma— and all creatures, Samanas and Brahmans, gods and men, and from that knowledge makes it known and teaches others. The Truth does he proclaim both in its letter and in its spirit, lovely in its origin, lovely in its progress, lovely in its consummation. A higher life doth he make known in all its purity and in all its perfectness.

A householder or one of his sons, or a man of inferior birth in any caste, listens to the truth he proclaims. On hearing the truth, faith in the Tathagata is awakened and when that faith is strengthened he thus considers within himself: Full of hindrance is the household life, a path defiled by passion, free as the air is the life of him who has renounced all worldly things. How difficult it is for the man who dwells at home to live the higher life in all its fullness, in all its purity, in all its perfection. Let me then, shave my head and face, let me clothe myself in the garment of a mendicant and go forth from a household life into the homeless life. Then before long, forsaking his portion of the family property, be it great or be it small; forsaking his relatives, be they many or few, he shaves his head, clothes himself in the mendicant's robe, and goes forth from the household life into the homeless state.

When he has thus become a recluse, he passes a life of restraint according to rules of the Patimokkha; uprightness is his delight, he sees danger in the least of those things he should avoid; he adopts and trains himself in the Precepts;

he encompasses himself with purity in word and deed; he sustains his life by means that are unselfish and kind; good is his conduct, guarded the door of his senses; mindful and self-possessed, he is altogether happy.

* * *

Now, Vasettha, wherein is his conduct good? Herein, O Vasettha, putting away all unkindness to sentient beings he abstains from destroying life. He lays aside the cudgel and sword and, full of humility and pity, he is compassionate and kind to all creatures that have life. Putting away the desire for things which are not his, he abstains from taking anything that is not freely given him. He has only what has been given him, therewith is he content, and he passes his life in honesty and in purity of heart. Putting away all thoughts of lust, he lives a life of chastity and purity. Putting away all thoughts of deceiving, he abstains from all prevarications; he speaks truthfully, from the truth he never swerves; faithful and trustworthy, he never injures his fellow men by deceit.

Putting away all judgment of others, he abstains from slander. What he hears he repeats not elsewhere to raise a quarrel; what he hears elsewhere he repeats not here to raise a quarrel. Thus he brings together those who are divided, he encourages those who are friendly; he is a peacemaker, a lover of peace, impassioned for peace, a speaker of words that make for peace. Putting away all bitter thoughts, he abstains from harsh language. Whatever is humane, pleasant to the ear, kindly, reaching to the heart, urbane, acceptable to the people, appreciated by the people—such are the words he speaks. Putting away all foolish thoughts, he abstains from vain conversation. He speaks in season, he speaks truthfully, consistently, wisely, with restraint. He speaks only when it is appropriate for him to speak, words that are profitable, well sustained, well defined, full of wisdom.

Besides being kind to all animate life, he refrains from injuring insects or even herbs. He takes but one meal a day; abstaining from food at all other times. He abstains from attending dances, concerts and theatrical shows. He abstains from wearing, using or adorning himself with garlands, scents and ointments, he abstains from large and soft beds. He abstains from accumulating silver or gold, from coveting great harvests, herds of cattle; he abstains from the getting of maids and women attendants, slaves either men or women; he abstains from gathering herds of sheep or goats, fowls or swine, elephants, cattle, horses and mares. He abstains from the getting of fields and lands.

He refrains from accepting commissions to carry messages, he refrains from all buying and selling, he abstains from the use of all trade deceptions, false weights, alloyed metals, false measures. He abstains from all bribery, cheating, fraud and crooked ways. He refrains from all banditry, killing or maiming, abducting, highway robbery, plundering villages, or obtaining money by threats of violence. These are the kinds of goodness he practices.

* * *

The true Samana, he who is seeking the way to the Brahma World, lets his mind pervade all quarters of the world with thoughts of Love; first one quarter then the second quarter, then the third quarter and so the fourth quarter. And thus the whole wide world, above, below, around, and everywhere, does he continue to pervade with thoughts of love, far-reaching, beyond measure, all-embracing.

Just, Vasettha, as a mighty trumpeter makes himself heard—and that without difficulty—in all four directions; even so of all things that have form or life, there is not one that he passes by or leaves aside; he regards them all with mind set free and filled with deep-felt love. Verily, Vasettha, this is the way to a state of union with Brahma. He lets his mind pervade one quarter of the world with thoughts of pity, sympathy, and equanimity, and so the second, and so the third, and so the fourth. And thus the whole wide world, above, below, around and everywhere, does he continue to pervade with heart of pity, sympathy and equanimity, far-reaching, beyond measure, all embracing.

Just, Vasettha, as a mighty trumpeter makes himself heard—and that without difficulty—in all four directions, even so of all things that have form or life, there is not one that he passes by or leaves aside, but he regards them all with mind set free and filled with deep-felt pity, sympathy and equanimity. Verily, Vasettha, this is the way to a state of union with Brahma.

Now what think you, Vasetta, will the Bhikkhu who lives thus be in possession of women and wealth, or will he not?

He will not, Gotama.

Will he be full of anger, or will he be free from anger?

He will be free from anger, Gotama.

Will his mind be full of malice, or free from malice?

Free from malice, Gotama.

Will his mind be lustful or pure?

It will be pure, Gotama.

Will he have self-mastery or will he not?

Surely he will, Gotama.

Vasettha, you say that the Bhikkhu is free from household cares and that Brahma is free from household cares. Is there then agreement and likeness between the Bhikkhu and Brahma?

There is, Gotama.

Very good, Vasettha! Then in sooth, that the Bhikkhu who is free from household cares should, after death, when the body is dissolved, become united with Brahma, who is the same—such a condition of things is in every way, possible.

And you say, Vasettha, that the Bhikkhu is free from anger, free from malice, pure in mind, and master of himself; and that Brahma is likewise free from anger, free from malice, pure in mind, and master of himself. Then in sooth, Vasettha, that the Bhikkhu who is free from anger, free from malice, pure in mind, and master of himself should after death, when the body is dissolved, become united with Brahma, who is the same—such a condition of things is in every way possible.

When the Blessed One had thus spoken, the two young Brahmans, Vasettha and Bharadvaga addressed the Blessed One, saying:—

Most excellent, Lord, are the words of thy mouth, most excellent! It is just as if a man were to set up what was thrown down, or to reveal that which was hidden away, or were to point out the right road to him who has gone astray, or were to bring a lamp into the darkness so that those who have eyes can see:—just even so, Lord, has the truth been made known to us by the Blessed One. And we betake ourselves, Lord, to the Blessed One, to the Truth, and to the Brotherhood, as our refuge. May the Blessed One accept us as disciples, as true believers, from this day forth, as long as life shall last.

TAKEN FROM THE COLLECTION OF MIDDLE DISCOURSES

Introspective Breathing Exercises

THUS have I heard. Once the Exalted One was staying near Savatthi, in the Eastern Grove, on the terrace of Migara's mother, together with many well-known elders of the Order, with many well-known disciples, with the Venerable Sariputto and the Venerable Mahamoggallano, the Venerable Mahakassapo and the Venerable Mahakaccayano, the Venerable Mahakotthito and the Venerable Mahakappino, the Venerable Mahacundo and the Venerable Anuruddho, the Venerable Revato and the Venerable Anando and with other well-known elders and disciples.

On this occasion the elders of the Order instructed and taught the novices. Some of the elders instructed and taught maybe ten of the new monks, other elders instructed and taught about twenty, still others of the elders instructed and taught thirty, and still others of the elders instructed and taught about forty of the novices. And these young monks, thus instructed and taught by the elders of the Order realized a great and gradually perceptible result.

And just at this time, it was a holy day on the fifteenth day of the month during the night of plain full moon, the Exalted One was seated in the midst of the assembly of monks under the canopy of heaven. And the Exalted One beheld the silent, calm assembly of monks and spoke to them as follows:

"I have become perfect, o Monks, on this Path, I have become perfect of mind, o Monks, on this Path: and you also, o Monks, you must become more and more perfect to achieve what you have not yet achieved, to attain what you have not yet attained, to realize what you have not yet realized. And now on the last autumnal full-moon day I will quit Savatthi."

When the monks living in the country heard: 'The Exalted

One, it is said, will soon quit Savatthi, he will leave Savatthi on the last autumnal full-moon day,' then these monks living in the country turned their steps towards Savatthi to visit the Exalted One.

The elder monks were still continuing to instruct and teach more and more in detail the new monks arriving. Some of the elder of the Order instructed and taught may be ten of the new monks, other elders instructed and taught about twenty, still others of the elders instructed and taught thirty, and still others of the elders instructed and taught about forty of the novices. And these young monks, thus instructed and taught by the elders of the Order realized a great and gradually perceptible result.

When the time was come, it was a holy day, on the fifteenth day of the month, on the last autumnal plain full-moon night the Exalted One took His seat in the midst of the assembly of monks under the canopy of heaven. And the Exalted One beheld the silent, calm assembly of monks and spoke to them as follows:

"Not a word is spoken, o Monks, by this assembly, not a word is uttered, o Monks, by this assembly, this assembly consists of pure kernel. Such is, o Monks, this fraternity of disciples, such is, o Monks, this assembly, that it is worthy of offerings, of oblations, of gifts and homage and is the noblest community in the world. Such is, o Monks, this fraternity of disciples, such is, o Monks, this assembly, that a small gift given to it becomes great, and a great gift given to it becomes greater still. Such is, o Monks, this fraternity of disciples, such is, o Monks, this assembly, that it is difficult to find one like it in the world. Such is, o Monks, this fraternity of disciples, such is, o Monks, this assembly, that one is glad to walk many miles to behold it, and even if it be only from behind.

"Such is, o Monks, this fraternity of disciples, such is, o Monks, this assembly, that, o Monks, there are among these disciples some monks who are Perfect Ones, who have reached the end of all illusion, who have arrived at the goal, who have accomplished the task, have cast off the burden, have won their deliverance, who have destroyed the fetters of existence, and who, through supreme knowledge, have liberated themselves: there are such monks, o Monks, among these disciples. There are, o Monks, among these disciples some monks who, after the destruction of the five downward leading fetters, will rise (to higher worlds) to attain extinction from there, not to return to that world anymore: there are such monks, o Monks, among these disciples. There are, o Monks, among these disciples some monks, who after the destruction of the three fetters, eased from desire, hatred and illusion, almost purified, will return only once more, and returning only once more to this world will make an end to suffering: there are such monks, o Monks, among these disciples. There are, o Monks, among these disciples some monks, who after the destruction of the three fetters have entered the stream, escaped from the downfall, consciously hastening towards full Awakening: there are such monks, o Monks, among these disciples.

"There are, o Monks, among these disciples some monks, who persevere assiduously as conquerors of the Four Foundations of Introspection: there are such monks, o Monks, among these disciples. There are, o Monks, among these disciples some monks, who persevere assiduously as masters of the Four Great Efforts: there are such monks, o Monks, among these disciples. There are, o Monks, among these disciples some monks, who persevere assiduously as conquerors of the Four Domains of Power, of the Five Faculties and the Five Attributes, the Seven Factors of Enlightenment and of the Noble Eightfold Path: there are such monks, o Monks, among these disciples.

"There are, o Monks, among these disciples some monks, who persevere assiduously in the practice of Boundless Kindness: there are such monks, o Monks, among these disciples. There are, o Monks, among these disciples some monks, who persevere assiduously in the practice of Boundless Compassion, Joyful Serenity and Perfect Equanimity: there are such monks, o Monks, among these disciples.

"There are, o Monks, among these disciples some monks, who persevere assiduously as conquerors of awe: there are such monks, o Monks, among these disciples. There are, o Monks, among these disciples some monks, who persevere assiduously in the perception of transitoriness: there are such monks, o Monks, among these disciples.

"There are, o Monks, among these disciples some monks, who persevere assiduously as conquerors of introspective breathing exercises. Inhalation and exhalation, o Monks, practised and cultivated introspectively causes the attainment of high recompense, of high advancement. Inhalation and exhalation, o Monks, practised and cultivated introspectively causes the unfoldment of the Four Foundations of Introspection; the Four Foundations of Introspection, practised and cultivated assiduously, cause the enfoldment of the Seven Factors of Enlightenment; the Seven Factors of Enlightenment, practised and cultivated introspectively, cause the enfoldment of Knowledge that liberates.

"But how, o Monks, must inhalation and exhalation be practised and cultivated introspectively that it causes high recompense, high advancement?

"A monk, o Monks, goes into a forest, or to the foot of a great tree, or to a lonely place, and there sits down, cross-legged, holding his body upright, and practises Introspection.

"He breathes in attentively, and attentively breathes out.

Drawing in a long breath, he knows: 'I am drawing in a long breath,' exhaling a long breath, he knows: 'I am exhaling a long breath.'

Drawing in a short breath, he knows: 'I am drawing in a short breath,' exhaling a short breath, he knows: 'I am exhaling a short breath.'

'Perceiving the whole body, will I breathe in, perceiving the whole body, will I breathe out,' thus he practises.

'Calming down this body compound, will I breathe in, calming down this body compound, will I breathe out,' thus he practises.

'Serenely feeling will I breathe in, serenely feeling will I breathe out,' thus he trains himself.

'Blissfully feeling will I breathe in, blissfully feeling will I breathe out,' thus he trains himself.

'Perceiving the thought connection, will I breathe in, perceiving the thought connection, will I breathe out,' thus he trains himself.

'Calming down this thought connection, will I breathe in, calming down this thought connection, will I breathe out,' thus he trains himself.

'Perceiving the thoughts will I breathe in, perceiving the thoughts will I breathe out,' thus he trains himself.

'Enlivening the thoughts will I breathe in, enlivening the thoughts will I breathe out,' thus he trains himself.

'Concentrating the thoughts will I breathe in, concentrating the thoughts will I breathe out,' thus he trains himself.

'Dissolving the thoughts will I breathe in, dissolving the thoughts will I breathe out,' thus he trains himself.

'Perceiving impermanence will I breathe in, perceiving impermanence will I breathe out,' thus he trains himself.

'Rejecting attraction will I breathe in, rejecting attraction will I breathe out,' thus he trains himself.

'Perceiving eradication will I breathe in, perceiving eradication will I breathe out,' thus he trains himself.

'Perceiving estrangement will I breathe in, perceiving estrangement will I breathe out,' thus he trains himself.

"Thus, o Monks, must inhalation and exhalation be practised and cultivated introspectively that it may bestow high recompense, high advancement.

"But how, o Monks, must inhalation and exhalation be practised and cultivated introspectively in order to establish the Four Foundations of Introspection?

"At a time, o Monks, when the monk drawing in a long breath knows 'I am drawing in a long breath,' exhaling a long breath knows 'I am exhaling a long breath,' drawing in a short breath knows 'I am drawing in a short breath,' exhaling a short breath knows 'I am exhaling a short breath'; 'Perceiving the whole body will I breathe in, perceiving the whole body will I breathe out,' thus trains himself; 'Calming down this body compound will I breathe in, calming down this body compound will I breathe out,' thus trains himself; at such a time, o Monks, the monk examining the body observes the body, unremittingly, with perspicacity and insight, after having conquered worldly desires and worry. I call this, o Monks, a transformation of the body, namely inhalation and exhalation. Thus, therefore, o Monks, at such a time, the monk examining the body observes the body, unremittingly, with perspicacity and insight, after having conquered worldly desires and worry.

"At a time, o Monks, when the monk thus trains himself: 'Serenely feeling will I breathe in, serenely feeling will I breathe out'; 'blissfully feeling will I breathe in, blissfully feeling will I breathe out'; 'perceiving the thought connection will I breathe in, perceiving the thought connection will I breathe out'; 'calming down this thought connection will I breathe in, calming down this thought connection will I breathe out'; at such a time, o Monks, a monk examining feeling observes feeling, unremittingly, with perspicacity and insight, after having conquered worldly desires and worry. I call this, o Monks, a transformation of feelings, while observing feelings, namely to observe attentively the feelings when breathing in and out; thus, therefore, o Monks, at such a time the monk examining feelings observes the feelings, unremittingly, with perspicacity and insight, after having conquered worldly desires and worry.

"At a time, o Monks, when the monk thus trains himself: 'Perceiving the thoughts will I breathe in, perceiving the thoughts will I breathe out'; 'enlivening the thoughts will I breathe in, enlivening the thoughts will I breathe out'; 'concentrating the thoughts will I breathe in, concentrating the thoughts will I breathe out'; 'dissolving the thoughts will I breathe in, dissolving the thoughts will I breathe out': at such a time, o Monks, a monk examining thoughts observes the thoughts, unremittingly, with perspicacity and insight, after having conquered worldly desires and worry. It is impossible, o Monks, this I declare, that a heedless man, who does not think clearly, could practise the in and out breathing introspectively. Thus, therefore, o Monks, at such a time, the monk examining thoughts observes the thoughts, unremittingly, with perspicacity and insight, after having conquered worldly desires and worry.

"At a time, o Monks, when the monk thus trains himself: 'Perceiving impermanence will I breathe in, perceiving impermanence will I breathe out'; 'rejecting attraction will I breathe in, rejecting attraction will I breathe out'; 'perceiving eradication will I breathe in, perceiving eradication will I breathe out'; 'perceiving estrangement will I breathe in, perceiving estrangement will I breathe out': at such a time, o Monks, a monk examining phenomena observes phenomena, unremittingly, with perspicacity and insight, after having conquered worldly desires and worry. And he recognizes with wisdom, how worldly desires and worry are being overcome, and attains peace. Thus, therefore, o Monks, at such a time, the monk examining phenomena observes phenomena, unremittingly, with perspicacity and insight, after having conquered worldly desires and worry.

"Thus must, o Monks, inhalation and exhalation be practised and cultivated introspectively in order to establish the Four Foundations of Introspection.

"And how, o Monks, must the Four Foundations of Introspection be practised and cultivated in order that they may effect the Seven Factors of Enlightenment?

"At a time, o Monks, when the monk examining the body observes the body, unremittingly, with perspicacity and insight, after having conquered worldly desires and worry, at such a time he has Introspection present immovable; at a time, o Monks, when the monk has Introspection present immovable, at such a time he has effected the Awakening of Introspection, he has accomplished the Awakening of Introspection, at such a time the Awakening of Introspection is being fully unfolded by him. Abiding thus reflective he fathoms the meaning, analyses it, penetrates into its depths; at a time, o Monks, when the monk abides thus reflective, fathoming the meaning with wisdom, analysing it, penetrating into its depths, at such a time he has effected the Awakening of Penetration, he has accomplished the Awakening of Penetration, at such a time the Awakening of Penetration is being fully unfolded by him. Thus fathoming the meaning with wisdom, analysing it, penetrating into its depths, he effects Energy immovable; at a time, o Monks, when the monk thus fathoming the meaning with wisdom, analysing it and penetrating into its depths, effects Energy immovable, at such a time he realizes the Awakening of Energy, he accomplishes the Awakening of Energy, at such a time the Awakening of Energy is being fully unfolded by him. Having realized Energy, a supramundane Serenity arises in him; at a time, o Monks, when the monk has realized Energy and supramundane Serenity arises in him, at such a time he has effected the Awakening of Serenity, he accomplishes the Awakening of Serenity, at such a time the Awakening of Serenity is being fully unfolded by him. Being filled with Serenity he becomes gentle in body and gentle in mind; at a time, o Monks, when the monk is filled with Serenity and is gentle in body, gentle in mind, at such a time he has effected the Awakening of Gentleness, he has accomplished the Awakening of Gentleness, at such a time the Awakening of Gentleness is being fully unfolded by him. Having subdued his body with serene Gentleness, his mind becomes concen-

trated; at a time, o Monks, when the monk has subdued his
body with serene Gentleness and when his mind has become
concentrated, at such a time he has effected the Awakening of
Concentration, he has accomplished the Awakening of Concentration, at such a time the Awakening of Concentration is
being fully unfolded by him. Having thus become of concentrated mind, he attains peace; at a time, o Monks, when the
monk has thus become concentrated of mind and has attained
peace, at such a time he has effected the Awakening of Even-
Mindedness, he has accomplished the Awakening of Even-
Mindedness, at such a time the Awakening of Even-Mindedness
is being fully unfolded by him.

"At a time, o Monks, when the monks examining feelings
observes the feelings, examining thoughts observes the thoughts,
examining phenomena observes phenomena, unremittingly,
with perspicacity and insight, after having conquered worldly
desires and worry, at such a time he has Introspection present
immovable; at a time, o Monks, when the monk has Introspection present immovable, at such a time he has effected the
Awakening of Introspection, he has accomplished the Awakening of Introspection, at such a time the Awakening of Introspection is being fully unfolded by him. Abiding thus reflective he
fathoms the meaning, analyses it, penetrates into its depths;
at a time, o Monks, when the monk abides thus reflective,
fathoming the meaning with wisdom, analysing it, penetrating
into its depths, at such a time he has effected the Awakening
of Penetration, he has accomplished the Awakening of Penetration, at such a time the Awakening of Penetration is being
fully unfolded by him. Thus fathoming the meaning with wisdom, analysing it, penetrating into its depths, he effects Energy
immovable; at a time, o Monks, when the monk thus fathoming the meaning with wisdom, analysing it and penetrating into
its depths, effects Energy immovable, at such a time he realizes
the Awakening of Energy, he accomplishes the Awakening of
Energy, at such a time the Awakening of Energy is being
fully unfolded by him. Having realized Energy, a supramundane Serenity arises in him; at a time, o Monks, when the
monk has realized Energy and supramundane Serenity arises
in him, at such a time he has effected the Awakening of Serenity, he accomplishes the Awakening of Serenity at such a time
the Awakening of Serenity is being fully unfolded by him. Be-

ing filled with Serenity he becomes gentle in body and gentle in mind; at a time, o Monks, when the monk is filled with Serenity and is gentle in body, gentle in mind, at such a time he has effected the Awakening of Gentleness, he has accomplished the Awakening of Gentleness, at such a time the Awakening of Gentleness is being fully unfolded by him. Having thus subdued his body with serene Gentleness, his mind becomes concentrated; at a time, o Monks, when the monk has subdued his body with serene Gentleness and when his mind has become concentrated, at such a time he has effected the Awakening of Concentration, he has accomplished the Awakening of Concentration, at such a time the Awakening of Concentration is being fully unfolded by him. Having thus become of concentrated mind, he attains peace; at a time, o Monks, when the monk has thus become concentrated of mind and has attained peace, at such a time he has effected the Awakening of Even-Mindedness, he has accomplished the Awakening of Even-Mindedness, at such a time the Awakening of Even-mindedness is being fully unfolded by him.

"Practising thus and cultivating thus, o Monks, the Four Foundations of Introspection, they cause the development of the Seven Factors of Enlightenment.

"And how, o Monks, must the Seven Factors of Enlightenment be practised and cultivated that they effect the Knowledge that liberates?

"A monk, o Monks, practises the Awakening of Introspection, effected in solitude, effected by detachment, effected by renunciation, ending in finality; practises the Awakening of Penetration, effected in solitude, effected by detachment, effected by renunciation, ending in finality; practises the Awakening of Energy, effected in solitude, effected by detachment, effected by renunciation, ending in finality; practises the Awakening of Serenity, effected in solitude, effected by detachment, effected by renunciation, ending in finality; practises the Awakening of Gentleness, effected in solitude, effected by detachment, effected by renunciation, ending in finality; practises the Awakening of Concentration, effected in solitude, effected by detachment, effected by renunciation, ending in finality; practises the Awakening of Even-Mindedness, effected in solitude, effected by detachment, effected by renunciation, ending in finality.

"Practising thus and cultivating thus, o Monks, the Seven Factors of Enlightenment, the Knowledge that liberates ensues."

Thus spoke the Exalted One. Well content were those monks with the words of the Exalted One.

SELECTIONS
FROM SANSKRIT SOURCES

Everything changes, everything passes,
Things appearing, things disappearing.
But when all is over—everything having appeared and
    having disappeared,
Being and extinction both transcended.—
Still the basic emptiness and silence abides,
And that is blissful Peace.

MAHA-PRAJNA-PARAMITA-HRIDAYA

THUS have I heard. At one time the Blessed One together with many of the highest Bodhisattvas and a great company of Bhikshus was staying at Rajagaha on Mt. Gridhrakuta. The Blessed One was sitting apart absorbed in Samadhi and the Noble Avalokitesvara was meditating on the profound Prajna-paramita. The Venerable Sariputra, influenced by the Blessed One absorbed in Samadhi, spoke thus to the Noble Bodhisattva Avalokitesvara:—If a son or daughter wishes to study the profound Prajna-paramita, how is he to do so?

The Noble Avalokitesvara replied to the Venerable Sariputra, saying:—If a son or daughter wishes to study the profound Prajna-paramita, he must first get rid of all ideas of egoselfness. Let him think thus: Personality? What is personality? Is it an enduring entity? or is it made up of elements that pass away? Personality is made up of the five grasping aggregates: form, sensation, perception, discrimination, consciousness, all of which are by nature empty of any self-substance. Form is emptiness, emptiness is not different from form, neither is form different from emptiness, indeed, emptiness is form. Also, sensation is emptiness, emptiness is not different from sensation, neither is sensation different from emptiness, indeed, emptiness is sensation. Also, perception is emptiness, emptiness is not different from perception, neither is perception different from emptiness, indeed, emptiness is perception. Also, discrimination is emptiness, emptiness is not different from discrimination, neither is discrimination different from emptiness, indeed, emptiness is discrimination. Also, consciousness is emptiness, emptiness is not different from consciousness, neither is consciousness different from emptiness, indeed, emptiness is consciousness.

Thus, O Sariputra, all things having the nature of emptiness have no beginning and no ending. They are neither faultless nor not faultless; they are neither perfect nor imperfect. In emptiness there is no form, no sensation, no perception, no discrimination, no consciousness. There is no eye, no ear, no nose, no tongue, no sensitiveness to contact, no mind. There is no sight, no sound, no smell, no taste, no touch, no mental process, no object, no knowledge, no ignorance. There is no destruction of objects, there is no cessation of knowledge, no cessation of ignorance. There is no Noble Four-fold Truths: no pain, no cause of pain, no cessation of pain, no Noble Path leading to the cessation of pain. There is no decay and no death, and no destruction of the notion of decay and death. There is no knowledge of Nirvana, there is no obtaining of Nirvana, there is no not obtaining of Nirvana.

Why is there no obtaining of Nirvana? Because Nirvana is the realm of no "thingness." If the ego-soul of personality was an enduring entity it could not obtain Nirvana. It is only because personality is made up of elements that pass away, that personality may attain Nirvana. So long as man is seeking highest perfect Wisdom, he is still abiding in the realm of consciousness. If he is to realize Nirvana, he must pass beyond consciousness. In highest samadhi having transcended consciousness, he has passed beyond discrimination and knowledge, beyond the reach of change or fear; he is already enjoying Nirvana. The perfect understanding of this and the patient acceptance of it is the highest perfect Wisdom that is Prajna-paramita. All the Buddhas of the past, present and future having attained highest samadhi, awake to find themselves realizing Prajna-paramita.

Therefore, O Sariputra, every-one should seek self-realization of Prajna-paramita, the Transcendent Truth, the unsurpassable Truth, the Truth that ends all pain, the Truth that is forever True. O Prajna-paramita! O Transcendent Truth that spans the troubled ocean of life and death: safely carry all seekers to the other shore of Enlightenment.

Listen to the Mantra, the Great, Mysterious Mantra:—*Gate, gate, paragate, parasamgate, bodhi, svaha!* Gone, gone, gone to that other shore; safely passed to that other shore, O Prajna-paramita! So may it be.

THE DIAMOND SUTRA

Introduction

(1) Thus have I heard. At one time the Lord Buddha was sojourning in the kingdom of Shravasti, staying in the Jeta-vana Grove which Anatha-pindika had given to the Brother-hood, and with him were assembled twelve hundred and fifty experienced Bhikshus.

As the hour drew near for the morning meal, the Lord Buddha and his disciples put on their street robes and carrying their alms bowls went toward the city of Shravasti and begged their food from door to door. After they had returned to the Jeta Grove, they laid aside their street garments, bathed their feet, partook of the morning meal, put away their begging bowls for another day, and afterward seated themselves about the Lord Buddha.

(2) The Venerable Subhuti rose from his seat in the midst of the assembly, arranged his robes so the right shoulder was exposed, kneeled upon his right knee, pressed the palms of his hands together and, bowing respectfully to the Lord Buddha, said:—

Tathagata, Honored of the worlds, our beloved Lord! May thy mercy be upon us to take good care of us and to give us good instruction.

The Lord Buddha replied to Subhuti, saying:—Indeed, I will take good care of every Bodhisattva-Mahasattva and give them the best of instruction.

Subhuti replied:—Honored of the worlds! We are very glad to listen to thy blessed instruction. Tell us what we shall say when good pious men and women come to us enquiring how they should begin the practice of seeking to attain Highest Perfect Wisdom (*Anuttara-samyak-sambodhi*). What shall we tell them? How are they to quiet their drifting minds and subdue their craving thoughts?

The Lord Buddha replied to Subhuti, saying:—You have made a good request, Subhuti. Listen carefully and I will answer your question so that all the Brotherhood will understand. As good and pious men and women come to you wishing to begin the practice of seeking to attain highest perfect Wisdom, they will simply have to follow what I am about to say to you, and very soon they will be able to subdue their discriminative thoughts and craving desires, and will be able to attain perfect tranquillity of mind.

The Practice of Charity
(The Dana Paramita)

(3) Then the Lord Buddha addressed the assembly. Every one in the world, beginning with the highest Bodhisattva-Mahasattvas, should follow what I am going to teach you, for this teaching will bring deliverance to everyone whether hatched from an egg, or formed in a womb, or evolved from spawn, or produced by metamorphosis, with or without form, possessing mental faculties or devoid of mental faculties, or both devoid and not devoid, or neither devoid or not devoid, and lead them toward perfect Nirvana. Though the sentient beings thus to be delivered by me are innumerable and without limit yet, in reality, there are no sentient beings to be delivered. And why, Subhuti? Because should there exist in the minds of Bodhisattva-Mahasattvas such arbitrary conceptions of phenomena as the existence of one's own ego-selfness, the ego-selfness of another, self-ness as divided into an infinite number of living and dying beings, or selfness as unified into one Universal Self existing eternally, they would be unworthy to be called Bodhisattva-Mahasattvas.

(4) Moreover, Subhuti, the Bodhisattva-Mahasattvas, in teaching the Dharma to others, should first be free themselves from all the craving thoughts awakened by beautiful sights, pleasant sounds, sweet tastes, fragrance, soft tangibles, and seductive thoughts. In their practice of charity, they should not be influenced by any of these seductive phenomena. And why? Because, if in their practice of charity they are uninfluenced by such things they will realize a blessing and merit that is inestimable and inconceivable. What think you, Subhuti? Is it possible to estimate the distance of space in the eastern heavens?

No, Blessed One! It is impossible to estimate the distance of space in the eastern heavens.

Subhuti, is it possible to estimate the limits of space in the northern, southern and western heavens? Or to any of the four corners of the universe, or above or below?

No, Honored of the worlds!

Subhuti, it is equally impossible to estimate the blessing and merit that will come to the Bodhisattva-Mahasattva who practices charity uninfluenced by any of these arbitrary conceptions. This truth should be taught in the beginning and to everybody.

(19) The Lord Buddha continued. What think you, Subhuti? If a disciple should bestow as alms an abundance of the seven treasures sufficient to fill the three thousand great worlds, would he thereby acquire a considerable blessing and merit?

Subhuti replied:—Honored of the worlds! Such a disciple would acquire a very considerable blessing.

The Lord Buddha said:—Subhuti, if such a blessing and merit had any substantiality, if it was anything other than a mere expression, the Tathagata would not have used the words, 'blessing and merit.'

(13 B) What think you, Subhuti? Are the atoms of dust that comprise the three thousand great universes very numerous?

Very numerous indeed, Blessed Lord!

Subhuti, when the Tathagata speaks of 'atoms of dust,' it does not mean that he has in mind any definite or arbitrary conception, he merely uses the words as a figure of speech. It is just the same with the words, 'the great universes,' they do not assert any definite or arbitrary idea, he merely uses the words as words.

(13 D) Subhuti, if any good and pious disciple, man or woman, for the sake of charity has been sacrificing his or her life for generation after generation as many as the grains of sand in the three thousand great universes, and another disciple has been simply studying and observing even one stanza of this Scripture and explaining it to others, his blessing and merit will be far greater.

(8) What think you, Subhuti? If a disciple bestowed in charity an abundance of the seven treasures sufficient to fill the three thousand great universes, would there accrue to that person a considerable blessing and merit?

Subhuti replied:—A very considerable blessing and merit. And why? Because what the Lord has referred to as 'blessing and merit' does not refer to any objective value or quantity; he only refers to them in a relative sense.

The Lord Buddha continued: If there is another disciple who, after studying and observing even a single stanza of this Scripture, explains its meaning to others, his blessing and merit will be much greater. And why? Because from these explanations Buddhas have attained Anuttara-samyak-sambodhi and their teachings are based upon this sacred Scripture. But, Subhuti, as soon as I have spoken of these Buddhas and their Dharmas, I must recall the words, for there are no Buddhas and no Dharmas.

(14 C) The Lord Buddha then continued. When a Bodhisattva-Mahasattva begins the practice of attaining Anuttara-samyak-sambodhi, he must give up, also, all clinging to arbitrary conceptions about phenomena. When engaged in thinking, he should definitely exclude all thoughts connected with the phenomena of sight, sound, taste, smell, touch, and all discriminations based upon them, keeping his thinking independent of all such arbitrary conceptions of phenomena. The mind is disturbed by these discriminations of sense concepts and the following arbitrary conceptions about them and, as the mind becomes disturbed, it falls into false imaginations as to one's self and its relation to other selves. It is for that reason that the Tathagata has constantly urged the Bodhisattva-Mahasattvas in their practice of charity not to be influenced by any arbitrary conceptions of phenomena such as sights, sounds, etc.

The Bodhisattva-Mahasattva should also bestow alms, uninfluenced by any preconceived thoughts as to self and other selves and for the sole purpose of benefiting sentient beings, always remembering that both the phenomena and sentient beings are to be considered as mere expressions. Nevertheless, Subhuti, the teaching of the Tathagata are all true, credible, immutable: they are neither extravagant nor chimerical. The same is true of the attainments of the Tathagatas—they should be considered as neither realities nor as unrealities.

Subhuti, if a Bodhisattva-Mahasattva, in practising charity, conceives within his mind any of these arbitrary conceptions discriminating himself from other selves, he will be like a man walking in darkness and seeing nothing. But if the Bodhisattva-Mahasattva, in his practice of charity, has no arbitrary conceptions of the attainment of the blessing and merit which he will attain by such practice, he will be like a person with good eyes, seeing all things clearly as in the bright sunshine.

If in future ages there should be any good and pious disciple, either man or woman, able to faithfully observe and study this Scripture, his success and attainment of inestimable and illimitable blessing and merit will be instantly known and appreciated by the Transcendental Eye of the Tathagata.

The Practice of Selfless Kindness
(Sila Paramita)

(23 B) Subhuti, when a disciple is moved to make objective gifts of charity, he should also practice the Sila Paramita of selfless kindness, that is, he should remember that there is no arbitrary distinction between one's own self and the selfhood of others and, therefore, he should practice charity by giving, not objective gifts alone, but the selfless gifts of kindness and sympathy. If any disciple will simply practice kindness, he will soon attain Anuttara-samyak-sambodhi.

Subhuti, by what I have just said about kindness, the Tathagata does not mean that a disciple when making gifts should hold in his mind any arbitrary conceptions about kindness, for kindness after all is only a word and charity should be spontaneous and selfless.

(24) The Lord Buddha continued:—Subhuti, if any disciple heaped together the seven treasures forming an elevation as high as Mount Sumeru and as many Mount Sumerus as there are in the three thousand great universes, and bestowed them in charity, his merit would be less than what would accrue to the disciple that simply observed and studied this Scripture and in the kindness of his heart explained it to others. The latter disciple would accumulate greater blessing and merit in comparison of a hundred to one, yes, of a hundred thousand myriads to one. Nothing can be compared with it.

(25) The Lord Buddha continued:—Do not think, Subhuti, that the Tathagata would consider within himself:—I will deliver human beings. That would be a degrading thought. Why? Because really there are no sentient beings to be delivered by the Tathagata. Should there be any sentient beings to be de-

livered by the Tathagata, it would mean that the Tathagata
was cherishing within his mind arbitrary conceptions of phenomena such as one's own self, other selves, living beings and
an universal self. Even when the Tathagata refers to himself,
he is not holding in his mind any such arbitrary thought. Only
terrestrial human beings think of selfhood as being a personal
possession. Subhuti, even the expression 'terrestrial beings' as
used by the Tathagata does not mean that there are any such
beings. It is used only as a figure of speech.

(28) The Lord Buddha continued:—Subhuti, if a disciple bestowed as alms an abundance of the seven treasures sufficient
to fill as many worlds as there are grains of sand in the Ganges
river, and if another disciple, having realized the principle of
the egolessness of all things and thereby had attained perfect
self-lessness, the self-less disciple would have more blessing and
merit than the one who merely practiced objective charity. And
why? Because Bodhisatta-Mahasattvas do not look upon their
blessing and merit as a private possession.

Subhuti enquired of the Lord Buddha:—What do the words
'Bodhisattva-Mahasattvas do not look upon their blessing and
merit as a private possession' mean?

The Lord Buddha replied:—As those blessing and merit
have never been sought in any covetous spirit by Bodhisattva-
Mahasattvas, so by that same spirit they do not look upon them
as a private possession, but as the common possession of all animate beings.

The Practice of Humility and Patience
(The Kshanti Paramita)

(9) What do you think, Subhuti? Supposing a disciple who
has attained the degree of *Crotapanna* (entered the stream),
could he make any such arbitrary assertion as, 'I have entered
the stream'?

Subhuti replied:—No, honored of the worlds! Because,
while, by that measure of attainment, it means that he has entered the Holy Stream, yet, speaking truly, he has not entered
anything, nor has his mind entertained any such arbitrary conception as form, sound, taste, odor, touch and discrimination.
It is because of that degree of attainment that he is entitled to
be called a Crotapanna.

What think you, Subhuti? Suppose a disciple has attained the degree of *Sakradagamin* (One more return), could he make any such arbitrary assertion as, 'I have attained the degree of Sakradagamin'?

No, Honored of the worlds. Because by the degree of Sakradagamin, it is meant that he is to be reborn but once more. Yet speaking truly, there will be no rebirth either in this world or in any other world. It is because he knows this that he is to be called a Sakradagamin.

What think you, Subhuti? Suppose a disciple has attained the degree of *Anagamin* (Never to return), could he hold within his mind any such arbitrary conception as, 'I have attained the degree of Anagamin'?

No, Honored of the worlds! Because by the degree of Anagamin it means that he is never to return, yet, speaking truly, one who has attained that degree never cherishes any such arbitrary conception and for that reason, he is entitled to be called, an Anagamin.

What think you, Subhuti? Suppose a disciple has attained the degree of *Arahat* (Fully enlightened), could he entertain within his mind any such arbitrary conception as, 'I have become an Arahat'?

No, Honored of the worlds! Because speaking truly, there is no such thing as a fully enlightened one. Should a disciple who has attained such a degree of enlightenment, cherish within his mind such an arbitrary conception as, 'I have become an Arahat,' he would soon be grasping after such things as his own selfhood, other selves, living beings and a universal self. O Blessed Lord! Thou hast said that I have attained the samadhi of 'non-assertion' and, therefore, have reached the climax of human attainment and, because of it, am an Arahat. If I had cherished within my mind the thought, 'I am an Arahat free from all desire'! my Lord could not have declared that Subhuti delights himself in the practice of silence and tranquillity. But, speaking truly, I have cherished no such arbitrary thought, so my Lord could truly say, 'Subhuti delights himself in the practice of silence and tranquillity.'

(10) What think you, Subhuti? When the Tathagata in a previous life was with Dipankara Buddha, did I receive any definite teaching or attain any definite degree of discipline because of which I later become a Buddha?

No, Honored of the worlds! When Tathagata was a disciple of Buddha Dipankara, speaking truly, he received no definite teaching nor did he attain any definite excellence.

What think you, Subhuti? Do the Bodhisattva-Mahasattvas embellish the Buddha-lands to which they go?

No, Honored of the worlds! And why? Because what the Lord means by the expression, 'embellishment of the Buddha-lands' is self contradictory, for Buddha-lands thus embellished could no longer be called Buddha-lands. Therefore, the expression, 'embellishment of the Buddha-lands'; is merely a figure of speech.

The Lord Buddha continued:—For this reason, Subhuti, the minds of all Bodhisattvas should be purified of all such conceptions as relate to seeing, hearing, tasting, smelling, touching and discriminating. They should use the mental faculties spontaneously and naturally, but unconstrained by any preconceptions arising from the senses.

Subhuti, supposing a man had a body as large as Mount Sumeru. What think you? Would his body be counted great?

Exceedingly great, Honored of the worlds! Because what the Lord Buddha really means by the expression, 'the greatness of the human body,' is not limited by any arbitrary conception whatever, so it can rightly be called, 'great.'

(14 B) In what has been said in the foregoing about the Third Paramita of Patience, the Tathagata does not hold in his mind any arbitrary conceptions of the phenomena of patience— he merely refers to it as the Third Paramita. And why? Because when, in a previous life, the Prince of Kalinga severed the flesh from my limbs and my body, even then I was free from any such ideas as my own self, other selves, living beings, a universal self. Because if, at the time of my suffering, I had cherished any of these arbitrary ideas, inevitably, I would have fallen into impatience and hatred.

Besides, Subhuti, I recall that during my five hundred previous lives, I had used life after life to practice patience and to look upon my life humbly as though it was some saintly being called upon to suffer humility. Even then my mind was free from any such arbitrary conceptions of phenomena as my own self, other selves, living beings, and a universal self.

(16) The Blessed One resumed:—Subhuti, should there be among the faithful disciples some who have not yet matured

their karma and who must first suffer the natural retribution of sins committed in some previous life by being degraded to a lower domain of existence and should they earnestly and faithfully observe and study this Scripture and because of it be despised and persecuted by the people, their karma will immediately be matured and they will at once attain Anuttara-samyak-sambodhi.

Subhuti, I recall that long ago, numberless asamkhyas of kalpas before the advent of Dipankara Buddha, without any fault having been committed by me, I served and worshipped with offerings and received spiritual instruction and discipline from eight hundred and four thousand myriads of Buddhas, yet in the far off ages of the last kalpa of this world, if a disciple shall faithfully observe, study and put into practice the teachings of this Scripture, the blessing that he by so doing will gain, will far exceed that acquired by me during those long years of service and discipline under those many Buddhas. Yes, it will exceed my poor merit, in comparison as ten myriads to one. Yes, even more; as uncounted myriads to one.

The Lord Buddha continued:—Subhuti, in contrast to what I have said as to the inestimable blessing that will come·to earnest disciples who observe and study and practice this Scripture in that far off last kalpa, I must tell you, that probably there will be some disciples who upon hearing this Scripture will become bewildered in their minds and will not believe it. Subhuti, you should remember that just as the Dharma of this Scripture transcends human thought, so the effect and the final result of studying it and putting it into practice is also inscrutable.

The Practice of Zeal and Perseverance
(The Virya Paramita)

(11) What think you, Subhuti? If there are as many Ganges Rivers as there are grains of sand in the River Ganges, will these rivers be very numerous?

Exceedingly numerous, my Lord.

Supposing there were these innumerable rivers, how immeasurable would be their grains of sand! And yet, Subhuti, if a good and pious disciple, either man or woman, should bestow as alms an amount of the seven treasures equal to those grains of sand, would the merit that would accrue to him be a considerable blessing and merit?

A very considerable merit, My Lord.

Subhuti, if another disciple after studying and observing even one stanza of this Scripture, should explain it to others his blessing and merit would be greater.

(12) Moreover, Subhuti, if any disciple in any place should teach even one stanza of this Scripture, that place would become sacred ground and would be held in reverence, and would be enriched by offerings from gods, devas and spirits, as though it was a sacred pagoda or temple. How much more sacred would the place become if a disciple studied and observed the whole of this Scripture! Be assured, Subhuti, that such a disciple will succeed in the attainment of Anuttara-samyak-sambodhi, and the place where this Scripture is reverenced will be like an altar consecrated to Buddha, or to one of his honored disciples.

(15) The Lord Buddha continued:--Subhuti, should there be any good pious disciple, man or woman, who in his zeal to practice charity is willing to sacrifice his life in the morning, or at noon-tide, or in the evening, on as many occasions as there are grains of sand in the river Ganges, even if these occasions recur for a hundred thousand myriad kalpas, would his blessing and merit be great?

It would be great, indeed, Lord Buddha.

Supposing, Subhuti, another disciple should observe and study this Scripture in pure faith, his blessing and merit would be greater. And if still another disciple, besides observing and studying this Scripture, should zealously explain it to others and copy it and circulate it, his blessing and merit would be far greater.

In other words, Subhuti, this Scripture is invested with a virtue and power that is inestimable, illimitable and ineffable. The Tathagata elucidates this Scripture only to those disciples who are earnestly and perseveringly seeking the perfect realization of Anuttara-samyak-sambodhi and attaining the Bodhisattva stages of compassion that characterize the Mahayana. As disciples become able to zealously and faithfully observe and study this Scripture, explain it to others and circulate it widely, the Tathagata will recognize and support them until they shall succeed in the attainment of its inestimable, illimitable and wonderful virtues. Such disciples will share with the Tathagata its burden of compassion and its reward of Anuttara-samyak-sambodhi.

And why, Subhuti, is this promise limited to the Mahayana disciples? It is because the Hinayana disciples have not yet been able to free themselves from such arbitrary conceptions of phenomena as one's own selfhood, other personalities, living beings and a universal self and, therefore, are not yet able to faithfully and earnestly observe and study and explain this Scripture to others.

Listen, Subhuti! Wherever this Scripture shall be observed and studied and explained, that place will become sacred ground to which countless devas and angels will bring offerings. Such places, however humble they may be, will be reverenced as though they were famous temples and pagodas, to which countless pilgrims will come to offer worship and incense. And over them the devas and angels will hover like a cloud and will sprinkle upon them an offering of celestial flowers.

The Practice of Tranquillity
(The Dhyana Paramita)

(17) Then Subhuti enquired of the Lord Buddha, saying: Supposing a good pious disciple, either man or woman, having begun the practice of attaining Anuttara-samyak-sambodhi (should still find his mind disturbed), how is he to keep his mind tranquil, how is he to wholly subdue his wandering thoughts and craving desires?

The Lord Buddha replied:—Subhuti, any good pious disciple who undertakes the practice of concentrating his mind in an effort to realize Anuttara-samyak-sambodhi, should cherish only one thought, namely, when I attain this highest perfect Wisdom, I will deliver all sentient beings into the eternal peace of Nirvana. If this purpose and vow is sincere, these sentient beings are already delivered. And yet, Subhuti, if the full truth is realized, one would know that not a single sentient being has ever been delivered. And why, Subhuti? Because if the Bodhisattva-Mahasattvas have kept in mind any such arbitrary conceptions as one's own self, other selves, living beings, or a universal self, they could not be called Bodhisattva-

Mahasattvas. And what does this mean, Subhuti? It means that there are no sentient beings to be delivered and there is no selfhood that can begin the practice of seeking to attain Anuttara-samyak-sambodhi.

What think you, Subhuti? When the Tathagata was with Buddha Dipankara did he have any such arbitrary conception of the Dharma as would warrant him in seeking to attain Anuttara-samyak-sambodhi intuitively?

No, Blessed Lord. As I understand what thou hast said to us, when the Lord Buddha was with Buddha Dipankara, he had no such arbitrary conception of the Dharma as would warrant him in seeking to attain Arnuttara-samyak-sambodhi intuitively.

The Lord Buddha was much pleased with this and said:— You are right, Subhuti. Speaking truly there is no such arbitrary conception of the Dharma as that. If there had been, Dipankara Buddha would not have foretold that in some future life, I would attain Buddhahood under the name of Shakyamuni. What does this mean, Subhuti? It means that what I attained is not something limited and arbitrary that can be called, 'Anuttara-samyak-sambodhi,' but is Buddhahood whose essence is identical with the essence of all things and is what it is—universal, inconceivable, inscrutable.

Supposing, Subhuti, there should still be a disciple who asserts that the Tathagata had some ideas about the Dharma that warranted him in seeking to attain Anuttra-samyak-sambodhi. Be it understood, Subhuti, that the Tathagata truly had no ideas of the Dharma that warranted him in seeking to attain Anuttara-samyak-sambodhi.

The Lord Buddha emphasized this by saying:—Subhuti, the Buddhahood to which the Tathagata attained is both the same as Anuttara-samyak-sambodhi and not the same. This is only another way of saying that the phenomena of all things is of one 'suchness' with Buddhahood and Anuttara-samyak-sambodhi, and that it is neither reality nor unreality but abides together with all phenomena in emptiness and silence, inconceivable and inscrutable. Subhuti, that is why I say that the Dharma of all things can never be embraced within any arbitrary conception of phenomena however universal that conception may be. That is why it is called the Dharma and why there is no such thing as the Dharma.

Subhuti, suppose I should speak of the largeness of the human body, what would you understand by it?

Honored of the worlds! I should understand that the Lord Buddha was not speaking of the largeness of the human body as an arbitrary conception of its phenomenality. I should understand that the words carried only an imaginary meaning.

Subhuti, it is just the same when Bodhisattva-Mahasattvas speak of delivering numberless sentient beings. If they have in mind any arbitrary conception of sentient being or of definite numbers, they are unworthy to be called Bodhisattva-Mahasattvas. And why, Subhuti? Because the very reason why they are called Bodhisattva-Mahasattvas is because they have abandoned all such arbitrary conceptions. And what is true of one arbitrary conception is true of all conceptions. The Tathagata's teachings are entirely free from all such arbitrary conceptions as one's own self, other selves, living beings or a universal self.

To make this teaching more emphatic, the Lord Buddha continued:—If a Bodhisattva-Mahasattva was to speak like this:—I will add embellishments to the Buddha-lands, he would be unworthy to be called a Bodhisattva-Mahasattva. And why? Because the Tathagata has explicitly taught that when a Bodhisattva-Mahasattva uses such words, they must not hold in mind any arbitrary conception of phenomena; they are to use such expressions merely as so many words.

Subhuti, it is only those disciples whose understanding can penetrate deeply enough into the meaning of the Tathagata's teachings concerning the egolessness of both things and living beings, and who can clearly understand their significance, that are worthy to be called Bodhisattva-Mahasattvas.

(18) The Lord Buddha then enquired of Subhuti, saying: What think you? Does the Tathagata possess a physical eye?

Subhuti replied:—Surely, Blessed Lord, he possesses a physical eye.

Does he possess the eye of enlightenment, Subhuti?

Certainly the Tathagata possesses the eye of enlightenment; he would not be the Lord Buddha otherwise.

Does the Tathagata possess the eye of transcendental intelligence?

Yes, Blessed Lord, the Tathagata possesses the eye of transcendental intelligence.

Does the Tathagata possess the eye of spiritual intuition?

Yes, Blessed Lord, the Tathagata possesses the eye of spiritual intuition.

Does the Tathagata possess the eye of a Buddha's love and compassion for all sentient life, Subhuti?

Subhuti assented and said:—Blessed Lord, thou lovest all sentient life.

What think you, Subhuti? When I referred to the grains of sand in the river Ganges, did I assert that they were truly grains of sand?

No, Blessed Lord, you only spoke of them as grains of sand.

Subhuti, if there were as many Ganges rivers as there are grains of sand in the river Ganges, and if there were as many Buddha-lands as there are grains of sand in all of these innumerable rivers, would these Buddha-lands be considered as very numerous?

Very numerous, indeed, Lord Buddha.

Listen, Subhuti. Within these innumerable Buddha-lands there are every form of sentient beings with all their various mentalities and conceptions, all of which are fully known to the Tathagata, but not one of them is held in the Tathagata's mind as an arbitrary conception of phenomena. They are merely thought of. Not one of this vast accumulation of conceptions from beginningless time, through the present and into the never ending future, not one of them is graspable.

(30) The Lord Buddha resumed:—Subhuti, if any good and pious disciple, either man or woman, were to take the three thousand great universes and grind them into impalpable powder and blow it away into space, what think you, Subhuti? do you think this powder would have any individual existence?

Subhuti replied:—Yes, Blessed Lord, as an impalpable powder infinitely dissipated, it might be said to have a relative existence, but as the Blessed One uses the words, it has no existence—the words have only a figurative meaning. Otherwise the words would imply a belief in the existence of matter as an independent and self-existent entity, which it is not.

Moreover, when the Tathagata refers to the 'three thousand great universes,' he could only do so as a figure of speech. And why? Because if the three thousand great universes really existed, their only reality would consist in their cosmic unity. Whether as impalpable powder or as great universes, what matters it? It is only in the sense of the cosmic unity of ultimate essence that the Tathagata can rightfully refer to it.

The Lord Buddha was much pleased with this reply and said:—Subhuti, although terrestrial human beings have always grasped after the arbitrary conception of matter and great universes, the conception has no true basis—it is an illusion of mortal mind. Even when it is referred to as 'cosmic unity' it is something inscrutable.

(31) The Lord Buddha continued:—If any disciple were to say that the Tathagata, in his teachings, has constantly referred to himself, other selves, living beings, an Universal Self, what think you Subhuti? would that disciple have understood the meaning of what I have been teaching?

Subhuti replied:—No, Blessed Lord. That disciple would not have understood the meaning of the Lord's teachings. For when the Lord has referred to them he has never referred to their actual existence; he has only used the words as figures and symbols. It is only in that sense that they can be used, for conceptions, and ideas, and limited truths, and Dharmas have no more reality than have matter and phenomena.

Then the Lord made this more emphatic by saying:—Subhuti, when disciples begin their practice of seeking to attain Anuttara-samyak-sambodhi, they ought thus to see, to perceive, to know, to understand, and to realize that all things and all Dharmas are no-things, and, therefore, they ought not to conceive within their minds any arbitrary conceptions whatever.

(32) The Lord Buddha continued:—Subhuti, if any disciple bestowed upon the Tathagatas as alms an abundance of the seven treasures sufficient to fill the innumerable and illimitable worlds; and if another disciple, a good and pious man or woman, in his practice of seeking to attain Anuttara-samyak-sambodhi should earnestly and faithfully observe and study even a single stanza of this Scripture and explain it to others, the accumulated blessing and merit of that latter disciple would be relatively greater.

Subhuti, how is it possible to explain this Scripture to others without holding in mind any arbitrary conception of things and phenomena and Dharmas? It can only be done, Subhuti, by keeping the mind in perfect tranquillity and in self-less oneness with the 'suchness' that is Tathagatahood. And why? Because all the mind's arbitrary conceptions of matter, phenomena, and of all conditioning factors and all conceptions and ideas relating thereto are like a dream, a phantasm, a bubble, a shadow, the evanescent dew, the lightning's flash. Every true disciple should thus look upon all phenomena and upon all the activities of the mind, and keep his mind empty and self-less and tranquil.

The Practice of Wisdom
(The Prajna Paramita)

(7) What think you, Subhuti? Has the Tathagata attained anything that can be described as Anuttara-samyak-sambodhi? Has he ever given you any such teaching?

Subhuti replied:—As I understand the teaching of the Lord Buddha, there is no such thing as Anuttara-samyak-sambodhi, nor is it possible for the Tathagata to teach any fixed Dharma. And why? Because the things taught by the Tathagata are, in their essential nature, inconceivable and inscrutable; they are neither existent nor non-existent; they are neither phenomena nor noumena. What is meant by this? It means that Buddhas and Bodhistattwas are not enlightened by fixed teachings but by an intuitive process that is spontaneous and natural.

(26) Then the Lord Buddha enquired of Subhuti:—What think you, Subhuti? Is it possible to recognize the Tathagata by the thirty-two marks of physical excellence?

Subhuti replied:—Yes, Honored of the worlds:—The Tathagata may be thus recognized.

Subhuti, if that is so then Chakravartin, the legendary king of the world (who also had the thirty-two marks of excellence) would be classed among the Tathagatas.

Then Subhuti, realizing his error, said:—Honored of the worlds! Now I realize that the Tathagata can not be recognized merely by his thirty-two marks of physical excellence.

The Lord Buddha then said:—Should anyone looking at an image or a likeness of the Tathagata, claim to know the Tathagata and should offer worship and prayer to him, you should consider such a person a heretic who does not know the true Tathagata.

(5) What think you, Subhuti? Is it possible even to see the Tathagata in the phenomena of his physical appearance?

No, Honored of the worlds! It is impossible even to see the Tathagata in the phenomena of his physical appearance. And why? Because the phenomena of his physical appearance is not the same as the essential Tathagata.

You are right, Subhuti. The phenomena of the physical appearance is wholly illusion. It is not until a disciple understands this that he can realize the true Tathagata.

(13 C) What think you, Subhuti? Can one grasp the Tathagata's personality by its thirty-two marks of physical excellence?

No, Blessed One! We can not grasp the Tathagata's wonderful personality by its thirty-two marks of excellence. And why? Because what the Tathagata has expressed as 'thirty-two marks of physical excellence' does not convey any definite or arbitrary assertions as to the qualities of a Buddha. The words are used merely as a figure of speech.

(29) The Lord said:—Subhuti, if any disciple were to say that the Tathagata is now coming or now going, or is now sitting up or is now lying down, he would not have understood the principle that I have been teaching. And why? Because while the word, Tathagata, means 'He who has thus come' and 'He who has thus gone,' the true Tathagata is never coming from anywere, nor is he going anywhere. The name, Tathagata, is merely a word.

(20) Again the Lord Buddha enquired of Subhuti, saying: Can the Tathagata be fully known through any manifestation in form (of either body or idea)?

No, Honored of the worlds! The Tathagata can not be fully known by any manifestation in form. And why? Because the phenomena of form is inadequate to incarnate Buddhahood. It can only serve as a mere expression, a hint of that which is inconceivable.

What think you, Subhuti? Can the Tathagata be fully known by any or all of his transcendental transformations?

No, Honored of the worlds! The Tathagata can not be fully known by even all of his transcendental transformations. And why? Because what the Tathagata has just referred to as 'transcendental transformations' is merely a figure of speech. Even the highest Bodhisattva-Mahasattvas are unable to fully realize even by intuition that which is essentially inscrutable.

(27) The Lord Buddha continued:—Subhuti, do not think the opposite either that when the Tathagata attained Anuttara-

samyak-sambodhi it was not by means of his possession of the
thirty-two marks of physical excellence. Do not think that.
Should you think that, then when you begin the practice of
seeking to attain Anuttara-samyak-sambodhi you would think
that all systems of phenomena and all conceptions about phenomena are to be cut off and rejected. Do not think that. And
why? Because when a disciple practices seeking to attain Anuttara-samyak-sambodhi, he should neither grasp after such arbitrary conceptions of phenomena nor reject them.

(21) The Lord Buddha then warned Subhuti, saying:—Subhuti, do not think that the Tathagata ever considers within his
own mind: I ought to enunciate a system of teaching for the
elucidation of the Dharma. You should never cherish such an
unworthy thought. And why? Because if any disciple should
harbor such a thought, he would not only be misunderstanding
the teaching of the Tathagata but he would be slandering him
as well. Moreover, what has just been referred to as 'a system
of teaching' has no meaning, as Truth can not be cut up into
pieces and arranged into a system. The words can only be used
as a figure of speech.

Thereupon the Venerable Subhuti, because of his enlightened and transcendental intelligence, addressed the Lord Buddha, saying:—Blessed Lord! In ages to come when any sentient
beings shall happen by chance to hear this Scripture will they
awaken within their minds the essential elements of faith?

The Lord Buddha said:—Subhuti, why do you still hold
within your mind such arbitrary conceptions? There are no
such things as sentient beings, neither are there any non-sen-
tient beings. And why, Subhuti? Because what you have in
mind as sentient beings are unreal and non-existent. When the
Tathagata has used such words in his teachings, he has merely
used them as figures of speech. Your question, therefore, is
irrelevant.

(22) Subhuti, again enquired:—Blessed Lord! When thou
didst attain Anuttara-samyak-sambodhi didst thou feel within
thy mind that nothing had been acquired?

The Lord Buddha replied:—That is it precisely, Subhuti.
When I attained Anuttara-samyak-sambodhi, I did not feel, as
grasped within my mind, any arbitrary conception of Dharma,
not even the slightest. Even the words Anuttara-samyak-sambodhi are merely words.

(23 A) Moreover, Subhuti, what I have attained in Anuttara-samyak-sambodhi is the same as what all others have attained. It is something that is undifferentiated, neither to be regarded as a high state, nor is it to be regarded as a low state. It is wholly independent of any definitive or arbitrary conceptions of an individual self, other selves, living beings or an Universal Self.

Conclusion

(6) Subhuti respectfully enquired of the Lord Buddha:— Honored of the worlds! In future days, if a disciple hears this teaching or a part of it—a section or a sentence—will it awaken true faith in his mind?

Subhuti, do not doubt it. Even at the remote period of five hundred years after the nirvana of the Tathagata, there will be those who, practicing charity and keeping the precepts, will believe in sections and sentences of this Scripture and will awaken within their minds a true pure faith. You should know, however, that such disciples, long ago, have planted roots of goodness, not simply before one Buddha shrine, or two, or five, but before the shrines of a hundred thousand myriad as-amkyas of Buddhas, so that when they hear sentences and sections of this Scripture there will instantly awaken within their minds a pure true faith.

Subhuti, the Tathagata knows that the sentient beings who awaken faith after hearing sentences and sections of this Scrip-ture will accumulate blessing and merit that are inestimable. How do I know this? Because these sentient beings must have already discarded such arbitrary conceptions of phenomena as one's own self, other selves, living beings and Universal Self. If they had not, their minds would inevitably grasp after such things and then they would not be able to practice charity nor keep the precepts.

Moreover, these sentient beings must have also discarded all arbitrary ideas relating to the conceptions of a personal self, other personalities, living beings and a Universal Self, because if they had not, their minds would inevitably grasp after such relative ideas. Futher, these sentient beings must have already discarded all arbitrary ideas relating to the conception of the non-existence of a personal self, other personalities, living beings and a Universal Self. If they had not, their minds would still be grasping after such ideas. Therefore, every disciple who is seeking Anuttara-samyak-sambodhi should discard, not only conceptions of one's own selfhood, other selves, living beings and a Universal Selfhood, but should discard, also, all ideas about such conceptions and all ideas about the non-existence of such conceptions.

While the Tathagata, in his teaching, constantly makes use of conceptions and ideas about them, disciples should keep in mind the unreality of all such conceptions and ideas. They should recall that the Tathagata, in making use of them in explaining the Dharma always uses them in the resemblance of a raft that is of use only to cross a river. As the raft is of no further use after the river is crossed, it should be discarded. So these arbitrary conceptions of things and about things should be wholly given up as one attains enlightenment. How much more should be given up conceptions of non-existent things (and everything is non-existent).

(14 A) As Subhuti listened intently to the words of the Lord Buddha, the teaching of the Scripture penetrated into the depths of his understanding and he fully realized that it was the true Path to enlightenment. The tears came to his eyes as he realized this and he said:—O Blessed Lord! I have never before realized this profound Scripture. Thou hast opened my eyes to its Transcendental Wisdom.

Honored of the worlds! What has been taught us concerning the true significance of phenomena carries no arbitrary or limited meaning. The teaching is, as you say, a raft that will carry us to the other shore. Noble Lord! when as at present, I have the chance of hearing this Scripture, it is not difficult for me to concentrate my mind upon it and to clearly understand its significance, and it awakens within my mind a pure faith. In future time—after five centuries—if there be any ready to hear it and ready to attain enlightenment, able to concentrate their minds upon it, able to realize a clear understanding of it, able to awaken a pure faith in it, such a disciple will hereby become a wonderful and preëminent disciple. And if there is such a disciple the reason he will be able to awaken a pure faith will be because he has ceased to cherish any arbitrary conceptions as to his own selfness, the selfhood of others, of living beings, of an Universal Self. Why is this so? It is because, if he is cherishing any arbitrary conception as to his own selfhood, he will be cherishing something that is non-existent. It is the same as to all arbitrary conceptions of other personalities, living beings, on an Universal Self. They are all expressions of things that are non-existent. If a disciple is able to discard all arbitrary conceptions of phenomena or about phenomena, he will immediately become a Buddha.

The Lord Buddha was much pleased with this reply, saying: True indeed! If a disciple having heard this Scripture is not surprised, nor frightened, nor does not shrink from it, you should know that he is worthy to be regarded as a truly wonderful disciple.

(13 A) Subhuti said to the Blessed One:—By what name shall this scripture be known, so that it will be understood and honored and studied?

The Lord Buddha replied:—This Scripture shall be known as the *Vajracchedika Prajna Paramita.* By this name it shall be reverenced, studied and observed. What is meant by this name? It means that when the Lord Buddha named it Prajna Paramita, he did not have in mind any definite or arbitrary conception and so he thus named it. It is the Scripture that is hard and sharp like a diamond that will cut away all arbitrary conceptions and bring one to the other shore of enlightenment.

What think you, Subhuti? Has the Tathagata given you any definite teaching in this scripture?

No, Blessed Lord! The Tathagata has not given us any definite teaching in this Scripture.

* * *

(32 B) When the Lord Buddha had finished the teaching recorded in this Scripture, the Venerable Subhuti, together with all the assembled Bhikshus and Bhikshuni and disciples both men and women, and all the devas and angels, greatly rejoiced and, thereafter, sincerely believing the teaching, heartily accepted it, faithfully observed it, and zealously practised it.

THE SURANGAMA SUTRA

Introduction

THUS have I heard. Upon a memorable occasion, the Lord
Buddha while staying at the Jetavana Meditation Hall in
the city of Sravasti delivered a discourse to twelve hundred
Great Disciples who were all great Arhats and free from all
intoxicants, that is, they were all perfectly emancipated from
sensual attachments and defilements. They were true heirs of
their Lord Buddha and worthy to share their Lord's responsibility for the ever-continuing preaching of the Lord's Dharma.
They had all transcended phenomenal existence and could
manifest their gracious presence by a Buddhist influence wherever they sojourned. They were so highly advanced in the transcendental attainments that they were perfectly qualified to receive the Dharma from their Lord and Master and had so
greatly profited from the Lord's teaching that they knew well
how, with the Lord Buddha, to themselves turn the mysterious
wheel of the true Dharma. They had kept the Precepts with
such strict observance and perfect purity as to be qualified as
perfect models for this triple world. They could assume innumerable appearance-bodies in response to the earnest prayer
of any sentient being to rescue them and to perfect their emancipation. They were also willing to extend their helping hands
into the future, so that all sentient beings in the future might
become emancipated and free from all their fetters of earthly
defilement.

Among the Great Bhikshus present, acting as leaders, were
the wise Sariputra, the Great Maudgalyayana, the Great Kaustila, Purna Metaluniputra, Subhuti, Upanishada, and many
others equally well known and highly regarded. In addition
there were present many Pratyeka-Buddhas, who had mastered
the teachings and perfected the practices, together with innumerable novice disciples. They all came to pay homage to Lord
Buddha and also to associate themselves with all the great
Bhikshus and their disciples in this great Dharma assembly.

which had gathered for the "Summer Devotion" where they could make public confession and practice Dhyana together.

Besides the great company of Bhikshus and Disciples that had gathered from far and near, there were present Bodhi-sattva-Mahasattvas from all the ten quarters of the Universe who had come to pay their highest respect to the Lord Shakya-muni Buddha as though it was an offering to a loving parent. Moreover, they came to entreat the Lord Buddha for some high teaching that would solve their mental puzzles and help them to get rid of the troublesome doubts which they occasionally experienced in their meditations.

Then the Lord Buddha ascended the Honorable Throne of Dharma and immediately became absorbed in profound con-templation with such noble solemnity and tranquillity that the whole company were spellbound by its profound silence and mystery. At the same time all the Bodhisattva-Mahasattvas, as numerous as the particles of sand in the river Ganges, with Manjusri the Great Bodhisattva at their head, gathered about the Lord Buddha and merged their deep meditation with the Lord Buddha's perfect Samadhi. Seldom, indeed, had any of them ever before experienced such serenity and quietness as then pervaded this Great Dharma Assembly. Wonderful music like the songs of the Kalavinka and Jiva-jiva birds seem to come from the Lord Buddha's perfect Samadhi and to fill the air with its heavenly music, and floating away to pervade the ten quarters of the Universe.

Upon this occasion, Prasenajit the King of Sravasti in cele-bration of the anniversary of his father's death, prepared a special feast of choice vegetables and dainties, and came per-sonally to call upon the Lord Buddha and to invite him and all the Great Bodhisattvas-Mahasattvas to attend a reception at the royal palace. At the same time the elders and wealthy laymen of the city added to the King's celebration by preparing jointly another feast and invited all the Disciples of the Lord Buddha to attend while the Lord and the Great Disciples were with the King. The Lord Buddha, knowing all about it, bade his Great Disciple Manjusri to first lead part of the Bodhisat-tvas-Mahasattva and Arhats to attend the Laymen's homes and to receive their offerings.

Ananda was the only one of the Great Disciples who was noticeably absent. Owing to a previous engagement in a distant district, he had not yet returned. He was quite alone and when he reached the Meditation Hall upon his return, he found it deserted, not a single disciple about, nor were there any offerings from their patrons in sight. Then Ananda, thoughtful as ever, took his alms bowl and entered into the city begging food from house to house in regular order, his only thought being to receive the offerings from all alike even to the last *danapati*. It mattered nothing to Ananda whether the offering was small or generous, attractive or repulsive, whether the giver was of the Kshatriya caste or the Candra caste, to him the all important thing was to practice kindness and compassion on all alike with no discrimination whatever. He sought only to attain the inestimable merit of delivering all sentient beings, treating them all alike.

Ananda had heard that the Lord on one occasion had rebuked Subhuti and Mahakatyayana for showing discrimination towards Arahats in their practice of begging. He greatly admired the Lord's liberal mind and determined that he would not commit the same fault himself. He was proud of his good name and did not wish to give cause for people having suspicions or for slandering about himself, so he quietly crossed the dried moat that surrounded the city, entered the city-gate with solemn gravity. He was a noticeable figure in his neat attire and solemn manner as if he was on a special mission to receive some ceremonial offering.

While Ananda was begging in orderly succession, he came to the house of a prostitute named Maudenka who had a beautiful daughter named Pchiti. This young maiden was attracted by Ananda's youthful and attractive person and pleaded earnestly with her mother to conjure the young monk by the magic spell of *"bramanyika."* This the mother did and Ananda coming under the spell of its magic became fascinated by the charm of the young maiden and entered the house and her room.

As soon as the feast was ended, the Lord Tathagata returned to the Meditation Hall in the Jeta Grove. King Prasenajit and his royal ministers and many of the prominent elders and wealthy laymen of the city returned with the Lord to listen further to his wonderful and precious teaching, the like of which they had never before heard. The Lord as usual first sitting quietly became absorbed in Samadhi, radiating from the crown of his head rays of soft and tender brightness, like lotus petals surrounded by innumerable leaves. In the center of the Lotus petals there was a vision of the Nirmanakaya Buddha sitting with feet crossed intuiting and radiating the intrinsic Dharani.

The Lord Buddha had known all along what was happening to Ananda and now called Manjusri and bade him repeat the Great Dharani at the place where Ananda was yielding to temptation. As soon as Manjusri reached the house, the magic spell lost its power and Ananda returned to self-control. Manjusri encouraged Ananda and Pchiti and they returned with him to meet the Lord Buddha.

CHAPTER ONE

The Many Manifestations of the Wonderful Essence-Mind, and of the Perfect Principle of the Three Excellencies within the All-Inclusive Unity of the Womb of Tathagata.

(False Mind vs True Mind.)

When Ananda came into the presence of the Lord Buddha, he bowed down to the ground in great humility, blaming himself that he had not yet fully developed the potentialities of Enlightenment, because from the beginning of his previous lives, he had too much devoted himself to study and learning. He earnestly pleaded with the Lord Buddha and with all the other Tathagatas from the ten quarters of the Universe, to support him in attaining perfect Enlightenment, that is, to support him in his practice of the Three Excellencies of Dhyana, Samadhi and Samapatti, by some most fundamental and expedient means.

At the same time, all of the Bodhisattvas-Mahasattva, as numerous as the sands of the river Ganges, together with all the Arhats, Pratyeka-Buddhas, from all the ten quarters, with one accord and with gladness of heart, prepared to listen to the instruction to be given to Ananda by the Lord Buddha. With one accord they paid homage to the Lord and then resuming their seats, waited in perfect quietness and patience to receive the sacred teaching.

Then the Lord Buddha spoke to Ananda, saying:—Ananda,

you and I are from the same ancestral blood and we have always cherished a fraternal affection for each other. Let me ask you a few questions and you answer me spontaneously and freely. When you first began to be interested in Buddhism what was it that impressed you in our Buddhist way of life and most influenced you to forsake all worldly pleasures and enabled you to cut asunder your youthful sexual cravings?

Ananda replied:—Oh, my Lord! The first thing that impressed me were the thirty-two marks of excellency in my Lord's personality. They appeared to me so fine, as tender and brilliant, and transparent as a crystal.

From that time I have constantly thought about them and have been more and more convinced that these marks of excellence would be impossible for anyone who was not free from all sexual passion and desire. And why? Because when anyone becomes inflamed by sexual passion, his mind becomes disturbed and confused, he loses self-control and becomes reckless and crude. Besides, in sexual intercourse, the blood becomes inflamed and impure and adulterated with impure secretions. Naturally from such a source, there can never originate an aureole of such transcendently pure and golden brightness as I have seen emanating from the person of my Lord. It was because of this that I admired my Lord and it was this that influenced me to become one of thy true followers.

The Lord Buddha then said:—Very good, Ananda! All of you in this Great Dharma Assembly ought to know and appreciate that the reason why sentient beings by their previous lives since beginningless time have formed a succession of deaths and rebirths, life after life, is because they have never realized the true Essence of Mind and its self-purifying brightness. On the contrary they have been absorbed all the time busying themselves with their deluding and transient thoughts which are nothing but falsity and vanity. Hence they have prepared for themselves the conditions for this ever returning cycle of deaths and rebirths.

Ananda, if you are now desirous of more perfectly understanding Supreme Enlightenment and the enlightening nature of pure Mind-Essence, you must learn to answer questions spontaneously with no recourse to discriminating thinking. For the Tathagatas in the ten quarters of the universes have been delivered from the ever returning cycle of deaths and rebirths by this same single way, namely, by reliance upon their intuitive minds.

It is because of the straight-forwardness of their minds and the spontaneity of their mentations that the Tathagatas have ever remained, from beginningless time to endless time, of one pure Suchness, undisturbed by any complexity within their minds nor any rising thoughts of discrimination.

Then the Lord Buddha said:—Ananda, I want to question you; please listen carefully. You have just said that at the time your faith in me was awakened, that it was due to seeing the thirty-two marks of excellence. Let me ask you: What was it that gave you the sensation of seeing? What was it that experienced the sensation? And who was it that experienced the feeling of being pleased?

Ananda replied:—My Lord! At the time I experienced the sensation of being pleased, it was both through my eyes and my mind. When my eyes saw my Lord's excellencies, my mind immediately experienced a feeling of being pleased. It was then that I made up my mind to become thy disciple so that I might be delivered from the cycle of deaths and rebirths.

The Lord said:—From what you have just said, Ananda, your feeling of being pleased originated in your eyes and mind. But if you do not know where lies the perception of sight and where the activities of the mind originate, you will never be able to subjugate your worldly attachments and contaminations. It is like a king whose city was pestered by robbers and who tried to put an end to the thieving but was unsuccessful because he could not locate the secret hiding place of the robbers. So it is in the lives of human beings who are always being troubled by worldly attachments and contaminations, causing their perception of sight to become inverted and unreliable and seducing their thoughts and causing them to wander about ignorantly and uncontrolled. Ananda, let me ask you? Referring to your eyes and mind, do you know their secret hiding place?

Ananda replied:—Noble Lord! In all the ten different orders of life, the eyes are in the front of the face, as are my Lord's clear lotus eyes, and mine also. The same is true of the other sense organs, they are on the surface of the body, but the mind is hidden within the body.

The Lord Buddha interrupted:—Ananda, you are now sitting in the Lecture Hall, are you not? And when you are looking out to the Jetavana Grove, can you tell me where the hall and the grove are situated?

Certainly, my Lord. This quiet and splendid Lecture Hall and the Jetavana Grove are both situated in Anathapindika's beautiful park.

Now, Ananda, what do you see first, the people in this hall or the park outside?

I first see my Lord, then I see the noble audience, and other things in turn, and only afterward do I see the grove and the lovely park outside.

True, Ananda! Now tell me, while you are looking outside at the grove and park, what is it that enables you to distinguish the different views that your eyes see?

Noble Lord! It is because the windows and doors of the lecture hall are open wide. That is why I can see the distant views from inside the hall.

Then the Blessed Lord, in view of the great audience, reached out his golden hand and softly stroked Ananda's head, at the same time speaking to both him and the great assembly, saying:—

There is a particular Samadhi called, The Highest Samadhi, which was the Lord Buddha's Crowning Experience, and by it he attained a perfect realization of all manifestations and transformations. It was a wonderful door that opened to the mysterious Path that all the Tathagatas of all the ten quarters of all the universes have followed. It is of this Highest Samadhi that I am going to speak. Listen very carefully.

Then Ananda and the great audience bowed to the ground in deep adoration and then resumed their seats and waited humbly for the Master's solemn teaching.

The Lord Buddha then addressed Ananda and the great assembly, saying:—

Ananda, you have just said that from the inside of the lecture hall you can look out to the grove and the distant park because the windows and doors are open wide. It is possible that there are some within this very audience that only see these outside things and who are unable to see the Lord Tathagata within.

Ananda interrupted:—But my Lord, how can it be that

anyone in this hall who can see the grove and streams without can fail to see the Lord within?

It does seem absurd, Ananda, but it is just that way with you. You say that your mind exists within your body and that it is quite clear of all obstructions, but if this clear mind really exists within your body, then you ought to see the inside of your body first of all. But there are no sentient beings who can do this, that is, see both the inside and outside of their bodies. Though they may not see all the inside things—such as the heart, stomach, liver, kidneys, etc.—but at least they ought to see the growth of the finger-nails, the lengthening of the hair, the knotting of the sinews, the throbbing of the pulse. If the mind is within the body, why does it not see these things? But if the mind is within the body and can not see the things within, how can it see the things without the body? So you must see that what you have said about the perceiving mind, abiding within the body, is untrue.

With a respectful bow, Ananda said to the Lord:—Listening to the words of my Lord, I begin to realize that my mind, after all, may be outside my body. It may be like a lamp. If the lamp is within the room, it will certainly illumine the room first and then shining through the open door and windows will illumine the yard outside. If it was like that, why is it that one seeing only outside objects does not see the things within? It must be that the mind is like a lamp placed outside of a room, for then it would be dark within. If one can clearly understand what his mind is, he would no longer be puzzled, but would have the same intelligence and understanding that the Buddhas have. Would it not be so, my Lord?

The Lord replied:—Ananda, this morning all of the Bhikshus followed me to the city of Sravasti begging for food in regular order and afterwards all returned to this Grove. I was fasting at the time, but the others ate the food. What think you, Ananda? If only one of the Bhikshus ate the food, would the others be satisfied of their hunger?

Ananda replied:—No, my Lord, and why? Because, although all of these Bhikshus are Arahats, yet their physical bodies are individually separated. How could it be, that one Bhikshu eating, could satisfy the hunger of all?

The Lord Buddha replied:—Ananda if your perceiving, understanding mind is really outside your body, then what the mind perceives could not be felt by the body, and what the body feels could not be perceived by the mind. Look at my hand, Ananda. When your eyes are looking at it, does your mind make any discriminations about it?

Yes, my Lord, it makes discriminations.

The Lord continued:—But if your mind and body are in mutual correspondence, how can it possibly be said, that the mind exists outside the body? Therefore, Ananda, you ought to know that what you have just said about the mind existing outside the body is impossible.

Then Ananda said:—According to what my Lord says, the perceiving mind does not exist within the body because it does not see the things within, neither does it exist outside the body, because the mind and body are in mutual correspondence and therefore cannot be isolated from each other. Yet it seems to me that the perceiving mind must be in some locality.

Then the Lord Buddha questioned Ananda further:—But Ananda, where is its abiding place?

Ananda replied:—My Lord, since this perceiving mind cannot know the inside of its own body, but can see outside objects, it seems to me now, that it must be concealed in the sense organ itself. It may be like a man covering his eyes with a crystal bowl; though his eyes are covered yet there is no hindrance to his sight—the eye can still see clearly and make distinctions as usual. The reason that it does not see the inside of the body is because it is a part of the organ of the eye, and the reason it can see outside objects clearly is because it is hidden in the organ of the eye.

But, Ananda, you have just said that this perceiving mind concealed within the organ of the eye is like a crystal bowl covering the eyes. Now suppose a man has covered his eyes with a crystal bowl, but is still able to see outer objects such as mountains, rivers, etc., tell me, does he see the crystal bowl, also?

Yes, my Lord, while the man is covering his eyes with the crystal bowl, he sees the crystal bowl, also.

The Lord said:—Ananda, if your mind is just the same as the crystal bowl covering the eyes, why does your mind, while seeing the outside mountains and rivers, not see your own eyes, too? Or, supposing your mind does see your eyes, then your eyes will be regarded as any other objective thing and they will no longer be regarded as a dependent organ. Or, if the mind cannot see everything, then how can it be said of the perceiving mind, that it is concealed within the organ of the eyes in the resemblance of a crystal bowl covering the eyes? Therefore, Ananda, what you have asserted, that this perceiving mind is concealed within the organ of the eyes like a crystal bowl covering the eyes, is impossible also.

Then Ananda said to the Lord Buddha:—Honored of the worlds! It may be like this:—As all sentient beings have their intestines inside the body and the opening outside the body, the intestines are hidden to their sight but the opening is visible. While I am standing before you and open my eyes, I see your brightness—this means to see the outside. When my eyes are closed, I see the hiddenness—this means to see the inside.

The Lord interrupted:—Ananda, when you close your eyes, you say you see the hiddenness, but this hidden condition, is it in an opposing direction to your eyes, or is it not? If it is directly opposed to your eyes, then the hiddenness must be in front of your eyes and then it cannot be thought of as a part of your inside. Or suppose it is meant as part of your inside, then when in any dark room, without the light of any such thing as sun, moon, or lamp, the whole dark space of the room might be regarded as your intestines or your heart. Or, if it is in a direction not opposite to your eyes, then how does it happen that the sight of your eyes is being affected at all?

Or, if you put aside this outside perception of sight and say that it is to be regarded as being in an inside opposite direction to your eyes, so that when you shut your eyes, you see darkness only, which would mean to see your inside body. But when you open your eyes and see the brightness, why do you not see your own face, also? If you do not see your own face, it would mean that the face is not in an inside opposite direction to your eyes. Or, supposing you can see your own face, then both this perceiving mind and the organ of sight must be in the open space, or they can no longer be thought of as being in an inside opposite direction.

If your perceptive mind is supposed to be in the open space, naturally it can not belong to the body, and then, when the Lord Tathagata is in sight of your face which would mean that he is a part of your body, your eyes will, of course, get the perception, but the others parts of your body could not get into consciousness at the same time.

Or, if you persistently claim that the body and the eyes have each a separate consciousness, then there would be two perceiving minds, which would mean that your single personality would see two Buddhas. Therefore you should understand that it is utterly absurd for you to say that to see into the dimness of the eyes is the same as seeing into the inside of the body.

Then Ananda said to the Lord Buddha:—I have constantly learned from the instruction of my Lord and from the teaching of all four classes of Thy disciples that all the existences of phenomena are simply the manifestation of the mind itself and vice versa that all the existences of mind are the manifestation of phenomena. Now it seems to me that this thinking mind is really the essence of my mind, and that wherever it happens to meet outer objects, there is a manifestation of mind. That is, the perceiving mind is neither inside, nor outside, nor between the body.

The Lord interrupted, saying:—What you are just saying—that all the manifestations of thoughts are simply meant as all the existences of phenomena and that wherever the mind happens to meet outer objects, there is its manifestations. But if your mind has no substantiality of its own, how can it meet any outer objects? Or, if it should be that in spite of the mind having no substantiality of its own, it might happen to meet outer objects, then there would be another newly assumed datum of nineteen spheres of mentation, namely, the six objects, the six sense organs, the six perceptions, plus this newly assumed normality of thought considered as a "thing in itself." And then there must be assumed a new datum of seven objects,—the object of sight, the object of hearing, of smelling, of tasting, of touching, of the unified object of thought, plus this outer "thing of itself." No, your suggestion is by no means the right interpretation.

Ananda, your interpretation that the perceiving mind has a substantiality of its own at the point where the object and thought meet, would put fetters to your mind, like putting fetters to your hands and feet. Let me ask you in this way: does your mental consciousness arise within or without your body? If it arises within, you should be able to know the inside of your body; if it comes from outside your body, you should be able to first see your own face.

Ananda replied:—My Lord! I see with my eyes and I perceive with my mind. That does not mean that they are interchangeable.

The Lord Buddha continued:—Ananda, if your eyes can see by themselves, then supposing you are within a room, can the door share the perception of seeing? If the door shares with the eyes this perception of seeing, then all dead bodies that still have eye organs intact, should continue to see things. If they can still perceive, how can it be said that they are dead bodies.

Ananda, if we grant that your perceiving mind has some kind of substantiality, is it one body or many bodies? Is it located in one place in your body or is it distributed all over the body? If it is one body, then if you bind one limb the others will feel bound. If they all feel bound, then there can be no sure knowledge of the exact place of the binding. Or, if the perception of being bound is located in one place, then the perceiving mind cannot be considered as one localized body. Or if the perceiving mind is considered to be many bodies or involved in many bodies, it would mean that there must be as many personalities, and the question would arise, which of these localized perceiving minds rightly belongs to you. Or if your mind is considered as being uniformally distributed over all parts of your body, then if your limb was tightly bound, then the whole body would feel the suffering. Or if not uniformally distributed, but only on some parts of the body, then if you touch your head and at the same touch your feet, one would know it and the other would not. We know that this is not so. Therefore, Ananda, you must see that your suggestion that wherever the mind happens to meet outer objects, there is localized a manifestation of mind is unreasonable.

Then Ananda said to the Lord Buddha:—Now I recall hearing my Lord Buddha say, at a time when he was teaching Brother Manjusri and other princes of the Dharma, that the mind neither abides inside nor outside the body. It seems to me, if it is inside and we cannot see the inside, and if it was outside we ought not to feel the outside. We know that we cannot see the inside of the body, so it must mean that the

mind is not abiding inside the body; it must mean that in
some way our mind and body are in mutual correspondence
with each other through the faculty of perception, and that
would mean that it is not abiding outside the body. Now, My
Lord, I see that since our mind and body are in mutual correspondence and yet we cannot see the inside of our body, it
must be that the perceiving understanding mind must be abiding between these things.

The Lord Buddha resumed:—Ananda, now you think that
the mind must be abiding between somethings. Let us consider
it. If it is abiding between somethings, there must be some
particular place where it is abiding. We can not conceive of an
indefinite abiding place. Now Ananda, supposing you guess
between what things it is located. Is it located between outside
things and our bodies? Then it would be on the surface of the
body and could not mean any place within the body. If it is
located between parts of our body, then it would be within
the body. Or, if it is between external things, what is its
standard of direction? Suppose we take the case of a man: if
he is standing between things looking toward the east, he must
be standing in the west; or if he is looking toward the west,
he must be standing in the east; or if he is looking toward the
south, he must be standing in the north. If the mind is between things but has no standard of direction, it is the same as
saying that it has no existence; or even if it has some standard
of direction, there can be no certainty about it (if by just
turning he can be either in east or west or north or south).
If the standard is uncertain, the mind will be confused
naturally.

Ananda replied:—What I said of the mind being "between
somethings," is not meant in that sense. On one occasion my
Lord has said:—"As causal conditions, eyes and sights are mutually attracted," but there must be something that is manifested in the consciousness that is dependent upon the eyes.
That is what I meant by the mind being "between somethings."
The eyes note discriminations while objects and sights are insensible things. As consciousness develops between them, the
conceiving mind must be localized between them.

The Lord Buddha interrupted, saying:—Ananda, if it is
stated that the mind is existing between the sense organ and
the object, then, let me ask, is the essence of mind separated

into two parts or not? If it is, the object and essential mind will be confusingly mingled, and as the object can not be exactly the same as essential mind which possesses the consciousness, they must be opposite to each other. How then can you say, that the mind exists between them?

If the statement that the mind is separated into two parts has no ground, then the statement that the insensible object is imperceptive, means just the same as saying that it has no essence itself and must be, therefore, imperceptible. So the expression "between somethings," has no meaning. Therefore, Ananda, you must admit that the statement that the mind exists between somethings, is an absurd statement that is incapable of interpretation.

Ananda then addressed the Lord Buddha, saying:—Noble Lord! Some time ago when my Lord was discussing the intrinsic Dharma with the four great Bodhisattva-Mahasattvas, Maudgalyayana, Subhuti, Purna, and Sariputra, I overheard my Lord to say, that the essence of the discerning, perceiving, conscious mind existed neither inside nor outside, nor between, in fact, that it had no location of existence. Since my Lord has interpreted this in his teachings just now, I have ceased to grasp any arbitrary conception as to the location of mind, but if this is true, and it is something intangible, in what sense can it be thought of as "my mind."

The Lord Buddha replied:—Ananda, as to what you have just said that the essence of the discerning, perceptive, conscious mind has no definite location anywhere, the meaning is clear; it is neither in this world, in the vast open spaces, neither in water, nor on land, neither flying with wings, nor walking, nor is it anywhere. But when you say that your mind no longer grasps any arbitrary conception of the existence of the phenomena of mind, what do you mean by it? Do you mean that the phenomena have no true existence, or that they have no tangible existence? If you mean that they have no true existence, that would mean that they are like hair on a tortoise, or like horns on a rabbit. But so long as you retain this notion of not grasping, you cannot mean perfect non-existence. But what do you mean? Of course if your mind is perfectly blank, it must mean, as far as you are concerned, absolute non-existence, but if you are still cherishing some arbitrary conception of phenomena, you must mean some kind of existence. How is it then, that so long as the notion of not-grasping of anything, as for instance, the notion of "my mind," that you mean its non-existence? Therefore, Ananda, you ought to see that what you have just said concerning the non-existence of anything just because you no longer cherish a conception of it within your mind, and that would mean the non-existence of a discerning, perceptive, conscious mind, would be quite absurd, would it not?

Thereupon, Ananda rose from his place in the midst of the assembly, adjusted his ceremonial scarf, knelt upon his right knee, placed the palms of his hands together, and respectfully addressed the Lord Buddha, saying:—

My Noble Lord! I have the honor of being thy youngest relative and thou hast always treated me with affectionate kindness. Although I am now only one of your many converts, thou dost still continue to show thy affection for me. But in spite of all I have gained mentally, I have not become liberated from contaminations and attachments and consequently I could not overcome the magic spell at the home of a harlot. My mind became confused and I was at the point of drowning in its defilement. I can see now that it was wholly due to my ignorance as to the right realization of what is true and essential Mind. I pray thee, Oh my Lord, to have pity and mercy upon me and show me the right Path to the spiritual graces of the Samapatti so that I may attain to self-mastery and become emancipated from the lure of evil myself, and be able to free all heretics from the bonds of their false ideas and craft.

* * *

When Ananda had finished his plea, he bowed humbly before the Lord Buddha, with hands and forehead touching the ground, and the whole audience, awed into intense excitement, waited with earnest and reverential hearts for the response of the Blessed One.

Suddenly in the Meditation Hall, filled with its awed and expectant throng, there appeared a most marvelous sight that transcended everything that had ever been seen before. The Hall was filled with a radiant splendor that emanated from the moon-life face of the Blessed One, like hundreds of thousands of sunbeams scintillating everywhere, and wherever the rays reached immediately there were seen celestial Buddha-lands. Moreover, the person of the Lord Buddha was vibrant with the six transcendental motions simultaneously manifesting and embracing all the Buddha-lands of the ten quarters of all the universes, as numerous as the finest particles of dust in the sunlight. And this all-embracing, blessed and transcendent glory united all these innumerable Buddha-lands into one single whole, and all the great Bodhisattvas of all these innumerable Buddha-lands were seen to be each in his own place with hands raised and pressed together expectantly waiting for the words of the Blessed One.

Then the Lord Buddha addressed the assembly, saying:— Ananda, from beginningless time, from life to life, all sentient beings have had their disturbing illusions that have been manifested in their natural development each under the conditioning power of his own individual karma, such as the seed-pod of the okra which when opening always drops three seeds in each group. The reason why all devoted disciples do not at once attain to supreme enlightenment is because they do not realize two primary principles and because of it some attain only to Arhatship, or to Pratyakaship, and some to even lower attainments, to the state of devas and heretics, and some to Mara kings and their dependents. The reason for these great differences is because, not knowing these two basic principles, they become confused in mind and fall into wrong practices. It is as if they were trying to cook fine delicacies by boiling stones or sand, which of course they could never do if they tried for countless kalpas.

What are these two fundamental principles, Ananda? The First Fundamental Principle is the primary cause of the succession of deaths and rebirths from beginningless time. (It is the Principle of Ignorance, the outgoing principle of individuation, manifestation, transformation, succession and discrimination.) From the working out of this Principle there has resulted the various differentiation of minds of all sentient beings, and all the time they have been taking these limited and perturbed and contaminated minds to be their true and natural Essence of Mind.

The Second Fundamental Principle is the primary cause of the pure unity of Enlightenment and Nirvana that has existed from beginningless time. (It is the Principle of integrating compassion, the in-drawing, unifying principle of purity, harmony, likeness, rhythm, permanency and peace.) By the in-drawing of this Principle within the brightness of your own nature, its unifying spirit can be discovered and developed and realized under all varieties of conditions. The reason why this unifying spirit is so quickly lost amongst the conditions is be-cause you so quickly forget the brightness and purity of your own essential nature, and amid the activities of the day, you cease to realize its existence. That is why, Ananda, you and all sentient beings have fallen through ignorance into misfortune and into different realms of existence.

Now, Ananda, you wish to know the right road to Sama-patti, so as to escape from the cycle of deaths and rebirths. Is it not so, Ananda? Then let me ask you some more questions. The Lord Tathagata raised one of his arms with hand and fingers clenched, saying:—Ananda, do you see this?

Yes, I see it, my Lord.

What do you see, Ananda?

I see my Lord raising one of his arms with hand clenched and its brightness blinds my eyes and warms my heart.

With what do you see it, Ananda?

I see it with my eyes, of course.

Then the Lord Buddha said:—Ananda, you have just an-swered me by saying that when the Tathagata by clenching his fingers made a shining fist, that its brightness shone into your eyes and warmed your heart. Very good. Now I will ask you:—While my fist is shining brightly and while you are looking at it closely, what is it that reveals the existence of your mind?

Ananda replied:—You are now asking me about the exist-ence of my mind. To answer that question I must use my thinking and reasoning faculty to search and find an answer. Yes, now I understand. This thinking and reasoning being is what is meant as "my mind."

The Lord Buddha rebuked Ananda sharply and said:—Surely that is nonsense, to assert that your being is your mind.

Ananda stood up with hands pressed together and said with astonishment:—Why, my Lord, if my being is not my mind, what else can be my mind?

The Lord Buddha replied:—The notion that your being is your mind, is simply one of the false conceptions that arises from reflecting about the relations of yourself and outside objects, and which obscures your true and essential Mind. It is because, since from beginningless time down to the present life, you have been constantly misunderstanding your true and essential Mind. It is like treating a petty thief as your own son. By so doing you have lost consciousness of your original and permanent Mind and because of it have been forced to undergo the sufferings of successive deaths and rebirths.

Ananda, in dismay and confusion, said to the Lord:—I am your beloved cousin and owing to my appreciation of your marks of excellence, you have permitted me to become your disciple. So, in regard to my mind, it is not simply that my mind has offered adoration to my Lord Tathagata, but it has also offered praise to all the Buddhas and learned Masters of all the innumerable Buddha Lands. More than that, it is my mind that has been attempting all manner of difficult practices with great resolution and courage. These are all activities of my mind as well as of myself. How can they be separated? Even my evil acts of slandering the Dharma, neglecting good practices, these also are activities of my mind as well as of myself. Myself is my mind. If these acts can be shown to be not the activities of my mind, then I would be mindless, just like any other image made from a log or from earth. Or, if I should give up my perceptions and consciousness, there would be nothing left that could be regarded as my self or as my mind. What do you mean, my Lord, when you say that my being is not my mind? As you can see, I am astonished and confused. And this audience, they are also in doubt. Pray have mercy upon us all and explain yourself clearly for we are only ignorant disciples.

Thereupon the Blessed Lord laid his hand affectionately upon the head of Ananda and proceeded to explain the true and Essence nature of Mind, desiring to awaken in them a consciousness of that which transcended phenomena. He explained to them how necessary it was to keep the mind free from all discriminating thoughts of self and not-self if they were to correctly understand it.

He continued:—Ananda and all my Disciples! I have always taught you that all phenomena and their developments are simply manifestations of mind. All causes and effects, from great universes to the fine dust only seen in the sunlight come into apparent existence only by means of the discriminating mind. If we examine the origin of anything in all the universe, we find that it is but a manifestation of some primal essence. Even the tiny leaves of herbs, knots of thread, everything, if we examine them carefully we find that there is some essence in its originality. Even open space is not nothingness. How can it be then that the wonderful, pure, tranquil and enlightened Mind, which is the source of all conceptions of manifested phenomena, should have no essence of itself.

If you must niggardly grasp this perceptive mind of discriminating consciousness that is dependent upon the different sense organs as being the same as Essential Mind, then the discriminative mind would have to forsake all those activities responding to any kind of form, sight, sound, odor, taste, touch, and seek for another and more perfect self-nature. You are now listening to my teaching and your minds are making discriminations by means of the sounds rising from my speaking, but when the sounds cease and all the perceptions arising from the sounds come to an end, still the mind goes on discriminating the memory of those sounds and you find it difficult to keep your mind in emptiness and tranquillity. This does not mean that I am instructing you not to grasp at these following activities, but I am instructing you to study their nature more closely. If your mind, after the object is removed from sight, still has its discriminating nature, does it necessarily mean that your discriminating mind has lost its substantiality? Does it not rather mean that you are now discriminating merely the shadows and reflections of unreal things which had their origin in objects in the presence of your sight? Objects certainly are not permanent; as they vanish, does your mind vanish, also, and become like hair on a tortoise, or a horn on a rabbit? If mind vanishes, then the Dharmakaya would be exterminated and who would be devoted to the practice of attaining perseverence in getting rid of the developments arising from the conceptions of phenomena? At this, Ananda and the great audience became more confused and speechless.

The Lord Buddha continued:—Ananda, if in this world disciples practiced meditation assiduously, though they attained all the nine stages of calmness in Dhyana, yet do not accomplish the attainment of Arhats free from the intoxicants arising from worldly contaminations and attachments, it is wholly due to their grasping this deceiving conception of discriminative thinking that is based on unrealities and mistaking the delusion as being a reality. Ananda, although you have learned a great deal, you are not yet ready for the maturity of Buddhahood.

*   *   *

When Ananda heard this solemn teaching, he became very sorrowful and with tears falling, with forehead, hands and feet touching the ground, he paid homage to the Lord. Then kneeling, he said:—

Noble Lord! Since I determined to follow thee and become thy disciple, I have always thought that I could rely upon thy supernormal strength and that it would not be difficult to put thy teachings into practice. I expected that the Lord would favor me with an experience of Samadhi in this body; I did not appreciate that the body and mind were different and could not be substituted for each other, so I have likely lost my own mind. Although I have become a disciple of Buddha, my heart is not yet absorbed in Enlightenment. I am like a prodigal son who has forsaken his father. I now see that in spite of my learning, if I am not able to put it into practice, I am no better than an unlearned man. It is like a man talking about food, but never eating and becoming satisfied. We are all entangled in these two hindrances: knowledge and learning, and vexation and suffering. I can now see that it is all due to our ignorance of the eternal and tranquil nature of true Mind. Pray, my Lord Tathagata, have mercy upon us all; show us clearly the mysterious, enlightening Mind, and open our true eye of Enlightenment.

Suddenly from the holy symbol on the breast of the Lord Tathagata, there shown forth a glorious, blazing brightness, which radiated forth brilliantly into hundreds and thousands of colored rays reaching to the ten quarters of the universes, which were instantly turned into innumerable Buddha-lands, and glorified all the holy shrines of the Tathagata, in all the ten quarters of the universes. And, finally, the scintillating splendor returned to rest on the crown of Ananda and upon the crown of each one in the assembly.

Then the Lord Buddha addressed Ananda, saying:—For the sake of all I will lift the luminous beacon of the Dharma so that by its light all sentient beings may realize the wonderful, mysterious nature of the pure enlightening Mind and acquire its true intrinsic Eye.

First, let me question you, Ananda. You saw my fist and it seemed bright to you. By what means did its brightness manifest itself? By what means was it seen, and by what means was the thought of brightness conceived?

Ananda replied:—My Lord, the brightness comes from the whole luminous body of my Lord which is as brightly shining as a valley filled with rubies. Your holy body, shining as it does, could not have originated except from Purity itself. Your hand being clenched was in the form of a fist, I saw it with my eyes, my mind conceived its brightness.

The Buddha said:—You say that it takes the movement of my fingers and the seeing of your eyes to give you the conception of a fist. Does that mean that the nature of the movement of the fingers and the seeing of the eyes and the thinking of the mind are all alike?

Ananda replied:—Yes, my Lord. If you had no hand, or I had no eyes, there could be no conception of a fist. There must be the meeting of the two conditions.

The Lord Buddha interrupted:—You state that the movement of the hand and the seeing of the eyes being in agreement, the mind conceives a fist. Is that wholly true? If a man loses his hand he loses it forever, but if a man loses his eyes, he does not wholly lose the sense of sight, nor does he lose the conception of a fist. Suppose you meet a blind man on the road and you ask him, "In your blindness, what do you see?" He will give you some such answer as this:—"I can only see darkness, nothing else." This means that the objects within the range of his former sight have become darkened; there is no loss of his conception of sight but the conception is of darkness.

Ananda asked:—My Lord, if the blind man can only perceive darkness, how can it mean that he still possesses the perception of sight?

The Buddha replied:—Ananda, this blind man of no eyes simply sees darkness just as any seeing man who is shut up in a dark room sees darkness. Close your eyes, Ananda, what do you perceive but darkness?

Ananda had to admit that as far as perceiving darkness was

concerned there was no difference between the blind man, the man in a dark room and himself with his eyes closed.

The Buddha resumed:—If the blind man seeing only darkness suddenly recovers his sight and again sees objects, we say that he sees them by means of his eyes. A lamp is suddenly brought into the dark room and we say that the man again sees objects by means of the lamp. That is not strictly true for while the lamp does reveal objects, it is the eyes that perceive them. If it were otherwise and the seeing belonged to the lamp then it would no longer be a lamp and the seeing would have no relation to him. In a true sense, however, it is neither the lamp nor the eyes that perceives objects.

Although this was the second instruction that Ananda had had on this subject, he did not yet understand it and sat dazed hoping for a clearer interpretation of it in the kind and gentle tones of the Master and he waited with a pure and expectant heart for the Blessed One's further explanation.

The Lord Buddha, in great kindness, let his hand rest kindly on the head of Ananda and said to him:—Ananda, at the beginning of my perfect Enlightenment I went to the Deer Forest at Sarnath where Kaundinya and his four disciples were staying and gave them my first teaching The teaching was this:—The reason why all sentient beings fail to attain enlightenment and Arhatship is because they have been led astray by false conceptions regarding phenomena and objects, which defiled their minds. Since that time they have understood the import of that teaching and have become enlightened.

Then Kaundinya rose from his seat and addressed the Lord, saying:—Blessed Lord! I am now the oldest in this assembly and am credited with having the best understanding of the Dharma. I attained Arhatship by realizing the significance of objective things. I was like a traveler seeking lodgings where I could satisfy my hunger and take my rest, but, like a traveler after he had satisfied his hunger and taken his rest, he could no longer stay there for a comfortable rest but must set out on another day's journey. If he was the inn-keeper he could do so, but the traveler is the symbol of impermanency. We may also draw a lesson from the sky. After a rain it is fresh and clear and the sun's rays penetrating the clouds light up the dust particles moving about in the air. We think of open space as a symbol of motionlessness and permanency, while we think of dust particles as symbols of motion and impermanency.

The Lord Buddha was much pleased by the words of Kaundinya and said:—So it is, so it is, Kaundinya! Then raising his hand, he opened his fingers and then closed them, saying:—What do you see, Ananda?

Ananda replied:—I see my Lord standing before the assembling opening and closing his beautiful fingers.

The Lord resumed:—As you watch the fingers of my hand opening and closing, does the perception of motion belong to my hand or to your eyes?

Ananda replied:—My Lord, while thy precious hand is opening and closing I recognize the motion as belonging to thy hand and not to my eyes.

The Lord enquired:—Ananda, what is in motion and what is still?

Ananda replied:—My Lord, it is thy fingers that are in motion, but as to the perception of my eyes, while it can not be said that it possesses the nature of absolute stillness, it can hardly be said that it is in motion.

The Lord Buddha was pleased with this reply and said: So it is, Ananda. Then the Lord Buddha caused a bright beam of light to dart from his hand and fall on Ananda's right side. Ananda quickly turned his head to look at it. Then the Lord caused another beam of light to fall on Ananda's left, and Ananda quickly turned his head to look at that. Then the Lord Buddha questioned Ananda, saying:—Ananda, what caused you to turn your head about?

My Lord, it was because I saw a shining beam of light springing from my Lord's hand and darting first to my right and then to my left, and I turned my head to look at it.

Ananda, you say that when your eyes followed the light, you turned your head from right to left. Tell me was it your head or the perception of your sight that moved?

My Lord, it was my head that moved. As to the perception of sight, while it can not be said that it has the nature of motionlessness, neither can it be said that it has no motion.

The Lord was pleased with this reply and said:—So it is, Ananda. When I was looking at you as sentient beings do, it was your head that was moving about but my perception of sight did not move, and when you were looking at me, it was my hand opening and closing, not your "seeing" that moved.

Ananda, can you not see the difference in nature in that which moves and changes, and that which is motionless and unchanging? It is body which moves and changes, not Mind. Why do you so persistently look upon motion as appertaining to both body and mind? Why do you permit your thoughts to rise and fall, letting the body rule the mind, instead of Mind ruling the body? Why do you let your senses deceive you as to the true unchanging nature of Mind and then to do things in a reversed order which leads to motion and confusion and suffering? As one forgets the true nature of Mind, so he mistakes the reflections of objects as being his own mind, thus binding him to the endless movements and changes and suffering of the recurring cycles of deaths and rebirths that are of his own causing. You should regard all that changes as "dust-particles" and that which is unchanging as being your own true Nature of Mind.

Then Ananda and all the assembly realized that from beginningless time, they had forgotten and ignored their own true nature, had misinterpreted conditional objects, and had confused their minds by false discriminations and illusive reflections. They felt like a little baby that had found its mother's breast, and became calm and peaceful in spirit. In this spirit they pressed their hands together and made devout obeisance to the Blessed One. They besought the Lord Tathagata to teach them how to make right distinctions between body and mind, between the real and the unreal, between that which is true and that which is false, between the manifested natures of deaths and rebirths on the one hand, and the intrinsic nature of that which is un-born and never dies on the other hand; the one appearing and disappearing, the other forever abiding within the essence of their own mind.

(Questions of King Prasenajit.)

His Highness King Prasenajit who was in the assembly, stood up and addressed the Lord Buddha, saying:—Honorable Lord, formerly before I had been under the instruction of my Lord, I visited Katyayana and Vairotiputra (two heretic teachers). They both taught that after one's death, the destruction of body and mind meant Nirvana. Afterwards, I have been occasionally with my Lord, I have had doubts within my mind and even now the matter is not clear. How can I clearly understand and realize this state of non-death and non-

rebirth. I think that all the disciples present who have not yet
attained Arhatship, are equally desirous of more perfectly understanding this profound teaching from my Lord Buddha.

The Lord addressed the King, saying:—Your Majesty! May
I have the honor of asking you some questions about your
present body. Is your Majesty's body as permanent and enduring as gold and steel, or is it impermanent and destructible?

Oh, my Lord, my present body of flesh will soon come to
destruction.

Your Majesty! While your body has not yet come to destruction, how do you know that it ever will?

My Lord, it is true that this body has not yet come to
total destruction, but as I have watched it and reflected about
it, I have seen it constantly changing and needing constant
renewal. It seems as though it was slowly being changed into
ashes, gradually decreasing and fading away. From this I am
convinced that it will ultimately come to destruction.

Yes, your Majesty, it is all too true. You are growing old
and your health is becoming imperfect. Tell me a little about
your present appearance as compared with your boyhood.

Your Lordship! When I was a boy, my skin was tender
and smooth, in young manhood my blood and energy were in
full supply, now as I am getting old, my strength is failing,
my appearance is languid and dull, my brain is dull and uncertain, my hair has become grey and white, my face wrinkled.
All these changes certainly show that I can not live much
longer. How can I compare my present with my youth?

The Lord Buddha replied kindly:—Your Majesty, do not be
discouraged, your appearance will not become decrepit as
quickly as all that.

Your Lordship! It is true that these changes have been going on so secretly that I have hardly felt them, but as winters
and summers pass I know that I have been gradually changing
into my present condition. At twenty I was young for my age
but my appearance was very different than at ten; at thirty I
was older; at forty, still older; and now after twenty years I
am sixty and am what I am. I recollect that at fifty years of
age I felt comparatively young and strong. Your Lordship! I
am conscious that these processes and changes are still going
on secretly and that in a brief time, perhaps ten limited years,
the end will come.

Moreover, your Lordship, as I think about these changes, I see that it is not a matter of changes in one or two decades, the process is going on yearly. And not only yearly, but month by month, yes, day by day. Now I think of it, the changes are going on faster than that even, breath by breath, changes incessantly going on faster than thought. In the end my body will be given over to destruction.

The Lord Buddha said:—Your Majesty from watching this process of change going on you have become convinced that ultimately your body will be given over to destruction. At the time of the destruction of your body, do you think there is anything within your body that is not destructible?

The King Prasenajit pressed his hands together and replied soberly:—Certainly, your Lordship, I do not know. I wish I did.

The Lord Buddha said: Your Majesty! I will now show you the nature of no-dying and no-rebirth. At the time you first saw the river Ganges, your Majesty, how old were you?

The King replied:—I can remember when my mother brought me there to worship the Dèva god. I was then just three years old. I can remember when we crossed the river; I can remember hearing it called the Ganges.

The Lord Buddha said:—Your Majesty! You were three years old at that time. As you have said, when ten years had passed, you were older, and down to the age of sixty the processes of change have been going on year after year, month after month, day after day and thought after thought. Your Majesty, you said that when you first saw the river Ganges, you were three years of age. Tell me, when you were thirteen years of age and saw the Ganges, how did it appear to you? Was the sight of it, your mind's perception of the sight, any different?

The King replied:—My sight of it was just the same as when I was three years of age. And now at my present age of sixty-two, while the sight of my eyes is not as good, my perception of the sight is just the same as ever.

The Lord Buddha continued:—Your Majesty! You have been saddened by the changes in your personal appearance since your youth—your greying hair and wrinkled face—but you say that your perception of sight compared with it when you were a youth, shows no change. Tell me, Your Majesty,

is there any youth and old age in the perception of sight?
Not at all, your Lordship.

The Lord Buddha continued:—Your Majesty! Though your face has become wrinkled, in the perception of your eyes, there are no signs of age, no wrinkles. Then, wrinkles are the symbol of change, and the un-wrinkled is the symbol of the un-changing. That which is changing must suffer destruction, of course, but the un-changing is naturally free from deaths and re-births. How is it, Your Majesty, that the un-changing perception of Mind still suffers the illusion of deaths and rebirths and you are still clinging to the teaching of the heretic, who claimed that after the death of the body, everyone was completely destroyed?

After listening to this wonderful instruction that implied that after one's death something survived to reappear in a new body, the King and the whole assembly were much cheered and filled with joy. It was a most interesting occasion.

(Questions by Ananda.)

Then Ananda, after paying the usual reverence to the Lord Buddha, rose in his place and addressed the Lord, saying:—

Noble Lord! If the perception of the eyes and ears is free from death and re-birth, why did my Lord say that we had forgotten our true nature of mind and acted in a state of "reversed confusion"? Pray, my Lord, have pity on us all and purify our contaminated minds and clear away our attachments to them.

Immediately the Lord Buddha stretched out his arm with fingers pointing downward in some mystic "mudra." He said to Ananda:—As you are looking at my fingers, are they in an upright position or in a reversed position?

Ananda replied:—My Lord! Most people in this world would say that they were in a reversed position, but because the fingers are arranged in some mystic mudra, I do not know which is the upright position and which is the reverse.

The Lord replied:—Ananda, if human beings regard this as in a reversed position, what would they regard as an upright position?

Ananda replied:—My Lord, if you were to turn the hand so that the fingers were pointing up, that they would call an upright position.

The Lord Buddha suddenly turned his hand and said to Ananda:—If this interpretation of positions, reversed or upright, is simply made by turning the hand so that the fingers are pointing either up or down without any change in the location of the hand, that is, as viewed by beings in this world, then you should know that the essence of the Lord Tathagata's true body, the pure Dharmakaya, may be interpreted differently by viewing it from different view points of attainment, as being either the Lord Tathagata's "True Omniscience" (upright position), or as the body of one's own mind, the "reversed position."

Now, Ananda, concentrate your mind on this and explain it to me;—When you say that your mind is in the reversed position, in what position is your body to be regarded? Is the body, also, in a reversed position?

At this question, Ananda and the whole assembly were confused and stared up at him with open mouths. What did he mean by a reversed position of both their body and mind?

In great compassion of heart, the Lord Buddha pitied Ananda and the great assembly. He spoke to them reassuringly, and his voice was like the subdued sound of the ocean's billows:—My good, faithful disciples! Have I not been constantly teaching you that all of the causes and conditions that characterize changing phenomena and the modes of the mind, and of the different attributes of the mind, and the independently developed conditions of the mind, are all simply manifestations of the mind; and all of your body and mind are but manifestations of the wonderful, enlightening, and true nature of the all-embracing and mysterious Essence of Mind.

My good, faithful disciples! Why do you so easily forget this natural, wonderful, and enlightening Mind of perfect Purity —this mysterious Mind of radiant Brightness? And why are you still bewildered in your realizing consciousness? Open space is nothing but invisible dimness; the invisible dimness of space is mingled with darkness to look like forms; sensations of form are mingled into illusive and arbitrary conceptions of phenomena; and from these false conceptions of phenomena, is developed the consciousness of body. So, within the mind, these jumblings of causes and conditions, segregating into groups and coming into contact with the world's external objects, there is awakened desire or fear which divides the mind and causes it to sink into either indulgence or anger. All of you have been accepting this confusing conception of phenomena as being your own nature of mind. As soon as you accepted it as your true mind, is it any wonder that you became bewildered and supposed it to be localized in your physical body, and that all the external things, mountains, rivers, the great open spaces, and the whole world, were outside the body. Is it any wonder that you failed to realize that everything you have so falsely conceived has its only existence within your own wonderful, enlightening Mind of True Essence.

In likeness you have abandoned all the great, pure, calm oceans of water, and clung to one bubble which you not only accept but which you regard as the whole body of water in all the hundreds of thousands of seas. In such bewilderment, you reveal yourselves as fools among fools. Though I move my fingers up or down, there is no change in the hand itself, but the world makes a distinction, and says that now it is upright, now it is reversed. Those who do this are greatly to be pitied.

Ananda was profoundly moved by this teaching and through the kindness of the Lord Buddha was delivered from his foolish bewilderment. He sincerely repented and pressing his hands together reverenced the Lord Buddha, saying:—My Noble Lord! Though I have been listening to the Lord's wonderful teaching and have realized that this wonderful Enlightening Mind is by nature perfect in itself and is the permanent ground of my changing mind, but, as I have been listening to this Teaching of the Dharma, I think of my concentrating mind. I know that it is of a higher order than my conditional mind, but I dare not recognize it as being the pure, original ground of my mind. Pray, my Lord, have pity upon us all and kindly declare to us the complete teaching and remove this root of suspicion and doubt, so that we may attain to supreme Enlightenment.

The Lord Buddha replied to Ananda, saying:—Ananda, from what you have just said, I can see that you have been listening to my teaching with your conditional mind, and so my teachings have become conditional, also. It shows that you have not yet fully realized the pure Essence of your mind. It is like a man calling the attention of another man to the moon by pointing his finger toward it. The other man ought to look at the moon, but instead he looks at the finger and by so doing, not only misses the moon but misses the finger, also. And why? Because he has taken the finger to be the moon. Not only that, he has failed to notice the difference between darkness and brightness. And why? Because he takes the dark finger to be the moon's brightness. That is why he does not know the difference between darkness and brightness. Ananda, you are just as foolish as that man.

The Lord Buddha continued:—Ananda, if you take that which discriminates my teaching as your mind, then when it lays aside its conceptions of the discriminated teaching, the mind should still retain its own discriminating nature, which it does not. It is like a traveller seeking an inn where he may rest for a short time but not permanently. But the inn-keeper lives there permanently, he does not go away. It is the same with this difficulty. If the discriminating mind is your true Mind, it should never change. How can it be your true Mind when, as soon as the sound of my voice ceases, it has no discriminating nature?

Ananda, this is true not only as regards discriminations of sound, but also of sight and all other sensations, and if the mind is free from all conceptions of phenomena, inherently it must be free from discriminations in its own nature. And even if there is no discriminated object before it, the mind is neither vacuity nor phenomena. If it can be, that when you leave off all the conditions of phenomena, there shall remain no discriminating nature of mind, then both your mind and its Essence will have one individual and original nature, which would be their own and true reality.

Ananda said to the Lord Buddha:—Noble Lord, if both my mind and its Essence have one originality, why does the wonderful, enlightening original Mind, which has just been proclaimed by the Lord Buddha as being one with my discriminating mind, not return to its original state? Have pity upon us, my Lord, and explain it more clearly.

The Lord Buddha replied, saying:—Ananda, as you look at me with this enlightening Essence of sight, its perception of sight is the same thing and yet is not the same as the Enlightening Mind of the wonderful Essence. It is just like a reproduction of the true moon—that is, it is not merely a shadow of the moon. Now, Ananda, listen and I will show you the originality that has no need of returning at all.

Let us consider this great Lecture Hall which opens toward the east: when the crimson sun rises, it is filled with a glorious brightness; but when it is mid-night and no moonlight, and the sky overcast by clouds and mist, then there is dense darkness. Again, because it has doors and windows, the interior is visible, but if there were no doors or windows, the perception of sight would be hindered. Where there is only space, then there is only a common emptiness, but when discriminations are made, they straight away condition the sight. When the air is shut in by walls, it soon becomes close and gloomy and permeated with dust; when clear fresh air comes in, the dust soon disappears and the room becomes clear and refreshing to the eyes.

Ananda, during your life you have experienced many changes; I am now going to return these changes to their respective originalities. What do I mean by their respective originalities, Ananda? I will explain. In this Lecture Hall, first let us return the brightness to the crimson sun. Why? Because if there were no sun, there would be no brightness. That is, the origin of the brightness is in the sun, so let us return the brightness to the sun. Let us do the same with the other conditions; darkness returns to the dim moon, passage of light returns to the doors and windows, hindrance to light returns to the dense walls of the house, conditions return to discriminations, space returns to emptiness, closeness and gloominess return to dust and clearness and freshness return to the purifying air. Thus all the existencies in the world may be included in these eight kinds of phenomena.

Now, Ananda, let us consider the perceiving mind which distinguishes these eight kinds of phenomena and which we have already found has its ground in the enlightening nature of the Essence of Mind; to which one of these eight phenomena shall it be returned? If you return the faculty of perceiving to brightness, then when there is no brightness, there will be no perception of darkness. Though there may be all degrees of illumination between brightness and darkness, perception in its self-nature possesses no differentials. (Therefore, we can not return perceiving, which belongs to our Essence of Mind to the phenomena of brightness or any other of the eight classes of phenomena noted above.) Thus we see that those things which can be returned to their originalities do not belong to your own true nature; and that which we can not return to its originality, is the only thing which truly belongs to us. This shows that your mind has its own mysterious nature of brightness and purity, and when you try to refer your mind to the various classes of phenomena, you simply deceive and bewilder yourself, and, by so doing, you have lost your own true nature and have suffered endless misfortunes, like a vagrant adrift on the ocean of deaths and rebirths. That is why, I look upon you as being most pitiable.

Ananda was still in doubt as to the true nature of his mind, and begged the Lord Buddha for further elucidation, saying:— My Lord, though I now can see that the nature of the mind's perceiving is constant and does not need to be referred to any originality in phenomena, but how can I fully realize that it is my true and essential nature?

The Lord Buddha replied:—Ananda, you have not yet attained to the pure state of freedom from the intoxicants, but you have, with the aid of my Transcendental Power, advanced to the first attainment of Dhyana and thus acquired the state of Perfect Intelligence. In the state of Freedom from Intoxicants, Anuruddha looking upon the countries of this world, sees them as clearly as he sees an amala fruit lying in the palm of his hand. In that state the Bodhisattva-Mahasattvas, looking beyond this world, have seen with like clearness, all the worlds, even hundreds of thousands of worlds. It is the same with the Tathagatas of the ten quarters of all the universes. Their sight reaches everywhere; they see clearly all the Buddha-lands of Purity, greater in number than the fine particles of dust. But the perception of the eyes belonging to ordinary sentient beings cannot pierce through the thickness of a tenth of an inch.

Let us consider the palaces of the Four Heavenly Kings! How great the distances. How different the conditions of water and earth and air. In those Heavenly Realms there may be seen similarities to light and darkness, and all other phenomena of this world, but that is because of the lingering memory of objects seen in this world. Under those Heavenly conditions, you would still have to continue making distinctions between yourself and objects. But, Ananda, I challenge you, by the perception of your sight, to detect which is my True Essence and which manifestation.

Ananda, let us go to the extreme limit of our sight—to the

palaces of the sun and moon—do you see anything there that belongs to our nature? Coming nearer to the Seven Golden Mountains that surround Mt. Sumaru, look carefully, what do you see? We see all sorts of brightness and glory, but nothing that belongs to our nature. Moving nearer, we come to the massing clouds, the flying birds, the hurrying winds, the rising of dust, the mountains, the familiar woods, trees, rivers, herbs, vegetables, animals, none of which belongs to our nature.

Ananda, regarding all these things, far or near, as perceived by the pure Essence of your perceiving eyes, they have different characteristics, but the perception of our eyes is always the same. Does this not mean, that this wonderful perception of sight is the true nature of our minds?

Ananda, if the perception of sight is not your own nature, but is to be regarded as an object, then since it is to be regarded as an object, my perception of sight is to be regarded as an object also, and you should be able to see my perception of sight. Moreover, if when you see the same thing that I do, you regard it as seeing my perception of sight, then since you have seen the sphere of my seeing, you should also see the sphere of my not seeing. Why can you not do so? Furthermore, if you falsely say that you see the sphere of my not seeing, it is then simply your own sphere of not seeing and it can not be the phenomena of my not seeing. And if not, how can it be that the phenomena of your not seeing is to be regarded as mine? Therefore, if you really do not see the sphere of my not seeing, then the selfness of this perception of sight can not be an object that can be seen with the eyes and touched with the hands. And if it is not an object, then why is it not your own true nature? If you still falsely regard your perception of sight as an object, the object should be able to see you, too. If you try to explain it in this way, the substantiality of an object and the selfness of the perception of sight of the object would be hopelessly jumbled together. No one would be able to tell which is subject and which object.

Ananda, as the nature of the perception of sight is universal, how can it be regarded as otherwise than your own true nature? What does it mean, Ananda, that you do not recognize the true nature that naturally belongs to you, and on the contrary, you are asking me to show you another reality?

Ananda said to the Blessed One:—Noble Lord! If the nature of the perception of my sight is my true nature and not any different, then when my Lord and I (in a Samapatti state) were visiting the transcendental, mystical, and magnificent palaces of the Four Heavenly Kings and were sojourning in the palaces of the sun and moon, the perception of our sight was then perfect and universal, reaching and including every part of the Saha world. But when we returned to this Jetavena Grove we see only this Hall—a still, quiet place with doors and windows—and when we look out from within, we are able to see only the veranda and eaves. Now I learn from my Lord, that the essence of the perception of sight naturally permeates the whole universe. If that is so, why is it that now our perception of sight only embraces this little hall and nothing more? What does it mean, my Lord? Does it mean that the perception of sight is reduced from universality to the finiteness of mortal mind? Or is it that the perception of sight is partitioned off by walls and houses? I do not see where the point of your explanation lies. Please explain it more clearly, for we are very ignorant and stupid.

The Lord Buddha replied:—As all things in the universe, either great or small, external or internal, are objects in the presence of our sight, so it would not be right to say that our perception of sight has the potentiality of enlarging and reducing. For instance, take an empty square vessel. When you consider the space in the square vessel, is that square space fixed or changeable? If it is fixed, then if you put a round vessel inside of it, the square space would not permit the admission of the round vessel; or if it is changeable, then the space in the square vessel would no longer appear square. You said that you did not see where the point lies. Well here is the point: it is the nature of space to be neither fixed nor changeable (and the same is true of the mind's perception), as I have stated before, so it is absurd for you to repeat your question.

Or, Ananda, (if you are still unconvinced) suppose you fill the square vessel with objects and then remove the vessel's squareness; are you still troubled as to the existence of shape in open space? Supposing that it is true that when we re-entered the Hall, the perception of our sight became limited, and when we look at the sun, it appears to lengthen to reach the surface of the sun. Or when we build a wall or a house, it appears to set apart or limit the perception of our sight, but when we make a hole in the wall, is the perception of our sight unable to look through and beyond? The point of my explanation is that changeableness is not an attribute of our perception of sight.

The Lord Buddha continued:—Ananda! Since beginningless time sentient beings have been led astray by mistaking the nature of their mind to be the same as the nature of any other object. As they thus lose their true and essential Mind their minds become bewildered by outer objects and the perception of their sight becomes changeable to conform to the dimensions of its visual field and to become limited strictly according to outer conditions. But if you can learn to see things by your true and essential Mind, right away you will become equal to all the Tathagatas—both your mind and your body will become perfectly enlightened and you will be in the same state of tranquillity and stillness as though you were sitting under the Bodhi tree. So perfectly universalized will your mind have become that even at the point of a single hair all the kingdoms of the ten quarters of the universe will be seen.

Ananda said:—Noble Lord, if the Essence of the perception of sight is my wonderful, enlightening Mind, then this wonderful Mind must be something which we can consider, and if the perception of sight is my true Essence, then what becomes of my present body and mind? I feel that both my body and mind have their separate existence, and yet this Essential perception of sight, even in its concentrated state of stillness, appears to make no discrimination of my body. If this Essential Nature of my perception of sight is truly my Mind then it should be able to show me in the presence of my sight, that it is my true self, but if it does, what becomes of my body, does it belong to me or not? This would seem to be contrary to what my Lord has previously said, that the object could not see the mind. We beg, my Lord to have pity upon us and enlighten our ignorant minds.

The Lord Buddha said:—Ananda, what you have just questioned, as to whether the perception of sight is something that can be considered as standing in your presence, is not true. If it was really present before your sight and you could really see it, then as the Essence of the perception of sight has a location, it will no longer be without a point of direction.

Suppose we were sitting in the Jetavana grove and our sight reached everywhere in the grove—to the streams, to the Royal Palace and its mansions, up to the sun and the moon and down to the River Ganges. All of these different phenomena, which we are supposing you are indicating with your hand as being within the purview of our sight, each has its distinctive characteristic; the grove is shady, the sun is bright, the wall is an obstacle to light, the opening in the wall is a passage for the light, and the same is true even of the smaller things, the trees, herbs, fine grasses etc. Though in dimensions they all differ from one another, so long as it has appearance, there is nothing that is beyond the range of our sight or description. If the perception of sight is present before your sight, you should be able to point to me, which is your perception of sight and describe it to me.

If it is space that is the perception of sight, you ought to know, and if we were to remove perception of sight, what would you substitute for space? If one of the many objects is the perception of sight and has now become the perception of sight, what other object will you substitute for the first? Suppose you look closely, analyze all the phenomena before you, pick out the essential and enlightening, pure and wonderful nature of the perception of sight, and show it to me just as describable and tangible as the other things.

Ananda said to the Lord:—My Lord! Standing in the Lecture Hall of this imposing building and looking out into the far distances, to the vista of the Ganges, up to the sun and the moon, looking everywhere my hand can point and my sight can reach, there is nothing in sight but objects, and I see nothing that is analogous to my perception of sight. It is just as my Lord has taught us. I am simply a junior Arhat not yet free from the intoxicants, but it is the same with the Bodhisattva-Mahasattvas, we are all alike unable to detect the presence of anything to be called the perception of sight among all the appearances of phenomena, nor are we able to point out an analogous something that transcends all objects.

The Lord Buddha was greatly pleased with this reply and said:—So it is, Ananda, so it is! There is neither the Essence of the perception of sight, nor any other essential nature transcending all objects. There is no such "thing" as the perception of sight. Now let me ask you some more questions.

Suppose Ananda, that you and I are again sitting in the Jeta grove, looking out over the gardens, even to the sun and moon, and seeing all the multitudinous objects, and no such thing as perception of sight can be pointed out to us. But, Ananda, among all these multitudinous phenomena, can you show me anything which does not belong to the perception of sight?

Ananda replied:—Noble Lord! True, I see every part of the Jeta grove, but see nothing which does not belong to perception of sight. And why? Because if the trees in the grove do not belong to the perception of sight, we could not call them trees. But if the trees belong to the perception of sight, why do we still call them trees? It is the same with space. If it does not belong to the perception of sight, we could not see space, and if it does belong to the perception of sight, why should we still call it space? I am convinced now that all objects whatsoever, be they little or big, wherever there are manifestations and appearances, all belong to the perception of sight.

Again, the Lord Buddha expressed agreement, saying:—So it is, Ananda, so it is!

Then all the junior disciples, except the older ones among them who had finished the practice of meditation, having listened to the discussion and not understanding the significance of the conclusion, became confused and frightened and lost control of themselves.

The Lord Tathagata, recognizing that the junior disciples were thrown into perplexity and discouragement by the teaching, took pity upon them and consoled them, saying to Ananda and to all of them:—

My good, pious disciples! Do not be disturbed by what has been taught. All that the supreme Teacher of the Dharma has taught are true and sincere words, they are neither extravagant nor chimerical. They are not to be compared with the puzzling paradoxes given by the famous heretic teachers. Do not be disturbed by what has been taught, but ponder upon it seriously and never give yourself up either to sadness or delight.

Thereupon the great disciple Manjusri, regarded by all as a Prince of the Lord's Dharma, took pity upon the confused ones among the Brothers, rose in his place and bowing with great reverence at the feet of the Lord Buddha, said to him:—

Blessed Lord! There are some among the Brothers in this Assembly who have not yet fully realized the significance of these two seemingly ambiguous interpretations relating to whether phenomena and space belong to perception of sight, which have been presented by my Lord Tathagata.

Blessed Lord! If the conditioning causes in the presence of our sight, such as phenomenal objects, space etc., are meant as belonging to the perception of sight, they should have relations to be pointed out; or, if they are not meant as belonging to the perception of sight, they should not be seen by our sight. The Brothers do not see the point of the teaching and, therefore, have become confused and frightened. It does not mean that the roots of the Brothers' goodness in previous lives are too weak for such profound teaching, but for them the explanation needs to be very plain. I pray the Blessed Lord to be kind enough to bring out the Truth more simply as to what relations there are lying between the phenomenal objects and the Essence of the perception of sight. What are their origins, and how is the ambiguity as to whether they belong or do not belong, to be gotten rid of.

Then the Lord Buddha replied:—Manjusri and all my good pious Disciples! The Tathagatas in the ten quarters of the universe, together with all the great Bodhisattva-Mahasattvas, as they are intrinsically abiding in Samadhi, regard all of the perceptions of sight, their causes and conditions, and of all conceptions of phenomena, as being visionary flowers in the air, having no true nature of existence within themselves. But they regard the perceiving of sight as belonging to the Essence of the wonderful, pure, enlightening Mind (Bodhi). Why should there be any ambiguity as to belonging or not belonging, between the perception of sight and the perceiving of objects?

Manjusri, let me ask you, supposing there is another Manjusri, just such as you are. What do you think? Is there truly another Manjusri? Or is it an impossible supposition.

Blessed Lord, it is just as you say, it is impossible. I am the true Manjusri; it is impossible to have another of me. And why? Because if it was possible to have another in perfect likeness, there would be two Manjusris, but I would still be the one and true Manjusri. There is no ambiguity of one or two.

The Lord Buddha was pleased with this reply and continued:—It is just the same with this wonderful, enlightening perception of sight, the seeing of objects, as well as objects themselves, they all intrinsically belong to the pure, perfect, Essential Mind of the wonderful, enlightening, Supreme Bodhi. But they have been discriminated as phenomena of sight, space, the perception of seeing, hearing etc. It is just like a man with defective eyes seeing two moons at the same time. Who can tell which is the true moon? Manjusri, there is only one true moon; there can be no ambiguity of one being true and the other untrue. Therefore, when one is looking upon these manifestations arising from the senses in contact with objects, he must remember that they are all illusion and then there will be no ambiguity. But if the feeling still persists that there is some ambiguity as to whether the essence of the perceiving mind is the wonderful, enlightening Mind of the True Essence or not, the wonderful enlightening Mind itself can free you from the ambiguity as to whether it is the True Mind or not.

Ananda said:—Noble Lord! My Lord Dharma has said that the perceptions and their causes are universally permeating the ten quarters, that by nature they are tranquil and permanent, and that their nature is devoid of deaths and rebirths. If this is so, then what is the difference between it and the heretical teachings, such as the doctrine of "emptiness," the doctrine of "naturalism," and similar teaching, all of which teach that there is a "True Ego" universally permeating the ten quarters? My Lord has also given teachings to the wise Saraputra, our Brother, and to many others, on Mount Lankara, in which he explained to them that, while the heretics were always talking about "naturalism," my Lord taught the principle of "causes and conditions," which was fundamentally different from the teachings of the heretical philosophers. Now when I learn from my Lord's teaching that this nature of perception of sight is also natural in its origin, is devoid of death and rebirth, and is perfectly free from all sorts of illusive reversions, it does not seem to belong to your principle of "causes and conditions." How can it be distinguished from the "naturalism" taught by the heretics? Pray explain this to us, so that we do not fall into their heresy, and so that we may realize the wonderful, enlightening, and intelligent nature of our True Mind.

The Lord Buddha replied, saying:—Ananda, I have already explained it to you and shown you the Truth, but you have not realized it. On the contrary your mind is bewildered and you have mistaken my teaching of Mind-essence, as being "naturalism." Ananda, if your perception of sight belonged to "naturalism," then we should examine into the essence of its nature. Let us do so. In this wonderful, enlightening perception of sight, what would you take as belonging to itself? Does your perception of sight take its brightness from its own nature? Does it take its darkness from its own nature? Does it take its limitlessness from its own nature? Or its being limited by impenetrable objects as belonging to its own nature?

Ananda, if brightness belongs to it by nature, then it should not see darkness. If its ability to see everywhere in space belongs to it, then it should not be hindered by impenetrable objects. The opposite of this is true also. If darkness belongs to its nature, then there should be no brightness in the perception of sight. How then could it see the phenomena of brightness?

Then Ananda said to the Lord Buddha:—Noble Lord! If this wonderful perception of sight can not be explained as belonging to the principle of "naturalism," then how can it be explained as belonging to the principle of "cause and condition"? When I come to study the question of how the perception of sight can arise from causes and conditions, my mind is still confused. I beg my Lord to explain it for us once more.

The Lord Buddha replied:—Ananda, as to what you have just asked me about the nature of cause and condition, I would rather ask you a few questions first. Supposing the nature of your perception of sight was before us now for our examination. How could it be manifested to us? Would it be because of its brightness? Or its darkness? Or because of the clearness of space? Or because of the impenetrability of objects?

If the perception of sight is manifested by reason of its brightness, then we could not see darkness, or vice versa. And the same would be true if our perception of sight was manifested by the clearness of space, or the impenetrability of objects. Again, Ananda. Is the perception of sight manifested by the condition of brightness? Or the condition of darkness? Or the condition of the clearness of space? Or under the condition of impenetrable objects? If it is manifested under the condition of brightness, then it could not see darkness. And the same would be true of the opposite, or of open space and its opposite, impenetrable objects.

Ananda, you ought to realize that the nature of this essentially wonderful, intelligent, enlightening, perception of sight belongs to neither cause nor condition, to neither nature nor phenomena, to neither the ambiguities of being or not being, or of nothingness or not nothingness. Neither does the conception of sight belong to any conception of phenomena, and yet it embraces all phenomena.

Now, Ananda, after all these arguments, how can you discriminate within your mind, and how can you make distinctions and give them all those worldly fictitious names? You might as well try to take a pinch of space, or rub space with your hand. You would use up your strength and the air in the space would remain undisturbed. How would it be possible for you to catch and hold even a tiny bit of space? The same is true of your perception of sight.

Then Ananda said to the Lord Buddha:—Noble Lord! If this wonderful, enlightening nature of perception of sight, belongs neither to its own nature, nor to causes and conditions, then why did my Lord once explain to the Bhikshus that the nature of perception of sight is under four kinds of conditions, namely, space, brightness, mind and eyes? What did you mean by that explanation?

The Lord Buddha replied, saying:—Ananda! What I said about the causes and conditions in this phenomenal world, was not my supreme, intrinsic Teaching. Let me ask you again, Ananda:—When the people of this world say they can see this and that, what do they mean by it, Ananda?

My Lord, they mean that by the light of the sun or the moon or a lamp, they are able to see, and when devoid of the light of sun, moon or lamp, they are unable to see.

Suppose, Ananda, there is no light and they are unable to see things, does that mean that they cannot see the darkness? If it is possible to see darkness when it is too dark to see things, it simply means there is no light; it does not mean they can not see. Supposing, Ananda, they were in the light and could not see the darkness; does that mean, also, that they can not see? Here are two kinds of phenomena, light and darkness, and of both you say, 'he can not see.' If these two kinds of phenomena are mutually exclusive, then he can not see at all and that would mean, as far as the perception of sight is concerned, a temporary discontinuance of existence. But the fact is not so. Therefore, it is quite clear that you must mean that he can not see at all. I am puzzled to know just what you do mean, when you say, "he can not see in the darkness."

Listen, now Ananda, to what I am going to teach you. When you are seeing light, it does not mean that the perception of sight belongs to light, and when you are seeing darkness, it does not mean that the perception of sight belongs to darkness. It is just the same when you see through clear space, or can not see through impenetrable objects. Ananda, you should understand the significance of those four things, for when you are speaking of the perception of sight you are not referring to the phenomena of seeing with the eyes, but to the intrinsic perception of sight that transcends the experiential sight of the eyes, and is beyond its reach. Then how can you interpret this transcendental perception of sight as being dependent upon causes and conditions, or nature, or a synthesis of all of them? Ananda, are you of all the Arahats so limited in understanding that you cannot comprehend that this Perception of Sight is pure Reality itself? This is a profound teaching and I want all of you to ponder upon it seriously. Do not become tired of it, nor indolent in realizing it. While it is the most profound of all teachings, it is the surest way to Enlightenment.

Still Ananda was not satisfied and said to the Lord Buddha:—Noble Lord! Although my Lord has explained to us the principles of causes and conditions, of naturalism, and all the phenomena of conformity. and non-conformity, yet we do not fully realize any of them, and now as we listen to the teachings of our Lord about Perception of Sight, we become more puzzled than ever. We do not understand what you mean when you say that our mental perception of sight is not our intrinsic Perception of Sight. Pray, my Lord, have mercy upon us; give us the true eye of Transcendental Intelligence and reveal to us more clearly our Intuitive Mind of Brightest Purity. At this Ananda was so far overcome that he broke into sobs and bowed down to the ground waiting for the Lord's further instruction.

Thereupon the Blessed One had pity for Ananda and for all the younger members of the Assembly, and solemnly recited the Great Dharani which is the mystic way to the full attainment of Samadhi.

Then he said:—Ananda! Though you have an excellent

memory, it seems to serve only to increase your knowledge. You are still a long way from the mysterious insight and reflection that accompany the attainment of Samapatti. Now, Ananda, listen carefully to me and I will teach you more particularly, not for your sake alone, but for the sake of all true disciples in the future, so that all alike may reap the fruit of Enlightenment.

The reason why all sentient beings in this world have ever been bound to the cycle of deaths and re-births is because of two reverse, discriminative and false perceptions of the eyes which spring up everywhere to bind us to this present life and keep us turning about in the cycle of deaths and re-births by every wind of karma. What are these two reverse perceptions of the eyes? One is the false perception of the eyes that is caused by individual and particular karma of any single sentient being. The other is the false perception of eyes that is caused by the general karma of many sentient beings.

Ananda, what is meant by the false perceptive karma that is caused by the individual and particular karma of single sentient beings? Supposing in this world there was someone who was suffering from inflamation of the eyes, so that when he looked at the light of a lamp in the night time, he would see a strange halo of different colors, surrounding the light. What do you think, Ananda? Is this strange bright halo caused by the lamp, or does it belong to the perception of the eyes? If it belongs to the lamp, then why do others with healthy eyes not perceive it? If it belongs to the perception of the eyes, then why does not every one see it? What is the strange sight only perceived by the single individual with the inflamed eyes?

Again, Ananda. If this halo that surrounds the light, exists independently of the lamp, then other objects near by should have like halos about them, screen, curtain, desk, table etc. If it exists independently of the perception of the eyes, then it ought not to be seen by the eyes at all. How is it, that only the inflamed eyes see it?

Ananda, you should know that the sight really belongs to the lamp, but the halo is caused by the inflamation of the particular eyes, for the halo and the perception are both under the condition of the inflammation, but the nature that perceives the effect of the inflammation of the eyes is not sick itself. So, in conclusion, it should not be said that the halo belongs ex-

clusively either to the lamp or to the perception of the eyes,
nor should it be said that it belongs neither to the lamp nor
to the perception of the eyes. It is just the same as the reflection of the moon in still water: it is neither the real moon
nor its double. And why? Because the reproduction of any
sight is always accounted for by causes and conditions, so that
the learned and intelligent do not say that the origin of any
sight that can be accounted for by causes and conditions, belongs to the object, nor does not belong to the object. It is the
same with the sight caused by the inflamed eyes, which should
not be said to be either independent of the perception of the
eyes nor not independent of the perception of the eyes. Would
it not be absurd to try and distinguish what part of the sight
belongs to the eyes and what part belongs to the lamp? Would
it not be more absurd to try and distinguish which part of the
sight does not belong to the lamp and which part does not belong to the inflamed eyes?

Ananda! Now let us consider, what is meant by false perception of eyes that is caused by the general karma of many
sentient beings. In this world there are many thousands of
kingdoms, great and small. Supposing we think that in one of
the smallest of these kingdoms, all of the people are under
the influence of a common bad condition of mind, that is, they
all see many sorts of unpropitious signs that are not seen by
any other people—two suns, two moons, or different eclipses of
the sun or moon, or halos about the sun or moon, or comets,
with or without tails, or flying meteors seen only for an instant,
or gloomy shadows like a great ear near the sun or moon, or
sometimes rainbows seen early or late. Supposing that all these
strange phenomena of evil omen are seen only by this small
kingdom, and have never been seen or heard of by any other
people. Now, Ananda, we will consider these two examples together. First let us refer to the individual and particular false
perception of eyes as seen by a single individual in the strange
halo about the night lamp. Though it appeared to belong to
the conditions in the presence of sight yet, after all, it belonged
to the perception of the inflamed eyes. The imaginary halo
meant only the sickness of the perception of eyes; it had nothing whatever to do with sight in itself. That is, the nature of
the perception of the eyes that sees an imaginary halo is not
responsible for the viewing mistakes. For instance, Ananda,

when you are viewing the whole appearance of a country,
seeing its mountains, rivers, kingdoms, people etc., they seem
to be discriminated particulars of fact, but in truth, they are
all made up by the original, beginningless, sickness of perceiving eyes. To both the visual condition of the eyes and the
perception of the eyes these particular sights seem manifested
in our presence, but to our intuitive, enlightened nature it is
seen to be, what it truly is, a morbid sight indicative of sick
eyes. So any and all perceptions of enlightened nature, for instance, even the particular perception of eyes itself, are seen
to be simply an obscuring mist. But our fundamental, intuitive,
enlightening Mind that perceives this perception of eyes and its
visual conditions can by no means be regarded as something
imaginary and morbidly sick. Therefore, we must be careful not
to plunge this intuitive nature that perceives this morbid mist
that is discriminated by the perception of inflamed eyes into
the same morbid mist. We must be careful to distinguish between the perception of our eyes and the intrinsic Perception
of Sight by our enlightened Mind that is conscious of the fallible perception of the eyes.

Since this intrinsic Sight is not identical with the perception
of the sight as perceived by the eyes, how can the perceptions
of morbid sight, such as your common seeing, hearing, perceiving and discriminating, how can you continue to call it your
True Mind, Ananda? Thus when you are regarding yourself,
or me, or any of the ten species of sentient beings in this
world, you are simply regarding the morbid mist of the perception of the eyes; it is not the true, unconditioned Sight.
The nature of this intrinsic Sight naturally manifests no morbid mist in its transcendental Perceiving and, accordingly, your
intrinsic Mind is not the same as your perceiving, experiential
mind.

Ananda! Let us now regard those sentient beings with their
general, common and false perception of eyes and compare them
with this one person who is suffering under his individual and
particular karma of false perception of eyes. This inflamed-eye
individual who perceived an imaginary halo about the light,
caused by the morbid mist in his perceiving mind, is perfectly
typical of all the people in that little kingdom who saw the
imaginary unpropitious signs in the heavens caused by the general and common karma of false perceptions of eyes. They are

alike developments of a false perception of sight since beginningless time. For instance, in this great world with its continents and oceans, in the social world with all its races of people and kingdoms, all of these sentient beings and all the natural phenomena all have their origin in the intuitive, enlightening, non-intoxicating, mysterious, intrinsic Mind, but they are all manifestations of the false, morbid conditions that belong respectfully to the perceptions of the eyes, ears, nose, tongue, touch, discrimination, emotion, thinking. All these sentient beings are ever subject to the sufferings of an unceasing cycle of deaths and rebirths according to the general principle of causes and conditions.

Ananda! If you can remain perfectly independent of these false perceptions and of all conformity and non-conformity to them, then you will have exterminated all the causes leading to deaths and rebirths and, besides, you will have attained a perfectly matured enlightenment that is of the nature of non-death and non-rebirth. This is the pure Intrinsic Mind, the ever abiding Intuitive Essence.

(Questions that arise in view of the sole Reality of Essential Mind.)

Then the Lord Buddha continued, saying:—Ananda! Though you had previously realized that the mysterious enlightening nature of Intuitive Essence was subject to neither cause nor condition nor nature, yet you were not clear as to its intuitive origin which is made up neither by conformity to causes and conditions, nor by non-conformity to them.

You still appear to be in bondage to the objects that are in your presence and are still constrained to conform to the false conceptions of the world, for you still cherish doubts within your mind when you hear that your enlightening Mind is not to be attained by conformity to the principle of cause and condition. Let me ask you some more questions. Tell me, Ananda. Regarding your present mysterious and pure Essence of the perception of your eyes, is it in conformity with brightness, or is it in conformity with darkness? Is it in conformity with the clearness of space, or is it in conformity with the impenetrability of obstacles? If it is in conformity with brightness, then when you are seeing the brightness which is manifested in your presence, can you detect what part of the brightness is mixed up with the perception of eyes? It is quite clear that there is the perception of eyes, but when you are seeing the brightness, do you notice what kind of appearance comes from the brightness to be mixed up with your perception of eyes? If the viewing of brightness does not belong to the perception of eyes, then how is it you can see brightness at all? If it does belong to the perception of eyes, then how is it that there is some nature that perceives the perception of eyes? If it is asserted that the perception of eyes is perfect by itself, then what part of it is in conformity with brightness? If brightness is perfect by itself, then it should be in conformity with the perception of eyes. Thus the perception of eyes must be a different thing from brightness. If they are blurred together, then each of them would lose something of its own nature. Since by blurring they lose something of their own natures, the perception of eyes would, by no means, be in conformity with brightness. And the same deduction can be made as to the other phenomena, darkness, space and impenetrable objects.

Again, Ananda. As regards your mysterious, pure Essence of the perception of Sight, is it compounded with brightness, or is it compounded with darkness, or with space, or with impenetrable objects? If the perception of sight is compounded with brightness, then, supposing you were in darkness, and the phenomena of brightness had disappeared so that it does not become mixed with darkness, how is it that you can still see darkness? Or, when you are seeing darkness and the perception of eyes does not combine with darkness, then when it combines with brightness, how can it see brightness, also? Since the perception of eyes has not seen brightness, then how is it that the perception of eyes can distinguish brightness from darkness. And the same deduction can be made with the other phenomena of darkness, space and impenetrable objects.

Then Ananda interposed, saying to the Lord Buddha:— Noble Lord! It seems to me that this mysterious, intuitive Nature and all of these conditioning objects and thoughts of the mind must be in some kind of mutual conformity, or mixed compound.

The Lord Buddha replied:—Ananda, you have just now asserted that the intuitive Nature is not in conformity nor in compound with other phenomena. I will ask you some more questions. As to what you have just said, that this Mysterious

Essence of the perception of Sight is neither in conformity nor in compound with other phenomena. Do you mean by this, that it is not in conformity with brightness, nor with darkness, nor space, nor impenetrable objects? If it is not in conformity with brightness, then the perception of eyes and brightness must have each their individual and exclusive sphere. Can you show the boundary line between them, which part belongs to perception of eyes and which to brightness? If within the sphere of brightness, there must be no admission of the perception of eyes, how could they influence each other as the perception of eyes would naturally not know the proper limits of manifested brightness. And if perception of eyes could not know, how could you? The same can be said of all other phenomena, darkness, space and impenetrable objects.

Again, Ananda. If it is true as suggested by you, that the Essence of this mysterious perception of Sight is neither in conformity or in combination with conditions, then do you mean that it is not in conformity with brightness, nor with darkness, nor space, nor impenetrable objects? If the perception of eyes is not in combination with brightness, then they would be like two diverging horns. They would be like the relation of the ear and brightness which do not influence each other at all. Since the perception of eyes does not know the exact location where brightness manifests itself, how can it make distinctions between combining and not combining? And the same can be said of the other phenomena, darkness, space and impenetrable objects.

Ananda, you have not yet realized that the True Nature of all transitory perceptions of sights of objects and fleeting illusions that become manifest when they are in the presence of objects and which disappear when out of the presence of objects, IS this mysterious, enlightening, intuitive Essence. This is true of all these five sense ingredients, six kinds of perceptions, and is true from all the twelve locations of contact between consciousness and objects, into the eighteen spheres of mentation in contact with objects through the sense organs. When they are in conformity or in combination with causes and conditions, they manifest these fleeting, illusive conceptions, and when they are disconnected from causes and conditions, the illusions disappear. As you do not realize the foregoing—that the true nature of the perceptions of the senses is the Intuitive Essence of Mind—how can you realize that all the phenomena of death and rebirth—their appearing, going to and fro, disappearing—is simply the permanent, mysterious, enlightening, unchanging, all-perfect, Wonderful Mind-Essence of Tathagata's Womb (wherein all is in perfect purity and unity and potentiality)?

If you still think that these conceptions of the senses and discriminations concerning them have some self-nature of their own then you should seek for it within the purity of this Permanent Reality, but not a sign of their individual characteristics or of conceptions concerning them will you find there.

Ananda! What is involved in the assertion that the five sense-ingredients and discriminations concerning them belong to the mysterious Mind-Essence of Tathagata's Womb? Suppose a man with good fresh eyes looks steadily into the bright shining space of the sky without glancing about or winking. After long staring, there arise contaminations of the eyes and in the emptiness of space, he sees fantastic blossoms and many other strange phantasms. These fantastic blossoms that the contaminated eyes see in the open space of the sky come neither from the sky nor from the eyes. If you suppose they come from the sky then, when they disappear, they must return to the sky. However, as soon as you have the notion of coming from and going to then the sky is no longer open space. If open space is not open space then the fantastic blossoms could not have come into manifestation nor disappear.

Ananda, you should know that all the sights of the eyes are like that. Since beginningless time, sentient beings have been regarding the purity of Intuitive Mind-Essence and their eyes have become contaminated and they see the myriads of sense conceptions and from liking them birth after birth and grasping them by force of habit the false conceptions of the senses have seemingly become real, and have set up a conception of Ananda and that which is not Ananda, and resent the coming in of the true Ananda.

If you suppose that these fantastic blossoms come from the eyes, they should also return to the eyes, but do they? If they come from the eyes naturally they would have the nature of perception of sight and, going out from these eyes, having the perception of sight, they should see their own eyes. If they did not have the nature of seeing when they went out, they would be the objects and would cast shadows on the sky, and when they return to the eyes they should cast shadows in their own eyes. According to our supposition, the eyes that saw the clear space of the sky were good, fresh eyes, now when they have seen the fantastic blossoms they have shadows in them; how can they be called, good, fresh eyes? Therefore, Ananda, you should know that the ingredients of sight are false and and illusion; they are neither manifested naturally by causes and conditions, nor do they arise spontaneously from their own nature.

Suppose, Ananda, a man sitting at ease, with hands and feet at rest, and all the bones of his body in harmony and comfort, with his mind in a state of tranquillity, neither happy nor unhappy, sitting almost unconscious of his own existence. With no especial purpose in mind, he rubs the palms of his two hands together and forthwith there arises from his hands perceptions of roughness, smoothness, coldness, warmness. So you should know that the ingredients of the perception of touch are fanciful and illusion, also. Ananda, all these fantastic feelings that arise from rubbing the hands together, neither come from the air nor from the palms of the hands. If it comes from the air, since it can touch the palms of the hands, why does it not touch the body elsewhere? What caused the selection? Or, if it comes from the palms, why does this feeling-perception not arise until the palms are pressed together? Because of its arising from the palms when they are pressed together, they naturally become conscious of each other, and when the palms are separated, the perception of touch naturally retreats into the body. Naturally there is something in the body that is passing to and fro, but how is it that the body has to wait until the hands are pressed together before it becomes conscious of a perception of touch? Therefore, Ananda, you should know that the perception ingredients of touch are fanciful and illusion that are neither manifested by causes and conditions, nor do they arise spontaneously from their own nature.

Ananda, suppose a man speaks of sour plums, he immediately is conscious of saliva flowing out from his tongue, or as he thinks of falling from a high cliff, he immediately feels a trembling in his feet. It is just the same with all thinking ingredients of perception. In this case it neither comes from the plum, nor from an actual plum going into his mouth. If sourness is manifested by a plum, then it must be speaking for itself, how is it that it was perceived in this case by some one speaking about it? Or, if the perception arises from the going into the mouth, then it should be heard by the mouth; why did the saliva have to wait until the ear heard of the sourness? If it was the ear that heard it why did not the saliva come out of the ear? The same is true of the effect of thinking of falling from a steep cliff. Therefore, Ananda, you should know that the thinking ingredients of perception are fanciful and illusion, they are neither manifested naturally by causes and condition, nor spontaneously by their own nature.

Ananda! A river flows on with no gaps between the water that goes before and the water that flows after, so is the current of the activity-ingredients of our perceptions. The nature of such an everflowing current of water neither arises from the air nor from the waters; it is neither of the nature of water or air, nor is it independent of them. If it arises from the air, then all the infinite spaces of the ten quarters of the universe would become torrents of water and the whole universe would suffer denudation. If it is manifested by means of water alone, then the substance and potentialities of water would be manifested for once only, it wouldn't be a current. If it arises from the nature of water, then when water is stilled, the current would be of some other substance than water. Therefore, Ananda, you should know that the action-ingredients of perception are not manifested naturally by causes and conditions nor spontaneously by their own nature.

Ananda, suppose a man fills a jar with air in his native country, plugs up the mouth of the jar and journeys many hundred of miles to a distant country, for the purpose of bringing some of his native air to that far country. This is in likeness to the conscious-ingredient of perception. When the jar is opened the air mingles with the other air and can neither be said to come from the native country nor to be the pure air of the far country. If it came from the native country, then the air there should be decreased, and the air in the far country increased, but on the contrary, when he opens the jar he sees nothing going in and nothing coming out. Therefore, Ananda, you should know that the conscious ingredients are fanciful and illusive; they are neither manifested naturally by causes and conditions, nor spontaneously by their own nature.

Then the Lord Buddha asked Ananda:—Ananda, if we

think of Ultimate Reality as the Womb of Tathagata from which every manifestation emerges, in what sense can it be said that the six sense perceptions belong to this true, mysterious Mind-Essence?

Let me explain this relation to you. Referring to what I said to you a little while ago, that long staring at the clear bright sky was the cause of contaminations in the perception of the eyes. In that teaching, both the perception of the eyes and the contaminated state were shown to be restraints placed upon the pure Wisdom (*Bodhi*) nature. It is because of this constraint placed upon it by the two opposing but false notions of brightness and darkness that the perception of sight, which perceives the phenomenal object, is spoken of as having the nature of perceiving sights. But this perception of sight, apart from brightness and darkness, has no substantiality of existence. I will show this to be a fact. Ananda, you know very well that this perception of sight is independent of brightness and darkness, nor does it have its origin in the sense organ (which only records sensation), nor does it arise from the surrounding space. Because, if it comes from brightness, then it could not perceive darkness; and if it comes from darkness, it ought not to perceive brightness any more. If it comes from the sense-organ, its sensations will vary, but it will know nothing of brightness or darkness. Such is the essence of the perception of sight that it has no nature of its own. Because, if it comes from space, then as it goes forth to view an object in its presence, so it should be able to view the eye-organ on its return. If it comes from space, moreover, then space must have its own organ of sight, and what relation would it have with your eyes? Therefore, Ananda, you should know that the perception of the eyes is false and fantastic and that it is neither manifested by causes and conditions, nor spontaneously by its own nature, (for it has no nature of its own).

(*The same is proven in the text, to hold true as to the un-substantiality and falsity of the perception of the other senses, of hearing, tasting, and smelling.*) . . . .

Ananda, supposing a man has one warm hand and the other cold, and they touch each other. If the coldness exceeds the warmth, then both hands will become cold, or if the warm hand is greater in force, both hands will become warm. Thus by means of this perception of two sensations at the same time, and of the one being greater than the other, the conditions are set up by the phenomena of contamination, the same being manifested by means of the contact of two hands in different degrees of warmth and coldness. This perception of two hands and their contaminations are both to be included in the contaminated state manifested on account of the constraint of the Wisdom nature. It is by means of the conflict between these two false notions of separation and contact that there is manifested the sense of touching, which perceives the notion of contact, which provides the basis of the perception of touching. If this perception of touching can be shown to be independent both of the unpleasant notion of separation and the pleasant notion of contact, then it has no substantiality of existence after all. I will now show this to be a fact. But first you should know that this perception of touch does not come from separation or contact, nor does it reveal its existence by means of a feeling of unpleasantness or of pleasantness, nor does it arise spontaneously from its own sense of touch, and, finally, it is not manifested from space, either. And why? Because if the perception of touch comes when it is in contact with something then when it is separated from something, the perception of touching should have disappeared but, as it is, it still perceives its separation. And the same is true in regard to the phenomena of unpleasantness and pleasantness for, if the perception of touch springs up from the sense of body there can be none of these four phenomena of separation; contact, unpleasantness and pleasantness. And, moreover, the perception of your body naturally has no nature of its own. If the perception of touch must be regarded as springing out of space, and space would be availing itself of the perception of touch, and then, what would be the relation between the perceptions arising out of space and the perceptions arising within our own bodies? Therefore, Ananda, you should know that the perception of the sense of touch is false and fantastic, that it is neither manifested by cause and condition, nor spontaneously by its own nature.

Then the Lord Buddha, continued:—Ananda, when a man becomes weary, he lies down to sleep; when his sleep is satisfied, he wakes up; when he opens his eyes, he sees objects and begins to think about them; when he loses his memory he becomes worried. These are to be considered as reversed conceptions of death and re-birth, and transformations and continuity, which develop in a more orderly succession and to which the mind becomes accustomed. These phenomena (analogous to the phenomena connected with the senses of seeing, hearing, smelling, tasting, touching) are connected with the mental or thinking sense. The perception of thinking (or the consciousness of thinking), with its contaminations is to be included with the other sense perceptions and their contaminations, as being restraints placed upon our Bodhi nature.

It is because of being placed between two false notions, such as death and re-birth, that the perception of thinking becomes manifested. The mind-sense, (considered as an object) in contact with the other senses receives notions of ideas, and thoughts and recollections, which being in reversed order (i.e. moving toward diversity) are ever moving away from True Mind (which is in a state of primal and unchanging unity and purity), and thus will never reach their source in the Wisdom of True Mind. This is characteristic of all conscious and discriminative thinking.

If this perception of thinking becomes separated from the dualism of phenomena, such as deaths and rebirths, waking and sleeping, etc., it loses all substantiality. I will now prove this to be a fact.

Ananda, you should know that this sense of thinking does not come from waking and sleeping, nor from deaths and rebirths, nor from its own nature, nor from space. And why? Because if the perception of thought comes from the awakened state, then when sleep predominates it should disappear completely, and who would be the one to awake? If the perception of thinking exists only when we are in the presence of something, then when nothing is present, it would be in resemblance to non-existence, and who is it that would suffer death? If it is manifested from death, then thinking would immediately disappear with the approach of death and, thus, who would be able to recognize his rebirth? If the perception of thinking springs from its own nature, then the two phenomena of waking and sleeping would be like the opening and closing of the lotus flower. If it is independent of both waking and sleeping, it would be like the visionary flowers seen in the air by inflamed eyes, which have no substantiality whatever. If it is manifested from space, it would naturally belong to the perception of space and what, then, would be its relation to our sense of thinking? Therefore, Ananda, you should know that the perception of thinking is false and fantastic, that it is not manifested by causes and conditions, nor spontaneously by its own nature.

* * *

Then the Lord Buddha continued, saying:—Again, Ananda, what is meant when it is said that the twelve locations of contact between consciousness and objects belong by nature to the Mysterious Mind-Essence considered as the Womb of Tathagata?

Ananda, suppose you are looking at the Jetavana grove and at all its beautiful springs and pools. What think you? Is it that all these sights develop the perception of the eyes, or is it, that the eye-sense develops the sights. If it is that the sense of the eyes develops sights, then when it sees space, as space is of different nature from sight, then sight should disappear. If the nature of sight disappears, then all the manifestations of sight would become as naught. If all the phenomena of sight become as naught, how can we be sure of the substantiality of space? And the reverse is true also, namely, if all the phenomena of space become naught, how can we be sure of the substantiality of the sights we see? Moreover, if the different sight-objects develop the perception of the eyes, then when the eyes look at space (as the nature of space is different from that of sight) then the perception of sights should immediately disappear. Should the perception of sight disappear, then all the sight-objects would become non-existent. How, then, can we be sure of the phenomena of space and sights? Therefore, Ananda, you should know that the perception of the eyes and the sight-objects it sees and space itself, are all devoid of location, which simply means that both the locations of the sight-objects and the perception of these eyes are alike false and fantastic being neither manifested by causes and conditions, nor spontaneously by their own nature.

(*The same is proven in the text, to hold true as to the unsubstantiality and falsity of the perception of the location of contact of the other sense-objects, also.*) . . . .

Ananda, suppose you have been conceiving within your mind under the conditions of some system of thought regarded as the cause of the conceptions of the sense, and that you have always discriminated among these conceptions by three attributes, namely, good thoughts, bad thoughts and disinterested thoughts. Are these attributes developed within the mind, or in some other locality independent of the mind? If they are developed within the intuitive sense of the mind, then they can not be the same things as the sense-objects themselves, nor as the influences that condition the mind. If this system of conceptions is considered as being developed in some other locality independent of the mind, then is the nature of its attributes to be rightly called, perceiving? If they are to be called perceiving, then it must be our mind that does the perceiving and not some other mind outside our mind. If the perception belongs to some other mind, as the mind is not an object, how can its perception be the same as your perception? Or, if it just means yourself, as being different from your mind, then that would mean that you are two different personalities, or at least that you have two different minds. If the nature of the attributes of our system of conceptions is unperceptive then, as this system (considered as an inner object) has none of the characteristics of sight, sound, odor, taste, touch, independence, conformity, coldness, warmness, where can we locate it? As it has no definite location either in space or form where, in all this terrestrial world can it have location? And since it is not a condition that influences the mind, how can it have a location, anyway? Therefore, Ananda, you should know that the system of sense-conceptions as well as the conceptions of thinking are devoid of any location. This means that the locations of contact of the conceptions within the mind and the system of sense-conceptions are alike false and fantastic; they are neither manifested by causes and conditions or spontaneously by their own nature.

* * *

The Lord Buddha continued to question Ananda, saying:— What is meant by the assertion that the eighteen spheres of mentation (sense-organs, sense-minds, and sense-perceptions) all belong to the mysterious Essence of Tathagata's Womb?

We have already shown that the perception of sight is dependent upon the eyes and their power of seeing in combination with the object of sight. Let me ask you, is this consciousness that is dependent upon the eyes, developed solely by means of the eyes and limited by the eyes, or is it developed solely by means of sight and bounded by sight? If the consciousness of sight is developed by means of the eyes only, then as it is independent of sight and space, it can not make any discrimination and thus, in spite of your consciousness, of what avail will it be? Moreover, as the perception of sight does not belong to colors—green, yellow, red, and white—it can not manifest any appearance and, thus, what shall be its boundary lines? Or if the perception of sight is developed by means of sight then, as there is only space and no sight, your consciousness of it will be annihilated and how can you know anything of the nature of space? And if, when the sight changes, you are conscious of the change, it would mean that the sight itself is changing. But as your consciousness does not change, what will be the line between it and your perception of sight? Or, if your consciousness is subject to change along with the changes of sight, then any phenomena of differences will disappear. Or, if your consciousness is permanent and unchangeable, then, as it is developed from sight, it should not recognize any location of space. Or, if consciousness is developed by both eyes and sight, then one part of your consciousness, the part developed from the eyes will be sensitive, and the other part developed from the sight will be insensitive. So, when the sense of your eyes and the sight are in contact, one part of your consciousness will be perceptive and one part unperceptive, it would mean that if these two parts of consciousness become separated from each other, then they must both be independent of the mind. And when the sense of your eyes and the sight are in separation, one part of your consciousness will return to your eyes and one part will return to the sight. That would mean that these two parts of your consciousness are in separate contacts with your eyes and the sight. Thus, the body and its attributes are confusingly mixed and what shall be their boundary lines?

Therefore, Ananda, you should know that these three localities where the perception of sight is under the conditions of the sense of the eyes and the sight, and where the perception of sight arises from your consciousness dependent upon eyes are all devoid of any substantial existence, so these three phenomena of the perception of sight, the sight itself, and the sphere of mentation about sight are neither manifested by causes and conditions, nor spontaneously by their own nature. . . . .

(*In the text, the same is proven to hold true as to the relation of the other senses, hearing, smelling, tasting, touching, and are omitted.*)

Again, Ananda, you have understood that the perceptions of the thinking mind are under the conditions of the thinking mind and of its conceptions of phenomena, and that it is manifested from the consciousness dependent upon the thinking mind. Is this consciousness that is dependent upon the thinking mind developed by means of the thinking mind and bounded by the thinking mind? Or is it developed by means of its conceptions of phenomena and bounded by its conceptions of phenomena? If it is developed by means of the thinking mind, then within your thinking mind, there must be some consciousness that discovers your thinking mind. Should there be no such kind of thoughts, the thinking mind would not have been developed. Should it then be independent of any such conditions, it would have no appearances of thinking and what, then, would be the use of consciousness? Moreover, in referring to your conscious mind and to all its attributes of thinking and discriminating are they in unity, or are they different things? If they are in unity with the thinking mind, then they are no different from the thinking mind and how could they have any other manifestations? If they are not in unity with the thinking mind, then they are different things and separated from one another, in which case the thinking mind would be unconscious of them. Should the thinking mind be unconscious of them, then how could the thinking mind be developed? If the thinking mind is conscious of them, then what is it that is conscious of the thinking mind? Thus, whether consciousness and its attributes are in unity with the thinking mind or in separation from it, there is no such kind of existence and how can consciousness then be bounded by spheres? If this consciousness that is dependent upon the thinking mind is developed by means of thoughts about phenomena, then all the phenomena of the world belong to the five sense objects. For instance, supposing you are attending to the five phenomena of sight, sound, odour, taste and touch, which are very distinctive in their manifestations, and if these five kinds of phenomena go with their respective sense organs, it shows that they are not managed by the thinking mind. If it is asserted that consciousness must be developed by conceptions of phenomena, then please concentrate your reflections and tell me what is the appearance in your thinking mind of these conceptions of phenomena. If you set aside all such phenomena as sight, space, motion, silence, transmissibility, non-transmissibility, combination, separation, death, rebirth, then you will never be able to think out the appearance of consciousness. As soon as consciousness appears, then all such phenomena as sight, space, motion, etc., will be manifested also; and as soon as consciousness disappears, all such phenomena as sight, space, motion, etc., will disappear, too. As there is, thus, no substantial existence of the objects of the phenomena of conception, which we are regarding as the cause of consciousness, it shows clearly that there is also no substantial nature and manifestation for the consciousness that is manifested by means of the objects of the phenomena of conception. Since consciousness possesses no substantial nature, manifestation, nor existence, how can its sphere be revealed? Therefore, Ananda, you should know that these three localities where the perception of the thinking mind, as being under the conditions of the sense of the thinking mind and of its conceptions of phenomena, develops its thinking process, the thinking process, the consciousness dependent upon it, and its sphere, are all devoid of any substantial existence. So these three phenomena, the perceptions of the thinking mind, its conceptions about them, and its sphere of thinking, are neither manifested by causes and conditions, nor spontaneously by its own nature.

(Relations of Perceptions to the Four Great Elements)

Then Ananda addressed the Lord Buddha, saying:—Noble Lord! You have always taught us that all the variety of changes in the world are manifested by means of conformity and combination of the Four Great Elements, according to the principle of causes and conditions. How is it that now, the Lord Tathagata rejects both the principle of naturalism and the principle of causes and conditions? I am confused as to what you are trying to teach. Pray, Noble Lord, have pity upon us once more and show us the true and perfect teaching of the Middle Way which is free from all ambiguous statements.

Thereupon the Blessed Lord addressed the disciples, saying:—Ananda, at first you disliked the Hinayana attainments of Arahatship and Pratyaka-Buddha, and devoted all your effort to seeking Supreme Enlightenment. How does it come that you are still troubling your mind with those fictitious statements and false conceptions of causes and conditions? Though it is true that you are quite learned, you are like the man who knew the names of drugs, but when medicines were brought to him he could not tell their different properties and virtues. Ananda, you are to be pitied. Now listen to me attentively and I will answer your question by explaining clearly the distinctions in detail. And not for you only, Ananda, but for the sake of all the disciples of the future who will practice Mahayana, so that all will be able to attain to the Ultimate Principle of Reality.

Ananda, by his perfect silence and attention, showed himself ready for the teaching from the Blessed Lord Buddha.

The Lord Buddha said:—Ananda, it is just as you have said, all the varieties and changes in this world are manifested by means of the conformities and combinations of the Four Great Elements (earth, water, fire, air). If the substance of these Great Elements is of the nature of non-conformity and non-combination, then they can not mingle together in conformity, just as space cannot be in conformity with sights. Or, if the great Elements are in conformity and combination with one another, they will be like all other transformations, which are forever in process of completing one another, but from beginning to end incessantly passing from death to rebirth, and from rebirth to death, like a blazing wheel.

Ananda! The manifestations of the Four Great Elements are like water being continually frozen into ice and just as repeatedly thawed into water again. Suppose we consider the nature of the earth element. In a crude and coarse form it covers the globe, but in a highly refined form it is the infinitesimal dust of space, and even everything that the eyes can see can be reduced into its seven primal elements. If we analyze this infinitesimal dust of space, we will more and more approximate the purity of space, but will not bring us its absolute vacuum. You should know, Ananda, that if this infinitesimal dust of space should be truly reduced to the purity and emptiness of space, it would be out of this inconceivable purity that the phenomena of sight is manifested also. You have just now asked me, how it is that by means of conformity and combination all sorts of transformations in this world are manifested. Let us first examine this most refined dust that is approximately close to the nature of open space and what do we find. Ananda, how much space, reduced to finest particles, do you think it would take in conformity and combination to become that most refined dust? No, however much space be condensed, its proximities can never become the proximities of finest dust, and however much finest dust be analyzed it can never become by conformity and combination the purity of space. Moreover, in regard to perceiving these finest particles of dust that approximate the purity of space, how many elements of the perception of sight will it take in combination to perceive pure space? And even if the phenomena of sights are combined together, it will not become space; and if the elements of space be combined, it will not become sights.

Indeed, Ananda, you are foolish to ask such questions, for in the Tathagata's Womb, the intrinsic nature of sight is the real emptiness of space, the true vacuum, while the intrinsic nature of space is the real sight, the true essence. In the Tathagata's Womb, space and sights are of perennial freshness and purity, permeating everywhere throughout the phenomenal universes, and are being forever manifested spontaneously and perfectly in accordance with the amount of karma accumulated under the conscious activity of sentient beings. However, people of the world being ignorant of this principle, become bewildered in the entanglements of cause and conditions and naturalism, which are wholly the discriminations of their mental consciousness, and are merely figurative words having no meaning in reality.

Ananda, now let us consider the nature of the water-element. By nature water is impermanent, whether in the current of rivers or in the waves of the sea. Where does water originate? The great masters of Magic in the City of Sravasti attempt to get it pure from the moon to mix with their magical medicines. They wait until there is bright moonlight and they hold out a receptacle, which they call the magical pearl, to receive this pure moon-water. What do you think about it, Ananda? Does this water come from the magical pearl, or does it come out of space, or does it really come from the moon? If the water comes from the moon, then the pearls in

any far distant place could be made to give out water, and all
the forests where these pearls are found, and all the lands
where they are found should effuse water, and it would be unnecessary, on a moonlight night, to carry a bucket to a well.
But if you had such a pearl and no water come from it, it
would be proof that water does not come from the moon.

Or if the water comes from the magical pearl, then the said
pearl should effuse water constantly and it would be unnecessary to wait for a bright moonlight. If the water comes from
the empty space between the moon and the pearl, then, as
space is boundless and if water was equally boundless, then all
sentient beings on earth or in sky would be in danger of drowning. Why is it that there are still living beings in water, earth
and air? Think carefully, Ananda; here is the moon moving
silently in the sky, the Master of Magic standing with the
magical pearl in his hand, and remember the vast space between the moon and the pearl,—they are neither in conformity
nor in combination. From where does the water come? Surely
it can not come from nowhere. And then, again, consider that
wherever a master of magic may be standing in the moonlight
in some one place there water appears, supposing there are
magicians all over the world and water is appearing everywhere,
what would that signify?

Ananda! Why is it that you still remain in ignorance that
in the Tathagata's Womb the intrinsic nature of water is the
real emptiness, while the intrinsic nature of space is the real
water-essence. In the Womb of Tathagata both water and
space abide in freshenss and purity and permeate everywhere
throughout the universes and is being manifested freely, and
perfectly corresponding to the accumulation of karma by the
conscious activity of sentient beings.

However, people of this world, being ignorant of this, and
by regarding water as being manifested by causes and conditions, or spontaneously by its own nature, have become bewildered. Whereas, all of these false presuppositions and prejudices are simply the discriminations made by their own
mental consciousness, and are merely figurative words having
no basis in reality.

Now, Ananda, let us consider the element of fire. Fire has
not its own individual nature, but is dependent upon other
considerations. If you were to look toward the city of Sravasti

at the time people are getting ready to prepare the noon meal, you would see every householder bring his lens into the sunlight to kindle a fire. They all do the same thing, but each acts individually. In like manner this assembly of twelve hundred and fifty Bhikshus gather here for one purpose, but each has his own individuality, each has his own body and his own family name, such as Sariputra born in a Brahmin family, Urbinzuru born in the family of Kasyapa, down to you, the last of all, Ananda, born in the family of Gotama. (All of these instances are examples of individuality under the conditions of conformity and combination.)

If the quality of fire is developed by means of conformity and combination, then as one holds out his lens to the heat of the sunlight in order to kindle a fire, does the fire come from the glass, or does it come from the wormwood fiber that the heat kindles, or does the fire come from the sun, Ananda? If the fire comes from the sun and kindles the wormwood fiber, why is not the whole forest of wormwood trees kindled also? If it comes from the lens and is hot enough to kindle the wormwood, why is the lens itself not burnt? As it is, there is no fire until your hand holds out the lens between the sun and the fiber. Again, Ananda, think carefully. Here are certain conditions that being present, fire arises: you are holding a lens in your hand, the sunlight is coming from the sun, the wormwood fiber has grown from the ground, but where does the fire come from, and how does it sojourn here? Moreover, the lens and the sun are separated from each other by a very great distance. There seems to be no conformity nor any combination, but it can not be that the fire comes from nowhere.

Ananda, why is it that you still remain in ignorance that in the Tathagata's Womb the intrinsic nature of fire is the real emptiness, while the intrinsic nature of space is the real fire-essence. In the Womb of Tathagata both fire and space abide in freshness and purity and permeate everywhere throughout the universes and are being manifested freely and perfectly corresponding to the accumulation of karma by the conscious activity of sentient beings. You should therefore know, Ananda, that wherever people in this world hold out lenses fire may be kindled, and as fire may be kindled everywhere, there is the place where fire originates. However, people of this world being ignorant of this, and by regarding fire as being manifested by causes and conditions, or spontaneously by reason of its own nature, have become bewildered. Whereas, all of these false presuppositions and prejudices are simply the discriminations made by their own mental consciousness, and are merely figurative words having no meaning in reality.

Ananda, let us now consider the nature of wind. It has no (visible) substantiality and it has no permanency either when in motion or in quietness. For instance, whenever you enter the assembly your garments are well arranged, but as you enter the lower corner of your robe is moving and a little breeze from it blows on the faces of the brothers sitting close by. What think you, Ananda, does this little breeze come from the lower corner of your robe, or does it come from the air-space between them, or does it come from the nearby faces? If it came from your garment, then it must have been in a moving state when you put it on, and why did not your garment fly away from you? If the breeze comes from the garments, then as I stand before you teaching the Dharma with my scarf hanging quietly from my shoulder, where is the breeze? Can you find its hiding place? Or if it comes from the space of air, why do your scarfs hang motionless? Moreover, as the nature of space is permanent, the breeze if it comes from space should be blowing constantly. As there is no breeze, does it mean that there is no space, either? If the breeze comes and goes, what is its appearance as it comes and goes? If it comes and goes, then space would have its deaths and rebirths, and could no longer be called space. If it is called space, how can it give out wind from its emptiness? If the breeze that is felt on one's face, comes from that face, then it should be felt by your face. As it is your garment, why does not the breeze blow toward you, why does it blow away from you? And again, Ananda, as you think about these things, the arrangement of your garment, the nearby faces, the stillness of the air, space taking no part in the moving breeze, what originates the breeze and just where does it come from? Moreover, the natures of the breeze and space are widely divergent, they are neither in conformity nor in combination with each other; and yet the breeze must come from somewhere; it is not its nature to come from nowhere.

Ananda! Why is it that you still remain in ignorance that in the Tathagata's Womb the intrinsic nature of wind is the real emptiness, while the intrinsic nature of space is the real wind-essence. In the Womb of Tathagata both wind and space abide in freshness and purity and permeate everywhere throughout the phenomenal universes and are being manifested freely, and perfectly correspond to the amount of karma accumulated by the conscious activity of sentient beings. And then, again, wherever a single person arranges his garment there comes out a breeze, and when all the world arrange their garments, wind arises everywhere. If wind comes out everywhere, where can be the particular locality that is the origin of wind?

However, people of the world, being ignorant of this, and by regarding wind as being manifested by causes and conditions, or spontaneously by its own nature, have become bewildered. Whereas, all of these false presuppositions and prejudices are simply the discriminations made by their own mental consciousness; they are merely figurative words that have no basis in reality.

Ananda, the nature of space possesses no form and is manifested by colors only. For instance, at a distance from the river all the newly built homes in the city of Sravasti, whether belonging to the Ksatriya family, or to some Brahman family, or to a Sudra, or to a Bradha, or to a Chandra family, each has to dig a well for their supply of water. As they dig up one foot of earth, there is one foot of air space left open, and so they go on digging even down to ten feet, but there is always the same number of feet of open space left open. The amount of open space left open is entirely in proportion to the amount of digging up of earth. What think you, Ananda? Does the space left open come from the earth that has been removed, or does it come by means of the digging, or does it just come by itself, without any cause? If it comes just simply by itself without any other cause, why do we have to remove the earth before it comes into sight? Instead of space we see the impassable earth everywhere. If it comes from the earth, then as the earth is dug up, we should see the space coming to take its place. If we do not see space coming in to take the place of the earth as it is being removed, how can we say that the space comes from outside of the earth? If there is neither coming out of earth nor coming in of space, then we might say that both earth and space are alike, but if there was no difference between them, there would be a sameness, but as the

earth is dug up, why does the space not come up also? Or if
the space comes out by the digging, then as space is dug up,
why should the earth come up too? If it does not come out
by digging, then while the earth is being removed, why do we
see space left in the hole? Ananda, you should concentrate
your mind, reflect, and give intense insight upon these conditions of digging, earth coming out, and space filling up the
place, trying to realize where the space comes from. As digging
is a matter of fact while space is a phenomena of emptiness,
there can be no correspondence between them, nor are they in
mutual accomodation, that is, they are neither in conformity
nor in combination with each other, and yet it can not be that
the nature of space comes from nowhere. Moreover, if the nature of space is perfect and permeates all the universes, then
you should know that, in our consideration, space together
with earth, water, fire, and wind, are to be regarded as the
Five Great Elements, whose essential nature is perfect, and all-
in-unity, and all alike belonging to the Tathagata's Womb, and
all alike devoid of deaths and rebirths.

Ananda, your mind appears to be still in a state of bewilderment, you do not realize even that essence of the Four
Great Elements belongs to the Womb of Tathagata. You should
carefully observe as to whether space comes out from some unseen place, or comes in from something seen outside, or does
it neither come out from or come into? You are ignorant
that within the Tathagata's Womb the intuition of Essence is
the real emptiness, while the intrinsic nature of space is real
Enlightenment. Within Tathagata's Womb they are ever in
freshness and purity, permeating everywhere throughout the
phenomenal universes, and are being manifested freely and
perfectly in correspondence to the amount of karma accumulated by the conscious activity of sentient beings.

For instance, Ananda, when there is one well dug, space is
manifested to the limit of one well, and when all the ten
quarters of the universes become empty, the space of emptiness
is manifested all throughout the universes, also. If the space of
emptiness is perfectly permeating everywhere throughout the
ten quarters of the universes, then where can the space of emptiness be seen and located? But the world is all in ignorance
and bewilderment because they have always regarded the space
of emptiness as being manifested by causes and conditions, or

spontaneously by its own nature, whereas, all of these false pre-suppositions and prejudices are simply discriminations made by their own mental consciousness; they are merely figurative words that have no basis in reality.

Ananda! The perception of sight is to be regarded in the same way. It has no substantiality of itself and its existence is dependent upon sights and space. For instance, here in the Grove of Jetavana it is daybreak in the morning and it becomes dark after sunset; at midnight, when there is moonlight, we have brightness and when there is no moonlight, there is darkness. The distinctions of brightness and darkness are noted by our perception of sight. What do you think, Ananda? Is this perception of sight in one unity with brightness, darkness and space, or is it not in unity with them? Is it of the same substantiality with them; is it of different substantiality from them; or is it not of different substantiality? If our perception of sight is in unity with brightness, darkness and space, then as brightness and darkness are in mutual correspondence as regards their appearing and disappearing, so when it is dark there is no brightness, and when it is light there is no darkness. If perception of sight is in unity with darkness, then when it is bright, it must follow that there is no perception of sight. Or if it is in unity with brightness, then when it is dark, there ought not to be any perception of sight either? If it disappears when it is both dark and bright, how can it note the difference between brightness and darkness? Or, if there is a difference between perception of sight and brightness and darkness, and perception of sight has no appearing and no disappearing, then how can they be in unity with them? If perception of sight is not in unity with brightness and darkness, then leaving brightness, darkness and space out of account, suppose you try to analyze this perception of sight and tell me what it appears like. Independent of brightness, darkness and space, perception of sight would be non-existent, like the tortoise's hair or the horns of a rabbit. Let us grant that these phenomena of brightness, darkness and space, are different from one another, then from which one of the three phenomena is perception of sight manifested? Brightness and darkness are in contrast with each other, how can it be said that perception of sight is in unity with both of them or with either one of them? If perception of sight is independent of all three of these different phenomena, it must be devoid of existence entirely, and if it is, how can it be asserted that it is not in unity with them? The spheres of space and sight by their nature are devoid of any limits, how can it be said that there are distinctions between them? If it is asserted that when perception of sight sees brightness and when it sees darkness that its nature does not undergo any change, how can it be said that there is no distinction between them?

Ananda! You should observe carefully, scrutinize the details, concentrate your attention, bring into use your profound insight, upon all these conditions of brightness when the sun is shining, darkness when there is no moon, sight passing through space unhindered and being hindered by the opaqueness of the great earth. In all these varied conditions by what means is perception of sight manifested? From all these things perception of sight appears to be false and empty, it is neither in conformity with brightness, darkness and space, nor in combination with them, and yet it can not be that perception of space comes from nowhere.

Ananda! If perception of sight, hearing, understanding, etc., has a nature that is unlimited and perfect, permeating everywhere throughout the universes, and by nature unchangeable, then you should know that the natures of the multitudinous and different perceptions, infinite, unmovable space, together with the movable elements of earth, water, fire, and wind, are to be regarded as the Six Great Elements. Their essential natures are perfect and in one unity, and they all belong to the Womb of Tathagata, and are devoid of deaths and rebirths. As your mind-essence has fallen out of attention, you have failed to realize that all your perceptions of sight, hearing, understanding and feeling, belong by reason of their nature to Tathagata's Womb. You should meditate upon this and note whether your perceptions of sight, hearing, understanding and feeling, belong to deaths and rebirths, or belong to one great unity. Do they belong to different natures, or belong to non-death and non-rebirth, or do they belong to not one unity and not different natures? You have never yet fully realized that within the Womb of Tathagata the essential nature of perception of sight is intuitive and enlightening, and that the intuition of the one and all embracing Essence, manifests its faculty of seeing, hearing, understanding and feeling everywhere, and that the essential nature of perception of sight, within Tathagata's Womb is ever in freshness and purity, permeating everywhere throughout the universes, and are being manifested freely and perfectly in correspondence to the amount of karma accumulated by the conscious activity of sentient beings.

For instance, referring to one of our sense organs, the sense of sight, the perception of sight reaches to every part of the phenomenal universes, and the same is true of all the sense organs, seeing, hearing, tasting, smelling, touching and consciousness, the wonderful qualities of their perception reaching everywhere and permeating everywhere throughout the ten quarters of all the phenomenal universes. However, all the people of the world being ignorant of this, and by regarding perception of sight as being manifested by causes and conditions, or spontaneously by its own nature, have become bewildered. Whereas, all these false presuppositions and prejudices are simply the discriminations made by their mental consciousness; they are merely figurative words and figures of speech that have no basis in reality.

Ananda! Consciousness has no originality of its own. It is an illusive manifestation developed by means of the six objects of sense. Suppose you were looking over this assembly, without making any particular distinctions, letting the different persons present be reflected in your mind as in a looking glass. Your consciousness would, nevertheless, make acknowledgement of the different ones, saying in orderly succession:—This is Brother Manjusri, this is Brother Purna, this is Brother Maudgalyayana, this is Brother Subhuti, this is Brother Sariputra, etc. What think you, Ananda? Is this discriminating consciousness manifested from the phenomena, or is it manifested from space, or is it manifested spontaneously without any cause?

If the nature of your consciousness is manifested from the perception of eyes, let us suppose there is no brightness, no darkness, no sight and no space. If these are not existent then, naturally, there will be no perception of sight, and if there is no perception of sight by your eyes, how can any consciousness arise? Or, if the nature of your consciousness is manifested from phenomena, but not from the perception of your eyes, then as there can be no perception of brightness, there can be no perception of darkness, either. If there is no perception of either brightness or darkness, there can be no sight and no space. If there is no phenomena of either sight or space, from what can consciousness be manifested? Or, if the nature of your consciousness is manifested from the emptiness of space, then, as there is no phenomena, so there can be no perception of eyes and nothing to distinguish, and of course, consciousness could not say, this is brightness, this is darkness, this is sight or this is space. If consciousness belongs to non-phenomena, then there will be no condition in its presence and, thus, all perceptions of sight, hearing, understanding, feeling, will be devoid of location and therefore of all existence. If there can be no existence under these two conditions of no phenomena and no perception of sight, is it possible to have existence under any other conditions? If it is possible, then the conditions must be different in nature from the phenomena of sight, or the phenomena of space and the resulting consciousness will be something different from consciousness based upon distinctions of sight, hearing, etc. Or if the nature of your consciousness is manifested spontaneously without any particular cause, why do you not see the bright moon in some abnormal way?

Ananda! You should ponder upon this question very carefully, concentrate your attention, make use of your profound insight, scrutinizing such details of conditions as the teaching that perception of seeing is dependent upon eyes, perception of phenomena is derived from conditions within one's presence, that existence means describable forms and that non-existence means the absence of phenomena. These conditions of consciousness:—from what cause are they developed? It can not be that they come from nowhere. As to those disciples who have not yet attained to the state of absorption into the Womb of Tathagata, their consciousness belongs to activity and the perception of sight to tranquillity, so accordingly, peception of sight and the consciousness dependent upon it are neither manifested by means of conformity to something, nor by combination with something; and it is just the same with the other perceptions of hearing, understanding, and feeling, and with their corresponding consciousness.

Ananda! If your conscious mind is not manifested from any source, then you should know that both discriminative consciousness and the different perceptions of seeing, hearing, understanding, and feeling, are all existing in perfection and tranquillity the nature of which is unmanifested from any outer source, and that all of them—perceptions, consciousness, together with earth, water, air, fire and space—are to be regarded as the Seven Great Elements. Their essential nature is perfect and in unity within the Womb of Tathagata and, therefore, they are free from deaths and rebirths.

Ananda! The reason you have never been able to realize that your perceptions of seeing, hearing, understanding and feeling, and your mental faculties for discriminating phenomenal objects and developing thoughts relating to them, all belong to your own Womb of Tathagata. You should meditate upon these questions, namely, whether the six different localities of consciousness, dependent upon the sense organs, are all one consciousness or different? Whether they exist in the emptiness of space or have phenomenal existence? Whether they are in a state of non-unity and non-difference, or in a state of non-space and non-existence? Naturally, you have never known that within your Womb of Tathagata the essential nature of consciousness is enlightening and intelligent, that your enlightened intuition is your true Essence of Consciousness, and that this wonderful intuition abides in tranquillity permeating everywhere throughout the phenomenal worlds and embracing all the ten quarters of the universes. Why do you still raise questions as to its locality of existence? Moreover, it is manifested freely and perfectly in correspondence with the amount of karma accumulated by the conscious activity of sentient beings. But the people of the world, being ignorant of this, and by regarding the nature of consciousness as being manifested by causes and conditions, or spontaneously by its own nature, have become bewildered. Whereas, all these false presuppositions and prejudices are simply the discriminations made by their conscious minds; they are but figurative words and figures of speech that have no basis in reality.

(Questions by Purna answered.)

Thereupon Ananda and all the assembly, having received this wonderful and profound instruction from the Lord Tathagata and having attained to a state of perfect accommodation of mind and perfect emancipation of mind from all remembrances, thinking and desires, became perfectly free in both body and mind. Each one of them understood clearly that the

Mind can reach to all the ten quarters of the universes and that their perception of sight can reach to all the ten quarters also. It was just as clear to them as though it was a blade of grass held in their hand. They saw that all the worldly phenomena was nothing but their own wonderful, intelligent, original Mind of Enlightenment embracing all the ten quarters of the universes. In contrast to this wonderful, all-embracing Mind of Enlightenment, their physical bodies begotten from their parents seemed like specks of dust blowing about in the open space of the ten quarters of the universes. Who would notice their existence or their non-existence? Their physical bodies were like a speck of foam floating about on a vast and trackless ocean, with nothing distinctive about them to indicate from whence they came, and if they disappeared, whither they went. They realized very clearly, that they, at last, had acquired their own wonderful Mind, a Mind that was Permanent and Indestructible.

Therefore the whole assembly with palms pressed together in adoration made obeisance to the Lord Buddha in greatest respect and sincerity as though for the first time they had realized his transcendent worth.

Then they together chanted the following verses, praising the glory of the Lord Tathagata and voicing their sincere devotion to him:

Oh, Most Blessed One! Thou who hast ever been absorbed in tranquil concentration of Dhyana, inspiring wonder and awe.

Oh, Honored of the Worlds! Thou art the King of Highest Samadhi!

Oh, Blessed Lord! We beseech Thee, to dissipate all our upset and confused conceptions that have been developing for milliards of kalpas, so that we may attain to the pure state of Dharmakaya.

Oh, Blessed Lord! We beseech Thee, that in this life we may attain to the glory of Supreme Enlightenment; and grant us, we beseech Thee, that in a following rebirth we may return to this world, for the deliverance of all sentient beings.

O Blessed Lord! As an expression of our gratitude to our Lord Buddha, we dedicate our lives to the emancipation of all sentient beings in all the worlds.

Oh, Blessed Lord! We beseech Thee to witness our vow to be the pioneers of Liberation to those confined to the five evil worlds of impurities.

Oh, Blessed Lord! So long as any sentient being shall fail to attain Buddhahood, we vow never to accomplish our own Nirvana.

Oh, Lord, the Greatest of Heros, Almighty, Most Compassionate! We beseech Thee to teach us through meditation, how to get rid of all the defilements of illusive thoughts, reflections and desires.

Oh, Blessed Lord! We beseech Thee to help us to attain to Highest Perfect Enlightenment, and to quickly develop the power to concentrate our minds in Dhyana, to the end that all sentient beings in all the universes may become tranquil and enlightened, also.

Oh, Blessed Lord! Though the purity of our minds may be disturbed by vagrant thoughts, we beseech Thee, Oh Lord, that our diamond-like Essential Mind may never again be disturbed.

Thereupon, Purna Metaluniputra rose from his seat, arranged his robe, knelt upon his right knee, with the palms of his hands together, addressed the Lord Buddha, saying:— Blessed Lord of Highest Majesty! Thou has fully enunciated the Dharma-teaching of first importance—the nature of our True Mind—and thou hast done it for the sake of all sentient beings. The Lord has honored me by looking upon me as being the foremost teacher of the Dharma among the Disciples, but as I listened to the perfect teaching of the Lord Tathagata, I seemed like a deaf person listening to a far away mosquito, too far away to be seen. Though the instruction of the Lord was clear and purified my mind of its illusions, nevertheless, I could not grasp all thy profound teaching nor was my mind completely freed from its doubts and suspicions.

Oh, Blessed Lord! There are among us many Brothers like Ananda who have attained a measure of realization and en-

lightenment, but have not yet been able to discard all of their
habitual sentiments, emotions and desires. Then there are some
of us, though we have completely discarded our habitual intoxicants, as we listened to the Lord's instruction, so profound
was it, that some of our doubts still remained, for which we are
humbly repentant.

Blessed Lord! The thing that troubles us, that we do not
fully understand, is this: If all of the sense organs, objects of
sense, ingredients of sensation, location of perception between
objects and consciousness, and spheres of mentation about objects, are all to be considered as manifestations of the Womb
of Tathagata which by its essential nature ever abides in freshness and purity, how have all the conditional phenomena of
rivers, mountains, earth, etc., which from beginningless time
have been going on in successively changing processes, how have
they ever come into manifestation?

And one more question. The Lord Tathagata has said that
all of the four great Elements of Earth, Water, Fire, and Wind,
are perfect and accommodating in their nature and are permeating everywhere throughout the phenomenal universes, how
can they be permeating everywhere and, at the same time, be
in perfect tranquillity?

Blessed Lord! If the nature of Earth is universal, how can
it, at the same time and in the same space, co-exist with water?
Or, if the nature of water is universal, how can fire exist at the
same time; that is, if water and fire are present universally in
the same space and at the same time, how is it that they do
not destroy each other? Or, as the nature of earth is dense and
impassable and the nature of space is empty and passable, how
can the two different and opposing natures be mutually universal at the same time? These things are too difficult for us
to comprehend, I pray the Lord Tathagata to have compassion
upon us and solve these puzzling questions.

Having finished his plea, the Disciple Purna with forehead,
hands and knees touching the ground, waited humbly and expectantly for the Lord Buddha to resume his instruction.

Then the Blessed Lord replies to Purna and to all the advanced Disciples who had attained to self-mastery and Arhatship, saying:—Today I will explain the essential nature of True
Transcendency, so that all of those who have attained the universalized nature of Arhatship, and all those who have attained

Arhatship but have not yet wholly discarded the conception of their own selfhood as being separate from the selfhood of others, to attain to the true seclusion for their practice of Dhyana and to the attainment of Nirvana. Please listen carefully to this teaching. Then Purna and all the other advanced Disciples waited humbly and expectantly for the Lord's instruction.

The Lord Buddha said:—Purna! Referring to your first question as to how the phenomena of rivers, mountains, earth etc., can come into manifestation if the sense organs, objects of sense, ingredients of sensation, location of perceptions between objects and consciousness, and spheres of mentation, are ever abiding in the freshness and purity of the Womb of Tathagata. In my previous instruction, I made clear to you that the Essential Intuitive Mind possessed its own mysterious Enlightening Nature, and that the attainment to this Essential Intuitive Mind unveils this mysterious Enlightening Nature. Did you not understand?

Purna replied:—Yes, Blessed Lord! I have tried to understand thy teaching interpreting this principle, but still it is not clear.

The Lord Buddha enquired of him:—Purna, when I spoke of the enlightening nature of Intuitive Mind, what did I mean by it? Did I mean that as our Essential nature is enlightening of itself so we called it "Intuitive Mind"? Or does it mean that as our Intuitive Mind is not enlightening by itself so we speak of it as "the Enlightened Mind of Intuition?"

Purna replied:—Blessed Lord! If this un-enlightened mind is to be regarded as the same as our Intuitive Mind, what would there be to be enlightened?

Purna, the Lord Buddha interrupted, if there is nothing to be enlightened then there would be no enlightening nature of intuition, either. So long as you cherish and discriminate such arbitrary conceptions as "there is some nature of non-intuitive," or "there is no nature of non-enlightening" you only reveal your ignorance—they do not belong to your enlightening mind of tranquillity and Intuition—for the Essential Nature of Intuition is naturally enlightening by itself. It is because of these arbitrary conceptions that these false expressions concerning the Enlightened Mind of Intuition, take their rise. However, Intuitive Mind is not enlightened by something else—it is self-

enlightening. As soon as it is supposed to be enlightened by
something else, there rises false conceptions as to this something
else and then following there rises fantastic conceptions of functions and processes. Because of this from the perfect unity of
Intuitive Mind innumerable varieties have been manifested and
as there are distinctions among them so classifications among
these varieties are developed. From this arises conceptions of
likes and unlikes, and then conceptions of non-likes and non-
unlikes, and the mind is thrown into a medley of bewildering
puzzles which in time become attached to the mind and contaminate it. At the end, these attachments and contaminations
within your mind develop the consciousness of differences between self and the not-self of objects and thus the pure mind
becomes entangled in the snarls of attachments and contaminations. Because of their defilement, there rises the disturbing
manifestation of an external world, but when they are stilled,
there remains only empty space, abiding in perfect unity. The
world is a medley of unreal and transitory diversities that contaminate the mind and it is out of these arbitrary conceptions
of phenomena that the very conception of unity and diversity
arises. But Essential Mind is wholly devoid of conceptions
and therefore recognizes neither unity nor diversity.

Moreover, Purna, these two opposites—the Pure Reality of
Intuitive Mind by its very self-nature ceaselessly drawing everything into its perfect Unity and Tranquillity, and the unreal
and transitory medley of diverse and conflicting differences forever tending to variety and multiplicities—these two opposing
conceptions arising from the discrimination of Ignorance bring
into existence a vibratory motion that by reason of desire and
grasping and the perpetuating influence of habit energy, accounts for all the basic conceptions of the primary Elements,
the solidity of Earth, the fluidity of Water, the heat of Fire and
the motivity of Wind. Amid them it is the nature of Fire to
move upward and the nature of Water to move downward, and
from these two Elements being in reciprocal development there
are the manifestations of rivers, and volcanoes and land. As
Water takes precedence, oceans appear and when Fire takes
precedence, continents and islands. The great ocean is also in
reciprocal development with the illusive conception of fire
within the mind, and reveals the fact that the blazing Fire is

arising continuously. The continents and islands are also in a reciprocal development with the false conception of water within the mind, revealing the fact that rivers and streams are ever flowing. Or if the false conception of water is running very slowly within the mind, and the flame of fire is in a high state of activity, then there rises the high mountains and volcanoes which after all are only combinations of the false conceptions of water and fire within the mind. So if we strike flint, sparks of fire shoot out, and if we melt rocks, they will become liquid. If the false conception of water within the mind predominates over the false conception of earth, then the phenomena of grass and trees rises. As grass and trees are also false conceptions of the mind, as soon as they are compressed they become water again. Thus all these false conceptions of phenomena have their reciprocal developments and successive manifestations within the mind, and by means of causes and conditions there rises the false conception of the reciprocal continuance of the world's existence.

Again, Purna! It is quite all right for you to have these false conceptions but the fault you have always committed is this, that you have cherished a false conception of the nature of Enlightenment which has conditioned your realization of truth. Because of this false assumption as to the nature of Enlightenment, the reasoning power of the intellectual mind can never go beyond the category of discriminated illusions. For instance:—the perception of hearing cannot go beyond the nature of sound, the perception of seeing cannot go beyond the nature of sights, and the same as to other perceptions. And thus the function of the mind is divided into its six divisions of sensitiveness of the sense organs, sensation, perception, discrimination, consciousness and discriminative thinking. As all of these activities of the mind rise from the first activities of the sense organs, so all the activities of the mind are but the working over of material that has originated within its own nature. These thoughts of the mind later become the foundation for the recurring cycles of deaths and rebirths in the manifestations of all the different orders of sentient life. Life that comes from eggs and gives suck to its young comes into entanglement and suffering by means of Karma accumulated by different sentient beings, and the spawns and life produced by metamorphosis come into transformations by means of separation and combination of their elements under the influence of causes and conditions.

* * *

After such a manner have the four orders of sentient life been ever wandering in the recurring cycles of deaths and rebirths wholly in close correspondence to the conditions of karma accumulated by them in previous lives. The lives that come from eggs were conceived by means of mutual intercourse that had been inspired by thoughts of each other; lives that are born from wombs, conceive by means of lust and concupiscence; lives that come from spawn come by the conjunction of conformable cells; lives that come by metamorphosis come by means of transformation and separation of cells. Because of these causes and conditions there rises the false conception of a reciprocal continuance of sentient lives.

Again, Purna! When mutual thinking and lustful desire combine the attraction is so intense that the two cannot be separated and, thus, parenthood and posterity will ever continue their reciprocal rebirths because of this lustful desire. So great is this lust and greed that it can not be restrained and thus, all these four great orders of life prey upon each other according to their relative strength—the bodies of the weak becoming the prey of the strong. Thus the killing of sentient beings is always because of greed in some form. When a man kills a sheep for food, the sheep gives rebirth to a man and the man gives rebirth to a sheep, and so the reciprocal killing goes on ever increasing without termination through innumerable kalpas of time. This awful suffering and retribution is all because of greed. So the proverb runs:—"You owe me your life, but I must repay the debt." Because of these causes and conditions all sentient lives have been fast bound to the cycle of deaths and rebirths after hundreds and thousands of kalpas. Another proverb says:—"You love my inner heart, but I love your outer beauty," so because of all these causes and condition, all sentient beings have been entangled in cycle of deaths and rebirths for hundreds and thousands of kalpas. All this suffering and retribution is based upon lust, greed and killing, and because of the causes and conditions arising from them, there is the false conception of the continuity of karmas and their inevitable fruit.

Again, Purna! The pure Essence of Mind leads toward enlightenment and peace, but these three deluding entanglements of lust, greed and killing, are the very reverse and lead toward entanglement, strife, suffering, deaths and rebirths and all rise from the illusive thinking of the discriminating mind. Because of this false thinking there becomes manifest all the false phenomena that fall within the range of the sense organs. Thus all these conditional phenomena of rivers, mountains, earth, etc., and their successive and endless changes arise, and all are based upon the illusions of the thinking mind without any other interpretation.

Purna addressed the Lord Buddha, saying:—Blessed Lord! If this wonderful Intuitive Mind of Essence by nature belongs to mystery, enlightenment and intelligence and is in the same state of permanency as the Tathagata's Mind of Essence without any decrease or increase in its perfection, how can there be, suddenly, the manifestation of the conditional phenomena of rivers, mountains, earth, etc.? Moreover, as the Lord Tathagata's Mind has attained to the state of Brightest Enlightenment and Transcendental Emptiness how can there appear within thy Mind, all of these limited and conditional and entangling conceptions of rivers, mountains, earth, etc.?

The Lord Buddha interrupted Purna to enquire:—Suppose a person comes to a strange and unknown village and becomes confused as to which is north and which is south. Is this confusion of mind derived from the mind's misconception or from the mind's right understanding?

Purna replied:—Blessed Lord! A person going astray under those conditions becomes confused as to the direction, neither because of his bewilderment, nor because of his right understanding. And why? Because as the confusion in his mind has. no real basis, how can it be said to have been caused by his bewilderment? And as the right understanding never changes nor makes a mistake, how can it be said that the bewilderment was caused by his right understanding?

The Lord Buddha then asked Purna:—Suppose the person who has lost his sense of direction recovers it by some chance. Does he still have misconceptions about the directions of this unknown village?

Purna replied: No, Blessed Lord.

The Lord Buddha continued:—It is just the same with the Tathagata in all the ten quarters of the universes. Your misconceptions about them have no basis in fact. The essential nature of your mind is the purity of perfect emptiness. Though your mind has ever been under illusions, in reality it can suffer no bewilderment; it only seems to be under a cloud of fascinating sentiments and false perceptions. As soon as the mind realizes that it is being deceived, the misconceptions disappear and its right understanding will never again be disturbed. The bewildered mind resembles a person who suffers from some optical hallucination and he thinks that he sees, for instance, fantastic forms of blossoms in empty space. But if his eyes clear, the fantastic blossoms vanish. Suppose there was by chance some simpleton who wanted to see the fantastic blossoms and went peering about. What would you think of such a person, Purna? Is he a fool? Or a half-witted man?

Purna replied:—In empty space there can be no blossoms, of course, but by means of false perceptions of seeing they certainly appear and disappear, that is, the perception of seeing is in a state of reversion. If the man continues peering about for the fantastic blossoms, he will soon become insane, and who can say then whether he is a fool or a half-wit?

The Lord Buddha replied:—Purna, it is all right for you to interpret the foolish man in that way, but why do you remain in doubt about the intelligence of the Tathagata's mysterious Enlightenment in realizing the emptiness of all phenomena? Why should you still see manifestations of rivers, mountains, earth, etc.?

Purna, the ordinary unenlightened mind resembles gold hid in its ore, but as soon as the gold is extracted, it can never again be hidden in its ore. It further resembles the condition of wood that is being burned into ashes: it can never again be changed back into wood. It is just the same with all the Buddha-Tathagatas' experience of Enlightenment and Nirvana.

Purna, you also asked me about the nature of the Four Great Elements—earth, water, fire and wind—if their nature is perfect and accommodating and permeates everywhere throughout all the phenomenal universes, why do not the nature of water and fire mutually destroy one another? And also, you asked about the natures of empty space and the great earth that are permeating everywhere throughout all the phenomenal universes, how can they keep their natures distinct and avoid becoming involved in each other?

As empty space is not made up of a mass of innumerable phenomena, it offers no objection to the manifestation of phenomena. Let me explain this. When the sun shines, the vast ethereal world becomes clear; when the sky is overcast with clouds, it becomes dark and gloomy; when the wind blows, there is motion; after a rain it is fresh and pure; when the atmosphere becomes laden with moisture, it becomes sultry; when there is much dust it becomes impure; after a shower has washed out the dust, it is clear and transparent. What do you think, Purna? Are all these conditional phenomena manifested by themselves, or by the empty space? If they are manifested by themselves, then when the sun is shining, the brightness belongs to the sun and in all the ten quarters of the universes, the brightness belongs to the sunshine. If this is the explanation, how is it that you still see the round sun in the sky. If the brightness belongs to the sky, then the sky should shine of itself, and how is it that the brightness never appears until the sun rises? If the brightness belongs to both the sky and sun, then which part of the brightness belongs to the sun and which part to the sky? Again, if the brightness is manifested by conformity and combination of the sky and sun, then when the sun goes down, thy sky should still retain part of the brightness. Why is it that after the sun sets, the night becomes dark? Therefore the brightness belongs neither to the sky nor to the sun. However, if there is neither sun nor sky, how can brightness become manifest? Therefore, we must conclude that brightness is neither dependent nor independent of either sky or sun.

Purna! It is just the same with the intelligence of the true mysterious Mind of Intuition. The Mind of Intuition has universal intelligence and because of it conception of space is embraced within it but undifferentiated and thus the manifestation of emptiness responds to the perception of your sight. Because the Four Great Elements are present within the pure universal intelligence of the Intuitive Mind, the manifestation of them responds to the perception of your sight. What is the significance of this, Purna? Take for instance the reflection of the sun in the water. Two persons, looking at the reflection, go away in opposite direction, one toward the east, the other toward the west, but the reflection of the sun in the water follows both of them. In the beginning they would have agreed that there was only one sun, but now we have two persons each asserting that the sun is following himself, therefore there must be two suns. But why then is there only one sun in the sky? All such deductions and assertions are false and empty because they have no basis of proof.

Purna! All the phenomena arising from sight are false and illusion—they are both indescribable and inexplicable. We might as well wish for the fantastic blossoms in the air to bear fruit. How foolish it is to seek the reason for their transient appearance and disappearance. Nevertheless, the Essential Nature of Perception of Sight is real and true, because it IS the mysterious, intelligent luminosity of the Intuitive Mind of Enlightenment. As the perception does not belong to the element fire or water, of what use is it for you to ask about the principle of their mutual involvement in each other's phenomena.

Purna! It is because you regard the conceptions of empty space and all the sights as being reciprocally overlapping and substituting for one another in the Tathagata's Womb, and so, accordingly, the Tathagata's Womb permeates everywhere throughout the phenomenal world in forms of emptiness and sights. And, therefore, from the Tathagata's Womb are manifested all such fantastic visions as the movement of wind, the transparency of the sky, the brightness of the sun, the gloominess of the clouds, etc. But it is because of the ignorance and stupidity of sentient beings they turn away from their own enlightening nature and hanker after worldly objects thus accumulating the defilements of attachments and contaminations. Thus arise the manifestations of the phenomenal world.

But I concentrate my mind so as to ignore all these contaminations and return to the mysterious, enlightening nature of non-death and non-rebirth so as to be in conformity with the Womb of Tathagata. Accordingly the Tathagata's Womb becomes the clear intelligence of the true and mysterious Mind of Intuition that throws its perfect reflection and insight into all the phenomenal world. Therefore, in Tathagata's Womb Oneness has the same meaning as Infinity, and Infinity has the same meaning as Oneness, the minimum is embraced in the maximum and the maximum in the minimum. The tranquillity and peacefulness of my concentration of mind in Samadhi prevails all over the ten quarters of the universes, my body embraces the vast spaces of the ten quarters, and even within a single pore of my skin there is a Buddha-land with a Buddha sitting on a seat no larger than a particle of dust, absorbed in Samadhi, but endlessly radiating therefrom all the forces of Life-giving Truth and ceaselessly drawing inward into its perfect unity all of its multitudinous manifestations. Since I have ignored and forgotten all worldly objects, I have fully realized this mysterious, enlightening Nature of the Pure Essence of Mind.

Nevertheless, the Womb of Tathagata is pure and perfect, all embracing but free from distinctions. In it is neither the finite mind, nor empty space, nor the earth, nor water, nor wind, nor fire, nor the senses, nor the whole body, nor sensations, nor perceptions, nor the sphere of conscious discriminations, nor the sphere of consciousness that is dependent upon the thinking mind. It is neither the enlightening nature of the Intuitive Mind, nor the non-enlightening nature of the intellectual mind, nor the mental state that discards all ideas relating to enlightenment and non-enlightenment. It is neither decay nor death, nor the state that discards all ideas of decay and death; it is neither suffering, the cause of suffering, the ending of suffering, nor the Noble Path leading to Enlightenment. It is neither Wisdom, nor attainment; neither the giving of gifts, nor the keepings of precepts, nor humble patience, nor zealous perseverance, nor the tranquil concentration of mind, nor Prajna (*paramita*), nor Emancipation (*paramitta*). It is neither Tathagata, nor Arhat, nor Highest Perfect Wisdom (*anuttara-samyak-sambodhi*), nor Pari-nirvana. It is neither eternity, nor happiness, nor ego-consciousness, nor purity, nor anything else. All these differentiations are but arbitrary conceptions—merely figures of speech—not only do they not convey the true meaning of Emancipation, neither do they convey the true meaning of every day life.

(*Note: Consider the relation of the radio instrument to the surrounding atmosphere. The air is burdened with all manner of vibrations, not kept distinct, but blended into some complex rhythm that is ceaselessly changing, from which the radio by its receiving mechanism selects the vibrations it desires and transforms them into what the ear interprets to be speech or music.*)

Nevertheless, if you rightly realize the true meaning of the Tathagata's Womb in its mysterious nature of the natural Enlightening Mind, you will also realize that this mysterious nature is also the thinking mind; empty space; earth, water, wind and fire; the sense organs, the whole body, sensations, perceptions, discriminations, the sphere of consciousness dependent upon the senses; enlightenment and non-enlightenment; the state that is neither enlightenment nor non-enlightenment; it is the state of decay and death, and the absence of all ideas about decay and death; it is suffering, the cause of suffering, the ending of suffering and the Noble Path that leads to enlightenment; it is Wisdom, it is all the transcendental attainments and graces (samapatti); it is the giving of gifts, keeping the precepts in selfless kindness, practising humble patience, and zealous perseverance, and tranquil concentration of mind and Wisdom and Emanciapation. It is Tathagata, the Arhats, Anuttara-samyak-sambodhi, and Pari-nirvana. It is Eternity, and Blissful Peace, and ego-consciousness, and Perfect Unity and Purity. And because Tathagata's Essential Mind contains all these, it not only conveys the true meaning of Emancipation but of every day life as well.

If you fully realize the intrinsic significance of Tathagata's Womb in its mysterious nature of Enlightening Mind, then you will realize that it embraces both the negative aspects and affirmative aspects as just outlined. You will realize that Tathagata's Womb and the pure Mind of Enlightenment and the Mind of Intuition (Alaya-vijnana) are of one Essence, radiant in Wisdom, integrant in Compassion, vibrant with Purpose and Life but unmanifest and in perfect balance and thus abiding in perfect and blissful Peace.

Purna! The mysterious nature of the Pure Enlightening Mind is profound and inconceivably mysterious, how can sentient beings in the Triple World, even the "salvation-for-themselves" Arhats and Pratyake-Buddhas, how can they with their limited minds fathom the Supreme Enlightenment of the Lord Tathagata? And how can they merge their mundane understanding with the inscrutable intelligence and insight of the Lord Tathagata? Consider the sweet harmonies that come from the violin, zither, harp or guitar. They do not come of themselves: they only come when some skilful musician plays upon them. It is the same with your minds and the minds of all sentient beings. Each one of you has full possession of the true Mind-Essence of Buddhahood whose transcendently glorious brightness may shine forth as quickly as the sweet harmonies come from the musical instruments when a Master's hand plays upon them. Nevertheless, as soon as you attempt to use your mind, the conditioning effects of your defilements, attachments and hindrances, at once reveal themselves. This is wholly due to your lack of diligence in your practice of seeking Supreme Enlightenment, as conditioned by your inclination toward the simpler teachings of the Hinayana school, and your self-complacency because of your imperfect attainments.

Then Purna addressed the Lord Buddha, saying:—Blessed Lord! I can see that thy true mysterious and pure Mind of Perfect Enlightenment and my own imperfect mind are one in Essence, but as the false conceptions within my mind have been accumulating since beginningless time, I have continued in the cycle of deaths and rebirths for innumerable kalpas. Though I have now acquired some measure of attainment, I have not yet attained Anuttara-samyak-sambodhi. Blessed Lord! Thou hast just taught us that as soon as we get rid of all illusions of thought that the mysterious Essential Mind of Permanency alone remains. May I enquire of thee, Lord Tathagata, by what causes do sentient beings cling to their illusions of thoughts which so over-shadow the mysterious Brightness of their Essential Mind and cause them to fall into the vast ocean of defilements?

The Lord Buddha replied:—Purna, although you have gotten rid of most of your uncertainties about the teaching of Emancipations, yet you still grasp the delusion of an arbitrary discrimination between Ignorance and Enlightenment. To clear this in your mind, I will ask you some questions about a present happening near us. You have doubtless heard about the insane man, Yayattadha in this very city of Sravasti. One morning he looked into a mirror and saw his head but it had no eyes nor eyebrows. He became very angry with his own head and blamed it as being the head of a goblin because it had no eyes nor eyebrows, and ran away quite crazy. What do you think, Purna? Did the man have any good reason for becoming crazy?

Purna replied:—It seems to me, Blessed Lord, that he had no other reason than this, that he was crazy already.

The Lord Buddha said:—Purna! Our mysterious Intuitive Nature is perfect and enlightening and its natural perfection is

intelligent and profound. Since the True Nature is free from all
illusions, so the illusions are naturally devoid of any reality, and,
therefore, have no source of existence. If they have no source
of existence, they are no longer illusions even. All these
thought-illusions have been raised by means of their own reciprocal manifestations and thus the piling up of delusion upon
delusions has been going on for kalpa after kalpa as many as
the particles of dust in the air. Though the Buddhas have
disclosed their falsity, yet sentient beings cannot at once realize
their falsity and return to their natural state of enlightenment.
The source of these delusions is nowhere else but within one's
own mind. As soon as you understand the source of a delusion,
the deluding conception loses its hold upon existence. If within
your mind you provide no source for these false conceptions,
there will be none to be discarded. Those who have attained
enlightenment are as if awakening from sleep, and their past
life seems only a dream. However clear one's memory may be,
it is impossible to reproduce any dreamed of object—no matter
under what conditions or causes. It would be more impossible
for you to grasp that which has no hold whatever upon its
own source of existence. Like the insane man of Sravasti who
ran away because of the wholly imaginary and fantastic
thoughts of his mind, with no other cause or conditions. If this
insanity was suddenly cured, his consciousness of his head would
just as suddenly be recovered, and no matter whether his insanity is cured or not, his head is on his body. Purna, the
illusions of the mind are just as fantastic and have no more
basis for existence. So if your mind is to remain tranquil and
undisturbed, there must be no discriminations of the three deluding phenomena of interrelating continuity, namely, the conception of the world's existence, the conception of the ego-personality, and the conception of karma and its forth-coming fruit.
If you cease all killing, robbery and lust, whose actions are the
cause of karma, then the three great causes for the existence of
interrelated continuity of existence will cease. Thus, within your
mind, your madness will clear of itself, and when your madness clears, Enlightenment is already present. For the essential
nature of your Transcendental, Pure and Enlightening Mind is
present everywhere, permeating the whole phenomenal world.
It is not acquired from any other person, nor by any method
of hard and diligent devotion to ascetic practices and attain-

ments. Sentient beings are like a man with a magic gem hidden in his garment of which he is ignorant. He becomes poor and ragged and hungry and wanders about to far countries. Although he is actually suffering from poverty, he still possesses the magic gem. One day a very wise man tells the poor man of his magic gem and forthwith the poor man becomes a millionaire. It is the same with your own nature of Intuitive Mind. You should forthwith realize that this magic gem of Enlightening Essence of Mind, is not to be acquired from some difficult source, but is already within your possession.

(Instructions to Ananda.)

Then Ananda from his place in the Assembly bowed down in reverence to the Lord Buddha and asked him:—Noble Lord! You have just taught us that if we get rid of the three causes of karma (killing, stealing and lust) that the three great causes for the interrelated continuity of existence will never appear again; that as soon as this madness is cleared away, Enlightenment will be acquired, not from some outside source, but will be revealed within the mind itself. This seems to come clearly under the principle of causes and conditions to which my Lord Buddha objects. As for myself, I certainly acquired realization by means of causes and conditions. And not only myself but all of us practicing junior Arhats and all our elder Brothers, the senior Arhats, the Venerable Maudgalyayana, Sariputra, Subhuti, and many others, after listening to the Lord's instruction, began their practicings of devotion, acquired their realization, and attained perfect non-recession; are these not causes and conditions? But, now, the Lord Buddha seems to be teaching that Enlightenment appears spontaneously and from no cause nor condition. To me this appears to be somewhat like the teaching of the heretic Kusali of Sravasti who teaches that naturalism is the supreme principle of all natures. Pray, my Lord, have great kindness toward us and clear away the uncertainty.

The Lord Buddha replied:—Ananda! In regard to the insane man in Sravasti should the causes and conditions of his insanity be removed, the nature of his non-insanity would be revealed and thus the heretical teaching of causes and conditions and of naturalism would fall short of the true interpretation. Ananda! If that insane man of Sravasti has his head according to the principle of naturalism, then as his head belongs to his nature so everything he thinks can not be otherwise interpreted than as being the natural manifestation of his mind, then why was he by causes and conditions frightened and became mad and run away? Or, if his natural head causes him to go insane by means of causes and conditions, then why does he not also lose his natural head, by means of causes and conditions? How since his own head has not been lost, but there rises in it the illusion of fright and madness, and his head shows not the slightest change, how is it to be said that the madness comes from causes and conditions? Does this not clearly explain that no principle of causes and conditions, or of naturalism, can reveal the true nature of mind? Or, if the man's insanity primarily belonged to his nature and he possessed madness and fright from the beginning, before he became suddenly mad and frightened, where did his madness conceal itself? Or, if by nature he is not insane and his head is normal, then why was he suddenly carried away by a fit of madness? Or, if he realized that his head was normal and that he had been carried away by a fit of madness, then the principles of both cause and condition and naturalism are mere talk. I have explained that as soon as the three conditions of killing, stealing and impurity have been gotten rid of, the mind becomes enlightened. When the mind of enlightenment is attained, then the mind of variability and ignorance disappears. But if you keep these conceptions in mind simply as arbitrary conceptions, then they are mere whimsical talk. When one has discarded the last arbitrary conception of death and rebirth, then he has attained to a state of perfect emptiness. As one is able to get rid of the thought that he is practicing meditation, then he is truly advancing toward enlightenment. Indeed, this is no whimsical talk. But even if the mind is free from the thought that one is practicing meditation, and one has advanced on the path of enlightenment, and even if one has attained to a perfect state of emptiness, it cannot be said that it has been accomplished according to a principle of naturalism. For so long as the mind cherishes any arbitrary conception, such as, that a perfect state of emptiness of mind belongs to the principle of naturalism, then there will develop along with it the arbitrary conception that as soon as the natural mind is developed that its variability and ignorance will disappear. This above all else is whimsical talk of a variable and ignorant mind. My teaching of the non-variability of the true Mind is a teaching that does not belong to whimsical speaking, neither does it belong to the principle of naturalism either. Or, if one thinks that the non-variability of true Mind is a kind of naturalism, that would be like mixing up natural phenomena into one all-inclusive compost and thinking of it under the category of combination and conformity, and the thinking of its opposite—non-combination and non-conformity—as being of the nature of originality. Such thnking is whimsical, indeed; it belongs to a habit of contrasting dualistic, and therefore false, conceptions. In regard to the nature of originality, it should be understood that, although it is invariable, yet it yields freely to conditions, so that it can not be regarded as coming under any law of naturalism. In regard to the phenomena manifested by combination and conformity, though they, also, yield to conditions, yet their body considered as a whole, suffers no change, so that these phenomena also, in their essence, do not come under the principle of combination and conformity. When interpreted in this way even these things are no longer whimsical words but are a true teaching, although they are a long way from Enlightenment and Nirvana.

Listen, Ananda! Although you hold in memory all the pure and profound teachings of the twelve classes of the Sacred Scriptures, if you use your learning only for flippant talk, of what value is it? To attain wisdom, you must practice mindfulness and concentration of mind in Dhyana for many, many kalpas. Although you have spoken glibly about the principles of causes and conditions, and naturalism,' and although you are commonly regarded as the most learned man in the assembly, your learning and thinking only increases your knowledge and you become more and more cultured with the multiplying of the kalpas, and as a consequence, you could not escape from the seductive allurement of Pchiti, the beautiful maiden. And why was it, Ananda, that by my transcendental power her sexual lust was immediately calmed and she became one of my most zealous disciples, and you found escape from your dangerous entanglement and receive this opportunity of instruction?

Therefore, Ananda, though you have kept in mind all the wonderful and systematic and profound teachings of the Tathagata for many kalpas, it would have been far better for you if you had practiced even for one day the lesson of resistance to the earthly passions of lust and hatred. Pchiti responded to her lesson and when her lust was quieted by my transcendental power she became a true Bhikshuni in our assembly. Both she and Yasdra, the mother of Rahula, have matured their karma of previous lives and now realize the causes of their sufferings in previous lives from yielding to loving desires and greediness. So each of you, after many kalpas of-suffering, by simply yielding to a single lesson have found emancipation. She has attained the stage of an Anagamin disciple and you have been assured of your future attainment of Arhat. Oh, Ananda, why do you still linger about, merely listening to my teachings, and deceiving yourself by thinking up foolish questions?

CHAPTER TWO

Interpretation of Non-Death and Non-Rebirth, the Wonderful Door of the Three Reflections and the Fundamental Cause of Practice.

(Questions by Ananda as to how to attain Enlightenment.)

After having listened to the Lord Buddha's instruction, Ananda and all the Disciples, discarding all their doubts and illusions, realized the true reality of their minds and, because of it, became calm and refreshed as never before. Ananda, as usual, being the natural spokesman, bowed down with great sadness at the feet of the Lord Buddha, and addressing him, said:—

Glorious Lord of great Compassion and Purity! Thou hast skilfully unveiled my heart and encouraged me by many expedient means even as thou hast delivered all who were drowning in the depths of the great Ocean of Suffering. Blessed Lord! Listening to thy sacred teaching we have come to understand that the Mysterious, Intuitive, Enlightening Mind of the Lord Tathagata's Womb is Universal and embraces all the Buddha-lands in its pure, tranquil, glorious, profound Enlightenment. But I have failed to enter into this Enlightenment and the Lord Tathagata has blamed me for it, saying that it was because of my very learning that I have been prevented from entering. I am like a man who has inherited a magnificent palace through the munificence of some heavenly king, but who is unable to take possession of it without first passing through the door of Enlightenment. We pray thee, Lord Buddha, because of thy great compassion to show us the way to enter into this inheritance of Enlightenment. Teach us, unenlightened as we are, how to give up the ideas we have accumulated by our learning and how to attain the goal of the Lord Tathagata's perfect Enlightenment. Show us the right starting point for our devotion and our disciplinary practice, show us how to get rid of all entangling conditions and thus to encourage all of us who are still practicing Arhats to concentrate our minds on the right path so that we may surely attain the intelligence and insight of our Lord Buddha. Then Ananda, having finished his plea, first bowed to the ground, and then together with all the great assembly, waited for the Lord Buddha to continue his sacred instruction.

Thereupon the Blessed Lord, taking pity upon his Disciples who were yet in the Pratyaka and practicing stage of Arhatship and for the sake of all later disciples in the decadent periods that were to follow his Nirvana, that they too might attain Supreme Enlightenment, gave the following instruction.

Ananda! When you have fully made up your minds to attain this true Mind of Enlightenment and have determined never to tire seeking for the Lord Tathagata's profound Samadhi, there are two definite principles for beginning practice that must from the first be fully understood and appreciated.

The first definite principle for beginning practice is this. If you are successfully to give up your old idea of Arhatship, that is, of gaining Enlightenment and Nirvana for yourself, and to begin the practice for attaining the ideal of Bodhisattvaship, that is, enlightenment for the sake of all sentient life, and to enter with perfect realization into the Buddha's perfect Intelligence and Insight, you must, first of all, (A) observe and see clearly that your starting point of motive and purpose is in full accord with the eventual fruit of Enlightenment. If, at the beginning, you take the varying and momentary thoughts of your mind as your starting point for seeking Buddha's perfect and un-varying Mind of Enlightenment, there is no such agreement.

From the beginning you must recollect that all conditional phenomena are transitory and passing. Have you any doubt of this? Can you think of any exception? Take for example, pure space. Have any of you ever heard of space coming to corruption and destruction? No, because pure space is free from conditions and, therefore, is indestructible.

Compare this with your body, Ananda. Within your body there is an element of hardness, of Earth; there is an element of fluidity, of Water; there is an element of warmth, of Fire; and an element of breathing and motion, the element of Wind. The body is in bondage to these Four Great Elements, and these four bonds divide your tranquil, mysterious, intuitive, enlightening Mind into such divisions as the sensations and perceptions of seeing, hearing, tasting, smelling and touching, and of the following conceptions and discriminations of thought, that cause your enlightening Mind to fall into the corresponding five defilements of this evil world from its beginning and will continue to do so to its end.

What are these five defilements, Ananda? What is their nature? Consider the difference between fresh, pure spring water, and such substances as dust, ashes and sand. If these are mixed, the water becomes dirty and opaque. It is just the same with the five defilements and the mind.

Ananda, when you look into the vast space that stretches beyond the universe, the nature of space and the nature of the perception of sight do not interfere with each other, but mingling together there is no boundary line to limit their individuality. But if there is only empty space, with no suns nor planets in it, then space loses its substantiality. And the conception of sight looking into space with nothing to see, loses its sensibility. But as there are these two arbitrary conceptions of false phenomena—suns and planets moving in space, and the false perception of sight, all interwoven together,—so there are all the uncounted false manifestations of differences in the universes. This is the first defilement of individuation which is the basis of ignorance.

Next, the substantiality of the body is made up of the Four Great Elements, and the processes of the mind—seeing, hearing, tasting, smelling, touching, perceiving, discriminating—mingling with the processes of the body and they become interwoven together into the false imaginations that are the second defilement, called the defilement of erroneous views concerning form.

Again, within your mind there are the processes of consciousness, such as memory, moods, emotions, incidental to the recitation of the daily ritual, desires, etc., and there is the pure intuition of the Intuitional Mind. They, also, mingle together and give rise to false imaginations which form the third defilement, the conditioning defilement of the two kinds of evil desires (klesas).

Again, your mind is continually in a process of change from morning to night and every time your thoughts change, you seek to manifest and perpetuate them by some sort of creative activity in this terrestrial world. And every time your actions, conditioned by your karma, take form, they transform sentient lives also. Thus these interwoven false imaginations and these objective illusions manifested by them make up the fourth defilement which is called the evil defilement of sentient beings grasping the things they desire.

Again, since your perceptions of seeing, hearing, touching, thinking, having no differences in their nature, but because of their attributes of form and appearance and individuation are placed in opposition and relation to one another revealing abnormal differences and distinctions which, in the pure Essence of Mind, are mutually accomodating, but which when manifested in form and appearance are found to be mutually incompatible. Thus there arise internal and external conflicts which, although imaginary, form the fifth defilement, the defilement of weariness, suffering, growing old and decrepitude.

Ananda! If you wish your sense perceptions and conscious understanding to be in harmony with the permanent joy of the Tathagata's natural purity, you must first pull up these roots of death and rebirth which have been surreptitiously planted by these five kinds of defilements, namely, the defilements of discriminating ignorance, of form, of desire, of grasping, of decrepitude, and then begin the practice of concentration of your attention on the pure and Essential Mind of non-death and non-rebirth. It is by means of your tranquillity of mind that you are able to transmute this false mind of death and rebirth into the true and clear Intuitive Mind and, by so doing, to realize the primal, enlightening and intuitive Essence of Mind. You should make this your starting point for practice. Having thus harmonized your starting point with your goal, you will be able by right practice to attain the true goal of perfect Enlightenment.

If you wish to tranquillize your mind and restore its original purity, you must proceed as if you were purifying a jar of muddy water. You first let it stand until the sediment settles to the bottom when the water will become pure, which corresponds with the state of mind before the defilements of the evil passions had troubled it. Then you carefully strain off the pure water which is the state of the mind after the five defilements of ignorance, form, desire, grasping, decreptitude, have been wholly removed. When the mind becomes tranquillized and concentrated into perfect unity, then all things will be seen, not in their separateness, but in their unity wherein there is no place for the evil passions to enter, and which is in full conformity with the mysterious and indescribable purity of Nirvana.

(B) The second definite principle for beginning practice is this:—If you are to successfully give up your old ideal of Arhatship and to begin the practice for attaining Bodhisattvaship, that is, of attaining Enlightenment for the sake of all sentient life, you must face with great courage the requirement for becoming a Bodhisattva-Mahasattva, namely, to abandon all dependence upon conditional phenomena which includes all conceptions relating to your own ego-selfness, and to examine carefully and with determination into the roots of all passionate desires (klesas); that is, as to who it is, or what it is, that develops these passionate desires, and who it is and what it is that suffers these karmas and rebirths through the beginningless kalpas.

Ananda! Unless from the very beginning of your practice for the attainment of Enlightenment, you do not look into the roots of these klesas, you will never be able to understand the deceptiveness of the sense organs and sense minds and the discriminating thoughts relating to them and to the objects of sense, and to the general topsy-turviness of mind. If you fail to discover and to understand this point, how will you otherwise be able to subdue your vagrant thoughts and vexations of mind, and be able to successfully ascend to the throne of Tathagata?

Ananda! If you watch a man untangle knots in a rope, you will notice that he first studies the interweaving of the rope to find out which strand to unloosen first. But space is different. Space has no body nor form, so there can be no knots in space to untangle. But in your organism there are six thieves:—eyés, ears, nose, tongue, body and discriminating mind, to steal away precious values of truth and leave you in bondage to false imagination. Consequently from beginningless time all sentient beings in this phenomenal world have developed knots and bonds and entanglements which render it impossible for them to transcend this world, until these knots be first disentangled.

Ananda! What do you understand when I speak of the world of sentient beings? Do I mean just thinking people? No, I mean the whole complicated process of change that has been going on endlessly and its ever-shifting manifestations and positions. For instance, the positions of the phenomena being momentarily manifested, we speak of as being east, or west, north, south, south-east, north-east, south-west and north-west, and also above and below. Moreover, this endless process of change has been going on in the past, is going on at present, and will be going on into the endless future. Because of the vast, incalculable number and permutations of these changes, everywhere and forever, the false and arbitrary conceptions of all sentient minds have been ever-flowing and interweaving together in a most bewildering process of manifestation and evolution and involution, and this ever-shifting and bewildering process of change makes up the world of sentient beings.

Though the nature of this world may be divided into the ten directions and their positions may be made definitely clear, but as people are ignorant and thoughtless and careless, they only think of these locations in a very general way and fail to realize that there is another direction than east and west and north and south which is of more importance because it takes in all the rest. This is the direction toward the center. Then they fail to remember that each of these directions is mutually related to a fourth direction of time that in its turn is in three directions, past, present and future. And each of these is related to the ten realms of existence and each of these has its ten points of direction, which makes in all twelve hundred, and each of our six senses has its own twelve hundred. Then you must remember that none of these senses see everything and always, so that their single and combined report to the perceiving and discriminating mind is never perfect nor complete. Each conception has its measure of merit and no more.

*   *   *

(*Then follows several pages elaborating this thought of the incompleteness and imperfection of all sense originating conceptions, which are here omitted.*)

Ananda! If you wish to discriminate rightly between the desire-current of your mind as it sets outwardly towards different forms and their inevitable suffering and death and rebirth, and the returning current of compassion that sets inward toward the source of non-death and non-rebirth at the center, you will have to test each one of them with the pure Mind Essence to find out which one is opposed to it and which one is in harmony with it. I have tried to bring this out clearly so that you may be able to distinguish them and be able to abandon the one that is deceiving and false and that has been accumulating karma since beginningless time, and to follow after and to develop your perfect and accommodating nature so that every day under every circumstance, you may part company from the deceiving and enslaving defilements. I have brought out this distinction very clearly in order to help your advancement by a more perfect daily practice.

As for the Tathagatas of the ten quarters of all the universes, they can practice in any one of the eighteen spheres of mentation and in any one of them find Supreme and Perfect Enlightenment, for to them there are no distinctions of attainment. But because of your ignorance and deterioration you become confused amid these eighteen spheres of mentation and are unable to regain your native intelligence. Therefore, I have made this clear statement so that you may all enter by this one door to Enlightenment, and may be able to attain to one unity of Mind free from all deceiving thoughts, and having gained this unity, all these perceptions of the senses will become purified simultaneously.

Then Ananda addressed the Lord Buddha, saying:—

Noble Lord! How is it that in making progress against the forth-going desire current of death and rebirth, that by entering the one door of deep concentration of mind, we purify all six of the perceiving sense-minds simultaneously?

The Lord Buddha replied:—Ananda! Having attained the degree of Crotapana, you are supposed to have gotten rid of all the delusions belonging to the sight perception of sentient beings and to have reached the enlightenment-stage of your sight faculty. However, you have not yet gotten rid of the fantastic habit of dividing things that by their nature are indivisible, which had developed in the sense organs since beginningless time. Such fantastic habits will be overcome as you reach the enlightenment stage of your practice, by the realization of the perfect unity of Mind Essence that transcends all divisions.

There still remains within your sense-mind individualized delusions arising from ignorance regarding the process of growing, continuing, changing, and disappearing, of the mind's perceptions. I now want to ask you, Ananda, whether these sense-minds are to be considered as six little minds, or as one unified Mind? If they are to be considered as only one unified Mind, how is it that the ear cannot see, or the eye hear, or the head walk, or the feet talk? Or if the sense-minds are definitely six in number, which one of your six senses is it that receives my teaching as I explain to you the mystery of this profound door of Dharma, and which one of them is it that accepts it?

Ananda replied:—My Lord! I received your teaching through my ears.

The Lord Buddha said:—Ananda, as my teaching is particularly heard by your hearing sense, what relation has it to your body and to your thinking mind? Having received my teaching with your ears, how was it that your mouth asked the question and your body rose up to show me reverence? You should think about this very carefully. There can be no doubt about the fact that the teaching was received at first by one of the senses, but there is a question as to whether the mind that perceived the teaching and accepted it was one or six. Ananda, you should clearly understand that your sense-minds, in truth, are neither one nor six. The confusing differentiation is explained by the fact that since from beginningless time the mind has fallen into the habit of seeing divisions where there are no divisions until it is in a chronic state of topsy-turviness, and among its illusions this arbitrary conception of one and six has arisen to cloud over your originally perfect and tranquil Mind-Essence. You have succeeded in discard-

ing all attachments and contaminations belonging to the six
sense-perceptions, but you have not yet regained a clear realization of the original and intrinsic unity of your true Mind.

The same is true as to space. When you leave objects out
of account and think only of clear space, you have no difficulty
in recognizing that space is a perfect unity. But when you
think of it in relation to objects, you note differences and also
divide up space. But space can not be divided simply for
your convenience; it is absurd to even question whether it is
unity or not-unity. It is the same with your six sense-minds—
whether they are one or six—they are pure Essence of Mind
which in its nature is as undifferentiated and universal as space.

By means of the opposing phenomena of brightness and
darkness, the natural unity and tranquillity of your mind is
disturbed and deceived, and perception of sight is registered
within the wonderful, perfect and Essential Mind. The essential
nature of this inner perception of sight is a reflection of outer
sights and by weaving different sights together there is manifested an undifferentiated, transcendental organ of sight that is
to be regarded as the real substantiality of the eye-sense. Moreover, there is a subsidiary of this transcendental eye-sense,
namely, consciousness dependent upon it, which consciousness
is not to be differentiated from the consciousness of the other
senses—of hearing, smelling, tasting and touching— and the
unity of which in the Mind's pure Essence, gives rise, within
the mortal mind, to wandering thoughts about every phenomena. Thus there is going on between the specialized sense-
organ and the unified transcendental sense-mind a constant succession of receiving and projecting, causing and being effected.

In like manner by means of the mutual conflict of the two
phenomena of motion and stillness, your natural tranquillity of
mind is contaminated and perception of hearing is manifested
within your wonderful perfect and Essential Mind. The essential nature of this inner perception of hearing reflects the
outer sounds and, by merging them together, manifests a transcendental organ of hearing, which is to be regarded as the real
substantiality of the ears. Moreover, there is a subsidiary of this
transcendental ear-organ, namely, the consciousness dependent
upon it and the other four objects of seeing, smelling, tasting,
and touching, which raises wandering thoughts after every phenomena of sounds.

And again, by means of the mutual conflict of the two phenomena of passibility and impassibility, your natural tranquillity of mind is contaminated and perception of smelling is manifested within your wonderful, perfect and Essential Mind. The essential nature of this inner perception of smelling reflects outer odours and, by merging them together, manifests a transcendental organ of smelling. The originality of this transcendental smelling-organ is to be thought of as the real substantiality of the nose. Moreover, there is a subsidiary of this transcendental smelling-organ, namely, the consciousness dependent upon it and the other four objects of seeing, hearing, tasting and touching, which raises wandering thoughts after every phenomena of smelling.

And again, by the interweaving of the two phenomena of variability and invariability, your natural tranquillity of mind is contaminated and perception of tasting is manifested within your wonderful, perfect and Essential Mind. The essential nature of this inner perception of tasting reflects the outer tastes and, by merging them together, manifests a transcendental organ of tasting. The originality of this transcendental organ of tasting is to be thought of as the real substantiality of the tongue. Moreover, there is a subsidiary of this transcendental tongue-organ, namely, consciousness dependent upon it and the other four objects of seeing, hearing, smelling and touching, which raises wandering thoughts after every phenomena of taste.

And again, by means of the irritation of the two phenomena of separation and touching, your natural tranquillity of mind is contaminated and perception of touching is manifested within your wonderful, perfect and Essential Mind. The essential nature of this inner perception of touching reflects the outer contacts and, by merging them together, manifests a transcendental feeling-organ. The originality of this transcendental feeling-organ is to be thought of as the real substantiality of the sense of touch. Moreover, there is a subsidiary of this transcendental feeling-organ, namely, consciousness dependent upon it and the other four objects of seeing, hearing, smelling and tasting, which raises wandering thoughts after every phenomena of feeling.

And again, by means of the reciprocal continuity of appearing and disappearing (birth and death), your natural tranquillity of mind is contaminated and manifests discriminating thoughts within your wonderful, perfect and Essential Mind. The essential nature of these discriminating thoughts reflects the conception of individualized phenomena and, by grouping the different phenomena together, there is formed a transcendental thinking-organ which is to be thought of as the real substantiality of the discriminating mind. Moreover, there is a subsidiary of the discriminating mind, namely, consciousness dependent upon it and upon the other five objects of seeing, hearing, smelling, tasting and feeling which raises wandering thoughts about any and all the phenomena of discriminating cognition.

These transcendental sense-organs, corresponding to the six physical sense-organs, are not six but one, and that One is the wonderful, mysterious, Essence-Mind of Intuition. In this unified transcendental Mind all sense-perceptions are perfectly accommodated in its perfect unity. When any one of the sense-conceptions is seen to be unreal and fantastic, then the transcendental sense-mind being perfectly accommodating and unified, realizes that all sense-perceptions are unreal and fantastic, and the transcendental mind-organ being the real substantiality of the physical mind-organ and the consciousness dependent upon it, projects its unified consciousness so that all the sense minds are purified at one and the same time.

Ananda! Such are the six kinds of transcendental sense-minds that are manifested by means of the intuitive, enlightening nature of your true Mind when it is possessed and deceived by the false perceptions of the different sense functions. As soon as you lose the true nature of the actual perceptions, you cling to false imaginations and the manifest false conceptions. Thus, when you ignore both brightness and darkness, there will be no substance to the perception of sight; when you ignore both motion and motionlessness, there will be no substance to the conception of hearing; when the discriminated notions of passibility and impassibility are ignored, the perception of smelling will have no substance; when there is no clinging to the notion of variability, the perception of taste will remain undeveloped; when there is no clinging to the notion of separation and contact, naturally there will be no perception of feeling; and when there is no clinging to the conception of an ego-self and of death and rebirth, there will be no further specialization and development of any of the six different sense perceptions, nor of their disappearance either, then where can a discriminating mind take up its abode?

If you simply do not follow after these twelve notions of conditioning phenomena, namely, motion and stillness, separation and contact, variability and constancy, appearing and disappearing, passing or impenetrability, brightness and darkness, or should ignore any pair of them, you will be free from bondage to all mental contaminations. You will become concentrated in mind, you will return to your natural Essence of Mind, you will manifest your original and innate enlightening brightness. As soon as you unveil your enlightening nature, by ceasing to cling to any pair of these conditioning phenomena, the other five contaminating attachments of sense perception will all lose their force and your mind will become perfectly free.

Ananda! When the intuitive and Essential Mind becomes free from contamination, it derives its discriminations and ideas, not by means of contact with objects in its presence, nor in the order and limited manner of the senses, but while it continues the use of the sense-organs for its purposes, henceforth the senses conceptions become universalized and mutually available.

Ananda, have you noticed in this assembly that Anaruddha sees things that his eyes can not see? This transcendental perception is temporarily reflected to him from the brightness of the Tathagata. The physical sense perception by its very nature is limited and does not possess any substantiality. For instance: The Arhats who have attained tranquillity and the Samapatti of perfect emancipation from desires and suffering, such as the great Katyayana who is present with us today, have long ago discarded the use of their thinking minds, which if clung to only serve to develop the arbitrary conception of an ego-self. They are perfectly intelligent but they apprehend knowledge, not by means of their thinking minds, but directly by intuition.

Ananda! When you have cut off all dependence upon the sense organs, your inner awareness will become as clear as crystal, manifesting its authentic brightness. Then all vagrant thoughts and transitory objects and the ever varying phenomena of this terrestrial world will melt away like ice when boiling water is poured upon it. In a moment, by a single act of true mindfulness, your inward awareness will become transcendental intelligence.

Ananda! It is as though a worldly man should focus all his senses in his eyes and after that see things only with his eyes. Then if he closes his eyes suddenly, there will be only a perception of darkness and all the other senses would become darkened, also. Such a man would become unconscious of any difference between his head and his feet. Now, if the man moves his hand over his body, although he does not see anything with his eyes, as soon as he discriminates his head from his feet by the sense of touch, the perception of all the sense organs will become as usual.

As brightness is a necessary condition for seeing, darkness prevents seeing, but if you can manifest the seeing faculty independent of brightness, darkness can never cause gloominess. When objects of sense experience are all ignored, then the transcendental brightness of Intuition will shine forth mysteriously, and you will have found the true source of cognition and tranquillity.

*   *   *

Ananda then said to the Lord Buddha:—Noble Lord! It has been said by thee, that if we wish to seek permanency of enlightenment, we must at the very beginning become acquainted with the different degrees of attainment, such as: Nirvana, Bodhi, Tathata, Mind Essence, Alaya Vijnana, the Emptiness of the Womb of Tathagata, the highest perfect Wisdom of the All-embracing Mirror. Though these are different in name, yet in nature, they are all pure, perfect and free, and their substantiality is as pure and as hard and as condensed as the diamond, which is pure and hard and permanent by nature. If the perception of seeing and hearing should omit all the conditions of brightness and darkness, motion and motionlessness, they would have none of their characteristic substantiality. The same would be true of the thinking mind. If it ignored all the perceptions of objects in its presence, there would be nothing left of it; it would be non-existent. Then how can we take the Samapatti of extermination of thoughts and desires as the starting point for our practices when we seek to acquire the Tathagata's seven fruits of permanency?

My Lord! If the phenomena of brightness and darkness are excluded, the perception of sight would disappear. If there are no conceptions of objects in its presence, the thinking mind would revert to nothingness, also. If its causes and results are considered carefully in this light, are you not forced to see that originally there is neither a thinking mind nor any attribute of it. If that is true then who is it that seeks to attain Supreme Enlightenment? At one time, my Lord Tathagata said that the mind was tranquil, perfect, permanent and Essential, in its nature, but later my Lord said that speaking truly all expressions referring to Mind were nothing but figures of speech. How, then, can it be said that even the Lord Tathagata is an authentic Teacher? If there is no Mind, how are we to use it to get rid of false conceptions and attain the true? Pray, my Lord, in great kindness enlighten our ignorance and stupidity.

The Lord Buddha replied:—Ananda, though you have learned many things by your wonderful brain, you have not yet fully attained to perfect mind-control. Your mind understands the causes and relations of your topsy-turvy thoughts, but when this true "topsy-turvy" thought is presented to you, you fail to understand it. I am afraid that your faith in my teaching is not well grounded. To help you clear away these uncertainties, I will ask you a few simple questions.

Then the Lord Buddha struck his gong and asked Ananda if he had heard the sound of it.

Ananda replied that he had. After the vibration of the sound had died away, the Lord Buddha enquired:—Do you still hear? Ananda replied that he no longer heard it.

The Lord Buddha struck the gong again and asked:—Did you hear the striking of the gong? Ananda replied:—Yes, Blessed Lord.

Then the Lord Buddha said to Ananda:—Why do you reply at one time that you hear and at another time that you do not hear?

Ananda replied at once:—Blessed Lord, when the gong was struck I heard the sound, but when the vibrations died away the sound ceased. That is what I meant when I said at one time that I heard, and at another that I did not hear.

Again, the Lord Buddha struck the gong and enquired of Ananda if he could still hear. Ananda replied that he could.

After a while when the sound had ceased, the Lord Buddha enquired again:—Do you still hear?

Ananda replied, a little impatiently:—No, Blessed Lord, the sound has ceased, how can I hear?

Then the Lord Buddha said:—Ananda, what is the meaning of it all? At one time you say you hear and at another time you say you do not hear?

Ananda replied: Blessed Lord when the gong is struck, there is sound. After a time the sound ceases, then there is no sound.

The Lord Buddha interrupted, saying: Ananda, why do you make such confused statements?

Ananda retorted:—Blessed One, why do you charge me with making confused statements, when I speak only of facts?

The Lord Buddha replied:—Ananda, why, indeed! When I asked whether you had heard the sound of the gong, you replied that you had heard it, but when I asked you if you could still hear, you replied at one time that you could, and at another time that you could not. You do not seem to realize that the sound of the gong, the hearing of the sound, and the perception of the hearing are three different things, for you replied without any recognition of the difference. That is why I said that you were making confused statements.

There is a difference between "sound" and "no-sound," and "hearing" and "no-hearing." Sound and no sound are momentary, while hearing and no-hearing are permanent. Sound and no-sound are imaginary, hearing belongs to the pure Essence of Mind. Ananda, you speak in error when you say there is no more hearing just because the sound ceases. If it is true that hearing ends with the cessation of noise, it would mean that the ear-organ had been destroyed. When the gong was struck again it would no longer have been heard, but you heard it so it means that you could hear all along. So you should recognize that your hearing of the sound and your not hearing of it are related to the existence or non-existence of the sound, and not to the perception of the ear. If you remember this, your hearing nature will not seem to you to become at one time existent and at another time non-existent.

Should the hearing nature really vanish, then by whom will the vanishing be realized? Therefore, Ananda, the sound-object within the scope of the hearing nature has its own death and rebirth. It is not when you note the existence of the sound or the non-existence of the sound, that you should think that your hearing nature is in existence or not in existence.

As your mind is still in a topsy-turvy condition, when it mistakes the sound to be the same as your hearing nature, it is no wonder that your mind is bewildered in the entanglements caused by mistaking the nature of permanency as being the same as destructibility. Therefore, it is not right for you to say that as soon as hearing is separated from such conditions as motion and motionlessness, impassability and passability, that the perception of hearing has no essential nature of its own. The hearing faculty can be likened to a sleepy fellow of this world, sleeping soundly on his bed. During his sleep, some of his family are batting their clothes as they wash them, and some were hulling rice by pounding it and the sound of the batting and the pounding mingle with his dreams and are but the rat-a-pan and the dum-dum of a drum. In his dream he wondered why the ding-dong should sometimes sound like coming from wood and sometimes like coming from stone. When he awoke, he immediately realized that the sound came from batting clothes on wood and pounding rice on stone. He told his family about his dream and how bewildered he was by such sounds coming from a drum.

Ananda! In his dream the man did not think of conceptions of motion and motionlessness in relation to the sounds, or of passability and impassability in relation to the organ of hearing, but though his body was asleep, yet the essential part of hearing was as clear as ever. By means of this illustration, you must see that in spite of the destruction of your body and the gradual exhaustion of the vitality of your life, that the essential nature of the hearing-conception is not destroyed nor caused to vanish.

Therefore, as all sentient beings from beginningless time have always hankered after beautiful sights and musical sounds, filling their thinking minds with thought after thought and causing it to be always active, and never realizing that by nature it was pure, mysterious, permanent and Essential, thus causing them, instead of following the path of permanency, to follow the current of transitory deaths and rebirths. Consequently there has been life after life ever recurring and ever filled with contaminations, impermanency and suffering.

Ananda, if you could only learn to get free from this bondage to deaths and rebirths and from this fear of impermanency, and learn to concentrate your mind on its true and permanent nature of Permanency, then the eternal Brightness would illumine you and all the individualized and discriminated perceptions of objective phenomena, sense-organs, false imaginations, self and not-self, would vanish, for the phenomena of the thinking mind are only empty and transitory things, the differentiated emotions of your mortal consciousness are only passing phenomena. If you can learn to ignore these two fundamental illusions—deaths and rebirths and the fear of impermanency—and hold fast to the Permanency that the Eye of Dharma perceives, then you need have no fear of failure in the attainment of Supreme Enlightenment.

* * *

Ananda addressed the Lord Buddha, saying:—Noble Lord! Though my Lord has shown us the negative teaching of our bondage to deaths and rebirths and their inevitable suffering, yet when we notice human beings struggling to untangle the knots that bind them to deaths and rebirths, we know that they will never be able to unsnarl the knots until they are given some clear and positive teaching that will lead them to Emancipation from the bondage and fear and suffering and to the attainment of Buddhahood. This need is also true of myself and of other practicing Arhats. Though we have acquired a measure of enlightenment and are honored as hermit sages yet, nevertheless, we are like men sick with remittent fever, we seem to gain only to fall back again into the old weakness and bondage and suffering. Pray, my Lord, have great mercy on our stupidity and be kind enough to show us in great detail and clearness how to untangle the knots that bind us. Your further teaching will not only help us, but will, through us, help all sentient beings of the future, so that we may all become free together and never again fall into the Three Great Realms of Passion, Anger and Infatuation.

As soon as Ananda had made this entreaty, the whole assembly with one accord paid to the Lord Buddha highest obeisance and waited in great expectation for further perfect teaching. Thereupon, the Blessed Lord having great pity, not only for Ananda and those present, but for the sake of all future disciples, sowed the good seed of Emancipation that would eventuate in the development of the Eye of Enlightenment. The Blessed Lord tenderly laid his golden hand of sandal wood fragrance upon the head of Ananda. Immediately all the innumerable Buddha-lands of all the ten quarters of the universe became rhythmic with the six kinds of mysterious vibrations, and all the Tathagatas existent in all these Buddha-lands emitted from the crowns of their heads rays of glorious splendor, and the rays of this glorious brightness simultaneously reached to the Jeta Grove where they were assembled and rested like a crown on the head of the Lord Tathagata. The whole assembly were overwhelmed with amazement and adoration and awe.

At the same time, mystic voices were heard coming from the innumerable Tathagatas in all the innumerable Buddha-lands and blending their varied tones into one melodious voice, seeming to say:—Well, indeed! Ananda! If you wish to understand your deep ignorance which is the secret of the knots that hold you fast bound in the cycle of deaths and rebirths, you must first understand your six sense-organs—eyes, ears, nose, tongue, body and discriminating mind, for if you wish to realize Supreme Enlightenment and its Samapatti graces of tranquillity, peace, joy, calmness, freedom, transcendency and permanency, they must be sought nowhere else but in these six sense-organs of your own body.

Although Ananda had heard this sacred teaching many times before, its full significance was not yet fully clear to him, so he knelt before the Lord Buddha and humbly entreated him, saying:—What does this mystic message that has come from all the Buddha-lands mean, when it says that both the secret of bondage to the cycle of deaths and rebirths, and the secret of the attainment of perfect peace, joy, transcendency and eternality, lie within my own sense-organs and nowhere else? What is its deep meaning?

The Lord Buddha interrupted, saying:—Ananda! The sense organs and their objects, and bondage and emancipation all belong to one single thing, which is your human conceptions which are false and deceptive and transitory, just like the fantastic blossoms seen in the air by clouded eyes. The perceptions of the senses arise from objects, and their phenomena are manifested under the conditions of the sense organs. All sense per-

ceptions, all discriminated ideas relating to them, all manifestations are mind-made and have no essential nature of their own—
they are as empty as the center of reeds—consequently, as soon
as you perceive anything, your seeing it, your discrimination of
it, your desire for it, your grasping it, become the knots that
bind you to ignorance and the cycle of deaths and rebirths. On
the contrary when your eyes perceive anything, if you let the
sensation of seeing pass unheeded, not letting any discriminating thoughts of judgment arise in your mind, this unties all
knots and is the genuine freedom that is non-intoxicating and
is Nirvana. This being true, how can any trace of conception
remain in your Mind? Indeed, it must not be allowed to remain to defile its pure Essence.

* * *

Then the Blessed One in order to emphasize his teaching
summed it up as follows:—

In comparison with Mind-Essence, all conditioned things
are as empty as space. Existing as they do under conditions,
they are false and fantastic; unconditioned things, having
neither appearance nor disappearance, are as imaginary as blossoms seen in the air. As we are obliged to use false expressions
to interpret the essence of things, so both the false expressions
and the essence of things as thus interpreted by the false expressions become a pair of falsities. It is clear to see that the
intrinsic Essence is neither the essence as interpreted, nor the
non-essence of the interpretation. How can it be asserted that
there is trueness in either the thing as perceived, or in the
phenomena of perceiving?

Therefore, as there is no reality at the heart either of the
sense-organs and of the objects seen, or of the perceiving consciousness, they must all be as empty as the heart of reeds. As
all the knots of the mind and all unloosening of knots has the
same basis of unreality, it matters not whether we think of
them as sacred or vulgar, there is but one path to emancipation and that is to escape from their bondage altogether.

If you are considering the nature of the center of reeds, it
matters not whether you interpret the center as emptiness or as
non-emptiness—either would be a misinterpretation. If anyone
is puzzled by the saying that both are false, it is because of
his ignorance. If one is not puzzled, it is because he has at-

tained emancipation. The unloosening of knots is a gradual process, one must begin with the knots of the five sense-organs, after which the knots of the sixth sense—the perceiving and discriminating mind—will loosen of themselves. Therefore, it is wise to begin with the sense organ that is most yielding and accomodating and by means of it, it will be easier to enter the true Stream of Life that flows into highest perfect Wisdom (*anuttara-samyak-sambodhi*).

Although the Alaya-vijnana (the universal or "storage" Mind) is immaculate in its self-nature, as it receives the seed of the false thinking, it becomes contaminated and becomes as wild and unmanageable as the current of a torrent. Because one easily falls into attachment to arbitrary conceptions, such as reality interpreted by false expressions and illusions of non-reality, I have not always interpreted things in this way. Since all conceptions of phenomena are nothing but activities of the mind, so, speaking truly, the mind is not a fantastic thing but it becomes a fantastic thing. If you are not in bondage to these contaminations of your own mind, there will be neither arbitrary conceptions of fantastic things, or of things that are not fantastic.

As there is no rising in your Essential Mind of such arbitrary conceptions as non-fantastic things, why should they be raised at all? This teaching is the wonderful "Lotus Flower." It is as gloriously enlightening as the diamond (*Vajra-raja*), as mysteriously potent as highest Samadhi. This is the Incomparable Teaching! Anyone practicing it with sincerity and earnestness will outdo the graduate disciples in a single moment, as suddenly as a rap on the door. Such a one will become Honored of all the Worlds! Indeed! This Teaching is the only path to Nirvana.

* * *

When the Lord Tathagata had finished this supreme instruction, whose profound and comprehensive thoughts had been expressed in well chosen words and beautiful style, Ananda and the whole assembly were enlightened and they praised the Lord Buddha for his sacred teaching.

But Ananda was not yet satisfied. In reverential manner and spirit, he addressed the Lord Buddha, saying:—Noble

Lord! Though I have listened carefully to my Lord's noble and compassionate teaching about the exclusive unity and oneness of the pure, mysterious and eternal Essence, I do not yet fully realize its meaning. It seems to teach that as soon as the six sense-organs have become emancipated from their contaminations and attachments that the remaining arbitrary conceptions of the thinking mind will fall way of themselves leaving only the one intrinsic Essence, and that this process of emancipation will proceed in an orderly and spontaneous fashion. Pray, my Lord, have great forbearance with us less advanced disciples and, for the sake of all future disciples, repeat this instruction in more detail, so that it may purify our minds and the minds of all future disciples.

The Lord Tathagata arranged his garments and taking a silk handkerchief proceeded to tie a knot in it and showed it to the assembly, saying, What is this?

With one accord, they replied:—It is a silk handkerchief in which you have tied a knot.

The Lord Tathagata tied another knot in the handkerchief and said:—What is this:

They replied:—It is another knot, Blessed Lord.

Again the Lord tied other knots until there were six. Then showing the handkerchief to the assembly, and indicating the knots one by one, he asked what is this? And what is this? And to each question Ananda and the other answered as before:—It is a knot.

Then the Lord Buddha said:—Ananda! When I showed you the first knot, you called it a knot, and when I showed you the second and the third and so on, you still insisted they were all knots.

Ananda replied:—Noble Lord! The handkerchief is made of silk threads of different colors and is woven into a single piece, but when it is tied into a knot, it is right to call it a knot, also, and if the Lord were to tie it into a hundred knots, each one would be a knot. However, my Lord, has only tied it six times—not seven or five—so there are only six knots. Why does my Lord seem to recognize only the first tying as a knot?

The Lord Buddha replied:—Ananda, you are right in saying that this beautiful handkerchief is one piece and that when I tied it six times there were six knots. Now look at it closely.

The silk handkerchief is the same piece of woven silk, the tying has not changed it in the slightest, except in appearance—it is still a handkerchief. Now think, Ananda. When the handkerchief was tied the first time, the first knot appeared; and then later and successively, the second knot and the third to the sixth. If I now take this sixth knot and begin to count them backward, the sixth knot becomes the first, does it not?

Ananda replied:—No, my Lord, when the handkerchief was tied six times, the last tying was the sixth knot; it can by no means be called the first knot. No matter what you say, there is no possibility of confusing the order of the knots—it is and always will be the sixth knot.

The Lord Buddha agreed to this, saying:—So it is, Ananda. The six knots may not all be exactly alike, but when you seek the root of their different forms, they are all arrangements of the single handkerchief. You can not confuse the single handkerchief, you may confuse the knots, their differences and order, but you can not confuse the handkerchief because it is a single whole. The same is true of your six sense-organs—they are knots tied in the essential unity of your mind and out of its unity there appears the variety.

The Lord Buddha continued:—Ananda, if you do not like to have knots tied in the handkerchief but prefer its original state, what would you do?

Ananda replied:—Noble Lord! As long as the knots exist in the handkerchief there will be the possibility of a discussion about them—which is first and which second—but when the knots are all untied, there can be no further discussion about them because they will all have disappeared and only the beautiful handkerchief will remain in its original state of oneness.

The Lord Buddha was pleased with this reply and said:—That is true, Ananda. The same is true about the relation of the six organs of sense to the Essential Mind. As the six sense-organs become freed from their contaminations, the remaining arbitrary conceptions of the discriminating mind will disappear also. It is because your mind, having become diseased and bewildered because of the false sense-conceptions accumulated since beginningless time, has developed many desires, attachments and habits. From these there have arisen, incident to the ever changing processes of life, arbitrary conceptions concerning self and not-self and as to what is true and what is not true. These arbitrary conceptions have not developed in a normal way from your pure Mind Essence, but in an abnormal way because of the prior false conceptions that had their origin in the sense-organs, like the sight of blossoms in the air that come to diseased minds. They falsely appear to have had their origin in the enlightening and Essential Mind but, in truth, they have arisen because of diseased conditions.

The same is true, also, of all conceptions, objective and component—universes, mountains, rivers, trees, sentient beings, and deaths and rebirths. Even discriminating thoughts of Mind-Essence and Nirvana, everything, all of which are nothing but phenomena analogous to blossoms seen in the air by diseased eyes and all of which have been manifested by the enslaved, bewildered and ever active, topsy-turvy mind.

Ananda then said to the Lord Buddha:—Noble Lord! If these ever-rising, changing, arbitrary conceptions of phenomena are like knots tied in a handkerchief, how can the knots be unloosed?

The Lord Tathagata took the handkerchief with the knots still tied in it and tugged at it in a blind, foolish way that only served to tighten the knots and asked Ananda if the knots could be unloosened in that way.

Ananda replied:—No, my Lord.

Then the Lord tugged at the knots in another wrong way and again asked if the knots could be unloosed in that way.

Ananda replied:—No, my Lord.

The Lord Buddha said:—I have tried now that way and now this way, but with no success in unloosening the knots. How would you untie them, Ananda?

Ananda replied:—My Lord, I would first study the knot and find out how it was tied, then it could easily be untied.

The Lord Buddha was pleased with this reply and said:—Right you are, Ananda! If you wish to untie a knot, you must first understand how it was tied. The lesson which I have been teaching you—that all things are manifested by causes and conditions—does not refer to these crude terrestrial phenomena of conformity and combination alone. but is the principle that the Tathagata has discovered from the Dharma of Emancipation which applies to both the terrestrial and transcendental worlds. For he knows the originality of all phenomena and accordingly he can make any manifestation he pleases to meet any situation or condition. He even knows each single drop of rain that falls on the sands of the River Ganges. For instance, in our presence there are all sorts of conditions—the straightness of pine trees, the crookedness of shrubs, the whiteness of storks, the blackness of magpies, etc.—the Tathagata knows the cause of each.

Therefore, Ananda, you may select any one of your six sense organs that you please, and if the bondage to that sense organ is destroyed, the arbitrary conceptions of all objects in the discriminating mind will be destroyed at the same time. Once being convinced that any single sense conception, or a thought based upon one, is unreal and fantastic, one's dependence upon sense conceptions in general is destroyed. After all the delusions of sense conceptions have been thus destroyed, there will remain only the true Essence of Mind.

Ananda! Let me ask you another question. This handkerchief has six knots tied in it. If I untie them can they all be untied at once?

No, my Lord. The knots were originally tied one by one in a certain order, so when we come to untie them we must follow the reverse order. For although the knots were made in one handkerchief, they were not made at one time and can not be untied at one time.

Again the Lord Buddha was pleased at the reply and said:—It is the same with the disentanglements of the conceptions of the six senses. The first knot of false conceptions that must be untied, is the one relating to the false conception of an ego-personality, one must first of all attain a realization of its utter non-reality. When this realization of the unreality of one's own ego-personality is perfectly attained it becomes enlightening, then the next knot to be untied is the one relating to personal attainments of any kind. This arbitrary conception must be untangled and its unreality fully realized. These two entanglements—belief in an ego-personality and the conception of personal attainment—must be utterly destroyed and never again permitted to rise to defile the true Essential Mind. This accomplishment may be called the Bodhisattva-Mahasattva's attainment of the Perseverance in the Dharma of non-rebirth through the Practice of their Samadhi.

* * *

(*NOTE. The following section is found at the close of the Sixth Chapter, where it is evidently out of place, and is inserted here, where it is more appropriate.*)

Having listened to this instruction from the Lord Buddha, Ananda rose in his place, and bowed down in profound obeisance to express both his gratitude and his sincere purpose to observe what had been said to them. He said to the Lord Buddha:—My Noble Lord! Referring to my Lord's teachings concerning the five sense-ingredients of the mind, thou hast taught us that at the base of the discriminating mind, there are five aggregates of conceptions all of which are unsubstantial and illusions, but which the mind assumes to be its own original mind. My Lord has not yet given us any detailed instruction as to how these five groups of conceptions are to be controlled under ordinary conditions. Are these sense-ingredients to be discarded at one time, or is it by gradual steps? And what are the boundary lines between the five groups? Have mercy upon us, my Lord, and instruct us clearly so that in the future we may be a guiding eye to all sentient beings in this last kalpa.

The Lord Buddha replied:—Ananda! The true Essence of the wonderful enlightening Mind is self-intuiting, perfectly accommodating, and pure. In its nature it has no such defilements as conceptions of deaths and rebirths, contaminations and taints, neither has it any such attribute as emptiness. All these are arbitrary conceptions that have arisen from prior false conceptions. But the original immaculate intuitive and enlightening Essence becomes defiled by the accumulating of these false conceptions and because of them manifests all the phenomena of the world. It is just like the insane Igratta who becoming ignorant of his true head was deceived by the shadow of a false head, which had no basis in fact and was wholly an hallucination. Upon this illusive conception he built up the causes and conditions that controlled him. So those who are ignorant of the real cause build up in their mind an imaginary cause. Even the nature of space which we think of as empty is an imaginary conception. So it is with every cause, condition and nature, it is always a mental illusion cherished by sentient beings.

Ananda! When you come to know where illusion has its rise, then you will clearly understand these universally false causes and conditions. If there are no illusions, of course, there would be no more talk about causes and conditions. And furthermore, if ignorant people had only true nature from which to make deductions, what would they have to talk about, anyway? Therefore I show you this interpretation in order to have you see clearly that at the base of the five-sense ingredients there are always false conceptions.

Ananda! Regarding your body. It is first begun by the conception of your parents, but if your karmic mind had not been in affinity with your parents' minds it would not have found lodgment in your parents' conception. As I have said, when any one thinks of vinegar, saliva immediately rises in the mouth; when one stands on the edge of a precipice, his feet begin to tremble. Therefore, Ananda, you ought to know that your present body is your first manifestation in substance of your false conceptions that have been accumulated in your karma. It may be called the first false conception of "firmness."

Again, in likeness to the trembling that comes to the feet when one stands on a lofty place, so in the presence of causes and conditions that can influence your body, there is corresponding reaction in the body. You have two kinds of conceptions always running about in your mind, a pleasant one that rises when these causes and conditions are propitious and to your advantage, and an unpleasant one that rises when the causes and conditions are disadvantageous or painful. This may be called the second false conception of "discrimination" or "knowledge."

By means of conceptions your physical body is always in bondage to the thinking mind, and this is because there is an affinity between the discriminating mind and the body. This is true of all the arbitrary conceptions of phenomena, of all manifestations of mental activities, of all the graspings of the physical body, they all react in response with the changing thoughts of the discriminating mind. For instance: when you are awakening, it simply means that you have begun to think again; when you are sleeping you dream according to some unconscious mental strain of passion that is agitating your mind. This may be called the third false conception of "accommodation" or "response" or "activity."

As the process of changes in everything is forever going on, there are secret and unconscious displacements throwing things out of balance, such as the growth of the nails, the rhythm of exhausting and expanding breathing, the wrinkling of the brow, the alternation of the days and nights, the causes of which we never bother about and never fully realize. Ananda, if all of these changes have no affinity with you, no relation to you, how is it that your body is ever responding to the corresponding changes that we call growth? Or if your body has affinity with them, why do you remain in ignorance of the reason for the affinity? The reason lies because all of these changing causes and conditions and reactions are but the shadows of the activities of your own mind and your own mind is but a shadow of Essential Mind as defiled by the mind's activities. This may be called the fourth false conception of "secrecy" and "silence."

Then by your practice of Dhyana there comes into your mind an enlightening essential point of tranquillity and stability, and you take that point of tranquillity as a permanently abiding place. If it has its location in the body, it cannot be other than the perceptions of seeing, hearing, smelling, tasting, feeling and thinking. If they are the true Essence, there would be no more falsity anywhere. But is that true? Supposing you saw some strange sight but for many years put it completely out of your mind, and then after a long time, you again saw the strange sight and it brought back to your memory all that you had seen before. Then within this tranquil Essence of Stability, does your thinking mind, which is always in activity as conditioned by its contaminations, does it have any precise account of it?

Ananda! You ought to know that this kind of limited tranquillity is not real or true. It is in likeness to the current of a deep river which, as you glance at it, seems to be quiet and motionless but in fact is steadily and relentlessly moving onward. If it does not have its source in the false conceptions of the senses, how is it that it receives all the habitual illusions? If it were not possible for your sense-organs, which had their source in the pure Essence of Mind but which had become differentiated through Ignorance, to return to their original pureness and oneness in Mind-Essence, how could these habitual illusions ever lose their existence? But now through your practice of Dhyana your sense-organs are losing their individual differences as they become increasingly merged into the pure Essence of Mind, and with this merging the habitual illusions lose their existence, also. In your present state of attainment these habitual illusions have become fine and inconspicuous, but they are not yet perfectly exterminated, so in such a state the mind will still be under a certain dependence upon the sense-organs and yet there will be times of insight and tranquillity. But this partial state of tranquillity is not the perfect state of Enlightenment for in that perfect state all dependence upon the senses is ended and with it all differentiations and discriminations that are based upon sense-conceptions will be ended also.

For instance, in our ordinary meditation before enlightenment we will often enter into it with a clear and tranquil mind, but the mind is still in a conditional state of false conceptions. This dependence upon a partial state of tranquillity as being the perfect attainment is the fifth refined and concentrated thought of "topsy-turviness" of mind.

Ananda! These five sense-ingredients are made up out of these five kinds of false conceptions. Your wish to know the boundaries of the spheres of causes is easily answered. Form and space are the boundary of sights; contact and separation are the boundaries of tangible things; remembering and forgetting are the boundaries of conceptions; appearing and disappearing (birth and death) are the boundaries of activities; false tranquillity and true tranquillity are the boundaries of consciousness.

These five sense-ingredients are developed by leaps and bounds. They are manifested by reason of consciousness, and they disappear by the discarding of sights. There is but one principle involved and may be immediately realized so the arbitrary conceptions of both principle and realization may be discarded at one and the same time, but the resultant memories of the conceptions can not be instantly discarded—they have to be gradually dissolved into emptiness by ignoring and forgetting them. I have now shown you how the knots in the kalpa handkerchief can be untangled. It should be clear to you. Do not ask again?

Now you ought to be prepared to interpret this principle, which is the source of false conceptions and is also the source of mental enlightenment, to all disciples of this latter period so as to enable them to realize the emptiness of their illusions, to develop their deep abhorrence of their own ego-personality, to understand that there is complete emancipation in Nirvana, so that they will no longer cling to this triple world of suffering.

Ananda! If any disciple should gather all the seven treasures sufficient to fill the open spaces of the ten quarters of all the universes, and offer them to all the innumerable Buddhas, and offer to them services of adoration with all his heart, what think you, Ananda? Would this disciple accumulate great merit by such an offering?

Ananda replied:—My Lord! It is impossible to comprehend the vastness of the open space of the universe, or to comprehend the amount of treasure sufficient to fill it. Once there was a disciple who acquired the rank of a great world-ruler by the gift of a few cash, how much more would be the merit to one making such an unthinkable offering of treasure to all the Buddhas of all the innumerable Buddha-lands.

The Lord Buddha said:—Ananda! The words and the instruction of all the Buddhas and Tathagatas are true and reliable, so if any Disciple should teach them to novice-disciples in the last kalpa, his sins would be annulled and would disappear with the speed of a single thought. This would be true if he had been able by only a single thought to show this Door of Dharma to a single human being, even if he had committed the four great offenses, or the ten minor offenses of a Bhikshu, or even had passed over into the hell of Avichi of this world. Yes, it would be true even if he had passed into the hells of Avichi in all the ten quarters of all the universes. His deed of merit—teaching novice disciples this door of Dharma—would change his memory of suffering in the hells of Avichi until they would seem to be memories of a happy paradise, and he would accumulate merit that would exceed the merit of the former disciple who gave the immeasurable treasure to all the Buddhas, by a hundred times, yes, by a thousand times, by myriads of times.

(NOTE. The text of the Second Chapter is now resumed.)

* * *

(Spiritual Experiences of Highest Bodhisattvas.)

Ananda and the assembly having listened to the Lord Buddha's instruction became thoroughly perfected in their intuitive intelligence and henceforth discarded all their suspicions and doubts. With one accord they bowed to the ground in humble obeisance and gratitude, saying:—Blessed Lord! This day both our bodies and minds have become transparently clear and we feel that we shall soon attain to a perfect state of freedom. Nevertheless, though we have realized thy teaching, that as soon as the six sense-organs have been liberated from their attachments and contaminations, the remaining arbitrary conceptions of the discriminating mind will disappear also, and the mind will attain to a state of perfect clarity, but we do not feel that we have as yet attained to this state of perfectly unified awareness.

Oh Blessed Lord! We have been wandering about in the desolate wilderness of this world for many kalpas, recognizing no sign of our Lord's parental love. We were as a nursing infant whose mother had left him for a time and who suddenly sees his loving mother returning to him. If we, by this extraordinary chance, should attain to Perfect Enlightenment and realize all of thy profound teachings so that they become a natural part of our minds, our own innate self-realization, then we feel it would be the same state that our Lord attained under the Bo-tree, which our Lord has not yet described to us. Pray, oh Lord, have great love for us and show us the way to thy secret and solemn Perfectness, so that we may receive it as our Lord's crowning instruction. When they had made this entreaty, they waited humbly and patiently, their devout and concentrated minds in profound tranquillity, for the Lord's final and most secret instruction.

Thereupon, the Blessed Lord revealed to the assembled highest Bodhisattva-Mahasattvas and Great Arhats free from all intoxicants, this most sacred teaching. He said:—

Honored Bodhisattva-Mahasattvas and Great Arhats! You have now been under my instruction for a long time and have attained to perfect emancipation. As an introduction to what

I am about to say, I want to enquire of each one of you as to how you attained Samadhi. When you began to realize, in the early stages of your devotion and practice, the falseness of the eighteen spheres of mentation in contact with objects by the sense organs, which one of the spheres first became thoroughly enlightened by means of which you attained to Samadhi?

The five Bhikshus, who were first converted, with Kaundinya at their head rose from their seats and bowed at the feet of the Lord Buddha and said:—When I and my four companions were at Sarnath and Kikuta, and had evidence of our Lord's enlightenment through our Lord's first sermon, we all realized the Four Noble Truths. As to the means for my first attainment of samadhi, I recall that after thou had approved my attainment of an advanced state of transcendental intelligence, my Lord Tathagata gave me the name of Aprajna (which means, "nothing is known"). It was while I was concentrating my mind in my practice of dhyana on the conception of the transcendental sound of the Dharma, that I attained my first experience of samadhi and became an Arhat.

This is my reply to my Lord's enquiry as to which one of the eighteen spheres of mentation in contact with sense organs, it was, that we arrived at samadhi. In my case it was through the mysterious sound of the Dharma.

* * *

Then Upanishad rose from his seat, bowed at the feet of the Lord Buddha and said:—Blessed Lord! I was also one of thy earliest disciples and a witness of my Lord's Enlightenment. I was in the habit of practicing meditation upon the impurity of my physical body. I became greatly disgusted with it and disliked it exceedingly. Later I realized that it is the nature of all living bodies to be impure, and that after my death my own corpse and bones would decay and then return to dust and vanish in thin air. It was by means of this realization that I attained to enlightenment and perfect emancipation, and it was the reason my Lord, after he had recognized my attainment of transcendental intelligence gave me the name of Nishad. It was because the sight of objects within my mind had all been discarded and it was by means of the realization that all sights of objects were as empty as clear space, that I attained Arhatship. As to the means by which I first attained samadhi, it was by reason of this attainment of transcendental sight and concentrating my mind on it, that I arrived at a perfect harmonization of the eighteen spheres of mentation in contact with sense-objects through the sense organs.

*　*　*

Then the boy called by the name of Gandha-prabasa-alam-kara, rose from his seat and bowed down to the Lord Buddha and said:—My Blessed Lord! One day, after I had been listening thoughtfully to thy teaching in regard to practising earnest insight into the true nature of all conditional things, I left thy presence when it was almost dark. The dining hall was quite deserted and the brothers were lighting incense before the great Altar, in the distance. Suddenly I noticed the sweet fragrance of the incense, and the thought came to me that the fragrance was neither wood, nor air, nor smoke, nor flame; when it was present it came from nowhere and when it vanished, there was no fixed place for its abode. It was by means of the insight that came to me at that time that all my arbitrary thoughts about the nature of things were discarded and I became perfectly emancipated from all attachments and contaminations. It was because of this attainment that my Lord Tathagata confirmed my attainment and gave me my name. Since then all discriminations of smells from objects have ceased and a realization of the meaning of transcendental fragrance has taken their place and has become developed and unified and mysteriously intuitional. Thus I attained to Arhatship by means of this pure insight directed toward sweet scents. As my Lord has asked us which of the sense activities was the channel for our individual accommodation and unification of the eighteen spheres of mentation in contact with sense objects, I reply that in my case, it was the attainment of perfect insight coming through the sense of smell.

*　*　*

Then Baisajagara and Baisajattama, together with their five hundred Brahmayika followers, rose from their seats and bowed down to the Lord Buddha, saying:—Blessed Lord! For many generations, we two brothers have been in a line of skilful and beneficent physicians, and during that time have tasted a vast number of different drugs, herbs, woods, metals, etc. We have learned to discriminate their different tastes—sour, bitter, salt, fresh, sweet, peppery, etc.—their different qualities in conformity and in combinations, their permanence or variability, their effect in initiating coldness or inflammation, or their action, such as poisonous or healing. After we had become thy disciples, we understood the true nature of the different discriminations of taste—neither belonging to existence nor to non-existence, neither to body nor to mind, nor independent of both body and mind. As we were meditating on the originality of all these differences in tastes, we became enlightened.

Our Lord Buddha confirmed our attainment and gave us the rank of Bodhisattva-Mahasattvas and we became princes of our Lord's Dharma in this great company of followers. As our Lord has enquired about our individual experience of perfect unification of our eighteen spheres of mentation in contact with objects through the sense-organs, ours was through the sense of taste.

* * *

Then Bhadrapala, with his sixteen personal followers all enlightened Bodhisattva-Mahasattvas, rose from their seats and bowed down to the Lord Buddha, saying:—Blessed Lord! I was first taught many aeons ago by Buddha Bhismagarjitasvararaga and was converted at that time. One day, which happened to be the bath holiday, I entered the bath and suddenly realized, through the sense of touch, the true originality of water: that it neither washed away dirtiness nor cleansed my physical body. With this insight I realized the true and essential nature of my heart and mind. With this realization, there seemed nothing abiding anywhere in existence but calmness and peacefulness. This experience remains in my consciousness even to this day. Since I have become a follower of my Lord and been reconverted by thy teachings, that early experience has continued to help me in attaining perfect emancipation from all attachments and contaminations. Because of it, my Lord approved my attainment and gave me the name of Bhadrapala, which means: "transcendental sense of touch, brightly enlightened." It was thus that I attained the permanent abidingness of a Dharma Prince. As my Lord has enquired of us as to our individual experience in first attaining perfect accommodation of the eighteen spheres of mentation in contact with sense-objects through sense-organs, I would testify that my attainment was accomplished through insight into the true originality of the sense of touch.

* * *

Then Maha-Kasyapa with the Bhikshuni Suvarna and other nuns of his spiritual family, rose from their seats and bowed down to the Lord, Buddha, saying:—Blessed Lord! In previous kalpas when Buddha Kandrasuryapradipa was living I served him faithfully and listened to his teaching and practiced it faithfully. After he passed into Nirvana, I continued to make offerings to his sacred relics and kept his image freshly gilded, so that his teaching, like a lamp, continued to illumine my life by its brightness. By my faithful reverence for his relics and his image, my mind was illumined by a purple-golden brightness that reflected itself in all my following lives and became a permanent purple-golden brightness within my body. This Bhikshuni Suvarna and her sister nuns began their practice with me in those by-gone days and have continued to be in my spiritual family ever since.

In the course of my previous lives, I gradually gained insight into the destructibility of all the six objects of sense in the Samsara world and observed their emptiness and transitoriness. I continued to practice concentration by means of this principle of the inherent emptiness and tranquillity of the essence of all things until no thought remained within my mind to disturb it. Thus, both my body and mind became emancipated from the accumulated defilements of a thousand kalpas and they disappeared as suddenly as the rap on a door. Thus I attained to Arhatship by means of the thoughts that arose from meditation upon the Dharma of Emptiness, and my Lord confirmed my attainment of enlightenment in all transcendental Truth and freedom from all the intoxicants of life, and has honored me with highest rank among his followers. As my Lord has enquired of us which one of our eighteen spheres of mentation in contact with objects through our sense-organs, it was, I would answer, it was through my meditation upon the originality of phenomena, that I first advanced toward enlightenment.

* * *

Then Anaruddha rose from his seat, bowed down to the

Lord Buddha and said:—Blessed Lord! When I first became a convert, I was inclined to sleepiness. My Lord rebuked me for the bad habit and warned me that if I continued it, I might become some kind of animal in my next birth. I took this rebuke to heart and for seven days kept my self from sleep entirely. From weeping and loss of sleep my eyes became over-wearied and I lost my sight. My Lord then taught me a better way for overcoming the bad habit and showed me how to recover my pleasant sight. From this experience I not only attained intuitive insight and enlightenment, but attained to the Diamond Samadhi, as well. Since then I have the transcendental power of seeing all the ten quarters of the universe, and I can see the spirit-essence of anything at any distance, as clearly as I see a fruit held in my hand. My Lord Tathagata recognized my attainment and confirmed my attainment of Arhatship. As my Lord has enquired of us about our personal experience in gaining perfect accommodation of the eighteen spheres of mentation in contact with objects through the sense-organs, I would testify that my first thoroughly perfect accommodation came to me through the return of sight to my sick eyes.

* * *

Then Suddhipanthaka rose from his seat and bowing down to the Lord Buddha, said:—Blessed Lord! Before I met thee, I had never recited scriptures or put their teaching into practice because my memory was very poor. After I met my Lord Buddha, I listened to his teaching and became converted. I tried to remember the teaching, even a single verse of it, by repeating it over and over even for a hundred days but failed. If I succeeded in remembering the first part, I would forget the last part, and if I remembered the last part, I would forget the first part. My Lord Tathagata took pity upon my stupidity, and taught me to sit quietly with empty and tranquil mind simply trying to regulate my in and out breathing. Since then I have always concentrated my mind on my breathing which has gradually become more and more gentle and peaceful. At the same time the defilements of my mind caused by conceptions of re-birth, continuance, change and death, gradually disappeared and my mind became enlightened. In time I acquired entire freedom from all attachments and contaminations and my mind became enlightened, so that I attained the degree of Arhat. I have since then become permanently tranquil under the influence of my Lord Buddha. Later my Lord confirmed my attainment of perfect emancipation. In reply to my Lord's enquiry, I witness that my approach to the unification of the eighteen spheres of mentation was by concentration of mind upon my in and out breathing, by reason of which I attained to perfect emptiness of thinking.

* * *

Then Gavampati rose from his seat and bowing down to the Lord Buddha, said:—Blessed Lord! Long ago in past kalpas, I made fun of holy disciples and by so doing committed the sin of blasphemy and drew upon myself the karma of chewing my cud like a cow, for many recurring lives. My Lord Tathagata in great kindness showed me the door of Dharma that leads to purity and humbleness of heart, whereby I was able to annihilate all my contaminations and arbitrary conceptions and to attain absorption in samadhi. From my long experience I was led to concentrate upon the nature of the tastes of the tongue, that they were neither a kind of matter, nor a kind of essence, and suddenly by one transcendental clearing of mind, I attained to perfect freedom from all the mind's attachments and contaminations, so that internally I was free from all arbitrary conceptions both of body and mind, and externally I was free from attachment to all worldly things, and lastly I was able to live remote from all the defilements of the triple world. I felt like a bird that had escaped from the confinement of its cage. The intuitive insight of my Dharma Eye had suddenly become purified and clear. This attainment of perfect emancipation was confirmed by my Lord Tathagata. In reply to his enquiry, I would answer, that my first thoroughly perfect accommodation of the eighteen spheres of mentation was by means of the return of my tasting faculty to its original intelligence.

* * *

Then Pilankapatha rose from his seat and bowing down to the Lord Buddha, said;—Blessed Lord! When I first tried to follow my Lord in the practice for enlightenment, I often heard his teaching that among all the world's attractions, there was nothing truly worthy of enjoyment because everything sooner or later led to suffering. One day when I was in the city begging food, with my mind fixed on the Dharma door, suddenly a poisonous point wounded my foot and my whole body throbbed with pain. This led me to remember that it was only because of sensations and perceptions that I felt pain. Although I felt the pain in my whole body, yet I was mindful that in my pure and Essential Mind there was no pain and no perception of feeling pain. I was mindful, also, that as there was only one body such as mine, how was it possible to have two different sets of feelings—pain in my foot because of the poison, and joy in my deeper mind because of my intuitive insight into the Dharma Door. Holding my mind in concentration on this question, suddenly my body and mind became empty of all arbitrary thoughts about things, and in three weeks, all attachments and contaminations vanished from my mind, and I attained the degree of Arhat, which was confirmed by my Lord when he noticed that I had advanced to perfect emancipation of mind. As my Lord has enquired of us as to our first perfect accommodation of the eighteen spheres of mentation in contact with objects through our sense-organs, I would answer that in my case, it was by the perfect unconsciousness of my physical body and my return to its primal state of perfect intuition of its intrinsic Essence of Mind.

* * *

Then Subhuti rose from his seat and bowing down to the Lord Buddha, said:—Blessed Lord! I attained to a pure state of mental freedom many kalpas ago and I recall that my rebirths have been as many as the sands of the Ganges. In this life while still in my mother's womb, I already realized the pure emptiness of Essential Mind and gradually, as I grew up, I progressively realized the pure emptiness of all the ten quarters of the universe, and there developed within my mind the wish that all sentient beings might also attain to the realization, each of his own Mind-essence. At last, through the inspiration of my Lord's teaching concerning the principle of the perfect and true emptiness of the wonderful, mysterious Mind Essence and of its highest perfect Wisdom, instantly, thereafter, I became absorbed into my Lord's gloriously radiant Ocean of Mind, so that my mind became like the mind of my Lord, sharing in a measure, his insight and his intelligence. Because of this attainment my Lord recognized my having attained to a perfect state of emancipation, that is, I had attained to the pure emptiness of Mind-Essence. In this attainment I am first among all this assembly. In reply to my Lord's enquiry, I reply, that my first thoroughly perfect accommodation of the eighteen spheres of mentation was the realization by means of the recollecting and mindfulness faculty, of the non-existence of all phenomena, by the exclusion from my thinking of all arbitrary conceptions of phenomena.

*   *   *

Then Sariputra rose from his seat and bowing down before the Lord Buddha, said:—Blessed Lord! Since many kalpas, as many as the sands of the Ganges, my mind has continued its purity and because of it, there have been many pure rebirths. As soon as my eyes perceived the differences in the ever-flowing process of changes both in this world and in the Way of Emancipation, my mind immediately understood them and, because of it, I acquired the attainment of perfect freedom. When I was on the road one day, I met the brothers Kasyapa who kindly explained the principle of the Lord's teaching—that everything rose from causes and conditions and therefore was empty and transitory—and I realized the infinitude of Pure Mind Essence. From that time I followed my Lord and my perception of mental sight became transcendental and perfectly enlightened, so that I instantly acquired an attainment of great fearlessness and confidence. Because of it I attained to the degree of Arhat and became, in fact, the first Prince of my Lord Buddha, begotten by the Lord's true words and nourished and transformed by his intrinsic Dharma. In reply to my Lord's enquiry as to our first experience of attainment, I would answer that my first thorough accommodation of the eighteen spheres of mentation in contact with objects through the sense-organs, was by reason of the transcendent brightness within my own mind whose shining beams illuminated my intelligence and reached as far as my insight could penetrate.

*   *   *

Then Samantabhadra rose from his seat and bowing down to the Lord Buddha, said:—I became a Prince of my Lord's

Dharma many long kalpas ago, and all of the innumerable
Tathagatas of the ten quarters of the universe, taught their
disciples, who had the qualifications for becoming Bodhisattva-
Mahasattvas, to practice the devotion of Samantabhadra's unceasing compassion for all sentient beings for his name's sake.
The transcendental and intrinsic hearing of my Essential Mind
became very pure and transparent, so that I could use it to
discriminate the understanding and ideas of all sentient beings.
Should there be any sentient beings in whatever quarter of
the universe—past, present or future—to develop the devotion
of Samantabhadra's unceasing compassion within his mind, I
would become aware of its vibrations through the transcendental sensitiveness of my hearing and I would thereupon ride
to them on the mysterious elephant of six tusks, in a hundred
thousand different manifestations of my likeness, at the same
time, to attend upon them each in his own place. Whatever
might be his hindrances, however deep or serious, able to appreciate my presence or not, I would be near him to lay my
hand upon his head, to give him encouragement and support,
peacefulness and comfort, so that he might accomplish his supreme attainment. As my Lord has enquired of us as to our
first attainment of accommodating our eighteen spheres of
mentation in contact with sense-objects through our sense-
organs, I would say that in my case it was through the intrinsic hearing of my Essential Mind and its spontaneous understanding and response.

* * *

Then Sandrananda rose from his seat and bowed down to
the Lord Buddha, saying:—Blessed Lord! I became a convert
under the instruction of my Lord Buddha. Since then, though
I have kept all the precepts, my mind continues in a constant
state of diffusion and I have not yet been able to attain samadhi. Consequently I have not yet acquired immunity from
the intoxicants of this world. My Lord taught brother Kaustila
and myself to concentrate attention on the tip of our nose, and
as I did this, I began to notice, after three weeks, that my in
and out breathing through the nose seemed to be like smoke
coming out of a chimney. At the same time my body and
mind became bright internally and I could see the whole world
becoming clear and transparent like a crystal ball. Later on,

the appearance of smoke coming from the nose gradually vanished and my breathing became luminous and shining. Then my mind became enlightened and I attained to a state of non-intoxication. My in and out breathing became brighter and seemed to pervade the whole universe. After that, I attained to the degree of Arhat and my Lord Buddha said that I will soon attain enlightenment. In reply to my Lord's enquiry, I would say, that my first accommodation to the eighteen spheres of mentation was through observing my in and out breathing through the nose, by reason of which, after long practice, it became bright and shining which as it developed eradicated all the intoxicants of attachment and contaminations.

* * *

Then Purna Metaluniputra rose from his seat and bowed down to the feet of the Lord Buddha, saying:—Blessed Lord! For an infinity of kalpas I have had great freedom in preaching the Dharmas of emptiness and suffering and because of it have realized my own Essence of Mind. In the course of my preaching I have interpreted profoundly and wonderfully the many Dharma Doors, with great confidence and with no feeling of fear, everywhere and before great assemblies. Because of my eloquence, my Lord has encouraged me to make use of it in propagating the Dharma by means of the wheel of my voice. Since these ancient days, since the Lord has been among us, I have offered my services in turning the Dharma Wheel, and have lately attained to the degree of Arhat by means of the development of my hearing by reason of which I am conscious of the transcendental sound of the Dharma, reverberating like the roar of a lion. Consequently, my Lord has honored me by regarding me as the greatest preacher of his Mysterious Dharma.

As my Lord has enquired of us which was our earliest accommodation of the eighteen spheres of mentation in contact with objects through sense organs, I would answer that my first thorough accommodation of mentation, was the subjugation of my internal attachments and enemies and the extermination of all intoxicants by means of the intrinsic sound of the Mysterious Dharma.

* * *

Then Uparli rose from his seat and bowed down to the Lord Buddha, saying:—Blessed Lord! I followed my Lord when he escaped from the palace and lived an ascetic life in the forest. For six years I watched him as he practiced asceticism and subjugated all Maras and heretics and exterminated all the intoxicants of worldly desires and cupidities. By the example of my Lord and by his instruction I became able to keep with purity all the Precepts, and the 3,000 rules of etiquette and the 80,000 refinements of the rules for the conduct of Buddhists, so that thereby both my body and mind became pure and tranquil, and I attained to Arhatship. I am regarded by all as the model of perfect behavior among all the Disciples.

As my Lord has enquired of us as to which was our most perfect accommodation of the eighteen spheres of mentation in contact with objects through the sense organs, I would answer that my first perfect accommodation of the eighteen spheres of mentation was the pure keeping of both my body and mind, so that my body acquired perfect health and my mind perfect intelligence.

* * *

Then the great Maudgalyayana rose from his seat and bowed down to the Lord Buddha, saying:—Blessed Lord! When I was begging on the road I met the three Kasyapa brothers who taught me the Lord Tathagata's profound principle of causes and conditions. I was greatly influenced by the teaching, and very soon acquired and realized particularly clear intelligence. My Lord was so kind as to bestow on me the true robe for my true body, my beard and head were shaved and I became a follower of my Lord. Since then my transcendental powers have become wonderfully developed, I have made visits to all the ten quarters of the universe, without hindrance by space, passing instantly from one Buddha-land to another without being conscious of how it was done. I thus attained the degree of Arhat and was accounted by all and by my Lord Tathagata as being highest among the disciples in perfect enlightenment, great purity of mind, spontaneity and fearlessness in manifestation of transcendental powers.

As my Lord has enquired of us which was our most perfect accommodation of the eighteen spheres of mentation in contact with objects through the sense organs, I would answer that my first perfect accommodation of the eighteen spheres of mentation was my mind becoming abstracted in tranquil reflection that mysteriously developed its enlightening brightness, as if my mind that had been a muddy stream had suddenly become clear and transparent like a crystal ball.

* * *

Then Ushusma with his hands pressed together, bowed in his place, and addressed the Lord Buddha, said:—Blessed Lord! I recall that in numerous past kalpas my heart was always full of lustful covetousness. At one time there was a Buddha called Akasaraga who taught that those who cherished lustful thoughts would be consumed in a burning flame. He taught me how to practice intuitive insight by reflecting upon parts of my body and skeleton and as to the susceptibility of my body to heat and cold. By this method my lustful thoughts were sublimated into burning torches of wisdom and intelligence. Since then I have been called, Ushusma, the blazing torch, and in due time I attained Arhatship owing to my samadhis radiating a blazing brightness. At that time I made a great vow that if any Bodhisattva-Mahasattva attained Buddhahood in my time, I would be his guardian knight, protecting him from all enemies and maras. As my Lord has enquired of us which was our most perfect accommodation of the eighteen spheres of mentation in contact with objects through the sense organs, I answer that my first thoroughly perfect accommodation was my keen insight into the states of coldness and warmth of my body, and the darkness and brightness of my mind by which there developed within my spirit a blazing glory of wisdom that illumined my mind until I attained my supreme enlightenment.

* * *

Then Bodhisattva-Mahasattva Dharanindhara, rose in his place and bowed at the feet of the Lord Buddha and saying:— Blessed Lord! I recollect that ages ago, when I was only a bhikshu, there appeared in the world the Tathagata Samantaprabhasa. He taught me to concentrate on the element of Earth, and I made the vow to always labor near the earth. Whenever I came to a place in the road that was too narrow or obstructed, or made impassable because of a gap, I made it my task, to widen it, clear it and to fill up the gaps, or remedy any other inconvenience that might be dangerous or cause trouble to travellers or passing carts. While I was busied with this laborious task, many Buddhas appeared and passed away. At other times, if I noticed any over-burdened, I would offer to help them carry their heavy loads, and when we reached our destination, I would lay the burden down carefully and go away without demanding any compensation. When the Buddha Vessabhu appeared there were frequent severe famines. At that time I often served as a carrier and no matter how far the distance, I never asked for more than one penny. Sometimes the cart and the ox would become mired in the muddy roads and I would use my transcendental strength to help drag the cart and thus relieve the poor ox. On one occasion the great King of the country prepared a vegetable feast in honor of Buddha Vessabhu, and I levelled the road over which he must pass in coming and waited upon him while he was there. The Buddha Vessabhu noticed me and instructed me, saying:— "First level your own mind, then every part of the earth will become level." Instantly I became enlightened and since then I have realized that the dust that made up the great earth and that made up my body were the same. I also realized that it was of the nature of dust particles not to be in contact with each other, and even when a sword cut through a body that it never came in contact with the particles of dust that made up the body. I also realized that it was an essential part of all phenomena that there was no re-birth, only an endless succession of non-rebirth. Thereby I attained Arhatship, and ever since there has been a constant advancement of attainment, until now I abide in the seat of a Bodhisattva-Mahasattva, and wherever in the ten quarters of the Universe a Buddha is to discourse on the wonderful lotus-like Dharma in his perfect insight and intelligence, I am the first to be present occupying a front seat and ready to corroborate his teaching. As my Lord has enquired of us what was our first thoroughly perfect accommodation of the eighteen spheres of mentation in contact with objects through the sense organs, that my first insight into the fact that there was no difference between the Earth Element of my body and the Earth Element of its sphere of mentation for they were both only fantastic manifestations from the Womb of Tathagata, and when my conception of their unreality was attained, my intelligence became perfectly clear and I realized supreme Enlightenment.

* * *

Then the lad Chandra-prabhasa, rose from his seat and bowed at the feet of the Lord Buddha and said:—Blessed Lord! I remember that many kalpas ago there was a Buddha named Apoyika who appeared in this world teaching all Bodhisattvas to practice concentration upon the nature of the Element Water and thus to attain Samadhi by that means. Following his instruction I meditated upon the fluidities within my body, concentrating my mind on the snivel and spittal, on the blood, the semen, the mucus, the urine, the pus exuding from sores, and my mind was filled with loathing. One day it came to me that the liquidity of the fragrant oceans in which the Fairy Isles of the Blest were immersed, were of the same essential nature as the disgusting fluids within my body. But for a long time I could not get rid of the idea of the substantial nature of my body. One day as I sat meditating in my room, a disciple of mine peeked through a crack into the room where I was seated and to his amazement it appeared to be filled with clear water with nothing else in sight. As he was an ignorant and foolish boy, he threw a broken tile into the room and ran away. When I emerged from meditation and resumed my normal consciousness, my mind was filled with a strange forboding and heartache. I mused to myself, "Why is it that I, who am released from all kinds of sickness and troublesome emotions, should suddenly be filled with forboding and heartac.e? Can it be, that I am slipping backward and am losing the attainment that I had gained?" When the boy no.iced my dejection he told me what he had seen and done. I bade him, that if ever again he peered into my room when I was absorbed in concentration of mind, and saw the same appearance of water, that he was to enter the room, pick up the broken tile, carry it out and throw it away. The boy being thus ordered, did as I said, and when I was in meditation returned and seeing the room filled with pure water, went into the room and seeing the broken tile, picked it up, went out quietly and threw it away. As I rose from my meditation and resumed my natural consciousness my mind was as calm and peaceful as ever.

But after that for a long time I never made any advancement in spiritual attainment. Aeons went by, Buddha after Buddha appearing and passing, still I continued to think of my body and never could put the idea of my self-ness out of my consciousness. After a long, long time, there appeared a Tathagata named Raga who had the transcendental power of being able to pass through mountains and oceans and any obstacle with perfect ease and freedom. From him I realized more perfectly the essential nature of my body and mind, that it was essentially like the fluidity of the Oceans of Fragrance that surrounded the Isles of the Blest. I came to realize that I had been all along throwing the broken shards of my thoughts of personality into the pure limpidity of my essential nature. From this experience and attainment, I received from my Lord the name of the Boy-Virgin, the ever Youthful One, cherishing no attachments and therefore free from all evolving conceptions, who being ever young yet was able to participate in the councils of the elders.

As my Lord has enquired of us which was our first and most thorough accommodation of the eighteen spheres of mentation in contact with objects through the sense organs, I would answer that it was by means of my concentration on the nature of the Element Water by which I came to realize the pure fluidity of my essential nature, by reason of which I have acquired the transcendental power in my states of concentration of passing through all things, to all places, in all times, and thus acquired the perseverance of non-rebirth, and accomplished my Enlightenment.

*   *   *

Then the Bodhisattva-Mahasattva Akshobhya rose from his seat and bowed to the feet of the Lord Buddha, saying:— Blessed Lord! My Lord Tathagata and I had already acquired a transcendental body of infinitude at the time, long ago during the advent of the Buddha Camatha-prabhasa. At that time I had in possession four precious pearls having the transcendental penetrating power of the Element of Fire, by reason of which everything was luminously clear to my intuitive insight, even to the farthermost Buddhalands of the most remote Universe. In the light of these magic pearls everything became as empty and transparent as pure space. Moreover, within my mind, there manifested a great mirror that was marvelously self-illuminating that radiated ten kinds of wonderful, glorious, far-reaching brightness, that illumined the ten quarters of the universes as far reaching as the infinitude of all embracing space. In this marvelous mirror were reflected all the royal continents of the Blessed and like the mingling of different colored lights, merged with my body into the pure brightness and clarity of infinite space, there being no hindrance to their entrance or passing. By this magical power, I was able to enter into all the Buddhalands and engage in all their Buddha-services of adoration with great ease and perfect accommodation. This transcendental power was due to my deep intuitive insight into the source of the Four Great Elements, by reason of which I was able to see that they were nothing but the appearing and disappearing of false imaginations, which were intrinsically as empty as pure space and with no more differentiation than pure space. And I realized that all the innumerable Buddhalands within and without the mind were of the same inconceivable purity. From this intuitive insight I consequently acquired the samadhi of perseverance of non-rebirth.

As my Lord has enquired of us which was our most thorough accommodation of the eighteen spheres of mentation in contact with objects through the sense organs, I would answer that in my case it was through my perfect intuitive insight into the infinity of open space as illumined by the Element of Fire, and by that power I attained to the highest Samadhi and the Transcendental power of Samapatti.

* * *

Then the Prince of the Lord's Dharma, Vejuria, arose from his seat and bowed down at the feet of the Lord Buddha and said:—Blessed Lord! I recall that many, many kalpas ago there appeared in the world a Buddha called Amitayus, teaching all Bodhisattva-Mahasattvas the intuitive and essential nature of the wonderful Essence of Mind, and urging them to concentrate their minds on the essential sameness of this Samsara world and all sentient beings in it, that they were all alike manifestations of the Element of Wind (or Ether) and its rhythmic-vibrations revealing and manifesting all else. In my practice of Dhyana I concentrated on this and reflected on how the great world was upheld in space, on how the great world

was kept in perpetual motion, on how my body was kept in
motion, moving and standing, on the rhythmic vibration of its
life established and maintained by breathing, upon the movement of the mind, thoughts rising and passing. I reflected upon
these various things and marvelled at their great sameness without any difference save in the rate of vibration. I realized that
the nature of these vibrations had neither any source for their
coming, nor destination for their going, and that all sentient
beings as numerous as the infinitessimal particles of dust in the
vast spaces, were each in his own way topsy-turvy balanced
vibrations, and that each and every one was obsessed with the
illusion that he was a unique creation. All sentient beings in
all the three thousand Great Chillicosms, are obsessed with this
hallucination. They are like innumerable mosquitos shut up in
a vessel and buzzing about in wildest confusion. Sometimes
they are roused to madness and pandemonium by the narrow
limits of their confinement. After meeting my Lord Buddha, I
attained to a state of intuitive realization and non-rebirth perseverance, whereupon my mind became Enlightened and I was
able to view the Buddhaland of Immovability in the Eastern
Heavens, which is the Pure Land of Buddha Amitayus. I was
acknowledged as a Prince of the Lord's Dharma and vowed to
serve all Buddhas everywhere, and because of my Enlightenment and great vow, my body and mind became perfectly
rhythmic and alive and sparkling, mingling with all other vibrations without hindrance to its perfect freedom.

As my Lord has enquired of us as to which was our first
thoroughly perfect accommodation of the eighteen spheres of
mentation in contact with objects through the sense-organs, I
will say that in my case it was through my intuitive insight
into the nature of the Element of Ether, and how by its balanced and rhythmic vibrations everything was embraced in perfect purity in the Enlightening Mind, and how concentrating
my mind upon it I attained Samadhi and in that Samadhi I
realized the perfect oneness of all the Buddhas in the purity
of the Wonderful Mind Essence, that is the Bliss-body of
Buddhahood.

* * *

Then Bodhisattva-Mahasattva Maitreya rose from his seat
and bowing down to the Lord Buddha said:—Blessed Lord! I

recall that many, many kalpas ago there was a Buddha appeared in this world called Chandra-surya-pradipa-prabhasa whom I followed as his disciple. At that time I was inclined to the worldly life and liked to associate with the nobility. The Lord Buddha, noticing it, instructed me to practice meditation concentrating my mind on its consciousness. I followed his instruction and attained samadhi. Since then I have served numberless other Buddhas using this same method and by it have now discarded all desire for worldly pleasures. By the time Buddha Dipankara appeared in the world I had attained to the supreme, wonderful, perfect Samadhi of Transcendental Consciousness. By this highest Samadhi I was conscious of infinite space, and realized that all of the Tathagata-lands whether pure or impure, existent or non-existent were nothing but the manifestation of my own mind. My Lord! Because of my perfect realization that all such skillful devices of the Tathagatas were nothing but evolvements of my own mental consciousness, the essential nature of my consciousness flowed out in innumerable manifestations of Tathagatas, and I came to be selected as the next Coming Buddha, after my Lord Shakyamuni Buddha.

As my Lord has enquired of us as to our first perfect accommodation of the eighteen spheres of mentation in contact with objects through the sense organs, I answer that my first perfect accommodation of the eighteen spheres of mentation was by my perfect realization that all the ten quarters of the universes were nothing but activities of my own consciousness. It was by that that my consciousness became perfectly enlightened and that the limits of my mind dissolved until it embraced all Reality. Forsaking all prejudices of conditional and unconditional assertions and denials, I acquired perfect nonbirth perseverance.

*   *   *

Then Maha-sthama-prapta, Prince of the Lord's Dharma, rose from his seat and bowed down to the feet of the Lord Buddha, together with the fifty-two members of his Brotherhood of Bodhisattva-Mahasattvas, and said:—Blessed Lord! I recall that in a past kalpa long ago, as many kalpas ago as there are grains of sand in the river Ganges, there appeared in this world a Buddha called, Amitabha-prabhasa Buddha, whose

Buddha-land was in the Eastern Heavens. In that kalpa there were twelve Tathagatas followed each other in close succession, the last one being called Buddha Chandra-surya-gomin, who taught me to practice meditation upon the name of Amitabha, saying: *Namo-Armitabha-Buddhaya.* The value of this practice lay in this: So long as one person practices his own method and another practices a different method, they balance off each other and meeting it is just the same as not meeting. Whereas if two persons practise the same method their mindfulness would become deeper and deeper, and they would remember each other and develop affinites for each other life after life. It is the same with those who practice concentrating on the name of Amitabha—they develop within their minds Amitabha's spirit of compassion toward all sentient life. Moreover, whoever recites the name of Amitabha Buddha, whether in the present time, or in future time, will surely see the Buddha Amitabha and never become separated from him. By reason of that association, just as one associating with a maker of perfumes becomes permeated with the same perfumes, so he will become perfumed by Amitabha's compassion, and will become enlightened without any other expedient means.

Blessed Lord! My devotion to reciting the name of Amitabha had no other purpose than to return to my original nature of purity and by it I attained to the state of non-rebirth perseverance. Now in this life, I have vowed to teach my disciples to concentrate their minds by means of reciting the name of Amitabha (*Namo-Amitabha-Buddhaya*), and also I teach them to wish to be born in his Land of Purity and to make that their only Refuge.

As my Lord has asked us which is our first perfect accommodation of the eighteen spheres of mentation in contact with objects through the sense organs, I answer that my first perfect accommodation of the eighteen spheres of mentation, was that I recognized no separation or differences among my six senses, but merge them into one transcendental sense from which arises the purity of Transcendental Wisdom, by reason of which I attained highest Samadhi and the graces of Samapatti.

* * *

Then the Bodhisattva-Mahasattva Avalokitesvara rose from his seat and bowing down to the Lord Buddha said:—Blessed

Lord! I recall that ages ago, as numerous as the sands of the river Ganges, that there was present in the world a Buddha called Avalokitesvara by whose instruction I was encouraged to begin seeking Enlightenment. I was taught to begin practising by concentrating my mind on the true nature of Transcendental hearing, and by that practice I attained samadhi. As soon as I had advanced to the stage of Entering the Stream, I determined to discard all thoughts discriminating as to where I was or had been. Later I discarded the conception of advancing altogether, and the thought of either activity or quietness in this connection did not again arise in my mind. Continuing my practice, I gradually advanced until all discrimination of the hearing nature of my self-hood and of the intrinsic Transcendental Hearing was discarded. As there ceased to be any grasping in my mind for the attainment of intrinsic hearing, the conception of Enlightenment and enlightened nature were all absent from my mind. When this state of perfect Emptiness of Mind was attained, all arbitrary conceptions of attaining to Emptiness of Mind and of enlightened nature, were discarded. As soon as all arbitrary conceptions of rising and disappearing of thoughts were completely discarded, the state of Nirvana was clearly realized. Then, all of a sudden, my mind became transcendental to both celestial and terrestrial worlds and there was nothing in all the ten quarters but empty space, and in that state I acquired two wonderful Transcendencies. The first was a Transcendental Consciousness that my mind was in perfect conformity with the Essential, Mysterious Enlightening Mind of all the Buddhas in all the ten quarters, and also it was in like perfect conformity with the Great Heart of Compassion of all the Buddhas. The second transcendency was that my mind was in perfect conformity with the minds of all sentient beings of the Six Realms and felt with them the same earnestness and longing for deliverance.

Blessed Lord! Because of my adoration for that Buddha Avalokitesvara, he taught me how to attain the Diamond Samadhi by the single method of concentrating my mind upon Transcendental Hearing. And moreover, he helped me to attain the same compassionate capacity that all the Tathagatas had, by reason of which I attained the thirty-two kinds of transformations that are instantaneously available in response to the

prayers for deliverance from any part of the world at any time.
. . . .

These transformations have all been attained and exercised
with perfect freedom and spontaneity in the mysterious Diamond Samadhi which I had attained by concentrating my mind
in the practice of Dhyana on the nature of Transcendental
Hearing.

Blessed Lord! I have also, because of the mysterious powers
that accompany the Diamond Samadhi and because of my being in perfect conformity and with the same earnestness and
longing for deliverance with all sentient beings, in the Six
Realms of all the ten quarters of all the universes, past, present and future, been able to bestow upon all sentient beings
the same Fourteen kinds of Fearlessness, which animate my
own mind. . . . .

As my attainment to the original nature of perfect accommodation is wonderfully developed from the hearing organ to
include all the sense organs and discriminating mind, my body
and mind profoundly and mysteriously embrace all the phenomenal world, so that if any disciple should recite my name,
his blessing and merit would be like and equal to that of any
Prince of the Lord's Dharma, whether he uses the same name or
some other name. Blessed Lord! The reason why their merit
is like and equal for one to recite my name, and for another to
recite some other name, is because of my practice of Dhyana by
which I acquired the True and Perfect Accommodation.

Blessed Lord! This is what is meant by the Fourteen kinds
of Fearlessness of Powers of Deliverance which bring blessing to
all sentient beings. But in addition to the acquirement of perfect accommodation by means of my attainment of Supreme
Enlightenment, I have also acquired another Four Kinds of
Inconceivable, Wonderful Transcendencies of Spontaneity.

The First is as it is because when I first attained to my
Transcendental Hearing my mind became abstracted into its
essential nature, and all the natural powers of hearing, seeing,
smelling, tasting, touching and understanding attained to a state
of pure, glorious, Enlightenment of perfect, mutuality and accommodation in one perfect unity of Awareness. Because of

this, I have acquired this great Transcendental Freedom, so that when I give deliverance to sentient beings, I can transform myself into wonderful appearances, and besides I can utter innumerable, mysterious, Dharanis. . . . .

Sometimes I appear in a form of kindness, or in a form of justice, or in a state of concentration, or in a state of intelligence. But in all, I do it for the sake of deliverance and protection of sentient beings so that they might acquire a like Great Freedom.

The Second inconceivable, wonderful Transcendency of Spontaneity is as it is because of my emancipation of hearing and thinking from the contaminations of the six sense-objects. It is as if sound were passing through walls without any hindrance. Thus I can skillfully transform into different kinds of appearances and recite different Dharanis, and can transform these appearances and recitation of Dharanis to give the Transcendental Power of Fearlessness to sentient beings. Thus in all the countries of the ten quarters I am known as the Giver of Transcendental Power of Fearlessness.

The Third inconceivable, wonderful Transcendency of Spontaneity is as it is because of my practice upon the pure, original Essence of perfect Accommodation, so that wherever I go, I lead sentient beings to willingness to sacrifice their lives and valuable possessions in order to pray for my compassion and mercy.

The Fourth inconceivable, wonderful Transcendency of Spontaneity is as it is because of my acquirement of the Buddha's Intrinsic Mind and because of my attainment of the supremacy so that I can give all different kinds of offerings to all of the Tathagatas of all the ten quarters of the universes.

As my Lord has enquired of us as to what was our first perfect accommodation of the eighteen spheres of mentation in contact with objects through the sense organs, I answer that my first perfect accommodation was when I attained to the state of perfectly accommodating reflection of Samadhi by means of my Intrinsic Hearing and Transcendental Mental Freedom from objective contaminations, so that my mind became abstracted and absorbed into the Divine Stream and thus acquired the Diamond Samadhi and attained Enlightenment.

Blessed Lord! In those far off days, my Lord the Buddha Avalokitesvara, praised me for my skillful acquirement of the

all-accommodating Door of Dharma, and in one of his great
Assemblies, he announced that I, too, should be called Avalokitesvara, The Hearer and Answerer of Prayer, the Bodhisattva
of Tenderest Compassion. As such my transcendental Hearing
reaches to the ten quarters of all the universes, and the name
of Avalokitesvara prevails over all extremes of human suffering
and danger.

* * *

(Manjusri's Summation)

Thereupon the Blessed Lord, sitting upon his throne in the
midst of the Tathagatas and highest Bodhisattva-Mahasattvas
from all the Buddha-lands, manifested his Transcendent Glory
surpassing them all. From his hands and feet and body radiated
supernal beams of light that rested upon the crowns of each
Tathagata, Bodhisattva-Mahasattva, and Prince of the Dharma,
in all the ten quarters of all the universes, in number more
numerous than the finest particles of dust. Moreover, from the
hands and feet and bodies of all the Tathagatas, Bodhisattva-
Mahasattvas and Princes of the Lord's Dharma, in all the ten
quarters of the universes, went forth rays of glorious brightness
that converged upon the crown of the Lord Buddha and upon
the crowns of all the Tathagatas, Bodhisattva-Mahasattvas and
Arhats present in the assembly. At the same time all the trees
of the Jeta Park, and all the waves lapping on the shores of its
lakes, were singing the music of the Dharma, and all the inter-
secting rays of brightness were like a net of splendor set with
jewels and over arching them all. Such a marvelous sight had
never been imagined and held them all in silence and awe. Unwittingly they passed into the blissful peace of the Diamond
Samadhi and upon them all there fell like a gentle rain the
soft petals of many different colored lotus blossoms—blue and
crimson, yellow and white—all blending together and being reflected into the open space of heaven in all the tints of the
spectrum. Moreover, all the differentiations of mountains and
seas and rivers and forests of the Saha World blended into
one another and faded away leaving only the flower-adorned
unity of the Primal Cosmos, not dead and inert but alive with
rhythmic life and light, vibrant with transcendental sounds of
songs and rhymes, melodiously rising and falling and merging
and then fading away into silence.

Then the Lord Tathagata addressed Manjusri, Prince of the Dharma, saying:—Manjusri! You have now heard what these Bodhisattva-Mahasattvas of greatest and highest attainments have testified regarding the expedient means that were involved, and the results seen in spiritual graces and powers of Samapatti, that followed in their devout lives and practices. Each one stated that the beginning was seen in the perfect accommodation of some one mental sphere in contact with its sense object, and from that followed the perfect accommodation of all the spheres of mentation and the attainment of Samadhi, Samapatti, and the perfect awareness of their Intuitive and Essential Mind. So we see that their devotions and practices, in spite of their variations, all eventuated in the same good result irrespective of their attainments and the times involved.

I want Ananda to fully understand and realize these different attainments of enlightenment and note which of them is adapted to him. And I wish, also, that after my Nirvana, as future disciples of this world wish to attain highest Anuttara-Samyak-Sambodhi, that from these experiences they may know which door of expedient means appears to each most easily entered.

Having listened to the kind instruction of the Blessed Lord, Manjusri, Prince of the Lord's Dharma, rose from his seat, bowed down to the Lord Buddha and, sobered by the influence of the Lord's profound dignity, uttered the following stanzas:—

* * *

The Nature of Enlightening Intuition—wide as the oceans—is perfectly limpid and accommodating, and this Enlightening Intuition of perfect accommodation is profound and inconceivably mysterious.

* * *

As soon as this original and perfectly limpid and all embracing Enlightening Intuition becomes reflected upon objects, it becomes illusive and loses its true Nature. Then as differentiations are manifested, space fantastically appears and by means of space, whole universes come into manifestation. Arbitrary conceptions seem to corroborate the existence of the universes and finally, that which becomes perceptive and sensible of the universe becomes regarded as a sentient being having an ego-personality.

* * *

The conception of empty space as existing in the Enlightening Nature of Mind Essence is but foam tossed about by the waves of a great sea. As it is under the conditions of this transient foam that the innumerable conceptions of universes and all that appertains to them which belongs to the intoxicant nature of sentient beings exists, as soon as this foam disappears, there is no more space and hence no more universes and all the three realms of sentient life, body, mind and ego-personality, vanish into nothingness.

* * *

As sentient beings wish to return to their origin where their nature will be in perfect unity there are many different ways that may be used as expedient means for attaining it. But there is one way, no matter what the conditions for practicing it may be—difficult or not difficult—that is available to all, that is accommodating to all, that, though the period of practicing may vary with different disciples, is sure to bring them to the goal. It is the Noble Path of the Blessed One that leads to the perfect Intuition of Samadhi.

* * *

Since the perception of sight and the arbitrary conceptions of sight in the novice's mind are entangled with the phenomena of objects of sight, he can seldom see things clearly and truly no matter how comprehensive and bright his thinking mind may be. It will always be difficult for him to seek perfect accommodation through the sense of sight.

* * *

Moreover, since the novice is easily attached to the sound of words, to a refined style of composition and speaking, to nice distinctions of meaning, he will find it difficult to realize the principle that one intrinsic unity embraces all phenomena, so how can he hope to attain by the sound of words, the essential nature of perfect accommodation?

* * *

The phenomena of fragrance and the smelling sensation are perceived by means of the conception of smelling so when the sensation and the perception are separated there can be no conception of fragrance. Since the novice does not realize the permanency of his intrinsic smelling nature, it will be difficult for him to attain the essential nature of perfect accommodation through the sense of smelling.

* * *

The quality of taste is not lasting, it exists only as we use it. So long as the novice makes distinctions of taste and does not realize the permanency of his intrinsic tasting nature, there is little ground for him to hope to attain the essential nature of perfect accommodation by means of his sense of taste.

* * *

Feeling arises from the contact of the body with something; when there is no contact there is no feeling. Since the novice finds it difficult to keep his mind unperturbed by contacts and does not realize the permanency of his intrinsic feeling nature, there is little ground for him to expect to attain the essential nature of perfect accommodation by means of the feeling faculty.

* * *

As soon as one admits conceptions of objects into his mind, there is the assumption that the objects exist. Since the novice does not realize that both cause and effect of existence go along with his discriminating nature, so there is little ground for him to hope to attain the nature of perfect accommodation by means of discriminative thinking.

* * *

Every novice has seen his essential nature but has not realized it. It is as though he saw the front only and failed to see the back, thus seeing only one half of the universe. There is little ground for him to expect to attain the essential nature of perfect accommodation by looking at the appearance of things.

* * *

Breathing is a spontaneous activity of the organism but it is conditioned by moods and emotions. The novice has not attained to a refined state of in and out breathing because the mind and the breathing are not yet united into an evenly balanced state of tranquillity which is difficult to attain so it will be difficult for him to attain the essential nature of perfect accommodation by merely concentrating his mind on his in and out breathing.

* * *

As the tongue of a novice is just like that of any other human being his sense of taste lasts only as long as he experiences the taste and when the taste disappears his consciousness of it dependent upon the tongue disappears with it, hence there is little ground for him to hope to attain the nature of perfect accommodation by means of the sense of taste.

* * *

As the novice develops his sense of feeling when in contact with something consciousness is dependent upon the body and disappears when separated from it. Consequently the feeling and not-feeling of his body do not belong to the Intuition of Perfect Accommodation, because the sphere of feeling and not-feeling and the capacity to feel can not be abstracted for separate realization. So there is no ground for one to hope to attain the essential nature of perfect accommodation by means of the sense of touch.

* * *

As the organ of the discriminating mind is filled with conflicting thoughts, the novice cannot know his own transparent and tranquil mind, and since his conflicting thoughts cannot entirely be gotten rid of, there is no ground for him to hope to attain the essential nature of perfect accommodation by means of his thinking mind.

* * *

As the consciousness dependent upon the eyes exists by means of the eye-organ, its sensations, and its consciousness of sight, when we come to examine its originality, there is no ground for confidence in it. And since the novice cannot prove to himself its validity, there is no ground for hope from the sense of sight for him to attain the essential nature of perfect accommodation.

* * *

The hearing nature of the Essential Mind reaches to all the ten quarters of the universes and is the source of some of the great Transcendental Powers, but since the novice has not attained to these transcendental powers, there is no ground for him to hope to attain the essential nature of perfect accommodation by means of his hearing nature.

* * *

In the practice of Dhyana, many novices seek concentration of mind by fixing attention on the tip of the nose, but as this is only a temporary means that is useful to some drifting and confused minds, it can never be relied upon as a permanent means for attaining the nature of perfect accommodation.

* * *

If a novice reflects upon the Four Great Elements beginning with Earth, his mind will always think of hardness and impenetrability which is simply conditional reflection and not enlightenment from his intuitive mind, so there is no reason for him to seek to attain the essential nature of perfect accommodation by that means.

* * *

If a novice disciple meditates upon the Element of Water, his mind will always be thinking of fluidity and impermanence which are simply relational reflections and not enlightenment from his intuitive mind, and since he is not free from the nature of water himself, it can not be the expedient means for him to practice concentration upon it expecting thereby that he will attain the essential nature of perfect accommodation.

* * *

If the novice meditates upon the Element of Fire, he simply comes to regard it with disgust and tries to avoid it.

Since he is not free from the nature of fire himself, it can not be the expedient means for him to practice concentration upon it expecting that thereby he will attain the essential nature of perfect accommodation.

*   *   *

If the novice disciple meditates upon the universal nature of the Element of Wind, his reflections can not be free from thoughts of the relativity of motion and rest; as his mind is occupied by thoughts of these relations, it cannot be supreme Enlightenment. How can it be that he can attain the essential nature of perfect accommodation by such means?

*   *   *

If a novice disciple meditates upon the notion of pure Space, his reflections will naturally become thin and hazy. Such reflections can not be of the nature of Enlightenment. How can it be said that he can attain the essential nature of perfect accommodation by such means?

*   *   *

If the novice disciple meditates upon the nature of consciousness, his reflections will partake of the nature of impermanence as his thoughts rise and pass away and become unreal and fantastic. How can it be said that he can attain to the essential nature of perfect accommodation by such means?

*   *   *

If the novice disciple meditates upon the teaching that all things are impermanent, then his reflections will belong to the cycle of deaths and rebirths. Thus the subject of his reflections will not be in conformity with the permanence of True Enlightenment. How can he ever attain the essential nature of perfect accommodation by such means?

*   *   *

There are sermons that are given without the sounds of words that are enlightening to those advanced disciples whose minds have been disciplined in previous lives, but which are useless to novices who are dependent upon words and definitions and style to keep up their interest; the novice can not depend upon them for his attaining the essential nature of perfect accommodation.

* * *

The keeping of the Precepts is a necessary part of the practice of Dhyana, but the novice can not depend upon them alone to bring him to the nature of perfect accommodation.

* * *

The seeds of Transcendental Powers are planted in previous lives, so the novice can not attain them in this life. The reason for this is because he is always making discriminations about phenomena in his consciousness dependent upon the thinking mind and as soon as he recollects any phenomena his mind becomes perturbed, so there is no chance of his attaining the essence of the nature of perfect accommodation by means of Transcendental Powers.

* * *

Just because the discriminating and thinking mind is temporarily peaceful because of fortuitous circumstances, it does not follow that its transient peace is the basic and permanent peace of the perfect accommodation of the pure mind essence.

* * *

Then Manjusri addressed the Lord Buddha, saying:— Blessed Lord! Since my Lord has descended from the Deva Realms to this Saha World, he has helped us most by his wonderful enlightening Teaching. At first we receive this Teaching through our sense of hearing, but when we are fully able to realize it, it becomes ours through a Transcendental and Intuitive Hearing. This makes the awakening and perfecting of a Transcendental Faculty of Hearing of very great importance to every novice. As the wish to attain Samadhi deepens in the mind of any disciple, he can most surely attain it by means of his Transcendental Organ of Hearing.

For many a kalpa—as numerous as the particles of sand in the river Ganges—Avalokitesvara Buddha, the hearer and answerer of prayer, has visited all the Buddha-lands of the ten quarters of the universe and has acquired Transcendental Powers of boundless Freedom and Fearlessness and has vowed to emancipate all sentient beings from their bondage and suffering. How sweetly mysterious is the Transcendental Sound of Avalokitesvara! It is the pure Brahman Sound. It is the subdued murmur of the sea-tide setting inward. Its mysterious Sound brings liberation and peace to all sentient beings who in their distress are calling for aid; it brings a sense of permanency to those who are truly seeking the attainment of Nirvana's Peace.

* * *

While I am addressing my Lord Tathagata, he is hearing, at the same time, the transcendental Sound of Avalokitesvara. It is just as though, while we are in the quiet seclusion of our Dhyana practice, there should come to our ears the sound of the beating of drums. If our minds, hearing the sounds, are undisturbed and tranquil, this is the nature of perfect accommodation.

* * *

The body develops feeling by coming in contact with something, and the sight of eyes is hindered by the opaqueness of objects, and similarly with the sense of smell and of taste, but it is different with the discriminating mind. Thoughts are rising and mingling and passing. At the same time it is conscious of sounds in the next room and sounds that have come from far away. The other senses are not so refined as the sense of hearing; the nature of hearing is the true reality of Passability.

* * *

The essence of sound is felt in both motion and silence, it passes from existent to non-existent. When there is no sound, it is said there is no hearing, but that does not mean that hearing has lost its preparedness. Indeed! When there is no sound, hearing is most alert, and when there is sound the hearing nature is least developed. If any disciple can be freed from these two illusions of appearing and disappearing, that is, from death and rebirth, he has attained the true reality of Permanency.

* * *

Even in dreams when all thinking has become quiescent, the hearing nature is still alert. It is like a mirror of enlightenment that is transcendental of the thinking mind because it is beyond the consciousness sphere of both body and mind. In this Saha world, the doctrine of intrinsic, Transcendental Sound may be spread abroad, but sentient beings as a class remain ignorant and indifferent to their own Intrinsic Hearing. They respond only to phenomenal sounds and are disturbed by both musical and discordant sounds.

* * *

Notwithstanding Ananda's wonderful memory, he was not able to avoid falling into an evil way. He has been adrift on a merciless sea. But if he will only turn his mind away from the drifting current of thoughts, he may soon recover the sober wiseness of Essential Mind. Ananda! Listen to me! I have ever relied upon the teaching of the Lord Buddha to bring me to the indescribable Dharma Sound of the Diamond Samadhi. Ananda! You have sought the secret lore from all the Buddha-lands without first attaining emancipation from the desires and intoxications of your own contaminations and attachments, with the result that you have stored in your memory a vast accumulation of worldly knowledge and built up a tower of faults and mistakes.

* * *

You have learned the Teachings by listening to the words of the Lord Buddha and then committing them to memory. Why do you not learn from your own self by listening to sound of the Intrinsic Dharma within your own Mind and then practicing reflection upon it? The perception of Transcendental Hearing is not developed by any natural process under the control of your own volition. Some time when you are reflecting upon your Transcendental Hearing, a chance sound suddenly claims your attention and your mind sets it apart and discriminates it and is disturbed thereby. As soon as you can ignore the phenomenal sound the notion of a Transcendental Sound ceases and you will realize your Intrinsic Hearing.

* * *

As soon as this one sense perception of hearing is returned to its originality and you clearly understand its falsity, then the mind instantly understands the falsity of all sense perceptions and is at once emancipated from the bondage of seeing, hearing, smelling, tasting, touching and thinking, for they are all alike illusive and delusive visions of unreality, and all the three great realms of existence are seen to be what they truly are, imaginary blossoms in the air.

* * *

As soon as the deceiving perception of hearing is emancipated, then all objective phenomena disappear and your Intuitive Mind of Essence becomes perfectly pure. As soon as you have attained to this Supreme Purity of Mind-Essence, its Intrinsic Brightness will shine out spontaneously and in all directions and, as you are sitting in tranquil dhyana, the mind will be in perfect conformity with Pure Space.

* * *

Ananda! As you return to the phenomenal world, it will seem like a vision in a dream. And your experience with the maiden Pchiti will seem like a dream, and your own body will lose its solidity and permanency. It will seem as though every human being, male and female, was simply a manifestation by some skillful magician of a manikin all of whose activities were under his control. Or each human being will seem like an automatic machine that once started goes on by itself, but as soon as the automatic machine loses its motive power, all its activities not only cease but their very existence disappears.

* * *

So it is with the six sense organs, which are fundamentally dependent upon one unifying and enlightening spirit, but which by ignorance have become divided into six semi-independent compositions and conformities. Should one organ become emancipated and return to its originality, so closely are they united in their fundamental originality, that all the other organs would immediately cease their activities also. And all worldly impurities will be purified by a single thought and you will attain to the wonderful purity of perfect Enlightenment. Should there remain some minute contamination of ignorance, you should practice the more earnestly until you attain to per-

fect Enlightenment, that is, to the Enlightenment of a
Tathagata.

* * *

All the Brothers in this Great Assembly, and you too, Ananda, should reverse your outward perception of hearing and
listen inwardly for the perfectly unified and intrinsic sound of
your own Mind-Essence, for as soon as you have attained perfect accommodation, you will have attained to Supreme
Enlightenment.

* * *

This is the only way to Nirvana, and it has been followed
by all the Tathagatas of the past. Moreover, it is for all the
Bodhisattva-Mahasattvas of the present and for all in the future if they are to hope for Perfect Enlightenment. Not only
did Avalokitesvara attain Perfect Enlightenment in long ages
past by this Golden Way, but in the present, I also, am one
of them.

* * *

My Lord enquired of us as to what expedient means each
one of us had employed to follow this Noble Path to Nirvana.
I bear testimony that the means employed by Avalokitesvara is
the most expedient means for all, since all other means must
be supported and guided by the Lord Buddha's Transcendental
Powers. Though one forsake all his worldly engagements, yet
he cannot always be practicing by these various means; they
are special means suitable for junior and senior disciples, but
for laymen, this common method of concentrating the mind on
its sense of hearing, turning it inward by this Door of Dharma
to hear the Transcendental Sound of his Essential Mind, is
most feasible and wise.

* * *

Oh Blessed Lord! I am bowing down before my Lord
Tathagata's Intrinsic Womb, which is immaculate and ineffable
in its perfect freedom from all contaminations and taints, and
I am praying my Lord to extend his boundless compassion for
the sake of all future disciples, so that I may continue to teach
Ananda and all sentient beings of this present kalpa, to have
faith in this wonderful Door of Dharma to the Intrinsic Hear-

ing of his own Mind Essence, so surely to be attained by this most expedient means. If any disciple should simply take this Intuitive Means for concentrating his mind in Dhyana Practice on this organ for Transcendental Hearing, all other sense organs would soon come into perfect harmony with it, and thus, by this single means of Intrinsic Hearing, he would attain perfect accommodation of his True and Essential Mind.

(Importance of Keeping the Precepts.)

Then Ananda and all the great assembly were purified in body and mind. They acquired a profound understanding and a clear insight into the nature of the Lord Buddha's Enlightenment and experience of highest Samadhi. They had confidence like a man who was about to set forth on a most important business to a far-off country, because they knew the route to go and to return. All the disciples in this great assembly realized their own Essence of Mind and purposed, henceforth, to live remote from all worldly entanglements and taints, and to live continuously in the pure brightness of the Eye of Dharma.

Then Ananda, rising in the midst of the assembly, straightened his robe, with the palms of his hands pressed together, knelt before the Lord Buddha. In the depths of his nature he was already enlightened and his heart was filled with happiness and compassion for all sentient beings and, especially, did he desire to benefit them by his newly acquired wisdom. He addressed the Lord Buddha, saying:—Oh my Lord of Great Mercy! I have now realized the True Door of Dharma for the attainment of Enlightenment, and have no more doubt about its being the only Door to Perfect Enlightenment. My Lord has taught us that those who are only starting the practice of Bodhisattvaship and have not yet delivered themselves, but who already wish to deliver others, that this is a sign of Bodhisattvaship. And when those who have attained Enlightenment have a deep purpose to enlighten others, that this is a sign of the Lord Tathagata's descent from the Pure Land for the deliverance of all the world. Although I have not yet delivered myself, I already wish to deliver all sentient beings of this present kalpa. Noble Lord! Sentient beings of this age and world are gradually becoming more and more alienated from my Lord's favor, and the propagation of heretical teachings, deceiving people and leading them astray, more and more flourishes. I want to persuade them to concentrate their minds in dhyana for the attainment of Samadhi. What can I do to help them arrange a True Altar to Enlightenment within their minds so that they may be kept far away from all deceiving temptations and in whose progress there shall be no retrogression or discouragement in the attainment of Enlightenment?

In response to this appeal, the Blessed One addressed the assembly:—Ananda has just requested me to teach how to arrange a True Altar of Enlightenment to which sentient beings of this last kalpa may come for deliverance and protection. Listen carefully as I explain it to you.

Ananda and all in this assembly! In explaining to you the rules of the Vinaya, I have frequently emphasized three good lessons, namely, (1) the only way to keep the Precepts is first to be able to concentrate the mind; (2) by keeping the Precepts you will be able to attain Samadhi; (3) by means of Samadhi one develops intelligence and wisdom. Having learned these three good lessons, one has gained freedom from the intoxicants and hindrances.

Ananda, why is concentration of mind necessary before one can keep the Precepts? And why is it necessary to keep the Precepts before one can rightly practice dhyana and attain Samadhi? And why is the attainment of Samadhi necessary before one may attain true intelligence and wisdom? Let me explain this to you. All sentient beings in all the six realms of existence are susceptible to temptations and allurements. As they yield to these temptations and allurements, they fall into and become fast bound to the recurring cycles of deaths and rebirths. Being prone to yield to these temptations and allurements, one must, in order to free himself from their bondage and their intoxication, concentrate his whole mind in a resolution to resist them to the uttermost. The most important of these allurements are the temptations to yield to sexual thoughts, desires and indulgence, with all their following waste and bondage and suffering. Unless one can free himself from this bondage and these contaminations and exterminate these sexual lusts, there will be no escape from the following suffering, nor hope of advancement to enlightenment and peacefulness. No matter how keen you may be mentally, no matter how much you may be able to practice dhyana, no matter to how high a degree of apparent samadhi you may attain, unless you have wholly annihilated all sexual lusts, you will ultimately fall into the lower realms of existence. In these lower Mara realms of existence there are three ranks of evil ones:—the Mara king, evil demons, and female fiends, and all of them have each his and her own double who disguise themselves as "angels of light" who have attained supreme Enlightenment.

After my Parinirvana, in the last kalpa of this world, there will be plenty of all these kinds of evil spirits everywhere. Some of them will beset you openly with avarice and concupiscence and others of them will pose as holy and learned masters. No one will escape their machinations to lure them into the swamps of defilement and thus to lose the Path to Enlightenment. Therefore, Ananda, and all of you, should persistently teach the people of this world to attain perfect concentration of mind, so that they may be enabled to keep the precept of purity and thus be able to practice dhyana successfully and attain Samadhi. This is the clear teaching of all the Blessed Buddhas of the past, and it is my instruction at the present and it will be the instruction of all Tathagatas of the future.

Therefore, Ananda, a man who tries to practice dhyana without first attaining control of his mind is like a man trying to bake bread out of a dough made of sand; bake it as long as he will, it will only be sand made a little hot. It is the same with sentient beings, Ananda. They can not hope to attain Buddhahood by means of an indecent body. How can they hope to attain the wonderful experience of Samadhi out of bawdiness? If the source is indecent, the outcome will be indecent; there will ever be a return to the never-ending recurrence of deaths and rebirths. Sexual lust leads to multiplicity; control of mind and Samadhi leads to enlightenment and the unitive life of Buddhahood. Multiplicity leads to strife and suffering; control of mind and dhyana leads to the blissful peace of Samadhi and Buddhahood.

Inhibition of sexual thoughts and annihilation of sexual lusts is the path to Samadhi, and even the conception of inhibiting and annihilating must be discarded and forgotten. When the mind is under perfect control and all indecent thoughts excluded, then there may be a reasonable expectation for the Enlightenment of the Buddhas. Any other teaching

than this is but the teaching of the evil Maras. This is my
first admonition as to keeping the Precepts.

The next important hindrance and allurement is the tendency of all sentient beings of all the six realms of existence
to gratify their pride of egoism. To gain this one is prone to
be unkind, to be unjust and cruel, to other sentient beings.
This tendency lures them into the bondage of deaths and rebirth, but if this tendency can be controlled they will no longer
be lured into this bondage for right control of mind will enable
them to keep the Precept of kindness to all animate life. The
reason for practicing dhyana and seeking to attain Samadhi is
to escape from the suffering of life, but in seeking to escape
from suffering ourselves, why should we inflict it upon others?
Unless you can so control your minds that even the thought
of brutal unkindness and killing is abhorrent, you will never be
able to escape from the bondage of the world's life. No matter
how keen you may be mentally, no matter how much you may
be able to practice dhyana, no matter to how high a degree of
Samadhi you may attain, unless you have wholly annihilated
all tendency to unkindness toward others, you will ultimately
fall into the realms of existence where the evil ghosts dwell.

There are three ranks of these ghosts:—the highest are the
mighty ghosts, the next are the Yaksha ghosts who fly in the
air, and the lowest are the Raksha ghosts that live under the
earth. Each of these ghosts has his double that disguises itself
as having attained enlightenment. After my Parinirvana in
the last kalpa these different kinds of ghosts will be encountered everywhere deceiving people and teaching them that they
can eat meat and still attain enlightenment. But how can any
faithful follower of the Lord Tathagata kill sentient life and
eat the flesh?

You of this great assembly ought to appreciate that those
human beings who might become enlightened and attain Samadhi, because of eating meat, can only hope to attain the
rank of a great Raksha and until the end of their enjoyment
of it must sink into the never ceasing round of deaths and rebirths. They are not true disciples of Buddha. If they kill sentient beings and eat the flesh, they will not be able to escape
from this triple world. Therefore, Ananda, next to teaching the
people of the last kalpa to put away all sexual lust, you must
teach them to put an end to all killing and brutal cruelty.

If one is trying to practice dhyana and is still eating meat, he would be like a man closing his ears and shouting loudly and then asserting that he heard nothing. The more one conceals things, the more apparent they become. Pure and earnest bhikshus and Bodhisattva-Mahasattvas, when walking a narrow path, will never so much as tread on the growing grass beside the path. How can a bhikshu, who hopes to become a deliverer of others, himself be living on the flesh of other sentient beings?

Pure and earnest bhikshus, if they are true and sincere, will never wear clothing made of silk, nor wear boots made of leather because it involves the taking of life. Neither will they indulge in eating milk or cheese because thereby they are depriving the young animals of that which rightly belongs to them. It is only such true and sincere bhikshus who have repaid their karmic debts of previous lives, who will attain true emancipation, and who will no more be bound to wander to this triple world. To wear anything, or partake of anything for self-comfort, deceiving one's self as to the suffering it causes others or other sentient life, is to set up an affinity with that lower life which will draw them toward it. So all bhikshus must be very careful to live in all sincerity, refraining from even the appearance of unkindness to other life. It is such true hearted bhikshus who will attain a true emancipation. Even in one's speech and especially in one's teaching, one must practice kindness for no teaching that is unkind can be the true teaching of Buddha. Unkindness is the murderer of the life of Wisdom. This is the second admonition of the Lord Buddha as to the keeping of the Precepts.

Then there is the Precept of not taking anything that does not rightfully belong to one, not coveting it or even admiring it. One must learn to keep this precept in all sincerity if he is to hope for escape from the chain of deaths and rebirths. The purpose of your practice of dhyana is to escape from the suffering of this mortal life. No matter how keen you may be mentally, no matter how much you may be able to practice dhyana, no matter to how high a degree of apparent Samadhi you may attain, unless you refrain from covetousness and stealing, you will fall into the realm of heretics.

There are three grades of these heretics:—the first grade are the spiritual heretics tempting one to rank and privilege and power and egoistic pride. The second grade are mental goblins tempting one to false ideas that will enhance one's knowledge and erudition. The third grade are the common heretics of this world who teach among human beings what is not the true Dharma. You will be beset by these heretics on every hand, within and without. And each one of these heretic goblins will have his double who disguises himself as one who has attained supreme enlightenment and who sets himself up as a teacher of highest truth. After my Parinirvana, in the last kalpa of this world, there will be plenty of these goblin-heretics about, hiding themselves within the very personalities of the saints, the better to carry out their deceiving tricks. Sometimes they gain control of some great and good master and teach under the prestige of his name. They often assert that they have received their Dharma from some notable Master, deceiving ignorant people, discouraging them and even causing them to go insane. In such deceptive ways do they spread their false and destructive heresies.

For all these various reasons, I teach my bhikshu-brothers not to covet comforts and privileges, but to beg their food, not here and there, or now and then, but to make it a regular habit so that they will be better able to overcome the greediness and covetousness that hinders their progress toward enlightenment. I teach them not to cook their own food even, but to be dependent upon others for even the poorest living so that they will realize their oneness with all sentient life and are but sojourners in this triple world. Under these conditions, how can bad men be tempted to put on our Buddhist garments and to offer the Dharma of all the Tathagatas as goods for sale? To do this is to accumulate all kinds of evil karma. Nevertheless, these heretics insist that their selfish and acquisitive acts are in conformity with Buddha's teaching and that Buddhism allows them to teach and act in these acquisitive ways. By so doing they defame the true Buddhist Bhikshus who have been tested and tried in some formal religious ceremony. On the contrary, they only reveal themselves as belonging to some heretical sect but, meanwhile, they have deluded and bewildered and turned astray or hindered many sentient beings so that they fall into the hells of suffering.

If after my Parinirvana there shall be bhikshus who undertake to practice dhyana and to attain Samadhi and who prove their sincerity and earnestness by some sacrifice before an image of the Tathagata, such as cutting off a part of their body, or burning a finger, or even burning one spot on their head with incense, such disciples immediately pay all their karmaic debts accumulated from beginningless time, and they will be immediately emancipated from the bondage of this triple world. Although such disciples will not at once attain Supreme Enlightenment, yet they reveal their right resolution and are on the right Path by the practice of dhyana.

But if they are not enough in earnest to sacrifice even the slightest comfort, even if they attain a measure of tranquillity, they will have to be reborn in a human body for the payment of the debts of previous lives. Thus I, myself, suffered for about three months to eat the rye in horse's fodder, so hungry was I, in recompense of the debt of an earlier life. Thus you must teach the people of this world who are practicing dhyana in the hope of attaining Samadhi, that they must abstain from stealing and covetousness.

Therefore, Ananda, if any of my disciples who are trying to practice dhyana, do not abstain from stealing and covetousness, their efforts will be like trying to fill a leaking pot with water; no matter how long they try, they will never succeed. So all of you, my bhikshu disciples, with the exception of your poor garments and your begging bowls should have nothing more in possession. Even the food that is left over from your begging after you have eaten should be given to hungry sentient beings and should not be kept for the next meal. Moreover, you should look upon your own body, its flesh, blood and bone, as not being your own but as being one with the bodies of all other sentient beings and so be ever ready to sacrifice it for the common need. Even when men beat you and scold you, you must accept it patiently and with hands pressed together bow to them humbly. Furthermore, you should not accept one teaching, or one principle, that is easy and agreeable, and reject the rest of the Dharma; you should accept all with equitable mind lest you misinterpret the Dharma to the new converts. Thus living, the Lord Buddha will confirm your attainment as one who has acquired the true Samadhi. As you teach the Dharma to others, be sure that your teaching is in agreement with the above so that it may be regarded as a true teaching of Buddha, otherwise it would be as heretical as the deceptive words of the goblin-heretics who are murderers of the life of Wisdom. This is the third admonition of the Lord Buddha as it relates to the Precepts.

Then there is the Precept of not deceiving nor telling lies. If the sentient beings of the six realms of existence should refrain from killing, stealing and adultery, and should refrain from even thinking about them, but should fail to keep the Precept of truthfulness and not be sincere in their practice of dhyana and their attainment of Samadhi, there would be no emancipation for them; they would fall into the ranks of the Maras who are satisfied with any slight attainment and who boast of it, or they would fall into the ranks of Maras who become prejudiced and egoistically assertive, and what is of more importance they would lose their seed of Buddhahood.

Such disciples presumptuously assume an attainment before they have attained it; they assume realization before they have realized it; they affect to be the most respected and competent masters, and speak to the people loftily, boasting:—"I have attained to the degree of Crotapanna, or to the degree of Sakradagamin, or to the degree of Anagamin, or to the degree of Arhat, or to the degree of Pratyaka-Buddha." They claim to have attained to the Ten Gradual Grounds of Tranquillity, or to the degree of those Bodhisattva-Mahasattvas who have attained to the stage of No Recension. Moreover, they covet the respect of people, they like to see them humble in their presence, they greedily watch for offerings from the people. Such disciples are to be regarded as no better than un-believers, no better than hardened Icchantikas. They not only lose their own seed of Buddhahood, they destroy the seed of Buddhahood in others. Such disciples progressively lose their nature of kindness and gradually lose the measure of understanding that they had attained and shall at last sink into the Sea of the Three Kinds of Suffering, namely, (1) the suffering of pain, (2) the loss of enjoyment, (3) the suffering of decay. They will not attain to Samadhi for a long, long time in after lives.

Nevertheless, Ananda, in the time after my Parinirvana, I urge all of you Bodhisattva-Mahasattvas and Arhats to choose to be reborn in the last kalpas wholly for the sake of delivering all sentient beings. You should make use of all manner of transformations, such as disciples, laymen, kings, lords, ministers, virgins, boy-eunuchs, and even as harlots, widows, adulterers, thieves, butchers, pedlers, etc., so as to be able to mingle with all kinds of people and to make known the true emancipation of Buddhism and the following peace of Samadhi. You must never speak of your own true rank of Bodhisattva-Mahasattva and Arhat, you must never reveal the Lord Buddha's Secret Cause of Attainment, nor speak without discretion before those who are not practicing meditation. Except toward the end of your mortal life, you may disclose to your most worthy disciples the secret teachings and instruction, lest the evil heretics disturb and lure them away by their lies. To teach the world to observe the Precept of truthful sincerity, to practice dhyana with sincerity and to attain a true Samadhi, this is the clear and true instruction of the Lord Buddha.

Therefore, Ananda, if any disciple does not abstain from deceit, he is like a man moulding human dung instead of carving sweet-smelling sandalwood. I have always taught my bhikshu Brothers to keep their intuitive minds in straightforward sincerity as their true Altar of Enlightenment, and at all times, whether walking, standing, sitting or lying down, there should be no falsehood in your life. How disgraceful is it for heretics whose lives are filled with deceit to present themselves as having attained supreme enlightenment. They are like poverty stricken people who pretend to be kings or wealthy merchants, only to shame and destroy their own lives. For any such disciple who dares to represent himself as a Prince of the Dharma, there will be a terrible retribution.

It has always been a truism that any disease in a seed will reveal itself in diseased and abortive fruit. Such a disciple, seeking to attain the Lord Buddha's Enlightenment can be likened to a man trying to bite his own navel. How impossible for them to attain true Enlightenment. But bhikshus whose lives are as straight as the chord of a bow will certainly attain Samadhi. They need never fear the wiles of the Maras. They are the bhikshus who are certain to attain the Bodhisattva-Mahasattva's supreme understanding and insight. Any lesson or instruction that is in agreement with the foregoing can be relied upon as being a true teaching of the Lord Buddha. Differing from it, it is simply a false teaching of the heretics who have always been murderers of the Life of Wisdom. This is the fourth admonition of the Lord Buddha.

(The Great Dharani.)

Ananda! As you have asked me as to the best method for concentrating the mind of those who have difficulty in following the common methods, I will now reveal to you the Lord Buddha's Secret Method for the attainment of Bodhisattva-Mahasattvahood. But you must remember that it is of first importance to fully observe the Four Precepts as explained above. To become a Bodhisattva-Mahasattva, one must have a nature as pure and clear and repellent as frost and ice, so that no false growths of leaves and branches shall sprout out from the true Mind, such as the three poisons of lust, hatred and infatuation; or the four wickednesses of the mouth: falsehood, slander, obscene words, and flattery.

Ananda! If any of the disciples in the last kalpa should be unable to overcome their old habits, you may teach them to recite this Dharani of mine. It is called, The Supreme Dharani of the Radiating Brightness of the Lord Buddha's Crowning Experience. It is the invisible transcendental power that rays out from the Tathagata's Wisdom Eye manifesting the unconditioned Essential Mind of the Lord Buddha. It is the transcendental radio-activity of Power and Glory that was revealed in me at the time of my Highest Samadhi, at the hour of my Perfect Enlightenment, as I sat amid the marvelous Lotus Blossoms under the Bodhi-tree.

Listen, Ananda! At the time you were helpless under the magic charm of the maiden Pchiti, what was it that released you and restored your control of mind? Your coming under her control was not a chance happening of this life, or of this kalpa alone: you had been in affinity with her for many a kalpa. Suddenly, when Manjusri repeated this Dharani, the bonds that bound you to her were destroyed, her passion for you was ended, and by once listening to my teaching she became enlightened. Although she was a prostitute and apparently had no interest in the Dharma, by the invisible power of my transcendental Dharani, she immediately attained to the perfection of all dhyana practice. What this Dharani did for her and for you, it can do for all others. Rest assured all my Bhikshu Brothers in this great assembly, you who are earnestly seeking Supreme Attainment, rest assured that, by the power of this Great Dharani, you will attain Buddhahood.

. . . .

Then Ananda bowed down to the feet of the Lord Buddha and said:—My Noble Lord! The reason I have not yet attained perfect Emancipation from arbitrary conceptions of phenomena, since becoming thy disciple, is because of my pride in being known as thy favorite cousin and because of my exceptional learning, so when I was brought under the spell of the old woman's magic, in spite of the conscious purpose of my mind, I was unable to free myself from it. Fortunately my Lord sent Brother Manjusri to deliver me by means of the spiritual power of my Lord's Great Crown Dharani. Unfortunately I had not mastered it and now pray, My Lord, to kindly repeat it again so that I and all the other practicing disciples in this assembly and, through us, all the disciples of the future who are still in the cycle of deaths and rebirths, shall all become free in both mind and body in the time of danger.

The whole audience having heard Ananda's sincere plea to the Lord, rose from their seats and made obeisance to the Lord and then waited attentively to hear the Lord's sacred Dharani. As they waited in solemn silence there appeared a most wonderful sight. From the crown of the Blessed One's head there streamed forth a glorious splendor in the likeness of a wonderful lotus blossom, and in the midst of the abundant foliage and seated in the cup of the blossom was the Lord Tathagata's Nirmanakaya (appearance body). From the crown of the Lord's head there radiated outward uncounted beams of light that shot outward in all the ten directions, and in each of the bright beams of light were figures of transcendently mysterious Vajra-gods permeating everywhere in the open spaces of the universes and suggesting the lightning-like potencies of all the transcendental powers. Each of the Vajra-gods was standing upright and alert with his symbol in his hand, ready and waiting but already victorious.

The assembly was transported with awe and fear and admiration. With one spontaneous movement their hearts went forth in an adoring prayer for its blessed, compassionate, and protective Providence to guard them from its awful but Beneficent Power.

As the vision faded away, the great assembly remained in solemn silence waiting to hear the Lord's Transcendental Dharani. The Lord Buddha standing in their midst, Brightness and Power radiating from the crown of his head, uttered the Great Crown Dharani.*

* Then follows several pages of the long and mysterious Dharani made up of Sanskrit words, Chinese paraphrases, names of Buddhas, Bodhisattvas, Devagods, etc., more or less of obscure meaning, all of which but the opening and closing lines are omitted. The lines in capital letters is considered the "heart" of the long Dharani and is commonly the part that is remembered and recited by those who cannot remember the whole.

THE GREAT DHARANI

Adoration to all Buddhas and Bodhisattvas;
Obeisance to their perfect Enlightenment and perfect tranquillity.
Adoration to all living Arhats;
Adoration to the millions of Disciples who make up the Sangha.

Adoration to those who have "entered the stream";
Adoration to those who have but "one more return";
Adoration to those who "will never more return to this world";
Obeisance to their perfect Righteousness.
Obeisance to the Tri-Ratna,—to Buddha, Dharma, Sangha!

Adoration to the Blessed Ones—exalted, firm, steady, powerful—the Kings among Tathagatas!
Obeisance to their Perfect Wisdom!
Adoration to the Blessed Amitabha Tathagata;
Adoration to the Blessed Akshobya Tathagata;
Obeisance to their Perfect Wisdom!

Adoration to the Blessed Master of Healing,
The Glorious Bhairaviya, the kingly Tathagata.
Adoration to the Blessed One, Sambhasana, the Sala tree
Among trees, the kingly Tathagata.
Adoration to the Blessed One, Shakyamuni Tathagata;
Adoration to their highest Perfect Wisdom!

Adoration to the Blessed Princes among Tathagatas,—
To the Blessed Pundarika Prince;
To the Blessed Vajra Prince;
To the Blessed Muni Prince;
To the Blessed Garbha Prince.

Adoration to the Heavenly Devas and Rishis—accomplished and disciplined executors of this Dharani—

Adoration to their transcendental power, their discipline, their resources.

Adoration to Brahman, to Indra, to the Blessed Rudra, and to their consorts, Indrani and Sahai.

Adoration to Narayana, Lord of this world, Lord of the five great Mudras, and to his consort.

* * *

OM! OH, THOU WHO HOLDEST THE SEAL OF POWER, RAISE THY DIAMOND HAND, BRING TO NAUGHT, DESTROY, EXTERMINATE!

OH, THOU SUSTAINER, SUSTAIN ALL WHO ARE IN EXTREMITY!

OH, THOU PURIFIER, PURIFY ALL WHO ARE IN BONDAGE TO SELF!

OM! MAY THE ENDER OF ALL SUFFERING BE VICTORIOUS!

OM! OH, THOU PERFECTLY ENLIGHTENED, ENLIGHTEN ALL SENTIENT BEINGS!

OH, THOU WHO ART PERFECT IN WISDOM AND COMPASSION, EMANCIPATE ALL BEINGS, AND BRING THEM TO BUDDHAHOOD! OM!

Adoration to Tathagata, Sugata, Buddha, of Perfect Wisdom and Compassion, Thou who hast accomplished, is accomplishing, and will accomplish, all these Words of Mystery! SVAHA! So be it!

(Final Words.)

When the Lord finished his recitation of the Great Crown Dharani, he resumed his instruction to Ananda, saying:—This mysterious *Agadha Dharani* of *Siddhartha Pdara* which is the quintessence of the Brightness and Power raying out from the Lord Buddha's Crown is One with the Brightness and Power emanating from all the Buddhas in all the ten quarters of all the universes. It is the *Sambhogakaya,* the Bliss-body of Buddhahood, radiantly Wise and Potential and ceaselessly Compassionate drawing all sentient life into its All-embracing Wholeness and Unity and Peacefulness. It was by means of this Transcendental Power, the quintessence of The Lord Buddha's Perfect Samadhi and Boundless Samapatti, that all the Tathagatas, past, present and future, of all the universes had attained *Anuttara Samyak Sambodhi,* had been able to subdue all the Maras and heretics, were sitting on their thrones in the Glorious Lotus Blossoms and forever giving response to the needs of all sentient life in all the kingdoms of existence, past, present and future.

By means of it all the Tathagatas were ceaselessly turning the Wheel of the Intrinsic Dharma; by means of it all the Tathagatas were in close fellowship with each individual disciple, comforting, encouraging, guiding, strengthening; no matter how immature disciples may be, they would be given assurance of their ultimate attainment of Buddhahood. By means of it, all the Tathagatas of the ten quarters have been able to give deliverance to those unfortunate disciples whose karma has brought them into suffering, even into the suffering of the lowest hells where are the hungry demons. Much more have been able by means of it to support and comfort the disciples in the midst of their common suffering of blindness, deafness and dumbness, the cruelty of enemies, separation from beloved ones, unfulfilled wishes, and the suffering arising from the ungratified desires of the five sense-ingredients. By means of it all the Tathagatas have been able to protect the disciples from harm by natural calamities, from war and robbery and famine and imprisonment; from violent storms, conflagrations, floods, drought, poverty. Whenever this Great Dharani is recited in faith, every suffering must give way and come to an end.

By means of it all the Tathagatas have supported the great Masters, to give their lectures with spontaneity and correctness, to supply their money necessities, to protect them from harm whether walking sitting or lying down, and to bring them to places of honor among the Bodhisattva-Mahasattvas as Princes of the Lord's Dharma. By means of it all the Tathagatas have been able to encourage beginners among the disciples, and those who have become frightened by the difficulties of the profound teachings of the Dharma.

By means of it all the Tathagatas have been able to attain their own Supreme Enlightenment, each under his own Spiritual Bodhi-tree, and finally to attain their Great Nirvana. And by means of this Great Dharani, after the passing of the Tatha-gatas, to consign to all disciples the duty and privilege of the practices of the Dharma so that it shall continue permanently in existence and the Precepts strictly observed and the disciples living in purity.

Should any disciple from morning until evening recite this Great Dharani without any omissions or additions, his merit will be unlimited even after innumerable kalpas. Should any of the practicing disciples who have not yet cut off their con-cern with deaths and rebirths, seriously attempt to attain Ar-hatship and to practice dhyana, without first relying on the power of this Great Dharani, it would be hopeless for him to avoid the deceptions and machinations of the Maras.

Ananda, should any sentient beings in any of the kingdoms of existence, copy down this Dharani on birch-bark or palm-leaves or paper made of papyrus or of white felt, and keep it safely in some scented wrapping, this man no matter how faint-hearted or unable to remember the words for reciting it, but who copies it in his room and keeps it by him, this man in all his life will remain unharmed by any poison of the Maras.

. . . .

(NOTE. *From now on the literary style changes from the convincing ra-tional character it has had and becomes more or less superstitious, irrational, unconvincing, and, to us of a more scientific age, is useless for our present purpose of winning by its spiritual power followers for the Lord Buddha. It is an ex-ample that is frequent in the Buddhist literature of the same apparent age, of "extending" or amplifying the text by including or interpolating additional matter that some less capable scribe thinks to be worth adding.*

At this point we are about two-thirds through the Text, in the midst of the Second Chapter, the balance of which is omitted. Chapter III is also omitted. Chapter IV is very short and is given entirely. It is devoted to the title of the Sutra and might well have been the end. Chapter V is devoted to a mythical description of the Seven Realms of Existence and is omitted. Chapter VI, while being more appropriate, also gives one the impression that it is something added. All but the closing paragraph is omitted.

CHAPTER IV

Giving the Title of This Great Sutra, so as to Reveal Its
Importance, Its Aim and Availability and Perfect
Accommodation.

At this time, Manjusri, Prince of the Lord's Dharma rose
in his place, bowed down to the Lord Buddha and addressed
him, saying:—

Our Blessed Lord! What shall we call this Instruction, so
that we and all future disciples may study it intelligently and
observe its teachings?

The Lord Buddha replied:—Manjusri! This Sutra should
be designated as The Lord Buddha's Crown of Siddhartha
Pdara; or the Pure and Ocean-wide Eye of all the Tathagatas
of the Ten Quarters; or as the Relationship-Cause of the
Emancipation of Ananda and the Bhikshuna Pchiti, so that
they Acquired their Enlightenment of Mind and entered into
the Ocean of Omniscience; or as the Perfect Teaching of the
Practices and Attainments of the Tathagata's Secret Path; or
as the Great, Immense and All-embracing Kingship of the
Wonderful Lotus; or as the Great Dharani of the Buddhas of
the Ten Quarters; or as the Initiating Lectures which Elucidate the Permanent Dhyana Practice of all the Bodhisattva-
Mahasattvas.

Manjusri! As you read this Great Sutra which I have interpreted with great care, you should consider and study all
these different titles, for each has its significance.

.   .   .   .

As the Lord Buddha finished his instruction as recorded in
this exceedingly long Sutra, there was great rejoicing in the
hearts of all those present, bhikshus and bhikshuni, lay disciples of both sexes, the heavenly Devas and Asuras, Bodhisattva-Mahasattvas of both this world and all the ten quarters
of the universe, Pratyaka-buddhas, Arhats, divine Gods, supernatural Cherubim, of the heavenly realms, newly converted
mighty Gods. All made sincere and humble obeisance to the
Lord Buddha and departed with grateful and joyful hearts.

THE END

THE LANKAVATARA SCRIPTURE
SELF-REALISATION OF
NOBLE WISDOM

CHAPTER I

Discrimination

THUS have I heard. The Blessed One once appeared in the Castle of Lanka which is on the summit of Mt. Malaya in the midst of the great Ocean. A great many Bodhisattva-Mahasattvas had miraculously assembled from all the Buddha-lands, and a large number of bhikshus were gathered there. The Bodhisattva-Mahasattvas with Mahamati at their head were all perfect masters of the various Samadhis, the tenfold Self-mastery, the ten Powers, and the six Psychic Faculties. Having been anointed by the Buddha's own hands, they all well understood the significance of the objective world; they all knew how to apply the various means, teachings and disciplinary measures according to the various mentalities and behaviors of beings; they were all thoroughly versed in the five Dharmas, the three Svabhavas, the eight Vijnanas, and the twofold Egolessness.

The Blessed One, knowing of the mental agitations going on in the minds of those assembled (like the surface of the ocean stirred into waves by the passing winds), and his great heart moved by compassion, smiled and said: In the days of old the Tathagatas of the past who were Arhats and fully-enlightened Ones came to the Castle of Lanka on Mount Malaya and discoursed on the Truth of Noble Wisdom that is beyond the reasoning knowledge of the philosophers as well as being beyond the understanding of ordinary disciples and masters; and which is realisable only within the inmost consciousness; for your sakes, I too, would discourse on the same Truth. All that is seen in the world is devoid of effort and action because all things in the world are like a dream, or like an image miraculously projected. This is not comprehended by the philosophers and the ignorant, but those who thus see things see them truthfully. Those who see things otherwise walk in discrimination and, as they depend upon discrimination, they cling to dualism. The world as seen by discrimination is like seeing one's own image reflected in a mirror, or one's shadow, or the moon reflected in water, or an echo heard in the valley. People grasping their own shadows of discrimination become attached to this thing and that thing and failing to abandon dualism they go on forever discriminating and thus never attain tranquillity. By tranquillity is meant Oneness, and Oneness gives birth to the highest Samadhi which is gained by entering into the realm of Noble Wisdom that is realisable only within one's inmost consciousness.

Then all the Bodhisattva-Mahasattvas rose from their seats and respectfully paid him homage and Mahamati the Bodhisattva-Mahasattva sustained by the power of the Buddhas drew his upper garment over one shoulder, knelt and pressing his hands together, praised him in the following verses:

As thou reviewest the world with thy perfect intelligence and compassion, it must seem to thee like an ethereal flower of which one cannot say: it is born, it is destroyed, for the terms being and non-being do not apply to it.

As thou reviewest the world with thy perfect intelligence and compassion, it must seem to thee like a dream of which it cannot be said: it is permanent or it is destructible, for being and non-being do not apply to it.

As thou reviewest all things by thy perfect intelligence and compassion, they must seem to thee like visions beyond the reach of the human mind, as being and non-being do not apply to them.

With thy perfect intelligence and compassion which are beyond all limit, thou comprehendest the egolessness of things and persons, and art free and clear from the hindrances of passion and learning and egoism.

Thou dost not vanish into Nirvana, nor does Nirvana abide in thee, for Nirvana transcends all duality of knowing and known, of being and non-being.

Those who see thee thus, serene and beyond conception, will be emancipated from attachment, will be cleansed of all de-

filement, both in this world and in the spiritual world beyond.

In this world whose nature is like a dream, there is place for praise and blame, but in the ultimate Reality of Dharmakaya which is far beyond the senses and the discriminating mind, what is there to praise? O thou most Wise!

* * *

Then said Mahamati the Bodhisattva-Mahasattva: O blessed One, Sugata, Arhat and Fully-enlightened One, pray tell us about the realisation of Noble Wisdom which is beyond the path and usage of the philosophers; which is devoid of all predicates such as being and non-being, oneness and otherness, bothness and not-bothness, existence and non-existence, eternity and non-eternity; which has nothing to do with individuality and generality, nor false-imagination, nor any illusions arising from the mind itself; but which manifests itself as the Truth of Highest Reality. By which, going up continuously by the stages of purification, one enters at last upon the stage of Tathagatahood, whereby, by the power of his original vows unattended by any striving, one will radiate its influence to infinite worlds, like a gem reflecting its variegated colors, whereby I and other Bodhisattva-Mahasattvas will be enabled to bring all beings to the same perfection of virtue.

Said the Blessed One: Well done, well done, Mahamati! And again, well done, indeed! It is because of your compassion for the world, because of the benefit it will bring to many people both human kind and celestial, that you have presented yourself before us to make this request. Therefore, Mahamati, listen well and truly reflect upon what I shall say, for I will instruct you.

Then Mahamati and the other Bodhisattva-Mahasattvas gave devout attention to the teaching of the Blessed One.

Mahamati, since the ignorant and simple-minded, not knowing that the world is only something seen of the mind itself, cling to the multitudinousness of external objects, cling to the notions of being and non-being, oneness and otherness, bothness and not-bothness, existence and non-existence, eternity and non-eternity, and think that they have a self-nature of their own, all of which rises from the discriminations of the mind and is perpetuated by habit-energy, and from which the, are given over to false imagination. It is all like a mirage in which springs of water are seen as if they were real. They are thus imagined by animals who, made thirsty by the heat of the season, run after them. Animals, not knowing that the springs are an hallucination of their own minds, do not realise that there are no such springs. In the same way, Mahamati, the ignorant and simple-minded, their minds burning with the fires of greed, anger and folly, finding delight in a world of multitudinous forms, their thoughts obsessed with ideas of birth, growth and destruction, not well understanding what is meant by existent and non-existent, and being impressed by the erroneous discriminations and speculations since beginningless time, fall into the habit of grasping this and that and thereby becoming attached to them.

It is like the city of the Gandharvas which the unwitting take to be a real city though it is not so in fact. The city appears as in a vision owing to their attachment to the memory of a city preserved in the mind as a seed; the city can thus be said to be both existent and non-existent. In the same way, clinging to the memory of erroneous speculations and doctrines accumulated since beginningless time, they hold fast to such ideas as oneness and otherness, being and non-being, and their thoughts are not at all clear as to what after all is only seen of the mind. It is like a man dreaming in his sleep of a country that seems to be filled with various men, women, elephants, horses, cars, pedestrians, villages, towns, hamlets, cows, buffalos, mansions, woods, mountains, rivers and lakes, and who moves about in that city until he is awakened. As he lies half awake, he recalls the city of his dreams and reviews his experiences there; what do you think, Mahamati, is this dreamer who is letting his mind dwell upon the various unrealities he has seen in his dream,—is he to be considered wise or foolish? In the same way, the ignorant and simple-minded who are favorably influenced by the erroneous views of the philosophers do not recognise that the views that are influencing them are only dream-like ideas originating in the mind itself, and consequently they are held fast by their notions of oneness and otherness, of being and non-being. It is like a painter's canvas on which the ignorant imagine they see the elevations and depressions of mountains and valleys.

In the same way there are people today being brought up

under the influence of similar erroneous views of oneness and otherness, of bothness and not-bothness, whose mentality is being conditioned by the habit-energy of these false-imaginings and who later on will declare those who hold the true doctrine of no-birth which is free from the alternatives of being and non-being, to be nihilists and by so doing will bring themselves and others to ruin. By the natural law of cause and effect these followers of pernicious views uproot meritorious causes that otherwise would lead to unstained purity. They are to be shunned by those whose desires are for more excellent things.

It is like the dim-eyed ones who seeing a hairnet exclaim to one another: "It is wonderful! Look, Honorable Sirs, it is wonderful!" But the hairnet has never existed; in fact, it is neither an entity, nor a non-entity, for it has both been seen and has not been seen. In the same manner those whose minds have been addicted to the discriminations of the erroneous views cherished by the philosophers which are given over to the realistic views of being and non-being, will contradict the good Dharma and will end in the destruction of themselves and others.

It is like a wheel of fire made by a revolving firebrand which is no wheel but which is imagined to be one by the ignorant. Nor is it not-a-wheel because it has not been seen by some. By the same reasoning, those who are in the habit of listening to the discriminations and views of the philosophers will regard things born as non-existent and those destroyed by causation as existent. It is like a mirror reflecting colors and images as determined by conditions but without any partiality. It is like the echo of the wind that gives the sound of a human voice. It is like a mirage of moving water seen in a desert. In the same way the discriminating mind of the ignorant which has been heated by false-imaginations and speculations is stirred into mirage-like waves by the winds of birth, growth and destruction. It is like the magician Pisaca, who by means of his spells makes a wooden image or a dead body to throb with life, though it has no power of its own. In the same way the ignorant and the simple-minded, committing themselves to erroneous philosophical views become thoroughly devoted to the ideas of oneness and otherness, but their confidence is not well grounded. For this reason, Mahamati, you and other Bodhisattva-Mahasattvas should cast off all discriminations leading to the notions of birth, abiding and destructions, of oneness and otherness, of bothness and not-bothness, of being and non-being and thus getting free of the bondage of habit-energy become able to attain the reality realisable within yourselves of Noble Wisdom.

*   *   *

Then said Mahamati to the Blessed One: Why is it that the ignorant are given up to discrimination and the wise are not?

The Blessed One replied: It is because the ignorant cling to names, signs and ideas; as their minds move along these channels they feed on multiplicities of objects and fall into the notion of an ego-soul and what belongs to it; they make discriminations of good and bad among appearances and cling to the agreeable. As they thus cling there is a reversion to ignorance, and karma born of greed, anger and folly, is accumulated. As the accumulation of karma goes on they become imprisoned in a cocoon of discrimination and are thenceforth unable to free themselves from the round of birth and death.

Because of folly they do not understand that all things are like maya, like the reflection of the moon in water, that there is no self-substance to be imagined as an ego-soul and its belongings, and that all their definitive ideas rise from their false discriminations of what exists only as it is seen of the mind itself. They do not realise that things have nothing to do with qualified and qualifying, nor with the course of birth, abiding and destruction, and instead they assert that they are born of a creator, of time, of atoms, of some celestial spirit. It is because the ignorant are given up to discrimination that they move along with the stream of appearances, but it is not so with the wise.

CHAPTER II

False-Imagination and Knowledge of
Appearances

Then Mahamati the Bodhisattva-Mahasattva spoke to the Blessed One, saying: You speak of the erroneous views of the philosophers, will you please tell us of them, that we may be on our guard against them?

The Blessed One replied, saying: Mahamati, the error in these erroneous teachings that are generally held by the philosophers lies in this: they do not recognise that the objective world rises from the mind itself; they do not understand that the whole mind-system also rises from the mind itself; but depending upon these manifestations of the mind as being real they go on discriminating them, like the simple-minded ones that they are, cherishing the dualism of this and that, of being and non-being, ignorant of the fact that there is but one common Essence.

On the contrary my teaching is based upon the recognition that the objective world, like a vision, is a manifestation of the mind itself; it teaches the cessation of ignorance, desire, deed and causality; it teaches the cessation of suffering that arises from the discriminations of the triple world.

There are some Brahman scholars who, assuming something out of nothing, assert that there is a substance bound up with causation which abides in time, and that the elements that make up personality and its environment have their genesis and continuation in causation and after thus existing, pass away. Then there are other scholars who hold a destructive and nihilistic view concerning such subjects as continuation, activity, breaking-up, existence, Nirvana, the Path, karma, fruition and Truth. Why? Because they have not attained an intuitive understanding of Truth itself and therefore they have no clear insight into the fundamentals of things. They are like a jar broken into pieces which is no longer able to function as a jar; they are like a burnt seed which is no longer capable of sprouting. But the elements that make up personality and its environment which they regard as subject to change are really incapable of uninterrupted transformations. Their views are based upon erroneous discriminations of the objective world; they are not based upon the true conception.

Again, if it is true that something comes out of nothing and there is the rise of the mind-system by reason of the combination of the three effect-producing causes, we could say the same of any non-existing thing: for instance, that a tortoise could grow hair, or sand produce oil. This proposition is of no avail; it ends in affirming nothing. It follows that the deed, work and cause of which they speak is of no use, and so also is their reference to being and non-being. If they argue that there is a combination of the three effect-producing causes, they must do it on the principle of cause and effect, that is, that something comes out of something and not out of nothing. As long as a world of relativity is asserted, there is an ever recurring chain of causation which cannot be denied under any circumstance, therefore we cannot talk of anything coming to an end or of cessation. As long as these scholars remain on their philosophical ground their demonstration must conform to logic and their textbooks, and the memory-habit of erroneous intellection will ever cling to them. To make the matter worse, the simple-minded ones, poisoned by this erroneous view, will declare this incorrect way of thinking taught by the ignorant, to be the same as that presented by the All-knowing One.

But the way of instruction presented by the Tathagatas is not based on assertions and refutations by means of words and logic. There are four forms of assertion that can be made concerning things not in existence, namely, assertions made about individual marks that are not in existence; about objects that are not in existence; about a cause that is non-existent; and about philosophical views that are erroneous. By refutation is meant that one, because of ignorance, has not examined properly the error that lies at the base of these assertions.

The assertion about individual marks that really have no existence, concerns the distinctive marks as perceived by the eye, ear, nose, etc., as indicating individuality and generality in the elements that make up personality and its external world; and then, taking these marks for reality and getting attached to them, to get into the habit of affirming that things are just so and not otherwise.

The assertion about objects that are non-existent is an assertion that rises from attachment to these associated marks of individuality and generality. Objects in themselves are neither in existence nor in non-existence and are quite devoid of the alternative of being and non-being, and should only be thought of as one thinks of the horns of a hare, a horse, or a camel, which never existed. Objects are discriminated by the ignorant who are addicted to assertion and negation, because their intelligence has not been acute enough to penetrate into the truth that there is nothing but what is seen of the mind itself.

The assertion of a cause that is non-existent assumes the causeless birth of the first element of the mind-system which later on comes to have only a maya-like non-existence. That is to say, there are philosophers who assert that an originally unborn mind-system begins to function under the conditions of eye, form, light and memory, which functioning goes on for a time and then ceases. This is an example of a cause that is non-existent.

The assertion of philosophical views concerning the elements that make up personality and its environing world that are non-existent, assume the existence of an ego, a being, a soul, a living being, a "nourisher," or a spirit. This is an example of philosophical views that are not true. It is this combination of discrimination of imaginary marks of individuality, grouping them and giving them a name and becoming attached to them as objects, by reason of habit-energy that has been accumulating since beginningless time, that one builds up erroneous views whose only basis is false-imagination. For this reason Bodhisattvas should avoid all discussions relating to assertions and negations whose only basis is words and logic.

Word-discrimination goes on by the coordination of brain, chest, nose, throat, palate, lips, tongue, teeth and lips. Words are neither different nor not-different from discrimination. Words rise from discrimination as their cause; if words were different from discrimination they could not have discrimination for their cause; then again, if words are not different, they could not carry and express meaning. Words, therefore, are produced by causation and are mutually conditioning and shifting and, just like things, are subject to birth and destruction.

There are four kinds of word discrimination, all of which are to be avoided because they are alike unreal. First there are the words indicating individual marks which rise from discriminating forms and signs as being real in themselves and, then, becoming attached to them. There are memory-words which rise from the unreal surroundings which come before the mind when it recalls some previous experience. Then there are words growing out of attachment to the erroneous distinctions and speculations of the mental processes. And finally, there are words growing out of inherited prejudices as seeds of habit-energy have accumulated since beginningless time, or which had

their origin in some long forgotten clinging to false-imagination
and erroneous speculations.

Then there are words where there are no corresponding objects, as for instance, the hare's horns, a barren woman's child,
etc.—there are no such things but we have the words, just the
same. Words are an artificial creation; there are Buddha-lands
where there are no words. In some Buddha-lands ideas are indicated by looking steadily, in others by gestures, in still others
by a frown, by a movement of the eyes, by laughing, by yawn-
ing, by the clearing of the throat, or by trembling. For instance, in the Buddha-land of the Tathagata Samantabhadra,
Bodhisattvas, by a dhyana transcending words and ideas, attain the recognition of all things as un-born and they, also,
experience various most excellent Samadhis that transcend
words. Even in this world such specialised beings as ants and
bees carry on their activities very well without recourse to
words. No, Mahamati, the validity of things is independent of
the validity of words.

Moreover, there are other things that belong to words,
namely, the syllable-body of words, the name-body of words,
and the sentence-body of words. By syllable-body is meant
that by which words and sentences are set up or indicated:
there is a reason for some syllables, some are mnemonic, and
some are chosen arbitrarily. By name-body is meant the object
depending upon which a name-word obtains its significance, or
in other words, name-body is the "substance" of a name-word.
By sentence-body is meant the completion of the meaning by
expressing the word more fully in a sentence. The name for
this sentence-body is suggested by the footprints left in the
road by elephants, horses, people, deer, cattle, goats, etc. But
neither words nor sentences can exactly express meanings, for
words are only sweet sounds that are arbitrarily chosen to represent things, they are not the things themselves, which in turn
are only manifestations of mind. Discrimination of meaning
is based upon the false-imagination that these sweet sounds
which we call words and which are dependent upon whatever
subjects they are supposed to stand for, and which subjects
are supposed to be self-existent, all of which is based on error.
Disciples should be on their guard against the seductions of
words and sentences and their illusive meanings, for by them

the ignorant and the dull-witted become entangled and helpless as an elephant floundering about in the deep mud.

Words and sentences are produced by the law of causation and are mutually conditioning,—they cannot express highest Reality. Moreover, in highest Reality there are no differentiations to be discriminated and there is nothing to be predicated in regard to it. Highest Reality is an exalted state of bliss, it is not a state of word-discrimination and it cannot be entered into by mere statements concerning it. The Tathagatas have a better way of teaching, namely, through self-realisation of Noble Wisdom.

* * *

Mahamati asked the Blessed One: Pray tell us about the causation of all things whereby I and other Bodhisattvas may see into the nature of causation and may no more discriminate it as to the gradual or simultaneous rising of all things?

The Blessed One replied: There are two factors of causation by reason of which all things come into seeming existence:— external and internal factors. The external factors are a lump of clay, a stick, a wheel, a thread, water, a worker, and his labor, the combination of all of which produces a jar. As with a jar which is made from a lump of clay, or a piece of cloth made from thread, or matting made from fragrant grass, or a sprout growing out of a seed, or fresh butter made from sour milk by a man churning it; so it is with all things which appear one after another in continuous succession. As regards the inner factors of causation, they are of such kinds as ignorance, desire, purpose, all of which enter into the idea of causation. Born of these two factors there is the manifestation of personality and the individual things that make up its environment, but they are not individual and distinctive things: they are only so discriminated by the ignorant.

Causation may be divided into six elements: indifference-cause, dependence-cause, possibility-cause, agency-cause, objectivity-cause, manifesting-cause. Indifference-cause means that if there is no discrimination present, there is no power of combination present and so no combination takes place, or if present there is dissolution. Dependence-cause means that the elements must be present. Possibility-cause means that when a cause is to become effective there must be a suitable meeting of conditions both internal and external. Agency-cause means that there must be a principle vested with supreme authority like a sovereign king present and asserting itself. Objectivity-cause means that to be a part of the objective world the mind-system must be in existence and must be keeping up its continuous activity. Manifesting-cause means that as the discriminating faculty of the mind-system becomes busy individual marks will be revealed as forms are revealed by the light of a lamp.

All causes are thus seen to be the outcome of discrimination carried on by the ignorant and simple-minded, and there is, therefore, no such thing as gradual or simultaneous rising of existence. If such a thing as the gradual rising of existence is asserted, it can be disproved by showing that there is no basic substance to hold the individual signs together which makes a gradual rising impossible. If simultaneous rising of existence is asserted, there would be no distinction between cause and effect and there will be nothing to characterise a cause as such. While a child is not yet born, the term father has no significance. Logicians argue that there is that which is born and that which gives birth by the mutual functioning of such causal factors as cause, substance, continuity, acceleration, etc., and so they conclude that there is a gradual rising of existence; but this gradual rising does not obtain except by reason of attachment to the notion of self-nature.

When ideas of body, property and abode are seen, discriminated and cherished in what after all is nothing but what is conceived by the mind itself, an external world is perceived under the aspects of individuality and generality which, however, are not realities, and, therefore, neither a gradual nor a simultaneous rising of things is possible. It is only when the mind-system comes into activity and discriminates the manifestations of mind that existence can be said to come into view. For these reasons, Mahamati, you must get rid of notions of gradation and simultaneity in the combination of causal activities.

* * *

Mahamati said: Blessed One, To what kind of discrimination and to what kind of thoughts should the term, false-imagination, be applied?

The Blessed One replied: So long as people do not understand the true nature of the objective world, they fall into the dualistic view of things. They imagine the multiplicity of external objects to be real and become attached to them and are nourished by their habit-energy. Because of this a system of mentation—mind and what belongs to it—is discriminated and is thought of as real; this leads to the assertion of an ego-soul and its belongings, and thus the mind-system goes on functioning. Depending upon and attaching itself to the dualistic habit of mind, they accept the views of the philosophers founded upon these erroneous distinctions, of being and non-being, existence and non-existence, and there evolves what we call, false-imaginations.

But, Mahamati, discrimination does not evolve nor is it put away because, when all that is seen is truly recognised to be nothing but the manifestation of mind, how can discrimination as regards being and non-being evolve? It is for the sake of the ignorant who are addicted to the discrimination of the multiplicity of things which are of their own mind, that it is said by me that discrimination takes its rise owing to attachment to the aspect of multiplicity which is characteristic of objects. How otherwise can the ignorant and simple-minded recognize that there is nothing but what is seen of the mind itself, and how otherwise can they gain an insight into the true nature of mind and be able to free themselves from wrong conceptions of cause and effect? How otherwise can they gain a clear conception of the Bodhisattva stages, and attain a "turning-about" in the deepest seat of their consciousness, and finally attain an inner self-realisation of Noble Wisdom which transcends the five Dharmas, the three Self-natures, and the whole idea of a discriminated Reality? For this reason is it said by me that discrimination takes its rise from the mind becoming attached to the multiplicities of things which in themselves are not real, and that emancipation comes from thoroughly understanding the meaning of Reality as it truly is.

False-imaginations rise from the consideration of appearances: things are discriminated as to form, signs and shape; as to having color, warmth, humidity, motility or rigidity. False-imagination consists in becoming attached to these appearances and their names. By attachment to objects is meant, the getting attached to inner and outer things as if they were real.

By attachment to names is meant, the recognition in these inner and outer things of the characteristic marks of individuation and generality, and to regard them as definitely belonging to the names of the objects.

False-imagination teaches that because all things are bound up with causes and conditions of habit-energy that has been accumulating since beginningless time by not recognising that the external world is of mind itself, all things are comprehensible under the aspects of individuality and generality. By reason of clinging to these false-imaginations there is multitudinousness of appearances which are imagined to be real but which are only imaginary. To illustrate: when a magician depending on grass, wood, shrubs and creepers, exercises his art, many shapes and beings take form that are only magically created; sometimes they even make figures that have bodies and that move and act like human beings; they are variously and fancifully discriminated but there is no reality in them; everyone but children and the simple-minded know that they are not real. Likewise based upon the notion of relativity false-imagination perceives a variety of appearances which the discriminating mind proceeds to objectify and name and become attached to, and memory and habit-energy perpetuate. Here is all that is necessary to constitute the self-nature of false-imagination.

The various features of false-imagination can be distinguished as follows: as regards words, meaning, individual marks, property, self-nature, cause, philosophical views, reasoning, birth, no-birth, dependence, bondage and emancipation. Discrimination of words is the becoming attached to various sounds carrying familiar meanings. Discrimination of meaning comes when one imagines that words rise depending upon whatever subjects they express, and which subjects are regarded as self-existent. Discrimination of individual marks is to imagine that whatever is denoted in words concerning the multiplicities of individual marks (which in themselves are like a mirage) is true, and clinging tenaciously to them, to discriminate all things according to such categories as, warmth, fluidity, motility, and solidity. Discrimination of property is to desire a state of wealth, such as gold, silver, and various precious stones.

Discrimination of self-nature is to make discriminations according to the views of the philosophers in reference to the self-nature of all things which they imagine and stoutly maintain to be true, saying: "This is just what it is and it cannot be otherwise." Discrimination of cause is to distinguish the notion of causation in reference to being and non-being and to imagine that there are such things as "cause-signs." Discrimination of philosophical views means considering different views relating to the notions of being and non-being, oneness and otherness, bothness and not-bothness, existence and non-existence, all of which are erroneous, and becoming attached to particular views. Discrimination of reasoning means the teaching whose reasoning is based on the grasping of the notion of an ego-substance and what belongs to it. Discrimination of birth means getting attached to the notion that things come into existence and pass out of existence according to causation. Discrimination of no-birth is to see that causeless substances which were not, come into existence by reason of causation. Discrimination of dependence means the mutual dependence of gold and the filament made of it. Discrimination of bondage and imagination is like imagining that there is something bound because of something binding, as in the case of a man who ties a knot and loosens one.

These are the various features of false-imagination to which all the ignorant and simple-minded cling. Those attached to the notion of relativity are attached to the notion of the multitudinousness of things which arises from false-imagination. It is like seeing varieties of objects depending upon maya, but these varieties thus revealing themselves are discriminated by the ignorant as something other than maya itself, according to their way of thinking. Now the turth is, maya and varieties of objects are neither different nor not different; if they were different, varieties of objects would not have maya for their characteristic; if they are not different there would be no distinction between them. But as there is a distinction these two—maya and varieties of objects—are neither different nor not-different, for the very good reason: they are one thing.

* * *

Mahamati said to the Blessed One: Is error an entity or not? The Blessed One replied: Error has no character in it making for attachment; if error had such a character no liberation would be possible from its attachment to existence, and the chain of origination would only be understood in the sense of creation as upheld by the philosophers. Error is like maya, also, and as maya is incapable from producing other maya, so error in itself cannot produce error; it is discrimination and attachment that produce evil thoughts and faults. Moreover, maya has no power of discrimination in itself; it only rises when invoked by the charm of the magician. Error has in itself no habit-energy; habit-energy only rises from discrimination and attachment. Error in itself has no faults; faults are due to the confused discriminations fondly cherished by the ignorant concerning the ego-soul and its mind. The wise have nothing to do either with maya or error.

Maya, however, is not an unreality because it only has the appearance of reality; all things have the nature of maya. It is not because all things are imagined and clung to because of the multitudinousness of individual signs, that they are like maya; it is because they are alike unreal and as quickly appearing and disappearing. Being attached to erroneous thoughts they confuse and contradict themselves and others. As they do not clearly grasp the fact that the world is no more than mind itself, they imagine and cling to causation, work, birth and individual signs, and their thoughts are characterised by error and false-imaginations. The teaching that all things are characterised by the self-nature of maya and a dream is meant to make the ignorant and simple-minded cast aside the idea of self-nature in anything.

False-imagination teaches that such things as light and shade, long and short, black and white are different and are to be discriminated; but they are not independent of each other; they are only different aspects of the same thing, they are terms of relation not of reality. Conditions of existence are not of a mutually exclusive character; in essence things are not two but one. Even Nirvana and Samsara's world of life and death are aspects of the same thing, for there is no Nirvana except where is Samsara, and no Samsara except where is Nirvana. All duality is falsely imagined.

Mahamati, you and all the Bodhisattvas should discipline yourselves in the realisation and patient acceptance of the truths of the emptiness, un-bornness, no self-natureness, and the non-duality of all things. This teaching is found in all the sutras of all the Buddhas and is presented to meet the varied dispositions of all beings, but it is not the Truth itself. These teachings are only a finger pointing toward Noble Wisdom. They are like a mirage with its springs of water which the deer take to be real and chase after. So with the teachings in all the sutras: They are intended for the consideration and guidance of the discriminating minds of all people, but they are not the Truth itself, which can only be self-realised within one's deepest consciousness.

Mahamati, you and all the Bodhisattvas must seek for this inner self-realisation of Noble Wisdom, and not be captivated by word-teaching.

CHAPTER III

Right Knowledge or Knowledge of
Relations

Then Mahamati said: Pray tell us, Blessed One, about the being and the non-being of all things?

The Blessed One replied: People of this world are dependent in their thinking on one of two things: on the notion of being whereby they take pleasure in realism, or in the notion of non-being whereby they take pleasure in nihilism; in either case they imagine emancipation where there is no emancipation. Those who are dependent upon the notion of being, regard the world as rising from a causation that is really existent, and that this actually existing and becoming world does not take its rise from a causation that is non-existent. This is the realistic view as held by some people. Then there are other people who are dependent on the notion of the non-being of all things. These people admit the existence of greed, anger and folly, and at the same time they deny the existence of the things that produce greed, anger and folly. This is not rational, for greed, anger and folly are no more to be taken hold of as real than are things; they neither have substance nor individual marks. Where there is a state of bondage, there is binding and means for binding; but where there is emancipation, as in the case of Buddhas, Bodhisattvas, masters and disciples, who have ceased to believe in both being and non-being, there is neither bondage, binding nor means for binding.

It is better to cherish the notion of an ego-substance than to entertain the notion of emptiness derived from the view of being and non-being, for those who so believe fail to understand the fundamental fact that the external world is nothing but a manifestation of mind. Because they see things as transient, as rising from cause and passing away from cause, now dividing, now combining into the elements which make up the aggregates of personality and its external world and now passing away, they are doomed to suffer every moment from the changes that follow one after another, and finally are doomed to ruin.

* * *

Then Mahamati asked the Blessed One, saying: Tell us, Blessed One, how all things can be empty, un-born, and have no self-nature, so that we may be awakened and quickly realise highest enlightenment?

The Blessed One replied: What is emptiness, indeed! It is a term whose very self-nature is false-imagination, but because of one's attachment to false-imagination we are obliged to talk of emptiness, no-birth, and no-self-nature. There are seven kinds of emptiness: emptiness of mutuality which is non-existence; emptiness of individual marks; emptiness of self-nature; emptiness of no-work; emptiness of work; emptiness of all things in the sense that they are unpredicable; and emptiness in its highest sense of Ultimate Reality.

By the emptiness of mutuality which is non-existence is meant that when a thing is missing here, one speaks of its being empty here. For instance: in the lecture hall of Mrigarama there are no elephants present, nor bulls, nor sheep; but as to monks there are many present. We can rightly speak of the hall as being empty as far as animals are concerned. It is not asserted that the lecture hall is empty of its own characteristics, or that the monks are empty of that which makes up their monkhood, nor that in some other place there are no elephants, bulls, nor sheep to be found. In this case we are speaking of things in their aspect of individuality and generality, but from the point of view of mutuality some things do not exist somewhere. This is the lowest form of emptiness and is to be sedulously put away.

By emptiness of individual marks is meant that all things

have no distinguishing marks of individuality and generality. Because of mutual relations and interactions things are super-ficially discriminated but when they are further and more care-fully investigated and analysed they are seen to be non-existent and nothing as to individuality and generality can be predicated of them. Thus when individual marks can no longer be seen. ideas of self, otherness and bothness, no longer hold good. So it must be said that all things are empty of self-marks.

By emptiness of self-nature is meant that all things in their self-nature are un-born; therefore, is it said that things are empty as to self-nature. By emptiness of no-work is meant that the aggregate of elements that makes up personality and its external world is Nirvana itself and from the beginning there is no activity in them; therefore, one speaks of the emptiness of no-work. By emptiness of work is meant that the aggregates being devoid of an ego and its belongings, go on functioning automatically as there is mutual conjunction of causes and con-ditions; thus one speaks of the emptiness of work. By empti-ness of all things in the sense that they are unpredicable is meant that, as the very nature of false-imagination is inexpres-sible, so all things are unpredicable, and, therefore, are empty in that sense. By emptiness in its highest sense of the emptiness of Ultimate Reality is meant that in the attainment of inner self-realisation of Noble Wisdom there is no trace of habit-energy generated by erroneous conceptions; thus one speaks of the highest emptiness of Ultimate Reality.

When things are examined by right knowledge there are no signs obtainable which would characterise them with marks of individuality and generality, therefore, they are said to have no self-nature. Because these signs of individuality and generality are seen both as existing and yet are known to be non-existent, are seen as going out and yet are known not to be going out, they are never annihilated. Why is this true? For this reason; because the individual signs that should make up the self-na-ture of all things are non-existent. Again in their self-nature things are both eternal and non-eternal. Things are not eternal because the marks of individuality appear and disappear, that is, the marks of self-nature are characterised by non-eternality. On the other hand, because things are un-born and are only mind-made, they are in a deep sense eternal. That is, things are eternal because of their very non-eternality.

Further, besides understanding the emptiness of all things both in regard to substance and self-nature, it is necessary for Bodhisattvas to clearly understand that all things are un-born. It is not asserted that things are not born in a superficial sense, but that in a deep sense they are not born of themselves. All that can be said, is this, that relatively speaking, there is a constant stream of becoming, a momentary and uninterrupted change from one state of appearance to another. When it is recognised that the world as it presents itself is no more than a manifestation of mind, then birth is seen as no-birth and all existing objects, concerning which discrimination asserts that they are and are not, are non-existent and, therefore, un-born; being devoid of agent and action things are un-born.

If things are not born of being and non-being, but are simply manifestations of mind itself, they have no reality, no self-nature:—they are like the horns of a hare, a horse, a donkey, a camel. But the ignorant and the simple-minded, who are given over to their false and erroneous imaginings, discriminate things where they are not. To the ignorant the characteristic marks of the self-nature of body-property-and-abode seem to be fundamental and rooted in the very nature of the mind itself, so they discriminate their multitudinousness and become attached to them.

There are two kinds of attachment: attachment to objects as having self-nature, and attachment to words as having self-nature. The first takes place by not knowing that the external world is only a manifestation of the mind itself; and the second arises from one's clinging to words and names by reason of habit-energy. In the teaching of no-birth, causation is out of place because, seeing that all things are like maya and a dream, one does not discriminate individual signs. That all things are un-born and have no self-nature because they are like maya is asserted to meet the thesis of the philosophers that birth is by causation. They foster the notion that the birth of all things is derived from the concept of being and non-being, and fail to regard it as it truly is,—as caused by attachment to the multitudinousness which arises from discriminations of the mind itself.

Those who believe in the birth of something that has never been in existence and, coming into existence, vanishes away, are obliged to assert that things come to exist and vanish away by causation—such people find no foothold in my teachings. When it is realised that there is nothing born, and nothing passes away, then there is no way to admit being and non-being, and the mind becomes quiescent.

* * *

Then Mahamati said to the Blessed One: The philosophers declare that the world rises from causal agencies according to a law of causation; they state that their cause is unborn and is not to be annihilated. They mention nine primary elements: Ishvara the Creator, the Creation, atoms, etc., which being elementary are unborn and not to be annihilated. The Blessed One, while teaching that all things are un-born and that there is no annihilation, also declares that the world takes its rise from ignorance, discrimination, attachment, deed, etc., working according to a law of causation. Though the two sets of elements may differ in form and name, there does not appear to be any essential difference between the two positions. If there is anything that is distinctive and superior in the Blessed One's teaching, pray tell us, Blessed One, what it is?

The Blessed One replied: My teaching of no-birth and no-annihilation is not like that of the philosophers, nor is it like their doctrine of birth and impermanency. That to which the philosophers ascribe the characteristic of no-birth and no-annihilation is the self-nature of all things, which causes them to fall into the dualism of being and non-being. My teaching transcends the whole conception of being and non-being; it has nothing to do with birth, abiding and destruction; nor with existence and non-existence. I teach that the multitudinousness of objects have no reality in themselves but are only seen of the mind and, therefore, are of the nature of maya and a dream. I teach the non-existence of things because they carry no signs of any inherent self-nature. It is true that in one sense they are seen and discriminated by the senses as individualised objects; but in another sense, because of the absence of any characteristic marks of self-nature, they are not seen but are only imagined. In one sense they are graspable, but in another sense, they are not graspable.

When it is clearly understood that there is nothing in the world but what is seen of the mind itself, discrimination no more rises, and the wise are established in their true abode which is the realm of quietude. The ignorant discriminate and work trying to adjust themselves to external conditions, and are constantly perturbed in mind; unrealities are imagined and discriminated, while realities are unseen and ignored. It is not so with the wise. To illustrate: What the ignorant see is like the magically-created city of the Gandharvas, where children are shown streets and houses, and phantom merchants, and people going in and coming out. This imaginary city with its streets and houses and people going in and coming out, are not thought of as being born or being annihilated, because in their case there is no question as to their existence or non-existence. In like manner, I teach, that there is nothing made nor unmade; that there is nothing that has connection with birth and destruction except as the ignorant cherish falsely imagined notions as to the reality of the external world. When objects are not seen and judged as they truly are in themselves, there is discrimination and clinging to the notions of being and non-being, and individualised self-nature, and as long as these notions of individuality and self-nature persist, the philosophers are bound to explain the external world by a law of causation. This position raises the question of a first cause which the philosophers meet by asserting that their first cause, Ishvara and the primal elements, are un-born and un-annihilate; which position is without evidence and is irrational.

Ignorant people and worldly philosophers cherish a kind of no-birth, but it is not the no-birth which I teach. I teach the un-bornness of the un-born essence of all things which teaching is established in the minds of the wise by their self-realisation of Noble Wisdom. A ladle, clay, a vessel, a wheel, or seeds, or elements—these are external conditions; ignorance, discrimination, attachment, habit, karma,—these are inner conditions. When this entire universe is regarded as concatenation and as nothing else but concatenation, then the mind, by its patient acceptance of the truth that all things are un-born, gains tranquillity.

CHAPTER IV

Perfect Knowledge, or Knowledge of
Reality

Then Mahamati asked the Blessed One: Pray tell us,
Blessed One, about the five Dharmas, so that we may fully
understand Perfect Knowledge?

The Blessed One replied: The five Dharmas are: appearance, name, discrimination, right-knowledge and Reality. By
appearance is meant that which reveals itself to the senses and
to the discriminating-mind and is perceived as form, sound,
odour, taste, and touch. Out of these appearances ideas are
formed, such as clay, water, jar, etc., by which one says: this
is such and such a thing and is no other,—this is name. When
appearances are contrasted and names compared, as when we
say: this is an elephant, this is a horse, a cart, a pedestrian, a
man, a woman, or, this is mind and what belongs to it,—the
things thus named are said to be discriminated. As these discriminations come to be seen as mutually conditioning, as empty
of self-substance, as un-born, and thus come to be seen as they
truly are, that is, as manifestations of the mind itself,—this is
right-knowledge. By it the wise cease to regard appearances
and names as realities.

When appearances and names are put away and all discrimination ceases, that which remains is the true and essential nature of things and, as nothing can be predicated as to the nature of essence, it is called the "Suchness" of Reality. This
universal, undifferentiated, inscrutable, "Suchness" is the only
Reality but it is variously characterised as Truth, Mind-essence,
Transcendental Intelligence, Noble Wisdom, etc. This Dharma
of the imagelessness of the Essence-nature of Ultimate Reality
is the Dharma which has been proclaimed by all the Buddhas,
and when all things are understood in full agreement with it,
one is in possession of Perfect Knowledge, and is on his way
to the attainment of the Transcendental Intelligence of the
Tathagatas.

* * *

Then Mahamati said to the Blessed One: Are the three
self-natures, of things, ideas, and Reality, to be considered as

included in the Five Dharmas, or as having their own characteristics complete in themselves.

The Blessed One replied: The three self-natures, the eightfold mind-system, and the twofold egolessness are all included in the Five Dharmas. The self-natures of things, of ideas, and of the sixfold mind-system, correspond with the Dharmas of appearance, name and discrimination; the self-nature of Universal Mind and Reality corresponds to the Dharmas of right-knowledge and "Suchness."

By becoming attached to what is seen of the mind itself, there is an activity awakened which is perpetuated by habit-energy that becomes manifest in the mind-system. From the activities of the mind-system there rises the notion of an ego-soul and its belongings; the discriminations, attachments, and notion of an ego-soul, rising simultaneously like the sun and its rays of light.

By the egolessness of things is meant that the elements that make up the aggregates of personality and its objective world being characterised by the nature of maya and destitute of anything that can be called ego-substance, are therefore un-born and have no self-nature. How can *things* be said to have an ego-soul? By the egolessness of persons is meant that in the aggregates that make up personality there is no ego-substance, nor anything that is like ego-substance nor that belongs to it. The mind-system, which is the most characteristic mark of personality, originated in ignorance, discrimination, desire and deed; and its activities are perpetuated by perceiving, grasping and becoming attached to objects as if they were real. The memory of these discriminations, desires, attachments and deeds is stored in Universal Mind since beginningless time, and is still being accumulated where it conditions the appearance of personality and its environment and brings about constant change and destruction from moment to moment. The manifestations are like a river, a seed, a lamp, a cloud, the wind; Universal mind in its voraciousness to store up everything, is like a monkey never at rest, like a fly ever in search of food and without partiality, like a fire that is never satisfied, like a water-lifting machine that goes on rolling. Universal mind as defiled by habit-energy is like a magician that causes phantom things and people to appear and move about. A thorough understanding of these things is necessary to an understanding of the egoless-ness of persons.

There are four kinds of Knowledge: Appearance-knowledge, relative-knowledge, perfect-knowledge, and Transcendental Intelligence. Appearance-knowledge belongs to the ignorant and simple-minded who are addicted to the notion of being and non-being, and who are frightened at the thought of being un-born. It is produced by the concordance of the triple combina-tion and attaches itself to the multiplicities of objects; it is characterised by attainability and accumulation; it is subject to birth and destruction. Appearance-knowledge belongs to word-mongers who revel in discriminations, assertions and negations.

Relative-knowledge belongs to the mind-world of the philos-ophers. It rises from the mind's ability to consider the rela-tions which appearances bear to each other and to the mind considering them, it rises from the mind's ability to arrange, combine and analyse these relations by its powers of discursive logic and imagination, by reason of which it is able to peer into the meaning and significance of things.

Perfect-knowledge belongs to the world of the Bodhisattvas who recognise that all things are but manifestations of mind; who clearly understand the emptiness, the un-bornness, the ego-lessness of all things; and who have entered into an under-standing of the Five Dharmas, the twofold egolessness, and into the truth of imagelessness. Perfect-knowledge differentiates the Bodhisattva stages, and is the pathway and the entrance into the exalted state of self-realisation of Noble Wisdom.

Perfect-knowledge (jnana) belongs to the Bodhisattvas who are entirely free from the dualisms of being and non-being, no-birth and no-annihilation, all assertions and negations, and who, by reason of self-realisation, have gained an insight into the truths of egolessness and imagelessness. They no longer dis-criminate the world as subject to causation: they regard the causation that rules the world as something like the fabled city of the Gandharvas. To them the world is like a vision and a dream, it is like the birth and death of a barren-woman's child; to them there is nothing evolving and nothing disappearing.

The wise who cherish Perfect-knowledge, may be divided into three classes: disciples, masters and Arhats. Common dis-ciples are separated from masters as common disciples continue to cherish the notion of individuality and generality; masters rise from common disciples when, forsaking the error of individuality and generality, they still cling to the notion of an ego-soul by reason of which they go off by themselves into retirement and solitude. Arhats rise when the error of all discrimination is realised. Error being discriminated by the wise turns into Truth by virtue of the "turning-about" that takes place within the deepest consciousness. Mind, thus emancipated, enters into perfect self-realisation of Noble Wisdom.

But, Mahamati, if you *assert* that there is such a thing as Noble Wisdom, it no longer holds good, because anything of which something is asserted thereby partakes of the nature of being and is thus characterised with the quality of birth. The very assertion: "All things are un-born" destroys the truthfulness of it. The same is true of the statements: "All things are empty," and "All things have no self-nature,"—both are untenable when put in the form of assertions. But when it is pointed out that all things are like a dream and a vision, it means that in one way things are perceived, and in another way they are not perceived; that is, in ignorance they are perceived but in Perfect-knowledge they are not perceived. All assertions and negations being thought-constructions are un-born. Even the assertion that Universal Mind and Noble Wisdom are Ultimate Reality, is thought construction and, therefore, is unborn. As "things" there is no Universal Mind, there is no Noble Wisdom, there is no Ultimate Reality. The insight of the wise who move about in the realm of imagelessness and its solitude is pure. That is, for the wise all "things" are wiped away and even the state of imagelessness ceases to exist.

CHAPTER V

The Mind System

Then Mahamati said to the Blessed One: Pray tell us, Blessed One, what is meant by the mind (*citta*)?

The Blessed One replied: All things of this world, be they seemingly good or bad, faulty or faultless, effect-producing or

not effect-producing, receptive or non-receptive, may be divided
into two classes: evil out-flowings and the non out-flowing
good. The five grasping elements that make up the aggregates
of personality, namely, form, sensation, perception, discrimination, and consciousness, and that are imagined to be good and
bad, have their rise in the habit-energy of the mind-system,—
they are the evil out-flowings of life. The spiritual attainments
and the joys of the Samadhis and the fruitage of the Samapattis that come to the wise through their self-realisation of Noble
Wisdom and that culminate in their return and participation in
the relations of the triple world are called the non out-flowing
good.

The mind-system which is the source of the evil out-flowings
consists of the five sense-organs and their accompanying sense-
minds (vijnanas) all of which are unified in the discriminating-
mind (manovijnana). There is an unending succession of sense-
concepts flowing into this discriminating or thinking-mind which
combines them and discriminates them and passes judgment
upon them as to their goodness or badness. Then follows
aversion to or desire for them and attachment and deed; thus
the entire system moves on continuously and closely bound together. But it fails to see and understand that what it sees
and discriminates and grasps is only a manifestation of its own
activity and has no other basis, and so the mind goes on erroneously perceiving and discriminating differences of forms and
qualities, not remaining still even for a minute.

In the mind-system there are three modes of activity dis-
tinguishable: the sense-minds functioning while remaining in
their original nature, the sense-minds as producing effects, and
the sense-minds as evolving. By normal functioning the sense-
minds grasp appropriate elements of their external world, by
which sensation and perception arise at once and by degrees in
every sense-organ and every sense-mind, in the pores of the
skin, and even in the atoms that make up the body, by which
the whole field is apprehended like a mirror reflecting objects,
and not realising that the external world itself is only a manifestation of mind. The second mode of activity produces effects
by which these sensations react on the discriminating mind to
produce perceptions, attractions, aversions, grasping, deed and
habit. The third mode of activity has to do with the growth,
development and passing of the mind-system, that is, the mind-

system is in subjection to its own habit-energy accumulated
from beginningless time, as for instance: the "eyeness" in the
eye that predisposes it to grasp and become attached to multi-
ple forms and appearances. In this way the activities of the
evolving mind-system by reason of its habit-energy stirs up
waves of objectivity on the face of Universal Mind which in
turn conditions the activities and evolvement of the mind-system. Appearances, perception, attraction, grasping, deed, habit,
reaction, condition one another incessantly, and the functioning
sense-minds, the discriminating-mind and Universal Mind are
thus bound up together. Thus, by reason of discrimination of
that which by nature is maya-like and unreal false-imagination
and erroneous reasoning takes place, action follows and its
habit-energy accumulates thereby defiling the pure face of Universal Mind, and as a result the mind-system comes into functioning and the physical body has its genesis. But the discriminating-mind has no thought that by its discriminations and attachments it is conditioning the whole body and so the sense-
minds and the discriminating-mind go on mutually related and
mutually conditioned in a most intimate manner and building
up a world of representations out of the activities of its own
imagination. As a mirror reflects forms, the perceiving senses
perceive appearances which the discriminating-mind gathers together and proceeds to discriminate, to name and become attached to. Between these two functions there is no gap, nevertheless, they are mutually conditioning. The perceiving senses
grasp that for which they have an affinity, and there is a transformation takes place in their structure by reason of which the
mind proceeds to combine, discriminate, apprise, and act; then
follows habit-energy and the establishing of the mind and its
continuance.

The discriminating-mind because of its capacity to discriminate, judge, select and reason about, is also called the thinking, or intellectual-mind. There are three divisions of its
mental activity: mentation which functions in connection with
attachment to objects and ideas, mentation that functions in
connection with general ideas, and mentation that examines
into the validity of these general ideas. The mentation which
functions in connection with attachment to objects and ideas
derived from discrimination, discriminates the mind from its
mental processes and accepts the ideas from it as being real

and becomes attached to them. A variety of false judgments are thus arrived at as to being, multiplicity, individuality, value, etc., a strong grasping takes place which is perpetuated by habit-energy and thus discrimination goes on asserting itself.

These mental processes give rise to general conceptions of warmth, fluidity, motility, and solidity, as characterising the objects of discrimination, while the tenacious holding to these general ideas gives rise to proposition, reason, definition, and illustration, all of which lead to the assertions of relative knowledge and the establishment of confidence in birth, self-nature, and an ego-soul.

By mentation as an examining function is meant the intellectual act of examining into these general conclusions as to their validity, significance, and truthfulness. This is the faculty that leads to understanding, right-knowledge and points the way to self-realisation.

* * *

Then Mahamati said to the Blessed One: Pray tell us, Blessed One, what relation ego-personality bears to the mind-system?

The Blessed One replied: To explain it, it is first necessary to speak of the self-nature of the five grasping aggregates that make up personality, although as I have already shown they are empty, un-born, and without self-nature. These five grasping aggregates are: form, sensation, perception, discrimination, consciousness. Of these, form belongs to what is made of the so-called primary elements, whatever they may be. The four remaining aggregates are without form and ought not to be reckoned as four, because they merge imperceptibly into one another. They are like space which cannot be numbered; it is only due to imagination that they are discriminated and likened to space. Because things are endowed with appearances of being, characteristic-marks, perceivableness, abode, work, one can say that they are born of effect-producing causes, but this can not be said of these four intangible aggregates for they are without form and marks. These four mental aggregates that make up personality are beyond calculability, they are beyond the four propositions, they are not to be predicated as existing nor as not existing, but together they constitute what is known as mortal-mind. They are even more maya-like and dream-like

than are things, nevertheless, as discriminating mortal-mind they
obstruct the self-realisation of Noble Wisdom. But it is only
by the ignorant that they are enumerated and thought of as
an ego-personality; the wise do not do so. This discrimination
of the five aggregates that make up personality and that serve
as a basis for an ego-soul and ground for its desires and self-
interests must be given up, and in its place the truth of imagelessness and solitude should be established.

*   *   *

Then said Mahamati to the Blessed One: Pray tell us,
Blessed One, about Universal Mind and its relation to the
lower mind-system?

The Blessed One replied: The sense-minds and their centralised discriminating-mind are related to the external world
which is a manifestation of itself and is given over to perceiving, discriminating, and grasping its maya-like appearances.
Universal Mind (*Alaya-vijnana*) transcends all individuation
and limits. Universal Mind is thoroughly pure in its essential
nature, subsisting unchanged and free from faults of impermanence, undisturbed by egoism, unruffled by distinctions, desires and aversions. Universal Mind is like a great ocean, its
surface ruffled by waves and surges but its depths remaining
forever unmoved. In itself it is devoid of personality and all
that belongs to it, but by reason of the defilement upon its
face it is like an actor and plays a variety of parts, among
which a mutual functioning takes place and the mind-system
arises. The principle of intellection becomes divided and mind,
the functions of mind, the evil out-flowings of mind, take on
individuation. The sevenfold gradation of mind appears:
namely, intuitive self-realisation, thinking-desiring-discriminat-
ing, seeing, hearing, tasting, smelling, touching, and all their
interactions and reactions take their rise.

The discriminating-mind is the cause of the sense-minds and
is their support and with them is kept functioning as it de-
scribes and becomes attached to a world of objects, and then,
by means of its habit-energy, it defiles the face of Universal
Mind. Thus Universal Mind becomes the storage and clearing
house of all the accumulated products of mentation and action
since beginningless time.

Between Universal Mind and the individual discriminating-mind is the intuitive-mind (*manas*) which is dependent upon Universal Mind for its cause and support and enters into relations with both. It partakes of the universality of Universal Mind, shares its purity, and like it, is above form and momentariness. It is through the intuitive-mind that the good non-out-flowings emerge, are manifested and are realised. Fortunate it is that intuition is not momentary for if the enlightenment which comes by intuition were momentary the wise would lose their "wiseness" which they do not. But the intuitive-mind enters into relations with the lower mind-system, shares its experiences and reflects upon its activities.

Intuitive-mind is one with Universal Mind by reason of its participation in Transcendental Intelligence (*Arya-jnana*), and is one with the mind-system by its comprehension of differentiated knowledge (*vijnana*). Intuitive-mind has no body of its own nor any marks by which it can be differentiated. Universal Mind is its cause and support but it is evolved along with the notion of an ego and what belongs to it, to which it clings and upon which it reflects. Through intuitive-mind, by the faculty of intuition which is a mingling of both identity and perceiving, the inconceivable wisdom of Universal Mind is revealed and made realisable. Like Universal Mind it can not be the source of error.

The discriminating-mind is a dancer and a magician with the objective world as his stage. Intuitive-mind is the wise jester who travels with the magician and reflects upon his emptiness and transiency. Universal Mind keeps the record and knows what must be and what may be. It is because of the activities of the discriminating-mind that error rises and an objective world evolves and the notion of an ego-soul becomes established. If and when the discriminating-mind can be gotten rid of, the whole mind-system will cease to function and Universal Mind will alone remain. Getting rid of the discriminating-mind removes the cause of all error.

* * *

Then said Mahamati to the Blessed One: Pray tell us, Blessed One, what is meant by the cessation of the mind-system?

The Blessed One replied: The five sense-functions and their discriminating and thinking function have their risings and complete endings from moment to moment. They are born with discrimination as cause, with form and appearance and objectivity closely linked together as condition. The will-to-live is the mother, ignorance is the father. By setting up names and forms greed is multiplied and thus the mind goes on mutually conditioning and being conditioned. By becoming attached to names and forms, not realising that they have no more basis than the activities of the mind itself, error rises, false-imagination as to pleasure and pain rises, and the way to emancipation is blocked. The lower system of sense-minds and the discriminating-mind do not really suffer pleasure and pain—they only imagine they do. Pleasure and pain are the deceptive reactions of mortal-mind as it grasps an imaginary objective world.

There are two ways in which the ceasing of the mind-system may take place: as regards form, and as regards continuation. The sense-organs function as regards form by the interaction of form, contact and grasping; and they cease to function when this contact is broken. As regards continuation,—when these interactions of form, contact and grasping cease, there is no more continuation of the seeing, hearing and other sense functions; with the ceasing of these sense functions, the discriminations, graspings and attachments of the discriminating-mind cease; and with their ceasing act and deed and their habit-energy cease, and there is no more accumulation of karma-defilement on the face of Universal Mind.

If the evolving mortal-mind were of the same nature as Universal Mind the cessation of the lower mind-system would mean the cessation of Universal Mind, but they are different for Universal Mind is not the cause of mortal-mind. There is no cessation of Universal Mind in its pure and essence-nature. What ceases to function is not Universal Mind in its essence-nature, but is the cessation of the effect-producing defilements upon its face that have been caused by the accumulation of the habit-energy of the activities of the discriminating and thinking mortal-mind. There is no cessation of Divine Mind which, in itself, is the abode of Reality and the Womb of Truth.

By the cessation of the sense-minds is meant, not the cessation of their perceiving functions, but the cessation of their discriminating and naming activities which are centralised in the discriminating mortal-mind. By the cessation of the mind-system as a whole is meant, the cessation of discrimination, the clearing away of the various attachments, and, therefore, the clearing away of the defilements of habit-energy in the face of Universal Mind which have been accumulating since beginningless time by reason of these discriminations, attachments, erroneous reasonings, and following acts. The cessation of the continuation aspect of the mind-system as a whole, takes place when there is the cessation of that which supports the mind-system, namely, the discriminating mortal-mind. With the cessation of mortal-mind the entire world of maya and desire disappears. Getting rid of the discriminating mortal-mind is Nirvana.

But the cessation of the discriminating-mind can not take place until there has been a "turning-about" in the deepest seat of consciousness. The mental habit of looking outward by the discriminating-mind upon an external objective world must be given up, and a new habit of realising Truth within the intuitive-mind by becoming one with Truth itself must be established. Until this intuitive self-realisation of Noble Wisdom is attained, the evolving mind-system will go on. But when an insight into the five Dharmas, the three self-natures, and the twofold egolessness is attained, then the way will be opened for this "turning-about" to take place. With the ending of pleasure and pain, of conflicting ideas, of the disturbing interests of egoism, a state of tranquillisation will be attained in which the truths of emancipation will be fully understood and there will be no further evil out-flowings of the mind-system to interfere with the perfect self-realisation of Noble Wisdom.

CHAPTER VI

Transcendental Intelligence

Then said Mahamati: Pray tell us, Blessed One, what constitutes Transcendental Intelligence?

The Blessed One replied: Transcendental Intelligence is the inner state of self-realisation of Noble Wisdom. It is realised suddenly and intuitively as the "turning-about" takes place in the deepest seat of consciousness; it neither enters nor goes out—it is like the moon seen in water. Transcendental Intelligence is not subject to birth nor destruction; it has nothing to do with combination nor concordance; it is devoid of attachment and accumulation; it transcends all dualistic conceptions.

When Transcendental Intelligence is considered, four things must be kept in mind: words, meanings, teachings and Noble Wisdom (*Arya-prajna*). Words are employed to express meanings but they are dependent upon discriminations and memory as cause, and upon the employment of sounds or letters by which a mutual transference of meaning is possible. Words are only symbols and may or may not clearly and fully express the meaning intended and, moreover, words may be understood quite differently from what was intended by the speaker. Words are neither different nor not different from meaning and meaning stands in the same relation to words.

If meaning is different from words it could not be made manifest by means of words; but meaning is illumined by words as things are by a lamp. Words are just like a man carrying a lamp to look for his property, by which he can say: this is my property. Just so, by means of words and speech originating in discrimination, the Bodhisattva can enter into the meaning of the teachings of the Tathagatas and through the meaning he can enter into the exalted state of self-realisation of Noble Wisdom, which, in itself, is free from word discrimination. But if a man becomes attached to the literal meaning of words and holds fast to the illusion that words and meaning are in agreement, especially in such things as Nirvana which is unborn and un-dying, or as to distinctions of the Vehicles, the five Dharmas, the three self-natures, then he will fail to understand the true meaning and will become entangled in assertions and refutations. Just as varieties of objects are seen and discriminated in dreams and in visions, so ideas and statements are discriminated erroneously and error goes on multiplying.

The ignorant and simple-minded declare that meaning is not otherwise than words, that as words are, so is meaning. They think that as meaning has no body of its own that it cannot be different from words and, therefore, declare meaning to be identical with words. In this they are ignorant of the nature of words, which are subject to birth and death, whereas meaning is not; words are dependent upon letters and meaning is not; meaning is apart from existence and non-existence, it has no substratum, it is un-born. The Tathagatas do not teach a Dharma that is dependent upon letters. Anyone who teaches a doctrine that is dependent upon letters and words is a mere prattler, because Truth is beyond letters and words and books.

This does not mean that words and books never declare what is in conformity with meaning and truth, but it means that words and books are dependent upon discriminations, while meaning and truth are not; moreover, words and books are subject to the interpretation of individual minds, while meaning and truth are not. But if Truth is not expressed in words and books, the scriptures which contain the meaning of Truth would disappear, and when the scriptures disappear there will be no more disciples and masters and Bodhisattvas and Buddhas, and there will be nothing to teach. But no one must become attached to the words of the scriptures because even the canonical texts sometimes deviate from their straightforward course owing to the imperfect functioning of sentient minds. Religious discourses are given by myself and other Tathagatas in response to the varying needs and faiths of all manner of beings, in order to free them from dependence upon the thinking function of the mind-system, but they are not given to take the place of self-realisation of Noble Wisdom. When there is recognition that there is nothing in the world but what is seen of the mind itself, all dualistic discriminations will be discarded and the truth of imagelessness will be understood, and will be seen to be in conformity with meaning rather than with words and letters.

The ignorant and simple-minded being fascinated with their self-imaginations and erroneous reasonings, keep on dancing and leaping about, but are unable to understand the discourse by words about the truth of self-realisation, much less are they able to understand the Truth itself. Clinging to the external world, they cling to the study of books which are a means only, and do not know properly how to ascertain the truth of self-realisation, which is Truth unspoiled by the four propositions. Self-realisation is an exalted state of inner attainment which transcends all dualistic thinking and which is above the mind-system with its logic, reasoning, theorising, and illustrations. The Tathagatas discourse to the ignorant, but sustain the Bodhisattvas as they seek self-realisation of Noble Wisdom.

Therefore, let every disciple take good heed not to become attached to words as being in perfect conformity with meaning, because Truth is not in the letters. When a man with his finger-tip points to something to somebody, the finger-tip may be mistaken for the thing pointed at; in like manner the ignorant and simple-minded, like children, are unable even to the day of their death to abandon the idea that in the finger-tip of words there is the meaning itself. They cannot realise Ultimate Reality because of their intent clinging to words which were intended to be no more than a pointing finger. Words and their discrimination bind one to the dreary round of rebirths into the world of birth-and-death; meaning stands alone and is a guide to Nirvana. Meaning is attained by much learning, and much learning is attained by becoming conversant with meaning and not with words; therefore, let seekers for truth reverently approach those who are wise and avoid the sticklers for particular words.

As for teachings: there are priests and popular preachers who are given to ritual and ceremony and who are skilled in various incantations and in the art of eloquence; they should not be honored nor reverently attended upon, for what one gains from them is emotional excitement and worldly enjoyment; it is not the Dharma. Such preachers, by their clever manipulation of words and phrases and various reasonings and incantations, being the mere prattle of a child, as far as one can make out and not at all in accordance with truth nor in unison with meaning, only serves to awaken sentiment and emotion, while it stupefies the mind. As he himself does not understand the meaning of all things, he only confuses the minds of his hearers with his dualistic views. Not understanding himself, that there is nothing but what is seen of the mind, and himself attached to the notion of self-nature in external things, and unable to know one path from another, he has no deliverance to offer others. Thus these priests and popular preachers who are clever in various incantations and skilled in the art of eloquence, themselves never being emancipated from such calamities as birth, old age, disease, sorrow, lamentation, pain and despair, lead the ignorant into bewilderment by means of their various words, phrases, examples, and conclusions.

Then there are the materialistic philosophers. No respect nor service is to be shown them because their teachings, though they may be explained by using hundreds of thousands of words and phrases, do not go beyond the concerns of this world and this body and in the end they lead to suffering. As the materialists recognise no truth as existing by itself, they are split up into many schools, each of which clings to its own way of reasoning.

But there is that which does not belong to materialism and which is not reached by the knowledge of the philosophers who cling to false-discriminations and erroneous reasonings because they fail to see that, fundamentally, there is no reality in external objects. When it is recognised that there is nothing beyond what is seen of the mind itself, the discrimination of being and non-being ceases and, as there is thus no external world as the object of perception, nothing remains but the solitude of Reality. This does not belong to the materialistic philosophers, it is the domain of the Tathagatas. If such things are imagined as the coming and going of the mind-system, vanishing and appearing, solicitation, attachment, intense affection, a philosophic hypothesis, a theory, an abode, a sense-concept, atomic attraction, organism, growth, thirst, grasping,—these things belong to materialism, they are not mine. These are things that are the object of worldly interest, to be sensed, handled and tasted; these are the things that attract one, that bind one to the external world; these are the things that appear in the elements that make up the aggregates of personality where, owing to the procreative force of lust, there arise all kinds of disaster, birth, sorrow, lamentation, pain, despair, disease, old age, death. All these things concern worldly interests and enjoyment; they lie along the path of the philosophers, which is not the path of the Dharma. When the true egolessness of things and persons is understood, discrimination ceases to assert itself; the lower mind-system ceases to function; the various Bodhisattva stages are followed one after another; the Bodhisattva is able to utter his ten inexhaustible vows and is anointed by all the Buddhas. The Bodhisattva becomes master of himself and of all things by virtue of a life of spontaneous and radiant effortlessness. Thus the Dharma, which is Transcendental Intelligence, transcends all discriminations, all false-reasonings, all philosophical systems, all dualism.

* * *

Then Mahamati said to the Blessed One: In the Scriptures mention is made of the Womb of Tathagatahood and it is taught that that which is born of it is by nature bright and pure, originally unspotted and endowed with the thirty-two marks of excellence. As it is described it is a precious gem but wrapped in a dirty garment soiled by greed, anger, folly and false-imagination. We are taught that this Buddha-nature immanent in every one is eternal, unchanging, auspicious. Is not this which is born of the Womb of Tathagatahood the same as the soul-substance that is taught by the philosophers? The Divine Atman as taught by them is also claimed to be eternal, inscrutable, unchanging, imperishable. Is there, or is there not a difference?

The Blessed One replied: No, Mahamati, my Womb of Tathagatahood is not the same as the Divine Atman as taught by the philosophers. What I teach is Tathagatahood in the sense of Dharmakaya, Ultimate Oneness, Nirvana, emptiness, unbornness, unqualifiedness, devoid of will-effort. The reason why I teach the doctrine of Tathagatahood is to cause the ignorant and simple-minded to lay aside their fears as they listen to the teaching of egolessness and come to understand the state of non-discrimination and imagelessness. The religious teachings of the Tathagatas are just like a potter making various vessels by his own skill of hand with the aid of rod, water and thread, out of the one mass of clay, so the Tathagatas by their command of skillful means issuing from Noble Wisdom, by various terms, expressions, and symbols, preach the twofold egolessness in order to remove the last trace of discrimination that is preventing disciples from attaining a self-realisation of Noble Wisdom. The doctrine of the Tathagata-womb is disclosed in order to awaken philosophers from their clinging to the notion of a Divine Atman as transcendental personality, so that their minds that have become attached to the imaginary notion of "soul" as being something self-existent, may be quickly awakened to a state of perfect enlightenment. All such notions as causation, succession, atoms, primary elements, that make up personality, personal soul, Supreme Spirit, Sovereign God, Creator, are all figments of the imagination and manifestations of mind. No, Mahamati, the Tathagata's doctrine of the Womb of Tathagatahood is not the same as the philosopher's Atman.

The Bodhisattva is said to have well grasped the teachings of the Tathagatas when, all alone in a lonely place, by means of his Transcendental Intelligence, he walks the path leading

to Nirvana. Thereon his mind will unfold by perceiving, thinking, meditating, and, abiding in the practise of concentration
until he attains the "turning about" at the source of habit-
energy, he will thereafter lead a life of excellent deeds. His
mind concentrated on the state of Buddhahood, he will become
thoroughly conversant with the noble truth of self-realisation;
he will become perfect master of his own mind; he will be like
a gem radiating many colors; he will be able to assume bodies
of transformation; he will be able to enter into the minds of
all to help them; and, finally, by gradually ascending the stages
he will become established in the perfect Transcendental Intelligence of the Tathagatas.

Nevertheless, Transcendental Intelligence (*Arya-jnana*) is
not Noble Wisdom (*Arya-prajna*) itself; it is only an intuitive
awareness of it. Noble Wisdom is a perfect state of imagelessness; it is the Womb of "Suchness"; it is the all-conserving
Divine Mind (*Alaya-vijnana*) which in its pure Essence forever
abides in perfect patience and undisturbed tranquillity.

CHAPTER VII

Self-Realisation

Then said Mahamati: Pray tell us, Blessed One, what is the
nature of Self-realisation by reason of which we shall be able
to attain Transcendental Intelligence?

The Blessed One replied: Transcendental Intelligence rises
when the intellectual-mind reaches its limit and, if things are
to be realised in their true and essence nature, its processes of
mentation, which are based on particularised ideas, discriminations and judgments, must be transcended by an appeal to
some higher faculty of cognition, if there be such a higher
faculty. There is such a faculty in the intuitive-mind (*Manas*),
which as we have seen is the link between the intellectual-
mind and Universal Mind. While it is not an individualised
organ like the intellectual-mind, it has that which is much better,—direct dependence upon Universal Mind. While intuition
does not give information that can be analysed and discrimi-

nated, it gives that which is far superior,—self-realisation through identification.

* * *

Mahamati then asked the Blessed One, saying: Pray tell us, Blessed One, what clear understandings an earnest disciple should have if he is to be successful in the discipline that leads to self-realisation?

The Blessed One replied: There are four things by the fulfilling of which an earnest disciple may gain self-realisation of Noble Wisdom and become a Bodhisattva-Mahasattva: First, he must have a clear understanding that all things are only manifestations of the mind itself; second, he must discard the notion of birth, abiding and disappearance; third, he must clearly understand the egolessness of both things and persons; and fourth, he must have a true conception of what constitutes self-realisation of Noble Wisdom. Provided with these four understandings, earnest disciples may become Bodhisattvas and attain Transcendental Intelligence.

As to the first; he must recognise and be fully convinced that this triple world is nothing but a complex manifestation of one's mental activities; that it is devoid of selfness and its belongings; that there are no strivings, no comings, no goings. He must recognise and accept the fact that this triple world is manifested and imagined as real only under the influence of habit-energy that has been accumulated since the beginningless past by reason of memory, false-imagination, false-reasoning, and attachments to the multiplicities of objects and reactions in close relationship and in conformity to ideas of body-property-and-abode.

As to the second; he must recognise and be convinced that all things are to be regarded as forms seen in a vision and a dream, empty of substance, un-born and without self-nature; that all things exist only by reason of a complicated network of causation which owes its rise to discrimination and attachment and which eventuates in the rise of the mind-system and its belongings and evolvements.

As to the third; he must recognise and patiently accept the fact that his own mind and personality is also mind-constructed, that it is empty of substance, unborn and egoless. With these three things clearly in mind, the Bodhisattva will be able to enter into the truth of imagelessness.

As to the fourth; he must have a true conception of what constitutes self-realisation of Noble Wisdom. First, it is not comparable to the perceptions attained by the sense-mind, neither is it comparable to the cognition of the discriminating and intellectual-mind. Both of these presuppose a difference between self and not-self and the knowledge so attained is characterised by individuality and generality. Self-realisation is based on identity and oneness; there is nothing to be discriminated nor predicated concerning it. But to enter into it the Bodhisattva must be free from all presuppositions and attachments to things, ideas and selfness.

* * *

Then said Mahamati to the Blessed One: Pray tell us, Blessed One, concerning the characteristics of deep attachments to existence and as to how we may become detached from existence?

The Blessed One replied: When one tries to understand the significance of things by means of words and discriminations, there follow immeasurably deep-seated attachments to existence. For instance: there are the deep-seated attachments to signs of individuality, to causation, to the notion of being and non-being, to the discrimination of birth and death, of doing and not-doing, to the habit of discrimination itself upon which the philosophers are so dependent.

There are three attachments that are especially deep-seated in the minds of all: greed, anger and infatuation, which are based on lust, fear and pride. Back of these lies discrimination and desire which is procreative and is accompanied with excitement and avariciousness and love of comfort and desire for eternal life; and, following, is a succession of rebirths on the five paths of existence and a continuation of attachments. But if these attachments are broken off, no signs of attachment nor of detachment will remain because they are based on things that are non-existent; when this truth is clearly understood the net of attachment is cleared away.

But depending upon and attaching itself to the triple combination which works in unison there is the rising and the continuation of the mind-system incessantly functioning, and because of it there is the deeply-felt and continuous assertion of the will-to-live. When the triple combination that causes the functioning of the mind-system ceases to exist, there is the triple emancipation and there is no further rising of any combination. When the existence and the non-existence of the external world are recognised as rising from the mind itself, then the Bodhisattva is prepared to enter into the state of imagelessness and therein to see into the emptiness which characterises all discrimination and all the deep-seated attachments resulting therefrom. Therein he will see no signs of deep-rooted attachment nor detachment; therein he will see no one in bondage and no one in emancipation, except those who themselves cherish bondage and emancipation, because in all things there is no "substance" to be taken hold of.

But so long as these discriminations are cherished by the ignorant and simple-minded they go on attaching themselves to them and, like the silkworm, go on spinning their thread of discrimination and enwrapping themselves and others, and are charmed with their prison. But to the wise there are no signs of attachment nor of detachment; all things are seen as abiding in solitude where there is no evolving of discrimination. Mahamati, you and all the Bodhisattvas should have your abode where you can see all things from the view-point of solitude.

Mahamati, when you and other Bodhisattvas understand well the distinction between attachment and detachment, you will be in possession of skillful means for avoiding becoming attached to words according to which one proceeds to grasp meanings. Free from the domination of words you will be able to establish yourselves where there will be a "turning about" in the deepest seat of consciousness by means of which you will attain self-realisation of Noble Wisdom and be able to enter into all the Buddha-lands and assemblies. There you will be stamped with the stamp of the powers, self-command, the psychic faculties, and will be endowed with the wisdom and the power of the ten inexhaustible vows, and will become radiant with the variegated rays of the Transformation Bodies. Therewith you will shine without effort like the moon, the sun, the magic wishing-jewel, and at every stage will view things as being of perfect oneness with yourself, uncontaminated by any self-consciousness. Seeing that all things are like a dream, you will be able to enter into the stage of the Tathagatas and be able to deliver discourses on the Dharma to the world of beings in accordance with their needs and be able to free them from all dualistic notions and false discriminations.

Mahamati, there are two ways of considering self-realisation: namely, the teachings about it, and the realisation itself. The teachings as variously given in the nine divisions of the doctrinal works, for the instructions of those who are inclined toward it, by making use of skillful means and expedients, are intended to awaken in all beings a true perception of the Dharma. The teachings are designed to keep one away from all the dualistic notions of being and non-being and oneness and otherness.

Realisation itself is within the inner consciousness. It is an inner experience that has no connection with the lower mind-system and its discriminations of words, ideas and philosophical speculations. It shines out with its own clear light to reveal the error and foolishness of mind-constructed teachings, to render impotent evil influences from without, and to guide one unerringly to the realm of the good non-outflowings. Mahamati, when the earnest disciple and Bodhisattva is provided with these requirements, the way is open to his perfect attainment of self-realisation of Noble Wisdom, and to the full enjoyment of the fruits that arise therefrom.

* * *

Then Mahamati asked the Blessed One, saying: Pray tell us, Blessed One, about the One Vehicle which the Blessed One has said characterises the attainment of the inner self-realisation of Noble Wisdom?

The Blessed One replied: In order to discard more easily discriminations and erroneous reasonings, the Bodhisattva should retire by himself to a quiet, secluded place where he may reflect within himself without relying on anyone else, and there let him exert himself to make successive advances along the stages; this solitude is the characteristic feature of the inner attainment of self-realisation of Noble Wisdom.

I call this the One Vehicle, not because it is the One Vehicle, but because it is only in solitude that one is able to recognise and realise the path of the One Vehicle. So long as the mind is distracted and is making conscious effort, there can be no culmination as regards the various vehicles; it is only when the mind is alone and quiet that it is able to forsake the discriminations of the external world and seek realisation of an inner realm where there is neither vehicle nor one who rides in it. I speak of the three vehicles in order to carry the ignorant. I do not speak much about the One Vehicle because there is no way by which earnest disciples and masters can realise Nirvana, unaided. According to the discourses of the Tathagatas earnest disciples should be segregated and disciplined and trained in meditation and dhyana whereby they are aided by many devices and expedients to realise emancipation. It is because earnest disciples and masters have not fully destroyed the habit-energy of karma and the hindrances of discriminative knowledge and human passion that they are often unable to accept the twofold egolessness and the inconceivable transformation death, that I preach the triple vehicle and not the One Vehicle. When earnest disciples have gotten rid of all their evil habit-energy and been able to realise the twofold egolessness, then they will not be intoxicated by the bliss of the Samadhis and will be awakened into the super-realm of the good non-outflowings. Being awakened into the realm of the good non-outflowings, they will be able to gather up all the requisites for the attainment of Noble Wisdom which is beyond conception and is of sovereign power. But really, Mahamati, there are no vehicles, and so I speak of the One Vehicle. Mahamati, the full recognition of the One Vehicle has never been attained by either earnest disciples, masters, or even by the great Brahma; it has been attained only by the Tathagatas themselves. That is the reason that it is known as the One Vehicle. I do not speak much about it because there is no way by which earnest disciples can realise Nirvana unaided.

* * *

Then Mahamati asked the Blessed One, saying: What are the steps that will lead an awakened disciple toward the self-realisation of Noble Wisdom?

The Blessed One replied: The beginning lies in the recognition that the external world is only a manifestation of the activities of the mind itself, and that the mind grasps it as an external world simply because of its habit of discrimination and false-reasoning. The disciple must get into the habit of looking at things truthfully. He must recognise the fact that the world has no self-nature, that it is un-born, that it is like a passing cloud, like an imaginary wheel made by a revolving firebrand, like the castle of the Gandharvas, like the moon reflected in the ocean, like a vision, a mirage, a dream. He must come to understand that mind in its essence-nature has nothing to do with discrimination nor causation; he must not listen to discourses based on the imaginary terms of qualifications; he must understand that Universal Mind in its pure essence is a state of imagelessness, that it is only because of the accumulated defilements on its face that body-property-and-abode appear to be its manifestations, that in its own pure nature it is unaffected and unaffecting by such changes as rising, abiding and destruction; he must fully understand that all these things come with the awakening of the notion of an ego-soul and its conscious mind. Therefore, Mahamati, let those disciples who wish to realise Noble Wisdom by following the Tathagata Vehicle desist from all discrimination and erroneous reasoning about such notions as the elements that make up the aggregates of personality and its sense-world or about such ideas as causation, rising, abiding and destruction, and exercise themselves in the discipline of dhyana that leads to the realisation of Noble Wisdom.

To practice dhyana, the earnest disciple should retire to a quiet and solitary place, remembering that life-long habits of discriminative thinking cannot be broken off easily nor quickly. There are four kinds of concentrative meditation (*dhyana*): The dhyana practised by the ignorant; the dhyana devoted to the examination of meaning; the dhyana with "suchness" (*tathata*) for its object; and the dhyana of the Tathagatas.

The dhyana practised by the ignorant is the one resorted to by those who are following the example of the disciples and masters but who do not understand its purpose and, therefore, it becomes "still-sitting" with vacant minds. This dhyana is practised, also, by those who, despising the body, see it as a shadow and a skeleton full of suffering and impurity, and yet who cling to the notion of an ego, seek to attain emancipation by the mere cessation of thought.

The dhyana devoted to the examination of meaning, is the one practised by those who, perceiving the untenability of such ideas as self, other and both, which are held by the philosophers, and who have passed beyond the twofold-egolessness,

devote dhyana to an examination of the significance of egolessness and the differentiations of the Bodhisattva stages.

The dhyana with Tathata, or "Suchness," or Oneness, or
the Divine Name, for its object is practised by those earnest
disciples and masters who, while fully recognising the twofold
egolessness and the imagelessness of Tathata, yet cling to the
notion of an ultimate Tathata.

The dhyana of the Tathagatas is the dhyana of those who
are entering upon the stage of Tathagatahood and who, abiding
in the triple bliss which characterises the self-realisation of Noble
Wisdom, are devoting themselves for the sake of all beings to
the accomplishment of incomprehensible works for their emancipation. This is the pure dhyana of the Tathagatas. When all
lesser things and ideas are transcended and forgotten, and there
remains only a perfect state of imagelessness where Tathagata
and Tathata are merged into perfect Oneness, then the Buddhas
will come together from all their Buddha-lands and with shining hands resting on his forehead will welcome a new
Tathagata.

CHAPTER VIII

The Attainment of Self-Realisation

Then said Mahamati to the Blessed One: Pray tell us more
as to what constitutes the state of self-realisation?

The Blessed One replied: In the life of an earnest disciple
there are two aspects that are to be distinguished: namely, the
state of attachment to the self-natures arising from discrimination of himself and his field of consciousness to which he is
related; and second, the excellent and exalted state of self-
realisation of Noble Wisdom. The state of attachment to the
discriminations of the self-natures of things, ideas and selfhood
is accompanied by emotions of pleasure or aversion according
to experience or as laid down in books of logic. Conforming
himself to the egolessness of things and holding back wrong
views as to his own egoness, he should abandon these thoughts
and hold himself firmly to the continuously ascending journey
of the stages.

The exalted state of self-realisation as it relates to an earnest disciple is a state of mental concentration in which he seeks to identify himself with Noble Wisdom. In that effort he must seek to annihilate all vagrant thoughts and notions belonging to the externality of things, and all ideas of individuality and generality, of suffering and impermanence, and cultivate the noblest ideas of egolessness and emptiness and imagelessness; thus will he attain a realisation of truth that is free from passion and is ever serene. When this active effort at mental concentration is successful it is followed by a more passive, receptive state of Samadhi in which the earnest disciple will enter into the blissful abode of Noble Wisdom and experience its consummations in the transformations of Samapatti. This is an earnest disciple's first experience of the exalted state of realisation, but as yet there is no discarding of habit-energy nor escaping from the transformation of death.

Having attained this exalted and blissful state of realisation as far as it can be attained by disciples, the Bodhisattva must not give himself up to the enjoyment of its bliss, for that would mean cessation, but should think compassionately of other beings and keep ever fresh his original vows; he should never let himself rest in nor exert himself in the bliss of the Samadhis.

But, Mahamati, as earnest disciples go on trying to advance on the path that leads to full realisation, there is one danger against which they must be on their guard. Disciples may not appreciate that the mind-system, because of its accumulated habit-energy, goes on functioning, more or less unconsciously, as long as they live. They may sometimes think that they can expedite the attainment of their goal of tranquillisation by entirely suppressing the activities of the mind-system. This is a mistake, for even if the activities of the mind are suppressed, the mind will still go on functioning because the seeds of habit-energy will still remain in it. What they think is extinction of mind, is really the non-functioning of the mind's external world to which they are no longer attached. That is, the goal of tranquillisation is to be reached not by suppressing all mind activity but by getting rid of discriminations and attachments.

Then there are others who, afraid of the suffering incident to the discriminations of life and death, unwisely seek Nirvana.

They have come to see that all things subject to discrimination have no reality and so imagine that Nirvana must consist in the annihilation of the senses and their fields of sensation; they do not appreciate that birth-and-death and Nirvana are not separate one from the other. They do not know that Nirvana is Universal Mind in its purity. Therefore, these stupid ones who cling to the notion that Nirvana is a world by itself that is outside what is seen by the mind, ignoring all the teachings of the Tathagatas concerning the external world, go on rolling themselves along the wheel of birth-and-death. But when they experience the "turning-about" in their deepest consciousness which will bring with it the perfect self-realisation of Noble Wisdom, then they will understand.

The true functioning of the mind is very subtle and difficult to be understood by young disciples, even masters with all their powers of right-knowledge and Samadhis often find it baffling. It is only the Tathagatas and the Bodhisattvas who are firmly established on the seventh stage who can fully understand its workings. Those earnest disciples and masters who wish to fully understand all the aspects of the different stages of Bodhisattvahood by the aid of their right-knowledge must do so by becoming thoroughly convinced that objects of discrimination are only seen to be so by the mind and, thus, by keeping themselves away from all discriminations and false reasonings which are also of the mind itself, by ever seeking to see things truly (*yathabhutam*), and by planting roots of goodness in Buddha-lands that know no limits made by differentiations.

To do all this the Bodhisattva should keep himself away from all turmoil, social excitements and sleepiness; let him keep away from the treatises and writings of worldly philosophers, and from the ritual and ceremonies of professional priestcraft. Let him retire to a secluded place in the forest and there devote himself to the practise of the various spiritual disciplines, because it is only by so doing that he will become capable of attaining in this world of multiplicities a true insight into the workings of Universal Mind in its Essence. There surrounded by his good friends the Buddhas, earnest disciples will become capable of understanding the significance of the mind-system and its place as a mediating agent between the external world and Universal Mind and he will become capable of

crossing the ocean of birth-and-death whicn rises from ignorance, desire and deed.

Having gained a thorough understanding of the mind-
system, the three self-natures, the twofold egolessness, and
established himself in the measure of self-realisation that goes
with that attainment, all of which may be gained by his right-
knowledge, the way will be clear for the Bodhisattva's further
advance along the stages of Bodhisattvahood. The disciple
should then abandon the understanding of mind which he has
gained by right-knowledge, which in comparison with Noble
Wisdom is like a lame donkey, and entering on the eighth
stage of Bodhisattvahood, he should then discipline himself in
Noble Wisdom according to its three aspects.

These aspects are: First, imagelessness which comes forth
when all things belonging to discipleship, mastership, and
philosophy are thoroughly mastered. Second, the power added
by all the Buddhas by reason of their original vows including
the identification of their lives and the sharing of their merit
with all sentient lives. Third, the perfect self-realisation that
thus far has only been realised in a measure. As the Bodhisattva succeeds in detaching himself from viewing all things,
including his own imagined egoness, in their phenomenality,
and realises the states of Samadhi and Samapatti whereby he
surveys the world as a vision and a dream, and being sustained
by all the Buddhas, he will be able to pass on to the full attainment of the Tathagata stage, which is Noble Wisdom itself.
This is the triplicity of the noble life and being furnished with
this triplicity the perfect self-realisation of Noble Wisdom has
been attained.

*　*　*

Then Mahamati asked the Blessed One, saying: Blessed
One, is the purification of the evil out-flowings of the mind
which come from clinging to the notions of an objective world
and an empirical soul, gradual or instantaneous?

The Blessed One replied: There are three characteristic out-
flows of the mind, namely, the evil out-flowings that rise from
thirst, grasping and attachment; the evil out-flowings that arise
from the illusions of the mind and the infatuations of egoism;
and the good non-outflowings that arise from Noble Wisdom.
The evil out-flowings that take place from recognising an ex-

ternal world, which in truth is only a manifestation of mind, and from becoming attached to it, are gradually purified and not instantaneously. Good behavior can only come by the path of restraint and effort. It is like a potter making pots that is done gradually and with attention and effort. It is like the mastery of comedy, dancing, singing, lute-playing, writing, and any other art; it must be acquired gradually and laboriously. Its reward will be a clearing insight into the emptiness and transiency of all things.

The evil out-flowings that arise from the illusions of the mind and the infatuations of egoism, concern the mental life more directly and are such things as fear, anger, hatred and pride; these are purified by study and meditation and that, too, must be attained gradually and not instananeously. It is like the amra fruit that ripens slowly; it is like grass, shrubs, herbs and trees that grow up from the earth gradually. Each must follow the path of study and meditation by himself gradually and with effort, but because of the original vows of the Bodhisattvas and all the Tathagatas who have devoted their merits and identified their lives with all animate life that all may be emancipated, they are not without aid and encouragement; but even with the aid of the Tathagatas, the purification of the evil out-flowings of the mind are at best slow and gradual, requiring both zeal and patience. Its reward is the gradual understanding of the twofold egolessness and its patient acceptance, and the feet well set on the stages of Bodhisattvahood.

But the good non-outflowings that come with self-realisation of Noble Wisdom, is a purification that comes instantaneously by the grace of the Tathagatas. It is like a mirror reflecting all forms and images instantaneously and without discrimination; it is like the sun or the moon revealing all forms instantaneously and illuminating them dispassionately with its light. In the same way the Tathagatas lead earnest disciples to a state of imagelessness; all the accumulations of habit-energy and karma that had been collecting since beginningless time because of attachment to erroneous views which have been entertained regarding an ego-soul and its external world, are cleared away, revealing instantaneously the realm of Transcendental Intelligence that belongs to Buddhahood. Just as Universal Mind defiled by accumulations of habit-energy and karma reveals multiplicities of ego-souls and their external worlds of false-imagination, so Universal Mind cleared of its defilements through the gradual purifications of the evil out-flowings that come by effort, study and meditation, and by the gradual self-realisation of Noble Wisdom, at the long last, like the Dharmata Buddha shining forth spontaneously with the rays that issue from its pure Self-nature, shines forth instantaneously. By it the mentality of all Bodhisattvas is matured instantaneously: they find themselves in the palatial abodes of the Akanistha heavens, themselves spontaneously radiating the various treasures of its spiritual abundance.

CHAPTER IX

The Fruit of Self-Realisation

Mahamati asked the Blessed One: Pray tell us, Blessed One, what is the fruitage that comes with self-realisation of Noble Wisdom?

The Blessed One replied: First, there will come a clearing insight into the meaning and significance of things and following that will come an unfolding insight into the significance of the spiritual ideals (*Paramitas*) by reason of which the Bodhisattvas will be able to enter more deeply into the abode of imagelessness and be able to experience the higher Samadhis and gradually to pass through the higher stages of Bodhisattvahood.

After experiencing the "turning-about" in the deepest seat of consciousness, they will experience other Samadhis even to the highest, the Vajravimbopama, which belongs to the Tathagatas and their transformations. They will be able to enter into the realm of consciousness that lies beyond the consciousness of the mind-system, even the consciousness of Tathagatahood. They will become endowed with all the powers, psychic faculties, self-mastery, loving compassion, skillful means, and ability to enter into other Buddha-lands. Before they had attained self-realisation of Noble Wisdom they had been influenced by the self-interests of egoism, but after they attain self-realisation they will find themselves reacting spontaneously to the impulses of a great and compassionate heart endowed with skillful and boundless means and sincerely and wholly devoted to the emancipation of all beings.

* * *

Mahamati said: Blessed One, tell us about the sustaining power of the Tathagatas by which the Bodhisattvas are aided to attain self-realisation of Noble Wisdom?

The Blessed One replied: There are two kinds of sustaining power, which issue from the Tathagatas and are at the service of the Bodhisattvas, sustained by which the Bodhisattvas should prostrate themselves before them and show their appreciation by asking questions. The first kind of sustaining power is the Bodhisattva's own adoration and faith in the Buddhas by reason of which the Buddhas are able to manifest themselves and render their aid and to ordain them with their own hands. The second kind of sustaining power is the power radiating from the Tathagatas that enables the Bodhisattvas to attain and to pass through the various Samadhis and Samapattis without becoming intoxicated by their bliss.

Being sustained by the power of the Buddhas, the Bodhisattva even at the first stage will be able to attain the Samadhi known as the Light of Mahayana. In that Samadhi Bodhisattvas will become conscious of the presence of the Tathagatas coming from all their different abodes in the ten quarters to impart to the Bodhisattvas their sustaining power in various ways. As the Bodhisattva Vajragarbha was sustained in his Samadhis and as many other Bodhisattvas of like degree and virtue have been sustained, so all earnest disciples and masters and Bodhisattvas may experience this sustaining power of the Buddhas in their Samadhis and Samapattis. The disciple's faith and the Tathagata's merit are two aspects of the same sustaining power and by it alone are the Bodhisattvas enabled to become one with the company of the Buddhas.

Whatever Samadhis, psychic faculties and teachings are realised by the Bodhisattvas, they are made possible only by the sustaining power of the Buddhas; if it were otherwise, the ignorant and the simple-minded might attain the same fruitage. Wherever the Tathagatas enter with their sustaining power there will be music, not only music made by human lips and played by human hands on various instruments, but there will be music among the grass and shrubs and trees, and in mountains and towns and palaces and hovels; much more will there be music in the hearts of those endowed with sentiency. The deaf, dumb and blind will be cured of their deficiencies and will rejoice in their emancipation. Such is the extraordinary virtue of the sustaining power imparted by the Tathagatas.

By the bestowal of this sustaining power, the Bodhisattvas are enabled to avoid the evils of passion, hatred and enslaving karma; they are enabled to transcend the dhyana of the beginners and to advance beyond the experience and truth already attained; they are enabled to demonstrate the Paramitas; and finally, to attain the stage of Tathagatahood. Mahamati, if it were not for this sustaining power, they would relapse into the ways and thoughts of the philosophers, easy-going disciples and the evil-minded, and would thus fall short of the highest attainment. For these reasons, earnest disciples and sincere Bodhisattvas are sustained by the power of all the Tathagatas.

* * *

Then said Mahamati: It has been said by the Blessed One that by fulfilling the six Paramitas, Buddhahood is realised. Pray tell us what the Paramitas are, and how they are to be fulfilled?

The Blessed One replied: The Paramitas are ideals of spiritual prefection that are to be the guide of the Bodhisattvas on the path to self-realisation. There are six of them but they are to be considered in three different ways according to the progress of the Bodhisattva on the stages. At first they are to be considered as ideals for the worldly life; next as ideals for the mental life; and, lastly, as ideals of the spiritual and unitive life.

In the worldly life where one is still holding tenaciously to the notions of an ego-soul and what concerns it and holding fast to discriminations of dualism, if only for worldly benefits, one should cherish ideals of charity, good behavior, patience, zeal, thoughtfulness and wisdom. Even in the worldly life the practice of these virtues will bring rewards of happiness and success.

Much more in the mind-world of earnest disciples and masters will their practice bring joys of emancipation, enlightenment and peace of mind, because the Paramitas are grounded on right-knowledge and lead to thoughts of Nirvana, even if the Nirvana of their thoughts is for themselves. In the mind-world the Paramitas become more ideal and more sympathetic; charity can no longer be expressed in the giving of impersonal gifts but will call for the more costly gifts of sympathy and understanding; good behavior will call for something more than outward conformity to the five precepts because in the light of the Paramitas they must practise humility, simplicity, restraint and self-giving. Patience will call for something more than forbearance with external circumstances and the temperaments of other people: it will now call for patience with one's self. Zeal will call for something more than industry and outward show of earnestness: it will call for more self-control in the task of following the Noble Path and in manifestating the Dharma in one's own life. Thoughtfulness will give way to mindfulness wherein discriminated meanings and logical deductions and rationalisations will give way to intuitions of significance and spirit. The Paramita of Wisdom (*Prajna*) will no longer be concerned with pragmatic wisdom and erudition, but will reveal itself in its true perfectness of All-inclusive Truth which is Love.

The third aspect of the Paramitas as seen in the ideal perfections of the Tathagatas can only be fully understood by the Bodhisattva-Mahasattvas who are devoted to the highest spiritual discipline and have fully understood that there is nothing to be seen in the world but that which issues from the mind itself; in whose minds the discrimination of dualities has ceased to function; and seizing and clinging has become non-existent. Thus free from all attachments to individual objects and ideas, their minds are free to consider ways of benefiting and giving happiness to others, even to all sentient beings. To the Bodhisattva-Mahasattvas the ideal of charity is shown in the self-yielding of the Tathagata's hope of Nirvana that all may enjoy it together. While having relations with an objective world there is no rising in the minds of the Tathagatas of discriminations between the interests of self and the interests of others, between good and evil,—there is just the spontaneity and effortless actuality of perfect behavior. To practise patience with full knowledge of this and that, of grasp and grasping, but with no thought of discrimination nor of attachment,—that is the Tathagatas Paramita of Patience. To exert oneself with energy from the first part of the night to its end in conformity with the disciplinary measures with no rising of discrimination as to comfort or discomfort,—that is the Tathagata's Paramita of Zeal. Not to discriminate between self and others in thoughts of Nirvana, but to keep the mind fixed on Nirvana,—that is the Paramita of Mindfulness. As to the Prajna-Paramita, which is Noble Wisdom, who can predicate it? When in Samadhi the mind ceases to discriminate and there is only perfect and love-filled imagelessness, then an inscrutable "turning-about" will take place in the inmost consciousness and one will have attained self-realisation of Noble Wisdom,—that is the highest Prajna-Paramita.

* * *

Then Mahamati said to the Blessed One: You have spoken of an astral-body, a "mind-vision-body" (*manomayakaya*) which the Bodhisattvas are able to assume, as being one of the fruits of self-realisation of Noble Wisdom: pray tell us, Blessed One, what is meant by such a transcendental body?

The Blessed One replied: There are three kinds of such transcendental bodies: First, there is the one in which the Bodhisattva attains enjoyment of the Samadhis and Samapattis. Second, there is the one which is assumed by the Tathagatas according to the class of beings to be sustained, and which achieves and perfects spontaneously with no attachment and no effort. Third, there is the one in which the Tathagatas receive their intuition of Dharmakaya.

The transcendental personality that enters into the enjoyment of the Samadhis comes with the third, fourth and fifth stages as the mentations of the mind-system become quieted and waves of consciousness are no more stirred on the face of Universal Mind. In this state, the conscious-mind is still aware, in a measure, of the bliss being experienced by this cessation of the mind's activities.

The second kind of transcendental personality is the kind assumed by the Bodhisattvas and Tathagatas as bodies of transformation by which they demonstrate their original vows in the work of achieving and perfecting; it comes with the eighth stage of Bodhisattvahood. When the Bodhisattva has a thorough-going penetration into the maya-like nature of things and understands the dharma of imagelessness, he will experience the "turning-about" in his deepest consciousness and will become able to experience the higher Samadhis even to the highest. By entering into these exalted Samadhis he attains a personality that transcends the conscious-mind, by reason of which he obtains supernatural powers of self-mastery and activities because of which he is able to move as he wishes, as quickly as a dream changes, as quickly as an image changes in a mirror. This transcendental body is not a product of the elements and yet there is something in it that is analogous to what is so produced; it is furnished with all the differences appertaining to the world of form but without their limitations; possessed of this "mind-vision-body" he is able to be present in all the assemblages in all the Buddha-lands. Just as his thoughts move instantly and without hindrance over walls and rivers and trees and mountains, and just as in memory he recalls and visits the scenes of his past experiences, so, while his mind keeps functioning in the body, his thoughts may be a hundred thousand yojanas away. In the same fashion the transcendental personality that experiences the Samadhi Vajravimbopama will be endowed with supernatural powers and psychic faculties and self-mastery by reason of which he will be able to follow the noble paths that lead to the assemblages of the Buddhas, moving about as freely as he may wish. But his wishes will no longer be self-centered nor tainted by discrimination and attachment, for this transcendental personality is not his old body, but is the transcendental embodiment of his original vows of self-yielding in order to bring all beings to maturity.

The third kind of transcendental personality is so ineffable that it is able to attain intuitions of the Dharmakaya, that is, it attains intuitions of the boundless and inscrutable cognition of Universal Mind. As Bodhisattva-Mahasattvas attain the highest of the stages and become conversant with all the treasures to be realised in Noble Wisdom, they will attain this inconceivable transformation-body which is the true nature of all the Tathagatas past, present and future, and will participate in the blissful peace which pervades the Dharma of all the Buddhas.

CHAPTER X

Discipleship: Lineage of the Arhats

Then Mahamati asked the Blessed One: Pray tell us how many kinds of disciples there are?

The Blessed One replied: There are as many kinds of disciples as there are individuals, but for convenience they may be divided into two groups: disciples of the lineage of the Arhats, and disciples known as Bodhisattvas. Disciples of the lineage of the Arhats may be considered under two aspects: First, according to the number of times they will return to this life of birth-and-death; and second, according to their spiritual progress. Under the first aspect, they may be subdivided into three groups: The "Stream-entered," the "Once-returning," and the "Never-returning."

The Stream-entered are those disciples, who having freed themselves from the attachments to the lower discriminations and who have cleansed themselves from the twofold hindrances and who clearly understand the meaning of the twofold egolessness, yet who still cling to the notions of individuality and generality and to their own egoness. They will advance along the stages to the sixth only to succumb to the entrancing bliss of the Samadhis. They will be reborn seven times, or five times, or three times, before they will be able to pass the sixth stage. The Once-returning are the Arhats, and the Never-returning are the Bodhisattvas who have reached the seventh stage.

The reason for these gradations is because of their attachment to the three degrees of false-imagination: namely, faith in moral practices, doubt, and the view of their individual personality. When these three hindrances are overcome, they will be able to attain the higher stages. As to moral practices: the ignorant, simple-minded disciples obey the rules of morality, piety and penance, because they desire thereby to gain worldly advancement and happiness, with the added hope of being re-born in more favorable conditions. The Stream-entered ones do not cling to moral practices for any hope of reward for their minds are fixed on the exalted state of self-realisation; the reason they devote themselves to the details of morality is that they wish to master such truths as are in conformity with the undefiled out-flowings. As regards the hindrance of doubt in the Buddha's teachings, that will continue so long as any of the notions of discriminations are cherished and will disappear when they disappear. Attachment to the view of individual personality will be gotten rid of as the disciple gains a more thorough understanding of the notions of being and non-being, self-nature and egolessness, thereby getting rid of the attachments to his own selfness that goes with those discriminations. By breaking up and clearing away these three hindrances the Stream-entered ones will be able to discard all greed, anger and folly.

As for the Once-returning Arhats; there was once in them the discrimination of forms, signs, and appearances, but as they gradually learned by right knowledge not to view individual objects under the aspect of quality and qualifying, and as they became acquainted with what marks the attainment of the practice of dhyana, they have reached a stage of enlightenment where in one more rebirth they will be able to put an end to the clinging to their own self-interests. Free of this burden of error and its attachments, the passions will no more assert themselves and the hindrances will be cleared away forever.

Under the second aspect disciples may be grouped according to the spiritual progress they have attained, into four classes, namely, disciples (*sravaka*), masters (*pratyekabuddha*), Arhats, and Bodhisattvas.

The first class of disciples mean well but they find it difficult to understand unfamiliar ideas. Their minds are joyful when studying about and practising the things belonging to appearances that can be discriminated, but they become confused by the notion of an uninterrupted chain of causation, and they become fearful when they consider the aggregates that make up personality and its object world as being maya-like, empty and egoless. They were able to advance to the fifth or sixth stage where they are able to do away with the rising of passions, but not with the notions that give rise to passion and, therefore, they are unable to get rid of the clinging to an ego-soul and its accompanying attachments, habits and habit-energy. In this same class of disciples are the earnest disciples of other faiths, who clinging to the notions of such things as, the soul as an eternal entity, Supreme Atman, Personal God, seek a

Nirvana that is in harmony with them. There are others, more materialistic in their ideas, who think that all things exist in dependence upon causation and, therefore, that Nirvana must be in like dependence. But none of these, earnest though they be, have gained an insight into the truth of the twofold ego-lessness and are, therefore, of limited spiritual insight as regards deliverance and non-deliverance; for them there is no emancipation. They have great self-confidence but they can never gain a true knowledge of Nirvana until they have learned to discipline themselves in the patient acceptance of the twofold egolessness.

The second class of masters are those who have gained a high degree of intellectual understanding of the truths concerning the aggregates that make up personality and its external world but who are filled with fear when they face the significance and consequences of these truths, and the demands which their learning makes upon them, that is, not to become attached to the external world and its manifold forms making for comfort and power, and to keep away from the entanglements of its social relations. They are attracted by the possibilities that are attainable by so doing, namely, the possession of miraculous powers such as dividing the personality and appearing in different places at the same time, or manifesting bodies of transformation. To gain these powers they even resort to the solitary life, but this class of masters never get beyond the seductions of their learning and egoism, and their discourses are always in conformity with that characteristic and limitation. Among them are many earnest disciples who show a degree of spiritual insight that is characterised by sincerity and undismayed willingness to meet all the demands that the stages make upon them. When they see that all that makes up the objective world is only manifestation of mind, that it is without self-nature, un-born and egoless, they accept it without fear, and when they see that their own ego-soul is also empty, un-born and egoless, they are untroubled and undismayed, with earnest purpose they seek to adjust their lives to the full demands of these truths, but they cannot forget the notions that lie back of these facts, especially the notion of their own conscious ego-self and its relation to Nirvana. They are of the Stream-entered class.

The class known as Arhats are those earnest masters who

belong to the once-returning class. By their spiritual insight they have reached the sixth and seventh stages. They have thoroughly understood the truth of the twofold egolessness and the imagelessness of Reality; with them there is no more discrimination, nor passions, nor pride of egoism; they have gained an exalted insight and seen into the immensity of the Buddha-lands. By attaining an inner perception of the true nature of Universal Mind they are steadily purifying their habit-energy. The Arhat has attained emancipation, enlightenment, the Dhyanas, the Samadhis, and his whole attention is given to the attainment of Nirvana, but the idea of Nirvana causes mental perturbations because he has a wrong idea of Nirvana. The notion of Nirvana in his mind is divided: he discriminates Nirvana from self, and self from others. He has attained some of the fruits of self-realisation but he still thinks and discourses on the Dhyanas, subjects for meditation, the Samadhis, the fruits. He pridefully says: "There are fetters, but I am disengaged from them." His is a double fault: he both denounces the vices of the ego, and still clings to its fetters. So long as he continues to discriminate notions of dhyana, dhyana practice, subjects for dhyana, right-knowledge and truth, there is a bewildered state of mind,—he has not attained perfect emancipation. Emancipation comes with the acceptance of imagelessness.

He is master of the Dhyanas and enters into the Samadhis, but to reach the higher stages one must pass beyond the Dhyanas, the immeasurables, the world of no-form, and the bliss of the Samadhis into the Samapattis leading to the cessation of thought itself. The dhyana-practiser, dhyana, the subject of dhyana, the cessation of thought, once-returning, never-returning, all these are divided and bewildering states of mind. Not until all discrimination is abandoned is there perfect emancipation. Thus the Arhat, master of the dhyanas, participating in the Samadhis, but unsupported by the Buddhas yields to the entrancing bliss of the Samadhis—and passes to his Nirvana.

Disciples and masters and Arhats may ascend the stages up to the sixth. They perceive that the triple world is no more than mind itself; they perceive that there is no becoming attached to the multiplicities of external objects except through the discriminations and activities of the mind itself; they perceive that there is no ego-soul; and, therefore, they attain a measure of tranquillisation. But their tranquillisation is not perfect every minute of their lives, for with them there is something effect-producing, some grasped and grasping, some lingering trace of dualism and egoism. Though disengaged from the actively functioning passions, they are still bound in with the habit-energy of passion and, becoming intoxicated with the wine of the Samadhis, they still have their abode in the realm of the out-flowings. Perfect tranquillisation is possible only with the seventh stage. So long as their minds are in confusion, they cannot attain to a clear conviction as to the cessation of all multiplicity and the actuality of the perfect oneness of all things. In their minds the self-nature of things is still discriminated as good and bad, therefore, their minds are in confusion and they cannot pass beyond the sixth stage. But at the sixth stage all discrimination ceases as they become engrossed in the bliss of the Samadhis wherein they cherish the thought of Nirvana and, as Nirvana is possible at the sixth stage, they pass into their Nirvana, but it is not the Nirvana of the Buddhas.

CHAPTER XI

Bodhisattvahood and Its Stages

Then said Mahamati to the Blessed One: Will you tell us now about the disciples who are Bodhisattvas?

The Blessed One replied: The Bodhisattvas are those earnest disciples who are enlightened by reason of their efforts to attain self-realisation of Noble Wisdom and who have taken upon themselves the task to enlighten others. They have gained a clear understanding of the truth that all things are empty, un-born, and of a maya-like nature; they have ceased from viewing things discriminatively and from considering them in their relations; they thoroughly understand the truth of two-fold egolessness and have adjusted themselves to it with patient acceptance; they have attained a definite realisation of image-lessness; and they are abiding in the perfect-knowledge that they have gained by self-realisation of Noble Wisdom.

Well stamped by the seal of "Suchness" they entered upon

the first of the Bodhisattva stages. The first stage is called the Stage of Joy (*Pramudita*). Entering this stage is like passing out of the glare and shadows into a realm of "no-shadows"; it is like passing out of the noise and tumult of the crowded city into the quietness of solitude. The Bodhisattva feels within himself the awakening of a great heart of compassion and he utters his ten original vows: To honor and serve all Buddhas; to spread the knowledge and practice of the Dharma; to welcome all coming Buddhas; to practise the six Paramitas; to persuade all beings to embrace the Dharma; to attain a perfect understanding of the universe; to attain a perfect understanding of the mutuality of all beings; to attain perfect self-realisation of the oneness of all the Buddhas and Tathagatas in self-nature, purpose and resources; to become acquainted with all skillful means for the carrying out of these vows for the emancipation of all beings; to realise supreme enlightenment through the perfect self-realization of Noble Wisdom, ascending the stages and entering Tathagatahood.

In the spirit of these vows the Bodhisattva gradually ascends the stages to the sixth. All earnest disciples, masters and Arhats have ascended thus far, but being enchanted by the bliss of the Samadhis and not being supported by the powers of the Buddhas, they pass to their Nirvana. The same fate would befall the Bodhisattvas except for the sustaining power of the Buddhas, by that they are enabled to refuse to enter Nirvana until all beings can enter Nirvana with them. The Tathagatas point out to them the virtues of Buddhahood which are beyond the conception of the intellectual-mind, and they encourage and strengthen the Bodhisattvas not to give in to the enchantment of the bliss of the Samadhis, but to press on to further advancement along the stages. If the Bodhisattvas had entered Nirvana at this stage, and they would have done so without the sustaining power of the Buddhas, there would have been the cessation of all things and the family of the Tathagatas would have become extinct.

Strengthened by the new strength that comes to them from the Buddhas and with the more perfect insight that is theirs by reason of their advance in self-realisation of Noble Wisdom, they re-examine the nature of the mind-system, the egolessness of personality, and the part that grasping and attachment and habit-energy play in the unfolding drama of life; they re-examine the illusions of the fourfold logical analysis, and the various elements that enter into enlightenment and self-realisation, and, in the thrill of their new powers of self-mastery, the Bodhisattvas enter upon the seventh stage of Far-going (*Durangama*).

Supported by the sustaining power of the Buddhas, the Bodhisattvas at this stage enter into the bliss of the Samadhi of perfect tranquillisation. Owing to their original vows they are transported by emotions of love and compassion as they become aware of the part they are to perform in the carrying out of their vows for the emancipation of all beings. Thus they do not enter into Nirvana, but, in truth, they too are already in Nirvana because in their emotions of love and compassion there is no rising of discrimination; henceforth, with them, discrimination no more takes place. Because of Transcendental Intelligence only one conception is present—the promotion of the realisation of Noble Wisdom. Their insight issues from the Womb of Tathagatahood and they enter into their task with spontaneity and radiancy because it is of the self-nature of Noble Wisdom. This is called the Bodhisattva's Nirvana—the losing oneself in the bliss of perfect self-yielding. This is the seventh stage, the stage of Far-going.

The eighth stage, is the stage of No-recession (*Acala*). Up to this stage, because of the defilements upon the face of Universal Mind caused by the accumulation of habit-energy since beginningless time, the mind-system and all that pertains to it has been evolved and sustained. The mind-system functioned by the discriminations of an external and objective world to which it became attached and by which it was perpetuated. But with the Bodhisattva's attainment of the eighth stage there comes the "turning-about" within his deepest consciousness from self-centered egoism to universal compassion for all beings, by which he attains perfect self-realisation of Noble Wisdom. There is an instant cessation of the delusive activities of the whole mind-system; the dancing of the waves of habit-energy on the face of Universal Mind are forever stilled, revealing its own inherent quietness and solitude, the inconceivable Oneness of the Womb of Tathagatahood.

Henceforth there is no more looking outward upon an external world by senses and sense-minds, nor a discrimination of particularised concepts and ideas and propositions by an intellectual-mind, no more grasping, nor attachment, nor pride of egoism, nor habit-energy. Henceforth there is only the inner experience of Noble Wisdom which has been attained by entering into its perfect Oneness.

Thus establishing himself at the eighth stage of No-recession, the Bodhisattva enters into the bliss of the ten Samadhis, but avoiding the path of the disciples and masters who yielded themselves up to their entrancing bliss and who passed to their Nirvanas, and supported by his vows and the Transcendental Intelligence which now is his and being sustained by the power of the Buddhas, he enters upon the higher paths that lead to Tathagatahood. He passes through the bliss of the Samadhis to assume the transformation body of a Tathagata that through him all beings may be emancipated. Mahamati, If there had been no Tathagata-womb and no Divine Mind then there would have been no rising and disappearance of the aggregates that make up personality and its external world, no rising and disappearance of ignorant people nor holy people, and no task for Bodhisattvas; therefore, while walking in the path of self-realisation and entering into the enjoyments of the Samadhis, you must never abandon working hard for the emancipation of all beings and your self-yielding love will never be in vain. To philosophers the conception of Tathagata-womb seems devoid of purity and soiled by these external manifestations, but it is not so understood by the Tathagatas,—to them it is not a proposition of philosophy but is an intuitive experience as real as though it was an amalaka fruit held in the palm of the hand.

With the cessation of the mind-system and all its evolving discriminations, there is cessation of all strain and effort. It is like a man in a dream who imagines he is crossing a river and who exerts himself to the utmost to do so, who is suddenly awakened. Being awake, he thinks: "Is this real or is it unreal?" Being now enlightened, he knows that it is neither real nor unreal. Thus when the Bodhisattva arrives at the eighth stage, he is able to see all things truthfully and, more than that, he is able to thoroughly understand the significance of all the dream-like things of his life as to how they came to pass and as to how they pass away. Ever since beginningless time the mind-system has perceived multiplicities of forms and conditions and ideas which the thinking-mind has discriminated and the empirical-mind has experienced and grasped and clung to. From this has risen habit-energy that by its accumulation has conditioned the illusions of existence and non-existence, individuality and generality, and has thus perpetuated the dream-state of false-imagination. But now, to the Bodhisattvas of the eighth stage, life is past and is remembered as it truly was—a passing dream.

As long as the Bodhisattva had not passed the seventh stage, even though he had attained an intuitive understanding of the true meaning of life and its maya-like nature, and as to how the mind carried on its discriminations and attachments yet, nevertheless, the cherishing of the notions of these things had continued and, although he no longer experienced within himself any ardent desire for things nor any impulse to grasp them yet, nevertheless, the notions concerning them persisted and perfumed his efforts to practise the teachings of the Buddhas and to labor for the emancipation of all beings. Now, in the eighth stage, even the notions have passed away, and all effort and striving is seen to be unnecessary. The Bodhisattva's Nirvana is perfect tranquillisation, but it is not extinction nor inertness; while there is an entire absence of discrimination and purpose, there is the freedom and spontaneity of potentiality that has come with the attainment and patient acceptance of the truths of egolessness and imagelessness. Here is perfect solitude, undisturbed by any gradation or continuous succession, but radiant with the potency and freedom of its self-nature which is the self-nature of Noble Wisdom, blissfully peaceful with the serenity of Perfect Love.

Entering upon the eighth stage, with the "turning-about" at the deepest seat of consciousness, the Bodhisattva will become conscious that he has received the second kind of Transcendental-body (*Manomayakaya*). The transition from mortal-body to Transcendental-body has nothing to do with mortal death, for the old body continues to function and the old mind serves the needs of the old body, but now it is free from the control of mortal mind. There has been an inconceivable transformation-death (*acintya-parinama-cyuti*) by which the false-imagination of his particularised individual personality has been transcended by a realisation of his oneness with the universalised mind of Tathagatahood, from which realisation there will be no recession. With that realisation he finds himself amply endowed with all the Tathagata's powers, psychic faculties, and self-mastery, and, just as the good earth is the support of all beings in the world of desire (karmadhatu), so the Tathagatas become the support of all beings in the Transcendental World of No-form.

The first seven of the Bodhisattva stages were in the realm of mind and the eighth, while transcending mind, was still in touch with it; but in the ninth stage of Transcendental Intelligence (Sadhumati), by reason of his perfect intelligence and insight into the imagelessness of Divine Mind which he had attained by self-realisation of Noble Wisdom, he is in the realm of Tathagatahood. Gradually the Bodhisattva will realise his Tathagata-nature and the possession of all its powers and psychic faculties, self-mastery, loving compassion, and skillful means, and by means of them will enter into all the Buddha-lands. Making use of these new powers, the Bodhisattva will assume various transformation-bodies and personalities for the sake of benefiting others. Just as in the former mental life, imagination had risen from relative-knowledge, so now skillful-means rise spontaneously from Transcendental Intelligence. It is like the magical gem that reflects instantaneously appropriate responses to one's wishes. The Bodhisattva passes over to all the assemblages of the Buddhas and listens to them as they discourse on the dream-like nature of all things and concerning the truths that transcend all notions of being and non-being, that have no relation to birth and death, nor to eternality nor extinction. Thus facing the Tathagatas as they discourse on Noble Wisdom that is far beyond the mental capacity of disciples and masters, he will attain a hundred thousand Samadhis, indeed, a hundred thousand nyutas of kotis of Samadhis, and in the spirit of these Samadhis he will instantly pass from one Buddha-land to another, paying homage to all the Buddhas, being born into all the celestial mansions, manifesting Buddha-bodies, and himself discoursing on the Triple Treasure to lesser Bodhisattvas that they too may partake of the fruits of self-realisation of Noble Wisdom.

Thus passing beyond the last stage of Bodhisattvahood, he becomes a Tathagata himself endowed with all the freedom of the Dharmakaya. The tenth stage belongs to the Tathagatas. Here the Bodhisattva will find himself seated upon a lotus-like throne in a splendid jewel-adorned palace and surrounded by Bodhisattvas of equal rank. Buddhas from all the Buddha-lands will gather about him and with their pure and fragrant hands resting on his forehead will give him ordination and recognition as one of themselves. Then they will assign him a Buddha-land that he may possess and perfect as his own.

The tenth stage is called the Great Truth Cloud (*Dharma-megha*), inconceivable, inscrutable. Only the Tathagatas can realise its perfect Imagelessness and Oneness and Solitude. It is Mahesvara, the Radiant Land, the Pure Land, the Land of Far-distances; surrounding and surpassing the lesser worlds of form and desire (*karmadhatu*), in which the Bodhisattva will find himself at-one-ment. Its rays of Noble Wisdom which is the self-nature of the Tathagatas, many-colored, entrancing, auspicious, are transforming the triple world as other worlds have been transformed in the past, and still other worlds will be transformed in the future. But in the Perfect Oneness of Noble Wisdom there is no gradation nor succession nor effort. The tenth stage is the first, the first is the eighth, the eighth is the fifth, the fifth is the seventh: what gradation can there be where perfect Imagelessness and Oneness prevail? And what is the reality of Noble Wisdom? It is the ineffable potency of the Dharmakaya; it has no bounds nor limits; it surpasses all the Buddha-lands, and pervades the Akanistha and the heavenly mansions of the Tushita.

Chapter XII

Tathagatahood Which Is Noble Wisdom

Then said Mahamati to the Blessed One: It has been taught in the canonical books that the Buddhas are subject to neither birth nor destruction, and you have said that "the Un-born" is one of the names of the Tathagatas; does that mean that the Tathagata is a non-entity?

The Blessed One replied: The Tathagata is not a non-entity nor is he to be conceived as other things are as neither born nor disappearing, nor is he subject to causation, nor is he without significance; yet I refer to him as "The Un-born." There is yet another name for the Tathagata, "The Mind-appearing

One" (*Manomayakaya*) which his Essence-body assumes at will in the transformations incident to his work of emancipation. This is beyond the understanding of common disciples and masters and even beyond the full comprehension of those Bodhisattvas who remain in the seventh stage. Yes, Mahamati, "The Un-born" is synonymous with Tathagata.

Then Mahamati said: If the Tathagatas are un-born, there does not seem to be anything to take hold of—no entity—or is there something that bears another name than entity? And what can that "something" be?

The Blessed One replied: Objects are frequently known by different names according to different aspects that they present,— the god Indra is sometimes known as Shakra, and sometimes as Purandara. These different names are sometimes used interchangeably and sometimes they are discriminated, but different objects are not to be imagined because of the different names, nor are they without individuation. The same can be said of myself as I appear in this world of patience before ignorant people and where I am known by uncounted trillions of names. They address me by different names not realising that they are all names of the one Tathagata. Some recognise me as Tathagata, some as The Self-existent One, some as Gautama the Ascetic, some as Buddha. Then there are others who recognise me as Brahma, as Vishnu, as Ishvara; some see me as Sun, as Moon; some as a reincarnation of the ancient sages; some as one of "the ten powers"; some as Rama, some as Indra, and some as Varuna. Still there are others who speak of me as The Un-born, as Emptiness, as "Suchness," as Truth, as Reality, as Ultimate Principle; still there are others who see me as Dharmakaya, as Nirvana, as the Eternal; some speak of me as sameness, as non-duality, as un-dying, as formless; some think of me as the doctrine of Buddha-causation, or of Emancipation, or of the Noble Path; and some think of me as Divine Mind and Noble Wisdom. Thus in this world and in other worlds am I known by these uncounted names, but they all see me as the moon is seen in water. Though they all honor, praise and esteem me, they do not fully understand the meaning and significance of the words they use; not having their own self-realisation of Truth they cling to the words of their canonical books, or to what has been told them, or to what they have imagined, and fail to see that the name they are using is only one of the many names of the Tathagata. In their studies they follow the mere words of the text vainly trying to gain the true meaning, instead of having confidence in the one "text" where self-confirming Truth is revealed, that is, having confidence in the self-realisation of Noble Wisdom.

*   *   *

Then said Mahamati: Pray tell us, Blessed One, about the self-nature of the Tathagatas?

The Blessed One replied: If the Tathagata is to be described by such expressions as made or un-made, effect or cause, we would have to describe him as neither made, nor un-made, nor effect, nor cause; but if we so described him we would be guilty of dualistic discrimination. If the Tathagata is something made, he would be impermanent; if he is impermanent anything made would be a Tathagata. If he is something un-made, then all effort to realise Tathagatahood would be useless. That which is neither an effect nor a cause, is neither a being nor a non-being, and that which is neither a being nor a non-being is outside the four propositions. The four propositions belong to worldly usage; that which is outside them is no more than a word, like a barren-woman's child; so are all the terms concerning the Tathagata to be understood.

When it is said that all things are egoless, it means that all things are devoid of self-hood. Each thing may have its own individuality—the being of a horse is not of cow nature—it is such as it is of its own nature and is thus discriminated by the ignorant, but, nevertheless, its own nature is of the nature of a dream or a vision. That is why the ignorant and the simple-minded, who are in the habit of discriminating appearances, fail to understand the significance of egolessness. It is not until discrimination is gotten rid of that the fact that all things are empty, un-born and without self-nature can be appreciated.

Mahamati, all these expressions as applied to the Tathagatas are without meaning, for that which is none of these is something removed from all measurement, and that which is removed from all measurement turns into a meaningless word; that which is a mere word is something un-born; that which is un-born is not subject to destruction; that which is not subject to destruction is like space and space is neither effect nor cause; that which is neither effect nor cause is something unconditioned; that which is unconditioned is beyond all reasoning; that which is beyond all reasoning,—that is the Tathagata. The self-nature of Tathagatahood is far removed from all predicates and measurements; the self-nature of Tathagatahood is Noble Wisdom.

* * *

Then Mahamati said to the Blessed One: Are the Tathagatas permanent or impermanent?

The Blessed One replied: The Tathagatas are neither permanent nor impermanent; if either is asserted there is error connected with it. If the Tathagata is said to be permanent then he will be connected with the creating agencies for, according to the philosophers, the creating agencies are something uncreated and permanent. But the Tathagatas are not connected with the so-called creating agencies and in that sense he is impermanent. If he is said to be impermanent then he is connected with things that are created for they also are impermanent. For these reasons the Tathagatas are neither permanent nor impermanent.

Neither can the Tathagatas he said to be permanent in the sense that space is said to be permanent, or that the horns of a hare can be said to be permanent for, being unreal, they exclude all ideas of permanency or impermanency. This does not apply to the Tathagatas because they come forth from the habit-energy of ignorance which is connected with the mind-system and the elements that make up personality. The triple world originates from the discrimination of unrealities and where discrimination takes place there is duality and the notion of permanency and impermanency, but the Tathagatas do not rise from the discrimination of unrealities. Thus, as long as there is discrimination there will be the notion of permanency and impermanency; when discrimination is done away with, Noble Wisdom, which is based on the significance of solitude, will be established.

However, there is another sense in which the Tathagatas may be said to be permanent. Transcendental Intelligence rising with the attainment of enlightenment is of a permanent nature. This Truth-essence which is discoverable in the enlightenment of all who are enlightened, is realisable as the regulative and sustaining principle of Reality, which forever abides. The Transcendental Intelligence attained intuitively by the Tathagatas by their self-realisation of Noble Wisdom, is a realisation of their own self-nature,—in this sense the Tathagatas are permanent. The eternal-unthinkable of the Tathagatas is the "suchness" of Noble Wisdom realised within themselves. It is both eternal and beyond thought. It conforms to the idea of a cause and yet is beyond existence and non-existence. Because it is the exalted state of Noble-Wisdom, it has its own character. Because it is the cause of highest Reality, it is its own causation. Its eternality is not derived from reasonings based on external notions of being and non-being, nor of eternality nor non-eternality. Being classed under the same head as space, cessation, Nirvana, it is eternal. Because it has nothing to do with existence and non-existence, it is no creator; because it has nothing to do with creation, nor with being and non-being, but is only revealed in the exalted state of Noble Wisdom, it is truly eternal.

When the twofold passions are destroyed, and the twofold hindrances are cleared away, and the twofold egolessness is fully understood, and the inconceivable transformation death of the Bodhisattva is attained—that which remains is the self-nature of the Tathagatas. When the teachings of the Dharma are fully understood and are perfectly realised by the disciples and masters, that which is realised in their deepest consciousness is their own Buddha-nature revealed as Tathagata.

In a true sense there are four kinds of sameness relating to Buddha-nature: there is sameness of letters, sameness of words, sameness of meaning, and sameness of Essence. The name Buddha is spelt: B-U-D-D-H-A; the letters are the same when used for any Buddha or Tathagata. When the Brahmans teach they use various words, and when the Tathagatas teach they use the very same words; in respect to words there is a sameness between us. In the teachings of all the Tathagatas there is a sameness of meaning. Among all the Buddhas there is a sameness of Buddha-nature. They all have the thirty-two marks of excellence and the eighty minor signs of bodily perfection; there is no distinction among them except as they manifest various transformations according to the different dispositions of beings who are to be disciplined and emancipated by various means. In the Ultimate Essence which is Dharmakaya, all the Buddhas of the past, present and future, are of one sameness.

* * *

Then said Mahamati to the Blessed One: It has been said by the Blessed One that from the night of the Enlightenment to the night of the Parinirvana, the Tathagata has uttered no word nor ever will utter a word. In what deep meaning is this true?

The Blessed One replied: By two reasons of deepest meaning is it true: In the light of the Truth self-realised by Noble Wisdom; and in the Truth of an eternally-abiding Reality. The self-realisation of Noble Wisdom by all the Tathagatas is the same as my own self-realisation of Noble Wisdom; there is no more, no less, no difference; and all the Tathagatas bear witness that the state of self-realisation is free from words and discriminations and has nothing to do with the dualistic way of speaking, that is, all beings receive the teachings of the Tathagatas through self-realisation of Noble Wisdom, not through words of discrimination.

Again Mahamati, there has always been an eternally-abiding Reality. The "substance" of Truth (*dharmadhatu*) abides forever whether a Tathagata appears in the world or not. So does the Reason of all things (*dharmata*) eternally abide; so does Reality (*paramartha*) abide and keep its order. What has been realised by myself and all other Tathagatas is this Reality (*Dharmakaya*), the eternally-abiding self-orderliness of Reality; the "suchness" (*tathata*) of things; the realness of things (*bhutata*); Noble Wisdom which is Truth itself. The sun radiates its splendor spontaneously on all alike and with no words of explanation; in like manner do the Tathagatas radiate the Truth of Noble Wisdom with no recourse to words and to all alike. For these reasons is it stated by me that from the night of the Enlightenment to the night of the Tathagata's Parinirvana, he has not uttered, nor ever will he utter, one word. And the same is true of all the Buddhas.

* * *

Then said Mahamati: Blessed One, you speak of the sameness of all the Buddhas, but in other places you have spoken of Dharmata-Buddha, Nishyanda-Buddha and Nirmana-Buddha as though they were different from each other; how can they be the same and yet different?

The Blessed One replied: I speak of the different Buddhas as opposed to the views of the philosophers who base their teachings on the reality of an external world of form and who cherish discriminations and attachments arising therefrom; against the teachings of these philosophers I disclose the Nirmana-Buddha, the Buddha of Transformations. In the many transformations of the Tathagata stage, the Nirmana-Buddha establishes such matters as charity, morality, patience, thoughtfulness, and tranquillisation; by right-knowledge he teaches the true understanding of the maya-like nature of the elements that make up personality and its external world; he teaches the true nature of the mind-system as a whole and in the distinctions of its forms, functions and ways of performance. In a deeper sense, The Nirmana-Buddha symbolises the principles of differentiation and integration by reason of which all component things are distributed, all complexities simplified, all thoughts analysed; at the same time it symbolises the harmonising, unifying power of sympathy and compassion; it removes all obstacles, it harmonises all differences, it brings into perfect Oneness the discordant many. For the emancipation of all beings the Bodhisattvas and Tathagatas assume bodies of transformation and employ many skillful devices,—this is the work of the Nirmana-Buddha.

For the enlightenment of the Bodhisattvas and their sustaining along the stages, the Inconceivable is made realisable. The Nishyanda-Buddha, the "Out-flowing-Buddha," through Transcendental Intelligence, reveals the true meaning and significance of appearances, discrimination, attachment; and of the power of habit-energy which is accumulated by them and conditions them; and of the un-bornness, the emptiness, the egolessness of all things. Because of Transcendental Intelligence and the purification of the evil out-flowings of life, all dualistic views of existence and non-existence are transcended and by self-realisation of Noble Wisdom the true imagelessness of Reality is made manifest. The inconceivable glory of Buddhahood is made manifest in rays of Noble Wisdom; Noble Wisdom is the self-nature of the Tathagatas. This is the work of the Nishyanda-Buddha. In a deeper sense, the Nishyanda-Buddha symbolises the emergence of the principles of intellection and compassion but as yet undifferentiated and in perfect balance, potential but unmanifest. Looked at from the in-going side of the Bodhisattvas, Nishyanda-Buddha is seen in the glorified bodies of the Tathagatas; looked at from the forth-going side of Buddhahood, Nishyanda-Buddha is seen in the radiant personalities of the Tathagatas ready and eager to manifest the inherent Love and Wisdom of the Dharmakaya.

Dharmata-Buddha is Buddhahood in its self-nature of Perfect Oneness in whom absolute Tranquillity prevails. As Noble Wisdom, Dharmata-Buddha transcends all differentiated knowledge, is the goal of intuitive self-realisation, and is the self-nature of the Tathagatas. As Noble Wisdom, Dharmata-Buddha is inscrutable, ineffable, unconditioned. Dharmata-Buddha is the Ultimate Principle of Reality from which all things derive their being and truthfulness, but which in itself transcends all predicates. Dharmata-Buddha is the central sun which holds all, illumines all. Its inconceivable Essence is made manifest in the "out-flowing" glory of Nishyanda-Buddha and in the transformations of Nirmana-Buddha.

* * *

Then said Mahamati: Pray tell us, Blessed One, more about the Dharmakaya?

The Blessed One replied: We have been speaking of it in terms of Buddhahood, but as it is inscrutable and beyond predicate we may just as well speak of it as the Truth-body, or the Truth-principle of Ultimate Reality (*Paramartha*). This Ultimate Principle of Reality may be considered as it is manifested under seven aspects: First, as *Citta-gocara*, it is the world of spiritual experience and the abode of the Tathagatas on their outgoing mission of emancipation. It is Noble Wisdom manifested as the principle of irradiancy and individuation. Second, as *Jnana*, it is the mind-world and its principle of intellection and consciousness. Third, as *Dristi*, it is the realm of dualism which is the physical world of birth and death wherein are manifested all the differentiations of thinker, thinking and thought-about and wherein are manifested the principles of sensation, perception, discrimination, desire, attachment and suffering.

Fourth, because of the greed, anger, infatuation, suffering and need of the physical world incident to discrimination and attachment, it reveals a world beyond the realm of dualism wherein it appears as the integrating principle of charity and sympathy. Fifth, in a realm still higher, which is the abode of the Bodhisattva stages, and is analogous to the mind-world, where the interests of heart transcend those of the mind, it appears as the principle of compassion and self-giving. Sixth, in the spiritual realm where the Bodhisattvas attain Buddhahood, it appears as the principle of perfect Love (*Karuna*). Here the last clinging to an ego-self is abandoned and the Bodhisattva enters into his self-realisation of Noble Wisdom which is the bliss of the Tathagata's perfect enjoyment of his inmost nature. Seventh as *Prajna* it is the active aspect of the Ultimate Principle wherein both the forth-going and the in-coming principles are alike implicit and potential, and wherein both Wisdom and Love are in perfect balance, harmony and Oneness.

These are the seven aspects of the Ultimate Principle of Dharmakaya, by reason of which all things are made manifest and perfected and then reintegrated, and all remaining within its inscrutable Oneness, with no signs of individuation, nor beginning, nor succession, nor ending. We speak of it as Dharmakaya, as Ultimate Principle, as Buddhahood, as Nirvana; what matters it? They are only other names for Noble Wisdom.

Mahamati, you and all the Bodhisattva-Mahasattvas should avoid the erroneous reasonings of the philosophers and seek for a self-realisation of Noble Wisdom.

Chapter XIII

Nirvana

Then said Mahamati to the Blessed One: Pray tell us about Nirvana?

The Blessed One replied: The term, Nirvana, is used with many different meanings, by different people, but these people may be divided into four groups: There are people who are suffering, or who are afraid of suffering, and who think of Nirvana; there are the philosophers who try to discriminate Nirvana; there are the class of disciples who think of Nirvana in relation to themselves; and, finally there is the Nirvana of the Buddhas.

Those who are suffering or who fear suffering, think of Nirvana as an escape and a recompense. They imagine that Nirvana consists in the future annihilation of the senses and the sense-minds; they are not aware that Universal Mind and Nirvana are One, and that this life-and-death world and Nirvana are not to be separated. These ignorant ones, instead of meditating on the imagelessness of Nirvana, talk of different ways of emancipation. Being ignorant of, or not understanding, the teachings of the Tathagatas, they cling to the notion of Nirvana that is outside what is seen of the mind and, thus, go on rolling themselves along with the wheel of life and death.

As to the Nirvanas discriminated by the philosophers: there really are none. Some philosophers conceive Nirvana to be found where the mind-system no more operates owing to the cessation of the elements that make up personality and its world; or is found where there is utter indifference to the objective world and its impermanency. Some conceive Nirvana to be a state where there is no recollection of the past or present, just as when a lamp is extinguished, or when a seed is burnt, or when a fire goes out; because then there is the cessation of all the substrata, which is explained by the philosophers as the non-rising of discrimination. But this is not Nirvana, because Nirvana does not consist in simple annihilation and vacuity.

Again, some philosophers explain deliverance as though it was the mere stopping of discrimination, as when the wind stops blowing, or as when one by self-effort gets rid of the dualistic view of knower and known, or gets rid of the notions of permanency and impermanency; or gets rid of the notions of good and evil; or overcomes passion by means of knowledge —to them Nirvana is deliverance. Some, seeing in "form" the bearer of pain are alarmed by the notion of "form" and look for happiness in a world of "no-form." Some conceive that in consideration of individuality and generality recognisable in all things inner and outer, that there is no destruction and that all beings maintain their being for ever and, in this eternality, see Nirvana. Others see the eternality of things in the conception of Nirvana as the absorption of the finite-soul in Supreme Atman; or who see all things as a manifestation of the vital-force of some Supreme Spirit to which all return; and some, who are especially silly, declare that there are two primary things, a primary substance and a primary soul, that react differently upon each other and thus produce all things from the transformations of qualities; some think that the world is born of action and interaction and that no other cause is necessary; others think that Ishvara is the free creator of all things; clinging to these foolish notions, there is no awakening, and they consider Nirvana to consist in the fact that there is no awakening.

Some imagine that Nirvana is where self-nature exists in its own right, unhampered by other self-natures, as the variegated feathers of a peacock, or various precious crystals, or the pointedness of a thorn. Some conceive being to be Nirvana, some non-being, while others conceive that all things and Nirvana are not to be distinguished from one another. Some, thinking that time is the creator and that as the rise of the world depends on time, they conceive that Nirvana consists in the recognition of time as Nirvana. Some think that there will be Nirvana when the "twenty-five" truths are generally accepted, or when the king observes the six virtues, and some religionists think that Nirvana is the attainment of paradise.

These views severally advanced by the philosophers with their various reasonings are not in accord with logic nor are they acceptable to the wise. They all conceive Nirvana dualistically and in some causal connection; by these discriminations philosophers imagine Nirvana, but where there is no rising and no disappearing, how can there be discrimination? Each philosopher relying on his own textbook from which he draws his understanding, sins against the truth, because truth is not where he imagines it to be. The only result is that it sets his mind to wandering about and becoming more confused as Nirvana is not to be found by mental searching, and the more his mind becomes confused the more he confuses other people.

As to the notion of Nirvana as held by disciples and masters who still cling to the notion of an ego-self, and who try to find it by going off by themselves into solitude: their notion of Nirvana is an eternity of bliss like the bliss of the Samadhis—for themselves. They recognise that the world is only a manifestation of mind and that all discriminations are of the mind, and so they forsake social relations and practise various spiritual disciplines and in solitude seek self-realisation of Noble Wisdom by self-effort. They follow the stages to the sixth and attain the bliss of the Samadhis, but as they are still clinging to egoism they do not attain the "turning-about" at the deepest seat of consciousness and, therefore, they are not free from the thinking-mind and the accumulation of its habit-energy. Clinging to the bliss of the Samadhis, they pass to their Nirvana, but it is not the Nirvana of the Tathagatas. They are of those who have "entered the stream"; they must return to this world of life and death.

* * *

Then said Mahamati to the Blessed One: When the Bodhisattvas yield up their stock of merit for the emancipation of all beings, they become spiritually one with all animate life; they themselves may be purified, but in others there yet remain unexhausted evil and unmatured karma. Pray tell us, Blessed One, how the Bodhisattvas are given assurance of Nirvana? and what is the Nirvana of the Bodhisattvas?

The Blessed One replied: Mahamati, this assurance is not an assurance of numbers nor logic; it is not the mind that is to be assured but the heart. The Bodhisattva's assurance comes with the unfolding insight that follows passion hindrances cleared away, knowledge hindrance purified, and egolessness clearly perceived and patiently accepted. As the mortal-mind ceases to discriminate, there is no more thirst for life, no more sex-lust, no more thirst for learning, no more thirst for eternal life; with the disappearance of these fourfold thirsts, there is no more accumulation of habit-energy; with no more accumulation of habit-energy the defilements on the face of Universal Mind clear away, and the Bodhisattva attains self-realisation of Noble Wisdom that is the heart's assurance of Nirvana.

There are Bodhisattvas here and in other Buddha-lands, who are sincerely devoted to the Bodhisattva's mission and yet who cannot wholly forget the bliss of the Samadhis and the peace of Nirvana—for themselves. The teaching of Nirvana in which there is no substrate left behind, is revealed according to a hidden meaning for the sake of these disciples who still cling to thoughts of Nirvana for themselves, that they may be inspired to exert themselves in the Bodhisattva's mission of emancipation for all beings. The Transformation-Buddhas teach a doctrine of Nirvana to meet conditions as they find them, and to give encouragement to the timid and selfish. In order to turn their thoughts away from themselves and to encourage them to a deeper compassion and more earnest zeal for others, they are given assurance as to the future by the sustaining power of the Buddhas of Transformation, but not by the Dharmata-Buddha.

The Dharma which establishes the Truth of Noble Wisdom belongs to the realm of the Dharmata-Buddha. To the Bodhisattvas of the seventh and eighth stages, Transcendental Intelligence is revealed by the Dharmata-Buddha and the Path is pointed out to them which they are to follow. In the perfect self-realisation of Noble Wisdom that follows the inconceivable transformation death of the Bodhisattva's individualised will-control, he no longer lives unto himself, but the life that he lives thereafter is the Tathagata's universalised life as manifested in its transformations. In this perfect self-realisation of Noble Wisdom the Bodhisattva realises that for Buddhas there is no Nirvana.

The death of a Buddha, the great Parinirvana, is neither destruction nor death, else would it be birth and continuation. If it were destruction, it would be an effect-producing deed, which it is not. Neither is it a vanishing nor an abandonment, neither is it attainment, nor is it of no attainment; neither is it of one significance nor of no significance, for there is no Nirvana for the Buddhas.

The Tathagata's Nirvana is where it is recognised that there is nothing but what is seen of the mind itself; is where, recognising the nature of the self-mind, one no longer cherishes the dualisms of discrimination; is where there is no more thirst nor grasping; is where there is no more attachment to external things. Nirvana is where the thinking-mind with all its discriminations, attachments, aversions and egoism is forever put away; is where logical measures, as they are seen to be inert, are no longer seized upon; is where even the notion of truth is treated with indifference because of its causing bewilderment; is where, getting rid of the four propositions, there is insight into the abode of Reality. Nirvana is where the twofold passions have subsided and the twofold hindrances are cleared away and the twofold egolessness is patiently accepted; is where, by the attainment of the "turning-about" in the deepest seat of consciousness, self-realisation of Noble Wisdom is fully entered into,—that is the Nirvana of the Tathagatas.

Nirvana is where the Bodhisattva stages are passed one after another; is where the sustaining power of the Buddhas upholds the Bodhisattvas in the bliss of the Samadhis; is where compassion for others transcends all thoughts of self; is where the Tathagata stage is finally realised.

Nirvana is the realm of Dharmata-Buddha; it is where the manifestation of Noble Wisdom that is Buddhahood expresses itself in Perfect Love for all; it is where the manifestation of Perfect Love that is Tathagatahood expresses itself in Noble Wisdom for the enlightenment of all —there, indeed, is Nirvana!

There are two classes of those who may not enter the Nirvana of the Tathagatas: there are those who have abandoned the Bodhisattva ideals, saying, they are not in conformity with the sutras, the codes of morality, nor with emancipation. Then there are the true Bodhisattvas who, on account of their original vows made for the sake of all beings, saying, "So long as they do not attain Nirvana, I will not attain it myself," voluntarily keep themselves out of Nirvana. But no beings are left outside by the will of the Tathagatas; some day each and every one will be influenced by the wisdom and love of the Tathagatas of Transformation to lay up a stock of merit and ascend the stages. But, if they only realised it, they are already in the Tathagata's Nirvana for, in Noble Wisdom, all things are in Nirvana from the beginning.

AWAKENING OF FAITH

MAHAYANA SHRADDHOTPADA SHASTRA

Preface

THIS Commentary upon the Mahayana Shradhotpadda Shastra is one of the most profound and wonderful books that has ever been written. It elucidates the significance of the Mahayana which is the Noble Path to Enlightenment and Nirvana, and by so doing it unveils the development of the Truth of Mind-Essence under the conditions of this Saha world. Its meaning is wide and profound, being as tranquil and peaceful as open space, and its potentialities as limitless and varied and vast as the boundless ocean. In its scope it includes divinities as well as humans, indeed, it reveals the origin of all individualized concepts. Because of its succinctness and profundity only a few are able to understand it.

In India, at the time of its writing some six hundred years after the Nirvana of our Lord Tathagata, the philosophic and religious culture of the times had developed and become segregated into many different schools and cults, so that all kinds of heresies and fallacies were flourishing everywhere. In only one thing did they agree and that was in a common attack and slanders about the True Teaching of Buddhism. At this crisis there came into prominence in India a scholar of outstanding virtue by the name of Ashvaghosha who rose to be the greatest controversalist of his time and who was able to subdue all opponents of Buddhism. As a Brahmin scholar he had studied all philosophies, but had become convinced that in the Truth of Mahayana he had found the ultimate ground of Truth and Faith and he cherished a deep and abiding faith in it. Although in the beginning a proud and egoistic Brahmin pedant, under the influence of his new faith he awakened a great heart of compassion and resolved that whenever opportunity came he would willingly interpret it to others. It was in this spirit of compassion for all the world, seeing them suffering under delusion, that he wrote this Commentary that by so doing he might broadcast the Three Treasures of Buddhism (Buddha, Dharma, Sangha, that is, Buddha, His Teaching, His Brotherhood) and revive their appeal. Any one who by reading it awakened a pure faith would be quickly turned away from his heretical preconceptions and enter upon the true Path. Since the time of the Lord Tathagata this Mahayana Teaching had only imperfectly been understood because its time of maturity had not yet fully come. In China it had not even been heard of. It was not until the times of the Later Liang Dynasty (505-552) that the Emperor Liang Wu-ti becoming interested in this Indian Teaching sent envoys to the Magadha country of India to secure copies of its Sanskrit Scriptures and to invite learned Masters to return with them to China. There these envoys met a great Sanskrit Master by the name of Kulananda, who afterward became better known as Paramartha. He had been a great student of Indian philosophies and religions during his academic life, but had later become wholly interested in the Teachings of the Mahayana and had become a Master of great insight into its Truths. He was eminently the Master the envoys were looking for and they invited him to return with them to be under the patronage of the Emperor. At first he refused to go, but under the urgent appeal of his own King, he at last consented and sailed for China with suitable attendants and a store of images and books.

He was received with great respect by the Emperor, but unfortunately within ten days a rebellion broke out, surrounded the palace and in less than eighty days the Emperor had died of starvation, leaving the Indian Master unprotected, but not without friends. At first he prepared to return to his native country, but certain of us including Lord Shaube of the Privy Council and the Generalissimo's office advised him to remain and provided him with a safe retreat in the Kien-shing Temple in Hengchow, Hunan Province.

In the Third Year of Shen-Seng (557) The Master began the translation of this Shastra and completed it in two years in one volume elucidating the Mahayana very vividly and clearly. Besides this he translated many other Scriptures, notably, Metaphysical Buddhism in twenty volumes, the Metaphysics of the Mahavagga in four volumes, and An Interpretation of the Nine Kinds of Consciousness in two volumes. Besides the Grand Master Paramartha, he was assisted by the Indo-Scythian Master Surnam and others, and I was one of the Chinese writers to put their interpretations into classical Chinese characters. From the commencement of the work to its ending, the task lasted two years. Since then this elucidation of the principle and practice of the Mahayana written by the Venerable Patriarch Ashvaghosha has prevailed in the scholarly world and most of the heretical scholars have submitted to the orthodox.

It was a cause of great regret to me that I was never able to meet the Venerable Patriarch personally, but I count it a good fortune to have had the chance to study his wonderful teaching and witness and praise its profound wisdom. I reverenced this Principle so much that I could hardly give up its study. In spite of my unlearnedness, I presumptuously accepted the honor of writing down the oral interpretations of my colleagues. If there ever should be greater scholars who by chance should read it, I would count it a great indebtedness if they would correct any errors.

Written by BHIKSHU CHIH-CHI *of the* LIANG DYNASTY.

Introduction

ADORATION to our Great Compassionate Savior, Omnipresent, Omniscient, Omnipotent!

ADORATION to his Potentiality and unmanifested Universality!

ADORATION to his Activity, perfectly balanced and accommodating!

ADORATION to the pure Essence of Mind, wide and deep as the sea!

ADORATION to its Store of infinite Virtues and Merit, that may be fully developed by earnest and true practising!

IN THY NAME I interpret the Mahayana for the sake of dispelling the suspicions and heretical prejudices of all sentient beings!

By the Awakening of their Faith in the Mahayana may I scatter Buddha seeds for an unending harvest!

* * *

This commentary is written wholly on the ground that there

is a way in which faith in the Mahayana can be developed. It was for this reason and no other that I was impelled to the writing of this interpretation of the Mahayana Principle. The interpretation is divided into five parts: 1) The introduction. 2) Terms used in the Mahayana. 3) The interpretation of the Mahayana. 4) The practising of the Mahayana. 5) The advantages of practising the Mahayana.

Part One

Introduction

Some one may enquire why I was led to write this Commentary. The reply is that there are eight kinds of causes and affinities that led me to undertake this task. My first and main purpose was to save all sentient beings from suffering and to bring them to eternal happiness. I had no desire to gain by it worldly fame, riches or honor. The second reason was a desire to present the true meaning of the Lord Tathagata's teachings so that all sentient beings might have the advantage of a true understanding of it at the very beginning. The third reason was to enable those who have made some advance on the Path to enlightenment to conserve their gain and not to later lose it. The fourth reason was to awaken and strengthen the faith of beginners on the path and to encourage them to a more earnest practice. The fifth reason was to show all those who are following the path expedient means for getting rid of the hindrances of bad karma, for keeping their minds free from the cravings and infatuations of egoism, and to keep free from the net of evil influences. The sixth reason was the wish to help all seekers to practice right methods for practising "stopping and reflecting" so as to guard them against the false view-points of both worldly minded people and Hinayana disciples. The seventh reason was to explain the expedient means of reciting the Divine Name of Amitabha Buddha and to prove to them that if they should recite the name of Amitabha with one-pointed mind that they would be sure to be reborn in Buddha's pure land, and once reborn there that they would never suffer retrogression. The eighth reason was to show to those whose faith was awakened by the reading of this treatise the inestimable advantages of the practice of Dhyana and to persuade them to an earnest perseverance in it. These are the reasons that led me to the writing of this commentary.

Again, some one may enquire why, so long as the Dharma was presented in the Sutras, a commentary was called for. My reply is this. It is true that the Buddha teachings are fully presented in the Sutras, but as the karmas and inherited tendencies of sentient beings vary widely, and their experiences and practises are different from one another, so the conditions of their awakening faith and their realization of its fruits will be different. During the presence of the Lord Tathagata in this world those sentient beings who were endowed with competent and intelligent minds as they listened to the Lord Buddha, whose words were transcendental both in their form and meaning, and which were interpreted with perfect accommodation, understood them, and there was no need at that time for such a treatise as this. But after the Nirvana of the Lord Tathagata conditions were different. The teachings had been reduced to written words and men's minds were less acute and more varied. Some were able to acquire an understanding of the teaching by their own study of them after a long time, and some after a short time. Some who lacked intellectual power would acquire an understanding after the study of long and erudite commentaries and some becoming confused by long and tiresome commentaries were helped by brief and concise ones. Because of these conditions I felt that a new and different commentary was called for and I felt impelled to present the Lord's Teachings in all their profound wisdom but to explain them briefly, succinctly, but clearly and adequately.

Part Two

Terms used in the Mahayana

Generally speaking the Mahayana employs two sets of terms. One set is used when speaking of the Dharma as Essence, the other when speaking of the Dharma as Principle. The Dharma is the mind of all sentient beings. This mind embraces all conceptions both relating to the phenomenal world and those relating to the mind world and leading to the purity and freedom of eternity. It is by means of the concepts of this mind that the principle of the Mahayana is being unfolded and comprehended. In one aspect it manifests the true essence of the Mahayana; in the other aspect it reflects the appearing and disappearing, because of causes and conditions, and unfolds the potentialities and activities of the principle of the Mahayana.

The concept of the principle of the Mahayana is capable of three kinds of interpretation. The first is its immensity, its all-embracing wholeness, in which all concepts are intrinsic but undifferentiated and of the same suchness neither decreasing nor increasing in quantity, but abiding in perfect purity and unity. The second is its immensity of potentiality; as the womb of Tathagata it is the fountain of all dharmas, of all natures and merits, even to infinities of infinity. The third is the immensity of its manifesting activities, giving rise to all manner of good causes and effects belonging both to this terrestrial world and to the mind world leading to the perfect purity and freedom of eternity. It is the path by which all the Buddhas have attained Nirvana, and by it the Bodhisattva-Mahasattvas will attain the sure ground of Tathagatahood.

PART THREE

The interpretation of the Mahayana

The interpretation of the Mahayana is divided into three sections. The first section treats of the unfolding of the true principle. The second is a refutation of false doctrines and prejudices. The third, relates to right practices leading to enlightenment.

SECTION ONE

First as to the unfolding of the true principle. The mind has two doors from which issue its activities. One leads to a realization of the mind's Pure Essence, the other leads to the differentiations of appearing and disappearing, of life and death. Through each door passes all the mind's conceptions so interrelated that they never have been separated and never will be.

What is meant by the Pure Essence of Mind? It is the ultimate purity and unity, the all-embracing wholeness, the quintessence of Truth. Essence of Mind belongs to neither death nor rebirth, it is uncreated and eternal. The concepts of the conscious mind are being individualized and discriminated by

false imaginations. If the mind could be kept free from discriminative thinking there would be no more arbitrary thoughts
to give rise to appearances of form, existencies and conditions.
Therefore from the beginning, all concepts have been independent of individuation, of names and mental moods and conditions. They are in their essential nature of an equal sameness,
neither variable nor breakable nor destructible. As they are of
one suchness, of one purity, it is spoken of as Mind-essence.

For the differentiations of words are but false notions with
no basis in reality. They have in their falsity only a relative
existence as false imaginations and thoughts arise and pass
away. Even as applying to Mind-essence words have no value,
for in Mind-essence there is nothing to be grasped nor named.
But we use words to get free from words until we reach the
pure wordless Essence. In Essence of Mind there is nothing
that can be taken away and nothing that can be added. All
concepts are an undivided part of Reality; they are not artificial but are unchangeable and ineffable and unthinkable. They
are the Essence of Mind itself. Some one may ask that if all
concepts are to be thus regarded, how are sentient beings to
make use of them to abstract their minds into the Mind's pure
Essence? The reply is that whenever any sentient being uses
words in relation to the mind's pure Essence he should remember their falsity and cherish no arbitrary conceptions, nor distinctions between themselves and the spoken words and the
thing spoken about. As they use words to express their
thoughts they should remember that words are wholly independent of the speaker and are not to be grasped as their own.
If any sentient being should be able to thus keep free from all
arbitrary conceptions, it would mean that they had attained
oneness with the pure Essence of all concepts.

Again, if we are to distinguish different aspects of Mind-
Essence, there is an emptiness aspect of its invariable Essence
for it can unfold its primal reality. And there is a non-emptiness aspect, for it has its own substantiality possessing all sorts
of merits of a non-intoxicant nature, that is, that it exists in its
own right. The first is an aspect of negation, the second an
aspect of affirmation. From the very beginning Mind-Essence
has never given any mutual response to any contaminated conceptions of differentiations, it has ever been free from discriminations among thoughts or phenomena, for it is perfect unity,

perfect purity. It should be clearly understood that the true nature of Mind-Essence does not belong to any individualized conception of phenomena or of non-phenomena; nor of the absence of phenomena, or of the absence of non-phenomena; nor of unity or of disunity; nor of the absence of unity or of disunity; in other words, it has no particularizing consciousness, it does not belong to any kind of describable nature. Individuations and the consciousness of them come into being only as sentient beings cherish false imaginations of differences and the mind makes discriminations among them, thought after thought rising with no mutual response among them, resulting in confusion and conflict and suffering. This is what is meant when speaking of Mind-Essence as being empty. But if the Truth is fully understood it will be seen that the conception of emptiness as it relates to Mind-Essence is itself, "empty." If the mind can be kept free from false imaginations there can be no conceivable meaning to the term, "emptiness."

On the other hand, Mind-Essence is by no means to be thought of as being empty of its own perfectly universalized nature; it is only empty in the sense that it includes in its true nature no elements of falsity, namely, it is the pure Dharmakaya, the very suchness of Truth. Since it has ever been permanent and invariable in its nature, and possessing the whole body of conceptions in perfectly undifferentiated purity it is the very acme of non-emptiness. At the same time, it must by no means be considered that Mind-Essence has its own transcendental phenomena; not at all, it has no conceivable or inconceivable phenomena of its own, it is perfect Emptiness, and can only be apprehended as the mind transcending its discriminating processes of thought and all imagery of selfness, becomes itself unified with the pure Suchness of Mind-Essence.

Then there is the appearing and dis-appearing aspect of Mind-Essence, that we think of as birth and death. In this connection we think of Mind-Essence as the Womb of Tathagata, but in fact nothing comes forth and nothing returns and there is no Womb of Tathagata, for the nature of appearing and disappearing coincides with the nature of non-appearing and non-disappearing. The pure Essence of Mind is neither unity nor plurality and yet we conceive it as the inconceivable Alaya-vijnana, the "storage" or Universal Mind. This Alaya consciousness embraces two significant aspects which can both receive and give forth all definitive concepts. The one aspect is that of Enlightenment,. the other that of Ignorance.

In its aspect of Enlightenment, Mind-Essence is free from all manner of individuation and discriminative thinking; it is all-embracing, extending to all immensities as vast as open space, as pure, as unchanging, as indefinable. It is the Dharmakaya of Tathagatahood. It is innate Enlightenment, but because it is Enlightenment, it foreshadows the appearing of Enlightenment, but innate Enlightenment and the appearing of Enlightenment are of one sameness; because there is the conception of Enlightenment, there is the conception of non-Enlightenment, and because of the conception of non-Enlightenment there is the conception of Enlightenment. Because of the conception of Enlightenment, and of non-Enlightenment, there is the conception of attaining Enlightenment, but Enlightenment, non-Enlightenment, attaining of Enlightenment are all of one sameness and unity. When the mind becomes conscious of its ultimate nature of Enlightenment, it speaks of it as Enlightenment; when it is not enlightened as to its ultimate nature, we think of it as Ignorance, but truly in the Alaya-vijnana there is no difference between them, there is only the perfect purity of the Dharmakaya.

Among human beings, Enlightenment appears in varying degrees of purity. Just as soon as a common person is conscious of a difference between right thoughts and false thoughts, between good thoughts and evil thoughts, it can be said that he has become enlightened, but it is a very rudimentary form of Enlightenment. Hinayana disciples as they begin their practice of Dhyana are conscious of their discriminating thoughts and at the same time are conscious that they have no validity; they are said to have attained Enlightenment, but it is a very crude form of Enlightenment. As they restrain their discriminative concepts, being conscious of their falsity their enlightenment becomes more refined. As they become Bodhisattvas, becoming more conscious of the grasping nature of discriminative thoughts and yet reminding themselves that even discriminative thoughts have no grasping quality in their self-nature, their Enlightenment has become partly accommodating. As Bodhisattvas advance along the stages, they more and more become sensitive to the arising of these false discriminations and more and more quickly react against them, and become more and more skillful in employing expedient means for checking their arising and ignoring them if they arise. Until at last they come to a state of awareness in which they are able to keep far away from even the most refined conceptions, knowing that Essential Mind is permanent and abiding in its purity. This is a state of perfect accommodation; it can be truly called Enlightenment. Therefore it is said in the Sutras, if any sentient being is able to keep free from all discriminative thinking, he has attained to the wisdom of a Buddha.

In the foregoing we have referred to the rising of conscious and discriminative thoughts, but speaking truly, there is no rising of thoughts of any kind, for conscious thinking is wholly subjective and imaginary. Most people are said to be lacking in Enlightenment. This is not because they have no thoughts, but because from the very beginning they have had a continuous stream of discriminations with no break in their succession. They are still abiding in a beginningless Ignorance. But when a Bodhisattva has completed the stages and has attained a state of no thinking, he is able to realize that all the phenomena of conscious mentation—its rising, growing, passing, disappearing—is the same as no thinking, that all the apparent changes are inherent but unmanifest in the Primal Enlightening Nature of Mind-Essence, and that the Primal state of Enlightenment is the Ultimate Enlightenment.

*　*　*

The question arises, how can these apparent differences arise out of the purity of Mind-Essence? The answer is, that it is because of the perfect accommodation of the Alaya-vijnana to its store of defilements that have been accumulated since beginningless time. These give rise to two classes of phenomena which are inseparable from its intrinsic nature of Enlightenment and yet are in mutual relationship with each other. In one class are phenomena relating to intellectual purity and moving toward Enlightenment, and in the other class are phenomena relating to karma and moving toward Ignorance.

By means of intellectual purity the Bodhisattva has been able to practice right methods and employ expedient means to transcend the influence of these defilements, to break away from their entanglements, destroy the enslaving power of conscious discriminations, and by intuition come into a realization of his

pure Dharmakaya. Though all the phenomena of the mind, its
perceptions, its discriminations, its consciousness, belong to the
nature of non-enlightenment, yet because the nature of non-
enlightenment is the same as the nature of Enlightenment, it is
neither destructible nor indestructible. It is like the waves on
the surface of the ocean raised by the passing wind, both are
involved but water does not of itself possess the nature of
movement, so when the wind ceases the waves subside and the
water returns to its natural tranquillity. It is the same with
sentient beings. Their pure Essential Mind has been disturbed
by the supposed wind of Ignorance, but neither mind nor Ignorance has any substance or form or phenomena of its own,
neither are they separated from each other. As disturbance does
not belong to the nature of Mind, so when its Ignorance is discarded, the disturbing phenomena of false imaginations and
discriminating thoughts will disappear also, for its power of intuition does not disturb its true nature in the least.

In the outward activities of the discriminating mind, karma
is the record of its habit-energy urging it on to further differentiation, but in the inconceivable integrating activities of Intuitional Purity, karma is the record of its unifying attractions
reducing multiplicities to unities and resulting in all manner of
transcendental syntheses and mysterious wonders, and effecting
within the minds of earnest disciples all manner of spiritual
benefits and powers, all of which because of their vows are
available to all sentient beings.

* * *

Likening Enlightenment to space or a clear mirror, a four-
fold significance relating to its greatness is revealed. The first
significance to be revealed is when by reason of removing all
objects to a distance from a mirror there is no reflection, so
when all disturbing mental conditions and all mental spheres
in contact with objects through the sense organs are done
away with there is no disturbance of the Mind's tranquillity.
This first significance, therefore, is a revelation of the greatness
of the Mind's Emptiness. The second significance is one of
greatness of its affirmation of trueness. No matter what the
phenomena or the conditions may be in the Saha world they
are reflected in the mirror of the Mind's pure Essence with perfect trueness and impartiality. There is nothing that enters and

nothing that departs, there is nothing that is lost nor destroyed, for in the true Essential Mind all conceptions are of one sameness that in its suchness abides unchanged and permanent. For true Essential Mind yields to no contaminations that can possibly contaminate it, and even its reflected contaminated conceptions have no effect upon it. Its intuitional nature is never disturbing and, on the contrary, is in possession of boundless non-intoxicant virtues that influence all sentient beings to draw them into the unity and purity of its pure Essence.

The third significance of Mind-Essence considered as a mirror, is an affirmation of the greatness of its freedom. Just as a mirror reflects freely all objects brought before it, so Essential Mind reflects all concepts freely without being contaminated by them. They go forth freely just as they are, separated from all hindrances and annoyances of knowledge, and all the phenomena of composition and conformity, for in Essential Mind all is pure and bright and free.

The fourth significance is an affirmation of compassionate helpfulness, for being free from all limitations of selfness, it draws all alike into its all-embracing purity and unity and peacefulness, illumining their minds with equal brightness so that all sentient beings have an equal right to Enlightenment, an equal chance to practice the ultimate principle of kindness, an equal surety that ultimately all sentient beings will attain Enlightenment, mature their root of merit and realize their inherent Buddha-nature.

* * *

Let us now consider further the real nature of non-Enlightenment. In the foregoing pages we have said that non-Enlightenment is related to Ignorance. This is true in the sense that the thinking mind, being confused by its false imaginations and discriminations, does not see clearly its own Mind-Essence, and the real sameness of all its conceptions. Just as soon as the mind notes differences because of its different sensations and sense perceptions, it immediately begins to unite them into conceptions, to name them, to discriminate them, to think about them, from which arises all manner of false judgments and self-consciousness. These discriminated thoughts have no substance of their own; they are not at all different from thought in its wholeness that by its Essential Nature is pure and enlightening. An ignorant man, one controlled by his discriminating mind, is like a man who has lost his way. When we speak of a man losing his way, we mean that he has a prior conception of a right way from which he has gone astray. Apart from this prior conception of a right way, of a place to which he wishes to reach, going astray has no meaning. It is just the same with sentient beings said to be un-enlightened. They have an innate affinity for Enlightenment, but because of their false imaginations and discriminations they go astray. Thus Ignorance and Enlightenment have only a relative meaning. If a man had no conception of Enlightenment, he would have no conception of Ignorance; and if he can get rid of his ignorance, he will have no conception of Enlightenment. It is by means of his discriminating mind that leads a man astray that he can also gain Enlightenment, therefore we can truly speak of the true and Enlightening Nature of a man's mind, but if he can free himself from all consciousness of his Enlightening Nature, then the significance of Enlightenment would vanish also.

* * *

Because of discriminating Ignorance, the mind gives rise to three kinds of conceptions which are in close mutuality and are inseparable from discriminations. The first is a conception of activity; the second is a conception of an actor; the third is a conception of a world of action. The first is called, karma. If there was only a state of pure Enlightenment, the mind would remain undisturbed and in tranquillity, but because of discriminating Ignorance the mind becomes disturbed, and this disturbance and its habit-energy we speak of as karma. As soon as the mind becomes disturbed by its discriminating differences, desire arises to be followed by suffering, all of which is embraced in the conception of Karma.

The second is called Egoism. As soon as the mind perceives differences, it awakens desire, grasping, and following suffering, and then the mind notes that some relate to himself and some to not-self, from which arises a conception of an actor, an ego-self. If the mind could remain undisturbed by differences and discriminations the conception of an ego-self would die away.

The third is a conception of a surrounding world that is not-self. Independent of an actor there is no meaning to an external world of things produced, acted upon and reacting. As one gets rid of the conception of self, the conception of an external world vanishes with it.

Again, because of discriminating Ignorance and the intimate relations of the conceptions of thinking, thinker and things thought about, there rises six kinds of mental phenomena. First, there are feelings of liking and disliking. Second, these feelings following in quick succession are fixed in memory and become intensified by a kind of habit-energy. Third, because of this habit-energy, there is a grasping after the agreeable and a shrinking from the disagreeable, thus abiding in either happiness or suffering. Fourth, because of the foregoing, there is a continuity or clinging that reacts on the thinker himself to condition his thoughts and he gives names and false meanings to things. Fifth, these false names and discriminating thoughts react upon his conception of an external world to condition his surroundings and build up a conditioning karma. Sixth, this karma going on accumulating from beginningless time develops a strong and stronger tendency to action that enslaves the thinker until he more and more loses his freedom. Thus we see that defiling thoughts and suffering do not exist in their own right but arise from the non-enlightenment of discriminating Ignorance.

Again, these two conceptions of Enlightenment and non-Enlightenment have a twofold relation. The first is a relation of similarity, the other a relation of dissimilarity. Just as different pieces of pottery made by a potter are similar in the sense that they are all made of clay, so with the different kinds of karma and karmaic illusions, the defiling as well as the purifying, they all have their only reality in the pure Essence of Mind. In this sense they are similar, as the Sutras say: All sentient beings are ever abiding in Nirvana. Nevertheless, the thing called Enlightenment is nothing that can be attained by practising, nor can it be created by human hands; it is intangible and ungraspable, having no form that can be seen or nature that can be described. The reason that Enlightenment can take on different manifestations of form and explicability is wholly because of the conditioning power of karma in correspondence with the defilements of the mind. Enlightenment and Wisdom in their true Nature have nothing to do with material forms or phenomena that it can become an object of sensation.

The relation of dissimilarity is this. Just as different objects made by the potter are infinitely diversified, so the manifestations of the mind's discriminating thoughts, both enlightening and defiling are infinitely varied. Just as karmas and karmaic conditions are varied, so the manifestations of their conditioning power are varied and dissimilar.

* * *

Again, what has been said in the foregoing about the appearing and disappearing, or what is known as birth and death, has its particular causes and conditions. We mean by this that sentient beings with their ever active discriminating and thinking minds are forever accumulating a body of false imaginations and notions which become defilements on the face of the Alaya-vijnana and give rise to self-consciousness and its propensity for desires and habits of grasping and clinging, all of which are dependent on the thinking mind without any self-nature of their own. This body of false notions having its dependence on the thinking mind and providing the causes and conditions for the evolution of mind is Ignorance. By it there arises the intuitive mind (*manas*), the intellectual mind (*mano-vijnana*) and the six sense-minds (the *vijnanas*). *Manas* having relations with both the Alaya-vijnana and the *mano-vijnana* mediates between them and gives rise to the conceptions of consciousness and the faculties of both intellection and intuition which lead respectfully to Ignorance and Enlightenment. As soon as the non-enlightening nature begins to rise there develops perceptibility, the manifesting power of discriminating thoughts, grasping upon conditions and causing a continuous evolution of changes and transformations, from which arises the consciousness of an ego-self and an external world of causes and conditions. This false notion of an ego-self is in possession of five aspects or names. The first is its activity-consciousness (*karma*-consciousness), which means that owing to the particularizing power of Ignorance, the non-enlightening potentialities of the mind are awakened and brought into activity. The second is the evolving-consciousness or power of transforming sensations into perceptions. The third is the reflecting-consciousness which reflects all kinds of perceptions originating in the contact of objects with the sense-organs and unites them into unities, spontaneously and without prejudice. The fourth is the discriminating-consciousness that classifies these unified perceptions as they are in relation to itself, into favorable or unfavorable, pure or defiled. The fifth is the memory-consciousness that retains all conceptions in mind and in mutual relations and synthetic response without any cessation. It keeps all the elements of karma accumulated from a beginningless past in activity and registering their full value. It compels the mind to endure the reactions of karma whether they be painful or pleasant to their full maturity; it brings past experiences into sudden remembrance and projects its false imaginations into the future. It is the cause of all the illusions of the triple-world, not one of which has any cause apart from the discriminating and thinking mind. Separated from the mind there are no objects of sense, all conceptions of them arise in the mind and are developed and manifested by the false activities of the mind. Not one of them has any self-substance of its own, they are all alike brought into manifestation and kept in continuity of relation by the false imaginations of Ignorance of sentient beings. They are, indeed, like reflections in a mirror which if grasped lead to hallucinations of a self and an external world, but which if allowed to pass, if the discriminating and thinking mind stops its thinking, leave the mind in tranquillity.

This memory consciousness because of the desiring and grasping nature of the mind becomes more and more ingrained in the mind. It develops and intensifies the false notion of an ego-self and exaggerates the supposed importance of its interests. This is the reason why the memory-consciousness is also thought of as the egoistic-consciousness, the separating-consciousness, because by reason of its activities the mind becomes more and more separated by its egoistic desires, prejudices and imaginary annoyances, from its true oneness in the pure Essence of Mind.

* * *

The relation of the conceptual, discriminating, thinking and conscious mind to Essential Mind, how it arises, develops and becomes established, is very difficult to understand. It is quite impossible for ordinary human beings, and even Hinayana disciples misunderstand it. Bodhisattvas who begin their practice of stopping thought and realizing truth in pure faith as they gain a degree of insight acquire a small degree of its understanding. Even those Bodhisattvas who have attained to the stage of immovability and constancy cannot understand it thoroughly, only Buddhas can understand it perfectly. Essential Mind is pure and immaculate by nature, it possesses Ignorance only as a superficial and transient defilement, but by reason of the defiling nature of Ignorance, it gives rise to all varieties and degrees of mental illusions and conceptions and discriminated appearances. But in spite of its relation to defiled minds, in its own Essentiality, it ever abides in unchanging and unchangeable purity. It is this profound relation of unchanging Purity to evolving impurities that is only understood by the highest perfect Wisdom of Buddhas. Because the mind does not realize the perfect purity of the all-embracing wholeness it falls into the habit of imagining differences where there are no differences, and thus the mind, being inharmonious with itself, becomes the puppet of Ignorance.

There are six different kinds of mental contaminations. The first is defilement by attachment by consent, from which disciples, Pratyekabuddhas, and Bodhisattvas of the early stages can be liberated, and Bodhisattvas as they attain the stage of "self-mastery" are kept far away. The second is defilement by attachments in spite of disapproval and resistance. This can be partially controlled as the Bodhisattva by his earnest practice gradually advances along the stages to the stage of "realization," when although still in touch with the discriminations and passions of outer things, realizes their emptiness. And as he further advances to the stage of "far-going" and leaves behind all thoughts and remembrances of discriminations, truly abiding in the inner world, can be wholly controlled. The third kind is defilement by attachment with consent to discriminations of the intellectual mind, the clinging to ideas and definitions. This can be gradually cleared away by the Bodhisattva's perfect and selfless keeping of the Precepts, and can be completely discarded after attaining a great heart of compassion and command of skillful and efficient means, which come to him as he gets rid of all arbitrary conceptions of phenomena, and passes from outward morality, to inner Wisdom and finally to perfect spirituality. The fourth kind is defilement of the intellectual mind in spite of disapproval and resistance. It can be purified as the Bodhisattva attains to the intrinsic ground of transcendental mental freedom. The fifth kind is defilement by the Bodhisattva still clinging to the notion of a perceiving and discriminating mind although no longer in bondage to it. This can be gotten rid of as he advances in transcendental mental freedom where there is no further thought of self or not-self, of self and otherness, as he passes beyond all duality, all incompleteness, and attains perfect equanimity. The sixth kind is the mental contamination that a Bodhisattva must accept of the general and universal karma until he passes into the Great Truth Cloud of Tathagatahood.

To review these paragraphs let us add the following observations. The common non-realization of the Essential purity and unity of the all-embracing Wholeness, can be partially discarded by the awakening of a pure faith, and then as the Bodhisattva ascends the stages by his earnest practice of Dhyana can be progressively discarded, until he attains to the highest stage of Tathagatahood when it will be perfectly discarded. The reference to the principle of mutuality of response or lack of it, means that the mind is always in contact with the various conceptions arising from the senses and which are being differentiated by means of contaminated or pure thoughts, and that the mind is sensitive to their relations of likeness and affinity. In regard to the principle of resistance, it means that the mind having the faculty of intuition that transcends all states of consciousness, all unconscious of their mutual resemblances and affinities, never makes any distinctions nor discriminations but reflects spontaneously their true nature. In regard to the reference to the principle of intellectual contaminations, it refers to the hindrances that obscure the forth-shining of the intrinsic Wisdom of the Mind's pure Essence. As regards the principle of Ignorance, it means the intellectual hindrance that obscures the free illumination of the general karma by the Light of Transcendental Intelligence. What is meant by this? It means that by means of mental contaminations and false imaginations the mind becomes disturbed and moved to different forms of manifesting activity which is contrary to its true nature of Equanimity. Pure concepts undefiled by the mind's discriminating judgments come and go unnoticed, but when disturbed by Ignorance they lose their quietness and enlightening nature and add to the world's karma.

* * *

Further, mind in its manifestation as birth and death has two appearances. First there is a crude state as seen in the minds of common people, and there a refined state as manifested in the minds of Buddhas. The mental state of a novice Bodhisattva may be said to be in a refined state of crudeness, and the mental state of an advanced Bodhisattva, in a crude state of refinement. But these two states of crudeness and refinement both exist because of the defiling power of Ignorance. As the thoughts of the mind appear and disappear the mind variously cherishes them and there develop causes and condition of affinities. The causes are the unenlightened nature of Ignorance, and because of there being affinities among the causes there develop varying conditions. If the cause should disappear, the affinities would disappear, and moreover, if the cause should disappear those parts of the mental attributes that are not in mutual response will disappear also. And because of the disappearing of the affinities, those parts of the mental attributes that are in mutual response will disappear, too.

It may then be asked, if all mental attributes should disappear what would become of the unceasing continuity of the mind? Or, if there should be some continuity of mind after its attributes had disappeared, how could we speak of the disappearing of the mental attributes? The reply is, as regards the disappearing of the mental attributes, it means the disappearing of the mind's arbitrary conceptions, not the disappearing of the mind's substantiality in Essential Mind. It is just the same as the relation of the wind and water and waves. Wind has the power to disturb water and by it to create waves, but if there is no water, the power remains potential and there are no waves. But so long as there is water and wind there will be waves. Again, if the wind loses its potential power of motion, there will be no waves even if the water remains. That is, it takes both wind and water to make waves. It is just the same with Ignorance and mind and discriminating thoughts. The reason that Ignorance is the cause of disturbing thoughts is because of the mind's Essential stability. If the mind should lose its stability, all sentient beings would disappear because there would be nothing for Ignorance to play upon. However, as the substantiality of the mind never disappears so the mind retains its continuity. But if Ignorance some day should disappear, then all arbitrary conceptions of form and phenomena would disappear with it, but it would not be the disappearing of the Mind's pure Wisdom.

* * *

There is a constant succession of thoughts both pure and
defiled that is taking place because of the interaction of four
elements. First, there is the Ultimate Principle of the Mind's
pure Essence; the second, is the cause of all the mind's contaminations, namely Ignorance; the third, is the discriminating
mind, or the karma-consciousness; the fourth, are the false
conditions of the external world, that is, the six objects of sense.

We may think of the interaction of these four elements as
a process of fumigation. Just like clothing that is perfectly
clean has no odour, but if packed away with fragrant herbs for
a long time the clothing becomes fumigated with the same fragrance. It is the same with these four elements, each tends to
fumigate the other as they come into relation with each other.
Pure Mind-Essence is by nature free of any contamination, but
by association with Ignorance its pure concepts become defiled.
Conversely, the impure concepts of Ignorance are in their nature free of any purity of karma, but having their substantiality
in the purity of Mind-Essence they come to partake of its
purity.

How can impure concepts continually arise by reason of the
habitual fumigation of Ignorance? It is because the Mind's
pure Essence has the potentiality for giving rise to all conceptual ideas and it follows from this that there develops the
principle of individuation and discrimination that we name Ignorance, and it is because of Ignorance giving rise to impure
concepts that there is the habitual fumigation of Mind-Essence.
By means of this habitual fumigation there develops the appearance of a false mind and it is by reason of this false mind
that there is the habitual fumigation of Ignorance. Since Ignorance does not realize the pure Concepts of Mind-Essence,
by its non-enlightening nature it gives rise continually to manifestations of false conditions. By means of there being these
false conditions affinities appear between them and the false
mind, continually reminding the mind of their existence and
thus fumigating it and giving rise continually to grasping and
activities and the laying up of all kinds of karma and all kinds
of suffering both mental and physical.

There are two ways by which the false conditions of an
external world fumigate the mind; first by continually increasing its thinking faculty, and second by continually strengthen-

ing its desires and graspings. The false mind has, also, two kinds of habitual ways for fumigating false conditions of the external world; first, to quicken the fundamental activity-consciousness by reason of which disciples, Pratyekabuddhas, Arhats and Bodhisattvas can endure all kinds of suffering and deaths and rebirths; second, to continually increase the discriminating-consciousness by reason of which common human beings suffer under their karma all manner of suffering. Again, the habitual fumigation of Ignorance has two other kinds of manifestation, first, a primary habitual fumigation by reason of which one's karma, or activity-consciousness, is being developed; second, an accompanying development of the desiring, or fondness for the agreeable objects of sense, consciousness. The first, by reason of its sufferings, awakens a dislike for the experiences of birth and death, the second, by its delights, urges it on to the grasping for more.

How are pure concepts constantly produced by the perfuming of Ignorance? It is because of there being the potentiality for pure concepts which reacts upon Ignorance awakening in the false minds a feeling of abhorrence of the sufferings of birth and death and prompts it to seek Nirvana with willingness and earnestness. This abhorrence for the suffering of birth and death and the seeking for Nirvana with earnestness, in turn reacts upon Mind-Essence. By reason of this, the thinking mind attains a conception of its Essential Nature and discriminates it from the changing and pain-producing nature of the experiential mind, to convince him of the latter's unreality and to enable him to practise right means for keeping away from its dissatisfying experiences and disturbances. Having become convinced that all external conditions and all the discriminations of the conscious mind have no true existence, it is led to make use of skillful means and appropriate activities to treat these false conditions and thoughts with indifference, neither fearing nor grasping nor desiring nor even thinking about them. Thus by means of the long continued fumigation of Ignorance by Mind-Essence, the state of Ignorance is gotten rid of altogether. As Ignorance is discarded the rising of all thoughts of individuation and discrimination are brought to an end. Because of the ceasing of all such thoughts there are no more conceptions of external things and conditions to appeal to one through the senses. Accordingly as conditions and discriminations come to an end, all the mental phenomena cease to disturb the mind and it becomes empty and tranquil. The dying down of all disturbance is the attainment of Nirvana, the state of perfect freedom.

Let us now further consider the reactions of the false mind and the pure concepts of the Mind's Essence. The habitual fumigation of the false mind by the Pure Concepts of Mind-Essence are of two kinds: first, there is the fumigation of the discriminating-consciousness by reason of which, disciples, Pratyekabuddhas and Arhats abhorring the suffering of life and death are supported according to their individual needs and possibilities in their purpose and effort to attain Perfect Enlightenment. Second, there is the habitual fumigation of the mind's states by reason of which the Bodhisattvas advance along the stages with zeal and courage and perfect faith until their goal of Nirvana is attained.

The habitual fumigation of Mind-Essence by the false mind are also of two kinds: first, there is the habitual fumigation of the potentialities of one's own true nature; the second, is the habitual fumigation of the mind's true activities which are no activity but are the spontaneous drawing-togetherness of the minds' disturbances and tensions. Since beginningless time, the mind has been fully possessed of its rightful non-intoxicating pure concepts which have been defiled and covered up by an inconceivable Karma to appear in all manner of forms and conditions. By means of the interaction of these two kinds of reaction, sentient beings are led to abhor the suffering of birth and death and to be willing to seek for the attainment of Nirvana, thus, it awakens faith in their true Essence of Mind and enables them to begin, and to continue the practice of devotion, and to endure the necessary restraints.

If the foregoing is true, that all sentient beings are possessed of their pure Mind-Essence and have been equally exposed to the habitual fumigation of its pure concepts, how is it that some of them awaken a pure faith and some do not. And how is it that there are so many and so great inequalities among sentient beings, and why is it that some continue in the dreary round of death and rebirth and only a few awaken a pure faith, practice expedient means with earnest diligence and attain to Nirvana? The reply is that while Essence of Mind in all alike is of one pure sameness, that because of the fumigating power of

Ignorance it has become differently defiled and therefore manifests its defilement in different ways and different degrees, so that their number is incalculable. So great is the variety of their personalities, their experiences, hindrances and suffering that only Buddha can comprehend them and embrace them all in perfect compassion.

As all sentient beings in spite of their common Buddha Nature are subject to the fumigation of Ignorance they would, except for the like constant fumigation of their pure Mind-Essence, fall deep and deeper into the defilements of Ignorance, but by reason of Buddha's compassion, they sooner or later meet causes and affinities that enable them to awaken a pure faith and attain emancipation from their bondage to Ignorance. Possessed of suitable causes and affinities any attainment is possible. It is the nature of wood to burn, but wood will not burn without suitable conditions are present and there is some exciting cause. Wood will not ignite itself or burn itself. Therefore, if sentient beings are to become emancipated and enlightened there must be present suitable causes and affinities. By nature sentient beings have affinity for emancipation and enlightenment, but without suitable causes and conditions they can not attain them. Even if they have a Buddha Nature but do not chance to meet a Buddha, or a good learned Master, or a Bodhisattva, they could not of themselves attain Nirvana. In like manner, no matter how suitable external conditions may be, if they were immune to the fumigation of the Mind's pure Concepts, so that there was no awakening of faith, how could they come to abhor the suffering of rebirths and deaths and willingly and earnestly seek the attainment of Nirvana? But if both causes and affinities are present, their Buddha Nature, the fumigating power of Mind Essence, the kind teaching and sympathy of Bodhisattvas, then there will come an abhorrence of the suffering of birth and death, the awakening of faith, the purpose to practice kindness and to press on toward Nirvana. Then after their karma has become matured, they will, all of a sudden, meet a Buddha or a Buddhisattva who will show them the benefits and joy of following the Path toward Enlightenment and Buddhahood.

There is an unceasing fumigation of the external activities of sentient beings, by the pure Concepts of the fundamental Essence of Mind. By means of this fumigation these external

activities take on a power of affinity for similar activities drawing them together into closer synthesis and harmony. This
power of affinity is manifested in innumerable ways, but for
convenience in considering it, we may think of it as of two
kinds. The first is affinity drawing dissimilar things together;
the second is affinity drawing likenesses together.

The affinity between dissimilar things is seen in the compassion which disciples upheld by the transcendental powers of
Buddhas and Bodhisattvas, from the very beginning of their
devotion to seeking Enlightenment, have had for all sentient
beings, wishing to develop and strengthen their better nature.
This compassion reveals itself whenever they meet or think of
their families, their parents, their relatives or servants or familiar friends, or even their bitter enemies. This compassion reveals itself in the awakening of aspirations to teach them and
to influence them by the four ways of charity, kind words, self-
forgetting kindnesses and sympathy. Such deeds of kindness
react upon their own natures to strengthen and deepen their
own faith and their own aspiration to benefit all sentient beings, and to draw them together in bonds of affectionate fellowship. This kind of affinity is of two kinds, one kind is immediate in the sense that its effects are seen in the present time;
the other kind is more remote in the sense that its effects continue and come to fruition long after in later rebirths. These
affinities may be further divided into two aspects, namely, an
increasing and developing affinity, and an unchanging affinity as
Enlightenment is attained and mutually enjoyed.

The affinity between similarities is seen in the Buddha's
recognition of their oneness with all sentient beings in the
purity of Mind-Essence; it is seen in the self-lessness of the
Buddha's compassion and self-yielding; it is seen in the Buddha's constant spontaneity in responding to human needs; and
because of it, human beings, by their potentiality for intuitive
Samadhi may realize Buddhahood even as Buddhas realize
their sufferings.

* * *

These interacting fumigations of Essence of Mind and activities may be considered as being divided into two aspects
as they are ready or unready for the reactions of habitual fumigation. The unready are those common disciples, Pratyekabud-

dhas and Arhats who having had sufficient faith to begin their practice but as they continued to receive the habitual fumigation under relations with their discriminated ideas and their consciousness dependent upon those ideas, they could neither discard those ideas, nor attain a state of mutual responsiveness with their Mind-Essence, nor continue their practice with spontaneity, nor be in mutual response with their activities. Such disciples and Bodhisattvas are to be classed as unready for Enlightenment.

Those who are ready for Enlightenment are those advanced Bodhisattvas who have discarded all discriminated ideas and consciousness dependent upon them, and are in mutual response with the Buddha's inconceivable activities which are no activity, and prosecute their devotional practices with spontaneity, and are relying sincerely and wholly on the fumigating power of their Mind's pure Essence to annihilate their Ignorance and bring them to Buddhahood. Such Dharmakaya Bodhisattvas are ready for Enlightenment.

This difference between the ready and the unready is explained as we understand that the impure concepts of the human mind have become defiled by the habitual fumigation of Ignorance since beginningless time which fumigation will continue until they attain to Buddhahood, when it will be totally discarded. On the contrary, the pure concepts of Mind-Essence having the power of fumigation within their own nature, while the impure concepts of the false mind are slowly being discarded, their pure conceptual Dharmakaya is being brought into manifestation in unceasing continuity.

The Threefold Nature of Mind-Essence

The self-substance of Mind-Essence is inconceivably pure and, therefore, all sentient beings, common people, disciples, Pratyekabuddhas, Arhats, Bodhisattvas and Buddhas are, in their essential nature of the same purity. In not one is it deficient, in not one is it in excess; nor has it any source of arising, nor time of disappearing; it is ever abiding, a permanent, unchangeable Reality. From its beginningless beginning it has been in full possession of all virtue and merit. It is in full possession of radiant Wisdom and luminosity, penetrating everywhere by the purity of its Concepts; seeing everything adequately and truly, its mind innately free and unprejudiced, ever abiding in blissful peace, pure, fresh, unchangeable, ever abounding, never segregating, never ceasing, never conceivable, an illimitable Fountain, a Womb of exuberant fertility, a Mind of perfect clarity and universality—the Tathagata's Truth-body, the all-embracing Dharmakaya.

The question might be raised, If Mind-Essence is free from all conceptions of phenomena, how can it be said to possess all kinds of merits and virtues? The reply is, that although it really possesses all kinds of merits and virtues, it does not possess them in the sense of grasping them. Mind-Essence in its nature of Purity is free from all individuation and discrimination and dualisms of any kind. All objects have but one flavor, the flavor of reality, but depending upon the principle of appearing and disappearing, by reason of its activity-consciousness, there are signs of individuation, discrimination, and opposing dualisms. It is true that the Mind embraces all Pure Concepts, and yet in reality it possesses no discriminative thoughts, but by means of its false defilements discriminative thoughts are developed, causing the mind to lose its Enlightenment, and to be given over to false imaginations and thus to become enslaved by all kinds of conditions and the puppet of Ignorance. If there should be no rising of discriminating thoughts, the mind, because of its Essence of Mind, would manifest Wisdom and Brightness. But if the mind gives rise to discriminations and prejudices, it soon becomes darkened and the prey of imaginary phenomena. So when one's Essence of Mind is kept away from all discrimination and prejudices, it radiates its inherent Brightness to all parts of the conceptual world. But if the mind becomes disturbed by its false imaginations, it would lose its true intuitional insight and understanding, and would become changing, unhappy, lacking self-control, impure, entangled, and the victim of innumerable vexations and hindrances. When the mind is not disturbed it reflects its potentiality for all pure merits and virtues. Thus it is seen that the possession of all pure merits and virtues is the natural and simple state of Mind-Essence undefiled by any thoughts of individuation or discrimination. It is the true Dharmakaya, the true Tathagata Womb.

Reference has been made to the Activity-Consciousness of Mind-Essence; what is the nature of its activity? The activity of the false mind is an outer activity bringing about changes and increased complexity and confusion, but the activity of the

Mind's pure Essence is an inner activity that brings about harmony, simplicity and unity. All Buddhas and Tathagatas from their very beginnings have developed hearts of Compassion and have spontaneously manifested the Paramitas of charity, unselfish kindness, humility and patience, zeal and perseverence, tranquillity and Wisdom, not for any gain to themselves but for the sake of all sentient beings. They have made great Vows, dedicating themselves to emancipating all sentient beings from their bondage in the world of sense. But the deliverance is effected not by outer acts but by an inner drawing of spirit that is not limited by time or conditions, but is ceaseless even to infinite ages of the future. The activity of Buddhas and Tathagatas is eternal because it is the oppostie of outer activities of the false mind which are subject to weariness and inertia. Its activities release and store up energy restoring the original purity and unity and peacefulness.

Tathagatas and Buddhas look upon sentient beings as being their own sameness not cherishing any conceptions of separation and individuation. To them all sentient beings together with themselves come from one and the same Mind-Essence in which there are no differences to be distinguished. As they possess such great Wisdom and command of skillful means all the defilements of Ignorance have been discarded. They have realized their oneness with the pure Dharmakaya in the possession of a ever-renewing and inconceivable potentiality for activity and karma that is ceaselessly being irradiated to all parts of the universes, and just as ceaselessly returning to its primal unity and purity and peacefulness. They do not grasp upon any arbitrary conceptions of their harmonizing and integrating activities, for why should they grasp after that which they already possess, the whole body of the potentialities of the Dharmakaya. Their activities are unconditioned by causes and circumstances, they flow out spontaneously as the imaginary needs of sentient beings arise.

These harmonizing activities of the Tathagatas, that are no activity in a worldly sense, are of two kinds. The first kind can be perceived by the minds of common people, disciples and Pratyekabuddhas and is known as Nirmanakaya, the appearance body of Buddha and his inscrutable activities. But common people, disciples and Pratyekabuddhas do not realize that the Nirmanakaya are being manifested by reason of their own consciousness and its false imaginations. They imagine that all sights arise from prior causes and conditions and they grasp them and seek to profit by them, thus they fail to understand their true significance. The second kind can only be perceived by the purified minds of the highest Bodhisattvas; they have no form that can be differentiated and described; it is the Dharmakaya in its aspect of Spirit and Principle. It is the Recompense Body of all the Buddhas, it is the abiding Bliss-body of Buddhahood, the inconceivable and inscrutable Sambhogakaya. This Sambhogakaya possesses a vast and boundless Potentiality, and the Blissful Peace in which it abides is adorned with inconceivably beautiful adornments, which are shadowed forth as its potential wisdom and compassion is manifested in spontaneously meeting the needs of human beings. It has no limitations of boundaries or quantity, it has no spheres nor points. Though it is responsive at any time of need, yet it ever abides in its permanent unchanging peacefulness, undiminished and unchanged. All its merits and virtues are being verified by means of such things as the Paramitas and other non-intoxicating perfumes. And, moreover, it is in full possession of boundless potentialities of joy and blissful peace. That is the reason it is called the Sambhogakaya.

That of the Dharmakaya which can be perceived by the minds of common people is only a shadow of it, and takes on different aspects according as it is considered from the different viewpoints of the six realms of existence. Their crude perception of it does not include any conception of its possibilities for happiness and enjoyment; they see only its reflection in the Nirmanakaya. Again, the conception of it which novice Bodhisattvas get is also only partial and unsatisfactory, but is true as far as it goes because of their sincere faith in their pure Mind-Essence. At least, they realize that its potentialities and embellishments are neither coming nor going, are free of all limitations, and are manifestations of, not parts of, the Pure Dharmakaya. But as the Bodhisattvas advance along the stages their minds become purified, their conceptions of it more profound and mysterious, their harmonizing activities more transcendental, until, when they have attained to the highest stage, they will be able to intuitively realize its true Reality. In that final realization all traces of their individual selfness and of the selfness of their brother Bodhisattvas will have faded away and only a realization of one undifferentiated Buddhahood will remain.

It may be asked then, If the Buddha's Dharmakaya is free from any perceptions or conceptions of form, how can they manifest themselves as sights and forms? The reply is, that the Dharmakaya is the very Essence of all sights and forms, and therefore, can manifest itself in sights and form. Both the mind and the sights that it perceives are in one and the same unity since beginningless time, because the essential nature of sights and forms is nothing but Mind-only. As the essence of sights possesses no physical form, it is the same as the Dharmakaya, formless and yet pervading all parts of the universes. The particular sights which Mind-Essence manifests are in their essential nature devoid of any limitations or points of definition. If conditions are suitable appearances may be manifested in any part of the universes, being solely dependent upon the mind for their appearing. Thus, there are vast Bodhisattvas, vast Sambhogakayas, vast embellishments, all of which are different from one another and yet are devoid of any spheres of limitation or points of definition, for Tathagatas are able to manifest themselves in bodily forms any where and at the same moment that other Tathagatas are manifesting themselves without any conflict or hindrance. This marvelous interpenetration is inconceivable by any consciousness dependent upon sense mind, but is a commonplace of the inconceivable, spontaneous activities of Mind-Essence.

SECTION TWO

Refutation of False Doctrines and Prejudices

Again, in order to awaken faith in the minds of sentient beings that they may turn from the cycle of deaths and rebirths and enter the path that leads to Enlightenment and Nirvana, it is necessary to show the falsity of the common conception of an ego-self and its aggregates of sensation, perception, discrimination and consciousness. If one is to become free from the bondage of these grasping aggregates then one must understand clearly their unreality. This obsession of an ego-personality may be considered in two ways. First, the aspects of it that arise from the physical organism; and second, the aspects of it that arise in the intellectual mind.

First let us consider the aspects of it that arise from the physical organism. These may be considered, as common minds think about them, under five heads. The first is the aspect of it as perceived by the sense-mind. According to the Sutras, Tathagatas are represented as existing in a state of emptiness and tranquillity. Common minds interpret this to mean that Tathagatas' minds are empty and tranquil, a physical analogy. They do not understand that it refers to the immaterial perceptions of the thinking mind, a metaphysical analogy, so they mistakenly consider that "emptiness" is a characteristic of Tathagatas. To disabuse their minds of this false conception, it is necessary to show that "emptiness" is a false conception arising in their own minds, existing only in relation to their senses and discriminating mind, and having no substantiality of its own. Its visible manifestation is to be recognized in the tendency of human beings to turn to the cycle of births and deaths and to continue therein. All these physical sights and mental perceptions and discriminations of them belong to the mind and have no existence apart from the mind. As soon as the mind understands this, even the conception of pure space is seen to be a false and arbitrary conception. And the same is true, also, of all sorts of physical conditions and conceptions about them, that common minds take for granted are in a state of existence, they are all simply the false arisings of the experiential mind, and when the mind understands the falsity of the conceptions, the objects themselves vanish into nothingness. Then, nothing would remain but the purity of Essential Mind radiantly present in all the ten quarters of the universes. This is the true significance of the Tathagata's intrinsic and all-embracing Wisdom.

The second aspect of egoism as perceived by the sense-minds relates to the conception of substantiality. In the Sutras it is stated that all conceptions of the world are in a state of emptiness. This is interpreted by common minds as meaning that it is in a state of physical emptiness but, in truth, it refers to a state of mental emptiness, a mental analogy. Common minds apply it to all their conceptions—their conceptions of Mind-Essence and Nirvana—and therefore think of them as empty of all "substantiality." To disabuse their minds of this false conception it is necessary to show that the Dharmakaya of Mind-Essence is not empty of its own true substantiality.

Mind-Essence is replete with its own merits and virtues, all-embracing, boundlessly potential, inconceivably vast and beautiful.

The third aspect, arises from the saying in the Sutras that the Tathagata's Womb is neither in a state of increasing nor in a state of decreasing, that its substantiality is embodied in an exhaustless store of Pure Concepts of merits and virtues. Common minds fail to understand the true significance of this and understand that it refers to some definite possession that is separate from the merits and virtues possessed by human beings. To disabuse their minds of this false conception, it is necessary to show that the true significance of Mind-Essence is its undifferentiated purity from all the differentiated conceptual defilements such.as the false concept of birth and death.

The fourth aspect, arises from the sayings in the Sutras that all the impure, contaminated concepts of deaths and rebirths belonging to the world exist because they come from Tathagata's Womb, a physical analogy, and that all concepts are not independent of Mind-Essence. However, as common people they do not understand the true significance of the sayings in the Sutras, and imagine that the self-nature of Tathagata's Womb is fully embodied in such concepts as deaths and rebirths belonging to the world. To disabuse their minds of this false understanding, it is necessary to show that Tathagata's Womb from beginningless time has only embraced the pure concepts of undifferentiated merit and virtue, all of which are neither independent of nor differentiated from the true significance of Mind-Essence. For all the contaminated concepts and vexatious differences and annoying discriminations, which are beyond all estimation, only exist as the false illusions of the thinking mind, not in its true essential Nature. More than this, they have never been in any kind of mutual response with Tathagata's Womb. Or, if it should be granted that the substantiality of Mind-Essence is embodied in the false concepts of birth and death, but that it could be discarded by intuitive realization, this would be, indeed, an absurdity.

The fifth aspect of egoism, arises from statements in the Sutras that births and deaths arise from Tathagata's Womb and that the attainment of Nirvana, also, arises from the same source. However, as common people they do not understand the true significance of these sayings in the Sutras, and they imagine that sentient beings have their beginnings and endings, and that the Nirvana attained by Tathagatas, also, has its beginnings and endings, and renewed births in this Saha world. To disabuse their minds of this false assumption, we have only to call attention to the fact that Tathagata's Womb is devoid of any beginnings or endings or relations of succession. And the same is true of Ignorance, also. Or, if it should be asserted that there are beings independent of this Saha world that have transcendental qualities, our reply would be, that the only basis for such assertions are the unprovable teachings of heretical books. Moreover, there are no endings to be conceived of as having relation to Tathagata's Womb, for the Nirvana attained by the Buddhas being in mutual sameness with Tathagata's Womb, has likewise no beginning and no ending.

Second let us consider the aspects of it arising from the immaterial, mental faculties. This refers to the clinging to the notions of personalities such as the immature disciples of the Hinayana reveal when they think the Tathagata has simply taught the non-existence of and ego-self as it relates to personalities, but who still cherish the notion of selfness as it relates to their attainment of Enlightenment and Nirvana. Just as common people are fearful of the physical suffering of life, so these disciples fear the notions of failure in their effort to attain Enlightenment and Nirvana, and they cling to the conception of a Nirvana for themselves. To disabuse their minds of these erroneous conceptions, be it known that just as the nature of physical cencepts arising from the sense reactions are devoid of any rebirths, so these metaphysical concepts derived from the intellectual mind are also devoid of any deaths for in their essence they are from the beginning in Nirvana.

If one is to become free from the grasping nature of these aspects of ego-selfness, he must clearly understand that all mental concepts, both the pure and the impure, exist only in a state of relativity, they have no self-hood in their own right. From their very beginnings they are neither matter nor mind, neither intelligence nor consciousness, neither existence nor nonexistence, they are wholly imaginary. But still having a kind of relative existence they are used by the Lord Tathagata as expedient means to guide sentient beings by means of words, into the path that leads to Enlightenment. The purpose of the Lord Tathagata is to emancipate sentient beings from the bondage of their thinking by means of their thinking, and to bring them back to their origin in Mind-Essence. But to let the mind dwell upon and grasp words and concepts only entangles the mind the more in the cycle of deaths and rebirths, and hinders it from merging into its true nature of Wisdom.

SECTION THREE

Right Practices Leading to Enlightenment

At the beginning, we must define what is meant by right practices leading to Enlightenment and to distinguish between the spontaneous activities attained by Buddhas and the crude practices laboriously undertaken by the Bodhisattvas at the beginning of their devotions. There are three motives that lead a novice to the beginning of his practices. The first is the awakening of faith in the Dharma. The second is some understanding as to what will be required of him if he is to attain a realization of the Dharma. The third is the unfolding insight that comes to him as he progressively attains a realization of Dharma.

First, let us consider the awakening and maturing of a pure faith in the Dharma. Every sentient being, no matter how unconcentrated his mind may be, has certain instinctive reactions of mind that make him sensitive to kindness, shrink from suffering, fear evil, dread retribution, confident in self-effort and attainment, and hopeful of something better. If by chance they should come in contact with a Buddha, give offerings to him, worship him or his image, they would develop their germ of faith and after ten thousand kalpas would have so far matured their faith that all Buddhas and Bodhisattvas would teach them how to start their devotions.

Or, because of a natural compassionate disposition, they may awaken faith in a conception of a Supernatural Compassionate One and start their devotional practices. Or, because of the absence of the Dharma, or fear that it might become lost, their faith may awaken and they begin devotional practices for the sake of preserving the true Dharma. All of these ways of beginning devotional practices are a manifestation of true faith. It will not be in vain nor will it suffer retrogression, but will develop under proper conditions, into right aspiration and right ways of practice until it merges into the true Samadhi of Buddhahood.

There may be others who, having a less developed kindness of disposition, but who have suffered extremes of vexations and sufferings for many kalpas, who by chance meet Buddhas and make offerings to them and worship them, they awaken faith, also, and start their devotions for the purposes of attaining a happy rebirth in this world, or among devas in some super-realm of heaven, or as an Arhat, or as a Pratyekabuddha in some Nirvana of their own.

There may be some even who wish to seek the true Mahayana attainment of Buddhahood but whose root of merit is deficient of stability, now earnest now heedless, now advancing now receding. These start devotional practices more or less on impulse, and lacking stability, when they meet difficulties or hindrances within their own minds, they turn aside from the true Mahayana path into the path of Hinayana disciples and Pratyekabuddhas.

From the foregoing we see that there are many reasons that move disciples to begin their practices of devotion, but they all are based on the awakening of faith. Let us now consider right reasons for beginning devotional practices. These are of three kinds; first, reasons based upon an intellectual understanding of the truth of Mind-Essence. This is the most straightforward reason. Second, reasons based upon an earnest purpose to keep the precepts and develop a good life. Third, reasons based upon a heart of compassion, that seeing the suffering among all sentient beings wishes out of the kindness of his heart to deliver them.

It may be inferred from what has been said that if a disciple has the true understanding of Mind-Essence and concentrates his mind on that, that he needs to do nothing further but to quietly wait for the unfolding of Enlightenment and Nirvana. The answer to this is, that a disciple is like a precious gem whose brilliance is hidden by a coating of impurities. If we are to enjoy the pure brilliance of the gem we must first resort to polishing. The true nature of Mind-Essence is immaculately pure but in the disciple it is hidden by accumulations of defilement that must be removed by expedient means if he is to attain Enlightenment. Therefore, besides having a true understanding of the Dharma, he must also keep the precepts and cherish a great heart of compassion.

There are four kinds of expedient means for beginning and continuing devotional practices if one is to be confident of attaining Enlightenment. The first, is to understand and cherish certain fundamental intellectual convictions. He should practice recollective mindfulness of the true nature of all concepts, that they are empty of any self-nature of their own, that they are devoid of any rebirth and free from all false prejudices and do not abide in the cycle of deaths and rebirths. He should practise recollective mindfulness upon the fact that concepts are purely relative being altered, united or destroyed by causes and affinities. He should practice recollective mindfulness as to the fact of karma and its inevitable maturing, and purpose to lay up a good karma by keeping with sincerity and faithfulness all the precepts and practising all the Paramitas, and to have all their practicing of recollective mindfulness and outward keeping of the precepts and inward keeping of the Paramitas motivated by a great heart of compassion. He should try to develop all merits and virtues; he should sympathise with all sentient beings and seek to awaken faith and aspiration in their minds. He must not think over much of Nirvana nor seek to grasp it for himself for in the Pure Concepts of Mind-Essence there are no desires, no graspings, no clingings.

The second kind of expedient means for practising is to develop feelings of shame and repentence after giving place to evil thoughts or doing evil acts, as a means for restraining one from yielding to them again, for Mind-Essence must be kept free from all evil defilements. The third kind is to develop one's root of kindness by the spontaneous and willing doing of all kinds of charity in cases of need, by making willing offerings to Buddha, Dharma and the Brotherhood. It is to praise Buddha and to beseech him to emancipate and enlighten all sentient beings. It is to practise expressing adoration and affection and dependence upon Buddha, Dharma and the Brotherhood, with perfect sincerity so as to increase one's faith and earnestness of practice in seeking for highest perfect Enlightenment, for it is only by the protecting and supporting power of Buddha, Dharma, Sangha, that he will be able to attain it. For to integrate oneself with the Pure Concepts of Mind-Essence one must be free from all hindrances both from without and within.

The fourth expedient means is the practising of compassion, the uttering of earnest wishes that all sentient beings may be taught and delivered, not a single one omitted even to infinite future, all to be brought to Nirvana, and that his merits may be devoted to that end. And to be in harmony with the pure concepts of Mind-Essence there must be no cessation or intermissions of his compassionate wishes and vows.

The essential nature of the Pure Concepts of Mind-Essence are its all-embracing inclusiveness, embracing all sentient beings in its perfect purity and unity with no shadow of individuation in either mind or the substance of compassion. Any Bodhisattva having made this solemn pranadana will attain to some measure of intuitive insight into the pure Dharmakaya of his Mind-Essence. As they by their intuition enter into pure Dharmakaya, they are enabled to make transcendental manifestations of eight kinds that will benefit all sentient beings. First, according to the purity and earnestness of their pranadana, after the example of Buddhas, they can descend from the heavenly palaces of the Tusita Realm, they can enter into a human womb, undergo a period of gestation, be born as a human, become a Bhikshu, attain Enlightenment, turn the wheel of the Dharma, pass into Nirvana. However, such Bodhisattvas can not be said to have attained to Dharmakaya, because they have not yet fully matured their karmas that had been inherited from infinite periods of past ages, so they still remain in mutual response with light sufferings in following rebirths, but enduring these light sufferings they are not in bondage to them because of their transcendental freedom and power belonging to their great pranadana. Some of these Bodhisattvas, it is said in the Sutras, must descend into the evil realms for a period, but this does not mean that they have retrograded, it only means that for the maturing of their remaining karma they must experience the suffering of those lower realms to cure them of any remaining shadow of indolence less they fall short of attaining true Bodhisattvahood, so that their courage and boldness may be adequate. Such Bodhisattvas by reason of this experience in the lower realms will start their devotional practices with renewed earnestness and will never again become timid or indolent, or have any fear of retrograding. Or if they should learn that in order to attain Nirvana they must endure hardship for immense kalpas, they would never slacken their zeal in practice or become cowardly and timid, for they have attained a pure faith in the teaching that all pure concepts, since beginningless time, are in their self-nature Nirvana itself.

Understanding and Practice.

As Bodhisattvas advance along the stages they attain a clearer understanding of the Dharma and of how to more perfectly practice it. As the first Asamkya Kalpa of their practice draws to a close, these advanced Bodhisattvas attain a transcendental understanding of the self-nature of the Pure Concepts of Mind-Essence and conform their practices to it. As they see that the essential nature of the Pure Concepts is free from all acquisitiveness, all stinginess and greediness, all covetousness, they bring their practising into conformity with it by practising the paramita of charity. As they see that the essential nature of the Pure Concepts of Mind-Essence are free from the defilement of all sensual desires, they bring their practising into conformity with it by practising the paramita of keeping the Precepts. As they see that the essential nature of the Pure Concepts is free from all resentment, all malice, all anger, they try to conform to it by practising the paramita of patience and humility. As they see that the essential nature of the Pure Concepts is free from all slothfulness and idleness and indifference, they try to conform to it by practising the paramita of zeal and perseverence. As they see that the essential nature of the Pure Concepts is free from all disturbance and confusion, the very perfection of permanence and peacefulness, they try to conform to it by practising the paramita of tranquillity. As they see that the essential nature of the Pure Concepts is free from all obscurity caused by segregation and individuation, and the darkness caused by Ignorance, and is luminous with the Brightness of Truth, they try to conform to it by practising the paramita of Wisdom.

Realization and Attainment

Let us now consider the unfolding insight that comes to a Bodhisattva as he attains the object of his faith and earnest practices. From the first awakening of his faith and beginning of his practice to his full realization and attainment there has been but one object in mind, enlightenment and Buddhahood for the sake of all sentient beings. But can this truly be called "an object"? If we think of it as a state or condition, that he as an ego-personality is to attain, it might be, but we have already found that the conception of an ego-personality is a false conception that the highest Bodhisattvas have already discarded. In the Pure Concepts of Mind-Essence there is no object and no subject, there is only the nature of Wisdom, the Pure Dharmakaya. It is this that highest Bodhisattvas realize and attain. In an instant of true realization they are offering gifts and worship to all the Buddhas in all the Buddha-lands of all the universes, they are beseeching the Buddhas to turn the wheel of the Dharma for the sake of all sentient beings, they are awakening faith in the minds of all beginners, they are supporting them and bestowing upon them all pure merits and virtue, and at the long last they are present when the realization comes to welcome them into the pure suchness of Enlightment, the pure Dharmakaya. And all this not as a glorified personality but as Buddhahood itself. However, on account of the timid and cowardly disciples, sometimes they will encourage them by such words as, "You will attain Enlightenment and Buddhahood after infinite ages," or on account of the indolent and sluggish disciples, they may urge them forward by many skillful devices, but in all cases the awakening of faith and the beginning of practice is equal in all cases, so their realization and attainment of Enlightenment is always on an equality. There are no Dharmas to bring one disciple quickly and another slowly to enlightenment, all Dharmas are of an equal potency, and all disciples must practice through many asamkyas of kalpas, and no Bodhisattva-Mahasattva has ever attained it in any less. It is only because of differences in the dispositions and environments of sentient beings that different skillful means are used and different advancements seem to be made, but in truth, in the pure Dharmakaya everything is in perfect balance and purity.

The Potential Merit and Virtue of Bodhisattva-Mahasattvas.

Again, when Bodhisattva-Mahasattvas awaken faith and make up their minds to begin spiritual devotions and discipline for the sake of all sentient beings, there come into potentiality great merits and virtues, which we will now consider under three heads. The first, is the True Mind for it embraces and cherishes no individuation nor discriminations nor partialities nor prejudices. The second, is the Mind of Perfect Wisdom for it unfolds all manner of skillful and expedient principles and means. The third, is the Mind of Perfect Compassion for it unfolds an activity or karma consciousness that is sympathetic toward all sentient beings, cherishing good-will toward them and spontaneously willing to satisfy their needs and benefit them in innumerable and inconceivable ways, appearing and disappearing with no thought of self. Furthermore, this kind of Bodhisattva-Mahasattva, having matured their merits and virtues, attain the ultimate perfection of Purity and Unity and Peacefulness, unimaginably supernal and harmonious and blissful, the Pure Dharmakaya. By the inscrutable integrancy of this Ultimate Purity, spontaneous and constant and ceaseless, Ignorance disappears. This is Ultimate, All-embracing Wisdom, the immaculate Womb of all Pure Dharmas and the awakening faith and beginning spiritual devotions and practices of all sentient beings. It is the Ultimate and Universal Breathing going forth in radiantly creative activity, drawing inward by intuitive sympathy and boundless good-will to the perfect purity and unity and peacefulness of the Pure Dharmakaya, and all for the benefit of all sentient beings that they may be One and fully realize their perfect Oneness.

It may be asked at this point, If the principle of individuation and discrimination is transcended by the vanishing of Ignorance, how can omniscience of Perfect Wisdom be attained by Bodhisattva-Mahasattvas? If an infinity of universes arises because of infinite space, and if because of an infinity of universes there are an infinity of sentient beings, and if because of infinite beings there are an infinitude of mentalities and predispositions and conditions and circumstances and differentiated activities, how can even a Bodhisattva-Mahasattva attain perfect understanding, or command of adequate skillful means, or highest perfect Wisdom? The explanation is, that all these infinity of infinities are fully embraced in the perfect self-awareness of the Bliss-body of Buddhahood which is the ineffable Dharmakaya, which is free of all differentiation or premonition of differentiation. But as sentient beings have falsely imagined illusions of objects and conditions and self-ness, and because of it discriminative thinking has arisen and egoism and grasping and clinging and karma. But all these false imaginations are not to be regarded as of the intrinsic self-nature of the Pure Dharmakaya, and provide no ground for infallibly understanding or perfectly realizing Truth itself. But by intuitively becoming identified with Truth, Highest Bodhisattva-Mahasattvas become free of all such differentiated thinking and prejudices and are free to react to the undifferentiated purity of their Mind-Essence. Their minds can reflect all false concepts but without stain or desire, by reason of which they attain perfect wisdom and command of expedient means and harmonizing activities. By entering intuitively and with sympathy and goodwill into the minds and desires and limitations of all sentient beings, they can elucidate the Dharmas and deliver all sentient beings. This is the reply to the question, How can purified Bodhisattva-Mahasattvas attain highest perfect Wisdom: It is because they understand and sympathize with the false imaginations of sentient beings and at the same time enter intuitively into the purity and unity of their Mind-Essence, not as standing apart and judging, but one with all sentient beings, themselves, the Buddhas, Mind-Essence, Dharmakaya itself, one and inseparable.

Still another question may arise. If all the Buddhas from remotest beginnings have had these transcendental powers of Wisdom, Compassion and command of unlimited expedient means for benefiting all sentient beings, how is it that sentient beings do not recognize and appreciate their good-will and beneficent activities and respond to them by awakening faith and beginning devotional practices and, in due course, attain enlightenment and Buddhahood? Instead, most sentient beings are indifferent and seem to prefer their own illusions to embrace the sufferings that follow Ignorance? The reply is that all Buddhas and Tathagatas and Bodhisattva-Mahasattvas having become identified with the pure Dharmakaya pervade all the universes equally and potently and spontaneously, but embracing in their pure Essence all sentient beings, also, and being in eternal relations with them and being of the same self-nature, they wait the willing and inevitable response that is a necessary part of the perfect purity and unity of the Dharmakaya. The minds of sentient beings are truly like a mirror, reflecting all Dharmas, but if the mirror is stained or defiled there will be no clear reflection. Not until the mirror of human minds and hearts is purified by the awakening of faith and the beginnings of spiritual practices, can they hope to see Buddhas, attain Enlightenment, and realize their own identity with Dharmakaya.

Part Four

Practice of the Mahayana

Thus far we have been elucidating the principles of the Mahayana. Now we will explain the practice of the Mahayana and to do so effectively we must begin by showing the part that faith plays in the Practice, especially in the beginning when the minds of the novice Bodhisattvas have not yet attained to right Samadhi. We will then proceed to explain what kind of faith a disciple should have and how to apply his faith in practice. There are four kinds of faith: First, the novice disciple must have faith in the fundamental, ultimate Principle of things, that it is perfect Wisdom and perfect Compassion, and perfect Oneness. He should think joyfully of his own identity with its pure Mind-Essence. Second, the disciple should have abounding faith in Buddhahood. This means that he should cherish a sincere faith in the merits and virtues of the Buddhas, that he should constantly remember them to feel his fellowship with them, to make offerings to them of adoration and gifts, to seek instruction and guidance from them. Third, the disciple should have an unshakable faith in the wisdom, the compassion, the power of the Dharma. This means that he should look to it and rely upon it as an infallible guide in his practice of its Paramita ideals. Fourth, the disciple should have an unfeigned, affectionate and abounding faith in the Brotherhood of Homeless-Bhikshus, caring for them, supplying their few needs, looking to them for instruction and sympathy in their own practice, that they may perfect their faith and move toward Buddhahood together.

There are six ways of practising faith. First, there is the way of Charity. Second, the way of unselfish kindness in Keeping the Precepts. Third, the way of Patience and Humility. Fourth, the way of Zeal and Perseverance. Fifth, the way of Tranquillity, stopping all discriminating thoughts and quietly realizing Truth itself. Sixth, the way of Wisdom.

First, the Way of Charity. The purpose of this practice is to eradicate one's own stinginess and cupidity. To effect this one should train himself to be generous. If any one comes to him begging, he should give him money or things as he has particular need, with discretion and kindness, as much as he can up to his ability and the other's need, so that the begging ones may be relieved and go away cheerful. Or, if the disciple come upon one in danger or hardship or an extremity of any kind, he should encourage him and help him as much as he can. Or, if one should come seeking instruction in the Dharma, he should humbly and patiently interpret it to him using expedient means, as much as he can interpret with clearness according to his ability. The disciple should practice Charity simply and unostentatiously, with no ulterior motive in mind of ambition, self-interest, reward, or praise, keeping in mind only this that the giving and receiving shall both tend in the direction of Enlightenment from them both alike and equally.

Second, the way of Keeping the Precepts. The purpose of this practice is to get rid of all selfish grasping after comforts, delights, and self-interests. It means not to kill any sentient being, not to steal, not to commit adultery, not to deceive nor slander nor to utter malicious words nor to flatter. If he is a layman, it means keeping away from all greedy actions, envy, cheating, mischief, injustice, hatred, anger, and all heretical views. If he is a Bhikshu, it means he should avoid all vexatious and annoying acts, he should keep away from the turmoil and activities of the worldly life and live in solitude and quietness, practising begging and disciplining himself to be content with least desires. He should feel regret over any slight fault and should always act with prudence and attentiveness. He should not neglect any of the Lord Tathagata's instructions, and should be always ready to defend any one suffering under suspicion or slander so as to restrain them from falling into further evil.

Third, the Way of Patience. This means to practice patience when vexed or annoyed by others and to restrain any rising thoughts of ill-will or vengeance. It means being patient when overtaken by any affront to one's pride, personal losses, criticisms, or praise, or flattery; it means being patient and undisturbed by either happiness or suffering, comfort or discomfort.

Fourth, the Way of Zeal. The purpose of this discipline is to restrain oneself from yielding to temptations to laziness and weariness. It disciplines one not to relax one's effort when he meets success and praise, but to ever renew one's resolution to seek enlightenment. It should strengthen one to keep far away from temptations to timidity or false modesty. One should ever remember past sufferings borne because of evil committed carelessly and to no benefit to himself, and by these recollections to renew his zeal and perseverence to make diligent practising of all kinds of meritorious and virtuous deeds that will benefit both others and himself and keep himself free from suffering in the future. In spite of his being a Bhikshu he may be suffering from unmatured karma of previous lives and thus still be open to the attacks of evil influences, or still be entangled in worldly affairs, or the responsibilities of a family life, or under some chronic illness or disability. In the face of all such burdensome hindrances, he should be courageous and zealous and unceaselessly diligent in his practisings during the day, and in the six watches of the night should be on his guard against idle thoughts by constantly repeating adorations to all the Buddhas with zeal and sincerity, beseeching the Buddhas to abide in the world to turn the Dharma wheel, to support all right efforts to practice, to encourage all kind acts, to awaken faith in the faithless, to encourage right vows and to return all merit for the Enlightenment of all sentient beings. Unless one is zealous and persevering in his practice, he will not be able to keep himself from increasing hindrances to cultivating his root of devotion.

Fifth, The Way of Tranquillity. The purpose of this discipline is twofold, to bring to a standstill all disturbing thoughts, and all discriminating thoughts are disturbing, to quiet all engrossing moods and emotions so that it will be possible to concentrate the mind for the practice of meditation and realization, and thus to be able to follow the practice willingly and gladly. Secondly, when the mind is tranquillized by stopping all thought, to practice "reflection" or meditation not in a discriminating way but in a more intellectual way of realizing the meaning and significance of one's thoughts and experiences, and also to follow this part of the practice willingly and gladly. By this twofold practice of "stopping and realizing", one's faith, that is already awakened, will become developed and gradually the two aspects of this practice will merge into one another— the mind perfectly tranquil but most active in realization. In the past, one naturally has had confidence in his faculty of discrimination, but this is now to be eradicated and ended.

For those who are practising "stopping", they should retire to some quiet place, or better live in some quiet place, sitting erect and with earnest and zestful purpose seek to quiet and concentrate the mind. While one may at first think of his breathing, it is not wise to continue it very long, nor to let the mind rest on any particular appearances or sights, or conceptions arising from the senses, such as the primal elements of earth, water, fire and ether, nor to let it rest on any of the lower mind's perceptions, particularizations, discriminations, moods or emotions. All kinds of ideation are to be discarded as fast as they arise, even the notions of controlling and discarding are to be gotten rid of. One's mind should become like a mirror, reflecting things but not judging them nor retaining them. Conceptions of themselves have no substance, let them rise and pass away unheeded. Conceptions arising from the senses and lower mind, will not take form of themselves, unless they are grasped by the attention, but if they are ignored there will be no appearing and no disappearing. The same is true of conditions outside the mind: they should not be permitted to engross one's attention nor hinder one's practice. As the mind can not be absolutely vacant, as thoughts rising from the senses and discriminating mind are discarded and ignored, one must supply their place by right mentation. The question then arises, what is right mentation? The reply is: right mentation is the realization of the mind itself, of its pure undifferentiated Essence. Even when we sit quietly with the mind fixed on its pure Essence, there should be no lingering notions of self, of self realizing, or any phenomena of realization. Pure Mind-Essence is ungraspable of any rising or appearing of individuation.

Sixth, the Way of Wisdom. The purpose of this discipline is to bring one into the habit of applying the insight that has come to him by the preceding ways of discipline. Even when one is rising, standing, walking, doing something, stopping, one should constantly concentrate his mind on the act and the doing of it, not on his relation to it or its character or its value. One should think: there is walking, there is doing, there is stopping, there is realizing; not, I am walking, I am doing this, it is a good thing, it is disagreeable, it is I who am gaining merit, it is I who am realizing how wonderful it is. Then come vagrant thoughts, feelings of elation or defeat and failure and un-happiness. Instead of all this, one should simply practice con-centration of the mind on the act itself, understanding it to be an expedient means for attaining tranquillity of mind, realiza-tion, insight and Wisdom, and to follow the practice in faith, willingness and gladness. After long practice the bondage of old habits becomes weakened and disappears, and in its place appears confidence, satisfaction, awareness and tranquillity.

What is this practice of Wisdom designed to accomplish? There are three classes of conditions that hinder one from ad-vancing along the path to Enlightenment: first, the allurements arising from the senses and external conditions and the dis-criminating mind; second, the inner conditions of the mind, its thoughts, desires and moods; these the earlier practices are de-signed to eliminate. The third class are the instinctive and fundamental, insidious and persistent, urgings, the will-to-live and enjoy, the will-to-protect one's life and personality, the will-to-propagate, which give rise to greed and lust, fear and anger, infatuation and pride of egoism. The practice of the Wis-dom Paramita is designed to control and eliminate these funda-mental and instinctive hindrances. By means of it the mind gradually becomes clearer, more luminous, more peaceful. In-sight clears, faith deepens and broadens, until they merge into the inconceivable Samadhi of the Mind's Pure Essence. As one continues the practice of Wisdom, one less and less yields to thoughts of comfort or discomfort, faith becomes surer, more pervasive, beneficent, joyous, and fear of retrogression vanishes.

But do not think that these consummations are to be at-tained easily or quickly; many rebirths may be necessary, many asamkyas of kalpas may have to elapse. So long as doubt, un-belief, slanders, evil conduct, hindrances of karma, weakness of faith, pride, laziness, a disturbed mind, persist, or their shadows linger, there can be no attainment of the Samadhi of the Bud-dhas. But once attained, in the luminous brightness of highest Samadhi, one will be able to realize with all the Buddhas, the perfect unity of all sentient beings with Buddhahood's Dharma-kaya. In the pure Dharmakaya, there is no dualism, neither shadow of differences. All sentient beings, if they are able to realize it, are already in Nirvana. The Mind's pure Essence is Highest Samadhi. The Mind's Pure Essence is *anuttara-samyak-sambodhi*, is Prajna Paramita, Highest Perfect Wisdom.

PART FIVE

The Advantages of Practising the Mahayana

There may be some disciples whose root of merit is not yet matured, whose control of mind is weak and whose power of application is limited, and yet who are sincere in their purpose to seek Enlightenment, these, for a time, may be beset and bewildered by maras and evil influences who are seeking to break down their good purpose. Such disciples, seeing seductive sights, attractive girls, strong young men, must constantly remind themselves that all such tempting and alluring things are mind-made, and if they do this, their tempting power will disappear and they will no longer be annoyed. Or, if they have visions of heavenly gods and Bodhisattvas and Tathagatas surrounded by celestial glories, they should remind themselves that they, too, are mind-made and unreal. Or if they should be up-lifted and excited by listening to mysterious Dharanis, to lectures upon the Paramitas, to elucidations of the great principles of the Mahayana, they must remind themselves that these also are emptiness and mind-made, that in their Essence they are Nirvana itself. Or, if they should have intimations within that they have attained transcendental powers, recalling past lives, or fore-seeing future lives, or reading other's thoughts, or freedom to visit other Buddha-lands, or great powers of eloquence, all of which may tempt them to become covetous for worldly power and riches and fame. Or, they may be tempted by extremes of emotion, at times angry at other times joyous, or, at times very kind-hearted and compassionate at other times the very opposite, or, at times alert and purposeful at other times indolent and stupid, at times full of faith and zealous in their practice at other times engrossed in other affairs and negligent. All of which will keep them vacillating, at times experiencing a kind of fictitious samadhi, such as the heretics boast of, but not the True Samadhi. Or later, when they are quite advanced and become absorbed in trance for a day, or two, or even seven, not partaking of any food but up-held by inward food of their spirit, being admired by their friends and feeling very comfortable and proud and complacent, and then later becoming very erratic, sometimes eating little, sometimes greedily, and the expression of their face constantly changing.

Because of all such queer manifestations and developments

in the course of their practisings, disciples should be on their guard to keep the mind under constant control. They should neither grasp after nor become attached to the passing and unsubstantial things of the senses or concepts and moods of the mind. If they do this they will be able to keep far away from the hindrances of karma. They should constantly remind themselves that the false samadhis and raptures of the heretics always have some imperfections about them and affinities with the triple world which lead the heretics to grasp after worldly fame, self-interest and self-pride, and becoming defiled by these graspings and prejudices and defilements, and becoming separated from their good Buddhist friends and learned masters, they miss the path of the Buddhas and quickly fall away into the path of the heretics.

The true Samadhi of Mind-Essence is free from all arbitrary conceptions, all prejudices, all attainments. There is only purity and blissful tranquillity. As the advanced Bodhisattva passes into true Samadhi all individualized concepts of body or mind vanish and only the pure awareness of truth in its undifferentiated wholeness remains, and the mind realizes its true freedom and peace, with no notions of egoism or individuality beclouding it.

As advanced Bodhisattvas practice this true Samadhi of Mind-Essence they will acquire in this present life ten great advantages: First, they will at all times be under the protection and support of all the Buddhas and Bodhisattvas who constitute the Eternal Sanga. Second, they will never fear evil. Third, they will attain clearing insight and intuitive understanding, and will cease to be confused or disturbed by false teachings. Fourth, they will no longer doubt the profound Dharma teaching, their predispositions and karma hindrances will gradually disappear. Fifth, the rising of instinctive desires, suspicious and malicious feelings will cease. Sixth, their faith in the purposive good-will of the Tathagatas and of the wisdom and compassion of Buddhahood will increase. Seventh, they will become courageous and serene in the face of the issues of life and death, escaping grief, and all feelings of contrition and despondency. Eighth, they will unfold a great heart of compassion themselves, their spirit will become gentle and mild, discarding all pride of egoism and untroubled by the acts of others. Ninth, they will cease to find pleasure in worldly things, and though they may not have attained samadhi, they will remain tranquil under ordinary conditions. Tenth, after they have attained Samadhi, they never again will be in bondage to sense-originating concepts.

* * *

Here ends this treatise interpreting the principles and practice of Mahayana Buddhism and designed to awaken faith in it. It is by means of these principles and practices that the Bodhisattvas are able to advance along the stages to the perfect attainment of Enlightenment and Buddhahood. All Bodhisattva-Mahasattvas of the past have by means of this Dharma awakened faith, undertaken devotional practices, continued them earnestly and perseveringly, and attained the goal of faith in Buddhahood. The same is true of all the Bodhisattvas of the present and the future, they are awakening faith and continuing the practices and will surely attain the consummation of their faith. Therefore, all sentient beings ought to awaken a like faith, and be diligent and faithful in studying and practising it.

I have now finished this interpretation of the Dharma, may any merit that arises from it, benefit all sentient beings and bring them to Buddhahood.

SELECTIONS
FROM CHINESE SOURCES

Oh for this one rare occurrence
Gladly would I give ten thousand pieces of gold!
A hat is on my head, a bundle on my back,
And my staff, the refreshing breeze and the full moon.

TAO-TEH-KING

ONE

THE TAO that can be "tao-ed" can not be the infinite TAO (that is, the way that can be followed can not be the ultimate, pathless Way). It is the same with the name of things: if things are explicable, the names we give them can not be the original Name. (That is) The source of the universe is hidden in non-existence; existence is only the mother of its evolution.

Since human beings are a small likeness of the great Universe, they can only realize their Taohood by making close imitations of it. Before one can attain the supreme perfection of Taohood, he must first realize its inmost mystery, that is, he must enter the door of this mystery of mysteries.

There are two ways for effecting this realization, both of which can be followed by the human organism. One way to realize the wonderful mystery of TAO is to put away all thoughts and desires. The other way is to concentrate both true intention and sincere devotion. These two ways of realization have different names but they both lead to a realization of the mystery that we call TAO.

TWO

Our minds naturally perceive the beauty of things on account of their beautifulness; so they also have a feeling of disgust for their ugliness on account of their ugliness. It is the same with goodness and badness. Everything in the world is mutually opposing and revealing itself.

So existence and non-existence are mutually related; the difficult and the easy are always in combination; the long and the short always qualify each other; the high and the low are always in opposition; the loud and the soft are loud and soft only in contrast with each other; the before and the behind are contrasted but always keep company.

Therefore the perfect Sage in avoiding the limitations of relativity resorts to no compulsion, nor does he make invidious comparisons in teaching his people. Whatever he does is done in harmony with the principle of TAO. Whatever he produces is not kept in his own possession; whatever he does is not exhibited with pride; whatever he accomplishes is not dwelt upon with self-conceit. Because he avoids possession, and pride and self-conceit, his accomplishments are kept in lasting memory.

THREE

If the perfect Sage would have his people give up their rivalries, he should not praise the competent ones. If he would have his people keep away from robbery and theft, he should not value precious things himself. If he would keep his mind undisturbed he should not covet desirable things. Thus the administration of the perfect Sage is designed to remove the desires of his people. He supplies them only with suitable nourishment and lessens their individual ideas by strengthening the common physical health. He ever tries to keep his people in ignorance and desirelessness so as to prevent the brainy ones from undertaking trouble-making activities. So long as he governs his people by the principle of *wu-wei* (non-assertion, or non-compulsion), things naturally arrange themselves into social order.

FOUR

TAO is invisible but permeates everywhere; no matter how one uses it or how much, it is never exhausted. It is wise for us to imitate its profoundness; that is, to keep ourselves in quiet confidence as being the unfailing source of all things. We should hide our wits and competencies; we should free ourselves from worldly entanglements; keep ourselves always in humility and courtesy; becoming ever more socialized and personally disinterested.

Should we attain all of these conditions, we would become as still and as transparent as the pure water of a spring. Then we would not recognize any spiritual forefather because no one would be worthy to be our ancestor except the perfect Father, the Great TAO.

FIVE

Heaven and earth are not fallible and unjust like humans: they are always impartial. They have no favorites in giving kindness to the world: they give life to humans with the same impartiality they give life to dogs and plants. The perfect sage is also impartial: he has no prejudices that would lead him to like this one and dislike that one; he treats all men as being of equal value. Moreover, there is nothing between heaven and earth but vast space. Heaven and earth resemble a bellows and a musical pipe: they are empty but inexhaustible; the more one plays on them the more they give out. The babbler is constantly being confounded but the dumb sage, constantly exercising concentration of mind, is competent to meet every chance and circumstance.

SIX

As rivers have their source in some far off fountain, so the human spirit has its source. To find his fountain of spirit is to learn the secret of heaven and earth. In this fountain of mystery, spirit is eternally present in endless supply. Anyone can avail himself of it for the refreshment and the unfolding greatness of his own spirit by the earnest practice of concentration, but to do so he must devote himself to the effort with *wu-wei* of mind and sensitive expectancy.

SEVEN

Heaven is eternal and earth is everlasting. The reason why heaven and earth are eternal is because they do not live for or by themselves: that is the reason they ever endure.

The perfect Sage, who puts his own interests behind him, is always the leader of his people. All the time he is looking after the welfare of his people and in doing so he preserves his own life. Is it not because he is disinterested that his own interests are conserved?

EIGHT

The highest virtue is like water: it benefits everything without exciting rivalries. We should be like water, choosing the lowest place which others avoid. We are then closely akin to TAO.

For our dwelling we should choose the place where we can be of most benefit to our neighbors; we should be kind and courteous, always choosing to be with good people; in speech we should only speak words of truth and kindness; in administration we should seek to keep things in peace and order; in affairs we should exercise our best abilities; in activities we should adjust ourselves as circumstances arise and change.

Inasmuch as we are never seeking pre-eminence, no one will hate us.

NINE

To stop one's desires is far better than to be continually satisfying them. Desire is like a knife: if it is continually being sharpened, it will soon wear away.

There are wealthy men with mansions filled with gold and jewels, but they must be on the watch all the time to protect them. The pride of wealth and position brings about its own destruction. As soon as one has gained merit and fame, he should withdraw into retirement. This is the TAO of Heaven.

TEN

During the daytime, our senses are kept busy in activities, but if we keep our minds concentrated, we will better preserve their potentialities. If, in our practice of concentration, we preserve humility and tenderness and retain our natural breathing, we will become like a little child. If, in our practice of concentration, our minds retain their purity, we will be kept free from faults.

If the perfect Sage truly loves his people and wishes to bring his state in to peace and order, he must practice *wu-wei*. If in our practice of concentration our heavenly eye is suddenly opened and we gain enlightenment thenceforth we shall be free from lust and greed. If we attain transcendental intelligence, our minds penetrating into every corner and into everything, then our minds will lose their self-consciousness.

A father begets children and sustains them while they are growing, nevertheless his children are not to be considered as his personal property, nor is his care of them to be done for any hope of reward, nor should his parental authority continue after they have reached manhood. This is the profoundest virtue of TAO.

ELEVEN

There are thirty spokes in a wheel, but its utility lies in the hole of the hub. The potter forms the clay into jars, but their

usefulness depends upon the enclosed space. A carpenter builds
the walls of a house and cuts out windows and doors, but the
value of the house is measured by the space within the walls.
Thus it may be said that existence is for accommodation but
non-existence is for utility.

Twelve

If a man indulges his desire for looking at the five beautiful
colors, his perception of their beauty will become dull; if a man
indulges a desire for listening to the five musical tones, his perception of their music will become dulled; if he indulges a desire for the five pleasant tastes, his perception of their delicious-
ness will become dull. If a man indulges a desire for racing
and hunting, he will lose his appreciation of tranquillity and
may become mad. So it is with the lure of hidden treasure
that tempts a man to do evil.

Therefore the perfect Sage aims at usefulness and is not deceived by the illusions of sense. A man in hunger desires food
to satisfy his hunger and is little concerned by its beauty and
delicacy.

Thirteen

Favor and disgrace are both to be feared; too great care of
the body and too great neglect of the body are both to be
feared. To be favored is humiliating, so to attain it is as much
to be dreaded as to lose it. That is what is meant by favor
and disgrace are alike to be feared.

Why do our greatest troubles lie in too great care of our
body? It is because one by so doing is all the time remembering that he has a body. As soon as I forget that I have a body
then the troubles of the body vanish.

Therefore, if a man is willing to give up his body for the
benefit of the state, he is worthy to be entrusted with the state.
It is the same with the perfect Sage who forgets his body in
the service of the people; he is best qualified to govern the
empire.

Fourteen

There is one thing in the universe that we can not see with
our eyes, nor hear with our ears, nor grasp by our perceiving
mind, which our senses fail to perceive or our mind fails to

grasp yet may be realized in meditation. When we look upward we can not see its brightness, when we look downward we can not perceive its existence. Although this mystery is always present there is no adequate name for it.

If we concentrate our mind upon it, our mind becomes unified with it and becomes as empty as open space. This is what may be called the form of the formless, the image of the imageless. It is as if we were in a trance. When we meet it we can not see its face and when we follow it we can not see its back. If, in dhyana, we tranquilize our minds by the *wu-wei* principle of TAO, some day we will realize our identity with its mystery. Then we are true apostles of TAO.

FIFTEEN

In olden times those who were competent to be Masters were intelligent, subtle, profound and spiritual. Their thoughts could not be easily fathomed. Since their thoughts were hard to comprehend, I will try to reveal their virtue by some explanation. They were as cautious as a man crossing a river in winter; they were as suspicious as a man who fears his neighbors; they were as circumspect as a guest in the presence of his host; they were as ready to adapt themselves as ice at the point of melting; they were as true and sound as the trunk of a perfect tree; they were as open and broadminded as a spacious valley; their thoughts were obscure like troubled waters.

Who can enlighten himself by slowly quieting the troubled waters of his mind? After gaining calmness of mind by concentration, who can gradually pass from its calmness into the activities of life and always retain the same calmness of mind? Only those who keep themselves from self-sufficiency and who control their lives by the principle of TAO. Being free from self-sufficiency, their spirit and energy will never fail, but will ever be refreshed and renewed.

SIXTEEN

At the moment when one is able to concentrate his mind to the extreme of emptiness and is able to hold it there in serene tranquillity, then his spirit is unified with the spirit of the universe and it has returned to its original state from which his mind and all things in the universe have emerged as appearance.

All things are in a recurring process of appearing and disappearing only to return to their original state. This may be called a kind of inertia, a drag on activity and manifestation, that brings all things back to their original state of composure. The original state is eternal. To understand this eternality of emptiness is enlightenment; without this enlightenment one's mind is engrossed in confusion and evil activity.

Understanding this truth of eternality makes one merciful; mercy leads one to be impartial; impartiality results in nobility of character; nobility is like heaven. To be heavenly means to have attained Taohood. To have attained Taohood is to become unified with eternity. One can never die even with the decay of his body.

SEVENTEEN

A great ruler, first of all, ought to know the necessities and habits of his people. Secondly, he should keep in close touch with them and praise the meritorious ones. Thirdly, he should give reason for them to respect his moral earnestness. Lastly, he should resort to punishment only to bring home to them the disgracefulness of evil.

When a ruler lacks faith in his people, his people will lack faith in him. A wise ruler is always careful in his choice of words and because of it his people respect him and give him credit for the natural success of his administration.

EIGHTEEN

When people no longer follow the great TAO, they originate the ideas of benevolence and righteousness. When knowledge and learning are cultivated there is hypocrisy. When relatives are unfriendly to one another, they adopt the teaching of filial piety and paternal affection. When a country is in confusion and discord, ideals of loyalty and patriotism arise.

NINETEEN

When people abandon the idea of becoming a sage and give up ambition for worldly knowledge and learning, then their innate goodness will have a chance to manifest itself and will develop a hundredfold. When there is no activity of thinking to interfere, there is nothing that the mind can not accomplish in the way of good self-development. If ideas of benevolence and righteousness are abandoned, then people will return naturally to the primal virtues of filial piety and parental affection. If craftiness and acquisitiveness are abandoned, then theft and robbery will naturally disappear.

The reason why I refer to this is because of the deficiency of these primal virtues in our present culture. Let us restrain our sensual desires and egoism and return to simplicity and naturalness.

TWENTY

Abandon your acquired learning and do not regret the loss. There is very little difference between 'yes' and 'no', but what a vast difference between a good man and a wicked man. There are some things (like suffering and death) which are universally feared and which it is natural to fear, but woe to those ignorant people who desire and grasp after amusements and defilements (the very things that cause suffering and death). People are busy with enjoyments as if they were celebrating a feast day, or as if they were flocking to the games. I, alone, am as fresh as the morning air, as pure as a babe in its mother's arms, as free as a homeless wanderer. Other people are admired and envied because of their cleverness; I, alone, am neglected. Am I (because of this) foolish at heart? No! Let them be as smart and aggressive as ever; I am content to remain retiring and obscure. Let them continue to be as sensible and prudent as ever; let me remain as neglected as a deaf-mute.

Nevertheless, I am as pure as the water in the ocean and as free as the driftwood upon its bosom. Let others have their means for acquiring wealth, I am content to be counted foolish and inefficient. I seem to stand in contrast to common people, empty and foolish, but I am nourished by food from Mother TAO.

TWENTY-ONE

All the innumerable forms of *teh* (power or virtue) correspond to the principle of TAO, but the nature of TAO is to be realized only in a state of mental concentration when the thinking mind is empty and quiescent and the intuitive mind is alert and receptive. Then the spirit reflects reality and realizes its true nature. When the spirit is in an advanced state of tranquillity, there will be opened a fountain of purest semen available for service which by its special signs can be recognized intuitively. Since the beginning, this generative vitality has ever been available for the creation and nourishment of all things. Moreover, the reason one can manifest the mystery of Originality is simply because of the fertilization of this same vitality called TAO.

TWENTY-TWO

Time will show that the humblest will attain supremacy, the dishonored will be justified, the empty will be filled, the old will be rejuvenated, those content with little will be rewarded with much, and those grasping much will fall into confusion.

Therefore, the perfect Sage who keeps his mind unified and humble will become the master of the world. As he has no prejudices, he becomes enlightened; as he does not assert himself, he will become exalted; as he does not praise himself, his merit will be recognized; as he is not proud of himself, his fame will endure; inasmuch as he does not seek supremacy, he will have no rivals.

True, indeed, is the old saying: "The humble will be exalted." Every one, with sincerity, should take refuge in humility.

TWENTY-THREE

To have an empty and transparent mind and to be unassertive is according to nature. A whirlwind never outlasts the morning, nor a violent rain the day. What causes the whirlwind and a violent rain? Is it not because of special condition of heaven and earth? If even nature can not keep up its disturbances for very long, how can a man expect to long assert himself?

Therefore, he who is devoting his life to the attainment of TAO, should be sincerely humble in mind and unassertive in his activities. If he is with those who are following TAO, he should show sympathy by following TAO himself. If he is with those who are practising *teh*, he should practise *teh*, also. If he is with those who have suffered loss, he should show sympathy with them in their loss.

For he who shows sympathy with those who are following TAO will thereby attain his own Taohood; he who shows sympathy with those who are practising *teh*, will rejoice in the acquirement of more *teh* himself, he who shows sympathy with those in loss will know better how to bear his own loss.

If one lacks faith in himself, it is because he lacks faith in TAO.

TWENTY-FOUR

He that stands on tiptoe can not long stand steady; he that is sitting astride can not walk; he that is prejudiced can not become enlightened; he that is self-assertive can not become distinguished; he that praises himself will not be given credit by others; he that takes pride in himself will not long be able to retain his safety and fame.

The comparison of these illustrations to TAO is like comparing offal to food, or like comparing superficial manners with true sympathy of heart. Even animals recognize the difference and show hatred. Therefore, one who has attained Taohood will never manifest these egoistic qualities. He will avoid thinking of himself and will remain humble at heart.

TWENTY-FIVE

There is a primal essence that is all-inclusive and undifferentiated and which existed before there was any appearance of heaven and earth. How tranquil and empty it is! How self-sufficing and changeless! How omnipresent and infinite! Yet this tranquil emptiness becomes the Mother of all. Who knows its name? I can only characterize it and call it TAO. Though it is quite inadequate, I will even call it the Great. But how boundless is its Greatness! It stretches away into the far distances (like a circle) only to return again.

How Great is TAO! But so is Heaven Great; and so is earth Great; and so is the perfect Sage Great. On the earth there are these four Greatnesses and among them is the perfect Sage. Men act in conformity with the laws of earth; earth acts in conformity with the laws of Heaven; Heaven acts in conformity with the laws of TAO; TAO acts in accordance with its own self-nature.

TWENTY-SIX

As the heavy is the foundation of the light, so the quiet is master of the passionate. Therefore, the perfect Sage in all the experiences of the day does not lose his serenity. Though he be surrounded by grandeur, he will keep himself unconcerned and simple.

But, alas, for those emperors, masters of ten thousand chariots, who recklessly ambitious for power, have grasped after riches and thereby have lost control of their empires. If a king be reckless and flippant, he will lose the respect of his subjects; if he give way to passion, he will lose control of his kingdom.

Twenty-seven

Good walkers need no guides; good speakers do not blame or reproach others; good managers need no rules nor diagrams; good locksmiths are competent to open any lock; good binders can unloose any kind of knot.

It is the same with the perfect Sage: he is always competent in giving advice to his people, so that not one becomes an outcast. He is competent in using things, so that nothing is useless to him. His insight detects hidden values. Therefore the competent man is the master of the incompetent, and the incompetent are as hands and feet to the competent. The incompetent who does not esteem his master and the competent who does not protect his hands and feet, though he otherwise be intelligent, is acting foolishly. Herein lies the value of intelligence.

Twenty-eight

He who realizes the foolishness of passionate action always keeps his mind concentrated and tranquil. Just as the valleys, because of their lowness, become the source of rivers, so the perfect Sage because of his characteristic humility returns to the simplicity of a little child.

He who realizes the true way of conserving his spirit will take good care of his body. Thereby he becomes an example to the world. His original vitality will never fail, and more, will return to its origin.

He who realizes the dignity of his personality, but retains his humility, is like the lowly valley. Being like a valley, he becomes filled with the original vitality and reverts to his original nature. But when he forsakes humility, he merely becomes cultivated and useful. The perfect Sage employs these cultivated and useful men to become his officials and chiefs.

Therefore a good administrator makes no reforms that will destroy the natural simplicity of his people.

TWENTY-NINE

If anyone desires to take and remake the empire under his own reforming plans, he will never be successful. The empire is a spiritual thing that cannot be remade after one's own ideas and he who attempts it will only make a failure. Even he who tries to hold it will lose it.

Under any system of holding or remaking the empire, the king must make use of different people and things; some of whom are honorable and precious and others are of less degree; some will be leaders and some will be only ornamental; some will be followers and some servants. Some people or things are strong and can be depended upon, others are fragile and will break or must be thrown away.

Therefore, the perfect Sage does not seek to take and remake the empire. He does not seek to enforce his own ideas upon it, but is content to give up extravagant comforts and indulgent egoism himself and thus to set the nation an example of returning to simplicity:

THIRTY

When a minister serves a ruler after the principle of TAO, he will not advise a resort to force of arms to become a great nation. Like returns to like. So briars and thorns grow rank where an army camps. Bad years of want and disorder follow a great war.

Therefore, the competent ruler, resolutely restraining his desires and ambition, dares not resort to force. Because he is resolute, he will not be boastful, nor haughty, nor arrogant; because he is resolute he will act only under necessity; because he is resolute, he will have no ambition to be powerful.

By the nature of things, when the strength of anything is fully developed, it immediately begins to decay. This means that strength is not in accordance with the principle of TAO. Being not in accordance with TAO, it will soon pass away.

THIRTY-ONE

Both arms and armor are unblessed things. Not only men come to detest them, but a curse seems to follow them. Therefore, the one who follows the principle of TAO does not resort to arms. It is significant that in peaceful times, the place of honor is on the left and in war times it is on the right. For as arms are unblessed things, they are not the things that men of good character resort to.

It is of first importance for a gentleman to preserve his serenity and dignity; even when victorious, a good soldier does not rejoice, because rejoicing over a victorious battle is the same as rejoicing over the killing of men. If he rejoices over the killing of men, he will never be victorious.

Thus, in propitious affairs, the place of honor is on the left, but in unpropitious affairs, the right is the place of honor. In times of war, lesser officers are on the left of the ranks, a place of honor, while the commanding general is on the right, a place of less honor. This means that war is considered as a funeral ceremony.

Therefore, after a battle the killing of many men should be honored by weeping and mourning, and the victor should be received as if he were attending a funeral ceremony.

THIRTY-TWO

TAO is eternal but is unnamable. Its simplicity, though considered as of the humblest, is most independent. Nothing in the world is able to bring it into subjection. If princes and kings retain simplicity heaven and earth are harmoniously unified and everywhere drop the sweet dew of their favor naturally and evenly.

As soon as things are given names, greed and grasping arise and, unless one understands when to stop, there will be no satisfying the desires. To know when to be satisfied and to restrain desire, is to know the secret of longevity. This is the principle of TAO. It resembles the great rivers that flow into the seas, but which have their origin in the little streams of the valleys.

THIRTY-THREE

He who understands others is intelligent; he who understands himself is enlightened. He who is able to conquer others is powerful; he who can control himself is more powerful.

He who is contented is richer than the richest. Those who have purpose are resolute, and those who keep tranquillity of mind have endurance. Those whose fame endures beyond death are immortal.

Thirty-four

Great TAO is all pervading! It is available everywhere, on the right hand and on the left. Everything is dependent upon it for existence and it never fails them. It does all this but claims no ownership. As TAO has no selfish desires and is perfectly humble, everything takes refuge in it. Because it does not care for ownership, it is regarded as the greatest. Because the perfect Sage never thinks of his greatness, he can attain true Greatness.

Thirty-five

The whole world is naturally drawn to him, who keeps this principle of TAO'S true Greatness. It goes to TAO and receives no harm; on the contrary it finds contentment, tranquillity and peace. To common people TAO'S principle of simplicity and humility seems weak and insipid; they desire and seek music and dainties. Indeed, TAO has no taste! When looked at, there is nothing to be prized; when listened for, it can scarcely be heard; but its satisfactions are inexhaustible.

Thirty-six

Before one can contract a thing, it must first be extended; before anything can be weakened, it must first be made strong; before anything can be wasted, it must be present; before one can take a thing by force, someone else must give it up. This is the profound principle which explains why the humble and yielding conquer the selfish and strong.

A fish should not be removed from its natural home in the deep pond, neither should the authority of the nation be entrusted to anyone, not even to the king's favorite.

Thirty-seven

TAO acts without assertion, yet all things proceed in conformity with it. If princes and kings would follow the principle of TAO, then all things would unfold according to their own nature. If there are troublesome desires arising from the habits of the people, they should be taught the principle of simplicity that characterizes the ineffable TAO.

Even the conception of the ineffable TAO's simplicity ought not to remain in one's mind. When quietness is attained, not by ideas and the satisfaction of desires but by the practice of *wu-wei*, the troubles of the world will right themselves.

THIRTY-EIGHT

The *teh* (power, or virtue) of the perfect Sage is not revealed intentionally. It naturally and spontaneously meets the needs of the world and, therefore, it is the true teh of TAO. The teh of inferiors simply makes an outside show of power which is assumed to be virtue, therefore, it falls short of the true teh.

The Teh of the perfect Sage does not interfere, it cooperates with open and sympathetic mind, while the teh of inferiors acts with intention and under conditions and is influenced by desires. The benevolence of the perfect Sage flows out naturally in acts of kindness and is unconditioned by desires, or ideas, or conditions; while righteousness, even of superior men, is done under conditioning desires and ideas. This evil is aggravated when these righteous ideas of superior men are made up into social codes, which if not obeyed willingly are enforced by law.

Therefore, when one loses TAO, he makes use of teh as a standard of living; when he loses Teh, he makes use of benevolence as a standard; when one loses benevolence, he makes use of righteousness; when he loses righteousness he makes use of social codes as his standard of conduct. Thus social codes take the place of loyalty and faith and there is the beginning of disorder. Cultural civilizations are a mere shadow of TAO and are the source of allurements and foolishness.

Therefore, the superior man of affairs conforms to the spirit of Teh and not to its reduction into codes of loyalty and righteousness. He abides in the reality of TAO and not in its shadow.

THIRTY-NINE

From the beginning there has been a law of unity. Heaven attained unity and thereby its perfect clearness; earth attained unity and thereby its solidity; spirit attained unity and thereby its subtilty; valleys attained unity and thereby became the source of rivers; everything in the world attained unity and thereby their power of growth; princes and kings attained unity and thereby attained to moral conduct. Everything unfolds by the same law into some form of unity.

For if heaven were not purity it would differentiate; if earth were not solidity it would crumble and fall apart; if spirit were not subtilty it would lose its vitality; if valleys were not ever flowing out, they would soon fill up; if things were not growing, they would soon come to destruction; when princes and kings decline in moral conduct, they soon lose the respect of their subjects and forfeit their kingdoms.

Unless nobles serve the interests of the common people, they are no longer noble; the high need the low for a foundation. The reason why princes and kings refer to themselves as "the forlorn," "the inferior," and "the unworthy," is because they understand the principle that nobles require common people as a basis for their nobility.

When a carriage is separated into its parts it is no longer a carriage, its unity is lost. The superior man should not desire to become cultivated and shine as a gem, neither should he become gross and dull as stones. There should be a unity of ideals and usefulness.

FORTY

To withdraw the mind from attention to outward things, to be thoughtful, to practice meditation, is to be in conformity with TAO. To be humble and of service to others is, also, being in conformity with TAO. Heaven and earth, and all things are manifestations of existence, but existence, itself, comes from non-existence. (It is to this potential non-existence that the mind should be directed).

FORTY-ONE

The superior man, as soon as he listens to TAO, earnestly practices TAO; an average man, hearing of TAO, sometimes remembers it and sometimes forgets it; an inferior man, hearing of Tao, ridicules it. If it were not thus ridiculed it would not be worth following as TAO.

There is an old saying:—"Those who are illuminated by TAO, are the most obscure; those who are advanced in TAO are the most timid; those who are indifferent to TAO are the most distinguished." The Teh of TAO resembles a deep valley; the most innocent appears to be most ashamed; the highest in teh appears the humblest; the most firmly established in teh appears the most remiss; the most straightforward seems to be the most fickle; the greatest polygon has no corners; the finest instrument is the latest to be perfected; the largest bell sounds rarely; the grandest phenomena are the inconceivable phenomena of spirit.

TAO is unseen and inscrutable. Nevertheless, it is precisely this TAO that alone can give and accomplish.

FORTY-TWO

TAO is inscrutable. From TAO proceeds the one (potentiality); one produces two (the positive and negative principles); this makes three. From these three proceed all things. All things, thus bear the imprint of the negative *yin* behind and embrace the positive *yang* in front. The primal principle of potentiality, as it becomes active, brings the negative and positive together and there is manifestation.

The things that are detested by common people, namely, to be called the forlorn, the inferior, the unworthy, are the very things that kings and princes take for titles. These are the very things that it is a gain to lose and a loss to gain.

I am teaching the same thing which is taught by others; others have said that the strong and aggressive do not come to natural deaths, but I make this saying the basis of my teaching.

FORTY-THREE

The tenderest things of creation prevail over the hardest. Something immaterial enters into the most impenetrable to preserve its unity. I, therefore, recognise the advantages of the principle of *wu-wei* and teach non-interference. There is no other doctrine that is grander than the doctrine of TAO, and no other teaching that is more universally potent than the teaching of *wu-wei*.

FORTY-FOUR

Which is more intimately precious: fame or life? Which is more valuable: life or treasure? Which gives the most trouble: gain or loss? One naturally seeks the things he most prizes; for that reason we should be careful to prize the right things, because grasping and hoarding invite waste and loss both to property and life.

A contented person is never dishonored. One who knows how to stop with enough is free from danger; he will therefore endure.

FORTY-FIVE

The enlightenment of the perfect Sage, because of its simplicity, appears as lacking, but his wisdom never fails. Perfect homogeneity appears as emptiness, but its potentiality is never exhausted. Extreme frankness appears as evasive, great skill as clumsiness, great eloquence as stammering. Motion conquers cold, while quietness conquers heat. Purity and tranquillity are the true characteristics of creation.

FORTY-SIX

When the world yields to the principle of TAO, its race horses will be used to haul manure; when the world ignores TAO, war horses are pastured on the public common.

There is no sin greater than yielding to desire. There is no misfortune greater than yielding to discontent. There is no greater folly than to yield to acquisitiveness. Thus, everyone should be contented for he that is contented is already rich.

FORTY-SEVEN

Not going out of the door, the sage has knowledge of the world. Not looking through the window, he perceives the TAO of heaven. The more one wanders about among objective things, the less he understands.

Therefore, the perfect Sage does not think about worldly affairs, but he understands the significance of all things. He does not boast of his ability, but his name is world famous. He works but without grasping and, therefore succeeds in whatever he undertakes.

FORTY-EIGHT

In regard to knowledge: the more one studies, the more he accumulates learning; while in regard to wisdom the more one practices TAO, the more his desires and thoughts are lessened, even to perfect emptiness of mind, all his innate excellencies will be developed and manifested. It is therefore necssary, if one is to keep control of his mind, to preserve its emptiness. But as soon as one desires to control his mind, he becomes incapable of doing so. It is by this perfect control of mind that the Sage gains the world's favor.

FORTY-NINE

The perfect Sage has no preconceived opinions; he accepts the opinions of his people as his own. The good he treats with fairness, the not-good he also treats with fairness and by so doing attains the teh of justice. The faithful he treats with good-faith, and the unfaithful he also treats with good-faith and so he attains the teh of faithfulness.

The perfect Sage is always concerned about the welfare of people and, indeed, it is for their sakes that his mind is burdened. All people show him respect and are obedient to him and, in return, he regards them as his children.

FIFTY

The moon from its first appearance to full moon, is in a state of appearing; from its fullness to its disappearance, it is in a state of disappearing. It is just the same with the life of a man: from babyhood to manhood he is growing up; from manhood to old age, he is failing. What does this signify? It means that it is only the spirit of man that shares the longevity of heaven and earth. Of all things, heaven and earth are endowed with perennial vitality.

Thus it may be said that those who have attained mastery over their spirit have set free this perennial vitality; when traveling will never suffer harm from rhinoceros or tiger, because the rhinoceros will find no place to horn him, nor the tiger for his claws; or in battle without weapons or armor, will soldiers be able to wound him. Why is this so? Because spirit transcends mortality.

FIFTY-ONE

Life comes from TAO; its nourishment comes from teh; its shape is formed by materiality; its accomplishments are owing to energy. Therefore among all men there are none who do not honor TAO and esteem teh. Honor for TAO and esteem for Teh is never by compulsion, it is always spontaneous. Men understand naturally that life comes from TAO and that teh nourishes them, raises them, nurtures them, completes, matures, rears, and protects them.

TAO gives life to them but does not exercise authority over them; teh forms them but makes no use of them, raises them but never interferes with them. This is the profound teh of the mysterious TAO.

FIFTY-TWO

When the potentiality of TAO manifests itself, it becomes the mother of all things. When one realizes that his life comes from this universal Mother, he will also realize his brotherhood to all her descendents. When one realizes his descent from the universal Mother and his brotherhood with all humanity, he will cherish his life and thus, to its end, will be kept in perfect health.

He who talks little and closes his sense gates will never become wearied to the end of life; he who talks much, and yields to the desires of his senses, and interferes with affairs, will be risking his life continually.

To be thoughtful and mindful is to be enlightened. To be humble and yielding is better than great strength. To use one's intelligence to seek enlightenment and to control one's body is to return to the nature of one's origin.

FIFTY-THREE

Should only one day be given me to carry out my wishes in explaining the principle of the Great TAO, I would condemn almsgiving as being a poisonous medicine, making people dependent. The Way of the Great TAO is wide and straight for men to follow, but most people prefer the bypaths.

When the royal palace is magnificent, fields become devastated and granaries empty. To wear ornaments and gay colors, to carry sharp swords, to indulge in dainties and excessive drinking, to hoard wealth and treasure, is simply to invite robbery. It is not the Way of the Great TAO.

FIFTY-FOUR

As a thing that is well planted is not easily uprooted and as a thing that is well guarded is not easily stolen, so if a family observes the principle of TAO, its descendents will ever hold their ancestors in honor.

He who practices TAO for himself will only gain teh for himself. He who practices TAO for the benefit of his family, his teh will pass to his descendents. If he practices TAO for the welfare of his community, his teh will be multiplied. If he practices TAO for the benefit of his country, his teh will become abundantly multiplied. If he practices the principle of TAO for the sake of the whole world, teh will become universal.

Therefore, he who practices TAO for himself will only himself be benefited. He who practices it for the sake of his family, will have his family benefited. He who practices it for his community will have his community benefited. He who practices TAO for the whole world will benefit the whole world.

How do I know all this? It comes from the practice of TAO.

FIFTY-FIVE

He who attains to the highest teh of simplicity and sincerity, may be compared to the ingenuousness of an infant. Poisonous insects do not sting their own young, wild beasts do not attack their own cubs, nor do birds of prey. A baby's bones may be weak and its muscles soft, but its spiritual vitality is perfect. An infant does not know about the relation of the sexes, but gradually its generative vigor will develop. Its spirit is virile, indeed! It may sob and cry all day but will not become hoarse. His unity as a child is perfect.

To understand how to preserve this unity and soundness, one must return to his original state of simplicity. To know how to return to one's original state is to be enlightened. To increase one's natural vigor means blessedness. To control one's breathing means strength. Things that are fully grown begin to decay, for growth is contrary to the principle of TAO. Things that are contrary to TAO soon pass away.

FIFTY-SIX

The wise keep silent; a babbler is not wise. Keep your mouth closed and guard the gates of sense. Hide your sharpness, free yourself from entanglements, conceal your personality, be socially minded and natural. Thus to harmonize one's life with the life of others is the teh of the profound TAO.

No one can befriend such a man, nor can they estrange him, nor endanger him, nor honor him, nor despise him. Such a man is naturally honored by all the world.

FIFTY-SEVEN

An empire is best administered by justice, an army by craft, and influence over people is gained by non-interference. The more people become selfish, the more the state is in disorder. The more people become artful and cunning, the more abnormal things become. The more laws and orders are multiplied, the more theft and violence increase.

Therefore, the perfect Sage reasons: If I practice *wu-wei*, that is, non-interference, the people will restrain themselves naturally. If I set an example of good behavior, people of themselves will become tranquil and prosperous naturally.

If I have no selfish desires myself, other people will become unselfish and simple.

FIFTY-EIGHT

If administrative restrictions be kept out of sight as much as possible, the people will become quiet, honest and sympathetic. If an administration becomes complex and officious, the people will become needy and turbulent.

Misery may be followed by happiness and happiness may lead to misery. Who can foretell the outcome of either misery or happiness? Is there no safe guide to normality? Indeed, normality itself soon becomes abnormal, and good conditions soon become unsatisfactory.

(Why is it necessary for justice to always become injustice, and for good conditions to always pass into evil?) It is because men have been under illusion for a long, long time. Therefore, the perfect Sage, though just himself, does not reprove another's injustice; though unselfish himself, he does not reprimand the covetousness of others; though he is straight forward, he does not offend others by disagreeable assertiveness, though wise, he does not make a show of his wisdom.

FIFTY-NINE

In governing people and in worshipping heaven, nothing surpasses the teh of self-restraint. The restraint of desire is like returning to the original TAO. Returning to one's origin means the recovery of one's vitality. When one has recovered his original vitality, nothing is unmanageable. If nothing is unmanageable then he retains his original tranquillity because he is unconscious of any limits. When he retains this state of tranquillity he may govern the country wisely. Moreover, when he is in a state of tranquillity, he will govern the country as a mother takes care of her children and by so doing long retain his usefulness. He will be like a plant having a strong stem and deep roots. He will manifest the longevity of TAO.

SIXTY

To govern a great state one should do it as a cook fries small fish, that is, without scaling or cleaning them.

If one rules an empire by the principle of TAO, evil spirits will lose their power. It is not because their power is any less, but because the people can no longer be harmed by them. It is not because of the harmlessness of the gods, but because of the harmlessness of the wise ruler. Since neither ghosts nor gods can harm people, if they have a wise ruler, they will return to that ruler good-will and they will abide in tranquillity.

SIXTY-ONE

A great state is like the current of a river; it is always flowing down the lower valleys. There is a bond of unity, also, in a great state that draws its people together, like the attraction of male to female.

The female wins the favor of a male by her quietude and quietude is always submissive. Thus a great state by its service to smaller states wins their allegiance. A smaller state by its submission to a great state wins an influence over it. Thus one wins by condescension, and the other by submission, and their interests are mutually conserved.

The great state likes to federate more states and have more people; the small state to guard its safety is willing to submit to the greater and enter its federation. Each by the same procedure gains its particular end. So it is a good policy for a great state to lead the way by itself first practicing humility.

SIXTY-TWO

TAO is an all-embracing mystery. It is treasure to good men and a refuge to bad men. Fine words are used in selling goods, but it is a noble life that wins the respect of others. Even though TAO is despised by common people, why should I be foolish as are they and ignore it?

In the establishment of a monarchy, (there are many things that are to be considered): the emperor is to bc enthroned, the three ministers are to be appointed, the precious gems that have been presented to the emperor are to be distributed, and the tribute war-horses are to be properly exhibited. But nothing is more important than the dedication of the throne to TAO. For what reason did the ancients so highly esteem TAO? Was it not because it was only by devotion to TAO that the hopes of the nation could be realized and the miseries of the people relieved?

That is why TAO is honored by all the world.

SIXTY-THREE

A man's first duty is to practice *wu-wei* and make use of his quiet hours to gain enlightenment. One should early learn to find sweetness in tasteless things; to discover greatness in small things; to be satisfied with few things.

One should respond to hatred with kindness; he should treat little affairs as though they were important. All the world's difficulties arise from slight causes, and all the world's great affairs have risen from small beginnings.

Therefore, the perfect Sage never asserts his greatness and by so doing attains to true greatness. Rash promises are easily made, but the simpler a thing looks, the harder it is to accomplish. This is a common experience, therefore the perfect Sage considers everything difficult and so to the end has no difficulties.

SIXTY-FOUR

That which is at rest can easily be taken hold of. That which has not yet become important, can be easily prevented. The fragile is easily broken, light things are easily scattered. It is wise to be prepared for difficulties and to establish order before there is disorder. A tree that it takes both arms to encircle grew from a tiny rootlet. A many storied pagoda is built by placing one brick upon another brick. A journey of three thousand miles is begun by a single step. If one attempts to govern either himself or another, he is bound to make a failure of it. If he tries to grasp anything, it slips away from him.

The perfect Sage, therefore, by practicing *wu-wei* and making no attempts, makes no failures, and because he does not grasp anything, he has nothing to lose. People in their eagerness are ever approaching success only to continually fail. If one is to succeed, he must be as careful to the end as at the beginning.

Therefore, the perfect Sage has no desire for things that are difficult to obtain, nor does he value them. He learns to be unlearned; he turns away from that which others greedily seek. In that spirit he helps all things toward their natural development but dares not attempt to force their development.

SIXTY-FIVE

In the olden days, those who were well versed in the principle of TAO, avoided teaching the people anything; instead they kept them in ignorance. The reason why people are difficult to govern is because they are educated. To govern a people by craftiness is a curse; to govern them by the principle of *wu-wei* is a blessing. He who understands the difference between these two ways of governing is a model ruler. If he knows how to become a model ruler, he has gained profoundness of teh.

The profoundness of Teh is deep, indeed, and far reaching! Because it is in harmony with the original nature of things, everything will be acting according to the law of its nature.

SIXTY-SIX

The rivers and seas become the kings of the myriad valleys because they are content with the low places. The perfect Sage rises above his people because of his humility; because he is first willing to follow them, he comes to leadership.

Although the perfect Sage is above his people, yet they feel no burden; he dominates them, but they cherish no resentment. Therefore the world rejoices to exalt the perfect Sage and never wearies of him. Because he does not seek to rival others, others have no desire to rival him.

SIXTY-SEVEN

The world calls it the Great TAO, but there is nothing with which to compare it. Why? Simply because of its greatness. If there were anything with which to compare it, TAO would immediately become, and remain so for a long time, the most insignificant thing in all the world.

TAO has three treasures that are inherent in its very nature. The first is compassion; the second is economy; the third is humility. Because of his compassion, a man becomes courageous. Because of his economy, a man becomes generous. Because of his humility, a man becomes a leader. Nowadays a man, because of disregarding compassion, merely becomes bold; because of discarding economy, he only becomes extravagant; because of discarding humility, he becomes arrogant. Such men are already in the process of dying.

If a soldier is compassionate, in battle he will be a conquerer and in defense secure. If a man is compassionate, Heaven will protect him because of its compassion.

SIXTY-EIGHT

He who excels as a soldier is the man who is not warlike. He who fights the best fight is the man who does not lose his temper. He who truly conquers an enemy does not lord it over him but treats him with respect. He who best employs people keeps himself humble.

This is what is meant by the teh of *wu-wei*. It is the way to bring out the good in others. It is the oldest principle that has ever been taught. It is in compliance with the nature of TAO.

SIXTY-NINE

It is taught in books of strategy: "Never be so rash as to start a war; at first, always be on the defense." "One should hesitate to advance an inch but be always ready to withdraw a foot." This means that it is better for an army to advance by craft rather than by aggressive operations. (It means for everybody) that there is a better way of attack than by hands, a better way of winning than by hostility, a better way of gaining than by resort to force. There is no greater mistake than to make light of an enemy. By making light of an enemy many a kingdom has been lost. When well matched armies come to conflict, the army that regrets the hostility between them, always conquers.

SEVENTY

The principle of TAO (*wu-wei*) is easy to understand and easy to put into practice, yet in all the world how few there are who understand it and put it into practice. Every word of common people has its object; every deed has its actor, but because these talkers and actors are ignorant, TAO is ignorant with them and does not interfere.

Since very few people know TAO, TAO is the more worthy of esteem. Therefore, the perfect Sage clothes himself in the cheap garments of poor people but keeps TAO, like a gem, hidden in his bosom.

SEVENTY-ONE

To recognize one's ignorance of unknowable things is mental health and to be ignorant of knowable things is sickness. It is only by grieving over knowable things that we are kept in mental health. The perfect Sage is free from the mental sickness of common people, because he understands his ignorance and grieves over it.

SEVENTY-TWO

When people are too ignorant to fear the things that are really fearful (greed, illusion and self-assertion), the greatest fear (of death) will soon over-power them. Do not be troubled because of the narrowness of your dwelling, do not become depressed because of the life you are compelled to live. If people cease to worry about their surroundings and their lives, their minds will become tranquil.

Therefore, the perfect Sage understands himself but never exhibits himself; he cherishes but never overvalues himself. He discards ostentation and pride, but keeps understanding and mindfulness.

SEVENTY-THREE

Courage carried to recklessness leads to death, while courage restrained and cautious leads to life. Of these two kinds of courage, one is harmful and one is beneficial. Why this is so, why some things are rejected by Heaven and some not, who can tell the reason? Therefore the perfect Sage looks upon all things as puzzling (and does not interfere with any).

The TAO of Heaven never seeks supremacy, yet it is always supreme. It speaks not but it is perfectly responsive. It issues no summons yet things come to it naturally. It appears to be open and simple, but hidden from view is a profound design. Indeed, the meshes of Heaven's net are wide, but no matter how wide or loose they may appear nothing escapes.

SEVENTY-FOUR

If people do not fear death, how can they be frightened by the death penalty? If people are afraid of death, I would seize the one who is not afraid of death and execute him. After that who would dare to disobey?

There is always an experienced officer to execute murderers. If an inexperienced person takes his place, it would be like an unskilled man taking the place of a skilled carpenter at his hewing: he is very likely to cut himself.

SEVENTY-FIVE

When a ruler appropriates too much of the taxes, starvation comes to the people. The reason why people are difficult to govern is because the ruler is thinking too much of his own interests. People make light of death because they are absorbed in the interests of life. The one who is not absorbed in life is wiser than he who esteems life.

SEVENTY-SIX

When a baby is born it is tender and fragile; when it grows to be a man and dies, it becomes hard and stiff. It is the same with everything. Herbs and trees when young and growing are tender and delicate, but when they become old and die, they become rigid and hard.

Therefore, those who are stiff and unyielding belong to the domain of death, while the tender and sympathetic belong to the realm of life. Those who are ruthless in battle do not gain the victory. When a tree becomes hard and rigid, it will soon decay. The large and hard are put at the bottom, the tender and delicate are placed on top.

SEVENTY-SEVEN

The TAO of Heaven resembles the stretching of a bow. The mighty it humbles, the lowly it exalts; the overflowing it diminishes, the insufficient it supplies.

The way of humans is not so. Humans take from the needy to further enrich the rich. The one who can take from his over-abundance and give to a needy world has attained Taohood. Therefore, the perfect Sage is not sparing of his services, nor does he look upon them as meritorious, nor does he make a display of them. Is this not so?

SEVENTY-EIGHT

Nothing is more fragile than water, yet of all the agencies that attack hard substances nothing can surpass water, nor take its place. Therefore the weak are conquerors of the strong, and the yielding are conquerors of the mighty. Everyone knows this but few practice it.

Therefore, the perfect Sage accepts the disgrace of his country and by so doing becomes a true patriot; he is a patient under the misfortunes of his country and because of it worthy to be its sovereign.

True words always seem paradoxical, but no other form of teaching can take its place.

SEVENTY-NINE

If nations hate each other but are making a treaty of peace, there will always remain some seeds of hatred. How can it be considered as a settlement?

The perfect Sage is always willing to accept the debit side of an account, for then he does not have to enforce payment from another. Those who have teh make unwritten contracts of faith; those who have no teh, make written contracts and hold them as evidence.

The TAO of Heaven makes no written contracts, but always helps the good man.

EIGHTY

In a small country with few people there will be in propor-tion many of exceptional merit and of competency but few vacancies for their services.

If people consider their death to be important, they will hesitate to go to distant countries. Though there be boats and carts they will have no occasion to use them. Though there be armor and weapons, there will be no occasion to don them. Let people return to the spirit of the olden days when they used knotted cords for their records; then they will take delight in simple food, be proud of their cheap clothes, content with their dwellings, and rejoice in their customs.

Neighboring states may be so close to each other that one can see them with their eyes, and their cocks and dogs can be mutually heard, but people will have no desire to go and come even to the end of their lives.

Eighty-one

Faithful words are often not pleasant; pleasant words are often not faithful. Well informed men do not dispute; men who dispute are not well informed. The wise man is not always learned; the learned man is not always wise.

The perfect Sage does not keep things in possession or in memory, but since he ever serves others he acquires the most after all. Since he continually gives to others, he will possess the most in the end.

The TAO of Heaven always benefits and harms no one. The perfect Sage by following TAO, that is, by practising *wu-wei* and serving others, will never be the cause of strife.

DHYANA FOR BEGINNERS

Preface

THE Tien-tai Sect hold four treatises on Dhyana in high regard. The first is entitled, Dhyana for Immediate Enlightenment. It was written for those who are seeking instantaneous enlightenment by means of one phrase or even one word. It is the record of lectures given at the Nuo-chien Monastery in King-chow, Hupeh Province, by Grand Master Chih-chi. It was written down by Chang-an, one of his disciples, and was compiled in ten volumes. The second treatise is entitled, Dhyana by Regular Steps. It is also based upon lectures by the Grand Master, but this time they were delivered at the N'rkwei Monastery and recorded by the disciple, Fah-chen. It was at first compiled in thirty volumes, but was afterward recompiled in ten volumes under the title, Dhyana Paramita, or the Ideal Dhyana. The third treatise was at first entitled, Dhyana by Irregular Steps. It was written down by the Grand Master at the request of Mao-shee, a Minister of the Grand Council (Chen Dynasty 548-581.) It was compiled in one volume and now goes under the title, the Six Wonderful Ways of Dhyana. The fourth treatise, the one that we are now to study, was written down by the Grand Master for the benefit and instruction of his own brother (Lieut. Col.) Chen-chin. It is undoubtedly a compendium of the Master's mature understanding of the Mahayana and is a sure key to enlightenment.

The different headings employed in this book, such as, "Stop and Realize," "Samapatti and Prajna" (Transcendental-powers and Wisdom), "Tranquillization and Reflection," "Serenity and Quietness," are all derived from the same source. If you trace out this source and terminus, or should trace out the practices and attainments of the Buddhas, they would all alike be found in this practice of Dhyana,—stopping thought about Truth and realizing Truth itself. It was just what the Grand Master of the Tien-tai Mountains had himself experienced in a vision of the Vulture Peak that had come to him when he was staying at the great Su Mountains, and was always after his chief inspiration. Briefly speaking, the Dhyana which our Master

Chih-chi had practiced, and the Samadhi which he had experienced, and the lectures which he had delivered with such eloquence, were nothing but the manifestation of this "Stop and Realize." Or, in other words, what the Master had been teaching us was simply the narrative of the operation of our own minds; and the profound teaching of the Tien-tai School, and the voluminous literature to be studied, are no more than an elaboration of this single subject. If we should disregard the conception of Dhyana, it would be impossible for us either to understand or to discuss the teachings of the Tien-tai School. Consequently, it is not only necessary for everyone who is following (Buddha) to study it, it is also necessary for him to practice it.

As we look outward upon the world, we see corruption everywhere—people hankering after amusements, seeking to gratify their own selfish comfort, trying to rationalize their prejudices, deliberately blinding their eyes to their own enlightenment. How few there are who comprehend the way to practice Dhyana! Instead of studying this book, they keep it hidden away in a bookcase and their labor is in vain. But again I bring the teaching to the "engraver of wooden blocks" for another republishing and I hope that everyone who reads it will profit by its teachings. Moreover, I hope that everyone who reads it will practise its teachings and gain thereby a personal realization of its immeasurable treasure. As my labor is now ended, I write these few lines as an introduction.

BHIKKSHU YUEN-TSO

Yu-hang (near Han-chow).
The first day of Mid-autumn,
the 2nd Year of Shao-sang (Tsung Dynasty, 956-1273).

DHYANA

Lectures Delivered by Grand Master Chih-chi of Tien-tai Mountains, at the Shiu-ch'an Temple.
(*Sui Dynasty, 581–618*)

"Avoid all evil, cherish all goodness, keep the mind pure. This is the teaching of Buddha."

There are many different paths to Nirvana, but the most important one for us is the path of *Dhyana*. Dhyana is the practice of mind-control by which we stop all thinking and seek to realize Truth in its essence. That is, it is the practice of "stopping and realizing." If we cease all discriminative thought it will keep us from the further accumulation of error, while the practice of realizing will clear away delusions. Stopping is a refreshment of the lower consciousness, while realizing may be compared to a golden spade that opens up a treasure of transcendental wealth. Stopping is an entrance into the wonderful silence and peacefulness of potentiality (*dhyana-samapatti*); while realizing is an entrance into the riches of intuition and transcendental intelligence (*matti-prajna*). As one advances along this path, he comes into full possession of all means for enriching himself and for benefiting others. In the *Lotus of the Wonderful Law Sutra*, it says:—

"Our Lord Buddha forever abides in the permanence of the Mahayana both as to his attainment of the realization of Truth and as to his enrichment with supernatural powers of intuition and transcendental intelligence. With these qualifications he brings deliverence to all penitent beings."

We may liken these two powers (*samapatti* and *prajna*) to the wheels of a chariot and the wings of an eagle. If a follower has only one, he is led into an unbalanced life. As the Sutra says:—

"Those who only practice the goodness and blessings of samapatti and do not learn wisdom are to be counted ignorant, while those who only practice wisdom and do not learn goodness and sympathy are to be counted as unbalanced." Though the errors eventuating from unbalance may differ from the errors of ignorance, they alike lead a person to the same false views. This explains clearly that if one is to attain Supreme Perfect Wisdom in an immediate way, he must hold the two powers in equal balance: he must be both prepared and ready. The Sutra says:—

"As intelligence is more especially developed by Arahats, the true nature of Buddhas is not perceived by them. The Mahasattva-Bodhisattvas, by possessing the ten enlightening factors of permanence, perceived the true nature of Buddhas, but if they do not perceive it truly it is because of their laying too much stress on intelligence. It is only the Buddhas and

Tathagatas that perceive it perfectly because their powers of
samapatti and prajna have been equally developed."

Hence, in conclusion, are we not right in drawing the in-
ference that the practice of Dhyana is the true gateway to
Supreme Perfect Enlightenment? Is it not the Noble Path that
all followers of Buddha must follow? Is not Dhyana the pole
star of all goodness and the Supreme Perfect Enlightenment?

If anyone thoroughly understands what has been said here
about Dhyana, he will appreciate that its practice is not an easy
task. However, for the sake of aiding beginners to clear away
their ignorance and hindrances and to guide them toward enlightenment, we will aid them all we can by explaining the
practice of Dhyana in as simple words as possible, but at best,
its practice will be difficult. It would be absurd to present its
profoundness otherwise. It will be explained under ten heads
which will be like the steps of a stairway that leads upward
to Enlightenment and Nirvana.

Those who are really seeking Truth, but are more advanced,
should not look upon this book with contempt because it is
written simply and for beginners. They should be humble and
prudent because of the difficulties they will encounter when
they come to its practice. It is possible that some will be able
to digest its teachings with great ease and, in the twinkle of
an eye, their hindrances will be abolished and their intelligence
will be boundlessly developed and so will be their supernormal
understanding, also. But if you just read over the literal meaning and do not enter into its significance, you will not be able
to find your way to enlightenment—the reading will be just
a waste of time. Such a reader will be likened to a poor man
who spends his time in counting another man's treasures and
being no richer for it himself.

The Ten Heads

1. External conditions. 2. Control of sense desires. 3. Abolishment of inner hindrances. 4. Regulation and adjustment.
5. Expedient activities of mind. 6. Right practice. 7. The development and manifestation of good qualities. 8. Evil influences. 9. Cure of disease. 10. Realization of Supreme Perfect
Enlightenment.

These ten headings indicate the stages of correct Dhyana

practice. It is imperative, if a follower of Buddha desires to be successful in the practice, that the stages be closely followed and their meaning be put faithfully into practice. If these ten stages are faithfully followed the mind will become tranquil, difficulties will be overcome, powers for concentrating the mind and for gaining insight and understanding will be developed, and in the future Supreme Perfect Enlightenment (*anuttara-samyak-sambodhi*) will be attained.

I

External Conditions

If a disciple undertakes the practice of Dhyana, and to put the lessons of this book into action, he must be in possession of five external conditions. (1) He must resolve to keep the Precepts (as to killing, stealing, sexual impurity, deceit, and use of intoxicants), as it is said in the Sutra that it is in obedience to the Precepts that all intelligence is developed and all suffering is brought to an end. So it is the duty of every disciple to keep the Precepts pure. However, there are three kinds of disciples who observe the Precepts under different conditions. The first kind are those who, before becoming converts, have not committed any of the "five highest offenses." Afterwards, happening to be in personal contact with some learned Master, they are taught the Three Holy Refuges and the Five Fundamental Precepts which are to be observed by every faithful follower of the Lord Buddha. If there is no hindrance developed after conversion they are next taught to keep the ten Additional Precepts of disciples. Afterwards, as they become Bhikshus and Bhikshuni, they are taught to observe the whole spirit of the Precepts. If after conversion they are able to keep the Precepts pure, both in letter and in spirit, they are counted worthy followers of Lord Buddha and will assuredly realise the Buddha-Dharma through their faithful practice of Dhyana. It is as if their robe was perfectly white and ready for dyeing.

The second kind of followers are those who keep the main Precepts but neglect many of the less important ones, but, because of their practice of Dhyana, are repentant. These are recognized as pure keepers of the Precepts, also, and they can progress in the practice of Dhyana and in the attainment of intelligence. It is as if their robe which had been stained and soiled could be worn again after washing and cleansing.

The third kind of followers are those who have been taught to keep the Precepts but who fail to keep even the important ones and who, on the contrary, are breaking both important as well as the less important. According to the rites of the Hinayana there is no way provided for removing the stain caused by the Four Main Violations (any kind of killing, theft, lust, and deceit). But in the Mahayana religious services are provided for the purification of such offences provided there is evidence of sincere penitence and remorse. The Sutra teaches that there are two kinds of "healthy" converts, namely, those who do not commit offences and those who having committed offences are sincerely repentant. The penitent should be in possession of ten indications of his sincerity:— (a) A clear understanding and acceptance of the cause and effect of his offense. (b) To be in a state of fear because of it. (c) To feel humiliation. (d) To search for means of purification, and when he finds them in the Mahayana Sutras to be willing to take advantage of them. (e) A frank confession of his guiltiness. (f) To break off the current of his thoughts relating to the offense. (g) To take advantage of the protective courage which the Dharma offers him. (h) To wish for the emancipation of all sentient beings and to renew his vow to help them all. (i) To keep continually in mind the non-existence of both offense and repentance.

If a penitent has these evidences of sincerity, he should prepare an altar with solemn adornments and purity. Then wearing clean, neat clothes, he should offer on this altar before Buddha's image an offering of flowers and incense. Then he should continue this practice as an evidence of his repentance for a period of one week, or three weeks, or a month, or three months, or even a year, or as long as the conception of guiltiness abides in the mind.

But, you may ask, how will we know that our offense has been cleared away? When we are making whole hearted repentance in agreement with the rites as indicated above, we will experience many different emotions that will bring testimony to our understanding. In the course of our practice of repentance we may feel both our body and mind to be in a state of briskness and lightness, and in our dreams we will see good visions. Or we shall happen to see wonderful signs of good omen, or feel our thoughts unfolding auspiciously. Or we shall feel our body as if it were a cloud drifting about in the free air, or as if, when we are practicing Dhyana, we were sitting in a shadow cast by our body. Under all these conditions we will gradually come to realize many aspects of Dhyana, or, all of a sudden, may realize enlightenment. We shall then understand the significance of all phenomena and, moreover, will gain a deeper conception of the meaning and import of the teachings we have heard from the Sutras. There will be no more griefs nor worries in our minds as we enter into a deeper enjoyment of the Dharma. We will recognize in all these experiences a manifestation and testimonial of our purification from the violation of the Precepts that has been a hindrance in our practice of Dhyana. Henceforth, keeping close to the Precepts, we can rightly practice Dhyana and it will be noticed by others that we have been purified. It is as if the robe that had been ragged and foul had been cleansed and mended and newly dyed.

If any one, having violated the main Precepts, feels that it will hinder his successful practice of Dhyana, let him go before Buddha's image and in earnest humility make a frank confession of his violation. This method of practicing repentance is not in accordance with the way shown in the Sutra, nevertheless, let him discontinue his recollections of guiltiness and resume his practice of Dhyana, sitting up straight with determination, recollecting that his wrong acts have no independent self-nature and keeping in mind the reality of the Buddhas in all the six regions. If his thoughts slip away from his practice, let him get up and go before Buddha's image and with humble and earnest heart, offer incense, repeat his confession, recite the Precepts and a Mahayana Sutra. The hindrances to the practice of Dhyana will be gradually cleared away, the temptation to violate the Precepts will be overcome, and he will progress in the practice of Dhyana. In the Wonderful Expedient Scripture it is written:—

"*Should anyone having committed crimes, come into great agony of spirit, and earnestly desire purification, there is no better way than the practice of Dhyana.*"

He should seek an open and quiet place, sitting up with

determined and concentrated mind, reciting Mahayana Sutras. In this way he will gradually get rid of thought of his guiltiness and in time will realize the usual Dhyana and Samadhis.

(2) The second external condition that one must possess if one is to hope for success in the practice of Dhyana, relates to clothing and food. We should consider clothing from three viewpoints. (a) If we have the fortitude to endure exposure we should follow the example of the great Masters of the Himalaya mountains and have but a single garment, just sufficient to cover one's nakedness. (b) If we move about in the world as itinerant monks, we should follow the example of Mahakasyapa and limit our garments to three and these old and castoff garments. (c) If we live in cold countries, we are permitted by Buddha to have an extra garment. As for a hundred other things that seem to be necessary, we are permitted to retain only one and be satisfied with that. If we permit our minds to become avaricious for many things, our thoughts will become disturbed and the many things will become a hindrance to gaining enlightenment.

Next, in regard to eating. There are four ways of living. (a) The first way is the way followed by the great Masters of the high mountains, who live on the herbs and seasonable fruits. (b) The second way is the way followed by the itinerant monks who live by begging their food and who are able to resist the temptation to live by the four wrong ways, namely, working for others for pay, living by astrology foretelling the changes and effects of the heavenly bodies in human affairs, by geomancy and fortune telling, and finally by flattery and dependence upon the rich and mighty. The danger of these ways of wrong living has been described by Sariputra. (c) The third right way of living is to take up one's abode in some secluded place and to depend in faith upon the gifts of generous laymen. (d) The fourth way of right living is to join some Brotherhood and participate in their communal life. If we are living in any one of these four ways of living, we are sure of all the food and clothing that is necessary. What does this mean? It means that if we lack any of these good conditions, our minds will not abide in peaceful quietude and that would be an impediment to enlightenment.

(3) The third external condition that one must possess if one is to hope for success in the practice of Dhyana, relates to

shelter. A retreat for a follower to be satisfactory must be quiet and free from annoyances and troubles of any kind. There are three kinds of places that are suitable for Dhyana practice: (a) A hermitage in the high and inaccessible mountains. (b) A shack such as would serve a begger or a homeless monk. These should be at least a mile and a half from a village where even the voice of a cowboy would not reach and where trouble and turmoil would not find it. (c) A bed in a monastery apart from a layman's house.

(4) The fourth external condition that one must possess if one is to hope for success in the practice of Dhyana, relates to freedom from entanglement in all worldly affairs. (a) It means to withdraw from all conditional engagements and social responsibilities. (b) It means to give up all worldly friends, relatives, and worldly interests. This means to cut off all social intercourse. (c) It means to give up all worldly business such as busies craftsmen, doctors, clerks, traders, fortune tellers, etc. (d) It means to give up all general study even of a seemingly good kind, such as reading, writing lectures or books, attending lectures, etc. For what reason should these things be given up? It is because if we are interested in these things our minds are not quiet and free for the practice of Dhyana and the attainment of enlightenment. Moreover, if our minds are disturbed or weary or not at peace, one can hardly practice Dhyana.

(5) The fifth external condition that one must possess if one is to hope for success in the practice of Dhyana, relates to association with people. We should keep in close relations with three kinds of noble minded people: The first kind are those outside the Brotherhood who supply us with our food and clothing, and who are competent in taking good care of us and in protecting us from annoyances and troubles. The second kind of noble minded people are the members of our Brotherhood with whom we live in intimacy and mutual forbearance and kindness. The third kind are our teachers and Masters who instruct us and guide us in the use of expedient means to meet both external and internal conditions, and to show us how to become interested and to enjoy ourselves in the practice of Dhyana.

This finishes the discussion of the control of external conditions. We will now turn to a discussion of internal conditions and how to control them.

II

Censorship Over Desires Arising
From the Senses

By the desires that should be placed under censorship are meant the kinds of desires that arise from the senses possessed by every living person, namely, the senses of seeing, hearing, smelling, tasting and touching. If we wish to be successful in the practice of Dhyana we must keep the desires arising from these senses under strict censorship. These five kinds of physical desires may easily lead one into foolishness and illusion and lustful cravings. If we clearly understand that our faults and feelings of guiltiness are but the outcome of these desires, we will no longer cherish them. In order to control these physical desires we must keep close watch over them.

(1) First is the censorship over the desires arising from the use of the eyes, among which we mention as of first importance, sexual desires that arise from seeing crystal eyes, slender brows, crimson lips, snow-white teeth, worldly adornments, garments of beautiful colors—green, yellow, red, white, purple, violet, and so on,—all of which will attract a fool's attention and awaken desires that are evil. It was the mere sight of his paramour's beauty that led King Bimbisara to risk his life in the enemy's country and to stay in the house of Lady Abrahmapara. So it was in the case of the King of Khotan who because of resentment arising from jealousy put many people to death. All such wickednesses have their rise from desires awakened by sight.

(2) Second is the censorship over the desires arising from the use of the ears, among which we mention, musical sounds from harp, twelve-stringed lute, and instruments using silk, bamboo, metal, stone, etc., and from the voices of dancing and singing girls, reciting, praising, etc. No sooner do we, disciples of Buddha, hear these sweet sounds than our hearts are stained and our minds entangled and we are led into evil acts. Such was the fact in the case of the five hundred disciples who lived in a monastery in the Himalayas when they heard the songs sung by a girl named Chindra. They lost their devotion to the practice of Dhyana and became delirious with exciting desires.

By all such causes and conditions we may know that sounds are the source of wickedness and guilt.

(3) Third is the censorship over the desires arising from the use of sense of smell. By this is meant the scent from sexually excited bodies, from beverages, from delicious foods, and from the fragrance from all kinds of smouldering perfumes. In our foolishness we do not recognize the true nature of smelling so no sooner do we smell a fragrance than we desire it and are captivated by it. This unlocks the prison door of moral defilement. Such was the fact in the case of a certain bhikshu. He was so captivated by the fragrance of lotus blossoms in a pond near his monastery that he neglected his practice of Dhyana to indulge his passion for it. The god of the pond rebuked him severely and said:—"Why do you steal my sweet perfume?" Because of our fondness for sweet fragrances we awaken sleeping desires and fall into moral defilement. By recognizing these causes and conditions we know that scents are the cause of evil acts.

(4) The fourth is the censorship over the desires arising from the use of the sense of taste, which means all kinds of sweet tastes in eating and drinking, such as, bitterness, sourness, sweetness, spiciness, saltness and freshness. All such pleasing tastes and flowers besides gratifying the tongue lure the heart into excesses and evil. Such was the fact in the case of a Lamaist monk in Tibet who was so fond of cheese, it is said, that at his death he was changed into a cheese-maggot. By all such instances we know that the sense of taste is the source of much guiltiness.

(5) Fifth is the censorship over the desires arising from the use of the sense of touch. Our body is very sensitive to softness, smoothness, warmth in winter, coolness in summer, etc. We are so ignorant as to the true nature of these sensations that our minds become upset and foolish by the touch of pleasing things, and our effort to attain enlightenment is obstructed and hindered. Such was the fact in the case of a "one-horned evil spirit" who lost his supernormal powers because of his craving after pleasing tangibles. By all such causes and conditions we see the folly and guiltiness of desiring pleasing tangibles and yielding to their seduction.

The several ways for censoring our desires that have been

given above are taken from the *Mahavibhasa* Sutra which, also, makes the following observation.—"*Notwithstanding the annoyances which the gratification of sensual desires brings to us, we go on craving for these desires.*" As these five sensual desires are gratified by anyone, he only becomes more intensely excited. It is like a burning house, the more fuel is added the hotter the flames become. Or, if these sensual desires are not gratified by anyone and he still clings to them, he is like a dog gnawing at rotten bones. Or, if these intensified desires become competitive, they are like birds fighting over their prey. Or, they burn us as though we were holding a blazing torch in the face of the wind. Or, they harm us as though we were treading on serpents. Or, they are like dreams from which we awake in a fright. Or, they have a life no longer than the sparks from a flint. They are looked upon as enemies, by wise men. Notwithstanding all this, we, like deluded fools, go on craving them as long as we live, not realizing that these annoyances and suffering will continue to trouble, after the death of the body, in a following rebirth.

These five kinds of sensual desire were grasped by animals before us and their baneful effects have come down to us. We are their slaves and by reason of their power we may be dragged down into the three lower realms. Even in the sacred moments of Dhyana and Samadhi they close in about us. What unbelievable enemies they are to us! We should flee from them instantly. The *Dhyana* Sutra speaks of them as follows:—

"*The continual sufferings of birth and death are due to thy sensual desires and lusts. When these thy children are grown they become thy enemies and all thy laborious work has been in vain and after the last breath thou art buried in the grave.*

"*How foul is thy dead body; how putrid is a dead corpse! Its nine cavities yield stinking fluids, but, thou, O fool, clingest to it as does a maggot to excrement.*

"*However, thou who art wisest, realizing the body's emptiness and transiency, will not be enslaved by the allurements of its desires but rising free from their fascinations will find thy true Nirvana.*

"*Thou shouldest follow the teaching of Buddha and, as thou sittest in Dhyana shouldest count thy breathing moment by moment with all thy mind and heart. This is the practice of the earnest bhikshu.*"

III

Inner Hindrances to be Abolished

There are five kinds of inner hindrances that must be abolished.

(1) The first kind are the hindrances of sensual desires that have their origin within the mind itself, because of memory or imagination. In the preceding chapter in discussing the external conditions, we referred to the sensual desires, also, but then we had in mind the bodily desires that had their origin in the physical contact of the senses with their objects. Now we are to consider the mental notions of these desires as they arise or linger within the mind itself. A follower of Buddha may be practicing Dhyana in a very solemn manner, but his mind may be filled with seductive notions of these craving sensual desires and their continual activity will effectually prevent good qualities from germinating. So when we become conscious of the presence of these sense-desire notions, we must get rid of them at once. For, as in the case of Jubhaga whose body was consumed by the inner fires of his concupiscence, so we must not be surprised if the flames of these inner desires consume all our good qualities. Those who cherish these inner desires will make little progress on the path that leads to enlightenment. Why is this so? It is because these inner desires are a stronghold of vexations that so engross the mind that they crowd out the very purpose to attain enlightenment. In the Sutra it is written:—

"Thou that seekest enlightenment must be a man of humility and modesty. Thou who holdest out the begging bowl that thou mayest give blessings to all sentient beings, how canst thou indulge in cheap desires for thyself and plunge into the sea of the five hindrances?

"How is it that thou, who has gotten rid of the external desires, hast forsaken all their pleasures and thrown them away without regret, shouldest now seek their shadow? Art thou a fool who returns to his own spittle?

"These notions of sensual desires which thou art hankering for inevitably lead to suffering. If they are gratified there is no satisfaction, and if they are not satisfied there is annoyance. In either case there is no happiness at all.

"What power hast thou to get rid of these pain-producing

desire-notions? When thou hast deeply enjoyed the happiness that arises from the successful practice of Dhyana, then thou wilt no longer be defrauded by these deluding notions."

(2) The second inner hindrance is the hindrance of hatred. This is a most fundamental factor in preventing one from attaining enlightenment. It is both the cause and condition for our fall into the evil existences. It is the enemy that keeps us from enjoying the Buddha's Dharma. It is the thief that steals away our thoughts of good-will toward all sentient beings. It is the fountain of evil words that burst out unchecked. Therefore, in the practice of Dhyana we should treat the mood of hatred as though it was a personality that was annoying not only yourself, but your relatives and enemies; and not only in the present but because of memory in both the past and the future. This makes nine annoyances which will keep alive this mood of hatred. Hatred gives rise to grievances and each added grievance gives rise to more annoyances. Thus hatred goes on disturbing the mind, and that is why we speak of it as fundamental hindrance. We should cut it away at the root and thus prevent it from spreading.

Suprapunna asked the Lord Buddha as follows:—

"What shall we get rid of if we want peace and happiness? What shall we do to get rid of sorrow? What is the poison that devours all our good thoughts?"

"Kill hatred and thou shalt have peace and happiness. Kill hatred and thou shalt have no more sorrow. It is hatred that devours all thy goodness."

Having become fully convinced of the evil of hatred, if one wishes to get rid of it, he must practice both compassion and patience.

(3) The third hindrance is the hindrance of laziness and sleepiness. Laziness means that our mind gets dull and inert; while sleepiness means that our five senses become relaxed, our body becomes immobile, and then we fall asleep. To attain enlightenment we need an alert mind and all such causes and conditions are hindrances that prevent us from experiencing the highest happiness both in our present life and in future lives, and the joy of the Pure Land, and the inconceivable peace of Nirvana. This hindrance is perhaps the most serious of all. Why? Because other hindrances come when we are awake mentally and we can at least make an effort to over-

come them, but the hindrance of laziness and sleepiness makes effort impossible. In sleepiness we are like a dead corpse with no perception and no consciousness.

Even our Lord Buddha and the Mahasattva-Bodhisattvas have had to combat sleepiness, as it is written in the following verses:—

"Get up! Do not lie there clasping a decaying corpse to thy bosom. Even though it passes under the name of man, it is only an aggregation of rubbish. It is as if thou hadst been poisoned by an arrow; in thy pain wouldst thou lazily lie down to sleep? It is as if thou wert tightly bound because thou hadst murdered some one; in thy calamity and fear wouldst thou lie down to sleep?

"This thief and kidnapper might well be our death if you do not repel him forcefully. It is like lying down with a poisonous snake, or it is like lying down in the midst of battle; under such desperate conditions how couldest thou think of indulging in a siesta?

"Thou shouldest realize that laziness and sleepiness leaves you in perfect darkness; it robs you of your intelligence, it dulls wits, it is a drag on your will, it obscures your heart's true purpose. How canst thou lie down to sleep when suffering such losses?"

It is because of these very serious causes and conditions that the mind is given its faculty for noticing and appreciating their danger, and for guarding against and warding off laziness and sleepiness. If laziness and sleepiness are the great foe of the practice of Dhyana, strange to say, the earnest practice of Dhyana is our best weapon against laziness and sleepiness.

(4) The fourth inner hindrance is recklessness and remorse. Recklessness is of three kinds. There is body haste, walking or rambling about with no especial purpose in mind, sports and make-believe and dancing about. Then there is haste and recklessness of lips. The lips seem to find enjoyment in just reciting and singing and disputing and boasting and discussing world affairs, all to no purpose, just for the thrill one gets out of it. The third is mind recklessness. This means careless thinking, idle day-dreams, the perversion of the mind's powers to selfish and acquisitive ends when they should be used for the attainment of enlightenment. Then there is the waste of the mind upon the unnecessary discrimination of external differ-

ences and the diversion of it into the enjoyment of worldly writings and artistic pursuits, or the frittering away of it in concentration upon sentimentality and emotionalism, and the absorption of it in contemplation of beautiful sights, music, delicacies, fragrance, softness, and the seductive rhythm and cadence of beautiful thoughts.

It is as if a person, who had made up his mind to strictly control his mind, deliberately forgets his purpose and lets his mind run along the easiest channel. What does it mean to be a reckless person? He is no better than an intoxicated elephant free of its chains, or a wild camel held by the nose. Concerning this hindrance, it is written in the Sutra:—

"O thou, who hast become a monk, hast shaved the head, hast gone begging from door to door, why dost thou indulge in light and reckless manners, when thou knowest that by such careless conduct and indulgence thou wilt imperil all the benefits of the Dharma that might be thine?"

As soon as we become aware of what we are risking by such reckless acts and habits we should give them up once for all. Because as soon as we become aware of our guiltiness and do not give them up then remorse will spring up and that will intensify the hindrance, where recklessness without remorse would not be so serious. Why is this? The reason is this: We may have reckless habits without thinking much about it and then remorse will not spring up to disturb the mind. It is in the quiet of Dhyana practice that remorse with its burden of sadness and regret and vexation rises to disturb the mind and prevent its concentration. That is why recklessness and remorse are so great a hindrance to the practice of Dhyana. There are two kinds of remorse, namely, one kind comes after recklessness as stated above, the other kind preceeds further recklessness. It is the fear that always shadows the life of a criminal. It is like an arrow that has penetrated so deep that it cannot be removed. As the Sutra says:—

"Because thou doest what thou oughtest not to do, and doest not what thou oughtest to do, thy life is replete with remorse and vexation, whereby thou shalt fall at thy death into an evil existence.

"If thou hast committed an offence and felt remorse for it and afterward art able to keep thy mind from its grievance, thy heart will be happy and peaceful, but be thou careful not

to reawaken the mind either to the offence or to the remorse.

"*There are two kinds of remorse in which the foolish man is accustomed to indulge. The first is for things done which ought not to have done; the second is for things which he ought to have done but which he did not do.*

"*The reason why both these kinds of remorse are foolish is because they do not express the true state of the mind, and because the offence having occurred it is too late for thee to undo it.*"

(5) The fifth inner hindrance is the hindrance of doubt. If the mind is clouded with doubt, how can it have any faith in the teaching? And if it has no faith in the teaching, how can it profit by it? It is as if one was going up a mountain for treasure but had no hands with which to bring back any of the treasure. There are some "honest doubts" which do not entirely hinder the practice of Dhyana, but there are three kinds of doubt that most effectually hinder the attainment of Samadhi. The first kind of doubt that hinders successful Dhyana is doubt of oneself. We may question whether we are the right one to attempt the Noble Path inasmuch as we are temperamentally gloomy and dull and our faults and offenses are many and serious. If in the very beginning we cherish such doubt as that, we will never attain any development of Samadhi. So, if we are to practice Dhyana, we should not be contemptuous of ourself. We should remind ourselves that it is impossible for anyone to fathom the depth that some root of goodness lies buried in our past lives.

The second kind of doubt is doubt of our Master. We may have been displeased with his manner or appearance and doubted whether he had attained any degree of enlightenment and would be able to guide us along the path. If we cherish such doubt or contempt for our Master it will certainly hinder our attainment of Samadhi. If we wish to get rid of this hindrance we should recall the words of the *Mahavibhasa* Sutra in its parable of the miser who kept his gold in a bag of rubbish. If we love the gold of enlightenment we, too, must keep it in our rubbish bag. Although our Master is not perfect as we think he ought to be, we should honor and trust him just the same, because he stands for us in Buddha's place.

The third kind of doubt is doubt of the Dharma. Nearly every one of us, no doubt, retains some measure of confidence in his own mental judgment, and, therefore, it will be hard for us at first to have faith in the teachings of the Master when they differ from what we think they ought to be, and it will be hard at first to put his teachings into practice humbly and faithfully. So long as we cherish doubts of our Master, we can not be much influenced by his teachings. This is clearly explained in the following stanzas:—

"Just as a man standing where roads cross and questioning which way he ought to go, so we are facing the true nature of things. If we cherish doubts as to our ability to know and to choose the right way, it is not likely that we will put much earnestness or zeal in our search.

"If, in our ignorance as we face the true nature of things, seeing bad and good, mortality and Nirvana, we doubt our Master, we resign ourselves to the bondage of life and death. We will be like a deer chased by a lion with no hope of escape.

"In thy ignorance, facing the true nature of things obscured by the world's appearances and changes, thou hadst better have faith in the good Dharma and follow its teachings with zeal and confidence. Standing where the ways of life cross, have faith and courage to choose the right."

Faith is the only entrance to Buddhism. Without faith all earnest study and constant effort will be of no avail. Just as soon as you are convinced that error always follows doubt, give up all doubt and enter the gateway of faith.

Some one may ask:—*"There are as many different kinds of error as there are grains of dust, why do you speak of giving up only five doubts?"* That is true, but these five doubts cover the whole field of greed, hatred and foolishness. Doubt, greed, hatred and foolishness, are the four bad ways that are fundamental. Beyond the gateway of doubt open all the paths, said to be eighty-four thousand in number, that lead to worldly suffering. If we close the gate of doubt we block the way to all evil.

For these reasons, the followers of Buddha should get rid of the five inner hindrances of greed, anger and hatred, laziness and sleepiness, recklessness and remorse, and doubt. Getting rid of these five hindrances is like having a debt remitted, it is like recovering from a painful sickness, it is passing from a famine-stricken country into a land of prosperity, it is like living in peace and safety in the midst of violence and enmity with no apparent reason for it. If we have given up all these hindrances our minds will be fresh and happy and our spirits will be tranquil and peaceful.

Just as the brightness of the sun may be obscured by smoke, or dust, or clouds, or mist, or Rahula or the Asuras may hide its brightness behind their palms, so the pure brightness of our minds may be obscured by these five hindrances.

IV

Regulating and Readjusting

When we, the followers of Buddha, begin to learn the practice of Dhyana, we do so because we wish to put into practice all the teachings of all the Buddhas of the Ten Quarters, past, present and future. We should, at the very beginning, besides desiring to attain supreme Enlightenment, make an earnest vow to emancipate all sentient beings. Our purpose to do this should be as firm and unchangeable as is gold or steel; we should be energetic and courageous even to the sacrifice of our lives; we should never be turned aside or backward even after we have attained all the Buddha-Dharmas. Having made this vow in all sincerity, we may sit up with right thoughts contemplating the true nature of all things, for all things, merit and demerit, memory and forgetfulness, the false consciousness that arises from the sense perception of objects and from the process of the mind, all kinds of impure outflowings of the mind and evil passions, all the laws in the triple world of cause and effect, of birth and death, and doing and not-doing, all are now within the grasp of the mind. This is written in the *Dasa-bhumika* Sutra which says:

"There is nothing in the triple world but the operation of our own minds. When thou dost realize that there is no personality in thy mind then thou wilt recognize that there is no reality in things as well."

If our thoughts do not become attached or influenced by things then action, deeds, birth and death, all cease and never have been. After recalling all these things, then begin the real practice of Dhyana in accordance with the orderly stages given here.

Now let us consider the fourth heading—What is meant by regulating and readjusting? It may be likened to the work of a potter. Before he can begin to form a bowl or anything else, he must first prepare the clay—it must neither be too soft nor too hard. Just as a violinist must first regulate the tension of the different strings—they must be in perfect tune—before he can produce harmonious music. So it is just the same in our case. Before we can control our mind for the attainment of enlightenment, we must first regulate and adjust the inner conditions.

To be able to secure the right regulation and readjustment of conditions for our practice of Dhyana there are five lessons to be learned. If these lessons are learned and applied, then Samadhi can be easily attained, otherwise a great deal of difficulty will be experienced and our tender root of goodness can hardly sprout.

(1) The first lesson relates to our habits of eating. Eating is necessary for the support of the body and mind in its search for enlightenment, but too much eating would clog the system and cause sickness that would be a distress and hindrance to our practice. On the other hand if we take too little food there will be an emaciated body, the distress of hunger, a feeble and unstable mind, a weak and uncertain purpose. Neither of these two extremes is the right way to attain the fruits of Dhyana. If we eat repulsive food our minds will be disturbed and our understanding confused and bewildered. If we take improper food we invite sickness and our strength of purpose fails. For these reasons we should be very careful of our eating. The Sutra says:—

"The strength of purpose to attain enlightenment will vary with the strength of thy body. Eating and drinking should be under restraint; thou shouldest keep thy mind tranquil by avoiding disturbing thoughts. When the mind is calm, thou will find satisfaction in zealous practice of Dhyana. These are the teachings of all the Buddhas."

(2) The second lesson relates to the regulation of laziness and sleep. Sloth is one of the besetting hindrances and no indulgence should be allowed it. If we give too much time to sleep we shall be wasting time that might be given to our practice, or that might better be employed in industry. Too much sleep brings dullness of mind and drowns our good qualities in deep seas of gloominess. We should recollect our impermanence and make good use of the time by restraining our laziness

and sleepiness. By so doing the brain is refreshed and the thoughts purified, and, as we realize Samadhi, the heart will be at rest as in a holy sepulchre. In the Sutra it is written:—

"In the evening and after midnight, thou shalt not forget thy practice of Dhyana."

Just because it is natural to be slothful and sleepy, we ought not to spend our lives in idle comfort—such a life is vain and fruitless. We should remember that the conflagration of impermanence is sweeping over the world and we should not yield to sloth and sleepiness in seeking deliverance.

(3) The third, fourth and fifth lessons relate to the right control of the body,—its physical state, its breathing, and its mental state. They are to be considered as the beginning, the middle and the ending of one regulation. In order to concentrate the mind in Dhyana, we must first regulate the condition and position of the body, then of its breathing, and finally of its mental states. This means that before we begin Dhyana we must keep close watch over our physical activities and states, such as walking, working, standing, sitting, etc., lest we become over-tired or excited and our breathing become rapid and forced. The mind then will be in no good condition to begin practice. It will be disturbed, vexed, clouded, and far from tranquil. We ought to take precautions against such a state at all times, whether we are expecting to practice Dhyana soon or not, so that our mind will always be fresh and transparent and in good condition. But, especially, before beginning Dhyana we should take careful thought as to the condition of the body. We should also take careful thought as to the place where we are to carry on the practice. We should find a place that will be free from disturbance and that will not offer any unnecessary difficulties to the practice.

Next we should consider the position of the body. We should cross the feet with the left foot on the right, draw the legs close to the body so that the toes are in line with the outside of the thighs. This is the half position. If you wish to take the full position, simply place the left foot on the right thigh and the right foot on the left thigh and at right angles to each other.[1] Next we should loosen the girdle and arrange the garments so that they will not become disarranged during

---

[1] The full position is impossible to most Europeans and can only be taken after long practice begun in youth.

practice. Next we place our left palm upon the right hand and place the hands on the left foot which we draw close to the body. Next we straighten up the body, swaying it several times to find its center, the backbone neither too bent nor too straight. Next we straighten our neck so that the nose is in a perpendicular line with the navel. Next open the mouth and breathe out all bad air from the lungs slowly and carefully so as not to quicken the circulation. Then close the mouth and breathe in fresh air through the nose. If the body is well regulated, once is enough, otherwise do it two or three times.

Next close the lips with tongue resting against the upper palate. Close the eyes easily simply to shut out unnecessary light. In this position sit firmly as if you were a foundation stone. Do not let your body, head, hands or feet move about. This is the best way for regulating the body for the practice of Dhyana. Do not be hurried about it nor unduly sluggish.

(4) The fourth lesson relates to the regulation of breathing. Breathing may be divided into four kinds,—blowing, panting, audible and silent, only the last of which can be said to be in a regulated adjusted state. By blowing is meant that we feel our breath being forcibly sent through the nose. By panting is meant that our breathing is too hurried and hard. By audible is meant that when sitting we can hear a faint sound of the breath as it passes through the nose. If we were standing or working we would not notice it, but in our practice it is enough to distract the mind. By silent breathing is meant that there is no sound, no compression, no force, simply the slightest feeling of the tranquillity of our breathing, which does not disturb the mind but rather gives to the mind a pleasant feeling of security and peace. Blowing disturbs concentration, panting gives it heaviness, audible breathing wearies it. We can attain Samadhi only with silent breathing.

This then is the lesson concerning breathing that we are to learn at the beginning of our practice of Dhyana. Wear loose clothes, let the wind blow over and refresh the body; imagine that every pore of the body is participating in the breathing. Let the breathing be neither forceful nor hasty, let it be gentle and natural and deliberate. By so doing the mind will be clear, sickness will be avoided, and there will be enjoyment in the practice and a successful issue from it.

(5) The fifth lesson relates to the regulation and adjust-

ment of the mind. There are three stages of this regulation, in entering Dhyana, in practicing it, and in retiring from it. In entering Dhyana the mind is to be brought into an empty and tranquil state. The uncontrolled and half-unconscious current of confused and vagrant thinking must be brought to a stop. Second, these vagrant thoughts must be prevented from again arising and all bad states of mind, such as discouragement or aimlessness, or lack of control, or too great tension, are to be avoided. Let us speak more at length about these bad mental states that are to be regulated and adjusted. When we are sitting erect and perfectly still the mind very easily falls into drowsiness and becomes inattentive and the head nods. At such moments it is advisable to focus the mind's attention on the tip of the nose but still keeping the mind empty and tranquil. This will prevent the mind from sinking into discouragement or aimlessness. Again, when we are sitting erect and perfectly still the mind very easily passes out of control and drifts about. The body becomes lax and all sorts of vagrant thoughts arise and pass away. At such times it is advisable to focus attention on the navel which tends to unify the mind and prevent confusion. So long as the restless activities of the mind are brought to a standstill there will naturally be tranquillity. That is, if our minds are regulated and adjusted there will be neither sinking nor drifting about.

As to the aspect of over strain, by this is meant that, because of our earnest effort to practice concentration we overdo the matter and use wrong means and the brain becomes tired and possibly there are fatigue pains in the head and chest. At such times we should relax our effort slightly and give up trying to forcibly eject the vagrant thoughts, letting them pass away more naturally, which they will do if for a moment we focus the mind on the navel.

As to the aspect of too great looseness of mind-control there is likely to be dullness and dispersion of attention, the body will lose its erectness, the mouth will open and the saliva drivel, and sleepiness will overcome it. On such occasions we should renew attention and effort toward mind-control by which the mind and body will be mutually helpful in attaining success. To attain this success there must be a progressive advance from a state of physical activity to a state of mental tranquillity. Just as the breathing is to become gentle and inaudible, so the current of the mind's activity is to become gentle and unnoticed. Just as we regulate the activities of the body, so we are to regulate and adjust the activities of the mind until there is tranquillity and peacefulness.

In the second teaching of the fifth lesson—regulating the mind as it abides in Dhyana—we are to employ three kinds of regulation. We are to use our brain to concentrate our mind at every moment of our sitting, and we are to use skillful means for extending the sittings from one hour, to two hours, to four hours, to even six hours out of the twenty-four. To be able to do this we must have perfect control over the condition of our bodies, our breathing and our minds, and must be able to regulate and adjust these conditions so that they will be in the best condition during the whole progress of the sitting. If, during the progress of the sitting, we become conscious that the body has relaxed into a loose or strained state, or a slouching attitude, we should immediately regulate and restore it to its former erect and attentive state. We have to do this again and again. Then, our body may be erect but our breathing may be wrong, constrained, panting, or audible. We must correct this at once, until it is gentle, continuous and silent.

Next, though both body and breathing may be regulated, the mind may be drifting, or sinking, or it may be too lax, or, too constrained. As soon as we become conscious of it, we should again bring it into adjustment as before. For the regulating of these three, body, breathing and mind, there is no fixed order, we should simply regulate and adjust whichever and whenever we notice any one of them to be in an improper state. As long as we sit in practice we should keep body, breathing and mind in perfect control and harmonious adjustment. If this is done there will be no relapses and no hindrance to the certain attainment of enlightenment.

In the third teaching of the fifth lesson—how to withdraw from Dhyana—there are three things to be attended to. First, we should gently relax the mind, open the mouth and exhale the air as though to empty it from every part of the body and arteries and veins. Then we should move our body little by little; next our shoulders, hands and neck; next our feet until they become flexible; then gently rub the body; next rub the hands until the blood circulates warmly; and not until then should we open our eyes and rub them with our warm hands. Finally sit quietly for a moment or two and then get up quietly and go away. If we proceed otherwise, if we break in suddenly upon our meditation and hurry away, the conditions of the body in Dhyana being different from the conditions of active life, there will be disharmony, perhaps a feeling of headache or of paralysis in the joints, which will linger in the mind as a feeling of annoyance and uneasiness that will prejudice the mind against a following sitting. Therefore, we should be attentive and careful in retiring from the practice. As we retire from a state of minimum activity of mind back to maximum activity of the body we should do it gradually and thoughtfully, carrying over into our ordinary life the practice of concentration of mind. There is a stanza that refers to this:—

"Thou shalt not only make rules for thy sitting, but thou shalt make rules for thy retirement from sitting so that there will be no jolt between the minimum activity of the mind and the maximum activity of the body. You should be like a good horseman who has perfect control of his horse."

It is also written in the Lotus of the Wonderful Law Sutra:—

"For the sake of the Enlightenment of all the Buddhas, the Bodhisattva-Mahasattvas assembled here have devoted their lives with zeal and perseverance. They have experienced the hundreds of thousands of myriads of kotis of Samadhis as they have entered Dhyana, abided in Dhyana and retired from Dhyana. They have attained transcendental powers, have practiced the practice of Brahma for long periods, have studied all the scriptures, for innumerable numbers of thousands of myriads of kotis of aeons."

V

Expedient Activities of Mind

In practicing Dhyana the mind should be possessed by five expedient activities or states. The first of these is an activity of wishfulness or purpose. It is willfulness in the sense of paramount desire, or preference of directive control. If we are to attain the object of Dhyana, we should wish and purpose to avoid all false and worldly thoughts and hindering states of mind and all confused and shifting attention, and should make the attainment of the object of Dhyana, namely the attainment of tranquillity, of transcendental knowledge and wisdom, the mind's paramount desire and purpose. The Lord Buddha said:—

"Of all thy good qualities, a wishful purpose is the principle cause."

The second expedient activity of the mind is characterized by an earnest and zestful spirit. It means to keep the precepts with a persevering earnestness of spirit; it means to give up the five hindrances, and to persevere in our practice with wholehearted zeal both in the evening and in the early morning. If you were trying to get fire from a twirling stick you would not expect to be successful if you did it intermittently; you must persist with increasing effort until the fire comes. So you must seek enlightenment with the same earnest zeal.

The third expedient activity of the mind is mindfulness and recollection. It means that we should always keep in mind the emptiness and deceptive aspect of the world with all its fraud and suffering, and should always cherish thoughts of the nobility and value of the enlightenment that comes from the practice of Dhyana. It is noble because it leads to the highest attainment of realization and wisdom and compassion. It opens up the capacity of the mind for the enjoyment of the highest powers of cognition, it gives one an intuition of the blessedness that follows the extinction of the intoxicants, it enables one to realize the highest joy when perfect wisdom is devoted to the deliverance of all sentient beings. This is what is meant by recollective mindfulness.

The fourth expedient activity of the mind is keenness of insight. We should ponder over a comparison of the enjoyments of the world with those that come with the practice of Dhyana. We should think with penetrating insight as to whether there is loss or gain, as to whether the gain from the practice of Dhyana is inconsiderable or of highest importance. The delights of the world are illusive and delusive, one needs keenness of insight to judge them rightly. The world's fascinations often obscures its suffering and unreality. If we consider it carefully and truly we are bound to see that desire for the world and its illusions is a loss and not a gain.

On the contrary, the same keenness of insight will convince

one that the practice of Dhyana brings one inestimable gain of intuitive realization and transcendental intelligence that are free from all intoxicants and are unconditioned. To live in a quiet and secluded place, to feel free from the bondage of life and death, its unhappiness and its suffering, to sit quietly in Dhyana, is of highest importance and value. Keenness of insight will keep these differences clear before the mind and will aid one in the earnest practice of Dhyana.

The fifth expedient activity of the mind is clearness and singleness. It means that we should understand clearly the true nature of the world as being pain-producing and abominable, and, at the same time, we should know well that the tranquillity and intelligence of the mind brought about by the practice of Dhyana is very precious and honorable. With this clearness and singleness of mind we should determine unreservedly to practice Dhyana with our mind as resistant as gold or diamond, so that we will be able to resist and cast off all evil influences of devas, maras and thirthakas, that might tend to discourage us. Even though we are unconscious of any marked success in our practice, clearness and singleness of mind will keep us from neglecting the practice or from turning back. A man before he begins a journey will have a clear idea as to where and why he is going and then after that will not be easily turned aside, so a man in his practice of Dhyana should have a clear and single mind, if he is to hope for success.

VI

Right Practices

In the practice of Dhyana there are two aspects to be considered. The first relates to the sitting, and the other relates to the circumstances and conditions.

1. First as the right practice of sitting. Dhyana can be practiced when one is walking, standing, sitting or reclining, but the position of sitting being the best for its practice, that is considered first. It may be considered under five different heads. (1) First, in its relation to the many and confused thoughts that fill the mind at the beginning of the practice. First we should practice stopping of thoughts in order to bring these many thoughts to a standstill and break off thinking altogether. If we have difficulty in doing this we should next

practice examination of thoughts. That is, to get rid of the many and confused thoughts that ordinarily crowd the mind at the beginning of Dhyana, we must practice "stopping and examining." We will explain this practice of "stopping and examining" in two ways. (a) As to "stopping." There are three ways of doing this. It can be done by recalling the wandering attention to some part of the body as the tip of the nose or the navel, by so doing the many and wandering thoughts drop out of attention and disappear. It says in one of the Sutras: *"Thou must keep thy mind under control without any relaxation; thou shouldest keep it under control as thou wouldest a monkey."* It can be done by bringing attention to only one thought when the other will pass away, after which the one thought can more easily be excluded. The Sutra says that of the six senses, the mental process is of highest importance; if we control the mind we control the other five senses and the perceptions that spring from them. Again it can be done by recalling the true nature of all objects of thought. We should recall that every object of thought arises from causes and conditions and therefore has no self-nature of its own. Recollecting this the mind will have no reason for grasping it and it will fall away. Referring to this the Sutra says:—

"There is no substance in phenomena for phenomena are made up of causes and conditions. Thou art called a disciple because thou dost recognize the true nature of all things and art able to stop thy mind from dwelling upon them."

When we begin to practice meditation, at first our thoughts continue and ramble about without any cessation. We try to realize their true nature and to employ different means for stopping them but the delusive thoughts continue to flow on. In this case we should reflect upon the history of the thought that has arisen:—in the past it must have taken some form that has now been exterminated; and we know that in its present form it has no actual existence; and in the future it will have no more reality. By this consideration we realize that the phenomena of thought has no reality by which it can be grasped, either in the past, present nor future, and so we exclude it from attention.

Although we may be convinced by our insight that this continuing stream of thoughts has no substantial existence and we are able in the main to exclude it from attention, but there still may remain a consciousness of flickerings of thought spring-ing up occasionally from moment to moment. In this case we should try to realize the true nature of consciousness by which we notice these momentary flickerings of thought. Conscious-ness arises when the six external objects of thought are brought into contact with the six senses and the six internal sense-minds react to them. So long as the six internal sense-minds are not in contact with the six external objects of sense, no conscious-ness of them will arise. Applying this to the consciousness of thoughts that we are convinced have no existence in the past, present nor future, we are forced to recognize that all such phenomena are mere assumptions of the mind. Being thus con-vinced as to the rising, extermination, and future unreality of thoughts, we exclude them from further attention and the mind becomes tranquil. As the mind becomes tranquil, we more and more become convinced as to the unreality of all thought, even the notion of our own existence. This is the ultimate principle of tranquillity and peacefulness that is embodied in the concep-tion of Nirvana where all thought comes to a natural and final end. In *the Lotus of the Wonderful Law* Sutra it is said that as soon as the mind becomes diffused we should bring it back into right mindfulness, and keep it under control of right mindfulness. This means that it is not by diffusion and scat-tering of thought that thought can be brought to a standstill but it is by concentration and mindfulness. The human mind is not an entity with its own phenomena that can be grasped and held by continued and forced effort, even right mindfulness is only an efficient means for controlling its activities. By this is meant that at the beginning of our practice of Dhyana we will find difficulty in controlling and excluding thought which if effected by too much violence may result in insanity. It is like becoming proficient in archery—we must take a long time for practice if we are to become proficient.

(b) Second, as to "stopping and examining," we will now consider the control of vagrant thoughts by examining, or ob-serving, or making insight. One way is by opposing bad state of mind with its corresponding good state, as for instance, thoughts of purity as opposing licentious thoughts and desires, thoughts of kindness as opposing hatred, thoughts of the five grasping aggregates that make up personality as opposing egoism, and thinking about the breath in controlling too much effort at the beginning, or controlling rising thoughts during the practice. Another way is to oppose definite things or thoughts with consideration of the causes and conditions that make them what they are, namely, empty, transitory and egoless. By doing this, the hold of these passing thoughts upon the attention will be broken and they will pass away as we note their vanity, and new thoughts will be less likely to arise. The discussion of this means of examining is referred to all through this treatise so we will say no more about it at this time. It is also stated in a Sutra:—

"All phenomena are impermanent, existing simply in our own minds, and so, as we see the unsubstantial character of all things, knowing them simply as objects of sense, thou shouldest devote no more thought to them."

(2) Second in the relation of the practice of Dhyana to such "sicknesses" of the mind as sinking and drifting. Often during the progress of the sitting the mind will become darkened or obscured or inattentive or unconscious or sleepy. On such occasions we should practice a reflecting insight; we should practice "stopping to stop them." This is a very brief suggestion for the treatment of these sicknesses of the mind's sinking and drifting, but in adopting it you should be careful to have the remedy fit the disease for there should be no inappropriateness.

(3) In the relation of the sitting practice of Dhyana we should take advantage of every means available to secure tranquillity of mind. As has been said, if the mind is disturbed or over active or sinking, we should practice stopping and examining. If the mind does not become tranquil, then we should practice "stopping to stop" our thoughts. If the body and mind then become calm and peaceful we have reason to believe that the remedy was suitable for the disease and we should use it as occasion demands. If in practicing Dhyana we feel the mind to be unsteady and not advancing toward tranquillity notwithstanding our practice of "stopping to stop," then we should try some form of insight. If, as soon as we employ insight, we notice that the mind is more serene and pure as well as tranquil and peaceful, then we know that insight was adapted to our need and we should employ it at once, in order to complete the pacification. This is a brief statement of the way to use adjustment means in the practice of stopping and reflecting.

But all these suggestions should be followed with care and discrimination if we are to expect the good results of a tranquil and peaceful mind and the following rewards of successful practice of Dhyana.

(4) The fourth relation of the practice of stopping and examining to our practice of Dhyana is the treatment of minimum thought in the concentration of mind. This means that after using stopping and insight for the suppression of confused and maximum thinking, we should now use it for the control of minimum thinking. As soon as our confused maximum thinking is tranquilized we attain a measure of concentration and because of that the mind enters into a more subtle state. Because the body and mind are comparatively tranquil and peaceful there is a feeling of exhilaration in which state it is easy for minimum thoughts of heretical prejudice to seep in. If we do not recognize this and do not adopt ways to prevent these false and deluding thoughts from arising they will easily increase and run into thoughts of egoism and craving desire. As soon as the mind begins to crave things it has already forsaken the idea of emptiness and has reinstated the idea that some things have a real existence. If we recall to mind the universal emptiness then these two vexations of sense-perception and desire will be eliminated and the mind will continue tranquil. This is the practice of stopping. But if these thoughts of sensation and craving continue to arise it proves that the mind is still in bondage, and we must try the other remedy of insight into the nature of these minimum thoughts. As soon as we recall their unsubstantial character we will cease to be attached to them; as soon as we cease desiring them they will quickly pass away being only the vexations of a moment. This is a brief account of the remedy of stopping and insight as applied to the minimum thoughts that arise in the course of our practice of Dhyana. There is a slight difference between stopping and insight which must be kept in mind when we come to passing out of concentration because a mistaken use of them at that time would be serious.

(5) The fifth relation of the practice of stopping and examining pertains to the need of establishing an equilibrium between Dhyana and intelligence. If, in the practice of Dhyana, we come into concentration of mind, either by the method of stopping or by the method of insight, and have no attainment

of intelligence, it is an ignorant form of concentration and can not cut away our bonds of mental habits. Again, we may have attained a little intelligence but not enough to develop into full intelligence or to wholly remove the bonds of defilement. In such a case we should apply the insight of analysis to our bonds and defilements, and by so doing would be able to get rid of them and thereafter would be able to realize concentration with intelligence and thus be able to employ the right ways for the attainment of enlightenment.

As we are sitting up and practicing Dhyana, especially by the means of insight, it is possible that all of a sudden we will be enveloped in a wave of intuition and intelligence, but as our power of concentration is still weak, our mind will be weak and fluctuating like a candle flame in the wind, so this measure of transcendental intelligence will not be lasting. Under this condition we must again go back to the method of stopping all thought. Then by the patient practice of stopping all thought, the mind will come to be like a candle in a closed room that burns steadily and brightly. This is a brief account of the methods of stopping and examining applied to securing equilibrium between concentration and intelligence, or concentration and realization. If we practice Dhyana with the body in right position and make good use of these five means for securing right conditions of the mind, choosing the one that is most appropriate at the time, we will soon become competent and will be able to make good use of our whole life.

2. We now come to a consideration of the second division of right practice of Dhyana. The first division had to do with right sitting and right conditions of mind control. This division has to do with the employment of stopping and examining in the circumstances to be encountered and to the conditions to be experienced. It is of first importance that we sit up in proper position but as the body is under bondage its condition is not always the same and the circumstances vary. We should learn to practice stopping and examining under whatever circumstances we are placed and in whatever condition we find ourselves. Otherwise the practice would be intermittent, the practicing mind would be checked by reverses, the bonds of desire and grasping would be renewed, and the defilement of habits would be intensified. Under these circumstances how can we expect to advance in our understanding of the Dharma or

in our powers of cognition? But if we keep our minds steadily under control and constantly employ the best means for practicing then we will steadily advance in our power of understanding and realizing.

Now, let us ask, what is meant by practicing stopping and examining in relation to conditions and experience? Under the heading of conditions and experience there are six conditions and six aspects of experience, making twelve items to be considered. (1) First as to the condition of acting, (2) while standing, (3) while sitting, (4) while reclining, (5) while doing things, (6) while speaking. In these conditions there are six aspects of behavior, namely, (7) as regards eyes toward sights, (8) of ears toward sounds, (9) of nose toward smells, (10) of tongue toward tastes, (11) of the body toward tangibles, (12) and of the mind toward ideas. We will now explain the relation of stopping and examining toward these six conditions and six aspects.

(1) Acting. When engaged in any activity we should ask this question:—For what reason am I engaged in this activity? If we are conscious that we are acting from some unworthy motive—because of discouragement, vexation, or some other evil instinct—we should cease the action. But if we are conscious that we are acting from some good motive, such as charity or some spiritual service, then we should go on with the activity. If we go on with the activity we should concentrate the mind on the pure activity with no ulterior purpose in mind. If we cease the activity, or the mind is disturbed by desires or angry or egoistic thoughts, then we should practice stopping. What is meant by this? It means that the mind should be tranquillized by getting rid of the thoughts which prompt the action. Action in itself is unwise as it leads to further multiplicity and increased confusion and dissatisfaction and suffering. Action is warranted by some good purpose and when the mind is convinced of this it will be quieted and if there is no good purpose in mind the activity will cease. The acting mind and all that eventuates from its activity have no reality that can be taken hold of. When this is fully understood, the disturbing activity of the mind will cease and with it the activity of the body. This is what is meant by practicing stopping under the conditions of action.

What is meant by practicing examining or insight under

these same conditions? This means that we should recall that the mind is crowded with impulses to activity which have no substance in themselves and which lead to vexation and disturbances good and bad. We should reflect upon this and realize that neither the acting mind or the following action has any true existence but are alike empty and vain. This is what is meant by the practice of examining under the condition of acting.

(2) Standing. If we are standing because we are vexed or disturbed or are seeking some selfish thing, then we should cease standing. But if we are standing for some good purpose we should remain standing but with tranquil mind. What is meant by standing? When a man is standing he is neither active nor at rest; he is simply "standing by," that is, in a position to begin activity or to sit down and relax. What is meant by practicing stopping and examining under these conditions of "standing by?" If in this condition we recall that by remaining in it we shall experience all manner of vexation and disturbance good and evil, and also recall that our standing-by-mind and all that arises from it by its manifestation in activity have no substance that can be grasped, then the deluding thoughts are quieted and activity ceases.

Now what is meant by practicing examining or insight under the condition of standing-by? It means that the mind being located in the brain is the cause of all the following vexations and disturbances both good and bad, which should lead us to reflect that not only are the vexatious and disturbing activities empty of any substance, but so, also, is the "personality" that seems to initiate the thoughts of standing-by and the thoughts of activity, and that all alike are emptiness and vanity. This explains the practice of examining.

(3) Sitting. We have already discussed the problem of the application of stopping and examining to the condition of sitting in the practice of Dhyana; we will now only refer to it briefly. First we should ask ourselves the question:—Why am I sitting here? If we are sitting because of vexation and a disturbed mind, we should not do it. But if it is for some good, unselfish purpose then we should take our seat with a concentrated but tranquil mind. What is meant by practicing stopping under the condition of sitting? When we are sitting, we should comprehend that by our sitting there will be all kinds of dis-

turbances and vexations, good and bad, and by so comprehending we will prevent the arising of delusive thoughts. This is the practice of stopping. By the practice of examining at the time of sitting, we mean, that at the time of encountering the vexations and disturbing experiences while we are sitting in practice, we should recall that it is by our sitting with legs crossed and body in right attitude, that we are encountering these vexations and disturbances, but that they have no substance and will pass away. And just as we reflect that the sitting-mind has no substance of its own, so the sitting "personality" has no existence and is nothing but vanity and emptiness. This is the practice of examining as applied to the condition of sitting.

(4) Reclining. We should keep in mind the question as to why we are lying down. If it is because we are lazy and sleepy we aught not to do it, but if it is the regular time for sleep, or because we truly need rest, then we should do so with tranquil mind. When we lie down we should take the position the lion takes—on his right side with his feet crossed. What is meant by stopping at this time? When we are about to rest or sleep, we should recall that various disturbances and vexations of mind will follow but that all of them are unsubstantial and unreal and with that recollection the mind will become tranquil. By this is meant the practice of stopping at the time of reclining.

What is meant by examining at the time of reclining? We should recall that it is by our hard labor and following weariness that we have become fatigued and our senses dulled. From this will follow many disturbances and vexations but that all of them, good and bad alike, are empty of any self-substance and are empty and vain. We should recall also that the reclining "personality" and all that arises from the condition of reclining are nothing but emptiness and vanity. This is the practice of examination under conditions of lying down.

(5) Doing things. When we are prompted to do things we should ask ourselves, why should we do them? If it is an instinctive act, or an evil, selfish act we should not do it. If it is a good act for the welfare of others then we should do it. During the act various vexatious and disturbing thoughts will arise both good and bad. To get rid of these thoughts we should practice stopping by means of realizing the emptiness

and vanity of all thoughts, by reason of which practice the deluding thoughts will disappear. This is the practice of stopping at the time of doing things.

The practice of examining at the time of doing things means that we should be mindful that we are doing things with our hands and body wholly under command of the mind and that as a result we are experiencing all manner of vexatious and disturbing thoughts. We should reflect upon this, and because these thoughts and acts have no substance of their own we should lose confidence in them. We should also recall that the doing—"personality" and all that arises from its doings are nothing after all but emptiness and vanity. This is what is meant by the practice of examining and insight under the condition of doing things.

(6) Speaking. While we are speaking we should keep in mind the reason for our speaking. If it is mere arguing, or vexatious discussion, or wild words prompted by instinctive moods, then we should keep silent, but if it is for some good, unselfish purpose, then we may speak. What is meant by the practicing of stopping at the time of speaking? If we recall that much vexatious disturbances arises from speaking, be it from good motive or bad motive, and comprehend that the speaking mind and all the vexations arising from its activitities have no substance that can be grasped, then our delusive thoughts will come to a natural end. This is what is called the practice of stopping at the time of speaking.

What is meant by the practice of examining at the time of speaking? In the practice of examining at the time of speaking we are to keep in mind that we are consciously and willfully giving our thoughts expression by forcing our breath through our throat, tongue, palate, teeth and lips, and that we have different sounding voices and different use of words, and that by our speaking we are giving rise to vexatious and disturbing feelings, both good and bad. We should reflect that the speaking-mind has no visible appearance, and that the speaking-personality and all the disturbances that arise from speaking, are nothing after all but emptiness and vanity. This is what is meant by the practice of examining at the time of speaking.

These six different occasions for employing the practice of stopping and examining may arise at any time and we are to use the practice whenever it is called for and in the manner as shown in the preceding five ways.

(7) We are to practice stopping whenever our eyes notice sights. This means that whenever our eyes catch sight of any object we are to recall that the apparent object has no more reality than the moonlight in the pond. So if it is a pleasing sight we are not to let desire for it arise in the mind, and if it is a repulsive sight we are not to let a feeling of aversion arise, and if it is an indifferent sight we are not to let ignorance of its meaning disturb the mind. This is what is meant by the practice of stopping at the time of catching sights by the eyes.

Now, what is meant by practicing examining in the act of seeing? We should keep in mind that whatever we see with our eyes is no more than vanity and emptiness. What do we mean by this? It means that if we are to seek for it, we could find no differentiated substance either in the internal organs or in the object, or in space, or in the light. Our consciousness of the supposed object is a phenomena that is dependent upon the reaction of the light upon the eye, a variety of other causes and conditions among which is the mental process that springs up in the mind because of the reaction by which we make distinctions between the various sights we see. Thus from the sights we see we experience all manner of vexations and disturbances, good and bad. We should immediately reflect that our sight-mindful thought has no visible appearance, and we should understand, also, that the sight-seeing personality and all that arises from sight-seeing are nothing after all but vanity and emptiness. This is what is meant by the practice of examining at the time of catching sights by our eyes.

(8) We are to practice stopping and examining at the time of hearing sounds by our ears. That is, just as soon as we are conscious of a sound we are to think of it as of no more value than an echo. If it is pleasing sound we are not to let it awaken any craving desire, and if it is discordant sound we are not to let it give rise to any fear or hatred, or if it is an indifferent sound we are not to be curious or disturbed. This is what is meant by the practice of stopping under hearing conditions.

What is meant by the practice of examining the conditions of hearing? We should immediately recall that every sound is an unreality. A sound is only the reaction of the hearing apparatus as it comes into contact with its appropriate field of vibration and the ear-mind is stimulated and the mental process distinguishes differences. By reason of this we have all kinds of vexatious and disturbing thoughts, both good and bad. This is what is involved in hearing. As we reflect that the hearing mind has no visible appearance, we should understand that the hearing personality and all that arises from hearing are nothing after all but emptiness and vanity. This is what is meant by the practice of examining under the conditions of hearing.

(9) We are to practice stopping and examining át the time of smelling. This is meant that whenever a scent is noticed, we are to think of it immediately as a make-believe bonfire. It it is a pleasant fragrance we are not to give away to a craving desire for it, if it is a disagreeable smell, we are not to let a feeling of aversion or dislike spring up, and, if it is an indifferent odor, any feeling of disturbance. This is what is meant by the practice of stopping at the time of smelling.

What is meant by the practice of examining at the time of smelling? We should immediately recollect that what we are smelling is unreal and deluding. Why? Because it is only a phenomena that is involved in the concurrence of the nose, its field of stimulation and the processes of the smelling-mind, by reason of which we perceive a consciousness of smell and the mind proceeds to differentiate it from other smells. From this there arises all manner of thoughts, vexatious and disturbing, both good and bad. As we reflect that our smelling has no substantial appearance, we should decide that our smelling-personality and all that arises from smelling are nothing after all but emptiness and vanity. This is what is meant by the practice of examining at the time of smelling.

(10) We are to practice stopping at the time of tasting. This means that whenever we taste anything we should immediately think of it as having no more substantiality than a dream experience. If it is a pleasing taste we should not crave it; if it is a repulsive taste, we should not be troubled by it; if it is an indifferent taste, we should ignore it. This is the practice of stopping under the condition of tasting. What is meant by the practice of examining at the time of tasting? It means that whenever we experience the sensation of taste we are immediately to remember that taste is nothing that has any reality about it. Why has it no reality? Because, although we distinguish six kinds of taste, there is no substantial difference

between them, they are all alike sensations that involve the tongue and its internal apparatus from which a sense-consciousness arises followed by a consciousness that is dependent upon the mental processes that notices differences, from which arise all manner of vexatious and disturbing thoughts both good and bad. As we reflect that our tasting-mind has no substantial appearance, we are forced to conclude that our tasting-personality and all that arises from tasting are nothing but emptiness and vanity. This is what is meant by the practice of examining at the time of tasting.

(11) We are to practice stopping and examining at the time of touching things. No matter what the hands or body touches we should think right away that it is unreal and visionary. If we receive pleasing sensations from what we touch we are not to become fond of it, and if the sensations are disagreeable and painful we are not to cherish dislike nor hatred for it, and if the sensations are indifferent we are not to try to make distinctions nor to carry them in memory. This is what is meant by stopping when in contact with tangibles.

What is meant by the practice of examining at the time of touching things? We should remember at once that all such feelings as heaviness and lightness, warmth and coldness, smoothness and roughness, have no reality except in connection with our thoughts, and that the six parts of our skeleton are only names. As these sensations are known to be only shame and visions, so we must recognize that the things and our body that gives rise to the sensations are unreal also. No sooner are causes and conditions blended than there arise sensations, perceptions and consciousness, and from these arise memory and distinctions and discriminations of happiness and suffering.

This is what is meant as the sensation of touch. At such times we are to reflect that the feeling-mind has no visible appearance and from that we should know that the feeling-personality and all that arises from tangibles are also empty and vain. This is what is meant by the practice of examining under the conditions of contact and the sensation of touch.

(12) We are to practice stopping and examining at all times when the mind is engaged in thinking, but as this subject has already been fully discussed at the beginning of this treatise, we will not dwell upon it further. At the time when we are sitting in the practice of Dhyana we may find ourselves

hindered by any one of these sense hindrances and should employ the corresponding means of relief, but as these have been now fully explained in the foregoing paragraphs we will not repeat them here. As any one of us becomes capable of applying these teachings to his practice of Dhyana, whether he be acting, standing, sitting, reclining, looking, listening, feeling, or consciousness, he may know that he is practicing Mahayana Dhyana truly. It is said in the *Maha-vagga Sutra*:—

"The Lord Buddha said to his disciple Sona, If Bodhisattva-Mahasattvas know how to act at the time of their acting, know how to sit at the time of their sitting, or even know how to wear the robe of a disciple at the time of wearing the robe, and how to enter the practice of Dhyana, at the time of entering, and how to retire at the time of retiring, then they may be rightfully called, Maha-Bodhisattva-Mahasattvas."

If we are able to practice the Mahayana at any time and place, as stated above, we are worthy to be known as the highest and supreme one in all the world and that none other is to be compared with us. It is said in the *Mahayana Shastra*:—

"To desire the happiness of the gods, thou must retire to the quiet forest, give up all they evil ways, free thyself from all lustful desires, and with tranquil mind practice Dhyana.

"Now, thou are craving for worldly things, lust, and riches and ambition, but such things can not give thee peace for there would be no satisfying of thy desires.

"But we, the wearers of the mended robes, live in quiet retirement with minds tranquil and concentrated at all times whether acting or standing or sitting and, by so doing, we are enlightening ourselves with wisdom, observing all things in their true nature.

"As we continue under these conditions, observing all phenomena with equitable and tranquil minds, our minds will gain serenity and understanding and insight that will transcend the possibilities of this triple world."

VII

The Development and Manifestation
of Good Qualities

As we become competent in the practice of stopping and insight, we will first come to an understanding of the emptiness and unreality of phenomena and then we will become able to avoid them as hindrances to our practice; then both our body and mind will become pure and serene. In this condition many kinds of good qualities will develop and manifest themselves. We will now briefly describe two different kinds of development of such good qualities.

The first kind is the development of external good qualities, such as the giving of alms, keeping the precepts, being filial to parents, respectful to elders, making offerings to images, observing the scriptural teachings, and many other good qualities. But as these good outward developments may be confused with similar outward developments of evil qualities, we must be on our guard. The distinction between good external developments and bad developments will not be considered at this time, but should be kept in mind. The second kind is the development of internal good qualities by which we mean the good qualities that develop and manifest themselves in the course of our Dhyana Practice. There are three groups of these good qualities:—

1. In the first group there are five of these good qualities:—

(1) The development of good qualities by right breathing. As we become competent in the practice of stopping and examining, both our body and mind will become regulated and adjusted and the delusions of our minds will cease. As our thinking gradually dies down, our minds will become tranquil and concentrated and the development and manifestation of good qualities will go on as far as they can go on under the conditions of this Karma-world of action. But it is not until we begin to advance along the ten stages of Bodhisattvahood that our bodies and minds come into a state of perfect tranquillity and our Dhyana-mind attains a state of safety and abiding peace. At this earlier stage of Dhyana, we do not at first notice any tangible result either of body or mind, but after one sitting or two sittings, or it may not be until after one day or two days, or after one month or two months, we will gradually become conscious that we are being forced to keep on with our practice, being convinced that as long as there is no interruption to our practice there will be a gradual gain even if there are no visible signs of gain. Then suddenly, we will become conscious that certain developments are taking place within our bodies and minds by which we are becoming more sensitive in

their reactions to conditions. We will notice slight differences of
pain and pleasure, heat and cold, heaviness and lightness,
smoothness and roughness. At the time of feeling these differences, our bodies as well as our minds will become very peaceful and tranquil, very quiet and happy, very joyous and pure.
It may be a very faint feeling at first and wholly indescribable
but it will be real nevertheless. This is what is meant by the
development of good qualities going on with out right breathing
at the time of our practice. It is what makes right breathing
of such fundamental importance in our practice of Dhyana.

Or, under the same conditions of the Karma-world before
we have begun to advance along the ten Bodhisattva stages,
all of a sudden we become conscious of our breathing and
notice its peaceful respiration, its extent and its transmission to
all the pores of the body. We will suddenly see with our
mental eyes that within the body are thirty-six good things.
It is as if the doors of a granary were opened and we saw
within the riches of sesame seeds and beans. It fills our minds
with awe and wonder and gladness, as well as peace and tranquillity, and calmness and bliss. Such is the wonderful development and manifestation of good qualities that goes on in our
practice of Dhyana coincident with right breathing.

(2) The development and manifestation of good qualities by
an examination of the essential impurity of that which we most
have loved—our bodies. If, in the state of Dhyana, under the
conditions of the Karma-world preceding an entrance along the
Bodhisattva stages, we reflect upon the emptiness and transiency
of both body and mind, suddenly we will have a vision of
bodies lying dead and becoming swollen and decaying, with pus
oozing out and maggots fattening on them, and scattered all
about the bones of other dead bodies. With this horrible vision
of the constitution of the bodies we have loved will come a
feeling of sadness and compassion. This is what is meant by
the development and manifestation of good qualities from insight into the impurity of all transient and component things.

Or, in the midst of our quiet practice, there will come a
recollection of the impurity of our own body: we will seem to
see our skeleton suspended before us. As we realize the significance of the five sensualities, we are filled with disgust at the
thought that we must submit to the death of the body. With
this thought we will lose all pride and confidence in our ego-

self and in the selfhood of others, and will gain a peaceful and quiet mind. This is the way good qualities develop and are manifested by the dissolving of attachments to things that were beloved, as we come to realize their impurity. The same thing is true of attachments to things outside of the body as we come to note their impurity, also. As attachments are dissolved, good qualities are developed.

(3) The development and manifestation of the good quality of compassion. If, in the state of Dhyana under the conditions of the Karma-world preceding an entrance upon the Bodhisattva stages, we practice realizing the good qualities of other people, there will come a feeling of great compassion for all sentient life. In this connection we will have vision and recollections of our parents, our close kinsmen, our intimate friends, and our hearts will be filled with inexpressible joy and gratitude. Then there will develop similar visions of compassion for our common acquaintances, even for our enemies, and for all sentient beings in the five realms of existence. When we rise from the practice of Dhyana after these experiences, our hearts will be full of joy and happiness and we will greet whoever we meet with kind and peaceful faces. This is the development and manifestation of the good quality of compassion. In like manner we will come to realize developments and manifestations of other good qualities such as kindness, sympathetic joy and equanimity.

(4) The development of the good quality of insight into causes and conditions. Owing to our practice of stopping and realizing in the state of Dhyana under the conditions of the Karma-world preceding an entrance upon the Bodhisattva stages, with both the body and mind tranquil, there will suddenly come to us a clear insight into the causes and conditions of our life in the triple aspects of past, present and future. At such times we will see clearly that there is no such thing as an ego-personality or an ego-nature of things, but that everything has arisen from the concatenation of causes and conditions of our own ignorance and activities. Under the conviction of this clear insight we will give up all of our conceptions of phenomena as having some attributes of reality, we will break away from our old prejudices, and we will attain to a more perfect concentration of mind with a correspondingly deeper peace and sense of mental security.

Then there will arise within our deepest consciousness a more comprehensive intelligence, our minds will find a purer joy in the Dharma, we will cease to be worried about our worldly conditions, we will accept with patience the fact that our personality is only the five grasping aggregates of form, sensation, perception, discrimination and consciousness, we will accept with patience the fact that our external world is wholly made up of the mental reactions between our six senses and their corresponding fields of contact, we will accept with patience the fact that all our physical experience is within the compass of our physical senses, the objects of sense and our sense-minds. This is what is meant by the development and manifestation of the good quality of insight into causes and conditions.

(5) The development and manifestation of the good quality of remembrance of all the Buddhas. In the state of Dhyana, under the conditions of the Karma-world preceding an entrance upon the Bodhisattva stages, and owing to our practice of stopping and realizing, when our minds and bodies are quiet and tranquil, then all of a sudden there comes into the memory a recollection of the inconceivable merits and purity of all the Buddhas. We recall their possession of the ten transcendental powers, of the four fearlessnesses of the eighteen characteristic marks of a Buddha; their attainment of the Samadhis and emancipations, and their command over all manner of skillful means and powers of transformations, which they use freely for the benefit of all sentient beings. All such kinds of transcendental powers and merits are beyond our human comprehension. As soon as we are dwelling in such remembrances of the Buddha's transcending attainments and merits, we feel springing up within our Dhyana-minds the development of a spirit of respect for all sentient life and a feeling of fraternity with them; we feel unfolding powers of samadhi, and a sense of joy and bliss pervades both body and mind that wraps us in a feeling of righteousness and safety. At such times we are never disturbed by the appearance of any bad developments nor evil manifestations. When we retire from our Dhyana practice, our body seems light and active and we feel so confident in the possession of good qualities, that we expect everyone whom we meet will respect us and respond to our good will. This is what

is meant by the development and manifestation of good qualities and powers of samadhi by our remembrance of all the Buddhas.

Or, if, on account of our practicing stopping and observing at the time of our Dhyana practice, we attain this purity and serenity of mind and body, then we will become conscious of the development within our minds of all kinds of ways of manifesting good qualities in the face of suffering, foolishness, pride, impurity, the disgusting things of the world, the impurity of food, death and the desire for survival after the death of the body. We will become conscious of and increasing love for Buddha, Dharma and the Brotherhood, of respect for the Precepts, of equanimity of mind, of a sense of awe for the celestial worlds, of the attainment of the four right viewpoints for our thinking, of the four right diligencies, of the four right powers of self-mastery, of the five factors and the five faculties, of the Noble Path, of the six Paramitas that lead to enlightenment, of all Wisdoms, and all transcendental powers of transformation, and we shall have powers of mind to distinguish every one of these things rightly and use them properly. The Sutra says that if we know our own mind on any one subject rightly, then we can attain anything we will.

2. The second conception of the internal developments relates to the faculty of distinguishing between trueness and falsity. It manifests itself in two ways. (1) The first relates to the development and manifestation of false forms of concentration. There is only one right way of practicing Dhyana but there are many false ways. According to our wrong ways of practicing there will be different corresponding signs. We may feel a tickling sensation over our bodies, or sometimes a feeling of heaviness as though our body were under pressure, or sometimes the very contrary, a feeling of lightness as if our body would float away, or sometimes a feeling as though the body was held down by bonds. Sometimes there will be a feeling of unbearable sleepiness, sometimes of coldness, sometimes of heat; sometimes there will be strange changing conditions, now and then the mind will become obscure and again it will be alive with many bad perceptions; or concerned with all kinds of troubles and the complicated affairs of others; or at times we may become lightheaded and optimistic, and at other times very

pessimistic; or sometimes we will be so filled with fright that our hair will stand on end, and then again, there will be times of exciting happiness as though we were intoxicated.

All such kinds of false developments may arise during the course of our practice, but we should pay no attention to them. If we become attached to any of these false developments, we will soon pass under the influence of ninety-five devils who will delude us into madness. When the gods or devils or evil spirits notice our susceptibility to these evil developments, they will sometimes give us increased meditating power so as to lead us on into deeper development of these evil manifestations. Sometimes they give one powers of knowledge and eloquence, sometimes magical gifts so that we will be able to stir up people all the more. Under these conditions foolish people think he has attained enlightenment and they give him their faith and obedience, but his deluded mind is in a disturbed condition and is really in the service of evil spirits in their efforts to lead the world into turmoil. Alas to him who yields himself to such evil developments and manifestations! He will decline in his practice of Dhyana and after his death will fall into evil existences.

But if we, true hearted followers of Buddha, notice that we are having these wrong developments and sham manifestations, then we should reject them forthwith. How may we reject them? Well, if we recognize them to be false and visionary, and take care not to think of them or grasp them or become attached to them, then they will soon vanish away. If we observe them with right insight, they will quickly pass away.

(2) The other way of drawing distinctions between falsehood and trueness is the discernment by the practice of development and manifestation of right Dhyana. If we are practicing right Dhyana there will come into development and manifestation all kinds of meritorious qualities that will approve themselves to our enlightened consciousness by their benefit to our Dhyana practice. The body will become bright and transparent, fresh and pure; our minds will become happy and joyous, tranquil and serene; hindrances to our practice will disappear and good thoughts will spring up to help us; our respect for the practice will increase and our faith in it will deepen; our powers of understanding and wisdom will become clear and trustworthy; both our body and mind will become

sensitive and flexible; our thought will be less superficial and more profound; our body will become tranquil; we will feel an instinctive disgust for the world's lusts. Under these conditions, our minds will become unconditioned and desireless, and both frankness and charm will characterize our daily life.

This is the true and right development and manifestation that should follow our practice of Dhyana. These reactions are similar to the reactions we feel when we are with people—if we are with bad people, we feel irritated and annoyed, but if we are with good people, we are mutually benefited and feel at ease. Stopping and observing at the time of our practice helps us to discern between the wrongness and the rightness of the developments that take place during the practice.

3. The third conception of the internal developments relates to making more use, in our practice of Dhyana, of stopping and observing as a continuing nourishment for these unfolding good qualities. If we wish to conserve and develop the good qualities, we must continually resort to the practice of stopping and observing. Sometimes it will be the practice of stopping that the situation needs, and at other times it will be observing that is needed. We should consider each situation separately by our enlightened insight and then apply the right remedy.

VIII

Beware of Evil Influences

(The word used in the title of this chapter in the Sanskrit is Mara which corresponds with the English, Satan or Devil. In the Chinese the word has the meaning of "killer" because it robs us of our treasure of merit and kills our life of wisdom. In the old days evil was usually personified as the doings of Mara the King of Evil and his hosts of demons, but in our day we think of it in impersonal terms of evil influences.) Our Lord Buddha accumulates all his store of merit and wisdom by delivering all sentient beings into Nirvana, while evil influences are always destroying the good qualities of sentient beings and keeping them in the dreary round of life and death. If we have patience to follow the Buddha's Noble Path we will clearly perceive the influence and danger of all evil things. These evil influences may be classified into four groups: (1) Vexation; (2) sensuality; (3) cruelty; and (4) "personal" evils. The first three are so common in our daily life and correspond so closely with the thoughts of our own minds that we will not make any further reference to them at present. They are to be driven off and kept off by our right thinking. But the evil influences that originate outside of our own minds, that we commonly think of as the doings of devils and goblins, require more attention.

There are three classes of these "personal" devils: (1) The first class are the evil influences that awaken fear. There are twelve of these and they seem to come during the different periods of the day and night. They make all sorts of transformations so that simple and innocent things take on the appearance of frightful things, or harmless women or girls appear as witches, or they are wholly imaginary. In the early morning from 3 to 5 things look like tigers; from 5 to 7 they take on harmless forms as deer or rabbits but they frighten us just the same. From 7 to 9 they are horrible things like dragons and turtles; from 9 to 11 they look like snakes; from 11 to 1 they take on the appearance of horses and mules and camels; from 1 to 3 they are sheep; from 3 to 5·they are monkeys; 5 to 7 in the twilight they are vultures and crows; from 7 to 9 in the shadows of night they look like dogs and wolves; from 9 to 11 they take on the appearance of pigs and disgusting things; from 11 to 1 they are scurrying rats and mice; from 1 to 3 they are big cows that frighten us. When we are tempted by these goblins or frightful things we must recall the hour of the night and the day and dismiss them from our thoughts. Just as soon as we see them as they truly are and call them by their right name, they will vanish away.

(2) The second class are the evil influences that awaken anger. They also employ transformations to gain their evil ends. They take on the form of worms and bugs creeping over our face or back and making sharp stings, or they tickle us, or suddenly they grab us, or make disturbing sounds, or jump out at us. At such times we should keep control of our minds and refuse to be annoyed, saying to ourselves, "I know who you are; you are only the little discomforts of life; you are only the annoying differences of opinion that try our patience and irritate us. But we are followers of Buddha, we keep the Precepts, you can not make us angry, you can not disturb us.

Sometimes it will be necessary, in order to keep control of our minds, to repeat a Sutra if we are monks, or repeat the Precepts if we are laymen. But these evil influences have no real power, they can only influence us as we let them. Careful reading of the scriptures will make this plain to us.

(3) The third class are the evil influences of illusion that bolster up our imaginary egoistic pride and self-complacency. They generally work through the conditions of our five sense objects, for the purpose of disturbing and breaking off our good and right thoughts. Their transformations may be divided into three groups. The first group are transformations of repulsive things, making them to appear to be desirable. The second group are transformations of pleasing things, making them to appear as undesirable. The third group are transformations of indifferent things, making them to appear different from what they are and by so doing serving to confuse and bewilder the mind.

All these transformations that serve to confuse and bewilder and deceive the mind are the work of demons and devils if anything is, because their arrows are sent against our highest thoughts and sentiments. They do not make a frontal attack, they attack from behind and underneath; they transform pleasing conditions, such as, forms of our parents and brothers and • friends; the conditions of simple and quiet living, the beautiful thoughts of Buddha, alluring us into imaginary conditions that have no substantial basis and which lead to suffering. They transform harmless things into an appearance of frightful beasts in order to deceive us and frighten us; or they transform indifferent conditions such as are usual and commonplace, in order to forestall and disturb our practice of Dhyana. They transform all kinds of pleasing and repulsive sights, all kinds of agreeable and distressing sounds, all kinds of fragrant and horrid odors, all kinds of delicious and distasteful flavors, all kinds of good and evil thoughts and conditions that make up the routine life of everyone, and thereby delude us and hinder us from following the Noble Path.

These transformations are too numerous to take up in detail, but we will group them under five heads. Anything which serves to transform the five objects of sense and the thoughts of the mind is the work of Mara's army of demons and goblins. The purpose of their activities is to annoy us, to delude us, to destroy our good qualities, to disturb our equanimity, to raise up hindrances against our practice of Dhyana. This is explained in the Sutra:

"*Be advised that sensual desires are the 1st Army of thine enemy; that discouragement and sadness are the 2nd Army; that hunger and thirst is the 3rd Army; that attachments are the 4th Army; that laziness and sleepiness are the 5th Army; that fear and fright are the 6th Army; that doubt and remorse are the 7th Army; that hatred is the 8th Army; that selfish love of comfort and praise are the 9th Army; that egoistic pride and complacency are the 10th Army. All of these armies of evil beset the follower of Buddha.*

"*But thou shalt say: "I will defeat all of these armies by the power of my Dhyana practice, and when I have attained Enlightenment I will deliver all mankind.*"

Now that we, the followers of Buddha, have become aware of all these evil influences, we must resist them with all determination. There are two ways of resisting them: The first way is by the practice of stopping. Just as soon as we become aware of any of these evil influences besetting us, we are to recall that each and every one of them is falsehood and delusion. If we do this, there will be no fear nor sadness, no aversion nor fondness, no discrimination nor rationalizing. If we practice stopping of thoughts the mind will become tranquil and the hosts of Mara will vanish away.

The second way of resisting evil influences is by the practice of insight and examination. If we instantly reflect that our perceiving and discriminating mind has no objective existence and that there is nothing for these evil influences to annoy and delude. If the evil thoughts still linger about, if we practice insight and right mindfulness we will, at least, not be vexed of them nor afraid of them. We should determine to keep the mind tranquil and steady even if we have to sacrifice our life to do so.

In our practice of right mindfulness we realize that the conception of Mara as the embodiment of evil and the conception of Buddha as the embodiment of goodness and truth is really one conception—the conception of manifestation—but that in ultimate reality they balance each other and there remains only the conception of Dharmakaya, the ultimate Essence that abides in emptiness and silence. In this sense there is no Mara to resist and no Buddha to take refuge in. But inasmuch as Mara is only the transformation of unreal appearances, and Buddha is the manifestation of the true nature of Dharmakaya, the transformations of Mara disappear, and the manifestations of the Buddha-Dharma are realized by us, all in the same moment.

Moreover, we need not be troubled if the transformed conditions of Mara do not vanish away, nor should we be pleased if they do vanish. Why? Because these evil influences that come to trouble us during our practice of Dhyana are not real wolves and tigers, neither is Mara a reality. As to our ignorance and foolishness and delusion by reason of which we become frightened or fond of unseen things, it is only our mind in state of illusion, diffusion, non-concentration and dementation. Thus our troubles, which we ascribe to evil influences, are only due to wrong states of our own minds. Our slowness in attaining enlightenment is not because of Mara's doings, but because of our own slackness in the practice of Dhyana.

Should these disturbing conditions persist through many months, and even years, we must patiently continue to seek to control the states of our own minds; we must do so with determination that knows neither fear nor pain. Falsehood must sooner or later yield to truth; the transformations that arise from evil influences must just as surely yield to an earnest purpose and steadfast effort.

But we are not to look lightly upon these disturbing influences, because the deeper they are and the stronger effort we make to uproot them, the greater will be the danger from them. We must learn to distinguish them clearly and fight them separately, or they will drive us mad. These morbid states of alternate happiness and gloomy discouragement are the cause of sickness and even death. Every follower of Buddha should have a competent Master or a wise and noble-hearted friend, for sooner or later he will encounter these evil influences.

Worse than sickness and madness, these besetting influences and transformed conditions, if not overcome, may change a follower of Buddha into a heretic and enemy of Buddha. It sometimes seems as though Mara was training a follower of

Buddha to become his own servant, by leading him into false kinds of concentration, false intelligence, false intuition, false supernatural powers, and magical spells, so that he may preach the Dharma with power and win many converts. And then later Mara seems to take delight in exposing his falsity and ruining his pseudo converts. The wiles of Mara and his hosts are innumerable and inexplicable. We have referred only to a few of them in order to warn the followers of Buddha to be on their guard against them constantly, and especially against this danger of heresy. The fundamental heresy of the reality of all phenomena is not of Mara's doing, that is basic, but all the rest belong to Mara. The Sutra says:—

"As soon as thou dost speculate discursively, thou art already caught in Mara's net. A follower of Buddha should neither yield to evil influences nor to the temptation of discursive discussion. This is the true Mudra that will protect him from all evil."

IX

Treatment of Sickness

As sickness rises from wrong conditions or maladjustments of good conditions, the followers of Buddha, by observing the Precepts, following the Noble Path and practicing Dhyana, should be largely if not wholly free from sickness. Wise control of the mind is the best preventative of sickness and is the best method of cure. If our body, mind and breathing are well regulated and our circumstances are in harmony with the teachings of Buddha, we should be able to throw off most sicknesses and heal most wounds. We should do everything we can to keep well because sickness is a discredit to our enlightenment besides being a hindrance to our practice of Dhyana.

There are two divisions of this subject that should be kept in mind. First, the nature of the sickness, its development and its symptoms. Second, methods of treatment. Under the first head we should distinguish between sickness caused by external conditions and sickness caused by irregularities within our own minds. In either case we should notice the beginning of sickness and try to prevent its becoming serious by remedying the conditions both external and internal as early as possible. What are the best remedies? The best remedy is the practice of stopping and insight. Stopping means removing dangerous conditions and ending bad habits. Insight means an examination of and reflection on the emptiness aspect of all phenomena. If we cease to let the mind dwell upon symptoms and hold it to a reflection upon the unreality of both body and ideas concerning its state, then the mind will speedily become tranquil and the symptoms will disappear. The reason for this is that most of our sicknesses come from irritations within the mind and if these can be controlled by right mindfulness, then the mind will become kind and tranquil and the sickness will disappear. Medicines made up of either minerals or herbs or both may be used if they have some correspondence with the sickness. The same thing is true, also, in the application of ways and means for practicing insight,—each practice must have correspondence with its mental sickness.

"In the treatment of sickness by some process of insight, it is necessary for us to do so in ten ways, if we are to expect good results. The ten ways are: (1) Faith. We must believe that the remedy is going to help us. (2) Application. We must make use of the remedy in the right way and the right time. (3) Diligence. It means to apply the remedy whole-heartedly, without relaxation until the sickness is cured. (4) Permanent conditions. This means that we are to keep the mind concentrated upon the Dharma. (5) Discernment of causes. (6) Expedient means. This means that we are to keep our right breathing, right practice, and right use of our thoughts in good adjustment and balance. (7) Long practice. This means that if we are benefited by the means or practice, we are to continue it faithfully without regard to the passing of time. (8) Choice of means. This means that we are to use observation to note whether a remedy is useful or harmful and be governed as to its continued use accordingly. (9) Maintenance and protection. This means that we are to protect the body by the best use of our mind. (10) Hindrances. This means that if we are benefited by our practice of Dhyana we shall not boast of it to others, and if we are unsuccessful in getting rid of hindrances we must not give rise to doubts and slanders. If we treat our sicknesses in these ways, no doubt we will have good results."

X

Realization of Supreme
Attainment

(Anuttara-samyak-sambodhi)

If we, followers of Buddha, in practicing stopping and insight as given in the preceding chapters, could see that all phenomena arise from our own minds, and that causes and conditions are merely pseudo-visions, then we would know, also, that all phenomena are nothing but emptiness. As we see that they are nothing but emptiness, then it will be impossible for us to retain the common conception of phenomena. By this new conception of phenomena as emptiness, it can be said, we have realized "the true viewpoint of reality." But from this viewpoint we are unable to see either the Supreme Perfect Attainment of the Buddha to whom we are devoted, nor are we able to see any sentient being that we can emancipate. This means the insight of emptiness attained by practicing the unreality of all phenomena and it also means "the insight of Ultimate Truth" both by the eyes of intelligence and the heart of realization. But if we come to a standstill in the practice of insight we soon descend into the state of a Pratyeka-buddha, who is content with his own attainment. As it is said in the Sutra:—

"All the Arhats sighed and said: 'When we listen to the preaching of our Lord Buddha, whether it be about the Pure Land or about our duty toward all sentient beings, why is it we are not interested and fail to enjoy it'?"

What does this verse signify? It signifies that to the Arhats all phenomena are nothing but emptiness and silence, neither birth nor death, neither greatness nor littleness, neither purity nor unconditionality. As they fix their minds on these negative conceptions, how can interest and enjoyment arise? You should clearly understand that if you attain concentration solely by fixing the mind on the unconditionality of emptiness, you will never be able to develop highest wisdom. It means that your attainment is one-sided, inasmuch as it is leaving out of focus the conception of Buddha. If the Mahasattva-Bodhisattvas keep all the Buddha Dharmas in mind and keep them in mind for the sake of all sentient beings, they will not fall into over-fondness for the unconditionality of emptiness and thus become satisfied with Nirvana for themselves.

From the very beginning the Mahasattva-Bodhisattva, beside his practice of insight into the emptiness of all phenomena, should also practice insight into the potentiality that abides in emptiness. If he does this he will realize with clearness that although the nature of mind is emptiness, as it comes into relations with suitable causes and conditions, it is potential of all phenomena though they are not real nor permanent, and though they manifest through different organs of seeing, hearing, perceiving, thinking, etc.

Notwithstanding his knowledge of the essential emptiness and silence of all phenomena, the Mahasattva-Bodhisattva, by the practice of rightly balanced insight, may practice all manner of activities in his conception of emptiness as though he were planting trees in the clouds, and also, he may distinguish in sentient beings all manner of relative qualities. As the desires of our nature are innumerable, so the ways of our preaching are innumerable, also. As we adapt our various arts of preaching to their various needs, we will be able to benefit all sentient beings in the six realms. This is what is meant by "the viewpoint of expedient adjustment to conditions," which is our insight from emptiness into potentiality. It is also called, "insight of equality," "the eyes of the Dharma," and "the garden of intuitive enlightenment." If we make this balanced insight our viewpoint we shall perceive, but with difficulty and dimly because our powers of intelligence are comparatively undeveloped, the true nature of Buddha potential in everything.

Although the Mahasattva-Bodhisattva has attained these two ways of insight, from the viewpoints of emptiness and potentiality, he has still not yet attained to perfect insight. Therefore, the Sutra says that these two ways of insight are to be used as expedient means for by them we may enter by a Middle Way into Supreme Attainment and therein abide in both conceptions of ultimate Truth,—Perfect Intelligence and Perfect Realization, Perfect Wisdom and Perfect Love—with our mind in tranquillity and peacefulness. Then our minds will no longer run in two channels but will cease their flow in Prajna's Ocean of Truth.

If the Mahasattva-Bodhisattva wishes to have all Buddha-Dharmas embraced in a single thought, he should practice in-

sight from the viewpoint of "cessation of the heretical separation of the two extremes"; this will enable him to walk by
right insight along a Middle Way. What does it mean to practice insight by the Middle Way? It means to look at the nature of our minds in a more comprehensive way. If we do
that we will see that the mind is neither true nor false, and
from that viewpoint we restrain our dependent thoughts. This
is what we mean by the right practice of insight.

If we are able to reflect upon so profound a conception as
the nature of our mind being *neither* emptiness nor potentiality, without cutting asunder our conceptions of emptiness and
potentiality, then the true nature of our mind will be wholly
and clearly comprehended as a manifestation of the Truth of
the Middle Way, and we can reflect upon both of these paths
of Reality (intelligence and intuitive realization), with readi-
ness and assurance. If we can see these two aspects of Reality
as the Middle Way in our own mind, then we can see them in
all phenomena. But we do not take these two aspects of Reality into our reflection upon the Middle Way, for we are unable
to find any trace of them in its nature. This is what is meant
by the practice of right insight into the Middle Way. It is
said in the *Madhyamika* Sutra:—

*"All phenomena which arise from causes and conditions are
nothing but emptiness, but we give them pseudo-names and
then think of a Middle Way."*

If we carefully examine the meaning of this stanza, we will
see that it not only embraces all conceptions of the differentiations of the Middle Way but it also shows the purpose of the
two preceding ways of expedient insight. We will also realize
that the right insight of the Middle Way reveals it to be both
the all-comprehending wisdom of Buddha's eyes and the all-
embracing love of his intuitive heart. If we keep our stand on
this right insight, then our powers of Dhyana and intelligence
will be in equality; we will clearly perceive the true nature of
Buddha, we will rest peacefully in the Mahayana; we will
advance with the steadiness and the speed of the wind; and
we will inevitably run into Prajna's Ocean of Truth.

If we do the deeds of Tathagata (the Ultimate Principle
that is what it is), abide in the palace of Tathagata, dress in
the robe of Tathagata, sit on the throne of Tathagata, then we
will be entering into all the imperial resources of Tathagata.

Then we will regain the purity of our six sense faculties and will no longer be defiled or become fond of the changing and passing phenomena of life. We will enter into the conditions of a Buddha, we will become able to understand all the Buddha-Dharmas, will attain the Samadhi of reciting the Sacred Name, will enter into the peaceful continuance of the Supreme Perfect Enlightenment, and will attain the highest Samadhi of the Transcendental Body. Then we may visit all Buddha Worlds, preach the Buddha-Dharmas to all sentient beings everywhere, purify and adorn all Buddha's Kshatra, make ambrosial offerings to all Buddhas everywhere, receiving and observing all the Dharma-scriptures, of all the Buddhas, possessing perfect ideals for all activities, and advancing along the Bodhisattva stages to Mahasattva-Bodhisattvahood. Then we will be of equal rank and in intimate friendship with Samantabhadra and Manjusri and will be in permanent possession of Dharma nature. Then all the Buddhas will praise us and prophesy our attainment of Buddhahood.

This was the progress of our Lord Buddha from his ascent into the glories of the Tusita Heaven, down to the entrance of his spirit into the womb of his mother Queen Maya, to his conversion to Buddhism, to his sitting under the Bodhi tree, to his rejection of Mara and his hosts, to his full attainment of enlightenment, to his preaching the Dharma, and to his Parinirvana. This means that we are in possession of two bodies, namely, a True Body and an Appearance Body, which are like a sound and its echo, a form and its shadow. The True Body abides in all directions and all times and in all worlds; the Appearance Body accomplishes all the deeds of a Buddha. This is our mission as Mahasattva-Bodhisattvas that was begun in our practice of Dhyana.

It is said in the *Avatamsaka Sutra* that as soon as novice Bodhisattvas begin their practice of Dhyana that they have already accomplished their full Enlightenment, and have comprehended that the intelligence embodied in the true nature of all phenomena is to be accomplished in no other way than by full Enlightenment. In another place the same Sutra says that new Mahasattva-Bodhisattvas in attaining oneness with Tathagata really attain innumerable bodies and that each body is Buddha.

In the Parinibanna Sutra it is said:—*"The beginnings as*

new Mahasattva-Bodhisattvas and the ultimate Buddha are indistinguishable, but in regard to responsibilities the new Mahasattva-Bodhisattva has the heavier burden."

In the Maha-vagga The Lord speaking to Sona Kutakanna said:—*Sona Kutakanna, there are some Mahasattva-Bodhisat-'tvas who, no sooner have they made their first practice of Dhyana than they are fitted to sit under the Bodhi-tree."*

We should realize that these novice Mahasattva-Bodhisattvas are really Buddhas in manifestation. This is signified in the *Wonderful Lotus Sutra,* also, in the case of the Naga Princess, who was a disciple of Manjusri and only eight years old, but who presented her priceless jewel to Lord Buddha as to an equal.

In all these Sutras the new Mahasattva-Bodhisattvas are represented as being already in possession of all Buddha-Dharmas. The same meaning is embodied in the *Maha-vagga* where it uses the first letter of the Sanskrit alphabet—Aum—to represent wholeness. It is so stated in the *Lotus Sutra,* where the purpose of our Lord Buddha's appearing in this world is presented as manifesting and emancipating the Buddha perception and understanding that is inherent in every sentient being. It is so stated in the *Nirvana Sutra,* that as we have received the nature of Buddha, so we ever abide in Maha-Nirvana.

This is a brief elucidation of the attainment of Supreme Perfect Wisdom through the practice of Dhyana by novice Mahasattva-Bodhisattvas. We will now refer to the attainment of Supreme Perfect Wisdom by the Buddhas.

As we cannot see the conditions that surround the perfect minds of Buddhas, we are limited in our understanding as to how they attain Supreme Perfect Wisdom to the teachings of the Sutras. In the Sutras we find only two ways in which Buddhas practice Dhyana. In the *Lotus of the Wonderful Law Sutra* we read these words:—"*(All the highest Mahasattva-Bodhisattvas) sincerely and earnestly and perseveringly praise the Wisdom of all the Buddhas."* This is their practice of realization in Dhyana. In their practice of Dhyana they abide in Samadhi. We get our understanding of their attainment of Supreme Perfect Wisdom through our own practice of realization.

In its interpretation of the meaning of Maha-Nirvana, the

Nirvana Sutra considers over a hundred phrases referring to the subject of emancipation. It interprets Nirvana as having the meaning of "stopping." That is, Buddhas attain Supreme Perfect Wisdom through the practice of "stopping." In this Sutra, Maha-Nirvana is spoken of as the "Permanent Tranquil Samadhi." Here Samadhi means "stopping."

In the *Lotus of the Wonderful Law Sutra,* though the Supreme Perfect Attainment is explained by deductions from the practice of realization, it is summarized in terms of "stopping." It is stated that even the conception of ultimate Nirvana as "Permanent Tranquil Samadhi" amounts to the same thing as "the full" realization of emptiness.

In the *Nirvana Sutra,* although Supreme Perfect Attainment is interpreted by deductions from "stopping," it is summarized in terms of realization, and therefore, takes the three ultimate qualities, Truth-Essence, Prajna-Potentiality, Blissful-Peace, as its Maha-Nirvana.

Although these two Sutras treat the subject of ultimate Nirvana differently, they both follow the two ways of "stopping and realizing," and they both explain Supreme Perfect Attainment in terms of "Stopping and realizing," which is the same thing as saying that they unite in looking upon Supreme Perfect Attainment as the common goal of both Intuition and Intelligence, of both Love and Wisdom.

We, the followers of Buddha, should humbly recognize and patiently accept the fact that the attainment of Bodhisattvaship, in the beginning, in the middle, and in the end, are alike inconceivable. The newly translated *Suvana-Prabhasa Sutra* says that the Buddhas of the past are inconceivable, the Buddhas of the Present possess inconceivable potentialities, the Buddhas of the future will never be destroyed. This is true because all Buddhas arrive at the Supreme Perfect Wisdom by the two ways of "stopping and realizing," and these are not two divergent ways but are one Middle Way whose goal is Highest Perfect Enlightenment.

In conclusion, I sincerely wish that all of you who are devoted to the practice of Dhyana will quickly get rid of the three poisons,—lust, anger, and foolishness; and the five hindrances,—coveteousness, fear, ignorance, conceit, and doubt. As long as the mind is burdened with these poisons and hindrances, no matter how hard you may try, you will never be benefited. As it is said in the *Prajna Sutra*:—

"*All the Buddhas attain their emancipation by means of their own minds, which are kept pure and transparent and undefiled, which are always fresh and clean, without stain of color, in all their six sense-fields. Thou, too, shouldest learn to keep thy mind in the same state, then thou, too, mayest attain the great Enlightenment.*"

SUTRA SPOKEN BY THE SIXTH PATRIARCH

CHAPTER I

Autobiography of Hui-Neng

ONCE when the patriarch had come to Paolam Monastery Prefect Wai of Shiu-chow and other officials came there to invite him to deliver public lectures on Buddhism in the hall of Tai-fan Temple in the city (Canton).

When the time came, there were assembled Prefect Wai, government officials and Confucian scholars about thirty each, bhikshu, bhikshuni, Taoists and laymen, nearly a thousand in all. After the Patriarch had taken his seat, the congregation in a body paid him homage and asked him to speak on the fundamental truths of Buddhism. Whereupon, His Eminence delivered the following address:—

Learned Audience, our self-nature which is the seed or kernel of Bodhi (the Wisdom that comes with enlightenment) is pure by nature and by making right use of it we can reach Buddhahood directly. Let me tell you something about my own life and how I came into possession of this inner teaching of our Ch'an School.

My father, a native of Fan-yang, was dismissed from his official post and banished to become a commoner in Sun-chow in Kwang-tung. My father died when I was quite young leaving my mother poor and miserable, to my great misfortune. We moved to Kwang-chow (now Canton) and lived in very bad circumstances. I was selling firewood in the market one day when one of my customers ordered some to be sent to his shop. Upon delivery and payment for the same as I went outside I found a man reciting a Sutra. No sooner had I heard the text of this Sutra than my mind became at once enlightened. I asked the man the name of the book he was reciting and was told that it was the "Diamond Sutra" (*Vajracchedika*). I asked

him where he came from and why he recited this particular
Sutra. He replied that he came from the Tung-tsan Monastery
in the Wong-mui District of Kee-chow; that the Abbot in
charge of this temple was Hwang-yan who was the Fifth Patriarch and had about a thousand disciples under him; and
that when he went there to pay homage to the Patriarch, he
found him lecturing on this Diamond Sutra. He further told
me that his Eminence was in the habit of encouraging the laity
as well as his monks to recite this scripture, as by so doing
they might realise their own essence-of-mind and thereby reach
Buddhahood directly.

It must be due to my good karma accumulated from past
lives that I heard about this and that later on I was given ten
taels for the maintenance of my mother by a man who advised me to go to Wong-mui to interview the Fifth Patriarch.
After arrangements had been made for my mother's support,
I left for Wong-mui which took me about thirty days to
reach.

I paid homage to the Patriarch and was asked where I
came from and what I expected to get from him. I replied that
I was a commoner from Sun-chow in Kwang-tung and had
travelled far to pay my respects to him, and then said, "I ask
for nothing but Buddhahood."

The Patriarch replied: "So you are a native of Kwang-
tung, are you? You evidently belong to the aborigines; how
can you expect to become a Buddha?"

I replied: "Although there are Northern men and Southern
men, but North or South make no difference in their Buddha-
nature. An aborigine is different from your Eminence phys-
ically, but there is no difference in our Buddha-nature."

He was going to speak further to me but the presence of
other disciples made him hesitate and he told me to join the
other laborers at their tasks. "May I tell Your Eminence," I
urged, "that Prajna (transcendental Wisdom) constantly rises in
my mind. As one cannot go astray from his own nature one
may be rightly called, 'a field of merit' (this is a title of honor
given to monks as a monk affords the best of opportunities to
others, 'to sow the seed of merit'). I do not know what work
Your Eminence would ask me to do."

"This aborigine is very witty," he remarked. "Go to the
work-rooms and say no more." I then withdrew to the rear

where the work of the monastery was carried on and was told by a lay brother to split firewood and hull rice.

More than eight months after, the Patriarch met me one day and said, "I know that your knowledge of Buddhism is very sound, but I have to refrain from speaking with you lest evil men should harm you. Do you understand?" "Yes, Sir, I understand," I replied. "And I will not go near your hall, lest people take notice of me."

One day the Patriarch assembled all his disciples and said to them: "The question of incessant rebirth is a very momentous one, but instead of trying to free yourselves from that bitter sea of life and death, you men, day after day, seem to be going after tainted merits only. Merit will be of no help to you if your essence of mind is polluted and clouded. Go now and seek for the transcendental wisdom that is within your own minds and then write me a stanza about it. He who gets the clearest idea of what Mind-essence is will be given the insignia of the Patriarch; I will give him the secret teaching of the Dharma, and will appoint him to be the Sixth Patriarch. Go away quickly, now, and do not delay in writing the stanza; deliberation is quite unnecessary and will be of no use. The one who has realised Essence of Mind can testify to it at once as soon as he is spoken to about it. He cannot lose sight of it, even if he were engaged in a battle."

Having received this instruction, the disciples withdrew and said to one another, "There is no use of our making an effort to write a stanza and submit it to His Eminence; the Patriarchship is bound to go to Elder Shin-shau, our Master, anyway. Why go through the form of writing, it will only be a waste of energy." Hearing this they decided to write nothing, saying, "Why should we take the trouble to do it? Hereafter we will simply follow our Master Shin-shau wherever he goes and will look to him for guidance."

Shin-shau reasoned within himself, "Considering that I am their Master, none of them will take part in competition. I wonder whether I should write a stanza and submit it to His Eminence, or not. If I do not, how can the Patriarch know how deep or how superficial my knowledge is? If my object is to get the Dharma, my motive is pure. If it is to get the Patriarchship, then it is bad; my mind would be that of a worldling and my action would amount to a theft of the Patriarch's holy seat. But if I do not submit the stanza, I will lose my chance of getting the Dharma. It is very difficult to know what to do."

In front of the Patriarch's hall there were three corridors the walls of which were to be painted by a court artist named Lo-chun, with pictures suggested by the Lankavatara Sutra depicting the transfiguration of the assembly, and with scenes showing the genealogy of the five Patriarchs, for the information and veneration of the public. When Shin-shau had composed his stanza he made several attempts to submit it, but his mind was so perturbed that he was prevented from doing it. Then he suggested to himself, "It would be better for me to write it on the wall of the corridor and let the Patriarch find it himself. If he approves it, then I will go to pay him homage and tell him that it was done by me; but if he disapproves it,—well, then I have wasted several years' time in this mountain receiving homage which I did not deserve. If I fail, what progress have I made in learning Buddhism?"

At midnight of that night, he went secretly to write his stanza on the wall of the south corridor, so that the Patriarch might know to what spiritual insight he had attained. The stanza read:—

"Our body may be compared to the Bodhi-tree;
While our mind is a mirror bright.
Carefully we cleanse and watch them hour by hour,
And let no dust collect upon them."

As soon as he had written it he returned at once to his room, so no one knew what he had done. In the quiet of his room he pondered: "When the Patriarch sees my stanza tomorrow, if he is pleased with it, it will show that I am (spiritually) ready for the Dharma; but if he disapproves of it, then it will mean that I am unfit for the Dharma owing to misdeeds in previous lives and karmic accumulations that so thickly becloud my mind. What will the Patriarch say about it? How difficult it is to speculate." He could neither sleep nor sit at ease; and so in this vein he kept on thinking until dawn.

In the morning the Patriarch sent for Lo, the court artist, to have the walls painted with pictures and went with him to the south corridor. The Patriarch noticed the stanza and said to the artist, "I am sorry to have troubled you to come so far, but the walls do not need to be painted now. The Sutra says,

'All forms and phenomena are transient and illusive'; we will leave the stanza here so that people may study the stanza and recite it. If they put its teachings into actual practice, they will be saved from the misery of being born in evil realms of existence. Any one who practices it will gain great merit." The Patriarch ordered incense to be burnt before it, and instructed all his disciples to pay homage to it and recite it, so that they might realise Essence of Mind. After his disciples had recited it, they all exclaimed, "Well done!"

That midnight the Patriarch sent for Shin-shau and asked if he had written the stanza. Shin-shau admitted that he had written it and then added: "I am not so vain as to expect to get the Patriarchship, but I wish Your Eminence would kindly tell me whether my stanza shows the least grain of wisdom."

"To attain supreme enlightenment," replied the Patriarch, "one must be able to know spontaneously one's own self-nature which is neither created nor can it be annihilated. From one momentary sensation to another, one should always be able to realise Essence of Mind; then all conceptions of the mind will be free of any graspings by the mind. As one thing is being realized as to its reality, so the mind will reflect all circumstances and conditions as being a state of naturalness. This means that the mind in its pure state is truthful. For if the mind is able to see things truthfully in their pure state it sees them to be the same as its own essential nature of Supreme Enlightenment. You had better return now and think it over for a couple of days and then submit another stanza. In case the new stanza shows that you have entered 'the door of enlightenment,' I will transmit to you the robe and the Dharma."

Shin-shau made obeisance to the Patriarch and went away. For several days he tried in vain to write another stanza, which upset his mind so much that he was as ill at ease as though he was in a nightmare; he could find comfort neither in sitting nor walking.

Two days after, it happened that a boy who was passing by the room where I was hulling rice, was loudly reciting the stanza written by Shin-shau. As soon as I heard it I knew at once that its composer had not yet realised Essence of Mind. Although at that time I never had had instruction about it, I already had a general idea of it. "What stanza is this," I asked the boy. "You aborigine," he said, "don't you know about it? The Patriarch told his disciples that the question of rebirth was a momentous one, and those who wished to inherit his robe and the Dharma should write him a stanza and the one who had the true idea of Mind-essence would get them and become the Sixth Patriarch. Elder Shin-shau wrote this 'formless' stanza on the wall of the south corridor and the Patriarch told us to recite it. He also said that those who put its teachings into actual practice would attain great merit and be saved from being born in the evil realms of existence."

I told the boy that I wished to learn the stanza also, so that I might have the benefit of it in future life. Although I had been hulling rice for eight months, I had never been to the hall, so I asked the boy to show me where the stanza was written, so that I might make obeisance to it. The boy took me there and as I was illiterate, I asked him to read it to me. A petty officer of the Kong-chow District, named Chang Fat-yung, who happened to be there, then read it clearly. When he had finished reading, I told him that I also, had composed a stanza and asked him to write it for me. "Extraordinary," he exclaimed, "that you, also, can compose a stanza."

"If you are a seeker of supreme enlightenment, you will not despise a beginner," I said.

"Please recite your stanza," said he, "I will write it down for you, but if you should succeed in getting the Dharma, do not forget to deliver me."

My stanza read as follows:

> By no means is Bodhi a kind of tree,
> Nor is the bright reflecting mind, a case of mirrors.
> Since mind is emptiness,
> Where can dust collect?

Later on seeing that a crowd was collecting, the Patriarch came out and erased the stanza with his shoe lest jealous ones should do me injury. Judging by this, the crowd took it for granted that the author of it had also not yet realised Mind-essence.

Next day the Patriarch came secretly to the room where the rice was being hulled and seeing me at work with the stone pestle, said, "A seeker of the Path risks his life for the Dharma. Should he do so?" Then he asked, "Is the rice ready?" "Ready long ago," I replied, "only waiting for the sieve." He knocked the mortar thrice with his stick and went away.

Knowing what his signal meant, in the third watch of the night, I went to his room. Using his robe as a screen so that no one would see us, he expounded the Diamond Sutra to me. When he came to the sentence, "One should use one's mind in such a way that it will be free from any attachment," I suddenly became thoroughly enlightened and realised that all things in the universe are Mind-essence itself.

I said to the Patriarch, "Who could have conceived that Mind-essence is intrinsically pure! Who could have conceived that Mind-essence is intrinsically free from becoming and annihilation! That Mind-essence is intrinsically self-sufficient, and free from change! Who could have conceived that all things are manifestations of Mind-essence!"

Thus at midnight, to the knowledge of no one, was the Dharma transmitted to me, and I consequently became the inheritor of the teachings of the "Sudden" School, and the possessor of the robe and the begging-bowl.

"You are now the Sixth Patriarch," said His Eminence. "Take good care of yourself and deliver as many sentient beings as possible. Spread the teaching; keep the teaching alive; do not let it come to an end. Listen to my stanza:

'Sentient beings who sow seed of Enlightenment
In the field of causation, will reap the fruit of
    Buddhahood.
Inanimate objects which are void of Buddha-nature
Sow not and reap not.' "

His Eminence further said: "When Patriarch Bodhidharma first came to China, few Chinese had confidence in him and so this robe has been handed down as a testimony from one Patriarch to another. As to the Dharma, as a rule it is transmitted from heart to heart and the recipient is expected to understand it and to realise it by his own efforts. From time immemorial, it has been the practice for one Buddha to pass on to his successor the quintessence of the Dharma, and for one Patriarch to transmit to another, from mind to mind, the esoteric teaching. As the robe may give cause for dispute, you will be the last one to inherit it. If you should again hand it down to a successor, your life would be in imminent danger. You must now leave this place as quickly as you can, lest some one should harm you."

I asked him, "Where shall I go?" and he replied, "Stop at Wei and seclude yourself at Wui."

As it was the middle of the night when I thus received the begging-bowl and the robe, I told the Patriarch that as I was a Southerner I did not know the mountain trails and it would be impossible for me to get down to the river. "You need not worry," he replied, "I will go with you." He then accompanied me to the Kiu-kiang landing where we got a boat. As he started to do the rowing himself, I asked him to be seated and let me handle the oar. He replied, "It is only right for me to get you across." (This is an illusion to the sea of birth and death which one has to cross before the shore of Nirvana can be reached.) To this I replied, " (So long as I was) under illusion, I was dependent on you to get me across, but now it is different. It was my fortune to be born on the frontier and my education is very deficient, but I have had the honor to inherit the Dharma from you; since I am now enlightened, it is only right for me to cross the sea of birth and death by my own effort to realise my own Essence of Mind."

"Quite so, quite so," he agreed. "Beginning with you (Ch'an) Buddhism will become very widespread. Three years from your leaving me I shall pass from this world. You may start on your journey now; go as fast as you can toward the South. Do not begin preaching too soon; (Ch'an) Buddhism is not to be easily spread."

After saying good-bye, I left him and walked toward the South. In about two months I reached the Tai-yu Mountain where I noticed several hundred men were in pursuit of me with the intention of recovering the robe and begging-bowl. Among them, the most vigilant was a monk of the name of Wei-ming whose surname was Chen. In lay-life he had been a general of the fourth rank. His manner was rough and his temper hot. When he overtook me, I threw the robe and the begging-bowl on a rock, saying, "This robe is nothing but a testimonial; what is the use of taking it away by force?" When he reached the rock, he tried to pick them up but could not. Then in astonishment he shouted, "Lay Brother, Lay Brother, (Hui-neng, although appointed the Sixth Patriarch, had not yet formally been admitted to the Order), I have come for the Dharma; I do not care for the robe." Whereupon I came from my hiding place and took the position on the rock of a Patriarch. He made obeisance and said, "Lay Brother, I beg you to teach me."

"Since the object of your coming is for the Dharma," said I, "please refrain from thinking about anything and try to keep your mind perfectly empty and receptive. I will then teach you." When he had done this for a considerable time, I said, "Venerable Sir, at the particular moment when you are thinking of neither good nor evil, what is your real self-nature (the word is, physiognomy)?"

As soon as he heard this he at once became enlightened, but he asked, "Apart from these sayings and ideas handed down by the Patriarchs from generation to generation, are there still any esoteric teachings?"

"What I can tell you is not esoteric," I replied, "If you turn your light inward, you will find what is esoteric within your own mind."

"In spite of my stay in Wong-mui," said he, "I did not realise my own self-nature. Now, thanks to your guidance, I realise it in the same way a water-drinker knows how hot and how cold the water is. Lay Brother, I am now your disciple." I replied, "If this is the case, then you and I are fellow disciples of the Fifth Patriarch. Please take good care of yourself." He paid homage and departed.

Some time after I reached Tso-kai, but as evil-doers were again persecuting me, I took refuge in Sze-wui where I staid with a party of hunters for fifteen years. They used to put me to watch their nets, but when I found living creatures entangled in them I would set them free. At meal time I would put vegetables in the same pan in which they cooked their meat. Some of them questioned me and I explained to them that I could only eat vegetables. Occasionally I talked to them in a way that befitted their understanding. One day I bethought myself that I ought not to pass so secluded a life all the time; I felt that the time had come for me to propagate the Dharma. Accordingly I left there and went to the Fat-shin Temple in Canton.

At the time I reached that temple, the monk Yen-chung, Master of Dharma, was lecturing on the Maha Parinirvana Sutra. It happened one day when a pennant was being blown about by the wind, that two monks entered into a dispute as to what was in motion, the wind or the pennant. As they failed to settle their difference, I suggested that it was neither; that what actually moved was their own mind. The whole group was surprised by what I said and the Master Yen-chung invited me to a seat of honor and questioned me about various knotty points in the Sutra. Seeing that my answers were precise and accurate, that they inferred more than book knowledge, he said to me, "Lay Brother, you must be an extraordinary man. I was told long ago that the inheritor of the Fifth Patriarch's robe and Dharma had come to the South; very likely you are the man?"

To this I politely assented. He made obeisence and courteously asked me to show to the assembly the robe and begging-bowl which I had inherited. He further asked what instructions I had received at the time the Fifth Patriarch had transmitted the Dharma to me.

I replied, "Apart from a discussion on the realisation of Mind-essence, he gave me no other instruction. He did not refer to Dhyana nor to Emancipation." The Master asked, "Why not?" I replied, "Because that would mean two kinds of Dharmas. That is not the Buddha Dharma, for the Buddha Dharma is not dual in its nature. He then asked, "What is the Buddha Dharma that is not dual in its nature?"

I replied, "The Maha Parinirvana Sutra which you are expounding teaches that Buddha-nature is the only way. For example: in that Sutra King-ko-kwai-tak, a Bodhisattva, asked the Buddha whether those who commit the four serious sins, or the five deadly sins, or are heretics, etc., would thereby root out their 'element of goodness' and their Buddha-nature. Buddha replied, 'There are two kinds of 'goodness-elements': an eternal element, and a non-eternal. Since Buddha-nature is neither eternal nor non-eternal, therefore, the Buddha's essential nature is not to be regarded as 'eradicated,' it is to be regarded as already, 'non-duality'. There are good natures and evil natures but Buddha's essential nature belongs to neither; it is non-dual. From the point of view and prejudices of ordinary people, there is a difference between the physical sense-ingredients and the mental and conscious ingredients, but enlightened men know that they are not dual in nature. It is that nature of non-duality that is Buddha-nature."

Master Yen-chung was pleased with my answer. Putting his hands together in token of respect, he said, "My interpretation of the Sutra is as worthless as a heap of debris, while your discourse is as valuable as pure gold." Subsequently he conducted a ceremony of initiation, receiving me into the order, and then asked me to accept him as a pupil.

Thenceforth under the Bodhi-tree I have discoursed about the teachings of the Fourth and Fifth Patriarchs. Since the Dharma was transmitted to me in Tung Mountain, I have gone through many hardships and often my life seemed to be hanging by a thread. Today I have had the honor of meeting Your Highness, and you, officials, monks and nuns, Taoists and laymen, in this great assembly. I must ascribe this good fortune to our happy connection in previous kalpas, as well as to our common accumulated merits in making offerings to various Buddhas in our past incarnations. Otherwise we would have had no chance of hearing the teachings of the "Sudden" School of Ch'an and thereby laying the foundation of our present success in understanding the Dharma.

This teaching is not a system of my own invention, but has been handed down by the Patriarchs. Those who wish to hear the teaching should first purify their own minds; and after hearing it, each must clear up his own doubts, even as the Sages have done in the past.

At the end of the address, the assembly felt rejoiced, made obeisance and departed.

CHAPTER II

Discourse on Repentance

At one time there was a large gathering of literary men and commoners gathered from Kwong-chow, Shiu-chow and other places, to listen to the Patriarch's words at his monastery of Tso-kai. The Patriarch ascended his platform and delivered the following address:—

Come, good people. In Buddhism we should start from our Essence of Mind. Let us purify our minds always and from one momentary sensation to another. Let us follow the Path by our own effort, recognise our own Essence-body, realise that our own mind is Buddha, and free ourselves by a voluntary observance of the disciplinary rules,—then this gathering will not be in vain. You have all come from distant places and your gathering here shows the affinity that exists among us. Let us now sit down together in the Indian fashion. First I will light the five kinds of incense that belong to your essential nature, then I will show you what is meant by "Formless Repentence."

When they were seated the Patriarch continued:—The first is the Sila Incense (Behavior), which symbolises that our minds are free from all taint of misdeeds, evil, jealousy, avarice, anger, spoilation and hatred. The second is Samadhi Incense, which symbolises that our mind is serene under all circumstances—favorable or unfavorable. The third is Prajna Incense, which means that our minds are free from all impediments; that we constantly seek to realise our Mind-essence with wisdom; that we refrain from all evil; that we do all kinds of good acts with no attachment to the fruit of such action; and that we are respectful toward our superiors, considerate of our inferiors, and sympathetic for the destitute and those in trouble. The fourth is the Incense of Liberation, which means that our minds are in such a perfectly free state that they cling to nothing and bother themselves neither with good nor evil. The fifth is the Incense of "Knowledge gained because of the attainment of Liberation." When our minds cling to neither good nor evil, we should take care not to let them go to the other extreme of vacuity and remain in a state of inertia. At this point we should study and seek to broaden our knowledge so that we can understand our own minds, thoroughly understand the principles of Buddhism, be considerate of others in our dealings with them, get rid of the idea of "self" and "existence," and realise that up to the time when we obtain enlightenment (*Bodhi*) our true nature (*Tathata*) is immutable.

Learned Audience:—This five-fold Incense perfumes us from within; we should not seek it without. Now I want to explain to you this Ritual of Repentance which is designed to expiate our sins whether committed in the present, the past or future lives; and whether physical, or by word, or by thought. (In Buddhist thought, sin is considered not in a legal sense as something to be punished, or forgiven, or atoned for by sacrifice, but in its cause-and effect aspect of Karma and its maturing.)

Please follow me carefully and repeat together what I am going to say. May we, disciples (from such and such a village), be always free from the taint of ignorance and delusion. We repent of all our past, present and future sins and evil deeds committed under delusion or in ignorance. May their karma be expiated at once and may they never rise again.

May we, disciples (from such and such a village), be always free from taint of arrogance and dishonesty. We repent of all our past, present and future evil deeds done in an arrogant or dishonest spirit. May their karma be expiated at once and may they never rise again.

May we, disciples (from such and such a village), be always free from taint of envy and jealousy. We repent of all our past, present and future evil deeds done in an envious or jealous spirit. May their karma be expiated at once and may they never rise again.

As you will notice, there are two aspects to this repentance ritual: One refers to repentance for past sin; we ought to repent for all our past sins and evil deeds committed under delusion or ignorance, arrogance or dishonesty, jealousy or envy, so as to put an end to all of them. This is one aspect of repentance. The other aspect refers to future conduct. Having realized the evil nature of our transgression we make a vow that hereafter we will put an end to all evil deeds committed under delusion or ignorance, arrogance or dishonesty, envy or jealousy, and that we will never sin again. This is the second aspect of repentance. On account of ignorance and delusion, common people do not always appreciate that in repentance they must not only feel sorry for their past sins, but must also refrain from sinning in the future. Since they often take no heed as to their future conduct, they commit the same sins over again almost before the past ones are expiated. How can we call that repentance?

Learned Audience: Having repented of our sins, we should take the following all-embracing vows: Listen very carefully:—

Our Mind-essence is potentially an infinite number of sentient beings. We vow to bring them all unto deliverance.

We vow to get rid of the evil passions of our minds, inexhaustible though they seem.

We vow to learn the countless systems of Dharma in our Mind-essence.

We vow to attain the Supreme Buddhahood of our Mind-essence.

We have now vowed to deliver an infinite number of sentient beings; but what does that mean? It does not mean that I, Hui-neng is going to deliver them. And who are these sentient beings, potential within our minds? They are the delusive mind, the deceitful mind, the evil mind, and such like—all these are sentient beings. Each of them has to be delivered by one-self by means of his own Essence of Mind; only by his own deliverance, is it genuine.

Now, what does it mean, "delivering oneself by one's own Essence of Mind?" It means the deliverance of the ignorant, delusive, and the vexatious beings that spring up within our own mind, by means of Right Views. With the aid of Right Views and Prajna, the barriers thrown up by these delusive and ignorant beings may be broken down; so that each of us will be in a position to deliver himself by his own efforts. The false will be delivered by truthfulness; the delusive by enlightenment; the ignorant by wisdom; and the malevolent by benevolence; such is genuine deliverance.

As to the vow; "to get rid of the inexhaustible evil passions," that refers to the transcendence of our unreliable and illusive thinking faculty by the transcendental Wisdom (Prajna) of our Mind-essence. As to the vow: "to learn the countless systems of Dharma"; there will be no true knowledge until we have been brought face to face with our Essence of Mind, by our conforming to the orthodox Dharma on all occasions. As to the vow, "to attain Supreme Buddhahood"; I wish to point out that when we are able to control our minds to follow the true and orthodox Dharma on all occasions, and when Prajna always rises in our minds, so that we can hold aloof from both ignorance and enlightenment, and can do away with falsehood as well as truth, then we may consider ourselves as having realised our Buddha-nature, or, in other words, having attained Buddhahood.

Learned Audience: we should always bear in mind that we are following the Path for thereby strength is added to our vows. Now, since we have all taken the four-fold vows, I will teach you the Ritual of the three-fold Guidance.

We take "Enlightenment" as our Guide, because it is the fruit of both merit (*Punya*) and Wisdom (*Prajna*).

We take "Orthodoxy" as our Guide, because it is the best way to get rid of desire.

We take "Purity" as our Guide, because it is the noblest quality of mankind.

Hereafter let Shakyamuni, the Enlightened One, be our guide and on no account should we listen to the suggestions of Mara, the evil one, or any heretic. We should testify to ourselves by constantly appealing to the "Three Gems" of our Essence of Mind, in which I advise you to take refuge. They are:

> Buddha, which stands for Enlightenment;
> Dharma, which stands for Orthodoxy;
> Sangha, which stands for Purity.

To take refuge in Enlightenment so that evil and delusive notions do not arise, so that desire decreases, discontent becomes unknown, and lust and greed no longer bind us—this is the fruitage of Punya and Prajna. To take refuge in Orthodoxy so that from momentary sensation to another we will be free from wrong views—this is the best means of getting rid of desires. To take refuge in Purity so that no matter under what circumstance we may be, we will not become contaminated by wearisome sense objects, by craving nor by desire— this is the noblest quality of mankind. To practise the "Three-fold Guidance" as thus outlined means to take refuge in one's Mind-essence. Ignorant people often take the "Three-fold Guidance" without understanding it. They say that they take refuge in Buddha: do they know where he is? If they cannot conceive Buddha, how can they take refuge in him? Would not such an assertion amount to self-deception? Each of you should examine this point for himself, so that his energy may not be misapplied through ignorance. The Sutra distinctly says that each should take refuge in the Buddha within himself. It does not refer to any other Buddhas, hence if we do not take refuge in the Buddha of our own Mind-essence, there is nowhere else for us to go. Having cleared this point, let each of us take refuge in the "Three Jewels" of his own mind. Within, each should control his own mind; without, each should be respectful toward others—this is the way to take refuge within ourselves.

I have a stanza, the reciting and practising of which will at once dispel the delusions and expiate the sins accumulated during many kalpas. This is the stanza:—

People under delusion accumulate tainted merit but tread
not the Path.

They are under the illusion that to accumulate merit
and to tread the Path are one and the same thing.

Their merit for alms-giving and offerings may be infinite,

But they fail to realise that the ultimate source of sin
lies in the greed, hatred and infatuation within their
own mind.

They expect to expiate their sin by the accumulation of
merit,

Without knowing that the felicities to be gained thereby
in future lives,

Have nothing to do with expiation of sin.

If we get rid of the sin within our own mind

Then it is a case of true repentance.

One who realises suddenly what constitutes true repentance in the Mahayana sense,

And who ceases to do evil and practises righteousness, is
free from sin.

* * *

Essence of Mind (Tathata) is the real Buddha,

While heretical views and the three poisonous elements
are Mara.

Enlightened by Right Views, we call forth the Buddha
within us.

When our nature is dominated by the three poisonous
elements, as the result of heretical views,

We are said to be possessed by Mara;

But when Right Views free our minds of these poison
elements,

Mara will be transformed into a real Buddha.

A follower of the Path who keeps constant watch on
his Mind-essence

Is in the same class with the many Buddhas.

Our Patriarchs transmitted no other system but this of
"Sudden Enlightenment."

If you are seeking Dharmakaya,

Search for it apart from the world of things and phenomena,

Then your mind will be pure and free.
Exert yourself in order to come face to face with Mind-
  essence and relax not;
For death may come suddenly and put an end to your
  earthly existence.

Learned Audience:—All of you should recite this stanza and
put it into practice. If you succeed in realising Essence of
Mind, then you may think of yourselves as being in my presence though you may be a thousand miles away. But should
you be unable to do so, though we were face to face with each
other, we would really be thousands of miles apart. In that
case what is the use of your taking the trouble to come here
from such a long distance? Take good care of yourselves. I
bid you good-bye.

Chapter III

Discourse on Prajna

On the following day Prefect Wai asked the Patriarch to give
another address. Having taken his seat, the Patriarch asked the
assembly to first purify their minds (by a period of dhyana-
silence) and then to join in reciting the Maha Prajna-paramita
Sutra, after which he gave the following address:—
Learned Audience: Prajna, the principle of wisdom, is inherent in every one of us. It is because of the delusions under
which our minds labor that we fail to realise its presence, and
that we have to seek the advice and the guidance of the more
highly enlightened before we can realise it in our mind's Essence. You should know that as far as Buddha-nature is
concerned, there is no difference between an enlightened man
and an ignorant one. What makes the difference is that one
realises it and the other is ignorant of it. Let me speak to
you now about the Maha Prajna-paramita Sutra, so that each
of you may attain wisdom. Listen carefully while I speak.
Learned Audience: There are many people who recite the
word, Prajna, the whole day long, who do not seem to know

that Prajna is inherent in their own nature. The mere talking about food will not appease hunger, but that is the very thing these people are doing. We may talk about the "Doctrine of Voidness" for myriads of kalpas, but merely talking about it will not enable one to realise it in his Mind-essence, and the talking will serve no good purpose in the end.

The name, Maha Prajna-paramita, is Sanskrit and means, "great Wisdom to reach the opposite shore." Now, what we ought to do with it is to carry it into practice with our mind; whether we recite it or do not recite it matters little. Mere reciting without mental practice, may be likened to a phantasm, a magical delusion, a flash of lighting, or a dew-drop. On the other hand, if we do both, then our mind will be in accord with what we repeat orally. Our very self-nature is Buddha, and apart from this nature there is no other Buddha.

What is Maha? Maha means, "great." The capacity of the mind is as great as that of space. It is infinite, it is neither round nor square, neither great nor small, neither green nor yellow, neither red nor white, neither above nor below, neither long nor short, neither angry nor happy, neither right nor wrong, neither good nor evil, neither first nor last. All Buddha-lands are as void as space. Intrinsically our transcendental nature is void and not a single dharma can be attained. It is the same with Mind-essence which is a state of the "voidness of non-voidity."

Learned Audience: when you hear me speak about the void, do not fall into the idea that I mean vacuity. It is of the utmost importance that we should not fall into that idea, because then when a man sits quietly and keeps his mind blank he would be abiding in a state of the "voidness of indifference." The illimitable void of the Universe is capable of holding myriads of things of various shapes and form, such as the sun and the moon, and the stars, worlds, mountains, rivers, rivulets, springs, woods, bushes, good men, bad men, laws pertaining to goodness and to badness, heavenly planes and hells, great oceans and all the mountains of Mahameru. Space takes in all these, and so does the voidness of our nature. We say that Essence of Mind is great because it embraces all things since all things are within our nature. When we see the goodness or the badness of other people, and are not attracted by it, nor repulsed by it, nor attached to it, then the attitude of our mind is as void as space. In that we see the greatness of our minds, therefore we call Mind-essence, Maha.

Learned Audience: When ignorant people have ideas they merely talk about them, but wise men keep them within their own minds and put them into practice. There is also a class of foolish people who sit quietly and try to keep their minds blank; they refrain from thinking of anything and then call themselves "great." Concerning this heretical view, I have no patience to speak. You should know that the capacity of the mind is very great since it pervades the whole Universe wherever the domain of Law extends. When we use the mind we can consider everything; when we use Mind to its full capacity, we shall know all.

Prajna comes from Mind-essence and not from any exterior source. Do not have any mistaken notion about that. To cherish mistaken notions about that is to make a "selfish use of True Nature." Once the "True Nature" of Mind-essence is realised, one will be forever free from delusion. Since the capacity of Mind is for great things, we should not busy it with trivial acts. (That is, the mind that can realise Mind-essence through the right practice of dhyana, ought not to be sitting quietly with a blank mind nor wasting its resources on idle talk.) Do not talk all day about "the void," without practising it in the mind. One who does this may be likened to a self-styled king who is really a commoner. Prajna can never be attained in that way and those who act like that are not my disciples.

What is Prajna? It means, Transcendental Wisdom. If we steadily, at all times and in all places, keep our thoughts free from foolish desire and act wisely on all occasions, then we are practising the Paramita of Prajna. One foolish notion is enough to shut-off Prajna; one wise thought will bring it forth again. People in ignorance or under delusion do not see this; they talk about it with their tongue but in their mind they are ignorant of it. They are always saying that they practice Prajna, and they talk incessantly about "vacuity," but they have not realised the True Void. Prajna is Wisdom's Heart; it has neither form nor characteristic. If we interpret it in this way, then it is, indeed, the Wisdom of Prajna.

What is Paramita? It is a Sanskrit word (commonly translated, "ideal") that means, "to the opposite shore." Figura-

tively it means, "beyond existence and non-existence." By clinging to sense things, existence and non-existence are like the
ups and downs of the billowy sea. Such a state, metaphorically
is called, "this shore"; while beyond existence and non-existence
there is a state characterised by non-attachment that has the
undisturbed calmness of running water, that is called, "the opposite shore." This is why Prajna is called, Paramita.

Learned Audience: People under illusion recite the Maha
Prajna-paramita with their tongue and, while they are reciting
it, erroneous and evil thoughts arise; but if they put it into
practice unremittingly they will come to realise its True Nature. To know this Dharma is to know the Law of Prajna;
and to practice it is to practice Ideal Wisdom. He who does
not practice it is an ordinary man; he who concentrates his
mind on its practice, even if it be but for a moment only, he
is the equal of Buddha. An ordinary man is Buddha! and defilement is Enlightenment (Bodhi). A passing foolish thought
makes one an ordinary man, while an enlightened thought
makes one a Buddha. A passing thought that clings to sense-
objects is defilement; a second thought that frees one from
attachment is Enlightenment.

Maha Prajna-paramita! The Great Transcendental-Wisdom
Ideal, supreme, most exalted, foremost. It neither stays, nor
goes, nor comes. By it Buddhas of the present, the past and
future generations attain Buddhahood. We should use this Perfect Wisdom to break up the five bundles of aggregates that
make up our personality, and thus get rid of the pollutions
and contaminations. To follow such a practice ensures the
attainment of Buddhahood. The three poisonous elements
(greed, anger and infatuation) will then be turned into good
conduct (sila) and self-realisation (samadhi) and wisdom
(Prajna). When one is free from defilement, Wisdom reveals
itself steadily and cannot be distinguished from Mind-essence.
Those who understand this Dharma will be free from idle
thoughts. To be free from discriminations, from clinging to
desires, from illusions; to set free one's true nature; to use
Prajna for contemplation; to take an attitude of neither indifference nor attachment towards all things—that is what is
meant by realising one's true Essence of Mind and (in its perfection) is the attainment of Buddhahood.

Learned Audience: If you wish to penetrate the deepest

mystery of the Dharma-world and experience the deepest realization (*samadhi*) of Prajna, you should practice Prajna by reciting and studying the Diamond Sutra (the *Vajracchedika*) which will enable you to realize Essence of Mind. You should know that the merit for studying this Sutra is distinctly set forth in the text in laudatory terms; it is immeasurable and illimitable and cannot be enumerated in detail. This Sutra expounds the highest thought of Buddhism and our Lord Buddha delivered it specially for the very wise and quick-witted. The less wise and the slow-witted doubt its credibility. Why? For example: When it rains through the power of the celestial Naga on the plains of India, cities, towns and villages are drifted about as if they were only leaves of the date tree; but should it rain on the great ocean, the level of the seas of the whole world would not be affected by it. When the followers of the highest school of Mahayana study the Diamond Sutra, their minds become enlightened as they realize that Prajna is immanent in their own Mind-essence. Since they have their own access to highest wisdom through the constant practice of concentration and contemplation (dhyana and samadhi) they realize that they no longer need to rely on scriptural authority.

The Prajna immanent in the minds of every one may be likened to the rain, the moisture of which refreshes every living thing, trees and plants as well as sentient creatures. When rivers and streams reach the sea, the water carried by them merges into the one body, which is a good analogy. When rain falls in a deluge, plants which are not deep-rooted are washed away and eventually they perish. It is the same with the slow-witted when they hear about the teachings of the "Sudden School." The Prajna immanent in them is exactly the same as that in very wise men, but when the Dharma is made known to them they fail to enlighten themselves. Why is it? It is because their minds are thickly veiled by erroneous views and deeply rooted infections, just as the sun is often thickly veiled by clouds and unable to show its splendor until the wind blows the clouds away. Prajna does not vary with different persons; what makes the seeming difference is the question whether one's mind is enlightened or is beclouded. He who does not realize his own Mind-essence, and rests under the delusion that Buddhahood can be attained by outward religious rites, is rightly called the slow-witted. He who knows the teachings of the "Sudden School," and who attaches no importance to ritual, and whose mind always functions under right views so that he is absolutely free of defilement and contamination, such an one may be said to have realized his Mind-essence.

Learned Audience: The mind should be framed in such a way that it will be independent of external and internal things, at liberty to come and go, free from attachment, thoroughly enlightened, without the least obscuration. He whose mind is thus framed is able to measure up to the standard of the Prajna Sutras. The sutras and the scriptures of both the Mahayana and the Hinayana, as well as the twelve sections of the canonical writings, were provided to suit the different needs and temperaments of various people. It is upon the principle that Prajna is latent in every man that the doctrines expounded in these scriptures are established. If there were no human beings, there would be no teachings; hence we know that all teachings are made for man and that all the Sutras owe their existence to preachers. Some men are wise, the so called superior men, and some are ignorant, the so called inferior men; the wise preach to the ignorant when they are asked to do so. Through this the ignorant may attain sudden enlightenment and their minds will become illuminated thereby; then they are no longer different from wise men. This does not mean that without enlightenment a man is in a class with human beings different from Buddhahood. The opposite is the truth, he has always been in the same class with Buddhas from the beginning. Ignorance does not separate him from Buddhahood, it only obscures his realization of his true Buddha nature.

A gleam of enlightenment is enough to make a living being the equal of a Buddha. Since all truth (Dharmas) is immanent in our minds, there is no reason why we should not realize intuitively the real nature of Mind-essence (tathata). The Bodhisattva Sila Sutra says, "Our Essence of Mind is intrinsically pure; if we knew our mind perfectly and realized what our self-nature truly is, all of us would attain Buddhahood." The Vimalakirti Nirdesa Sutra says, "At once they become enlightened and regain their true mind."

When the Fifth Patriarch preached to me I became enlightened immediately after he had spoken and spontaneously I realized the real nature of Mind-essence (tathata). For this reason it is my particular object to propagate the teaching of the "Sudden" School so that learners may know enlightenment at once and realize their true nature by introspection of mind. Should they fail to enlighten themselves they ought to ask some very pious and learned Buddhist who understands the teachings of this highest school to show them the right way. The office of a pious and learned Buddhist who guides others to realize Essence of Mind, is an exalted position. Through his assistance one may be initiated into all meritorious Dharmas. The wisdom of Buddhas, past, present and future, as well as the teachings of the twelve sections of the canon are immanent in the mind, but in case we fail to enlighten ourselves, we have to seek the guidance of the pious and learned. On the other hand those who enlighten themselves need no extraneous help. It is wrong to insist upon the idea that we cannot obtain liberation without the assistance of the pious and learned. It is by our innate wisdom that we enlighten ourselves, and even the extraneous help and instruction of a pious and learned friend would be of no use so long as one is deluded by false doctrines and erroneous views. As we introspect our minds with Prajna, all erroneous views will disappear of themselves, and just as soon as we realize Essence of Mind we will immediately arrive at the Buddha stage.

When we use Prajna for introspection we are illuminated within and without and are in position to know our own nature. To realize our own nature is to obtain fundamental liberation. To obtain liberation is to attain the Samadhi of Prajna, which is intuitive insight. What is intuitive insight? Intuitive insight to see and to realize all dharmas (things as well as truths) with a mind free from attachment. In action Prajna is everywhere present yet it "sticks" nowhere. What we have to do is to so purify the mind that the six aspects of consciousness (sight, sound, smell, taste, touch, mentation) in passing through their six sense-gates will neither be defiled by nor attached to their six sense-objects. When our mind works freely without any hindrance and is at liberty "to come" or "to go," then we have attained the intuitive insight of Prajna, which is emancipation. To enable one to attain such a mental state of freedom is the function of intuitive insight. To refrain from thinking of anything, in the sense that all mental activity is suppressed, is to be Dharma-ridden; this is an extremely erroneous view. (Discriminative thought which leads to desire and attachment, or to aversion and defilement, is to be controlled in the interests of intuitive thought which leads to self-realization and freedom.)

Those who understand the way of intuitive insight will know everything; they will have the experience that all the Buddhas have had, and they will attain Buddhahood. In the future, if an initiate of my school should make a vow in company with his fellow-disciples to devote his whole life without retrogression to the practice and commemoration of the teachings of this "Sudden" School, in the same spirit as if he were serving the Buddha, he would attain without failure the Path that leads to Bodhisattvahood and Buddhahood. He should transmit from heart the instructions handed down from one Patriarch to another, and no attempt should be made to conceal the orthodox teaching.

Learned Audience: I have a Stanza for all of you to recite. Both laity and monks should put its teachings into practice, without which it would be useless to remember the words alone. Listen to this stanza:—

> A master of the Buddhist canon
> As well as the teachings of the Dhyana school
> Should teach nothing but the Dharma for realizing Essence of Mind.
> We can hardly classify dharmas into "sudden" and "gradual,"
> But some men will attain enlightenment quicker than others.
> For example: this system for realizing Essence of Mind
> Is beyond the comprehension of the ignorant.
> We may explain it in ten thousand ways,
> But all these explanations may be traced back to one principle.
> To illumine our gloomy mind, stained by defilement,
> We should constantly set up the Sun of Wisdom.
> Erroneous views keep us in defilement,
> But right views remove us far from it.
> But when we are in a position to discard both defilement and purity
> Then are we absolutely free.
> Bodhi is immanent in our Mind-essence;
> Any attempt to look for it elsewhere is foolish.

Within our defiled minds, purity is to be found,
And once our mind is set right, we are free from the
  bonds
Of defilement, of evil karma, of expiation.
If we are treading the Path of Enlightenment,
We need not be worried by stumbling-blocks.
If we keep an eye constantly on our own faults,
We cannot go far astray from the right path.
Every species of life has its own way of salvation;
They will not be antagonistic one to another.
If we leave our own path and seek for another way
Of salvation, we shall never find it.
Though we plod on till death overtake us
We shall find only penitence at the end.
If one wishes to find the true way,
Right action will lead him to it directly.
If one has not a mind to aim at Buddhahood,
One will grope in the dark and never find it.
He who treads the Path in earnest
Sees not the mistakes of the world.
If we find fault with others,
We ourselves are also in the wrong;
When other people are in the wrong we should ignore it;
It is wrong for one to find fault with others.
By getting rid of the habit of fault-finding,
We get rid of one source of defilement.
When neither hatred nor love disturb the mind,
Serene and restful is our sleep.
Those who intend to be teachers of others
Should themselves be skillful in the various expedients
  that lead to enlightenment.
When the disciple is free from all doubts
Then it indicates that his Mind-essence is unclouded.
This world is the Buddha-world
Within which enlightenment may be sought.
To seek enlightenment by separating from this world
Is as foolish as to search for a rabbit's horn.
Right views are called "transcendental,"
Erroneous views are called "worldly,"
But when all views, both right and erroneous, are dis-
  carded,

Then the essence of Wisdom manifests itself.
Kalpa after kalpa a man may be under illusion,
But once enlightened, it takes him but a moment to
attain Buddhahood.

* * *

After hearing what the Patriarch had to say, Prefect Wai, the government officials, Taoists, monks, and laymen, were all enlightened. They made obeisance in a body and exclaimed unanimously, "Well done! Well done! Who would have expected that a Buddha would be born in Kwongtung?"

CHAPTER IV

Discourse on Dhyana and Samadhi

The Patriarch, on another occasion, addressed the assembly as follows:—

Learned Audience: Samadhi and Prajna are fundamental. But you must not be under the wrong impression that they are independent of each other, for they are not two entities, they are inseparably united. Samadhi is the quintessence of Prajna, while Prajna is the activity of Samadhi.

At the very moment Prajna is realized, Samadhi is simultaneously attained. At the very moment that Samadhi is realized, Prajna is attained. A disciple should not think that there is a distinction between first comes Samadhi, then comes Prajna, and first comes Prajna, then comes Samadhi. To think that way would imply succession and cause and effect, whereas, they are simultaneous. For one whose tongue is ready with good words but whose heart is impure, Samadhi and Prajna are useless because they are not in balance. On the other hand, when one is good in mind as well as in word, and when the outward appearance and inner feelings are in harmony with each other, then Samadhi and Prajna are in balance.

To an enlightened disciple (who has realized Prajna in Samadhi) discussion about it is unnecessary. To argue about Prajna or Samadhi as to which comes first, places one in the same position with those who are under delusion. Argument implies a desire to win, it strengthens egoism, it binds one to belief in the idea of "a self, a being, a living being and a person." But we may liken Samadhi and Prajna to a glowing lamp and its light: with the glowing lamp there is light; without it there is darkness. Light is the quintessence of the glowing lamp, the glowing lamp is the expression of light. In name they are two things, but in reality they are one and the same. It is the same with Samadhi and Prajna.

The Patriarch continued: To practice samadhi is to make it a rule to have the mind in concentrated attention on all occasions (that is, not to let the mind wander from the thing in hand),—no matter what we are doing, walking, standing, sitting or reclining. The Vimalakirti Nirdesa Sutra says: "Straightforwardness is the holy place, the Pure Land." Do not let your mind be "crooked" and try to be straightforward with your lips only. People should practice straightforwardness but should not attach themselves to anything. People under delusion believe obstinately that there is a substance behind appearances and so they are stubborn in holding to their own way of interpreting the samadhi of specific mode, which they define as, "sitting quietly and continuously without letting any idea arise in the mind." Such an interpretation would class us with inanimate objects; it is a stumbling-block to the right Path and the Path should be kept open. How can we block the Path? By attachment to any definite thought; if we free our minds from attachments, the Path will be clear, otherwise we are in bondage. If that practice of "sitting quietly without letting any idea arise in the mind," is correct, why on one occasion was Saraputra reprimanded by Vimalakirti for sitting quietly in the forest? (That is, it is not thinking that blocks the Path, but attachment to definite thoughts.)

Some teachers of concentration instructed their disciples to keep a watch on their minds and secure tranquillity by the cessation of all thought, and henceforth their disciples gave up all effort to concentrate the mind and ignorant persons who did not understand the distinction became insane from trying to carry out the instruction literally. Such cases are not rare and it is a great mistake to teach the practice.

It has been the tradition of our school to make "non-objectivity" as our basis, "idea-lessness" as our object, and "non-attachment" as our fundamental principle. "Non-objectivity" means, not to be absorbed in objects when in contact with objects; "idea-lessness" means, not to be carried away by any particular idea in our exercise of the mental faculty; ("non-attachment" means, not to cherish any desire for or aversion to any particular thing or idea). "Non-attachment" is the characteristic of Mind-essence.

We should treat all things—good or bad, beautiful or ugly—as void (of any self-substance). Even in time of dispute and quarrel, we should treat intimates and enemies alike and never think of retaliation. In the thinking faculty, let the past be dead. If we allow our thoughts, past, present and future, to become linked up into a series, we put ourselves under restraint. On the other hand, if we never let our mind become attached at any time to any thing, we gain emancipation. For this reason we make "non-attachment" our fundamental principle.

To free ourselves from dependence upon externals is called, "non-objectivity." In as far as we are in position to do this, the path of the Dharma is free. That is why we make "non-objectivity" our basis.

To keep our mind free from defilement under all circumstances is called "idea-lessness." Our mind should always stand aloof and on no account should we allow circumstances to influence the functioning of the mind. It is a great mistake to suppress all thinking. Even if we succeed, and die immediately thereafter, still, there is rebirth. Mark this, pilgrims of the Path! It is bad enough for a man to commit blunders by cherishing false ideas of the Dharma, how much worse to teach others. Being deluded, he is blind himself, and in addition he misrepresents and puts to shame the Buddhist scriptures. Therefore we make "idea-lessness" our object.

There is a type of man who is under delusion who boasts of his realization of Mind-essence; but being influenced by circumstances ideas rise in his mind, followed by erroneous views, which in turn become the source of attachment and defilement. In Essence of Mind, intrinsically, there is nothing to be attained. To boast of attainment and to talk foolishly of merits and demerits is erroneous and defiling. For this reason we make "idea-lessness" the object of our school.

(If "idea-lessness" is not the cessation of all thought) what ideas should we get rid of, and on what ideas should we focus our mind? We should get rid of all "pairs of opposites" of all conceptions of goodness and badness (that is, of all discriminative thinking). We should focus our mind on the true nature of reality. (The word used is "Tathata," which means, "True Nature," or Mind-essence, or Prajna, or "Oneness," or "Suchness," or anything else that is ultimate.) Tathata (considered as the ultimate "suchness" of Mind-essence) is the quintessence of "idea"; "idea" is the manifestation of Tathata. It is the function of Tathata to give rise to "ideas." It is not the sense-organs that do so. Tathata (considered as the Intellective Principle) reproduces its own attribute, therefore, it can give rise to "idea." Without Tathata, sense-organs and sense-objects would disappear immediately. Because it is an attribute to Tathata to give rise to ideas, our sense-organs, in spite of their functioning in seeing, hearing, touching, smelling, and knowing, are not tainted and defiled under all circumstances. (It is the cherishing of "attachments" that defiles.) Our true-nature is "self-manifesting" all the time. (The Path to self-realization of Mind-essence through Samadhi and Prajna is present to all, even though for some it may be blocked for a time by "attachments.") Therefore, the Sutra says: "He who is an adept in appreciation of that which lies behind things and phenomena, is established upon the Ultimate Principle (Prajna).

* * *

The Patriarch one day preached to an assembly as follows:

In our system of Dhyana, we neither dwell upon our mind nor upon its purity; neither do we seek to suppress its activity. As to dwelling on the mind: the (functional) mind is primarily delusive and as we come to realize that it is only a phantasm we see that there is no reason for dwelling upon it. As to dwelling upon its purity: our nature is intrinsically pure, and just as far as we get rid of discriminative thinking, there will remain nothing but purity in our nature; it is these delusive ideas that obscure our realization of True reality (Tathata). If we direct our mind to dwell upon purity, we are only creating another delusion: the delusion of purity. Since delusion has no abiding place, it is deluding to dwell upon it. Purity has neither shape nor form, but some people go so far as to invent the "Form of Purity" and then treat it as a problem for solution. Holding such an opinion, these people become purity-ridden and their Essence of Mind is thereby obscured. Those who are training themselves for serenity of mind, in their contact with the many types of men, should not notice the faults of others. They should be indifferent as to whether others are good or bad, or whether they deserve merit or demerit. To assume a discriminatory attitude toward others is to invite perturbation of mind. An unenlightened man may seem outwardly unperturbed, but as soon as he opens his mouth and criticises others and talks about their merit or demerit, their ability or weakness, their goodness or badness, he shows that he has deviated from the right course. On the other hand, to dwell upon our own mind and its purity is also a stumbling-block in the true Path.

* * *

At another assembly the Patriarch spoke as follows: What is dhyana? It means, first, to gain full freedom of mind and to be entirely unperturbed under all outward circumstances, be they good or otherwise. What is the difference between Dhyana and Samadhi? Dhyana is the effort to be mentally free from any attachment to outer objects. Samadhi is the realization of that freedom in inward peace. If we are attached to outer objects the inner mind will be perturbed. When we are free from attachment to all outer objects, the mind will be at peace. Our Essence of Mind is intrinsically pure; the reason we become perturbed is simply because we allow ourselves to be carried away by the circumstances we are under. He who is able to keep his mind serene, irrespective of circumstances, has attained true Samadhi.

To be free from attachment is Dhyana; to realize inner peace is Samadhi. When we are able to hold the mind concentrated, and to rest in inner peace, then we have attained both Dhyana and Samadhi. The Bodhisattva Sila Sutra says: "Our Essence of Mind is intrinsically pure." Learned Audience: let us each realize this for himself from one momentary sensation to another. Let us practice it by ourselves, let us train ourselves, and thus by our own effort attain Buddhahood.

CHAPTER V

Discourse on the Three-Bodies of Buddha

Some time after the foregoing Discourse on Repentance had been delivered to "commoners," when the Patriarch had gathered his disciples together for instruction, a senior disciple, Fathoi, said to the Patriarch, "Sir, will you please leave to posterity certain instruction whereby people under delusion may realize their Buddha-nature?"

"Listen to me," replied the Patriarch. It is possible for those who are under delusion to realize their Buddha-nature, provided they acquaint themselves with the nature of ordinary sentient beings. Without such knowledge, to seek Buddhahood would be in vain, even if one spent aeons of time in doing so.

First, let me show you how to get acquainted with the nature of the sentient beings within your mind, whereby one can realize the Buddha-nature latent in everyone. Knowing Buddha means nothing else than knowing sentient beings. It is sentient beings who are blind to the fact that they are potentially Buddhas, whereas a Buddha sees no difference between himself and other beings. When sentient beings realize their Essence of Mind, they are Buddhas. If a Buddha is under delusion as to his Essence of Mind, he is then only an ordinary being. Seeing everything as equal in Essence of Mind makes ordinary beings Buddhas. Seeing inequalities in Essence of Mind transforms a Buddha into an ordinary being. When one's mind is crooked or depraved, then he is only an ordinary being with Buddha-nature latent within him. On the other hand, if one concentrates his mind on equality and straightforwardness, even for one moment only, then he is a Buddha.

Within our mind there is Buddha, and that Buddha within is the real Buddha. If Buddha is not to be found within our mind, then where shall we seek for the real Buddha? Doubt not that Buddha is within your own mind, apart from which nothing can exist. Since all things and phenomena are the product of mind, the Sutra says: "When mental activity rises, various things exist; when mental activity ceases, various things exist not."

Our physical body may be likened to an inn where we can

remain only temporarily, we cannot make it a refuge. The Trikaya of Buddha is to be found within our Mind-essence which is the common possession of everybody. It is because the mind of an ordinary man labors under delusion that he does not know his own inner nature, the result is that he ignores the Trikaya that is within himself and seeks for it without. Please listen; I am going to show you that you can realize the Trikaya within yourself, which being a manifestation of Mind-essence cannot be found anywhere else.

> Within our physical body we take refuge in the Pure Dharmakaya (Essence-body) of Buddha;
> Within our physical body we take refuge in the Perfect Sambhoga-kaya (the Bliss-body) of Buddha;
> Within our physical body we take refuge in the Myriad Nirmanakaya (Bodies of transformation,) of Buddha.

What is the Pure Dharmakaya? Our Mind-essence is intrinsically pure, that is, all things are manifestations of mind. Good deeds and evil deeds are but the manifestation of good thoughts and evil thoughts respectively. Thus within Essence of Mind all things, like the azure of the sky and the radiance of the sun and moon which, when obscured by passing clouds, may appear as if their brightness had been dimmed, but as soon as the clouds are blown away, their brightness reappears and all objects are again fully illuminated. Foolish thoughts may be likened to the clouds while sagacity and Wisdom are the moon and the Sun. When we become attached to discriminated objects, our Mind-essence becomes clouded by drifting thoughts which prevent sagacity and Wisdom from sending forth their light. We were fortunate that we found learned and pious teachers to make known the orthodox Dharma to us so that we may, by our own effort do away with ignorance and delusion, and by so doing we will become enlightened both within and without, and our true nature within our Essence of Mind will manifest itself. This is precisely what happens with those who come face to face with their Essence of Mind. This is what is called the Pure Dharmakaya of Buddha.

To take refuge in the true Buddha is to take refuge in our own Essence of Mind. He who takes refuge within himself must first get rid of the evil-mind and the jealous-mind, the flattering and crooked-mind, deceit, and falsehood, and fallacious views, egotism, snobbishness, contemptuousness, arrogance, and all other evils that may arise at any time. To take refuge within ourselves is to be always on the alert to prevent our own mistakes and to refrain from criticism of other's faults. He who is humble and patient on all occasions and is courteous to every one, has truly realized his Mind-essence, so truly in fact that his Path is free from further obstacles. This is the way to take refuge in (the Buddha of) oneself.

What is the Perfect Sambhogakaya? Let us take the illustration of a lamp. Since the light of a lamp can dissipate darkness that has been there for a thousand years, so a ray of Wisdom can do away with ignorance that has lasted for ages. We need not bother about the past, for the past is gone and is irrecoverable. What demands our attention is the present and future, so let our thoughts, from one momentary sensation to another, be clear and pure and let us see face to face our Mind-essence. Goodness and evil are opposite to each other, but in essence they cannot be dualistic. This non-dualistic nature is called "true nature," it can neither be contaminated by evil, nor affected by goodness. This is what is called the Sambhogakaya of Buddha. One single evil thought clouding our Essence of Mind will undo the good merit accumulated in aeons of time; while a good thought can expiate all our sins though they be as many as the sands of the river Ganges. To realize our Essence of Mind from one momentary sensation to another and without intermission until we attain Supreme Enlightenment (Bodhi) so that we are in a perpetual state of Right Mindfulness, is the Sambhogakaya.

Now, what is the Myriad Nirmanakaya? When we subject ourselves to the least differentiation or particularisation, transformation takes place: otherwise all things would be as void as space, as they inherently are. By letting our minds dwell on evil things, hell arises. By letting our minds dwell upon good acts, paradise is manifested. Dragons and snakes are the transformations of venomous hatred; while Bodhisattvas are compassionate thoughts made manifest. The various heavens are the projection of Prajna; while underworlds are the transformations of ignorance and infatuation. Un-numbered, indeed, are the transformations of Mind-essence. People under delusion are as if asleep; they do not understand; their minds naturally turn toward evil and, as a rule, they practice evil. But should they turn their minds from evil to righteousness, even for one moment, Prajna shines forth. This is what is called the Nirmanakaya of the Buddha of Mind-essence.

The Dharmakaya is intrinsically self-sufficient. To see our own Essence of Mind clearly and without interruption, is the Sambhogakaya of Buddha. To let our mind dwell on the Sambhogakaya, so that Prajna radiates forth in manifestation is Nirmanakaya. To attain enlightenment by one's own effort and to practice by one's self the goodness that is inherent in our Essence of Mind, is a genuine case of "taking refuge." Our physical body consisting of flesh and skin, etc., is nothing more than a tenement or an inn; it is no place of refuge. Let us realize the Trikaya of our own Mind-essence, then we shall know the Buddha of our own nature.

In closing let me leave with you a stanza, entitled: "The Real Buddha of Mind-essence." Accordingly as they heed it people of future generations who can understand its meaning will realize their Mind-essence and attain Buddhahood. This is the stanza:—

> Those who understand the Mahayana teaching
> And are thus able to realize Mind-essence
> Should reverently and fervently seek for a realization of
>   Dharmakaya.
> The Dharmakaya, the Sambhogakaya, the Nirmana-
>   kaya—
> These three Bodies emanate from Oneness.
> He who is able to realize this fact intuitively
> Has sown the seed and will reap the fruit of Enlight-
>   enment.
> It is from Nirmanakaya that our "pure nature" emerges;
> Within the former the latter is always to be found.
> Guided by its "pure nature" Nirmanakaya follows the
>   right path,
> And will some day culminate in a Body of Bliss, perfect
>   and infinite.
> Pure Nature is hidden by our sensual instincts;
> By getting rid of sensuality, we realize Pure Dhar-
>   makaya.
> When our temperament is such that we are no longer
>   the slave of the five sense-objects,

And when we have realized Mind-essence, even for one
moment, then Tathata is known to us.

Those who are so fortunate as to be followers of the
Sudden School

Shall suddenly, in this life, see the Blessed One in their
own Mind-essence.

He who has not realized Essence of Mind and seeks for
Buddha without,

Is on a wrong path and is acting foolishly.

He who seeks Buddha by practising certain doctrines

Knows not the place where the real Buddha is to be
found.

He who is seeking to realize Buddha within his own
mind,

He only is sowing the seed of Buddhahood.

CHAPTER VI

Dialogues Suggested by Various
Temperaments and Circumstances

Upon the Patriarch's return to the village of Tso-hau in
Shiu-chow from Wong-mui, where the Dharma had been transmitted to him, he was an unknown man. At that time, it was
a Confucian scholar, named Liu Chi-luk, who first gave him a
warm welcome and appreciation. It came about in this manner.
Chi-luk had an aunt, named Wu Chun-chong who was a Buddhist nun, who was in the habit of reciting the Maha Parinirvana Sutra. One day the Patriarch heard her reciting it, and
after listening for only a short time, grasped the profound
meaning of the Sutra, and began to explain it to her, whereupon she brought the book and asked him the meaning of certain passages.

"I am not very well educated," he replied, "but if you wish
to understand the purport of the book, I will do the best I
can." "How can you understand the meaning of the text,"
she rejoined, "if you do not know the words?" To this he re-

plied: "The profound teaching of the various Buddhas, has nothing to do with the written language."

This answer surprised her very much, and recognising that he was no ordinary man, she spoke of him freely to the pious elders of the village, saying: "He is a sage. We should get his permission to supply him with food and lodgings, and urge him to remain with us."

Whereupon a descendant of Marquis Wu of the Ai Dynasty, named, Tso Shuk-leung, came one afternoon with other villagers to offer homage to the Patriarch. At that time the historic Po-lam Monastery, which had been devastated by war at the end of the 'Chu Dynasty, was reduced to a heap of ruins. The villagers rebuilt it on the old site, and asked the Patriarch to make it his home. Afterwards it became a very famous temple.

* * *

The monk, Fat-Hoi, a native of Hook-kong in Shu-chow, in his first interview with the Patriarch, asked the meaning of the well-known saying, "The spontaneous realization of Mind-Essence is the state of attaining Buddhahood." The Patriarch replied:—When one has attained to the state of mind in which there are no rising thoughts, simultaneously he has realized his Essence of Mind and attained Buddhahood. To realize that all phenomena are a manifestation of mind is just the same as realizing Mind-Essence. When one realizes that no rising thought should be annihilated, he is on his way to attaining Buddhahood, and to know how to be free from all discriminations of thought and conceptions of phenomena is the same as attaining Buddhahood. If I were to give you a full explanation, it would take the full time of a kalpa. Listen to this stanza:

"Prajna is what mind is; Samadhi is what Buddha is.
The spontaneous realization of Mind is Prajna;
Attaining the state of Buddhahood
Is what Samadhi is.
In practising Prajna and Samadhi, let each keep pace
    with the other,
Then our thoughts will be pure.
This teaching can be understood
Only through the 'habit of practice.'

Samadhi functions, but inherently it is not.
The orthodox teaching is, to practice Prajna as well as
    Samadhi."

After considering what the Patriarch had said, Fat-hoi was
enlightened and he praised the Patriarch in the following
stanza:

"That which mind is, Buddha is; how true it is, indeed!
I put myself to shame by not understanding it.
Now I understand the principle of Prajna and Samadhi,
Both of which I shall practice to set myself free from
    all confining forms."

* * *

The monk Fat-tat, a native of Hung-chow, who joined the
order at the early age of seven, used to recite the Lotus of the
Good Law Sutra. When he came to offer homage to the Patriarch, he failed in offering due respect to him, for which the
Patriach reproved him, saying, "If you object to offer due respect, would it not be better to omit the salutation entirely?
There must be something in your mind that makes you feel
that way. Please tell me what you do in your daily religious
exercise?"

"I recite the Lotus of the Good Law (*Saddharma Pundarika*) Sutra," replied Fat-tat; "I have read the whole text
three thousand times."

"If you had fully understood the meaning of the Sutra,"
remarked the Patriarch, "You would not have assumed such a
lofty bearing, even if you had read it ten thousand times.
When you understand it, you will be following the same Path
with me. But now, all that you have accomplished is to make
yourself conceited. Moreover, you do not seem to realize that
you are in the wrong. Listen to this stanza:

"Since the object of ceremony is to curb arrogance,
Why did you fail to offer due respect?
To take pride in oneself, is a source of sin,
But to learn to treat any attainment as 'void,' is to at-
    tain incomparable merit."

The Patriarch then asked him for his name, and upon being
told that his name was Fat-tat (which means "law-understand-

ing"), he remarked, "Your name is Fat-tat, but you have not yet understood the Law." Then the Patriarch intending to conclude the interview, recited the following stanza:

> "Your name is Fat-tat.
> Diligently and faithfully you recite the Sutra.
> Lip-repetition of the text ends with its pronunciation,
> But he whose mind is enlightened, by grasping its meaning, becomes a Bodhisattva.
> On account of conditions of affinity which may be traced to our past lives,
> Let me explain this to you.
> If you can only understand that Buddha speaks no words,
> Then the Lotus will blossom from your mouth.
> (Truth is inscrutable and ineffable; words fail,
> But the Lotus blossoms and radiates its perfume.)

Having heard this stanza, Fat-tat became ashamed and apologised to the Patriarch. He added, "Hereafter I will be humble and polite on all occasions. It is true: I do not quite understand the meaning of the Sutra as I recite it, so I am often doubtful as to its proper interpretation. From your profound knowledge and high Wisdom, will you kindly give me a short explanation?"

The Patriarch replied: "Fat-tat, the Good Law is quite clear; it is your mind that is not clear. The Sutra is free from doubtful passages; it is only your mind that makes them seem doubtful. Do you know the principal object of the Sutra?"

"How can I know, Sir," replied Fat-tat, "since I am so dull and stupid? All I know is to recite it word by word."

The Patriarch then said, "Will you please recite the Sutra? I am unable to read it myself. Then I will explain its meaning to you."

Fat-tat recited the Sutra loudly. When he came to the section entitled, "parables," the Patriarch stopped him, saying, "The theme of this Sutra is to set forth the aim and object of a Buddha's incarnation into this world. Though parables and illustrations are numerous in it, none of them go beyond this pivotal point. Now, what is that aim? and what is that object? The Sutra says, 'It is for a sole object, it is for a sole aim, but truly a lofty object and a lofty aim, that a Buddha appears in this world.' Now that sole object, that sole aim, that is so exalted, is the realization of Buddha-knowledge.

"Common people attach themselves to external objects, thinking them to be real, and within, they fall into the wrong idea that external things come to an end. When they are able to free themselves from attachment to objects when in contact with objects, and to free themselves from the fallacious view that 'Emptiness' means annihilation, then they are free from illusions without and delusions within. He who understands this and whose mind is thus suddenly enlightened, is said to have opened his eyes to the sight of Buddha-Knowledge.

"The word, 'Buddha' is equivalent to 'Enlightenment' and is dealt with under four heads:—Opening the eyes for the sight of Enlightenment-knowledge; seeing the sight of Enlightenment-knowledge; understanding Enlightenment-knowledge; becoming firmly established in Enlightenment-knowledge. If we are able, upon being taught, to grasp and thoroughly understand the teaching of Enlightenment-knowledge, then our inherent quality of 'true-nature' will have an opportunity to manifest itself. You should not misinterpret the text and come to the conclusion that Buddha-knowledge is something special to Buddha and not common to us, just because you happen to find in the Sutra these passages: 'To open the eyes for the sight of Buddha-knowledge,' 'To see the sight of Buddha-knowledge, etc.' Such a misinterpretation would be slandering Buddha and blaspheming the Sutra. Since one is (potentially) a Buddha, he is already in possession of this Enlightenment-knowledge, and there is no occasion for him to open his eyes for it. You should therefore accept the interpretation that Buddha-knowledge is the Buddha-knowledge of your own mind and not that of any other Buddha.

"Being infatuated with sense-objects and thereby shutting themselves from their own light, all sentient beings, tormented by outer circumstances and inner vexations, act voluntarily as slaves to their own desires. Seeing this, our Lord Buddha took the trouble of rising from his Samadhi in order to exhort them by earnest preaching of various kinds to suppress their desires and to refrain from seeking happiness from without, so that they may enter into their rights of Buddhahood. For this reason the Sutra says, 'To open the eyes for Buddha-knowledge etc.' I advise people to thus constantly open their eyes for the Buddha-knowledge within their own minds. But in their perversity they commit sins under delusion and ignorance; they are kind in words but wicked in mind; they are greedy, malignant, jealous, crooked, flattering, egoistic, offensive to men and destructive to inanimate objects. Thus they open their eyes to 'common-people-knowledge' instead. Should they rectify their heart so that wisdom rises spontaneously, the mind is under introspection and the practice of doing good takes the place of evil. Thus they would initiate themselves into Buddha-knowledge.

"You should, therefore, from one momentary sensation to another, open your eyes, not for 'common-people-knowledge,' which is worldly, but for the Buddha-knowledge that is supramundane. On the other hand, if you stick to the arbitrary concept that mere recitation as a daily exercise is good enough, then you are infatuated, like the yak by its own tail."

Fat-tat then said: "If that is so, then we only have to know the meaning of the Sutra and there will be no further necessity for reciting it. Is that right, Sir?" The Patriarch replied, "There is nothing wrong with the Sutra that you need to refrain from reciting it. Whether sutra-reciting will enlighten you or not, or benefit you or not, all depends upon yourself. He who recites the Sutra with his tongue and puts its teachings into actual practice with his mind, masters the Sutra. Listen to this stanza:

"When we are ignorant of the true meaning of the Saddharma-pundarika Sutra, our mind is being turned by the Sutra.
When we realize the true meaning of the Sutra, our mind turns the Sutra.
To recite the Sutra for a long time without understanding its meaning is the wrong way;
To recite the Sutra without holding any arbitrary conception of it is the right way.
To recite the Sutra with a pure mind is the true reciting, to do otherwise is wrong.
He whose mind is above affirmation and negation
Rides permanently in the Buddha vehicle."

Having heard this stanza, Fat-tat was enlightened and was unconsciously moved to tears. "It is quite true," he exclaimed, "heretofore I have been unable to master the Sutra, rather it has been my master."

Fat-tat then raised another difficulty. "The Sutra says, 'From various disciples up to Bodhisattva, though they were to speculate with their combined effort, they would be unable to comprehend Buddha-knowledge.' But you, sir, give me to understand that if an ordinary man realizes his own mind, he is said to have attained Buddha-knowledge. I am afraid, Sir, that with the exception of those gifted with superior mental dispositions, others may doubt your remark. Further, the Sutra mentions three kinds of carts: goat carts (the vehicle of disciples); deer carts (for Arahats); and bullock carts (for Bodhisattvas). How are these to be distinguished from the White Bullock carts of the Buddhas? Will you please tell me?"

The Patriarch replied: "The Sutra is quite plain on this point; it is you who fail to understand it. The reason why disciples, Arahats and Bodhisattvas fail to comprehend Buddha-knowledge is because they speculate about it (with their thinking mind which is limited and polluted); they may combine their efforts, but the more they speculate the farther they are from Truth. (Buddha-knowledge is to be realized within, not thought about as though it was something external.) It was not to Buddhas but to ordinary men that Buddha Gautama preached this Sutra. You do not seem to appreciate that since we are already riding in the White Bullock cart of the Buddhas, that there is no necessity for us to look for other vehicles. Moreover, the Sutra plainly teaches that there is only the one Buddha vehicle; that there are no others, no second, no third. It is because there is only one vehicle that Buddha had to preach to us with innumerable skillful means such as various reasons and arguments, various parables and illustrations, etc. Do you not understand that the other three vehicles are makeshifts, useful for the past only; while the sole vehicle, the Buddha vehicle, is for the present because it is ultimate?

"The Sutra teaches to dispense with the makeshifts and depend on the ultimate. Having resorted to the ultimate, you will find that even the very name 'ultimate' disappears. You should appreciate that you are the sole owner of these treasures and that they are entirely subject to your disposal. (This is in allusion to another Parable, the Buddhist Prodigal Son, in the Sutra.) But moreover, it is not until you are able to free yourself from the arbitrary conceptions that there are any treasures belonging to the Father or to the son, or subject to so and so's disposal, that you really know the right way to recite the Sutra. When you so understand it, the Sutra will be in your hand from eternity to eternity, and from morning to midnight you will be reciting the Sutra all the time."

Being thus awakened, Fat-tat praised the Patriarch in a transport of joy with the following stanza:—

> "The delusion that I had attained great merit by reciting the Sutra three thousand times
> Is all dispelled by a single utterance of the Master of Tso-kai.
> He who has not yet understood the object of the Buddha's incarnation
> Is unable to suppress the wild passions accumulated in many lives.
> The three vehicles are makeshifts only;
> And the three stages in which the scholars expound the Dharma are ingeniously spoken, indeed;
> But how few appreciate that it is within the burning house itself
> That the Truth of Dharma is to be found."

The Patriarch then told him that before he had rebuked him for being a "sutra-reciting monk," but that hereafter he would praise him for the same reason. After that interview, Fat-tat was able to grasp the profound meaning of Buddhism, and yet he continued to recite the Sutra as before.

* * *

The monk, Chi-tong, a native of Shau-chow of An-fung, had read over the Lankavatara Sutra nearly a thousand times, but could not understand the meaning of the Trikaya nor the four Prajnas. One day he called upon the Patriarch for an explanation of them.

"As to the 'Three Bodies,'" explained the Patriarch, "The Pure Dharmakaya is your nature; The Perfect Sambhogakaya is your wisdom; and the Myriad Nirmanakayas are your actions. If you deal with these three bodies apart from your Mind-essence, they would be bodies without wisdom. If you realize that these three: self-nature, self-wisdom and self-action, have no substance of their own (being only manifestations of Mind-essence) then you have attained the enlightenment of the four Prajnas. Listen to this stanza:—

> "The Three-bodies are inherent in our Essence of Mind,
> By the radiation of which the four Prajnas are manifested.
> Thus, without closing your eyes and your ears to shut out the external world,
> You may reach Buddhahood directly.
> Now that I have made this plain to you,
> If you believe it implicitly, you will be forever free from delusion.
> Follow not those who seek for 'enlightenment' from without:
> Such people talk about Bodhi all the time, but do it vainly."

For the second time, Chi-tong asked, "May I know something about the four Prajnas?" "If you understand the Three-Bodies," replied the Patriarch, "you should know the four Prajnas as well; your question is quite unnecessary. If you deal with the four Prajnas apart from the Three-Bodies, there would be Prajnas without bodies; in such a case, they would not be Prajnas. (Prajna is the Ultimate Principle of the Three-Bodies, which is Ultimate Reality.) The Patriarch then uttered this stanza:—

> "Mirror-like Wisdom is pure by nature;
> Wisdom that comprehends all things equally, frees the mind from all impediments;
> All-discerning Wisdom sees things intuitively;
> All-performing Wisdom, like Mirror-Wisdom, is free from prejudice.
> Perception-consciousness of the five-sense-vijnanas,
> And the Universal Consciousness of the Alaya-vijnana,
> Are not 'transmuted' to Prajna, until the Buddha-stage;
> While the intellective-consciousness of the Manas,
> And the discriminative-consciousness of the Manovijnana,
> Are 'transmuted' in the Bodhisattva-stage.

> When you are able to free yourself entirely from at-
> tachments to sense-objects as these 'transmutations'
> take place,
> Then you will forever abide in the never-ceasing Naga
> Samadhi."

Suddenly Chi-tong realized the Prajna of his Mind-essence
and submitted the following stanza to the Patriarch:—

> "Intrinsically, the Three-Bodies are within our Essence of
> Mind.
> When our mind is enlightened, the four Prajnas will
> appear.
> When 'Bodies' and Prajna appear as one identity,
> Then are we able to respond to the appeal of all beings,
> no matter what form they take.
> To make an effort to find the Trikaya and the four Praj-
> nas is to take an entirely wrong course;
> To try to 'discriminate' and 'grasp' them is to misun-
> derstand their intrinsic nature.
> Through you, Sir, I am now able to realize the pro-
> fundity of their meaning;
> Henceforth, I may discard for ever their false and arbi-
> trary names."

* * *

The monk, Chi-sheung, a native of Kwai-kai of Shun-chow,
joined the order in his childhood and was very zealous in his
efforts to realize Mind-essence. One day he came to pay homage to the Patriarch and was asked by the latter whence and
for what he came. Chi-sheung replied:—

"I have recently been at the White Cliff Monastery in
Hung-chow, to study with the Master Ta-tung who was good
enough to teach me how to realize Mind-essence and thereby
to gain Buddhahood, but as I still have some doubts, I have
travelled far to come here to pay my respects to you. Will
you kindly clear away my doubts, Sir?"

The Patriarch asked, "What instruction did he give you?
Will you please repeat it?

Chi-sheung replied: "After staying there three months without receiving any instruction, and being zealous for the
Dharma, I went alone one night to his chamber and asked

him, what my essence of mind was. He asked me, 'Do you see the illimitable void?' 'Yes, I do,' I replied. Then he asked me whether the void had any particular form, and on replying that the void must be formless and therefore can not have any particular form, he said: 'Your Essence of Mind is exactly like the void. To realize that there is nothing to be seen, is Right View. To realize that nothing is knowable, is True Knowledge. To realize that it is neither green nor yellow, neither long nor short; that it is pure by nature; that its quintessence is perfect and clear; is to realize Essence of Mind and thereby to attain Buddhahood. This is also called, Buddha-knowledge.' As I do not quite understand this teaching, will you please enlighten me, Sir?"

"His teaching indicates," said the Patriarch, "that he still retains the arbitrary concepts of 'Views' and 'Knowledge'; that explains why he failed to make it clear to you. Listen to this stanza:—

> "To realize that nothing can be seen, but to retain the concept of 'invisibility'
> Is somewhat like passing clouds obscuring the face of the sun.
> To realize that nothing is knowable, but to retain the concept of 'unknowability'
> May be likened to the clear sky disfigured by a flash of lightning.
> To let these arbitrary concepts arise spontaneously in the mind
> Indicates that you have not yet realized Essence of Mind,
> And that you have not yet found the skillful means to realize it.
> If you realize for one moment that these arbitrary concepts are wrong,
> Then your own spiritual light will shine forth unhindered."

Having heard this, Chi-sheung at once felt that his mind was enlightened. Thereupon, he submitted to the Patriarch, the following stanza:—

> "To allow the concepts of 'invisibility' and 'unknowability' to rise spontaneously in the mind

Is to seek Bodhi without freeing oneself from the arbi-
trary concepts of phenomena.
He who is puffed-up by the slightest impression, 'I am
now enlightened'
Is no farther advanced than one under delusion.
Had I not put myself at the feet of Your Eminence,
I would have remained bewildered, ignorant of the right
way to go."

One day Chi-sheung asked the Patriarch, "Buddha preached
the doctrine of 'Three Vehicles' and also that of the 'Supreme
Vehicle.' I do not understand them; will you please explain
them to me?"

The Patriarch replied, " (In trying to understand these) you
should introspect your own mind and ignore outward things
and phenomena. The distinction of these four vehicles does
not exist in the Dharma itself, but in the differentiations of
people's minds. To see and to hear and to recite the Sutras,
is the Small Vehicle. To know the Dharma and to understand
its meaning is the Middle Vehicle. To put the Dharma into
actual practice, is the Great Vehicle. To understand all
Dharmas (intuitively), to become part of them, to be free from
all attachments, to be independent of things and phenomena;
to be in possession of nothing, that is the Supreme Vehicle.

"Essence of Mind is always a state of tranquillity. Since
the word 'vehicle,' means, 'motion,' discussion is out of place.
All depends on intuitive self-practice. Do not ask any more
questions."

Chi-sheung made obeisance and thanked the Patriarch and,
thereafter served as one of the Patriarch's personal attendants
until his death.

* * *

The monk, Chi-wang, a follower of the Dhyana school, had
a consultation with the Fifth Patriarch and afterward considered
himself to have attained Samadhi. For twenty years he confined himself to a small temple and all the time kept the
Dhyana posture. Un-chak, a disciple of the Sixth Patriarch, on
a pilgrimage to the northern bank of the Hoang-ho, heard
about him and called at his temple.

"What are you doing here?" enquired Un-chak.

"I am abiding in Samadhi," replied Chi-wang.

"Abiding in Samadhi, did you say?" Observed Un-chak. "I wish to enquire whether you are doing it consciously or unconsciously? If you are doing it unconsciously, it would mean that it is possible for all inanimate objects, such as earthen ware, stones, trees and weeds, to attain Samadhi. On the other hand, if you do it consciously, then any animate object or sentient being might abide in Samadhi, also."

Chi-wang then said, "When I am in Samadhi, I know neither consciousness nor unconsciousness."

"In that case," observed Un-chak, "it is a perpetual quietude, in which there is neither abiding nor leaving. A state of samadhi in which you can abide or come out of at will, can not be a perfect Samadhi."

Chi-wang was nonplussed. After a long time, he asked, "May I know who is your teacher?"

"My teacher is the Sixth Patriarch, of Tso-kai," replied Un-chak.

"How does he define Dhyana and Samadhi?" enquired Chi-wang.

"According to his teaching," replied Un-chak, "the Dharma-kaya is perfect and serene and unchanging; its quintessence and its function are in a state of 'Suchness.' The five aggregates are intrinsically void and the six sense-objects are non-existent. There is neither abiding nor leaving in Samadhi; there is neither quietude nor perturbation. The nature of Dhyana is non-abiding, so we should seek to transcend the state of 'abiding in the calmness of Dhyana.' The nature of Dhyana is uncreative, so we should transcend the notion of 'creating a state of Dhyana.' Essence of Mind is like space without the limitations of space."

After this interview, Chi-wang went to Tso-kai to interview the Sixth Patriarch. Upon being asked whence he came, Chi-wang told the Patriarch the details of his conversation with Un-chak.

The Patriarch said, "What Un-chak said is quite right. Let your mind be in a state like the illimitable void, but do not think of it as 'vacuity.' Let the mind function freely, but whether it is in activity or at rest, let it abide nowhere. Forget all discriminations: see no distinction between a sage and an ordinary man; ignore the distinction between subject and object; let Essence of Mind and all phenomena and objects be alike in a state of 'Suchness.' Then you will truly be in Samadhi all the time."

Chi-wang was thereby fully enlightened. What he had considered for the past twenty years as an attainment, now all vanished. He remained with the Patriarch for a time and then returned to Ho-Pei where he taught many people, monks as well as laymen.

* * *

The monk, Chi-tao, a native of Nam-hoi of Kwong-tung, came to the Patriarch for instruction, saying, "Since I joined the order, I have read the Maha Parinirvana Sutra for more than ten years, but I have not yet grasped its teaching. Will you please teach me."

"What part of it do you not understand?" enquired the Patriarch.

"It is this part, Sir: 'All things are impermanent and so they belong to the Dharma of Becoming and Cessation. When both Becoming and Cessation cease to operate, Cessation of Change with its bliss of Perfect Rest (Nirvana) arises.' "

"What obscurity is there in that?" enquired the Patriarch.

Chi-tao replied, "All beings have two bodies: the physical body and an essence body. The former is impermanent—it exists and it deceases. The latter is permanent, but it knows not and feels not. Now the Sutra says, 'When both Becoming and Cessation cease to operate, the bliss of Perfect Rest and Cessation of Change arises.' I can not understand which body ceases to exist, and which body enjoys the bliss. It cannot be the physical body that enjoys, because when it dies, the material elements disintegrate and disintegration is suffering, the very opposite of bliss. If it is the essence body that ceases to exist, it would be in the same 'unfeeling' state as inanimate objects, such as the grass, trees and stones. Who, then, will be the enjoyer?

"Moreover, essence-nature is the quintessence of 'Becoming and Cessation' whose manifestation is the union of the five 'aggregates' (body, sensation, perception, consciousness and intellection). That is to say, from one essence, five functions arise. This process of Becoming and Cessation is everlasting. When function and operation 'arise' from the quintessence, it becomes; when operation and function are 'absorbed' back into the quintessence, it ceases to exist. If reincarnation is admitted, there will be no Cessation of Changes, as in the case of sentient beings. If reincarnation is out of the question, then things will remain forever in a state of lifeless quintessence, like the case of inanimate objects. When this is the case, under the limitations and restrictions of Nirvana, even existence would be impossible to all things, much less enjoyment."

"You are a Bhikkhu," said the Patriarch, "how can you adopt the fallacious views of Eternalism and Annihilationism that are held by heretics, and venture to criticise the teaching of the Supreme Vehicle? Your argument implies that apart from the physical body, there is an essence body; and that Perfect Rest and Cessation of Change may be sought apart from 'Becoming and Cessation.' Further, from the statement, 'Nirvana is everlasting rest,' you infer that there must be somebody to play the part of enjoyer.

"It is exactly these fallacious views that makes people crave for sentiate existence and worldly pleasure. These people are the victims of ignorance; they identify the union of the five aggregates as the 'self' and regard all other things as 'not-self'; they crave for individual existence and have an aversion to death; they are drifting about from one momentary sensation to another in the whirlpool of life and death without realising the emptiness of mundane existence which is only a dream and an illusion; they commit themselves to unnecessary suffering by binding themselves to rebirth; they mistake the state of everlasting joy of Nirvana to be a mode of suffering; they are always seeking after sensual pleasures. It was for these people, victims of ignorance, that the compassionate Buddha preached the real bliss of Nirvana.

"Never for a moment was Nirvana either the phenomena of Becoming and Cessation, or the ceasing of Becoming and Cessation. It is the perfect manifestation of Rest and Cessation of Change, and at the 'time' of manifestation, there is no such thing as manifestation. It is called 'everlasting' Joy because it has neither enjoyer nor non-enjoyer.

"There is no such thing as 'one quintessence and five manifestations.' You are slandering Buddha and blaspheming the Dharma, when you go so far as to state that under the limita-

tion and restriction of Nirvana, living is impossible to all beings.
Listen to this stanza:—

"The Supreme Maha Parinirvana
Is perfect, permanent, calm, radiantly illuminative.
Common and ignorant people miscall it death,
While heretics arbitrarily declare it to be annihilation.
Those who belong to the Small Vehicle and to the
    Middle Vehicle
Regard Nirvana as 'non-action.'
All these are merely intellectual speculations,
And they form the basis of the sixty-two fallacious views.
Since they are merely names, invented for the occasion,
They have nothing to do with Absolute Truth.
Only those of super-eminent mind
Can understand thoroughly what Nirvana is,
And take an attitude toward it of neither attachment
    nor indifference.
They know that the five aggregates,
And the so-called 'self' arising from the aggregates,
Together with all external forms and objects,
And the various phenomena of words and voice,
Are all equally unreal, like a dream or an illusion.
They make no discrimination between a sage and an
    ordinary man,
Nor do they have any arbitrary concept of Nirvana.
They are above 'affirmation' and 'negation';
They break the barriers between the past, the present
    and the future.
They use their sense organs when occasion requires,
But the concept of 'using' does not arise.
They may particularise on all sorts of things,
But the concept of 'particularisation' arises not.
Even during the cataclysmic fire at the end of a kalpa,
When ocean beds are burnt dry;
Or during the blowing of catastrophic winds, when
    mountains topple;
The everlasting bliss of Perfect Rest and Cessation of
    Change that is Nirvana
Remains the same and changes not."

The Patriarch then said to Chi-tao, "I am trying to describe to you something that intrinsically is ineffable, in order to help you to get rid of fallacious views. If you do not interpret my words too literally you may perhaps know a wee bit of Nirvana."

Chi-tao became highly enlightened and, in a rapturous mood he made obeisance and departed.

CHAPTER VII

Sudden Enlightenment and Gradual Attainment [1]

Contemporaneous with the Patriarch when he was living at Po-lam Monastery was Grand Master Shin-shau who was preaching in Yuk-chuen Monastery of King-nam. At that time the two schools of Hui-neng in the South and of Shin-shau in the North were both flourishing. As the two schools were dis-

---

[1] NOTE BY EDITOR. When Hui-neng, who afterward became the Sixth Patriarch, came to Wong-mui to interview the Fifth Patriarch, he was a comparatively uneducated country boy and not yet a member of the order of monks. He did not remain there very long but before he left his insight into the Dharma had been recognised by the Patriarch and he was initiated into the Patriarchate and given the insignia of the robe and begging bowl. While he remained at Monastery he served as a lay-helper in the granary, hulling rice. At the same time he was there, the Master (or Dean as we would call him) of the Monastery was Shin-shau, a notably learned monk of the Dhyana School. After Hui-neng left Ung-mui he lived in retirement for a number of years, Shin-shau, in disappointment at not receiving the appointment of Sixth Patriarch, returned to his home in the North and founded his own School which later, under Imperial patronage, came into great prominence. But after the death of Shin-shau, the School steadily lost prestige and later dropped out of importance. But the different principles of the two schools, "Sudden Enlightenment" of the Sixth Patriarch's Southern School and "Gradual Attainment" of Shin-shau's Northern School, have continued to divide Buddhism and do so to-day. The principle in dispute is as to whether enlightenment comes as a "gradual attainment" through study of the scriptures and the practice of dhyana, or whether it comes suddenly in some ecstatic samadhi, or, as the Japanese say, in some sudden and convincing and life-enhancing "satori." It is not a question of quickness or slowness in arriving at it: "gradual attainment" may arrive sooner than "sudden enlightenment." It is the question whether enlightenment comes as the culmination of a gradual process of mental growth, or whether it is a sudden "turning" at the seat of consciousness from an habitual reliance on the thinking faculty (a looking outward), to a new use of a higher intuitive faculty (a looking inward).

tinguished from each other by the names, Sudden, and Gradual, some Buddhist scholars were troubled as to which school to follow.

One day the Patriarch addressed his assembly as follows:—

"So far as the Dharma is concerned, there can be only one school. If a distinction is made, it exists in the fact that the founder of one school was a Northern man, and the founder of the other was a Southern man. While there is only one system of Dharma, some disciples realise it quicker than others but the reason why the names, 'Sudden' and 'Gradual,' are given is because some disciples are superior to others in their mental dispositions. So far as the Dharma is concerned, the distinction of Sudden and Gradual does not exist."

(Between the two leaders there was mutual respect but) the followers of Shin-shau often criticised the Patriarch. They discredited him by saying that he was illiterate and could not distinguish himself in any respect. Shin-shau, on the other hand, admitted that he was inferior to the Patriarch in one respect, namely, that Hui-neng thoroughly understood the teachings of the Mahayana, even if he had attained that wisdom without the aid of a teacher. "Moreover," he added, "my Master, the Fifth Patriarch, would not have personally transmitted the robe and bowl to him without good cause. I regret that, owing to the patronage of the Court, which I by no means deserve, I am unable to travel far to receive instruction from him personally. You should go to Tso-kai to consult him. Do not tarry."

One day, Shin-shau said to his disciple, Chi-shing, "You are clever and witty; I wish you would go to Tso-kai and attend the lectures there. Try your best to keep in mind what you hear, so that on your return you may repeat it to me."

Acting on his teacher's instruction, Chi-shing arrived at Tso-kai. Without saying anything about where he came from, he joined the company attending the Patriarch's lectures. When the Patriarch came to address the assembly, he said, "Some one has come here secretly to learn my teaching and later to plagiarise it." Chi-shing at once came forward, made obeisance, and told the Patriarch what his mission was.

"You come from Yuk-chuen Monastery, do you?" said the Patriarch. "Then you must be a spy."

"No, I am not," replied Chi-shing. "Why not?" asked the

Patriarch. "If I had not told you, I would have been a spy,"
said Chi-shing. "Since I have told you who I am, I am no
spy."

"Tell me, how does your teacher instruct his disciples?"
asked the Patriarch.

"He often tells them to concentrate their minds in a meditation on 'purity'; to keep up the dhyana position constantly,
and not to lie down."

Said the Patriarch, "To concentrate the mind on a meditation on 'purity' is an infirmity and is not Dhyana. To restrict
oneself to the crosslegged position all the time is logically unprofitable. Listen to this stanza:—

"A living man sits and does not lie down;
But a dead man lies down and does not sit.
On this physical body of ours, why should we impose
the task of sitting crosslegged?"

Making obeisance a second time, Chi-shing remarked,
"Though I have studied Buddhism for nine years under Grand
Master Shin-shau, my mind was not awakened for enlightenment, but as soon as you speak to me, my mind is enlightened.
As the question of continuous re-birth is an important one, I
wish you would take pity on me and give me instruction as
to that question."

The Patriarch said, "I understand that your Master gives his
disciples instruction as to 'disciplinary rules' (*sila*), meditation
(*dhyana*), and Wisdom (*Prajna*). Will you please tell me how
he defines these terms?"

"According to his teaching," replied Chi-shing, "to refrain
from all evil action, is Sila; to practise whatever is good, is
Prajna; and to purify one's mind, is Dhyana. This is the way
he teaches us. May I ask what your system is?"

The Patriarch replied, "If I should tell you that I had a
system of Dhyana to transmit to others, I would be deceiving
you. What I try to do to my disciples, is to liberate them from
their own bondage, by such device as each case requires. To
use a name, which after all is nothing but a makeshift, it may
be called 'Samadhi.' The way your Master teaches Sila, Dhyana, Prajna, is wonderful; but my way is different."

"How can it be different, Sir, when there is only one form
of Sila, Dhyana and Prajna?"

"The teaching of your Master," replied the Patriarch, "is
for the guidance of the general followers of the Mahayana; my
teaching is for the more advanced followers. It is because some
realise the Dharma quicker and deeper than others, that there
is a difference of interpretation. Listen while I explain and see
if you think my instruction is the same as his. In expounding
the Dharma, I do not deviate from the authority of my intuitive mind. To do otherwise would indicate that the expositor's
Mind-essence was obscured, and that he was competent to
teach only the phenomenal side of the Dharma (but not its
essence). The true teaching of Sila, Dhyana and Prajna, should
be based on the principle that the function of all things derives
its virtue from its essence. Listen to this stanza:—

> "To free the mind from all improprieties is the Sila of
> Mind-essence;
> To free the mind from all perturbations is the Dhyana
> of Mind-essence.
> That which neither increases nor decreases is the
> 'diamond' of Mind-essence.
> 'Going' and 'coming' are only phases of Samadhi."

Having heard this instruction, Chi-shing felt humiliated and
thanked the Patriarch for the instruction.

The Patriarch continued: "The teaching of your Master on
Sila, Dhyana and Prajna, is fitted for minds of wise men, it is
true, but my teaching is intended for minds of a more advanced type. He who has realised Mind-essence, himself, may
dispense with such doctrines as Bodhi, Nirvana, and Knowledge
of Emancipation. It is only those who do not possess a single
system of Dhyana, who can formulate all systems of Dhyana;
these who understand what this means, may rightly use such
terms as Buddhakaya, Bodhi, Nirvana, Knowledge of Emancipation. To those who have realised Mind-essence, it makes no
difference whether they formulate all systems of Dhyana, or
dispense with all of them. (Because of this non-attachment)
they are at liberty to come or to go; they are free from all
obstacles and impediments. As circumstances arise, they take
appropriate action; they give suitable answers according to the
varying temperament of their questioner. They see with a comprehensive glance that all 'Bodies of Transformation' are inseparable from Essence of Mind. They attain liberation, psychic

powers, and Samadhi, which enables them to perform the arduous task of universal salvation as easily as if they were only playing. Such are the men who have realised Mind-essence."

"By what principle are we guided in dispensing with all systems of Dhyana?" was Chi-shing's next question.

The Patriarch replied:—"When our Mind-essence is free from improprieties, infatuations and perturbations; when we look inward from each momentary sensation to another, with Prajna; and when we no longer cherish attachment to objects, or to words, or to ideas; then are we forever emancipated. Why should we formulate any system of Dhyana when our goal may be reached no matter whether we turn to the right or to the left? Since it is by our own effort that we realise Mind-essence, and since the realisation and practise of Dhyana are both spontaneous and instantaneous, the formulation of any system of Dhyana is unnecessary. All Dharmas are intrinsically Nirvanic, how can there be gradation in them?"

Chi-shing made obeisance and volunteered to be an attendent of the Patriarch, in which capacity he served faithfully.

* * *

Since the two Dhyana Schools, that of Hui-neng in the South and Shin-shau in the North, were flourishing at the same time, in spite of the tolerant spirit shown by both Masters who hardly knew what egotism was, there naturally developed a strong sectarian feeling among the disciples. Calling their own Master, Shin-shau, the Sixth Patriarch on no better authority than their own wishes, the followers of the Northern School were jealous of the rightful owner of that title whose claim was supported by the possession of the insignia, the robe etc., and was generally acknowledged. (In order to get rid of the rightful Patriarch) they sent a lay member of the order whose secular name was Chang Hang-chong, a native of Kiang-si, and who as a young man had been fond of adventure, to get rid of him.

With his psychic power of mind-reading, the Patriarch was able to know of the plot. One evening Chang entered the Patriarch's room intending to carry out his instructions. The Patriarch, after placing ten taels near his side, bent his neck forward and waited the blow. Chang made three attempts, but strange to say no wound was made. Then the Patriarch spoke to him, saying,

> "A straight sword is not crooked;
> A crooked sword is not straight.
> I owe you money only, but life I do not owe you."

Chang was taken by surprise and, remorseful and penitent, he asked for mercy and volunteered to join the order at once, but the Patriarch handed him the money and said: "If my followers should learn of it, they would harm you; you must not remain here. Some other time come to see me in disguise and I will take good care of you." As directed, Chang ran away that night and subsequently joined the order under another Master. Upon being fully ordained, he proved himself to be a very diligent monk.

One day recollecting what the Patriarch had said, he made the long journey to see him and to pay him homage. "Why have you waited so long?" said the Patriarch, "I have been expecting you all the time."

Said Chang, "Since that night you so graciously pardoned my crime, I have become a monk and have studied Buddhism diligently. I can only show my gratitude adequately by spreading the Dharma for the deliverance of all sentient beings." Then he asked a question as to the meaning of "eternal and non-eternal," which the Patriarch answered and then said, "You have now thoroughly realised Mind-essence; hereafter you may call yourself, Chi-chai."

Chi-chai made obeisance and departed.

Chapter VIII

Royal Patronage

An edict dated the 15th day of the First Moon of the 1st year of Shin Lung, issued by the Empress Dowager Chek Tin and the Emperor Chung Chung, read as follows:—

"Since we have invited Grand Masters Wei-on and Shin-shau to stay in the Palace and receive our offerings, we have continued to study under them as far as we could find time after attending to our imperial duties. Out of sheer modesty, these two Masters recommended that we should seek the advice of Dhyana Master Hui-neng of the South, who had inherited the secret Dharma and the robe of the Fifth Patriarch as well as the 'Heart Seal' of the Lord Buddha.

"We hereby send Eunuch, Sit Kan, as the courier of this Edict to invite His Eminence to come, and we trust His Eminence will graciously favor us with an early visit, etc., etc."

On the ground of illness, the Patriarch sent a reply declining the royal invitation and craved permission to be allowed to spend his remaining years in the "forest."

(In due time Sit Kan, the imperial envoy, arrived at Tsokai and interviewed the Patriarch as follows):

"In the capitol, Dhyana experts unanimously advise people to meditate in the 'crosslegged' position to attain Samadhi; they say that this is the only way to realise the 'Norm' and that it is impossible for any one to obtain liberation without going through this meditation exercise. May I know your way of teaching, Sir?"

"The Norm is to be realized by the mind," replied the Patriarch, "it does not depend upon the crosslegged position. The Vajracchedika Sutra says that it is wrong 'for any one to assert that Tathagata comes or goes, sits or reclines.' Why? Because Tathagata's Dhyana of Purity implies neither coming from anywhere nor going to anywhere, neither becoming nor annihilation. All Dharmas are calm and void, such is Tathagata's Seat of Purity. Strictly speaking, there is no such thing as 'attainment'; why should we bother ourselves about the crosslegged position?"

"Upon my return," said Sit Kan, "Their Majesties will ask me to make a report. Sir, will you kindly give me some hints as to your essential teachings, so that I may make them known, not only to Their Majesties, but also to all Buddhist scholars at the Capital. As the flame of one lamp may kindle hundreds of thousands of others, the ignorant will be enlightened and light will produce light without end."

"The Norm implies neither light nor darkness," replied the Patriarch. "Light and darkness signify the idea of alternation. (It is not correct to say) 'light will produce light without end'; since light and darkness are a pair of opposites, there must be an end as well as a beginning. The Vimalakirti Nirdesa Sutra says, 'The Norm has no analogy; it is not a relative term.'"

"Light signifies wisdom, and darkness signifies defilement. If a pilgrim of the Path does not get rid of defilement by wisdom, how is he going to free himself from the 'wheel of birth and death,' which is beginningless?"

The Patriarch continued, "Defilement (*klesa*) is wisdom (*bodhi*); The two are the same and are not different from each other. To break up klasa by Bodhi is only a teaching of the followers of the 'Small' and 'Middle' vehicles. To those of keen intellect and superior mental attainment, such teaching is disapproved."

"What, then, is the teaching of the Mahayana?"

"From the point of ordinary men," replied the Patriarch, "enlightenment and ignorance are two separate things. Wise men who thoroughly realise Mind-essence, know that they are of the same nature. This sameness of nature, that is, this non-duality of nature, is what is called 'true nature'; it neither decreases in the case of an ordinary man and ignorant person, nor increases in the case of an enlightened sage; it is undisturbed in an annoying situation, and is calm in Samadhi. It is neither eternal, nor not-eternal; it neither goes, nor comes; it is to be found neither in the interior, nor in exterior, nor in the space intervening between. It is beyond existence and non-existence; its nature and its phenomena are always in a state of 'tathata;' it is both permanent and immutable. Such is the Norm."

Sit Kan asked, "You speak of it as beyond existence and non-existence. How do you differentiate it from the teaching of the heretics, who teach the same thing?"

The Patriarch replied: "In the teaching of the heretics, non-existence means the 'end' of existence, while existence is used in contrast with non-existence. What they mean by 'non-existence' is not actual annihilation, and what they mean by 'existence' really does not exist. What I mean by 'beyond existence and non-existence' is this: intrinsically it exists not, and at the present moment it is not annihilated. Such is the difference between my teaching and the teaching of the heretics. If you wish to know the essentials of my teaching, you should free yourself from all thought—good ones as well as bad ones—then your mind will be in a state of purity, ever calm and serene, the usefulness of which will be as apparent as the sands of the Ganges."

This preaching of the Patriarch, awoke Sit Kan to full enlightenment. He made obeisance to the Patriarch and bade him, adieu. Upon his return to the Palace, he reported to Their Majesties, what the Patriarch had said.

In that same year on the 3d day of the 9th Moon, an Edict was issued commending the Patriarch in the following terms:—

"On the ground of old age and poor health, the Patriarch declined our invitation to the Capital. Devoting his life, as he does, to the practice of Buddhism for the benefit of us all, he is, indeed, 'a field of merit' for the nation. Following the example of Vimalakirti who recuperated in Vaisali, he widely spreads the Mahayana-teaching, transmitting the doctrines of the Dhyana School, expounding especially the 'non-dual' Dharma. Through the medium of Sit Kan to whom the Patriarch imparted the 'Buddha-knowledge,' we are fortunate enough to have an opportunity to understand clearly his teachings of Higher Buddhism. This must be due to the accumulated merit and our 'root of goodness' planted in past lives, otherwise we would not be contemporaries of His Eminence.

"In appreciation of the graciousness of the Patriarch, we find ourselves hardly able to express our gratitude. (As a token of our great regard for him) we present him herewith a Korean Mo-la robe and a crystal bowl. The Prefect of Shiu-chow is hereby ordered to renovate his monastery, and to convert his old residence into a temple which is to be named, Kwok-yen. By royal favor, etc., etc."

CHAPTER IX

Final Words and Death of the Patriarch

On the 1st day of the 7th Moon, the Patriarch assembled his disciples and addressed them as follows:—

"I am going to leave this world by the 8th Moon. Should any of you have doubts about the teaching, please ask me soon, so that I may clear them away before I go. You may not find any one to teach you after I am gone." (The sad news moved many of them to tears. The Patriarch spoke to them at some length) and then added: —

"Under all circumstances you should free yourselves from

attachment to objects; toward them your attitude should be neutral and indifferent. Let neither success nor failure, neither profit nor loss, worry you. Be ever calm and serene, modest and helpful, simple and dispassionate. The Dharma is nondual as is the mind also. The Path is pure and above all 'form.' You are especially warned not to let the exercise for concentration of mind, fall into mere quiet thinking or into an effort to keep the mind in a blank state. The mind is by nature pure, there is nothing for us to crave or give up."

Realising that the Patriarch would pass away in the near future, Elder Fat-hoi after prostrating himself twice asked, "Sir, upon your entering into Parinirvana, who will be the inheritor of the robe and the (secret) Dharma?"

"(As for the Dharma) all my sermons from the time I preached in the Tai-fan Monastery up to now, may be copied out for circulation. You should take good care of it and hand it down from generation to generation for the salvation of all sentient beings. He who preaches in accordance with its teaching preaches the Orthodox Dharma. I have already made known to you, all the Dharma I know.

"As to the transmission of the robe, this practice is to be discontinued. Why? Because you all have implicit faith in my teaching, you are all free from doubts, therefore, you are all able to carry out the lofty object of our school. It is in accordance with the meaning of the stanza, handed down by Bodhidharma, the First Patriarch, that the robe be no longer handed down to posterity. The verse says:—

> " 'The object of my coming to China,
> Was to transmit the Dharma of deliverance to all under
>   delusion.
> In five petals, the flower will be complete;
> Thereafter, fruit will come to maturity naturally.'

"Do your best each of you; go wherever circumstances lead you. Listen to this stanza:—

> "With those who are sympathetic
> You may have discussion about Buddhism.
> As to those whose point of view differs from ours,
> Treat them politely and try to make them happy.
> Disputes are alien to our school,
> They are incompatible with its spirit.

To be bigoted and to argue with others in disregard of
this rule
Is to subject one's Mind-essence to the bitterness of this
mundane existence."

* * *

On the 8th day of the 7th Moon, the Patriarch suddenly
gave an order to his disciples to get a boat ready for his return
to Sun-chow, (his native place). They entreated him earnestly
to remain where he was, but in vain.

"It is only natural," said the Patriarch, "death is the inevitable outcome of birth. Even the Buddhas as they appear in
this world must manifest an earthly death before they enter
Parinirvana. There will be no exception with me; my physical
body must be laid down somewhere. Fallen leaves go back to
the place where the root is."

* * *

On the 3rd day of the 8th Moon of the Year Kwai Tsau,
the 2nd year of the Sin Tan Era, after eating with his disciples
at the Kwok-yen Monastery (Sun-chow), the Patriarch spoke
as follows:—

"Please sit down in order of seniority; I am going to say
good bye to you. After my passing away, do not follow the
worldly custom of crying and lamenting. Neither should messages of condolence be accepted, nor should mourning be worn.
These things are contrary to orthodox teaching; he who does
them is not my disciple. What you should do is to know your
own mind and realise your own Buddha-nature, which neither
rests nor moves, neither becomes nor ceases to be, neither comes
nor goes, neither affirms nor denies, neither remains nor departs.
I repeat this to you that you may surely realise your Mind-
essence. If you carry out my instructions after my death and
practise them, then my going away will make no difference
with you. On the other hand, if you go against my teachings,
even if I remained with you, no benefit would be yours." Then
he uttered this stanza:—

"Undisturbed and serene, the wise man practises no
virtue;
Self-possessed and dispassionate, he commits no sin;
Calm and silent, he gives up seeing and hearing;
Even and upright his mind abides nowhere."

Having uttered the stanza, he sat reverently until the third watch of the night, then he said abruptly, "I am going now," and in a moment passed away. At that time, a peculiar fragrance pervaded the room and a lunar rainbow appeared to link the earth and heaven; the trees in the grove turned pale and the birds and animals cried mournfully.

* * *

In the 11th Moon of that year, the question of the Patriarch's resting place gave rise to a dispute among the government officials of Kwong-chow, Shiu-chow and Sun-chow, each party being anxious to have the remains of the Patriarch removed to his own district. The Patriarch's disciples together with other Bhikkhus and laymen, took part in the controversy. Being unable to come to any agreement, they burnt incense and prayed to the Patriarch to indicate by the drift of the smoke the place he himself would like to rest. As the smoke turned directly to Tso-kai, the sacred shrine together with the inherited robe and bowl were accordingly removed back there on the 13th day of the 11th Moon.

Next year on the 25th day of the 7th Moon, the body was taken from the shrine and re-embalmed and placed in the stupa, and by imperial order, tablets were erected to record the life of the Patriarch.

The Patriarch inherited the robe when he was 24; he was ordained at 39; and died at the age of 76. For thirty-seven years he preached to the benefit of all sentient beings. Forty-three of his disciples inherited the Dharma; while those who attained (a measure of) enlightenment and thereby got out of the rut of the ordinary life were too many to be numbered. The robe transmitted by the First Patriarch, Bodhidharma, as the insignia of the Patriarchship, the Mo La robe and the crystal bowl presented by the Emperor Chung Chung, the Patriarch's image carved by Fong-pin, and other sacred things, were given into the care of the keeper of the stupa. They were to be kept permanently at Po-lam Monastery to guard the welfare of the temple. The Sutra spoken by the Patriarch was published and circulated to make known the principles of the Dhyana School. All these steps were taken for the prosperity of the "Three Jewels," Buddha, Dharma and Sangha, as well as for the general welfare of all sentient beings.

SELECTIONS
FROM TIBETAN SOURCES

Better is it to live the solitary life of a monk
Than to return again and again to the dreary round
of life's distractions.
The true disciple of the Buddha, having freed himself
from the fetters of sense,
Seeks in solitude that serenity of mind
Which is necessary to the attainment of Wisdom.

* * *

I pray Thee, O gracious Lord,
Grant that this mendicant may cling successfully to
solitude,
Making solitude his paradise.

THE LIFE AND HYMNS OF MILAREPA

Milarepa's Belief

MY *Guru* said, My son, what beliefs or convictions hast thou arrived at regarding these Truths; what experiences, what insight, what understanding hast thou obtained? And he added, Take thy time and recount them to me.

Upon this, with deep and sincere humility, I knelt, and joining the palms of my hands, with tears in mine eyes, extemporaneously sang to my *Guru* a hymn of praise, offering him the sevenfold worship—as a prelude to submitting the narrative of mine experiences and convictions:

1

To the impure eyes of them Thou seekest to liberate,
Thou manifestest Thyself in a variety of shapes;
But to those of Thy followers who have been purified,
Thou, Lord, appearest as a Perfected Being; obeisance to
   Thee.

2

With Thy Brahma-like voice, endowed with the sixty
   vocal perfections,
Thou preachest the Holy Truths to each in his own
   speech,
Complete in their eighty-four thousand subjects;
Obeisance to Thy Word, audible yet inseparable from
   the Voidness.

3

In the Heavenly Radiance of *Dharma-Kaya* Mind,
There existeth not shadow of thing or concept,
Yet It pervadeth all objects of knowledge;
Obeisance to the Immutable, Eternal Mind.

4

In the Holy Palace of the Pure and Spiritual Realms,
Thou Person illusory, yet changeless and selfless,
Thou Mother Divine of Buddhas, past, present, and
    future,
O Great Mother Damema, to Thy Feet I bow.

5

(O *Guru*), to Thy children spiritual,
To Thy disciples who Thy word obey,
To each, with all his followers,
Obeisance humble and sincere I make.

6

Whate'er there be, in all the systems of the many worlds,
To serve as offerings for the rites divine,
I offer unto Thee, along with mine own fleshly form;
Of all my sins, may I be freed and purified.

7

In merits earned by others, I rejoice;
So set the Wheel of Truth in motion full, I pray;
Until the Whirling Pool of Being emptied be,
Do not, O Noble *Guru*, from the world depart.

I dedicate all merit from this Hymn,
Unto the Cause of Universal Good.

Having, as a prelude, sung this hymn of seven stanzas, I
then continued: Inseparable from Dorje-Chang Himself art
thou, my *Guru*, with thy consort, and thine offspring. In virtue
of thy fair and meritorious deeds, and of the power of the
waves of grace proceeding from thy boundless generosity, and
of thy kindness beyond repayment, I, thy vassal, have imbibed
a little knowledge, in the sphere of understanding, which I
now beg to lay before thee. Out of the unchanging State of
Quiescence of Eternal Truth, be pleased to listen unto me for a
little while.

I have understood this body of mine to be the product of
Ignorance, as set forth in the Twelve *Nidanas*, composed of
flesh and blood, lit up by the perceptive power of conscious-

ness. To those fortunate ones who long for Emancipation, it may be the great vessel by means of which they may procure Freedom and Endowments; but to those unfortunate ones, who only sin, it may be the guide to the lower and miserable states of existence. This, our life, is the boundary-mark whence one may take an upward or downward path. Our present time is a most precious time, wherein each of us must decide, in one way or the other, for lasting good or lasting ill. I have understood this to be the chief end of our present term of life. Here, again, by holding on to Thee, O powerful Lord and Saviour of sentient beings like myself, I hope to cross over this Ocean of Worldly Existence, the source of all pains and griefs, so difficult to escape from. But to be able to do so, it is first of all necessary for me to take refuge in the Precious Trinity, and to observe and adopt in a sincere spirit the rules prescribed. In this, too, I see the *Guru* to be the main source and embodiment of all good and happiness that can accrue to me.

Therefore do I realize the supreme necessity of obeying the *Guru's* commands and behests, and keeping my faith in him unsullied and staunch. After such realization, then deep meditation on the difficulty of obtaining the precious boon of a free and well-endowed human birth, on the uncertainty of the exact moment of death, on the certain effect of one's actions, and on the miseries of *sangsaric* being, cannot fail to compel one to desire freedom and emancipation from all *sangsaric* existence; and to obtain this, one must cleave to the staff of the Noble Eightfold Path, by which only may a sentient being obtain that emancipation. Then, from the level of this Path, one must pass on, by degrees, to the Higher Paths, all the while observing one's vows as carefully as if they were one's own eyes, rebuilding or mending them should they become in the least impaired. I have understood that one who aimeth at his individual peace and happiness adopteth the Lower Path (the *Hinayana*). But he, who from the very start, devoteth the merit of his love and compassion to the cause of others, I understand belongeth to the Higher Path (the *Mahayana*). To leave the Lower Path and to enter upon the Higher Path, it is necessary to gain a clear view of the goal of one's aspirations, as set forth by the unexcelled Immutable Path (the *Vajra-Yana*).

Again, to gain a clear view of the Final Goal, it is essential to have a perfectly well-accomplished *Guru,* who knoweth every branch of the four kinds of initiatory rites without the slightest misunderstanding or doubt regarding them; he alone can make the Final Goal thoroughly explicit to a *shishya.* The ceremony of initiation conferreth the power of mastering abstruse and deep thoughts regarding the Final Goal. In meditating on the Final Goal, step by step, one hath to put forth all one's energies, both of grammatical and logical acumen; as well as, through moral and mental reasoning and internal search, to discover the non-existence of the personal Ego and, therefore, the fallacy of the popular idea that it existeth. In realizing the non-existence of the personal Ego, the mind must be kept in quiescence. On being enabled, by various methods, to put the mind in that state as a result of a variety of causes, all (thoughts, ideas, and cognitions) cease, and the mind passeth from consciousness (of objects) into a state of perfect tranquillity, so that days, months, and years may pass without the person himself perceiving it; thus the passing of time hath to be marked for him by others. This state is called *Shi-nay* (Tranquil Rest). By not submitting oneself to the state of total oblivion and unconsciousness (of objects), but by exerting one's intellect or faculty of consciousness in this state, one gaineth the clear ecstatic state of quiescent consciousness.

Although there be this state, which may be called a state of superconsciousness (*Lhag-tong*), nevertheless, individuals, or ego-entities, so long as they are such, are incapable of experiencing it. I believe that it is only experienced when one hath gained the first (superhuman) state on the Path to Buddhahood. Thus, by thought-process and visualization, one treadeth the Path. The visions of the forms of the Deities upon which one meditateth are merely the signs attending perseverance in meditation. They have no intrinsic worth or value in themselves.

To sum up, a vivid state of mental quiescence, accompanied by energy, and a keen power of analysis, by a clear and inquisitive intellect, are indispensable requirements; like the lowest rungs of a ladder, they are absolutely necessary to enable one to ascend. But in the process of meditating on this state of mental quiescence (*Shi-nay*), by mental concentration, either on forms and shapes, or on shapeless and formless things, the very first effort must be made in a compassionate mood, with the aim of dedicating the merit of one's efforts to the Universal Good. Secondly, the goal of one's aspirations must be well defined and clear, soaring into the regions transcending thought. Finally, there is need of mentally praying and wishing for blessings on others so earnestly that one's mind-processes also transcend thought. These, I understand, to be the highest of all Paths.

Then, again, as the mere name of food doth not satisfy the appetite of a hungry person, but he must eat food, so, also, a man who would learn about the Voidness (of Thought) must meditate so as to realize it, and not merely learn its definition. Moreover, to obtain the knowledge of the state of superconsciousness (*Lhag-tong*), one must practice and accustom oneself to the mechanical attainment of the recurrence of the above practices without intermission. In short, habituation to the contemplation of Voidness, of Equilibrium, of the Indescribable, and of the Incognizable, forms the four different stages of the Four Degrees of Initiation,—graduated steps in the ultimate goal of the mystic *Vajra-Yana* (or Immutable Path). To understand these thoroughly, one must sacrifice bodily ease and all luxuriousness, and, with this in mind, face and surmount every obstacle, being ever willing to sacrifice life itself, and prepared for every possible contingency.

As for myself, I have not the means to a recompense thee, my *Guru* and the Reverend Mother,—my benefactors; your loving kindness is beyond my power to repay by any offer of worldly wealth or riches. So I will repay you by a lifelong devotion to meditation, and I will complete my final study of your Teachings in the 'Og-min Heaven.

> To my *Guru*, the Great Dorje-Chang,
> To Damema, the Mother of all Buddhas,
> And to all Princes Royal, the *Avataras*,
> I make as offering, to Their ears, this essence of my
>   learning gleaned.
>
> If there be heresy or error in my speech,
> I pray that They will kindly pardon it,
> And set me then upon the Righteous Path.
>
> Lord, from the sun-orb of Thy Grace,
> The radiant Rays of Light have shone,

And opened wide the petals of the Lotus of my Heart,
So that it breatheth forth the fragrance born of Knowl-
    edge,
For which I am for ever bounden unto Thee;
So will I worship Thee by constant meditation.

Vouchsafe to bless me in mine efforts,
That good may come to every sentient being.
Lastly, I ask forgiveness, too, for any lavishness of words.

Then my *Guru* replied, I have conferred upon thee the Supreme, Mystic, Ear-Whispered Truths, as revealed by the
Deities and transmitted to me by my Lord Naropa. To no
other of my disciples have I imparted them; nay, not even to
the foremost. To thee I have handed them on in an entire and
perfect manner, like unto a vessel filled to the very brim.

Then he invoked the Tutelary Deities to bear witness to the
truth of these statements.

The *Guru* having delivered this deeply impressive discourse
sang the following song extempore:

To desire much, bringeth a troubled mind;
(So) store within thy heart (these) precepts wise:
Many *seeming* Thats are not *the* That;
Many trees bear nought of fruit;
All Sciences are not the Wisdom True;
Acquiring these is not acquiring Truth.
Much talking is of little profit.

That which enricheth the heart is the Sacred Wealth;
Desirest thou wealth? then store thou this.
The Doctrine which subdueth passions vile is the Noble
    Path;
Desirest thou a safe path? then tread thou this.
A contented heart is the noblest king;
Desirest thou a noble master? Then seek thou this.

Forsake the weeping, sorrow-burdened world;
Make lonely caves thy home paternal,
And solitude thy paradise.
Let Thought riding Thought be thy tireless steed,
And thy body thy temple filled with gods,
And ceaseless devotion thy best of drugs.

To thee, thou energetic one,
The Teaching that containeth all of Wisdom I have
given;
Thy faith, the Teaching, and myself are one.
And may this Perfect Seed of Truth, thus to my son
entrusted,
Bring forth its foliage and its fruit,
Without corruption, without being scattered, without
withering.

Having sung this, the *Guru* placed his hand upon my head,
and said, My son, thy going away breaketh my heart; but
since all composite things are alike liable to dissolution it cannot be helped. Yet remain with me a few days more; examine
thy texts, and if thou find in them uncertainties, have these
cleared. I obeyed, and on my remaining for some days my uncertainties touching the texts were cleared up.

Then my *Guru* asked me, Son, hast thou seen, and dost
thou believe? I replied, Yes, Lord and *Guru,* impossible is it
not to believe; I myself will emulate Thee in devotion, till I,
too, obtain these powers.

He answered, That is well, my son. And now thou art fitted to take thy departure, for I have shown to thee the mirage-like nature of all existing things. Realize this fact for thyself, going into retreat in mountain recessess, lonely caves,
and the solitudes of wildernesses.

Having done this, I paid him due worship, and expressing
a wish for a future meeting started home. I reached there
after three days, feeling somewhat elated at the development
in the art of controlling the breath which this betokened.

Thus did all come about—mine obtaining the Truth in
its entirety, my thorough study of it, and, while thus engaged,
my being impelled by a significant dream to take leave of my
Guru and return home.

Milarepa's Visit to Old Home

The news of the death of my mother and the disappearance
of my sister filled my heart with despair and sorrow. I hid

myself in a nook till past sunset, where I wept bitterly. After sunset I went to the village, and lo! I beheld my house exactly in the condition I had seen in my dream. The fine house, which used to be like a temple, was in a most dilapidated and ruinous condition. The set of sacred volumes had been damaged by the rain leaking in, and thick layers of dust and earth fallen from the (ruined) roof covered them; they were serving as nests and sleeping-places for birds and mice. Wherever I looked, desolation and ruin met me, so that I was overwhelmed with despondency. Then groping my way towards the outer rooms I found a heap of earth and rags, over which a large quantity of weeds and grass had grown. On shaking it up I found it to be a heap of human bones, which instinctively I knew to be my mother's. A deep and unutterable yearning seized me. So unbearable was the thought that I should never more see my mother that I was about to lose consciousness, when I remembered my *Guru's* Teachings; and, communing spiritually with my mother's spirit and the divine spirits of the saints of the Kargyutpa Sect, I made a pillow of my mother's bones and remained in an undistracted state of tranquility, in clear and deep meditation, whereby I realized that it was indeed possible to save both my father and mother from the pain and miseries of *sangsaric* existence. After passing seven days and nights thus, I rose from the *samadhi*.

Thence, upon reflection, I came to the conclusion that there was no permanent benefit to be obtained in any state of *sangsaric* existence. So I made up my mind to dispose of my mother's bones in the approved way, namely, to have them pulverized and mixed with clay and then moulded into miniature reliquaries, called *tsha-tshas*. I would offer the volumes of Scripture in payment for having this done; and, as for myself, I would go away to the Dragkar-Taso Cave and there pass my whole time in constant meditation. I determined to sit there night and day, till death should put an end to my life. I vowed that if any thought of worldly ambition should allure me, I would commit suicide rather than allow myself to be overcome by it. I prayed to the Tutelary Deities and *Dakinis* to cut short my life if ever I should come to think of an easy sort of devotion.

Making these mental resolves over and over again, I gathered up my mother's bones; and then, upon removing the heap

of dust and dirt that had accumulated upon the volumes of
Scripture, I saw that their letters were still clear. Carrying the
volumes on my back and my mother's bones in my lap, I
started forth. An unutterable anguish wrung my heart to its
very core. Henceforth, the world had nothing to tempt me or
to bind me to it. I repeated my vows to devote my life to a
rigid course of asceticism in the realization of the Truth, and
resolved to adhere to them firmly. In an almost frenzied mood
I sang the following verses of firm resolution to myself:

> O Gracious Lord, Thou the Immutable,
> O Marpa the Translator, according to Thy Words
>   Prophetic,
> A teacher of the transitoriness of things I've found
> Within my native land—prison of temptation;
> And by Thy Blessing and Thy Grace, may I
> From this noble teacher, experience and faith obtain.

> All phenomena, existing and apparent,
> Are ever transient, changing, and unstable;
> But more especially the worldly life
> Hath no reality, no permanent gain (in it).
> And so, instead of doing work that's profitless,
> The Truth Divine I'll seek.

> First, when my father lived, the (grown-up) son lived
>   not;
> Next, when I was born (and grown), my father did not
>   live.
> Had both together met, little would have been the profit,
>   even then;
> So I will go to gain the Truth Divine,
> To the Dragkar-Taso Cave I'll go, to practise meditation.

> When my mother lived, myself, the son, was long away;
> When I come home, I find my mother dead.
> Had both together met, little would have been the profit,
>   even then;
> So I will go to gain the Truth Divine,
> To the Dragkar-Taso Cave I'll go, to practise meditation.

When my sister was at home, myself, her brother, was
   away;
When I, her brother, come back home, I find my sister
   gone astray.
Had both together met, little would have been the profit,
   even then;
So I will go to gain the Truth Divine,
To the Dragkar-Taso Cave I'll go, to practise meditation.

When the Scriptural Texts were there, no veneration had
   they;
When the veneration came, they lay damaged by the
   rain.
Had both together (earlier) met, little would have been
   the profit, even then;
So I will go to gain the Truth Divine,
To the Dragkar-Taso Cave I'll go, to practise meditation.

When the house stood firm, the master was away;
When the master came, the house was fallen in ruin.
Had both remained together, little would have been the
   profit, even then;
So I will go to gain the Truth Divine,
To the Dragkar-Taso Cave I'll go, to practise meditation.

When the field was fertile, the farmer was away;
When the farmer came, the field was choked with weeds.
Had both remained together, little would have been the
   profit, even then;
So I will go to gain the Truth Divine,
To the Dragkar-Taso Cave I'll go, to practice meditation.

Native land, and home, and all possessions,
I know you all to be but empty things;
Any thoughtless one may have you.
As for me, the devotee, I go to win the Truth Eternal

O Gracious Father, Marpa the Translator,
May I succeed in meditation in the solitude.

Milarepa's Temptations in Solitude

Zesay (to whom I had been betrothed in my childhood), hearing about my being there, came with some nice food and drink to meet me. She wept copiously and embraced me. When she had told me of the manner of my mother's death and about my sister's straying, I was greatly saddened, and wept bitterly. I said to her, How constant thou art, that thou shouldst not have married yet. She said, People were so afraid of thy Deities that no one dared to ask my hand in marriage, nor would I have married even had any one proposed to me. That thou hast taken to this religious life is admirable; but what dost thou intend doing with thy house and field? I understood her desire, and thinking that since, by the grace of my *Guru* (Marpa the Translator), I had given up worldly life altogether, praying for her might suffice from a religious point of view, but that I should say something to her which might settle her doubts from a worldly standpoint. So I said to her, If thou meet my sister, give them to her; until she cometh, thou mayst enjoy the field thyself; and, if my sister be dead, then thou canst have both the house and the field for thine own. She asked me, Dost thou not want them thyself? And I replied, I shall find my food as the mice and birds do theirs, or I shall fast and starve, therefore I need not the field; and, as I shall dwell only in caves and lonely solitudes, I have no need of a house. I realize that even though I should possess the whole world, at my death I should have to give up everything; and so it will confer happiness in this and the next life if I give up everything now. I am thus pursuing a life which is quite opposite to that followed by the people of the world. Give up thinking of me as a living person.

She then asked me, Is thy practice also opposed to that of all other religious persons? And I replied, I am of course opposed to those hypocrites who have assumed a religious garb only for the sake of the honour attending it, and—their aim being merely the acquisition of wealth, fame, and greatness— have succeeded in getting by heart the contents of a volume or two; and who, having strong party feelings, strive for victory for their own party and defeat for the opposite party. But as for those who are sincere devotees, although they be of different sects and creeds, if their principle be not like the one mentioned above, then there cannot be much disagreement between the aim of the one or the other, so I cannot be opposed to any of them. On the whole, if they are not as sincere as myself, then they must, of course, be opposed to my creed.

On this, she said, Then how is it that thy practice is so poor and miserable—much worse than that of the meanest beggar? I have never seen anyone like this before. To what particular doctrine of the Mahayana Sect dost thou belong? I told her that it was the highest creed of the Mahayana; that it was called the Path of Total Self-Abnegation, for the purpose of attaining Buddhahood in one lifetime; and that to attain Buddhahood thus we must scatter this life's aims and objects to the wind.

She said, Indeed, I see that the practice of thy doctrine and theirs is quite opposite; and from what I hear and see of thee it appeareth that the practice of the *Dharma* is not altogether a very easy matter; theirs would have been an easier path to tread. I replied, The *yogi* who still retaineth a love of the world would not attain to mine ideal of a sincere devotee. I am of opinion that even those sincere Truth-seekers who still cling to the yellow robe retain a little love of worldly fame and honour; and even though they do not retain it, yet I am convinced that there is (between me and them) a vast difference in regard to the speed and efficacy of attaining Buddhahood. This, however, thou wilt not comprehend just now. So, if thou think thou canst, thou shouldst devote thyself to a religious life; but if thou feel unequal to the task, then thou canst enjoy the house and field as I have already said, and hadst better go home. She replied, I cannot accept thy house and field which thou shouldst give to thy sister. I should like to be a devotee, but such a devotee as thou art I cannot be. Having said this she went away.

Mine aunt, coming to learn that I did not care about my house and field, after a while began to think that since I professed a determination to adhere to my *Guru's* command, she might perhaps be able to obtain them for herself. So she visited me, bringing with her a quantity of barley-flour, butter, *chhang,* and other food, and said, Some time ago I treated thee unkindly, being steeped in ignorance; but as thou, my nephew, art a religious person, thou must pardon me. If thou wilt allow me, I will cultivate thy field, and supply thee with food. To this I agreed, saying, So be it; please supply me with the flour of twenty measures of barley per month; the rest thou canst enjoy; thou mayst cultivate the field. She went away delighted with the bargain. For two months she supplied the flour as agreed; then she came again and said, People say that if I cultivate thy field perhaps thy Tutelary Deities may injure me because of thy magical power. When I satisfied her, saying, Why should I practice sorcery now? Rather wilt thou be acquiring merit if thou continue to cultivate the field and supply me as thou art doing, she at once said, In that case, wilt thou kindly reassure me by taking an oath that thou wilt not practice sorcery any more. Thou canst have no objection to doing so. I was not sure what she intended doing; But, as I considered it consistent with my calling to please others, I reassured her by taking the oath in accordance with her wish, at which she went away quite pleased.

All this while, in spite of mine unremitting perseverance in meditation, I was unable to obtain signs of any improvement or growth in my knowledge or experience of Ecstatic Warmth; and I was becoming anxious as to what I should do next. One night I dreamt that I was engaged in ploughing a very stiff and hardened plot of land, which defied all mine efforts; and, despairing of being able to plough it, was thinking of giving up the task. Thereupon, my beloved *Guru* Marpa appeared in the heavens and exhorted me, saying, Son, put forth thine energy and persevere in the ploughing; thou art sure to succeed, despite the hardness of the soil. Then Marpa himself guided the team; the soil was ploughed quite easily; and the field produced a rich harvest. The dream gave me great pleasure on my waking up.

Thereby the thought arose in me that dreams, being illusory reproductions of one's own thoughts, are not regarded as real even by stupid and ignorant boors, and that when I thus allowed a dream to affect my temper I must be more silly than the greatest fool. But as it seemed to be a sign that if I continued to meditate with zeal and perseverance mine efforts would be crowned with success, I was filled with pleasure and in that mood I sang this song to impress the true interpretation of the dream clearly on mine own memory:

I pray to Thee, O Gracious Lord!
Grant that this mendicant may cling successfully to
    solitude.

I put upon the field of Tranquil Mind
The water and manure of a constant faith,
Then sow it with unblemished seed of a heart immacul-
    ate,
And over it, like pealing thunder, reverberateth sincere
    prayer;
Grace of itself upon it falleth, like a shower of rain.

Unto the oxen and the plough of Undistracted Thought
I add the ploughshare of (Right) Method and of
    Reason.
The oxen, guided by the undeluded person,
And with firm grasp of undivided purpose,
And by the whip of zeal and perseverance goaded on,
Break up the hardened soil of Ignorance, born of the
    Evil Passions Five,
And clear away the stones of the hardened, sin-filled
    nature,
And weed out all hypocrisies.

Then, with the sickle of the Truth of *Karmic* Laws,
The reaping of the Noble Life is practised.
The fruits, which are of Truths Sublime,
Are stored within the Granary to which no concepts can
apply.
The gods engage in roasting and in grinding this most
    precious food,
Which then sustaineth my poor humble self
Whilst I for Truth am seeking.

The dream I thus interpret:
Words bring not forth True Fruit,
Mere expositions do not yield True Knowledge.
Yet those who would devote themselves unto the life
    religious,
In meditation must exert their utmost zeal and persever-
    ance;

And if they will endure hardships and strive most zealously,
And seek with care, the Most Precious can be found.

May all who are sincerely seeking Truth
Untroubled be by obstacles and interruptions on the
Path.

Having sung this, I made up my mind to go and carry on
my meditation in the Dragkar-Taso Cave. As I was about to
start, mine aunt came up with sixty measures of barley-flour,
a ragged dress of skins, one piece of good cloth, and some butter and grease mixed up into a ball, and said, My nephew,
these are in payment of thy field, which thus is disposed of.
Take them and go away to a place far beyond my sight and
hearing, for the neighbours are saying to me, Thopaga hath
wrought much mischief upon us before this; and if thou must
still have dealings with him and serve him, we are certain that
he will do us more harm and perhaps kill the remaining people
of the place. Rather than this, we will kill both of you. So it
is safer for thee to flee away into some other country. If
thou do not go, why should they sacrifice me? But there is
not the least doubt that they will kill thee.

I knew that the people would not speak in that fashion,
and so I said to her, If I were not faithful to my religious
vows, I would not refrain from practising sorcery to regain possession of my field, especially as I have not sworn to refrain
from doing so under these circumstances. Being possessed of
such magical powers, I could with the greatest ease stretch thee
out a pale corpse in an instant; yet I will not do so, for on
whom should I practise my patience if not on those who have
wronged me? If I should die to-night, what could I do with
the field, or with these few articles themselves? Patience is
said to be the shortest path to obtain Buddhahood, and thou
mine aunt art the very person on whom I must practise my
patience. Moreover, ye, mine aunt and mine uncle, have been
the means of bringing me to this life (of renunciation). I am
sincerely grateful to both of you, and in return for these deeds
of yours I will ever pray for you, that ye may obtain Buddhahood in your future lifetime. Not only can I give to thee the
field, but the house, too. Then I explained to her everything

explicitly, and ended by saying, As for me—whose life is devoted to the search for Truth—I require only my *Guru's* instructions and nothing more; so thou art welcome to both the field and the house. And I sang to her the following song:

> O Lord, my *Guru*, by Thy Grace do I the life ascetic live;
> My weal and woe are known to Thee!
>
> The whole *Sangsara*, being e'er entangled in the Web of *Karma*,
> Whoever holdeth fast to it severeth Salvation's Vital Cord.
>
> In harvesting of evil deeds the human race is busy;
> And the doing so is to taste the pangs of Hell.
>
> The affectionate expressions of one's kith and kin are the Devil's Castle;
> To build it is to fall into the Flames (of Anguish).
>
> The piling up of wealth is the piling up of others' property;
> What one thus storeth formeth but provisions for one's enemies.
>
> Enjoying wine and tea in merriment is drinking juice of aconite;
> To drink it is to drown Salvation's Vital Cord.
>
> The price mine aunt brought for my field are things wrung out of avarice;
> To eat them would entail a birth amongst the famished ghosts.
>
> The counsel of mine aunt is born of wrath and vengeance;
> To utter it entaileth general disturbance and destruction.
>
> Whatever I possess, both field and house,
> Take all, O aunt, and therewith, happy be.

I wash off human scandal by devotion true;
And by my zeal I satisfy the Deities.

By compassion I subdue the demons;
All blame I scatter to the wind,
And upward turn my face.

O Gracious One, Thou the Immutable,
Vouchsafe Thy Grace, that I may pass my life in solitude successfully.

Until I have attained to *Siddhi,* unto this solitude will
  I hold fast;
Of starvation though I die, I'll not go to seek alms given
  in faith or dedicated to the dead,
For that would be to choke myself with dust.
E'en though of cold I die, I'll not descend to beg for
  garments.
E'en though of misery and sorrow I should die, I'll not
  descend to join in pleasures of the worldly life.
Though I fall ill, e'en unto death, I'll not descend to
  seek one dose of medicine.
And not one movement of my body will I give to any
  worldly purpose;
But body, speech, and heart I dedicate to winning Buddhahood.

May the *Guru,* Gods, and *Dakinis* enable me to keep my
  vows,
And may they bless mine efforts;
May the *Dakinis* and Faith Protecting Deities fulfill my
  wishes,
And render me all needed aid.

(I added): Should I break these vows—seeing that it is
better to die than to live a life without seeking to acquire
Truth—may the Divine Beings, who protect the Faith, cut my
life short immediately, and may my *Guru's* and *Deva's* grace
combine in directing my next life to religious pursuits and endow it with the firmness and intellect necessary to enable it
to surmount all obstacles (on the Path) and triumph over
them.

Having thus vowed, I sang this song, consecrating my vows:

Offspring of Naropa and of the Saving Path,
May (I), the hermit, cling successfully to solitude.

May pleasures of the world illusory not tempt me;
But may Tranquillity of Meditation be increased;

May I not lie steeped in Unconsciousness of Quietude;
But may the Blossom of the Superconsciousness bloom
   forth in me.

May various mind-created worldly thoughts not vex me;
But may the foliage luxuriant, of Uncreatedness, burst
   forth in me.

May I, in hermitage, be troubled not with mental
   conflicts;
But may I ripen fruit of Knowledge and Experience.

May Mara and his hosts disturb me not;
But may I find self-satisfaction in the Knowledge of
   mine own (True) Mind.

May I doubt not the Path and Method I pursue;
But may I follow in the footsteps of my Father
   (Spiritual).

O Gracious Lord, Embodiment of the Immutable,
Thy Blessings grant, that I (the mendicant), may firmly
   hold to solitude.

* * *

About a year after that, some hunters of Tsa, having failed
to secure any game, happened to come strolling by the
cave. . . . . . They said, Living upon such food, and wearing
such garments as thou hast on now, it is no wonder that thy
body hath been reduced to this miserable plight. Thine appearance becometh not a man. Why, even if thou should serve as
a servant, thou wouldst have a bellyful of food and warm clothing. Thou art the most pitiable and miserable person in the
whole world. I said, O my friends, do not say that. I am one
of the most fortunate and best amongst all who have obtained

the human life. I have met with Marpa the Translator, of Lhobrak, and obtained from him the Truth which conferreth Buddhahood in one lifetime; and now, having entirely given up all worldly thoughts, I am passing my life in strict asceticism and devotion in these solitudes, far away from human habitations. I am obtaining that which will avail me in Eternity. By denying myself the trivial pleasures to be derived from food, clothing, and fame, I am subduing the Enemy (Ignorance) in this very lifetime. Amongst the World's entire human population I am one of the most courageous, with the highest aspirations. But ye!—born in a country where the Noble Doctrine of the Buddha prevaileth, yet have not so much as listened to one religious discourse, let alone devoting your lives to it; but, on the other hand, ye are striving your utmost to gain the lowest depths and the longest terms of an existence in the Infernal Regions! Ye are accumulating sins by the pound and stone, and vying with each other in that! How foolish and perverted are your aims in life! I not only rejoice in the prospect of Eternal Bliss, but enjoy these things which give me contentment and self-approbation.

I then sang to them a song about my Five Comforts:

Lord! Gracious Marpa! I bow down at Thy Feet!
Enable me to give up worldly aims.

Here is the Dragkar-Taso's Middle Cave,
On this the topmost summit of the Middle Cave,

I, the *Yogi* Tibetan called Repa,
Relinquishing all thoughts of what to eat or wear, and this life's aims,
Have settled down to win the perfect Buddhahood.

Comfortable is the hard mattress underneath me,
Comfortable is the Nepalese cotton-padded quilt above me,
Comfortable is the single meditation-band which holdeth up my knee,
Comfortable is the body, to a diet temperate inured,
Comfortable is the Lucid Mind which discerneth present clingings and the Final Goal;
Nought is there uncomfortable; everything is comfortable.

If all of ye can do so, try to imitate me;
But if inspired ye be not with the aim of the ascetic life,
And to the error of the Ego Doctrine will hold fast,
I pray that ye spare me your misplaced pity;
For I a *Yogi* am, upon the Path of the Acquirement of
   Eternal Bliss.

The sun's last rays are passing o'er the mountain tops;
Return ye to your own abodes.
And as for me, who soon must die, uncertain of the
   hour of death,
With self-set task of winning perfect Buddhahood,
No time have I to waste on useless talk;
Therefore shall I into the State Quiescent of *Samadhi*
   enter now.

On hearing the song, they said, Thou art singing of various comforts, yet, in fact, thou dost really possess a very nice voice. As for us, we cannot rough it as thou art doing. Then they went off home.

On the occasion of an annual feast-day in Kyanga-Tsa, they chanced to sing this song together. It happened that my sister Peta was also there, having gone to obtain some food and drink. She, upon hearing the song, said to them, Sirs, the man who sang that must be a very Buddha himself. One among the hunters said, Ha! Ha! see how she praiseth her own brother; and another said, Whether he be Buddha or animal, it is thy half-starved brother's song; he is on the point of death from hunger. On this, Peta said, Oh! my parents are dead long ago; my relatives have become mine enemies; my brother hath roamed away, and I myself am reduced to a beggar's life: what is the need of gloating over my miseries? And she burst out weeping. Zesay came up just then, and comforted her by saying, Do not weep. It is quite possible that it is thy brother; I also met him some time ago. Go thou to the Dragkar-Taso Cave, and find out if he be there still. If he be, then both of us will go to see him.

Thus being led to believe the statement, she came to me at the Dragkar-Taso Cave with a jugful of *chhang* and a small vessel full of flour. On first seeing me from the entrance of the cave, she was frightened. My body was emaciated by the privations and hardships; mine eyes were deeply sunken into the sockets; my bones showed prominently; my color was of a bluish green; my muscles were all shrunken and shrivelled; a growth of bluish-green hair covered my skeleton-like form; the hairs of my head were stiff, and formed a formidable wig; and my limbs appeared as if they were about to break. Altogether, I was a sight which inspired her with such a dreadful fright that she took me to be a *bhuta*. But recollecting that she had heard that her brother was on the point of death from starvation, she half doubted whether it was really myself. At last she mustered up courage, and asked me, Art thou a human being or a *bhuta?* I answered, and said, I am Mila Thopaga. She, recognizing my voice, came in and embraced me, crying, Brother, brother! and then fainted away for a while. I, too, knowing her to be Peta, felt both glad and sorry at the same time. Applying the best means of restoring her, I at last succeeded in doing so. But she put her head between my knees, and, covering her face with both her hands, gave way to another flood of tears, sobbing forth the following: Our mother died in great trouble with a keen yearning to see thee. No one came near us; and I, being unable to bear the great privations and loneliness in our own house, left it to go a-begging in distant lands. I thought that thou wert also dead. I should, however, have expected that if thou were alive to have found thee in better circumstances than these. But, alas! thy circumstances are such. Thou seest what mine own destiny is! Could there be any one on the earth more wretched than ourselves! Then she repeatedly called upon the names of our parents, and continued wailing bitterly. I tried my best to console her. At last, I, too, felt very sad, and sang this song to my sister:

Obeisance to my Lords, the *Gurus!*
Grant that this *Yogi* may hold fast to solitude.

O sister, thou art filled with worldly sentiments and
    feelings;
(Know thou that worldly) joys and griefs are all imper-
    manent.
But I, alone by taking on myself these hardships,
Am sure to win Eternal Happiness;
So harken thou unto thy brother's song:

To repay the kindness of all sentient beings,
They having been our parents, to the life religious I did
  give myself.

Behold my lodgings; like those of jungle beasts are they;
Any other person would be timid in them.

Behold my food; 'tis like the food of dogs and pigs;
It would excite in others nausea.

Behold my body; 'tis like a skeleton;
Even an enemy would weep on seeing it.

In my behaviour, I am like a madman;
O sister, thou art moved thereby to disappointment and
  to sorrow;
Yet if thou could observe my mind, 'tis the *Bodhi* Mind
  itself;
The Conquerors rejoice at seeing it.

Sitting upon this cold rock underneath me, I meditate
  with zeal,
Enough to bear the tearing of my skin off or my flesh
  from off its bones;
My body, both inside and out, like nettles hath become;
A greenish hue, which changeth not, it hath assumed.

Here in this solitary rocky cave,
Though with no chance of driving melancholy from my
  mind,
Unchangedly I ever hold adoration and affection
For the *Guru,* True-Embodiment of the Eternal Buddhas.

Thus persevering in my meditation,
I doubtlessly shall gain Transcendent Knowledge and
  Experience;
And if, in this, I can succeed,
Prosperity and happiness is won within this lifetime, as
  I go along;
And, in my next birth, Buddhahood I'll win.

Therefore, my sister, Peta dear,
To woeful sorrows give not way,
But also give thyself to penances, for religion's sake.

When Peta had heard this, she said, It would be admirable were it as thou sayest, but it is difficult to believe it true. For were it as thou representest it to be, other devotees would practise at least part of such hardships, even if they could not bear all that thou hast borne. But I have not seen even one who is undergoing such privations and penances. Saying this, she gave me the *chhang* and the food she had brought. I felt very much strengthened and refreshed by partaking of it, and my devotions during the night were more earnest and spiritual.

The next morning, after Peta's departure, I experienced a sharp feeling of excitement and physical pain; and a variety of pious and impious ideas and thoughts sprang up in my mind. I tried mine utmost to concentrate my mind upon meditation, but it was of no avail. Some days after this, Zesay paid me a visit, bringing some well-cured and seasoned meat and butter, and a goodly supply of *chhang* and flour. She was accompanied by Peta. They met me while I was going to fetch water. I being stark naked (for I had no clothes), they were both ashamed; and yet, despite their bashfulness, they could not help weeping at mine utter poverty. They offered me the meat, butter, flour, and *chhang*. While I was drinking the *chhang*, Peta said, O my brother, whichever way I observe thee, thou dost not look at all like a sane human being. Pray have recourse to soliciting of alms, and do partake of the food of men. I will try to find some cloth and bring it over to thee. Zesay added, Do have recourse to alms, begging for your food, and I, also, will come to offer thee a cloth. But I said, With the uncertainty of the time of death looming over me, I see not the use of going a-begging for food, nor could I afford to lose the time in doing so. Even if I were to die of the cold, it would for the sake of Truth and Religion; and, therefore, I should have very little cause for regret. I could not be satisfied with that show of devotion which is practised amid a circle of merry relatives and friends, revelling in unlimited quantities of food and drink, and clothed in fine raiment—all obtained at the cost of real and sincere devotion. Nor do I need thy clothes and visits. I will not pay heed to thine advice of going a-begging for food. Peta said, How then, my brother, can thy heart be satisfied? It seemeth to me that something more wretched than this would satisfy thee, but even thine ingenuity seemeth to fail in devising anything more painful and abstemious. I replied that the three Lower *Lokas* are much more miserable than this; yet most sentient beings are doing their best to obtain the miseries of these three states of existence. As for me, I am satisfied with these present afflictions. So saying, I sang the song of what would constitute my Satisfactions:

> Obeisance to the Body of my Lord, the *Guru!*
> O grant that I may cling successfully to solitude.
> My happiness unknown unto my relatives,
> My sorrowing unknown unto mine enemies—
> Could thus I die, amid this Solitude,
> Contented would I be, I the devotee.

> My growing old unknown unto my betrothed,
> My falling ill unknown unto my sister—
> Could thus I die, amid this Solitude,
> Contented would I be, I the devotee.

> My death unknown to any human being,
> My rotting corpse unseen by birds—
> Could thus I die, amid this Solitude,
> Contented would I be, I the devotee.

> My putrid flesh sucked by the flies,
> My dissolving muscles eaten by the worms—
> Could thus I die, amid this Solitude,
> Contented would I be, I the devotee.

> With no human foot-print by my door,
> With no mark of blood within (the Cave)—
> Could thus I die, amid this Solitude,
> Contented would I be, I the devotee.

> With none to crowd about my corpse (or bier),
> With none to lament o'er my death—
> Could thus I die, amid this Solitude,
> Contented would I be, I the devotee.

With none to ask where I had gone,
And with no place which one might point to as my
  goal—
Could thus I die, amid this Solitude,
Contented would I be, I the devotee.

Thus, may this prayer about the manner of my death
Amid this uninhabited Solitude
Bear fruit, and, for all beings good, be granted as I wish;
Then satisfied I'll die, I the devotee.

On hearing this Zesay said, Thy first sayings and thy present actions agree. Therefore this song is worthy of admiration.
Then Peta said, Whatever thou mayst say, my brother, as for
me, I cannot bear to see thee in such utter want of clothes and
food. I will do my best to find a cloth for thee, and will come
over with it. Thy devotion would not run away if thou
shouldst have a sufficiency of good food and clothing, but seeing that thou wilt not go to beg for alms, it is probable that
thou wilt die without any one near thee, in this solitude, of
starvation and cold, just as thou desirest. Should I, however,
find that thou art not dead, I will come to bring thee some
sort of a cloth, which I will try to get. Having said this, they
both went away.

On my partaking of the good food, my physical pains and
my mental disturbances increased so much that I was unable to
go on with my meditation. In this predicament, thinking that
there could not be a greater danger than the inability to continue my meditation, I opened the scroll given me by my *Guru*.
I found it to contain the manner of treating the present ail-
ment, thus clearing the obstacles and dangers on the Path, and
turning the Vice to Virtue, and increasing the Spiritual Earnestness and Energy. It was mentioned in the scroll that I should
use good wholesome food at this time. The perseverance with
which I had meditated had prepared my nerves for an internal
change in the whole nervous system, but this had been re-
tarded by the poor quality of my food. Peta's *chhang* had
somewhat excited the nerves, and Zesay's offerings had fully
affected them. I now understood what was happening; and, on
studying the contents of the scroll, I found it contained the
accessory means and exercises (both physical and mental),
which I at once began to practise. Thereupon, I saw that the

minuter nerves of my system were being straightened out; even the knot of the *Sushumna-Nadi* (median nerve) was loosening below the navel; and I experienced a state of supersensual calmness and clearness resembling the former states which I had experienced, but exceeding them in its depth and ecstatic intensity, and therein differing from them. Thus was a hitherto unknown and transcendent knowledge born in me. Soaring free above the obstacles, I knew that the very evil (or danger) had been turned to good. What till now had been regarded as objective discrimination shone forth as the *Dharma-kaya*. I understood the *Sangsara* and *Nirvana* to be dependent and relative states; and that the Universal Cause is Mind, which is distinct from the ideas of Interestedness or Partiality. This Universal Cause, when directed along the Path of Disbelief (or Selfishness), resulteth in the *Sangsara;* while if it be directed along the path of Altruism, it resulteth in *Nirvana*. I was perfectly convinced that the real source of both *Sangsara* and *Nirvana* lay in the Voidness (of the Supra-mundane Mind). The knowledge I now had obtained was born of my previous energetic devotions, which had served as its main cause; and it only awaited the accident, at the crisis, of the wholesome and nourishing food, and the timely prescription contained in the scroll, to bring it forth. My belief in the methods of the Mantrayanic doctrines, which teach that a real transcendent knowledge can be obtained by proper care of the body and without giving up nourishing food and comfortable clothing, was thus firmly established. I also saw that Peta and Zesay had greatly contributed to the final development of the hitherto latent qualities, and therefore mine obligation to them was great. So by way of proving my gratitude, and to consecrate their pious deeds to an Eternal and Inexhaustible Purpose, I sang this hymn (of prayer), which embodieth the Essence of the Dependence and Relativity of Facts:

> Obeisance to the Feet of Marpa of Lhobrak!
> Grant that this hermit may hold fast to Solitude successfully.
>
> Upon the charity of righteous laymen,
> Success for them and me dependeth;
> This body, delicate and brittle, and difficult to gain,
> By meeting food, is nourished and sustained.

The life-sustaining principle, upsprouting from the earth,
And ambrosial showers from the heavenly dome of blue,
Join together and confer a blessing on all sentient beings;
And in a life religious this is employed the best.

The transient body, nourished by one's parents,
And the Sacred Teaching of the Sacred *Guru,*
Join together and then favour the religious life;
Wherein, in Perseverance, lieth true success.

The rocky cave, amid the uninhabited solitude,
And devotion zealous and sincere,
Join together and bring forth the Issue of Success;
Of Knowledge Spiritual doth this consist.

In the stoical and patient fortitude of Milarepa's medi-
      tation,
And the faith of beings of the *Lokas* Three,
Lieth opportunity of Universal Usefulness;
Of this, the essence is Compassion.

The *yogi* who, in rocky caves, doth meditate,
And laymen who provide his sustenance,
Do each thus win the chance of gaining Buddhahood;
Of this, the essence is the Consecration.

In the Sacred *Guru's* grace,
And the active meditation of the zealous *shishya,*
Lieth opportunity to uphold the Truth (the Hierarchy);
Of this, the essence is the Purity of Faith.

In the Rites Initiatory, which confer and bless with Oc-
      cult Power,
And in the prayer, earnest and sincere (of the devotee),
Lieth opportunity of meeting speedily (Spiritual Com-
      munion);
Of this, the essence is the Benediction.

Lord Dorje-Chang, O Thou the Immutable,
The weal and woe of this mendicant Thou knowest.

This hymn having been sung, I zealously persevered in my meditations.

Now I thought that I could efficiently help all sentient beings if I liked, so I resolved to devote myself to helping others; but I had a direct command from my Tutelary Deity to go on devoting my whole life to meditation, as my *Guru* had commanded. By that alone I should serve the Cause of the Buddhistic Faith; and, also, in serving all sentient beings thereby, I could do no better; such was the command I received. Thereupon, I thought that by dedicating my whole life to meditation, I should be setting an example to future devotees, who would thus be led to spend their life in devotion, after giving up all worldy aims and prospects; and that would conduce to the Cause of the Buddhistic Faith and to the benefit of all sentient beings. So I resolved go spend my whole life in meditation.

* * *

I also went on towards Brin (Drin), where I heard about both Lapchi-Chubar (Mt. Everest?) and Kyit-Phug (Pleasant Cave), also known as Nyima-Dzong (Sunny Castle), of which I chose the latter. . . . Now I must go to a most solitary region and seek a cave there. So, according to my *Guru's* command, I resolved to go to Lapchi-Chubar. While I was about to start on my way thither, my sister Peta came to offer me a piece of blanket-cloth, woven of wool which she had collected from the leavings of others. She had taken it to Dragkar-Taso, and not finding me there, had come searching for me, inquiring from every one; and hearing, at Gungthang-Tot, that a hermit resembling a caterpillar which feedeth upon nettles had passed from Palkhung towards La-Tot-Lho (Upper Hills Facing South), she had come tracking my very footprints. At Tingri, she had seen Lama Bari-Lotsawa (Th Great Bari Translator) seated upon a high seat, with an umbrella over him, dressed in silks of five different colours, and surrounded by his disciples, some of whom blew conchs, cymbals, clarionets, and flutes, with an great crowd round about, all offering him tea and *chhang*. Upon seeing this, Peta thought, Other devotees and religious folk enjoy these things, but my brother's religion is a source of misery and trouble to himself and shame to his relatives. If I now meet my brother, I shall try mine utmost to persuade him to become a disciple of this Lama. Thinking thus, she asked some among the assembly there whether they had heard or seen aught of me, and, being told that I was at Brin, she had come inquiring after me right up to Kyit-Phug, where I then was. Upon seeing me, she at once said, O brother, it will never do to go on in this starving, naked condition, which thou sayest is thy mode of living a religious life. Thou art past shame and common decency! Make a lower garment of this blanket, and go to the Lama Bari-Lotsawa, who is a Lama indeed, but quite different in style and practice from thyself. He hath a throne under him, and an umbrella over him; he is clad in silken garments, and his lips are always dipped in tea and *chhang*. He is surrounded by his disciples and followers, who walk in front of him, blowing trumpets by pairs. He assembleth a crowd wherever he goeth, and collecteth their offerings in large quantities, thus benefiting his relatives; and is one who can be boasted of as a most eminent Lama. I would have thee try to enter his service and follow him as his disciple. Even if thou be accepted as his meanest disciple, that would be better than this sort of life. Thy penurious devotion and my luckless life will scarcely do in this world. We cannot sustain life. And then she began to weep bitterly, deploring our lot.

I tried to console her by saying, Peta, do not speak in that fashion. Thou regardest my naked condition with shame, because I have cast aside clothing and coverings. I am proud that I have obtained the Truth through my being a man; and there is no shame in that. I was born thus; therefore there is no shame in it. But those who knowing certain acts to be sinful commit them, thereby breaking their parents' hearts, and those coveting property dedicated to *Gurus* and the Trinity, committing various acts of deception and meanness to attain their selfish aims, cause pain and suffering to other beings, and hurt themselves in the end. They are objects of loathing and abhorrence to every righteous being among gods and men; and they alone should feel shame. . . . Moreover, if thou think that I am meditating in this penurious condition just because I cannot earn or obtain food and clothing, thou art quite mistaken. I am frightened at the pains and tribulations of this *Sangsara*. I feel them as keenly as though I had been cast alive into flames. Worldly acquisitions of wealth and the need of clinging to them, as well as the pursuit of the Eight Worldly Aims, I regard with as much loathing and disgust as a man who is suffering from biliousness regardeth the sight of rich food. Nay, I regard them as if they were the murderers of my father; therefore is it that I am assuming this beggarly and penurious mode of life. Moreover, my *Guru,* Marpa the Translator, bade me to give up all worldly concerns, aims, and objects; to bear the loss of food, clothing, and name; to live in various solitary places (not fixing myself to one place permanently); and to carry on my devotions most energetically, giving up all prospects in this life. Such being my *Guru's* commandments, I am fulfilling them. By thus obeying my *Guru's* commandments, I shall not only be able to confer temporal ease and comfort on those who are my followers, but I shall earn eternal happiness for every sentient being, including myself. I gave up all thoughts of this life, because I saw that there is no certainty as to when death may come upon me. If I were to think of acquiring wealth and ease, I should be able to acquire as much as Lama Bari-Lotsawa himself is acquiring; so what need is there to speak of his meanest follower! But I desire Buddhahood in this very life-time; therefore am I devoting myself to devotion and meditation in such an energetic way. Peta, do thou also give up all worldly aims, and come with thy brother, who is older, to pass thy life in meditation at Lapchi-Kang. If thou can give up worldly thoughts and come to pass thy life in meditative devotions, the sun of thy temporal and eternal happiness will thus shine in full splendour. Give ear to thy brother's song. Then I sang this song:

> O Lord, Protector of all Sentient Beings, Thou the
>   Eternal Buddha!
> Since Thou, by worldliness unsullied hath remained,
> And blessed Thy *Shishyas* with Thy Grace,
> I bow down at Thy Feet, O Marpa the Translator!
>
> My sister Peta, listen unto me,
> Immersed in worldly wishes as thou art.
>
> The pinnacle of gold, placed on an umbrella, at the top,
>   for one;
> The fringe of Chinese silk, arranged in tasteful folds,
>   below, for two;

The ribs outspread, like a peacock's gorgeous feathers, in
  between, for three;
The polished handle of red teak-wood, at the bottom,
  for four:
These four, if needed, thine elder brother could procure.

But these are worldly things, and I've eschewed them,
And, by my thus eschewing worldliness, my Sun of Hap-
  piness shineth gloriously.
Likewise, do thou, O Peta, all worldliness eschew,
And come to meditate in Lapchi-Kang:
Let us together go to Lapchi-Kang; to meditate.

The white conch-shell's far-sounding note, for one;
The practised blower's full and potent breath, for two;
The silken ribbons (on the conch), plaited in fine plaits,
  for three;
The vast assembly of celibate priests (summoned thus),
  for four:
These four, if needed, thine elder brother could procure.

(*Chorus*)

The charming, pretty little temple, just above a village
  placed, for one;
The fluent speech, of youthful novices, for two;
The splendid kitchen, well arranged, with goodly stock
  of Chinese tea, for three;
The busy hands, of many youthful novices, for four:
These four, if needed, thine elder brother could procure.

(*Chorus*)

The well-liked trade, in necromantic seership, and in
  astrology, for one;
The correctness and the modesty of a pastor's acts, for
  two;
The performance of the *pujas*, for enjoying them, for
  three;
The psalms melodious, sung with a view to turn the
  heads of the laity, for four:
These four, if needed, thine elder brother could procure.

(*Chorus*)

A building, massive, beautiful, and tall, of brick, for one;
A field, extensive and fertile, for two;
A well-stocked store, of food and wealth, for three;
A numerous retinue, and crowd of servitors, for four:
These four, if needed, thine elder brother could procure.

(*Chorus*)

But if thou can not give up worldliness,
And can not come to Lapchi-Kang,
No liking have I for thy sentimental, sisterly affections.
These talks of worldly things disturb my meditation.
I being born, know I must die; uncertain of the hour of
    death,
No time have I to postpone my devotion;
Uninterruptedly will I devote myself to meditation.
The teachings of my *Guru*-Father are beneficial to the
    mind;
Thus, contemplating that which bringeth benefit,
I'll earn the Great Happiness of Deliverance;
Therefore to Lapchi-Kang I'm going.

Do thou, my sister, cling to worldliness,
Acquire sins by the pound and stone,
Strive to remain, for all the time thou canst, in the
    Sangsara,
And strive to win thyself a birth in the Three Lower
    Worlds.

Yet if thou fear the *Sangsara* in the least,
Renounce, in this life now, the Eight *Sangsaric* Aims,
And let us go together, unto Lapchi-Kang,
Let us, the twain, brother and sister, be high-destined
    ones,
And go together to the Ranges of the Lapchi-Kang.

On my singing thus, Peta said, I see that thou meanest
ease and comfort by worldliness, my brother. As for that, both
of us have so little to give up. All these fine-sounding truths
and sermons are merely excuses to cloak thine inability to be
as well off as Lama Bari-Lotsawa; but, as for me, I will not

go to Lapchi-Kang, where I shall have nothing to eat, nor anything to wear: it would be unendurable misery, which I need not go to seek at Lapchi. I do not even know where it is; and I would entreat thee, my brother, to remain permanently in one place, instead of rushing about and clinging to uninhabited cliffs and rocks, like an animal pursued by dogs. I could find thee more easily then. The people of this place seem disposed to regard thee with veneration, so it would be best if thou remain here permanently. . . .

It is quite clear that thou wilt not do anything such as I wish thee to do, yet I cannot give thee up. So please use these; and I will do what I can to obtain more. Having said this, she was about to go away. I, however, wishing to turn her heart towards religion, induced her to remain as long as the provisions might last, so that even though she did not earn merit by practising devotion, she would for that much time, at least, be free from committing sin. As long as she thus lived with me, I talked to her about religious subjects and about the Law of *Karma*. At last, I succeeded in turning her heart towards the Faith, to some extent. . . .

I have obtained spiritual knowledge through giving up all thought of food, clothing, and name. Inspired with zeal in my heart, I bore every hardship and inured myself to all sorts of privations of the body; I devoted myself to meditation in the most unfrequented and solitary places. Thus did I obtain knowledge and experience; do ye also follow in the path trodden by me, and practise devotion as I have done. . . .

* * *

At the time when Jetsun had fulfilled the various duties mentioned above, there lived, in the interior of Brin (Drin), a learned Lama named Tsaphuwa, very rich and influential, who was accustomed to take the highest seat in the assemblies of the people of Brin. This man feigned great reverence for Jetsun, while at heart he was bursting with envy of him, and desirous of exposing what he took to be Jetsun's ignorance, by putting difficult questions to Jetsun in a public gathering of his own supporters. In this wise he asked Jetsun many and various questions, all the while pretending that it was for the clearing of his own doubts.

Then, in the first month of the autumn of the Wood-Tiger

year, there happened to be a grand marriage feast to which Jetsun was invited, and he was placed on the highest seat at the head of the first row of guests, and the *Geshe* Tsaphuwa was seated next to him. The *Geshe* bowed down to Jetsun, expecting that Jetsun would bow down to him in return. Jetsun, however, did not do so; for never having bowed down to, nor returned the obeisance of any person save his own *Guru*, he did not depart from his usual custom on this occasion.

Much chagrined, the *Geshe* thought to himself, What! shall so learned a *pandit* as I am bow down to an ignoramus like him, and he not condescend to return the salutation! I shall certainly do my best to lower him in the esteem of the public. And, producing a book on philosophy, he addressed Jetsun thus: O Jetsun, please be so good as to dissipate my perplexities by going through this book and explaining it to me word by word.

Upon this, Jetsun answered, As for the mere word-by-word explication of these dialectics, thou thyself are sufficiently expert; but to realize their true import it is necessary to renounce the Eight Worldly Ambitions, lopping off their heads, to subdue the illusion of belief in the personal ego, and, regarding *Nirvana* and *Sangsara* as inseparable, to conquer the spiritual ego by meditation in mountain solitudes. I have never valued or studied the mere sophistry of word-knowledge, set down in books in conventionalized form of questions and answers to be committed to memory (and fired off at one's opponent); these lead but to mental confusion and not to such practice as bringeth actual realization of Truth. Of such word-knowledge I am ignorant; and if ever I did know it, I have forgotten it long ago. I pray that thou wilt give ear to the song which I am about to sing, to show my reasons for forgetting book-learning. And then Jetsun sang this song:

> Obeisance to the honored Feet of Marpa the Translator!
> May I be far removed from arguing creeds and dogmas.
>
> E'er since my Lord's Grace entered in my mind,
> My mind hath never strayed seeking various distractions.
>
> Accustomed long to contemplating Love and Pity,
> I have forgot all difference between my self and others.

Accustomed long to meditating on my *Guru* as enhaloed
o'er my head,
I have forgot all those who rule by power and by
prestige.

Accustomed long to meditating on my Guardian Gods
as from myself inseparable,
I have forgot the lowly fleshly form.

Accustomed long to meditating on the Whispered Chosen
Truths,
I have forgot all that is said in written and in printed
books.

Accustomed, as I've been, to the study of the Common
Science,
Knowledge of erring Ignorance I've lost.

Accustomed, as I've been, to contemplating the Three
Bodies as inherent in myself,
I have forgot to think of hope and fear.

Accustomed, as I've been, to meditating on this life and
the future life as one,
I have forgot the dread of birth and death.

Accustomed long to studying, all by myself, mine own
experiences,
I have forgot the need of seeking the opinions of friends
and brethren.

Accustomed long to application of each new experience to
mine own growth spiritual,
I have forgot all creeds and dogmas.

Accustomed long to meditating on the Unborn, the In-
destructible, and the Unabiding,
I have forgot all definitions of this or that particular
Goal.

Accustomed long to meditating on all visible phenomena
as the *Dharma-Kaya,*
I have forgot all mind-made meditations.

Accustomed long to keep my mind in the Uncreated
State of Freedom,
I have forgot conventional and artificial usages.

Accustomed long to humbleness, of body and of mind,
I have forgot the pride and haughty manner of the
mighty.

Accustomed long to regard my fleshy body as my hermitage,
I have forgot the ease and comfort of retreats in monasteries.

Accustomed long to know the meaning of the Wordless,
I have forgot the way to trace the roots of verbs and
source of words and phrases;
May thou, O learned one, trace out these things in standard books.

Milarepa's Final Words

Now hear my principal testament, of which none save my
chief disciples and lay followers, male and female, should be
informed. . . .

As to how ye are to carry the religious teachings into practice in your everyday life, bear in mind the following: Some
there may be among you who are proud of their apparent
sanctity, but who, at heart, are really devoted to acquiring
name and fame in this world; they dispense a hundred necessary and unnecessary things in charity, hoping thereby to reap
a liberal return. This, though displeasing to the Divinities
gifted with divine vision, is persevered in by selfish beings of
obscured vision. The hypocrisy of thus hankering after the
rich juices of this world, while outwardly appearing pious and
devout, because unable to face the ridicule of the world (which

might otherwise come to know of the hankering), is like partaking of delicacies and rich food mixed with deadly aconite. Therefore, drink not the venom of desire for worldly fame and name; but casting aside all the fetters of worldly duties, which but lead to this desire, devote yourselves to sincere and earnest devotion.

The disciples then inquired if they could engage in worldly duties, in a small way, for the benefit of others, and Jetsun said, If there be not the least self-interest attached to such duties, it is permissible. But such (detachment) is indeed rare; and works performed for the good of others seldom succeed if not wholly freed from self-interest. Even without seeking to benefit others, it is with difficulty that works done even in one's own interest (or selfishly) are successful. It is as if a man helplessly drowning were to try to save another man in the same predicament. One should not be over-anxious and hasty in setting out to serve others before one hath oneself realized Truth in its fullness; to do so, would be like the blind leading the blind. As long as the sky endureth, so long will there be no end of sentient beings for one to serve; and to every one cometh the opportunity for such service. Till the opportunity comes, I exhort each of you to have but the one resolve, namely, to attain Buddhahood for the good of all living things.

Be lowly and meek. Clothe yourselves in rags. Be resigned to hardships with respect to food and dress. Renounce all thought of acquiring worldly renown. Endure bodily penance and mental burdens. Thus gain knowledge from experience. That your study and penance be directed towards the right path, it is necessary to hold these injunctions in your hearts.

Having so spoken, Jetsun sang this hymn:

Obeisance at the Feet of Lordly Marpa the Translator!

If ye who would be devotees, and Wisdom win,
Do not procure and serve a *Guru* wise,
Though ye have faith and meekness, small will be the Grace.

If ye do not obtain the Initiation deep and mystic,
The words alone, the *Tantras* hold, will merely serve as fetters.

If ye keep not the *Tantric* Scriptures as your witness,
All practice of the rites will be but many snares.

If ye do not the Chosen Teachings meditate,
Mere renunciation of the worldly life will be but vain
  self-torture.

If ye subdue not evil passions by their antidote,
Mere verbal preachings will be but empty sounds.

If ye know not the Subtle Methods and the Path,
Mere perseverance will bear but little fruit.

If ye know not the Secret and the Subtle Methods,
Mere exercise of zeal will make the Pathway long.

If ye do not acquire great merit,
And work for self alone, *sangsaric* being will continue.

If ye do not devote unto Religion all your worldly goods
  amassed,
Much meditation will not gain much Knowledge.

If ye do not acquire contentment in yourselves,
Heaped-up accumulations will only enrich others.

If ye do not obtain the Light of Inner Peace,
Mere external ease and pleasure will become a source of
  pain.

If ye do not suppress the Demon of Ambition,
Desire of fame will lead to ruin and to lawsuits.

The desire to please exciteth the Five Poisonous Passions;
The greed of gain separateth one from dearest friends;
The exaltation of the one is the humiliation of the
  others.

Hold your peace and no litigation will arise;
Maintain the State of Undistractedness and distraction
  will fly off;

Dwell alone and ye shall find a friend;
Take the lowest place and ye shall reach the highest;
Hasten slowly and ye shall soon arrive;
Renounce all worldly goals and ye shall reach the highest
    goal.

If ye tread the Secret Path, ye shall find the shortest
    way;
If ye realize the Voidness, Compassion will arise within
    your hearts;
If ye lose all differentiation between yourselves and
    others, fit to serve others ye will be;
And when in serving others ye shall win success, then
    shall ye meet with me;
And finding me, ye shall attain to Buddhahood.

To me, and to the Buddha, and the Brotherhood of my
    disciples
Pray ye earnestly, without distinguishing one from the
    other.

Thus did Jetsun sing. And then he said, Seeing that I may
not have much longer now to live, observe my teachings and
follow me.

After saying this, Jetsun sank in to the quiescent state of
Samadhi. Thus did Jetsun pass away at the age of eighty-
four years, on the fourteenth day of the last of the three winter
months of the Wood-Hare Year (A.D. 1135), at dawn.

THE SUPREME PATH,
THE ROSARY OF PRECIOUS GEMS

Obeisance to the Honored *Guru!*

The Foreword

L ET him who desireth deliverance from the fearful and difficult-to-traverse Sea of Successive Existences, by means of the precepts taught by the inspired Kargyutpa Sages, render due homage to these Teachers, whose glory is immaculate, whose virtues are as inexhaustible as the ocean, and whose infinite benevolence embraceth all beings, past, present, and future, throughout the Universe.

For the use of those who share in the quest for Divine Wisdom there follow, recorded in writing, the most highly esteemed precepts, called The Supreme Path, the Rosary of Precious Gems, transmitted to Gampopa, either directly or indirectly, through that Inspired Dynasty of *Gurus,* out of their love for him.

THE TWENTY-EIGHT CATEGORIES OF YOGIC PRECEPTS

I. The Ten Causes of Regret

The devotee seeking Liberation and the Omniscience of Buddhahood should first meditate upon these ten things which are causes of regret:

(1) Having obtained the difficult-to-obtain, free, and endowed human body, it would be a cause of regret to fritter life away.

(2) Having obtained this pure and difficult-to-obtain, free, and endowed human body, it would be a cause of regret to die an irreligious and worldly man.

(3) This human life in the *Kale-Yuga* (or Age of Darkness) being so brief and uncertain, it would be a cause of regret to spend it in worldly aims and pursuits.

(4) One's own mind being of the nature of the *Dharma-*

Kaya, uncreated, it would be a cause of regret to let it be swallowed up in the morass of the world's illusions.

(5) The holy *guru* being the guide on the Path, it would be a cause of regret to be separated from him before attaining Enlightenment.

(6) Religious faith and vows being the vessel which conveyeth one to Emancipation, it would be a cause of regret were they to be shattered by the force of uncontrolled passions.

(7) The Perfect Wisdom having been found within oneself in virtue of the *guru's* grace, it would be a cause of regret to dissipate it amidst the jungle of worldliness.

(8) To sell like so much merchandise the Sublime Doctrine of the Sages would be a cause of regret.

(9) Inasmuch as all beings are our kindly parents, it would be a cause of regret to have aversion for and thus disown or abandon any of them.

(10) The prime of youth being the period of development of the body, speech, and mind, it would be a cause of regret to waste it in vulgar indifference.

These are The Ten Causes of Regret.

II. The Ten Requirements Come Next

(1) Having estimated one's own capabilities, one requireth a sure line of action.

(2) To carry out the commands of a religious preceptor, one requireth confidence and diligence.

(3) To avoid error in choosing a *guru,* the disciple requireth knowledge of his own faults and virtues.

(4) Keenness of intellect and unwavering faith are required to tune in with the mind of the spiritual preceptor.

(5) Unceasing watchfulness and mental alertness, graced with humility, are required to keep the body, speech, and mind unsullied by evil.

(6) Spiritual armour and strength of intellect are required for the fulfilment of one's heart's vows.

(7) Habitual freedom from desire and attachment is necessary if one would be free from bondage.

(8) To acquire the Twofold Merit, born of right motives, right actions, and the altruistic dedication of their results, there is need of unceasing effort.

(9) The mind, imbued with love and compassion in thought

and deed, ought ever to be directed to the service of all sentient beings.

(10) Through hearing, understanding, and wisdom, one should so comprehend the nature of all things as not to fall into the error of regarding matter and phenomena as real.

These are The Ten Requirements.

III. The Ten Things to be Done

(1) Attach thyself to a religious preceptor endowed with spiritual power and complete knowledge.

(2) Seek a delightful solitude endowed with psychic influences as a hermitage.

(3) Seek friends who have beliefs and habits like thine own and in whom thou canst place thy trust.

(4) Keeping in mind the evils of gluttony, use just enough food to keep thee fit during the period of thy retreat.

(5) Study the teachings of the Great Sages of all sects impartially.

(6) Study the beneficent sciences of medicine and astrology, and the profound art of omens.

(7) Adopt such regimen and manner of living as will keep thee in good health.

(8) Adopt such devotional practices as will conduce to thy spiritual development.

(9) Retain such disciples as are firm in faith, meek in spirit, and who appear to be favoured by *karma* in their quest for Divine Wisdom.

(10) Constantly maintain alertness of consciousness in walking, in sitting, in eating, and in sleeping.

These are The Ten Things to be Done.

IV. The Ten Things to be Avoided

(1) Avoid a *guru* whose heart is set on acquiring worldly fame and possessions.

(2) Avoid friends and followers who are detrimental to thy peace of mind and spiritual growth.

(3) Avoid hermitages and places of abode where there happen to be many persons who annoy and distract thee.

(4) Avoid gaining thy livelihood by means of deceit and theft.

(5) Avoid such actions as harm thy mind and impede thy spiritual development.

(6) Avoid such acts of levity and thoughtlessness as lower thee in another's esteem.

(7) Avoid useless conduct and actions.

(8) Avoid concealing thine own faults and speaking loudly of those of others.

(9) Avoid such food and habits as disagree with thy health.

(10) Avoid such attachments as are inspired by avarice.

These are The Ten Things to be Avoided.

V. The Ten Things Not to be Avoided

(1) Ideas, being the radiance of the mind, are not to be avoided.

(2) Thought-forms, being the revelry of Reality, are not to be avoided.

(3) Obscuring passions, being the means of reminding one of Divine Wisdom (which giveth deliverance from them), are not to be avoided (if rightly used to enable one to taste life to the full and thereby reach disillusionment).

(5) Illness and tribulations, being teachers of piety, are not to be avoided.

(6) Enemies and misfortune, being the means of inclining one to a religious career, are not to be avoided.

(7) That which cometh of itself, being a divine gift, is not to be avoided.

(8) Reason, being in every action the best friend, is not to be avoided.

(9) Such devotional exercises of body and mind as one is capable of performing are not to be avoided.

(10) The thought of helping others, howsoever limited one's ability to help others may be, is not to be avoided.

These are The Ten Things Not To Be Avoided.

VI. The Ten Things One Must Know

(1) One must know that all visible phenomena, being illusory, are unreal.

(2) One must know that the mind, being without independent existence (apart from the One Mind), is impermanent.

(3) One must know that ideas arise from a concatenation of causes.

(4) One must know that the body and speech, being compounded of the four elements, are transitory.

(5) One must know that the effects of past actions, whence cometh all sorrow, are inevitable.

(6) One must know that sorrow, being the means of convincing one of the need of the religious life, is a *guru*.

(7) One must know that attachment to worldly things maketh material prosperity inimical to spiritual progress.

(8) One must know that misfortune, being the means of leading one to the Doctrine, is also a *guru*.

(9) One must know that no existing thing has an independent existence.

(10) One must know that all things are interdependent.

These are The Ten Things One Must Know.

VII. The Ten Things to be Practised

(1) One should acquire practical knowledge of the Path by treading it, and not be as are the multitude (who profess, but do not practice, religion).

(2) By quitting one's own country and dwelling in foreign lands one should acquire practical knowledge of non-attachment.

(3) Having chosen a religious preceptor, separate thyself from egotism and follow his teachings implicitly.

(4) Having acquired mental discipline by hearing and meditating upon religious teachings, boast not of thine attainment, but apply it to the realization of Truth.

(5) Spiritual knowledge having dawned in oneself, neglect it not through slothfulness, but cultivate it with ceaseless vigilance.

(6) Once having experienced spiritual illumination, commune with it in solitude, relinquishing the worldly activities of the multitude.

(7) Having acquired practical knowledge of spiritual things and made the Great Renunciation, permit not the body, speech, or mind to become unruly, but observe the three vows, of poverty, chastity, and obedience.

(8) Having resolved to attain the Highest Goal, abandon selfishness and devote thyself to the service of others.

(9) Having entered upon the mystic *Mantrayanic* Pathway,

permit not the body, the speech, or the mind to remain un-sanctified, but practise the threefold *mandala*.

(10) During the period of youth, frequent not those who cannot direct thee spiritually, but acquire practical knowledge painstakingly at the feet of a learned and pious *guru*.

These are The Ten Things to be Practised.

VIII. The Ten Things to be Persevered in

(1) Novices should persevere in listening to, and meditating upon, religious teachings.

(2) Having had spiritual experience, persevere in meditation and mental concentration.

(3) Persevere in solitude until the mind hath been *yogically* disciplined.

(4) Should thought-processes be difficult to control, persevere in thine efforts to dominate them.

(5) Should there be great drowsiness, persevere in thine efforts to invigorate the intellect (or to control the mind).

(6) Persevere in meditation until thou attainest the imperturbable mental tranquillity of *samadhi*.

(7) Having attained this state of *samadhi*, persevere in prolonging its duration and in causing its recurrence at will.

(8) Should various misfortunes assail thee, persevere in patience of body, speech, and mind.

(9) Should there be great attachment, hankering, or mental weakness, persevere in an effort to eradicate it as soon as it manifesteth itself.

(10) Should benevolence and pity be weak within thee, persevere in directing the mind towards Perfection.

These are The Ten Things to be Persevered in.

IX. The Ten Incentives

(1) By reflecting upon the difficulty of obtaining an endowed and free human body, mayest thou be incited to adopt the religious career.

(2) By reflecting upon death and the impermanence of life, mayest thou be incited to live piously.

(3) By reflecting upon the irrevocable nature of the results which inevitably arise from actions, mayest thou be incited to avoid impiety and evil.

(4) By reflecting upon the evils of life in the round of successive existences, mayest thou be incited to seek Emancipation.

(5) By reflecting upon the miseries which all sentient beings suffer, mayest thou be incited to attain deliverance therefrom by enlightenment of mind.

(6) By reflecting upon the perversity and illusory nature of the mind of all sentient beings, mayest thou be incited to listen to, and meditate upon, the Doctrine.

(7) By reflecting upon the difficulty of eradicating erroneous concepts, mayest thou be incited to constant meditatìon (which overcometh them).

(8) By reflecting upon the predominance of evil propensities in this *Kali-Yuga* (or Age of Darkness), mayest thou be incited to seek their antidote (in the Doctrine).

(9) By reflecting upon the multiplicity of misfortunes in this Age of Darkness, mayest thou be incited to perseverance (in the quest for Emancipation).

(10) By reflecting upon the uselessness of aimlessly frittering away thy life, mayest thou be incited to diligence (in the treading of the Path).

These are The Ten Incentives.

X. The Ten Errors

(1) Weakness of faith combined with strength of intellect are apt to lead to the error of talkativeness.

(2) Strength of faith combined with weakness of intellect are apt to lead to the error of narrow-minded dogmatism.

(3) Great zeal without adequate religious instruction is apt to lead to the error of going to erroneous extremes (or following misleading paths).

(4) Meditation without sufficient preparation through having heard and pondered the Doctrine is apt to lead to the error of losing oneself in the darkness of unconsciousness.

(5) Without practical and adequate understanding of the Doctrine, one is apt to fall into the error of religious self-conceit.

(6) Unless the mind be trained to selflessness and infinite compassion, one is apt to fall into the error of seeking liberation for self alone.

(7) Unless the mind be disciplined by knowledge of its own immaterial nature, one is apt to fall into the error of diverting all activities along the path of worldliness.

(8) Unless all worldly ambitions be eradicated, one is apt to fall into the error of allowing oneself to be dominated by worldly motives.

(9) By permitting credulous and vulgar admirers to congregate about thee, there is liability of falling into the error of becoming puffed up with worldly pride.

(10) By boasting of one's occult learning and powers, one is liable to fall into the error of proudly exhibiting proficiency in worldly rites.

These are The Ten Errors.

XI. The Ten Resemblances Wherein One May Err

(1) Desire may be mistaken for faith.

(2) Attachment may be mistaken for benevolence and compassion.

(3) Cessation of thought-processes may be mistaken for the quiescence of infinite mind, which is the true goal.

(4) Sense perceptions (or phenomena) may be mistaken for revelations (or glimpses) of Reality.

(5) A mere glimpse of Reality may be mistaken for complete realization.

(6) Those who outwardly profess, but do not practise, religion may be mistaken for true devotees.

(7) Slaves of passion may be mistaken for masters of *yoga* who have liberated themselves from all conventional laws.

(8) Actions performed in the interest of self may be mistakenly regarded as being altruistic.

(9) Deceptive methods may be mistakenly regarded as being prudent.

(10) Charlatans may be mistaken for Sages.

These are The Ten Resemblances Wherein One May Err.

XII. The Ten Things Wherein One Erreth Not

(1) In being free from attachment to all objects, and being ordained a *bhikshu* into the Holy Order, forsaking home and entering upon the homeless state, one doth not err.

(2) In revering one's spiritual preceptor one doth not err.

(3) In thoroughly studying the Doctrine, hearing discourses

thereon, and reflecting and meditating upon it, one doth not err.

(4) In nourishing lofty aspirations and a lowly demeanour one doth not err.

(5) In entertaining liberal views (as to religion) and yet being firm in observing (formal religious) vows one doth not err.

(6) In having greatness of intellect and smallness of pride one doth not err.

(7) In being wealthy in religious doctrines and diligent in meditating upon them one doth not err.

(8) In having profound religious learning, combined with knowledge of things spiritual and absence of pride, one doth not err.

(9) In being able to pass one's whole life in solitude one doth not err.

(10) In being unselfishly devoted to doing good to others, by means of wise methods, one doth not err.

These are The Ten Things Wherein One Erreth Not.

XIII. The Thirteen Grievous Failures

(1) If, having been born a human being, one give no heed to the Holy Doctrine, one resembleth a man who returneth empty-handed from a land rich in precious gems; and this is a grievous failure.

(2) If, after having entered the door of the Holy Order, one return to the life of the householder, one resembleth a moth plunging into the flame of a lamp; and this is a grievous failure.

(3) To dwell with a sage and remain in ignorance is to be like a man dying of thirst on the shore of a lake; and this is a grievous failure.

(4) To know the moral precepts and not apply them to the cure of obscuring passions is to be like a diseased man carrying a bag of medicine which he never useth; and this is a grievous failure.

(5) To preach religion and not practise it is to be like a parrot saying a prayer; and this is a grievous failure.

(6) The giving in alms and charity of things obtained by theft, robbery, or deceit, is like lightning striking the surface of water; and this is a grievous failure.

(7) The offering to the deities of meat obtained by killing animate beings is like offering a mother the flesh of her own child; and this is a grievous failure.

(8) To exercise patience for merely selfish ends rather than for doing good to others is to be like a cat exercising patience in order to kill a rat; and this is a grievous failure.

(9) Performing meritorious actions in order merely to attain fame and praise in this world is like bartering the mystic wish-granting gem for a pellet of goat's dung; and this is a grievous failure.

(10) If, after having heard much of the Doctrine, one's nature still be unattuned, one is like a physician with a chronic disease; and this is a grievous failure.

(11) To be clever concerning precepts yet ignorant of the spiritual experiences which come from applying them is to be like a rich man who hath lost the key of his treasury; and this is a grievous failure.

(12) To attempt to explain to others doctrines which one hath not completely mastered oneself is to be like a blind man leading the blind; and this is a grievous failure.

(13) To hold the experiences resulting from the first stage of meditation to be those of the final stage is to be like a man who mistaketh brass for gold; and this is a grievous failure.

These are The Thirteen Grievous Failures.

XIV. The Fifteen Weaknesses

(1) A religious devotee showeth weakness if he allow his mind to be obsessed with worldly thoughts while dwelling in solitude.

(2) A religious devotee who is the head of a monastery showeth weakness if he seek his own interests (rather than those of the brotherhood).

(3) A religious devotee showeth weakness if he be careful in the observance of moral discipline and lacking in moral restraint.

(4) It showeth weakness in one who hath entered upon the Righteous Path to cling to worldly feelings of attraction and repulsion.

(5) It showeth weakness in one who hath renounced worldliness and entered the Holy Order to hanker after acquiring merit.

(6) It showeth weakness in one who hath caught a glimpse of Reality to fail to persevere in *sadhama* (or *yogic* meditation) till the dawning of Full Enlightenment.

(7) It showeth weakness in one who is a religious devotee to enter upon the Path and then be unable to tread it.

(8) It showeth weakness in one who hath no other occupation than religious devotion to be unable to eradicate from himself unworthy actions.

(9) It showeth weakness in one who hath chosen the religious career to have hesitancy in entering into close retreat while knowing full well that the food and everything needed would be provided unasked.

(10) A religious devotee who exhibiteth occult powers when practising exorcism or in driving away diseases showeth weakness.

(11) A religious devotee showeth weakness if he barter sacred truths for food and money.

(12) One who is vowed to the religious life showeth weakness if he cunningly praise himself while disparaging others.

(13) A man of religion who preacheth loftily to others and doth not live loftily himself showeth weakness.

(14) One who professeth religion and is unable to live in solitude in his own company and yet knoweth not how to make himself agreeable in the company of others showeth weakness.

(15) The religious devotee showeth weakness if he be not indifferent to comfort and to hardship.

These are The Fifteen Weaknesses.

XV. The Twelve Indispensable Things

(1) It is indispensable to have an intellect endowed with the power of comprehending and applying the Doctrine to one's own needs.

(2) At the very beginning (of one's religious career) it is indispensably necessary to have the most profound aversion for the interminable sequence of repeated deaths and births.

(3) A *guru* capable of guiding thee on the Path of Emancipation is also indispensable.

(4) Diligence combined with fortitude and invulnerability to temptation are indispensable.

(5) Unceasing perseverance in neutralizing the results of evil deeds, by the performance of good deeds, and the fulfilling of the threefold vow, to maintain chastity of body, purity of mind, and control of speech, are indispensable.

(6) A philosophy comprehensive enough to embrace the whole of knowledge is indispensable.

(7) A system of meditation which will produce the power of concentrating the mind upon anything whatsoever is indispensable.

(8) An art of living which will enable one to utilize each activity (of body, speech, and mind) as an aid on the Path is indispensable.

(9) A method of practising the select teachings which will make them more than mere words is indispensable.

(10) Special instructions (by a wise *guru*) which will enable one to avoid misleading paths, temptations, pitfalls, and dangers are indispensable.

(11) Indomitable faith combined with supreme serenity of mind are indispensable at the moment of death.

(12) As a result of having practically applied the select teachings, the attainment of spiritual powers capable of transmuting the body, the speech, and the mind into their divine essences is indispensable.

These are The Twelve Indispensable Things.

XVI. The Ten Signs of a Superior Man

(1) To have but little pride and envy is the sign of a superior man.

(2) To have but few desires and satisfaction with simple things is the sign of a superior man.

(3) To be lacking in hypocrisy and deceit is the sign of a superior man.

(4) To regulate one's conduct in accordance with the law of cause and effect as carefully as one guardeth the pupils of one's eyes is the sign of a superior man.

(5) To be faithful to one's engagements and obligations is the sign of a superior man.

(6) To be able to keep alive friendships while one (at the same time) regardeth all beings with impartiality is the sign of a superior man.

(7) To look with pity and without anger upon those who live evilly is the sign of a superior man.

(8) To allow unto others the victory, taking unto oneself the defeat, is the sign of a superior man.

(9) To differ from the multitude in every thought and action is the sign of a superior man.

(10) To observe faithfully and without pride one's vows of chastity and piety is the sign of a superior man.

These are The Ten Signs of a Superior Man. Their opposites are The Ten Signs of an Inferior Man.

XVII. The Ten Useless Things

(1) Our body being illusory and transitory, it is useless to give over-much attention to it.

(2) Seeing that when we die we must depart empty-handed and on the morrow after our death our corpse is expelled from our own house, it is useless to labour and to suffer privations in order to make for oneself a home in this world.

(3) Seeing that when we die our descendants (if spiritually unenlightened) are unable to render us the least assistance, it is useless for us to bequeath to them worldly (rather than spiritual) riches, even out of love.

(4) Seeing that when we die we must go on our way alone and without kinsfolk or friends, it is useless to have devoted time (which ought to have been dedicated to the winning of Enlightenment) to their humouring and obliging, or in showering loving affection upon them.

(5) Seeing that our descendants themselves are subject to death and that whatever worldly goods we may bequeath to them are certain to be lost eventually, it is useless to make bequests of the things of this world.

(6) Seeing that when death cometh one must relinquish even one's own home, it is useless to devote life to the acquisition of worldly things.

(7) Seeing that unfaithfulness to the religious vows will result in one's going to the miserable states of existence, it is useless to have entered the Order if one live not a holy life.

(8) To have heard and thought about the Doctrine and not practised it and acquired spiritual powers to assist thee at the moment of death is useless.

(9) It is useless to have lived, even for a very long time, with a spiritual preceptor if one be lacking in humility and devotion and thus be unable to develop spiritually.

(10) Seeing that all existing and apparent phenomena are ever transient, changing, and unstable, and more especially that the worldly life affordeth neither reality nor permanent gain, it is useless to have devoted oneself to the profitless doings of this world rather than to the seeking of Divine Wisdom.

These are The Ten Useless Things.

XVIII. The Ten Self-Imposed Troubles

(1) To enter the state of the householder without means of sustenance produceth self-imposed trouble as doth an idiot eating aconite.

(2) To live a thoroughly evil life and disregard the Doctrine produceth self-imposed trouble as doth an insane person jumping over a precipice.

(3) To live hypocritically produceth self-imposed trouble as doth a person who putteth poison in his own food.

(4) To be lacking in firmness of mind and yet attempt to act as the head of a monastery produceth self-imposed trouble as doth a feeble old woman who attempteth to herd cattle.

(5) To devote oneself wholly to selfish ambitions and not to strive for the good of others produceth self-imposed trouble as doth a blind man who alloweth himself to become lost in a desert.

(6) To undertake difficult tasks and not have the ability to perform them produceth self-imposed trouble as doth a man without strength who trieth to carry a heavy load.

(7) To transgress the commandments of the Buddha or of the holy *guru* through pride and self-conceit produceth self-imposed trouble as doth a king who followeth a perverted policy.

(8) To waste one's time loitering about towns and villages instead of devoting it to meditation produceth self-imposed trouble as doth a deer that descendeth to the valley instead of keeping to the fastnesses of the mountains.

(9) To be absorbed in the pursuit of worldly things rather than in nourishing the growth of Divine Wisdom produceth self-imposed trouble as an eagle when it breaketh its wing.

(10) Shamelessly to misappropriate offerings which have been dedicated to the *guru* or to the Trinity produceth self-imposed trouble as doth a child swallowing live coals.

These are The Ten Self-Imposed Troubles.

XIX. The Ten Things Wherein one Doeth Good to Oneself

(1) One doeth good to oneself by abandoning worldly conventions and devoting oneself to the Holy *Dharma*.

(2) One doeth good to oneself by departing from home and kindred and attaching oneself to a *guru* of saintly character.

(3) One doeth good to oneself by relinquishing worldly activities and devoting oneself to the three religious activities,— hearing, reflecting, and meditating (upon the chosen teachings).

(4) One doeth good to oneself by giving up social intercourse and dwelling alone in solitude.

(5) One doeth good to oneself by renouncing desire for luxury and ease and enduring hardship.

(6) One doeth good to oneself by being contented with simple things and free from craving for worldly possessions.

(7) One doeth good to oneself by making and firmly adhering to the resolution not to take advantage of others.

(8) One doeth good to oneself by attaining freedom from hankering after the transitory pleasures of this life and devoting oneself to the realization of the eternal bliss of *Nirvana*.

(9) One doeth good to oneself by abandoning attachment to visible material things (which are transitory and unreal) and attaining knowledge of Reality.

(10) One doeth good to oneself by preventing the three doors to knowledge (the body, the speech, and the mind) from remaining spiritually undisciplined and by acquiring, through right use of them, the Twofold Merit.

These are The Ten Things Wherein one Doeth Good to Oneself.

XX. The Ten Best Things

(1) For one of little intellect, the best thing is to have faith in the law of cause and effect.

(2) For one of ordinary intellect, the best thing is to recognize, both within and without oneself, the workings of the law of opposites.

(3) For one of superior intellect, the best thing is to have thorough comprehension of the inseparableness of the knower, the object of knowledge, and the act of knowing.

(4) For one of little intellect, the best meditation is complete concentration of mind upon a single object.

(5) For one of ordinary intellect, the best meditation is unbroken concentration of mind upon the two dualistic concepts (of phenomena and noumena, and consciousness and mind).

(6) For one of superior intellect, the best meditation is to remain in mental quiescence, the mind devoid of all thought-processes, knowing that the meditator, the object of meditation, and the act of meditating constitute an inseparable unity.

(7) For one of little intellect, the best religious practice is to live in strict conformity with the law of cause and effect.

(8) For one of ordinary intellect, the best religious practice is to regard all objective things as though they were images seen in a dream or produced by magic.

(9) For one of superior intellect, the best religious practice is to abstain from all worldly desires and actions, (regarding all *sangsaric* things as though they were non-existent).

(10) For those of all three grades of intellect, the best indication of spiritual progress is the gradual diminution of obscuring passions and selfishness.

These are The Ten Best Things.

XXI. The Ten Grievous Mistakes

(1) For a religious devotee to follow a hypocritical charlatan instead of a *guru* who sincerely practiseth the Doctrine is a grievous mistake.

(2) For a religious devotee to apply himself to vain worldly sciences rather than to seeking the chosen secret teachings of the Great Sages is a grievous mistake.

(3) For a religious devotee to make far-reaching plans as though he were going to establish permanent residence (in this world) instead of living as though each day were the last he had to live is a grievous mistake.

(4) For a religious devotee to preach the Doctrine to the multitude (ere having realized it to be true) instead of meditating upon it (and testing its truth) in solitude is a grievous mistake.

(5) For a religious devotee to be like a miser and hoard up riches instead of dedicating them to religion and charity is a grievous mistake.

(6) For a religious devotee to give way in body, speech, and mind to the shamelessness of debauchery instead of observing carefully the vows (of purity and chastity) is a grievous mistake.

(7) For a religious devotee to spend his life between worldly hopes and fears instead of gaining understanding of Reality is a grievous mistake.

(8) For a religious devotee to try to reform others instead of reforming himself is a grievous mistake.

(9) For a religious devotee to strive after worldly powers instead of cultivating his own innate spiritual powers is a grievous mistake.

(10) For a religious devotee to be idle and indifferent instead of persevering when all the circumstances favourable for spiritual advancement are present is a grievous mistake.

These are The Ten Grievous Mistakes.

XXII. The Ten Necessary Things

(1) At the very outset (of one's religious career) one should have so profound an aversion for the continuous succession of deaths and births (to which all who have not attained Enlightenment are subject) that one will wish to flee from it even as a stag fleeth from captivity.

(2) The next necessary thing is perseverance so great that one regretteth not the losing of one's life (in the quest for Enlightenment), like that of the husbandman who tilleth his fields and regretteth not the tilling even though he die on the morrow.

(3) The third necessary thing is joyfulness of mind like that of a man who hath accomplished a great deed of far-reaching influence.

(4) Again, one should comprehend that, as with a man dangerously wounded by an arrow, there is not a moment of time to be wasted.

(5) One needeth ability to fix the mind on a single thought even as doth a mother who hath lost her only son.

(6) Another necessary thing is to understand that there is no need of doing anything, even as a cowherd whose cattle

have been driven off by enemies understandeth that he can do nothing to recover them.

(7) It is primarily requisite for one to hunger after the Doctrine even as a hungry man hungereth after good food.

(8) One needeth to be as confident of one's mental ability as doth a strong man of his physical ability to hold fast to a precious gem which he hath found.

(9) One must expose the fallacy of dualism as one doth the falsity of a liar.

(10) One must have confidence in the Thatness (as being the Sole Refuge) even as an exhausted crow far from land hath confidence in the mast of the ship upon which it resteth.

These are The Ten Necessary Things.

XXIII. The Ten Unnecessary Things

(1) If the empty nature of the mind be realized, no longer is it necessary to listen to or to meditate upon religious teachings.

(2) If the unsulliable nature of the intellect be realized, no longer is it necessary to seek absolution of one s sins.

(3) Nor is absolution necessary for one who abideth in the State of Mental Quiescence.

(4) For him who hath attained the State of Unalloyed Purity there is no need to meditate upon the Path or upon the methods of treading it, (for he hath arrived at the Goal).

(5) If the unreal (or illusory) nature of cognitions be realized, no need is there to meditate upon the state of non-cognition.

(6) If the non-reality (or illusory nature) of obscuring passions be realized, no need is there to seek their antidote.

(7) If all phenomena be known to be illusory, no need is there to seek or to reject anything.

(8) If sorrow and misfortune be recognized to be blessings, no need is there to seek happiness.

(9) If the unborn (or uncreated) nature of one's own consciousness be realized, no need is there to practise transference of consciousness.

(10) If only the good of others be sought in all that one doeth, no need is there to seek benefit for oneself.

These are The Ten Unnecessary Things.

XXIV. The Ten More Precious Things

(1) One free and well-endowed human life is more precious than myriads of non-human lives in any of the six states of existence.

(2) One Sage is more precious than multitudes of irreligious and worldly-minded persons.

(3) One esoteric truth is more precious than innumerable exoteric doctrines.

(4) One momentary glimpse of Divine Wisdom, born of meditation, is more precious than any amount of knowledge derived from merely listening to and thinking about religious teachings.

(5) The smallest amount of merit dedicated to the good of others is more precious than any amount of merit devoted to one's own good.

(6) To experience but momentarily the *samadhi* wherein all thought-processes are quiescent is more precious than to experience uninterruptedly the *samadhi* wherein thought-processes are still present.

(7) To enjoy a single moment of *Nirvanic* bliss is more precious than to enjoy any amount of sensual bliss.

(8) The smallest good deed done unselfishly is more precious than innumerable good deeds done selfishly.

(9) The renunciation of every worldly thing (home, family, friends, property, fame, duration of life, and even health) is more precious than the giving of inconceivably vast worldly wealth in charity.

(10) One lifetime spent in the quest for Enlightenment is more precious than all the lifetimes during an aeon spent in worldly pursuits.

These are The Ten More Precious Things.

XXV. The Ten Equal Things

(1) For him who is sincerely devoted to the religious life, it is the same whether he refrain from worldly activities or not.

(2) For him who hath realized the transcendental nature of mind, it is the same whether he meditate or not.

(3) For him who is freed from attachment to worldly luxuries, it is the same whether he practise asceticism or not.

(4) For him who hath realized Reality, it is the same

whether he dwell on an isolated hill-top in solitude or wander hither and thither (as a *bhikshu*).

(5) For him who hath attained the mastery of his mind, it is the same whether he partake of the pleasures of the world or not.

(6) For him who is endowed with the fullness of compassion, it is the same whether he practise meditation in solitude or work for the good of others in the midst of society.

(7) For him whose humility and faith (with respect to his *guru*) are unshakable, it is the same whether he dwell with his *guru* or not.

(8) For him who understandeth thoroughly the teachings which he hath received, it is the same whether he meet with good fortune or with bad fortune.

(9) For him who hath given up the worldly life and taken to the practice of the Spiritual Truths, it is the same whether he observe conventional codes of conduct or not.

(10) For him who hath attained the Sublime Wisdom, it is the same whether he be able to exercise miraculous powers or not.

These are The Ten Equal Things.

XXVI. The Ten Virtues of the Holy Dharma (or Doctrine)

(1) The fact that there have been made known amongst men the Ten Pious Acts, the Six *Paramita*, the various teachings concerning Reality and Perfection, the Four Noble Truths, the Four States of *Dhyana*, the Four States of Formless Existence, and the Two Mystic Paths of spiritual unfoldment and emancipation, showeth the virtue of the Holy *Dharma*.

(2) The fact that there have been evolved in the *Sangsara* spiritually enlightened princes and Brahmins amongst men, and the Four Great Guardians, the six orders of *devas* of the sensuous paradises, the seventeen orders of gods of the worlds of form, and the four orders of gods of the worlds without form showeth the virtue of the Holy *Dharma*.

(3) The fact that there have arisen in the world those who have entered the Stream, those who will return to birth but once more, those who have passed beyond the need of further birth, and *Arhants*, and Self-Enlightened Buddhas and Omniscient Buddhas, showeth the virtue of the Holy *Dharma*.

(4) The fact that there are Those who have attained *Bodhic*

Enlightenment and are able to return to the world as Divine Incarnations and work for the deliverance of mankind and of all living things till the time of the dissolution of the physical universe showeth the virtue of the Holy *Dharma*.

(5) The fact that there existeth, as an outcome of the all-embracing benevolence of the *Bodhisattvas,* protective spiritual influences wḥich make possible the deliverance of men and of all beings showeth the virtue of the Holy *Dharma*.

(6) The fact that one experienceth even in the unhappy worlds of existence moments of happiness as a direct outcome of having performed little deeds of mercy while in the human world showeth the virtue of the Holy *Dharma*.

(7) The fact that men after having lived evilly should have renounced the worldly life and become saints worthy of the veneration of the world showeth the virtue of the Holy *Dharma*.

(8) The fact that men whose heavy evil *karma* would have condemned them to almost endless suffering after death should have turned to the religious life and attained *Nirvana* showeth the virtue of the Holy *Dharma*.

(9) The fact that by merely having faith in or meditating upon the Doctrine, or by merely donning the robe of the *bhikshu,* one becometh worthy of respect and veneration showeth the virtue of the Holy *Dharma*.

(10) The fact that one, even after having abandoned all worldly possessions and embraced the religious life and given up the state of the householder and hidden himself in a most secluded hermitage, should still be sought for and supplied with all the necessities of life showeth the virtue of the Holy *Dharma*.

These are The Ten Virtues of the Holy *Dharma*.

XXVII. The Ten Figurative Expressions

(1) As the Foundation Truth cannot be described (but must be realized in *samadhi*), the expression Foundation Truth is merely figurative.

(2) As there is neither any traversing nor any traverser of the Path, the expression Path is merely figurative.

(3) As there is neither any seeing nor any seer of the True State, the expression True State is merely figurative.

(4) As there is neither any meditation nor any meditator of the Pure State, the expression Pure State is merely figurative.

(5) As there is neither any enjoying nor any enjoyer of the Natural Mood, the expression Natural Mood is merely figurative.

(6) As there is neither any vow-keeping nor any vow-keeper, these expressions are merely figurative.

(7) As there is neither any accumulating nor any accumulator of merits, the expression Twofold Merit is merely figurative.

(8) As there is neither any performing nor any performer of actions, the expression Twofold Obscuration is merely figurative.

(9) As there is neither any renunciation nor any renouncer (of worldly existence), the expression worldly existence is merely figurative.

(10) As there is neither any obtaining nor any obtainer (of results of actions), the expression results of actions is merely figurative.

These are The Ten Figurative Expressions.

XXVIII.   The Ten Great Joyful Realizations

(1) It is great joy to realize that the mind of all sentient beings is inseparable from the All-Mind.

(2) It is great joy to realize that the Fundamental Reality is qualityless.

(3) It is great joy to realize that in the infinite, thought-transcending Knowledge of Reality all *sangsaric* differentiations are non-existent.

(4) It is great joy to realize that in the state of primordial (or uncreated) mind there existeth no disturbing thought-process.

(5) It is great joy to realize that in the *Dharma-Kaya,* wherein mind and matter are inseparable, there existeth neither any holder of theories nor any support of theories.

(6) It is great joy to realize that in the self-emanated, compassionate *Sambhoga-Kaya* there existeth no birth, death, transition, or any change.

(7) It is great joy to realize that in the self-emanated, divine *Nirmana-Kaya* there existeth no feeling of duality.

(8) It is great joy to realize that in the *Dharma-Chakra* there existeth no support for the soul doctrine.

(9) It is great joy to realize that in the Divine, Boundless Compassion (of the *Bodhisattvas*) there existeth neither any shortcoming nor any showing of partiality.

(10) It is great joy to realize that the Path to Freedom which all the Buddhas have trodden is ever-existent, ever unchanged, and ever open to those who are ready to enter upon it.

These are The Ten Great Joyful Realizations.

(The Conclusion)

Herein, above, is contained the essence of the immaculate words of the Great *Gurus,* who were endowed with Divine Wisdom; and of the Goddess Tara and other divinites. Among these Great Teachers were the glorious Dipankara, the spiritual father and his successors, who were divinely appointed for the spreading of the Doctrine in this Northern Land of Snow; and the Gracious *Gurus* of the Kahdampa School. There were also that King of *Yogins,* Milarepa, to whom was bequeathed the learning of the Sage Marpa of Lhobrak and of others; and the illustrious Saints, Naropa and Maitripa, of the noble land of India, whose splendour equalled that of the Sun and Moon; and the disciples of all these.

Here endeth *The Supreme Path, the Rosary of Precious Gems.*

May this Book radiate divine virtue; and may it prove to be auspicious.

Mangalam.

SELECTIONS
FROM MODERN SOURCES

The scripture of the saviour of the world
Lord Buddha—Prince Siddartha styled on earth—
In Earth and Heavens and Hells Incomparable,
All-honoured, Wisest, Best, most Pitiful;
The Teacher of Nirvana and the Law.

*   *   *

Om mani padme hum, the Sunrise comes!
The Dewdrop slips into the shining Sea!

Sir Edwin Arnold
The Light of Asia.

A MAN who wishes to become my disciple must be willing to give up all direct relations with his family, with the social life of the world and all dependence upon wealth. A man who has given up all such relations for the sake of the Dharma and has no abiding place for either his body or his mind has become my disciple and is to be called a homeless brother.

Though his feet leave their imprints in my footsteps and his hands carry my garment, if his mind is disturbed by greed, he is far from me. Though he dresses like a monk, but does not accept the teaching, he does not see me. But if he has removed all greed and his mind is pure and peaceful, he is very close to me though he be thousands of miles away. If he receives the Dharma he sees me in the Dharma.

2. My disciples, the homeless brothers, observe four rules and about them build their lives. First, they wear old and cast-off garments; second, they get their food by faith; third, their home is where night finds them; fourth, they use the special medicine laid down by the brotherhood.

To carry a bowl in hand and go from house to house is a beggar's life, but he is not compelled to do it by others, he is not forced into it by circumstances or by temptation, he does it of his own free will because he thinks that a life of faith will keep him away from the delusions of life, will help him to avoid suffering, and will lead him toward enlightenment.

The life of a homeless brother is not an easy life; one ought not to undertake it if he can not keep his mind free from greed and anger, and if he can not control his mind and his five senses.

3. To believe oneself to be a homeless brother and to be able to answer when he is asked about it, one must be able to say:—"I am willing to undertake whatever is necessary to be a homeless brother. I will be sincere about it and will try to accomplish the purpose for becoming one. I will be grateful

to those who help me by donations and will try to make them happy by my earnestness and good life."

To be a homeless brother one must train himself in many ways:—He must be sensitive to shame and dishonor when he fails; he must keep his body, lips and mind pure if his life is to be pure; he must guard the gates of the five senses; he must not lose control of his mind for the sake of some passing pleasure; he must not praise himself nor rebuke others; and he must not be idle nor given to much sleep.

In the evening he should have a time for quiet sitting and meditation and a little walk before retiring. For peaceful sleep he should rest on the right side with his feet together and his last thought should be of the time when he wishes to rise in the early morning. In the early morning he should have another time for quiet sitting and meditation and a little walk after it. During the day he should always maintain an alert mind, keeping both body and mind under control, resisting all tendency to greed, anger, laziness, sleepiness, inattention, regret and suspicion, and all worldly desires. Thus, with concentrated mind, he should radiate excellent wisdom and aim at perfect enlightenment only.

4. If a homeless brother, forgetting himself, lapses into greed, gives way to anger, cherishes resentment, jealousy, conceit, self-praise, or insincerity, he is carrying a keen two-edged sword only covered by a thin cloth. One is not a homeless brother simply because he wears a monk's rags and carries a begging bowl; he is not a homeless brother just because he recites scriptures glibly; he is only a man of straw.

Even if his intention is honest, if he can not control his worldly desires, he is not a homeless brother, no more than an infant is. Only those who are able to concentrate and control the mind, who manifest wisdom, who have removed all worldly desires, and whose only purpose is to attain enlightenment, only these can be called a true homeless brother.

A true homeless brother determines to reach his goal of enlightenment even though he loses his last drop of blood and his bones crumble into powder. Such an one, trying his best, will finally attain the goal of a homeless brother and give evidence of it by his ability to do the meritorious deeds of a homeless brother.

5. The mission of the homeless brother is to carry forward the

light of the Dharma. He must preach to everybody, he must wake up sleeping people, he must correct false ideas, he must give people a right viewpoint; he must not wait for people to come to him, he must go everywhere, risking his own life even to do so.

The mission of a homeless brother is not an easy one, so he who aspires to it should wear Buddha's clothes, sit on Buddha's seat and enter into Buddha's room. To wear Buddha's clothes means to be humble and to practice endurance. To sit on Buddha's seat means, to see everything as emptiness, to have no abiding place, no attachments; to enter into Buddha's room means, to share his all-embracing compassion, to have sympathy with everybody. To be able to enter into Buddha's all-embracing compassion, one must sit on Buddha's seat of emptiness, must wear his garment of humility, and must patiently teach all people.

6. Those who wish to teach the Buddha's Dharma acceptably must be concerned about four things:—First, he must be concerned about his own behavior; second, he must be concerned about the people he will approach and teach and what words he will use; third, he must be concerned about his motive for teaching and the end he wishes to accomplish; fourth, he must be concerned about the great compassion for Buddha.

To be a good teacher of the Dharma, first of all, a homeless brother must have his feet well set on the ground of endurance, he must be modest, he must not be eccentric or desire publicity, he must constantly think of the emptiness aspect of things, he must avoid thinking of things as this good and that bad, as this easy and that hard, he must not become attached to anything. If he is thus concerned, he will be able to behave well.

Secondly, he must exercise caution in approaching people and situations. He must avoid people who are living evil lives or people of authority; he must avoid women. Then he must approach people in a friendly way; he must always remember that things rise from a combination of causes and conditions, and standing at that point, he must not blame people, or abuse them, or speak of their mistakes, or hold them in light esteem.

Thirdly, he must keep his mind peaceful, considering Buddha as his spiritual father, considering other homeless brothers who are training for enlightenment as his teachers, look upon everybody with great compassion and then teach anybody with friendly patience.

Fourthly, he must let his spirit of compassion have free course, even as Buddha did, unto the uttermost. Especially he should let his spirit of compassion flow out to those who do not know enough to want to be enlightened. He should wish that they might want to be enlightened, and then he should follow his wishes with an unselfish effort to awaken their interest.

Lay Members

1. It has already been explained that to become a disciple of Buddha one must believe in the three treasures:—Buddha, Dharma; and the Brotherhood. To become a lay member one must have an unshaken faith in Buddha, must believe in his teachings and study them and put them into practice, and must cherish the Brotherhood. To cherish the Brotherhood means, to feel themselves a part of its fellowship, honoring and sustaining the homeless brothers, making regular donations for their support, and seeking their instruction.

Lay members should follow the five precepts for good behavior:—not to harm any sentient life, not to steal, to live a pure and restrained life, not to lie or deceive, and not to use intoxicants.

Lay members should not only believe in the teachings and study themselves, but they should, as far as they are able, explain them to others, especially to their relatives and friends, trying to awaken in them a similar faith in Buddha, Dharma and the Brotherhood, so that they too may share in Buddha's mercy.

Lay members should always keep in mind that the reason why they believe in the three treasures and why they keep the precepts is to enable them ultimately to attain enlightenment and for that reason they should avoid becoming attached to worldly desires while still living in the world of desire.

Lay members should always keep in mind that sooner or later they will be obliged to leave their parents and families and pass away from this life of birth and death; therefore, they should set their minds on the world of enlightenment wherein nothing passes away.

2. Lay members should awaken an earnest undisturbed faith in

Buddha's teachings and as far as they do this they will realize within their minds a quiet and undisturbed happiness that will shine out on all their surroundings and be reflected back to them. This mind of faith is pure and gentle, always patient and enduring, never argues, never causes suffering to others, always keeps in mind the three treasures,—Buddha, Dharma and the Brotherhood.

Since by faith you are resting in the bosom of Buddha, you are kept far away from a selfish mind and from attachment to your possessions. You will have no fear about your future support and no fear that anyone will harm you. Since you have faith in the truth and the holiness of the Dharma, you can express your thoughts freely and without fear. Since you have faith in Buddha's Pure Land, you need have no fear of death.

Since your mind is filled with compassion for all people, you will make no distinctions among them but will treat all alike, and since your mind is free from likes and dislikes it will be pure and equitable, happy to do any good deed.

Whether you live in adversity or in prosperity will make no difference to the increase of your faith. If you cherish humility, if you respect Buddha's teachings, if you are consistent in speech and action, if you are guided by wisdom, if your mind is as resistant as a mountain, then you will make steady progress on the path to enlightenment. And though you are forced to live in a difficult situation and among people of impure minds, if you cherish faith in Buddha you can lead them toward better deeds.

3. Therefore, everyone should make the wish to hear Buddha's teaching the paramount wish of his heart. If anyone should tell him that it would be necessary to go through fire to gain enlightenment then he should be willing to pass through fire. There is a satisfaction in hearing the Buddha's name that is worth passing through a world filled with fire to gain.

If one wishes to follow the Buddha's teaching he must not be egoistic nor self-willed, but should cherish feelings of goodwill toward all alike, he should respect those who are worthy of respect, he should serve those who are worthy of service and treat all others with uniform kindness. After this manner lay members are to train their own minds first and not be disturbed as to how other people act. In this manner they are to receive the Buddha's teaching and put it into practice, not envying other people, nor being influenced by other teachings, not considering other ways.

Those who do not believe in Buddha's teaching have a narrow vision and consequently a disturbed mind. But those who believe in Buddha's teaching believe that there is a great wisdom and a great compassion encompassing everything and in that faith they are undisturbed by trifles.

4. Those who hear and receive the Dharma know that their lives are transient and that their bodies are merely aggregations of sufferings and the source of all evil, so they do not become attached to them. At the same time they do not neglect to take good care of their bodies, not because they wish to enjoy the physical life of the body, but because the body is necessary for the attainment of wisdom and for their mission of explaining the Dharma. If they do not take good care of their bodies they can not live long. If they do not keep well and live long, they can not practice the Dharma personally nor explain it to others.

If a man wishes to cross a river he is very careful of his raft. If he has a long journey to make he takes good care of his horse. So if a man wishes to attain enlightenment he takes good care of his body.

Those who are disciples of Buddha must wear suitable clothing to protect the body from the extremes of heat and cold and to hide its shame, but they should not wear them for decoration. They must eat suitable food to nourish the body so that they may hear and receive and explain the Dharma, but they should not eat for mere enjoyment. They must live in houses of enlightenment to be protected from the thieves of worldly passion and from the storms of evil teaching, but they should use the house for its real purpose and not for display or the concealment of selfish practices.

Thus you should value things and use them solely in their relation to enlightenment and the Dharma. You should not become attached to them for selfish reasons but only as they serve a useful purpose in carrying the Dharma to others. Therefore your mind should dwell on the Dharma even when you are living with your family. You should care for them with a wise and sympathetic mind, seeking to awaken faith in their minds by many methods.

5. Lay members of Buddha's Brotherhood should study the fol-

lowing lessons every day:—How to serve their parents, how to live with wife and children, how to control oneself, how to manifest Buddha.

To best serve parents they must learn to practice kindness toward all animate life. To live with wife and children happily they must keep away from lust and thoughts of selfish comfort. While hearing the music of the family life they must not forget the sweeter music of the Dharma, and while living in the shelter of the home, they should often seek the safer shelter of Dhyana practice where wise men find refuge from all impurity and all disturbance.

When laymen are bestowing charity they should remove all greed from their own hearts; when they are in the midst of a crowd, their minds should be in the company of wise men; when they face misfortune, they should keep the mind tranquil and free from hindrances. When they take refuge in Buddha, their desire should be for his wisdom; when they take refuge in the Dharma, their desire should be to realize its truth which is like a great ocean of wisdom; when they take refuge in the Brotherhood, their desire should be to share its peaceful fellowship unobstructed by any selfish interests.

When they wear clothes they must not forget to put on also the garment of goodness and humility. When they take an injection, they must wish to discharge all greed, anger and foolishness of mind. When they are toiling on an up-hill road, they should think of it as the road to enlightenment that will carry them beyond the world of delusion. When they are following an easy road, they should guard the mind against sloth and pride and should take advantage of its easier conditions to make a greater progress toward Buddhahood.

When they see a bridge, they must wish to tell people of the bridge of the Dharma; when they meet a sorrowful man, they should have feelings of hatred for the bitterness of this ever changing world; when they see a greedy man, they should have a great longing to keep free from the illusions of this life and to share in the true riches of enlightenment; when they see savory food, they must be on guard; when they see distasteful food, they should wish that greed might never return.

During the intense heat of summer, they must wish to be away from the heat of worldly desires and gain the fresh coolness of enlightenment. During the cold of winter, they must think of the warmth of Buddha's great compassion. When they recite the sacred scriptures, they must try not to forget them and must be very earnest to put their teaching into practice. When they think of Buddha, they must cherish a deep wish to have eyes like Buddha. As they fall asleep at night they should wish that their body, lips and mind might be purified and refreshed; when they awake in the morning, their first wish should be that during that day their minds might be clear to understand everything.

6. Laymen, although understanding that everything is characterized by "emptiness," do not treat the things that enter into a man's life lightly, but they receive them for what they are and then try to make them fit for enlightenment. Laymen must not think that the world of man's life is meaningless and filled with confusion, while the world of enlightenment is full of meaning and peaceful. Rather, they should taste the way of enlightenment in all the affairs of the world. If one looks upon the world with eyes dimmed in ignorance, he will see it filled with error, but if he looks upon it with clear wisdom, he will see it as the world of enlightenment itself.

The fact is, there is only one world,—there are not two worlds, one meaningless and the other full of meaning, one good, the other bad—People think there are two worlds by the activities of their own minds. If they could get rid of these false judgments and keep their minds pure with the light of wisdom, then they would see only one world and that world bathed in the light of wisdom.

7. Laymen who believe in Buddha taste this universal purity of oneness in everything, and in that mind they feel compassion for everyone and humbly desire to serve them. Therefore, laymen should cleanse their minds from all proudness and cherish minds of humility and courtesy and service. Their minds should be like the fruitful earth that nourishes everything without partiality, that serves without complaint, that endures patiently, that is always zealous, that finds its highest joy in serving all poor people by planting in their minds the seeds of Buddha's Dharma.

Thus the mind that has compassion on poor people, becomes a mother to all people, honors all people, looks upon all people as his personal friends, respects them as though they were his parents. Therefore, though thousands of people have hard feelings and cherish ill-will toward lay believers, they can do them no harm, for what harm is a drop of poison in the waters of an ocean.

8. A lay member will add to his happiness by habits of recollection and reflection and thanksgiving. He will come to realize that his faith is Buddha's compassion itself, that it is one thing, and that it has been given to him as a present by Buddha.

There are no seeds of faith in the mud of worldly passion, but seeds of faith may be sown there because of Buddha's compassion and they will purify the mind until it has faith to believe in Buddha.

As has been said, the fragrant Candana can not grow in the forest of Eranda. In like manner the seeds of faith in Buddha can not grow in the bosom of delusion. But actually the flower of joy is blooming there, so we must conclude that while its blossoms are in the bosom of delusion, its roots are elsewhere, namely, its roots are in the bosom of Buddha, or in other words, faith in Buddha is the gift of Buddha, and grows independent of conditions.

If a lay believer is later carried away by self-pride, he will become jealous, envious, hateful and harmful, because his mind has again become defiled with greed, anger and foolish infatuation, but if he return to Buddha, he will accomplish an even greater service for Buddha. It is, indeed, a marvel.

PRACTISING THE SEVENTH STAGE
OF BUDDHA'S NOBLE PATH

SITTING quietly with empty and tranquil mind, breathing gently, deliberately, evenly, slowly; realizing that however necessary the process of breathing is to the life of the organism, it is not the self, neither is it anything that a self can accomplish by volition or effort. It is a spontaneous activity that goes on best as we rest quietly, restraining all rising thoughts, keeping the mind fixed on its pure essence, realizing that the organism and all its activities is only a skillful device, an efficient means, which Buddhahood employs in fulfillment of its nature to emancipate and enlighten all sentient beings. As such it is a manifestation of Buddhahood's love and wisdom; it is Buddhahood taking form within one's own mind as a coming Buddha.

Sitting quietly with humble and patient mind, with earnest and disciplined mind, waiting for the clouds of karma and the defilements of the mind to clear away so that the clear brightness within may shine forth, illumining the mind, revealing that self is nothing, that mind-essence is everything. Sitting quietly realizing the mind's pure essence. Realizing its all-embracing wholeness, its inconceivable purity and unity, its boundless potentiality for radiation and integration; radiation going forth in rays and vibrations of cosmic energy; manifesting itself in particles, electrons and atoms; and by the phenomena of light, heat and electricity. Integration drawing everything inward to purity and unity; the going forth and the drawing inward being so perfectly balanced that all abides in the original emptiness and silence. Sitting quietly with empty and tranquil mind, realizing the universal emptiness and eternal silence; realizing it, but yielding to its radiating potency, continually being reborn in this Saha-world of suffering.

* * *

Sitting quietly, breathing gently, deliberately, evenly, slowly; realizing that the organism if it is to become enlightened and

634

brought to Buddhahood requires something more than breathing, namely, it requires nutrition. This need is supplied by the
organism going forth in search of food which the mouth proceeds to masticate and salivate, the stomach to digest, the intestines to assimilate the wholesome into the blood and to reject
the waste. But this process of transmuting food into nutritious
blood is not the self, neither is it anything that a self can accomplish by volition or effort. It is a spontaneous activity
that goes on best as we rest quietly, restraining all rising
thoughts, keeping the mind fixed on its pure essence, realizing
that the organism and all its activities is only a skillful device,
and efficient means, which Buddhahood employs in fulfillment
of its nature to emancipate and enlighten all sentient beings
and bring them to Buddhahood. As such it is a manifestation
of Buddhahood's love and wisdom; it is Buddhahood taking
form within one's own mind as a coming Buddha.

Sitting quietly with humble and patient mind, with earnest
and disciplined mind, waiting for the clouds of karma and the
defilements of the mind to clear away so that the brightness
within may shine forth, illumining the mind, revealing that
self is nothing, that mind essence is everything. Sitting quietly
realizing the mind's pure essence. Realizing its all-embracing
wholeness, its inconceivable purity and unity, its boundless potentiality for radiation and integration; radiation going forth
in chemical reactions among the atoms, manifesting themselves
as molecules and physical substances, and by the phenomena of
dynamics, gravitation and inertia; integration drawing everything inward to unity and purity; the going forth and the
drawing in being so perfectly balanced that all abides in the
original emptiness and silence. Sitting quietly with empty and
tranquil mind realizing the universal emptiness and eternal
silence; realizing its unbornness, its imagelessness, its egolessness; realizing it, but yielding to its radiating potency, continually being reborn in this Saha-world of suffering.

* * *

Sitting quietly, breathing gently, deliberately, evenly, slowly;
realizing that the organism, if it is to become enlightened and
brought to Buddhahood, requires something more than nutrition, namely, it requires vital energy. To satisfy this need the
muscles and glands and ganglia of the lower abdomen receive

the nutritious blood and transmutes it into vital energy by reason of which the material blood becomes living tissue. But this process is not a self neither is it anything that a self can accomplish by volition or effort; it is a spontaneous activity that goes on best as we rest quietly restraining all rising thoughts, keeping the mind fixed on its pure essence, realizing that the organism and all its activities is only a skillful device, an efficient means, which Buddhahood employs in the fulfillment of its nature to emancipate and enlighten all sentient beings and bring them to Buddhahood. As such it is a manifestation of Buddhahood's love and wisdom; it is Buddhahood taking form within one's own mind as a coming Buddha.

Sitting quietly with humble and patient mind, with earnest and disciplined mind, waiting for the clouds of karma and the defilements of the mind to clear away so that the pure brightness within may shine forth, illumining the mind, revealing that self is nothing, that mind essence is everything. Sitting quietly realizing the mind's pure essence; realizing its all-embracing wholeness, its inconceivable purity and unity, its boundless potentiality for radiation and integration; radiation going forth into more and more complex forms of life—protoplasm, bacteria, cellular life and organic—manifesting itself in the phenomena of birth, growth, reproduction, decay and death. Integration drawing everything into unity and purity; the going forth and the drawing in being so perfectly balanced that all abides in the original emptiness and silence. Sitting quietly with empty and tranquil mind, realizing the universal emptiness and eternal silence; realizing its unbornness, its imagelessness, its egolessness; realizing it, but yielding to its radiating potency, continually being reborn in this Saha-world of suffering.

* * *

Sitting quietly, breathing gently, deliberately, evenly, slowly; realizing that the organism, if it is to become enlightened and brought to Buddhahood requires something more than vital energy, namely, it requires awareness. This need is supplied by the dual system of nerves and their ganglia which receive the current of vital energy and transmute it into instinctive awareness. By this process the organism becomes aware of its needs and how to supply them, and of its dangers and how to protect itself. But this process transmuting energy into awareness is not the self, neither is it anything that a self can accomplish by volition and effort; it is a spontaneous activity that goes on best as we rest quietly, restraining all rising thoughts, keeping the mind fixed on its pure essence, realizing that the organism and all its activities is only a skillful device, an efficient means, that Buddhahood employs in fulfillment of its nature to emancipate and enlighten all sentient beings and bring them to Buddhahood. As such it is a manifestation of Buddhahood's love and wisdom; it is Buddhahood taking form within one's own mind as a coming Buddha.

Sitting quietly with humble and patient mind, with earnest and disciplined mind, waiting for the clouds of karma and the defilements of the mind to clear away, so that the pure brightness within may shine forth illumining the mind, revealing that self is nothing, that essence of mind is everything. Sitting quietly realizing the mind's pure essence. Realizing its all-embracing wholeness, its inconceivable purity and unity, its boundless potentiality for radiation and integration; radiation going forth in instinctive will-to-live, to-enjoy, to-propagate; becoming manifest in instinctive acts of greed, lust and self-assertion; and in the phenomena of natural selection, variation, conflict, suffering and survival. Integration drawing everything inward to unity and purity; the going forth and the drawing in being so perfectly balanced that all abides in the original emptiness and silence. Sitting quietly realizing the universal emptiness and eternal silence. Realizing its unbornness, its imagelessness, its egolessness; realizing it, but yielding to its radiating potency continually being reborn in this Saha-world of suffering.

* * *

Sitting quietly, breathing gently, deliberately, evenly, slowly; realizing that the organism, if it is to become enlightened and brought to Buddhahood requires something more than instinctive awareness, namely, it requires consciousness and discrimination. This need is supplied by the system of sense organs and the lower mind, which in contact with their appropriate fields receive the current of nervous energy and awareness and transmute it into sensations and perceptions, which the lower mind proceeds to unite, to name and to discriminate, from which arises consciousness and the ideas of self and not-self. But this process of transmuting nervous energy into consciousness and the idea of self is not the self, neither is it anything which a self can accomplish by volition or effort. It is a spontaneous activity which goes on best as we rest quietly, restraining every rising thought, ignoring every risen thought, keeping the mind fixed on its pure essence, realizing that the organism and all its activities is only a skillful device, an efficient means, which Buddhahood employs in fulfillment of its nature to emancipate and enlighten all sentient beings and bring them to Buddhahood. As such it is a manifestation of Buddhahood's love and wisdom; it is Buddhahood taking form within one's own mind, as a coming Buddha.

Sitting quietly with humble and patient mind, with earnest and disciplined mind, waiting for the clouds of karma and the defilements of the mind to clear away so that the pure brightness within may shine forth, illumining the mind, revealing that self is nothing, that mind-essence is everything. Realizing the mind's pure essence. Realizing its all-embracing wholeness, its inconceivable purity and unity, its boundless potentiality for radiation and integration; radiation going forth in discrimination of thoughts relating to self and not self, that awaken likes and dislikes; and the phenomena of desire, grasping, acts of greed, lust, hatred, to be accumulated in memory, habits and karma. Integration drawing everything inward to unity and purity; the going forth and the drawing in being so perfectly balanced that all abides in the original emptiness and silence. Sitting quietly realizing the universal emptiness, the eternal silence; realizing its unbornness, its imagelessness, its egolessness; realizing it, but yielding to its radiating potency being continually reborn in this Saha-world of Suffering.

* * *

Sitting quietly, breathing gently, deliberately, evenly, slowly; realizing that the organism, if it is to become enlightened and brought to Buddhahood, requires something more than conscious discriminations, namely, it requires intellection and knowledge. This need is supplied by the upper mind, the cerebrum, which receives the stream of conscious discriminations and transmutes them into intellectual knowledge. By this the mind becomes aware that the myriad, myriad things which the senses perceive and the conscious mind discriminates and thinks about are empty and transient—dreams that have been caused by its own greed, anger and infatuation, as conditioned by karma and the mind's defilements, and as expressed by body, lips and mind; it becomes aware that the only reality is the mind's pure essence, the dharma of whose self-nature is the ultimate principle. It becomes aware that as ultimate principle, mind is irradiant, going forth in discriminations of thought that manifest themselves in activities and appearances of form and phenomena. It becomes aware that mind as ultimate principle is also integrant drawing all these differentiations into more and more harmonious relations and into final identity with itself. It becomes aware that mind, whether as essence, as principle, as activity and manifestation, is of one undivided sameness.

But this process of transmuting discriminated thoughts into intellection and knowledge is not the self, neither is it anything that a self can accomplish by volition or effort; it is a spontaneous activity that goes on best as we rest quietly, restraining all rising thoughts, ignoring all risen thoughts, keeping the mind fixed on its pure essence, realizing that the organism and all its activities is only a skillful device, an efficient means, that Buddhahood employs in fulfillment of its nature to enlighten all sentient beings and bring them to Buddhahood. As such it is Buddhahood's love and wisdom becoming manifest; it is Buddhahood taking form within one's own mind, as a coming Buddha.

Sitting quietly with humble and patient mind, with earnest and disciplined mind, waiting for the clouds of karma and the defilements of the mind to clear away so that the pure brightness within may shine forth illumining the mind, revealing that self is nothing, that mind-essence is everything. Sitting quietly realizing the mind's pure essence. Realizing its all-embracing wholeness, its inconceivable purity and unity, its boundless potentiality for radiation and integration; radiation going forth as pragmatic thoughts concerning social relations, ethics, industry, economics, politics; going forth as scientific research as to the origin, the nature and the laws of physical things; going forth in philosophical speculations as to the nature of the soul, life after death, eternal life, a personal God,

Universal Self; all of which tend toward multiplicity, complexity, confusion, unrest of mind and pride of egoism; to karma and rebirth in the Saha world. Integration drawing everything toward unity and purity and peacefulness; the going forth and the drawing in being so perfectly balanced that all abides in the original emptiness and silence. Sitting quietly realizing this universal emptiness and eternal silence. Realizing its unbornness, its imagelessness, its egolessness; realizing it, but yielding to its radiating potency, continually being reborn in this Saha-world of suffering.

*   *   *

Sitting quietly, breathing gently, deliberately, evenly, slowly; realizing that the organism, if it is to become enlightened and brought to Buddhahood, requires something more than intellectual knowledge, namely, it requires wisdom. Knowledge about Truth is not Truth itself; if one is to attain wisdom, he must realize Truth itself, and that requires another process than intellection, namely, it requires intuition. By intuition the mind becomes identified with Truth and attains wisdom by itself becoming Truth. But this process transmuting intellection into intuition, and knowledge into wisdom, is not the self, neither are all the processes of the body and mind working together harmoniously a self; they are after all only an aggregation and concatenation of fortuitous causes and conditions and are not a self, nor are they anything that a self can accomplish by volition or effort. It is only a spontaneous activity that goes on best as we rest quietly, restraining all rising thoughts, ignoring all risen thoughts, keeping the mind fixed on its pure essence, realizing that the organism with all its activities, is only a skillful device, an efficient means, which Buddhahood employs in fulfillment of its nature to emancipate and enlighten all sentient beings and bring them to Buddhahood. As such it is a manifestation of Buddhahood's love and wisdom; it is Buddhahood taking form within one's own mind as a coming Buddha.

Sitting quietly with humble and patient mind, with earnest and disciplined mind, waiting for the clouds of karma and the defilements of mind to clear away so that the pure brightness within may shine forth, illumining the mind, revealing that self is nothing, mind-essence is everything. Sitting quietly realizing the mind's pure essence! Realizing that the mind's pure essence is the Universal Essence that is prior to everything, that embraces everything, that is everything; and realizing that what is mind is Buddhahood. Sitting quietly realizing that this life of birth and death with all its greed, anger and infatuation is the pure essence of mind and the Bliss-body of Buddhahood; that all the outer things of manifestation and form and phenomena are unreal and imaginary; that all the inner things of desire and aversion, of fear and anger, of infatuation and pride of egoism are unreal and imaginary; that all the activities of the mind discriminating this and that, big and little, good and bad, self and not-self, are unreal and imaginary; that all the states of the mind, its judgments and feelings and emotions, are unreal and imaginary; that only the mind's pure essence is real and abiding, and that is Buddhahood abiding in blissful Peace.

Sitting quietly realizing that all the changes and processes of the body and mind that are going on with no volition or effort on our part are bringing the organism into perfect Oneness with Buddhahood. Sitting quietly realizing this perfect Oneness:— realizing its all-embracing wholeness, its inconceivable unity and purity, its boundless potentiality for Wisdom and Compassion; Wisdom going forth in individuations of Ignorance and discriminations of knowledge that eventuate in multiplicities of thought, desires, activities, karma, rebirth in the Saha World of suffering. Compassion drawing everything together eventuating in the patient endurance of suffering, the awakening of faith, mind-control, clearing insight, maturing of karma, birth in the Pure Land, attainment of Buddhahood. The going forth and the drawing in being so perfectly balanced that all abides in the original emptiness and silence.

Sitting quietly, realizing the basic emptiness and eternal silence; realizing its unbornness, its imagelessness, its egolessness. Realizing that in its perfect purity and unity there is neither self nor not-self, neither Ignorance nor Enlightenment, neither a Saha World of Suffering nor a Pure Land of Bliss, but, potentially, all are present in fullness. Realizing that in its perfect unity this Saha World of Suffering is the Pure Land of Bliss; realizing that what is radiation is integration, that what is Wisdom is Compassion. Wisdom-Compassion urging one to yield to its radiating potency that it may go forth for the enlightenment of all sentient beings; Compassion-Wisdom supporting one as he advances along the Bodhisattva Stages, submitting to its integrating potency, for the sake of Buddhahood. In the long last, having yielded to Compassion and submitted to Wisdom, attaining Buddhahood—its highest perfect Wisdom, its unceasing Compassion, its blissful Peace; becoming Pure Essence—its emptiness, its silence.

ALL HAIL! THE BLISS-BODY OF BUDDHAHOOD!

Namo Sambhogakaya Buddhaya.

(*To be memorized and repeated daily.*)

SUMMARY
OF BUDDHA'S DHARMA

SUMMARY OF BUDDHA'S DHARMA

Introduction

THE Buddha's Dharma ought not to be considered as a system of philosophic or intellectual thought, much less as a system of ethical idealism. Strictly speaking, even less is it a religion based upon authority. It is simply a way of life which Buddha called the Eightfold Noble Path and the Middle Way, and which he said would lead him who followed it to emancipation of body, to enlightenment of mind, to tranquillity of spirit, to highest Samadhi. That is, it is a system of mind-control leading to highest perfect cognition. He did not make it up—it is the record of his own experience under the Bodhi-tree, when he himself attained Enlightenment.

The summary is introduced by what is known as the Twelve Nirdanas, or the Chain of Simultaneous Dependent Originations (*paticca-samutpada*). Then he taught the Four Noble Truths upon which he based the Eightfold Noble Path. These are all briefly summarized.

The Twelve Nirdanas

1. Because of Ignorance (*avidya*) the principle of individuation as discriminated from Enlightenment which is the principle of unity and sameness the primal unity becomes divided into thinking, thinker and discriminated thoughts by reason of which there appear the "formations" of karma.
2. Because of these "forms" (*samsara*), the principle of consciousness emerges.
3. Because of the principle of consciousness (*vijnana*), mentality and body emerge.
4. Because of mentality and body (*nama-rupa*), the six sense minds and organs appear.
5. Because of the six sense minds and organs (*shadayat-ana*), sensations and perceptions arise.
6. Because of sensations and perceptions (*spasha*), feelings and discriminations arise.

645

7. Because of feelings and sensations (*vedana*), thirst and craving arise.

8. Because of thirst and craving (*trishna*), grasping and clinging appear.

9. Because of grasping and clinging (*upadana*), conception takes place.

10. Because of conception (*bhava*), the continuing process of existence goes on.

11. Because of the continuing process of existence (*jeti*), growth, sickness, old age, decay and death take place.

12. Because of sickness, old age and death (*jana-marana*), "sorrow, lamentation, pain, grief and despair arise. Thus arises the whole mass of suffering." In all this

> "No doer of the deeds is found,
> No one who ever reaps their fruit.
> Empty phenomena are there.
> Thus does the world roll on.
> No god, no Brahma, can be found,
> No maker of this wheel of life.
> Empty phenomena are there,
> Dependent upon conditions all."

The Four Noble Truths

1. The universality of suffering.
2. The cause of suffering rooted in desire.
3. By ending desire, suffering comes to an end.
4. The way to end desire and hence to end suffering, is to follow the Eightfold Noble Path.

The Eightfold Noble Path

1. RIGHT IDEAS: the Twelve Nirdanas and the Four Noble Truths. Not only should one understand them but he should make them the basis of all his thinking and understanding of life, he should make them the basis for a life of patient and humble acceptance and submission.

2. RIGHT RESOLUTION: He should make it the purpose of his life to follow the Noble Path. In loyalty to this purpose he should be willing to give up anything that is contrary to it, or which hinders his progress. He should be willing to pay any cost of comfort, or self denial, or effort, in order to

attain its goal. He should not do this for any selfish motive but that he might devote the merit of its attainment to all animate life. And finally he should make his great Vow (*Pranadana*) not to enter Nirvana until all others may enter with him.

3. RIGHT SPEECH: Speech is the connecting link between thought and action; words often obscure the Truth within one's own mind, and often give a false impression to those that hear them. It is important therefore, that one should restrain his speech. It should always be characterized by wisdom and kindness. Undue loudness, over emphasis, and excitement should be avoided. Speech should not be prompted by prejudice, fear, anger, nor infatuation, nor self interest. Careless, idle and flippant words should be avoided. All invidious distinctions, and discriminations, and dogmatic assertions and negations, should be avoided. Words that are liable to cause hard feelings, such as repeating scandal, mean or angry words, words that deceive or cause misunderstandings, or that tend to arouse passion and lust, should never be uttered. In general speech should be limited to asking and answering necessary questions, and because speech is so easily conditioned by crowd psychology, all formal speech before groups, audiences and crowds should be avoided.

4. RIGHT BEHAVIOR. Besides behaving according to the general rules of propriety, one should be especially careful to keep the Five Precepts:—Not to kill but to practice kindness and harmlessness toward all animate life. Not to steal or covet what does not belong to one, but to practice charity and going without things oneself. Not to commit adultery but to practice purity of mind and sexual self-control. Not to lie but to practice honesty and sincerity in thought, word and deed. Not to partake of alcoholic drinks or drugs, or anything that weakens one's mind-control, but to practice abstinence and self-control.

The reason that Buddha made keeping the Precepts so important was not so much for ethical reasons as for its bearing on mind development and its goal of the attainment of highest cognition and enlightenment. Or can not progress toward this high goal if he is living a wicked or self-indulgent life. Even the keeping of the Precepts is only a beginning, for as disciples advance on the Path and undertake the homeless life, there are other five Precepts that must also be observed, namely, Not to use ointments or condiments and not to eat between meals. Not to wear jewelry or expensive clothes, but to practice humility. Not to sleep on soft beds but to resist all tendency to sloth and sleepiness. Not to attend entertainments, dances, concerts or to take part in games of chance; keeping the mind at all times under strict control. Not to have anything to do with money or precious things, but to practice poverty.

5. RIGHT VOCATION. One must not engage in any business or profession that involves cruelty or injustice to either men or animals. His life must be free from acquisitiveness, deceit or dishonesty. He must have nothing to do with war, gambling, prostitution. It must be a life of service rather than a life of profit and indulgence. For those who wish to devote their entire attention to attaining enlightenment it must be a Homeless Life, free from all dependence or responsibility for property, family life or society.

The ideal life, therefore, for one who has resolved to follow the Noble Path is the Homeless Life. But before one is willing and able to do this, he should come as near to it as possible while living the ordinary life of a householder. Being engaged in the family, social and economical life of the world, he will often find it difficult to do much more than keep the Precepts, but as he advances on the Path he can at least in part observe the other precepts, and as fast as it becomes possible, he can separate from his family and business, and undertake to live more simply and abstemiously and devote more time to his devotional practices. If there is any personal or family property it should gradually be disposed of, so that being free from family and property responsibilities, he may more exclusively undertake the Homeless Life.

In cutting himself off from all relations and responsibilities with the household and worldly life, the Homeless Brother does so with the single purpose of devoting himself to the attainment of enlightenment and Buddhahood, not for selfish reasons but that he may share his attainment and merit with whoever may need his instruction or help. In making his decision to follow the Homeless Life he does so in perfect faith that the Lay Brothers and other Homeless Brothers will take good care of him.

Some may think that this homeless, mendicant life might have been possible and rewarding under the primitive and simple conditions of patriarchal life, but that it would be impossible and foolish and futile under the more complex conditions of our modern, acquisitive, comfort seeking, excitement-loving conditions, founded as they are upon scientific materialism and enforced by conventions, laws, courts and police. If we count one's comfort and convenience important, it probably is. But are they of first importance? Is not enlightenment, the ending of suffering, the attainment of peace, of far more importance? If they are then any discipline, any deprivation, any inconvenience, any suffering even, is fully warranted. It would be different if there was any easier method known, but Buddha, who was perfectly enlightened, presented it as the only possible Path. Is it not for us who are seeking enlightenment and peace of mind, and who are following Buddha, to have faith in his Noble Path and give it a fair trial? It is noticeable, however, that doubt as to its reasonableness and possibility is not voiced by those who have tried it but by those whose habits and comforts would be curtailed and interfered with.

The Buddha's Dharma is too deep and inclusive to be translated into writing and even less to be completely understood and fully realized by the study of the Scriptures alone. It must be carried out into practice, systematically, earnestly, persistently. The source of all truth is within one's own mind and heart, by the practice of Dhyana, it issues forth in unutterable treasures of compassion and wisdom.

But more significant than that, it is by means of dhyana practised by free minds in undisturbed solitude that the deeper realizations of Truth issue forth spontaneously in unseen spiritual ways to implant intimations and seeds of faith and hope in the minds of others. Thus one, who in the midst of the world's unrest, craving and suffering, has found wisdom and peace, radiates from his being a serenity and compassion and wisdom that emancipates and enlightens others. He is already a Buddha. Being one with Buddha in the blissful peace of Samadhi, he will be radiating compassion and wisdom toward this Saha world of suffering and drawing in to his peace the world's woe. He has learned the secret of the Dharma breathing—going forth, drawing in—in eternal rhythm.

6. RIGHT EFFORT. As one advances along the Path, he
needs something more than ethical Precepts to guide and ac-
tivate his progress, namely, he needs spiritual ideals. To meet
this need, the Dharma presents Six Paramitas: (1) Dana Paramita. One should cherish a spirit of unselfish charity and good
will that will prompt him to the giving of material gifts for
the relief of need and suffering, being especially thoughtful of
the needs of the Homeless Brothers, and always remembering
that the greatest gift is the gift of the Dharma. (2) Sila Paramita. This same spirit of good-will towards others, the clearing sense of his oneness with all sentient beings, will first
prompt him to greater sincerity and fidelity in keeping the
Precepts himself for their sakes. Next it wil' lead him to ignore and forget his own comfort and convenience in offering
wherever needed the more intangible gifts of compassion and
sympathy and personal service. (3) Kshanti Paramita. This
Paramita of humility and patience will help him to bear without complaint, the acts of others without fear or malice
or anger. It will help him to bear the common ills of life, the
difficulties of the Path and the burden of his karma. It will
keep him free from both elation or discouragement as he meets
the extremes of success or failure, and will help him to always
maintain an equitable spirit of serenity and peacefulness. (4)
Virya Paramita. This Paramita of zeal and perseverance will
keep one from becoming indolent, careless and changeable.
This Paramita is not intended so much to prompt one to outward acts of charity and propaganda as it is wholly concerned
with these inner states of mind that affect one's control
of mind and attainment of highest cognition and unceasing
compassion. The results of behavior are not all outward and
apparent; they also affect one's inner habits and dispositions
and are surely registered in one's karma. One does not truly
attain until he becomes earnest and faithful in both outward
behavior and inner states of mind. Therefore, one should be
earnest and persevering and faithful in cherishing right ideas,
right purposes, right effort, right devotional practices, right
vows. (5) Dhyana Paramita. This Paramita of tranquillity
prompts one to practice one-pointedness of mind. One should
always keep his mind concentrated on the task in hand, undistracted by thoughts of policy, or its relation to one's selfish
advantage or comfort. It will often prompt one to a course

far different from the old competitive, acquisitive, exciting habits of the worldly life. One must often disregard personal comfort and advantage in an effort to be truly sympathetic and charitable. But so long as one acts from motives of sympathy and kindness the mind will be undisturbed by consequences, and so long as one has no desires, he will be undisturbed by conditions. So long as the mind is free from greed, anger, fear and egoism, it rests in peace. The mind should be trained, therefore, to be concentrated on spiritual ends. (6) Prajna Paramita. This Paramita prompts one to be yielding to the suggestions of wisdom. Thus far we have been considering aspects of spiritual behavior that are more or less under the control of one's own mind, but now in this Wisdom Paramita, we should cease from all self-direction of will and effort and, remaining tranquil in spirit, should yield ourselves in effortless ways, a free channel for the flow of mingled wisdom and compassion.

7. RIGHT MINDFULNESS. This stage of the Noble Path is the culmination of the intellective process and the connecting link with the intuitive process. The goal to be reached is the establishment of a habit of looking at things truthfully, at their meaning and significance rather than at their discriminated appearances, and relations. This is quite different and an advance from the instinctive reactions of the will-to-live, to enjoy, to propagate. It is also quite different and a further advance beyond the habit of considering things by their differences and relations. The senses can give one sensations and perceptions which the lower mind unites and names and discriminates, but they have little value in truth. Things seem real but they are not, they seem good and bad, big and little, right and wrong, but they are not. They often seem necessary but they are not. This consciously discriminated stream of appearances is only food for the higher intellectual mind to digest and assimilate, which by doing enables one to cognize more truthfully the realness or falsity of these first impressions. But the conclusions of the intellectual mind are not final for it can only arrive at a knowledge of relations among things which we think are true. If one is to gain an immediate awareness of Truth, he must transcend the intellectual mind, also. To make the highest and best use of the intellectual mind, however, it is necessary to first practice "recollective

mindfulness," which is the Seventh Stage of the Noble Path.

The Seventh Stage is usually translated, Mindfulness. It consists in recollecting and meditating upon the conclusions of the intellectual mind, seeking to understand their true meaning and significance.

8. RIGHT DHYANA. The Eighth Stage of the Noble Path is called in Sanskrit, Dhyana. It is a difficult word to translate into English because of its unfamiliar content of meaning. The nearest term is "concentration of mind" although in Pali this stage is named, "rapture." There are, thus, two aspects to it: the first is its active aspect of concentration, the second is a passive aspect of realization, or rapture. Having tranquillized the mind by the practice of the Seventh Stage of Mindfulness, to practice the Eighth Stage of Dhyana, one should sit quietly with empty and tranquil mind, but with attentive and concentrated mind, keeping the mind fixed on its pure essence. If attention wavers and vagrant thoughts arise, one should humbly and patiently regulate the mind anew, again and again, stopping all thinking, realizing Truth itself.

In doing this breathing plays an important part. Right breathing consists in breathing gently, deliberately, evenly. Think of it as filling the whole body to the top of the head, then gently pressing it downward to the abdomen, let it quietly pass away. Ordinarily we think of its course as being in a straight line, up and down, but it is better to think of it as a circle or loop always moving in one direction—upward to the head, downward to the abdomen, upward to the head and so on. Then forgetting the breathing, think of this circle moving more and more slowly and growing smaller and smaller until it comes to rest at a point between the eyes, the "wisdom eye" of the ancients, between the pineal and pituitary glands of the moderns. Hold the attention there, realizing its perfect balance and emptiness and silence.

At first it may be advisable to hold some simple thought conception in mind, such as counting the out-going breaths, or repeating Buddha's name, or some "koan" puzzle that can only be solved intuitively. But avoid thinking about them, keeping the mind fixed on its pure essence. In the primitive days of Buddhism, masters encouraged their disciples to keep in mind the abhorrent and painful aspects of the body, and the empty and transitory nature of all component things; but in later times and Western lands, not liking to think of disgusting and negative things, we more often go to the other extreme and think of the beautiful, noble and rewarding things of life, of wisdom and compassion and purity and solitude and joy and peace. But the right way is to avoid both extremes, keeping the mind fixed on its pure essence, unperturbed by any differentiations whatever.

In the course of this discipline, various psychic effects appear—colors, sounds, visions, raptures, etc., and beginners are apt to become elated or discouraged by them, and to measure their success or failure by their appearing or not appearing. But this is all wrong. All these transitory psychic experiences should be ignored and forgotten; they are only mile-stones on the path and will be left behind as we move upward toward emancipation and enlightenment and perfect equanimity. The goal is not some entrancing rapture, or indescribable vision; it is highest perfect Wisdom and a great heart of Compassion and blissful Peace. Then ceasing all thought, realize its unceasing calm and silence.

The Four Jnanas, or Holy States

1. COMPASSION. As the mind progresses towards Enlightenment, it becomes aware of clearing insight and sensitiveness as to the essential unity of all animate life, and there awakens within him a great heart of compassion and sympathy drawing all animate life together, harmonizing differences, unifying all dualisms.

2. JOY. With the disappearing of all sense of difference between self and others and all dualisms, the heart becomes filled with a great rapture of gladness and joy.

3. PEACE. Gradually as the difference between suffering and happiness fades away, this feeling of gladness and joy is transmuted into perfect tranquillity and peacefulness.

4. EQUANIMITY. Gradually even the conception of difference and likeness vanishes and all notions of even joy and peace drop out of sight, and the mind abides in the blissful peace of perfect Equanimity.

The Ten Bodhisattva Stages

For a long time the above Four Holy States engrossed the attention of the Pali Scriptures and Southern Buddhists, but gradually there appeared among Northern Buddhists and in the Sanskrit Scriptures a new vision of the goal of the Buddha's Noble Path. The enjoyment of the Four Raptures for one's self to their culmination in Nirvana, seemed less worthy and satisfying, and meditation on the deeper implications of the Buddha's Dharma, led the great Mahayana Masters to the vision of the Ten Stages of Bodhisattvahood.

1. *Pramudita*. Based upon the perfect practice of the Dana Paramita, the Bodhisattva enters the stage of gladness and Joy.

2. *Vimala*. Based upon the Sila Paramita, the Bodhisattva enters upon the perfect practice of purity wherein there is neither joy nor the absence of joy but the mind abides in perfect Peace.

3. *Prabhakari*. Based upon the perfect practice of the Kshanti Paramita, the Bodhisattva enters upon the stage of self-luminous humility in which there is absent even the conception of joy or peace,—the stage of perfect Equanimity, of effortless, self-shining patience.

4. *Archismati*. Based upon the perfect practice of the Virya Paramita, the Bodhisattva enters upon the stage wherein there is conviction and purpose and zeal and determination and perseverance. It is the stage of unceasing, in-drawing, effortless "Energy."

5. *Sudurjaya*. Based upon the perfect practice of the Dhyana Paramita, the Bodhisattva enters upon the overcoming stage of self-mastery and the attainment of tranquillity that is based upon unshakable confidence.

6. *Abhimukhi*. Based upon the perfect practice of the Prajna Paramita, the Bodhisattva enters upon the realization stage of Samadhi. While still being in touch with the passions and discriminations of the Saha world, he turns his mind inward by his faculty of intuitive insight to the realization of the intrinsic emptiness and silence of the mind's pure essence.

7. *Durangama*. The Bodhisattva, having attained highest Samadhi, leaves behind all remembrance of discriminations and wholly abiding in the Mind's Pure Essence, he attains within his mind a "turning about" from which he never again recedes. It is the stage of "far-going."

8. *Acala*. This is the "immovable stage," in which the Bodhisattva attains the Samapatti graces and transcendental powers. Having attained a clear understanding of all inner and

outer conditions, his mind accepting things as they are, he neither desires to return to the world or to enter Nirvana. He has no desire or purpose except to live a pure life of *anutpatika-dharma-kshanti-gocaya*—a life of patient submissive acceptance.

9. *Sadhumati*. This is the state of perfect identity with *anuttara-samyak-sambodhi*—highest perfect Wisdom. In this state the Bodhisattva has passed beyond all thought of individuation, or discrimination, or integration; he has passed beyond all dualisms, all incompleteness, and is abiding in perfect balance and equanimity realizing the blissful peace of unceasing Samadhi. But still he retains in mind a memory of the world's ignorance and suffering, unreal as it is in fact, but untainted and undisturbed by it, his mind overflowing with compassion, he goes forth in wisdom and love for its emancipation and enlightenment.

10. *Dharmamegha*. In this highest state, the Bodhisattva becomes wholly identified with the Great Truth Cloud and, like a cloud saturated with Truth and Compassion, he becomes Tathagata, his life perfectly integrated with the lives of all, and goes forth to sprinkle the rain of the Good Law by which the seed of enlightenment takes root in the minds of all sentient beings and in the long last brings them to Buddhahood.

Nirvana

In the more primitive type of Buddhism as still held in Ceylon and Burma, the end of the Path is the attainment of Arhatship and, when life passes, to Nirvana. What then is Nirvana? The root meaning of the word is the extinguishment of a fire when the fuel is all consumed. That is, in Southern Buddhism, when the fires of earthly passion die down, and the disciple becomes an Arhat, free from all desire, and life passes, he is said to have attained Nirvana, or Parinirvana. In Northern Buddhism, Nirvana has a more philosophic meaning: it means the state where not only the fires of earthly passion have died down and earthly life has passed, but all karmic desire for individual life is extinguished and the disciple has passed into the unitive life of Buddhahood.

The term, *pratyekabuddha* as used by both schools, means a disciple or an arhat who is selfishly desiring Nirvana for his own satisfaction. Such a disciple, according to the Mahayana

school has ceased to follow the Path at the seventh stage of
Bodhisattvahood and "passes to his nirvana." But after a Bodhisattva attains the eighth stage there is, thereafter, "no more
recension," and he goes on to the attainment of highest perfect Wisdom which constrains him, instead of passing to Nirvana, to return to the Saha world of Ignorance and suffering
for its liberation and enlightenment. Hence the saying in the
Lankavatara Sutra: "For Buddhas there is no Nirvana."

The question may be asked, how, in this world of ignorance,
suffering and death, we are to recognize these "returning" Buddhas and Tathagatas? Please recall that Bodhisattvas as they
attain the ninth and tenth stages of Bodhisattvahood lose all
individuation as human personalities to become identified with
Buddhahood in the Great Truth Cloud, and as "formless"
Tathagatas attain boundless potentiality and command of skillful means and transcendental powers of self-mastery and ef-
ficiency, and as the integrating principle of Buddhahood, are
able to take any form they think best, or to be present
wherever there is need to support and to draw all sentient beings to enlightenment and Buddhahood. By our practice of
Dhyana, as we attain moments of intuitive Samadhi, we integrate our lives with this ever present Buddha-nature, and
when we attain highest perfect Samadhi, we become one with
all the Buddhas, enjoying their blissful peace, and becoming
able ourselves to return to this Saha-world of suffering for its
emancipation and enlightenment.

American and European Buddhists, before they can commonly attain Enlightenment and Buddhahood, will need their
own method for practicing the Eighth Stage of the Noble Path,
but such a Right Method can not be formulated until
the Buddha that is taking form within our own minds, comes.
Some among us must first attain the Seventh and Eighth of
the Bodhisattva Stages and himself have experienced the Durangama Samadhi of "Far-going" and the Acala Samadhi of
"No-recension" before he will be worthy of being employed
as a skillful device and convenient means for formulating such
a Right Method for practicing the Eighth Stage of the Noble
Path. "When He comes, we shall be like Him, for we shall
see Him as He is." "Even so come, Lord Maitreya!"

APPENDIX

SCRIPTURES SELECTED FROM PALI SOURCES

LIFE OF THE HISTORIC BUDDHA. Page 3

This selection is the first chapter of the book entitled, THE ESSENCE OF BUDDHISM, written by the late P. Lakshmi Narasu and published by Srinivasa Varadachari & CO., Madras, India, Second Edition, 1912. The earliest accounts of the life of Buddha are crowded with legendary and mythical material and all modern accounts consist of selections from these sources the value of which consists in the judgment with which the selection has been made. Mr. Narasu's account is usually credited to have been written with great sympathy and good judgment.

THE WORD OF BUDDHA. Page 22

This selection is an epitome of the Buddha's teachings as recorded at length in the voluminous Pali Scriptures, which was made by the Venerable Bhikkhu Nyanatiloka, the German Abbot of a large and important colony and monastery located at Dodanduwa, Ceylon. The epitome is published in a pamphlet with many valuable notes and elucidations which are omitted in this version. It was published in 1935. We are very grateful to the Venerable Nyanatiloka for his permission to use it in this connection.

TEVIGGA SUTTA. Page 61

The Tevigga Sutta is the last Sutta of the first division of the Digha Nikaya which is called the *Silakkhandha Vaggo* be-. cause the whole of the twelve dialogs deal from one point of view or another with *"sila"* or Right Conduct. It was translated by T. W. Rhys-Davids and was published in Volume XI of the Sacred Books of the East in 1900.

This version is somewhat changed in choice of words and a few unimportant omissions to make it easier reading for Americans. The reader is referred to Volume XI for valuable Introduction and foot notes. Acknowledgement is gratefully made to the Clarendon Press of Oxford, for the use of this Scripture.

"In this Scripture we have Right Conduct used as a sort of *argumentum ad hominem* for the conversion of two earnest young Brahmans. They ask, which is the true path to a state of union (in the next birth) with God (Brahma) after arguing, in a kind of Socratic dialog, that on their own showing the basis of facts they themselves admitted, the Brahmans could have no real knowledge of Brahma, Gotama maintains that union with God, whom they admitted to be pure and holy, must be unattainable by men impure and sinful and self-righteous however great their knowledge of the Vedas may be. And he then lays down, not without occasional beauty of language, that system of Right Conduct that must be the only direct way to a real union with God."

118th DISCOURSE FROM THE COLLECTION OF THE MIDDLE DISCOURSES. Page 73

This Discourse is translated by the Venerable Chao Kung (Trebitch Lincoln) whose temple-hermitage is just outside of Tientsin, China. The number of his disciples varies of course but he has had as many as fifteen made up of both men and women, largely European but including some Chinese. We are indebted to Venerable Chao Kung for his kind permission to use this translation which was made for his personal instruction, the printing being made from his manuscript copy.

The Discourse opens with certain introspective breathing Exercises, and then is founded upon four psychological Categories,—Observing and examining body; Observing and examining sensations and feelings; Observing and examining thoughts; Observing and examining phenomena. These are next examined by Seven Stages, or Factors, leading to Enlightenment:—Introspection, Penetration, Energy, Serenity, Gentleness (or non-assertion), Concentration, and Even-mindedess (or Equanimity).

THE MAHA PRAJNA PARAMITA HRIDYA. Page 85

This Sutra forms part of the Great Pragna Paramita Sutra and is the shortest of all its sections. It is memorized and daily repeated by practically all Buddhist Bhikshus of the Mahayana School of Buddhism. It has been translated from the Sanskrit into Chinese at various times by Kumarajiva (400 A.D.), Hiouen-tsang (649 A.D.), Sh-hu (980 A.D.), Pragna (785-810). It has been translated into English either from the Sanskrit or Chinese a number of times, notably by Max Muller in the Sacred Books of the East, Volume XLIX, and by Dr. Daisetz Teitaro Suzuki, in his Manual of Zen Buddhism, Eastern Buddhist Society, 1935. This English Version was made by Dwight Goddard from various English translations.

THE DIAMOND SUTRA.   Page 87

The Sanskrit title of this Sutra is *Vajracchedika Sutra*. It is Number 9 of the Great Prajna Paramita Sutra, the author of which is unknown. It was written in the First Century and has been translated into the Tibetan and Chinese a number of times. This translation was made from Kumarajiva's translation from the Sanskrit into Chinese (384-417 A.D.) by Bhikshu Wai-tao and Dwight Goddard in 1935.

Its theme is that all definitive things, phenomena and ideas are subjective and unreal, being merely manifestations of one's own mind; that even the highest conceptions of the Dharma and of Tathagata are mind-made and "empty." Max Muller writes of it, "In contradistinction to fallacious phenomena, there is the true essence of mind; underlying the phenomena of mind there is unchanging principle." Based upon this theme, the Sutra teaches how to practice the Six Paramitas.

At some time in its literary history the "leaves" of the text must have become displaced for it is at present in a confused development. The editor has numbered the sections according to the original order, and then has re-arranged them to present the Scripture in as readable and logical an order as possible.

SCRIPTURES SELECTED FROM SANSKRIT SOURCES

THE SURANGAMA SUTRA.   Page 108

The name of this Sutra is usually translated, The Buddha's Great Crown Sutra, being an Elucidation of The Secret of the Lord Buddha's Supreme Attainment, and the Practice of all the Bodhisattvas. It was originally written in Sanskrit by an unknown writer during the First Century A.D. It was translated from the Sanskrit into Chinese by the Great Indian

Master Paramartha about 717 A.D. The English translation was made by Bhikshu Wai-tao and Dwight Goddard, during the years 1935-1937. The part presented here is only about one-third of the original text, the balance being omitted for various reasons. For instance, Chapter Three is omitted because it is obviously an "extension" by some lesser scribe. Chapters Five and Six are omitted because, while evidently being by the same author, the theme and treatment are quite different and independent.

The most important of these omissions, however, is that of the Great Dharani itself. At the time at which the Sutra was written and for many years afterwards it was probably its most important feature, and it is still chanted with great emotion in all Tibetan, Chinese and Japanese Monasteries. In omitting it from this English version the reader is entitled to a few words of explanation.

In the first place let us have a clear idea of what a *dharani* is. It is a more or less meaningless chain of words or names that is supposed to have a magical power in helping the one who is repeating it at some time of extremity. It may be very short, like the Sanskrit word *"aum,"* which the Tibetans repeat ad infinitum, or it may be very long, like this one we are now considering, or the one in the Lankavatara Sutra. Generally, however, they are quite short like the one in the Prajna-Paramita-Hridaya Sutra:—*"Gate, gate, paragate, parasamgate, bodhi svaha."* A Dharani is supposed to embody the quintessence of the spiritual power emanating from some great teacher or spiritual benefactor. It is a kind of carrier for spiritual "radio-activity," an appeal for "absent treatment." A great Master or Bodhisattva gives his instruction under quiet conditions with a sincere purpose of enlightening and benefiting his disciples, but in times of extremity when his Master is absent and the disciple feels his strength failing, he is encouraged by repeating the name and words of his Master. Doubtless there is a measure of superstition in its practice, but there is also a great deal of practical usefulness and provable value in it.

All religions have had their Dharani. The Pure Land Buddhists repeat:—*"Namo Omito Fu"* more or less constantly. The Nichiren Buddhists repeat:—*"Nemo myoho renge kyo,"* in which case its repetition holds the mind to the superlative spiritual power inherent in The Lotus of the Wonderful Dharma Scripture. The Mohammedans repeat in the same fashion the words:—"Allah is one God and Mohammed is his Prophet." Christians, whether they are conscious of it or not, in repeating the Lord's Prayer, are repeating a Dharani in which they have implicit faith. They are not thinking so much of the meaning of the words as they are voicing their faith in the supernal power of the Heavenly Father. Catholics have a number of these Dharani, "the *Pater Noster*," "*Ora Pro Nobis*," and "*Ave Maria*," for instance. Even the benediction, "In the Name of the Father, the Son and the Holy Spirit. Amen," and the various creeds, the Nicean, and the Alexandrian, are used as Dharani, as is seen by the fact of the general dislike of altering or amending them.

In omitting this long Dharani, therefore, we are not deprecating the great reality of the Spiritual Power that it symbolizes, nor are we denying its practical usefulness in serving to concentrate the mind's attention; in fact, in thus explaining at length why we omit it, we are emphasizing its basic value in holding a disciple's attention to the true source of Power in which by this practice of repeating Dharani he is identifying his spirit. Our Sutra is wholly given up to establishing the fact that this boundless Potentiality of Spiritual Power is resident in the Mind's Pure Essence, to which all appeal, whether in calm or tempest should be made.

The following Preface and Introduction was prepared for the English Version by Bhikshu Wai-tao and Dwight Goddard. It is here given in full.

The author and date of this profound Scripture, that is commonly known by its Sanskrit name, THE SURANGAMA Sutra, and by its Chinese name *Ta Fo Ting-shou Leng Yen Ching* (Buddha's Great Crown Sutra), is unknown, but it was undoubtedly written in Sanskrit about the First Century of the Christian Era. It was highly regarded by the kings of Southern India as being of supreme value for the protection of their country and they issued orders forbidding it to be carried out of their domains with the death penalty for anyone who should attempt it.

When the great Hindu Master Paramartha felt that the time had arrived for the propagation of this profound teaching in the great and powerful Empire of China, it is said that he made a gash in his arm and secreted the Sutra in the wound, which probably meant that he concealed it in the lining of his sleeve, and thus carried it safely by sea to Southern China. There he met an exiled Minister of State of the Tang Dynasty, by the name of Wang Yung, who aided him in translating it into Chinese. This was in the First Year of the Emperor Chien-Lung, about 717 A.D., it taking two years to do the work. The fact becoming known to the Chinese Emperor, he sent Censors to enquire into the matter who reported that the writing was of such importance that the translation ought not to have been undertaken without first getting the approval of the Government. The exiled Minister was punished and Paramartha was obliged to return to his native Country taking the Sanskrit text with him. How the translation was preserved is unknown.

Since the transmission of this wonderful Scripture to China, it has always been venerated by Buddhists of all Sects, and even the great among Taoist scholars have treated it with respect and studied it with care. Would that this English Version might receive the same respect in the English-reading world which it has received for two thousand years in the Orient.

The theme of the Sutra unfolds the necessary steps for attaining Supreme Enlightenment and Highest Samadhi. It is presented in the form of instruction given by the Blessed One to a great assembly of Bhikshus and highest Bodhisattva-Mahasattvas and especially to his favorite Bhikshu, Ananda, who had recently been unable to resist the lure of a prostitute, and by asking him questions, leads up to an elucidation of his own crowning experience of Highest Samadhi. In the course of the instruction there are seen many miraculous visions of glory radiating outward from the personality of the Lord Buddha and just as marvelously returning inward to rest upon his brow in a crown of glory.

The Sutra gives in great detail and precision the necessary mental preparation and steps that must be followed in the practice of Dhyana (concentration of mind and intuitive insight) for the attainment of Supreme Enlightenment. The successive steps are given in such detail and are so intelligently interpreted that if faithfully followed from their beginning in counting the breaths to their goal, one will surely attain Enlightenment and Samadhi.

The Sutra is divided into three main divisions corresponding to the three aspects of Dhyana, namely, (1) Steps relating to the aspect of tranquillizing the mind by the exclusion of all concepts originating in the senses and all discriminating thoughts based upon them. (2) The subjective aspect of intuitive realization of Truth itself, which is known as Samadhi. (3) The aspect known as Samapatti which is concerned with the transcendental graces and powers that are revealed in Supreme Enlightenment and made available by Samadhi.

In the first division the author brings out clearly the different components that make up the different activities of the mind and condition its manifestations, namely, the sense organs, the discriminating mind, the intellectual mind, their sensations, interactions and reactions, the six kinds of perceptions and conceptions, the twelve locations of contact between consciousness and its objects, the eighteen spheres of mentation down through the various sense-minds, sense-objects, the objects themselves, and finally the relation of the objects to the four great elements. He brings out the difference between false imaginations of the discriminating mind and the true knowledge of Essential Mind. By so doing he indicates and proves incontrovertibly the emptiness, transiency and unreality of all sense-originated concepts and all their combinations and permutations.

He then shows that because of and by means of these numerous divisions of manifestations and all dualistic thinking about them, the natural mind falls into a labyrinth of illusions which makes up the continuum of consciousness and its world of sentient beings and their accumulation of conditioning karmas. However, as all these causes and conditions are simply visions in the air, by one right attainment of intuitive realization the mind breaks through the entanglement of illusions and unveils its true nature of Enlightenment. This is the First Great Lesson for the Practice of intuitive meditation known as Dhyana.

After the mind has discarded all its dependence upon these entangling illusions and has gained confidence in its true and essential Mind, the Sutra teaches its Second Great Lesson:—

the attainment of Samadhi, which is the subjective aspect, or the intuitive realization of the intrinsic and eternal and perfectly unified nature of Essential and True Mind. The Sutra shows the source of vexations and how to untangle the knots that are made up by the six kinds of conceptions and reinforces the lesson by asking the great Disciples to relate their different experiences in untangling the knots in their own minds during their individual progress in realization and the attainment of Samadhi. It shows the extreme individuation among sentient beings and their worlds of experience and then sets forth the sixty transcendental powers available for the arduous practice of attainment. It points out advantageous ways for attaining the requisite control of mind and finally reveals the Great Dharani, or mystic combination of names and words, that symbolizes the power of his own supreme experience. It shows the six great realms of existence from the highest realm of spontaneity and freedom to the lowest of inconceivable bondage and sufferings. And then he shows the unreality of all these conceptions (*naiva-samjnana-samjna-yatana*) and the inconceivable unity and purity of Truth itself.

The Third Great Lesson has to do with the attainment of Highest Perfect Wisdom (*anuttara-samyak-sambodhi*) and the dangers originating in the evil Maras that beset its attainment even in heavenly places. As his parting gift of advice to his disciples and to all future disciples, he gives them ways by which these evil influences lurking in the conceptions arising from the five senses and the six sense-minds may be avoided and the supreme attainment realized by one's own efforts, but when that fails, by faith in the transcendental power of the Great Dharani.

It is Buddha's great gift to us that the teaching of this great Sutra has been preserved to our time. We may no longer listen to the charm of the Buddha's voice, but we may still study and meditate upon his teaching as elucidated in this wonderful Scripture. We must preserve it and pass it on even to the last kalpa for the benefit of all future beings. For the more scientifically trained minds of our Western World, its culminating resort to faith in a Great Dharani seems irrational and superstitious and negating the more important lesson of self-responsibility and self-effort. For that reason it is omitted in this Version. But in a deeper sense of embodying within its symbolic structure the intrinsic power of the inner working of the Ultimate Spiritual Principle that is drawing all sentient beings into some perfect Unity that is both Highest Perfect Wisdom and All-embracing Compassion, it is most profoundly true and our feeble efforts of self-help must always at last resort be supplemented by an appeal in faith to the Transcendental Power of the Self-nature of Truth itself as embodied and made available in the supreme experience of Shakyamuni Buddha.

If any good and earnest disciple, be he man or woman, with pure faith observes, studies and puts in practice this great Teaching, should he later become entangled in the five defilements of this evil world, but still keep up his practice of concentration of mind, he will surely be delivered and will move forward in the enjoyment of a life of purity, joy and tranquillity, to its goal in Samadhi.

THE LANKAVATARA SCRIPTURE.   Page 277

This Sutra was written in Sanskrit, but nothing is known as to the author or time of its writing. Its original Sanskrit form has been lost, but references to it indicate that it must have been tremendously long. It is generally felt that the present text must have been compiled early in the First Century, probably a little earlier than the Awakening of Faith Shastra, which doctrinally it greatly resembles. The earliest date we have of it, is the date of its first translation into Chinese by Dharmaraksha about A.D. 420 and which was lost before 700. Three other Chinese translations have been made of it: one by Gunabhadra in 443; one by Bodhiruchi in 513; and one by Shikshananda in 700.

The only English translation of it is Dr. Suzuki's made in 1929 and published by the Eastern Buddhist Society, Tokyo, and by Routledge, London, 1932. Dr. Suzuki's translation is very scholarly and exact, but owing to the nature of the text is considerably confused and "extended." With the encouragement of Dr. Suzuki, the present Editor undertook a rearrangement of it, omitting the extensions, verse portions, and other parts, in the interests of easier reading. The result of his effort is the present version. It is only about one-third the length of Dr. Suzuki's translation.

In the early days of Dhyana Buddhism in China, this Sutra was highly honored and together with the Diamond Sutra and the Awakening of Faith Shastra had largely to do with giving form to Chinese Mahayana. The theme of it is to elucidate the profoundest experience that comes to the human spirit. It everywhere deprecates dependence upon words and doctrines and urges upon all the wisdom of making a determined effort to attain this highest experience. It begins with a study of the origin and development of cognition and advances from Ignorance, to false imagination, knowledge of relations, knowledge about reality, a study of the mind system, transcendental intelligence, intuition and realization of Noble Wisdom. Then it proceeds to show the development of the mind along the stages of Bodhisattvaship in correspondence with the clearing cognition, until full realization and Buddhahood is attained.

AWAKENING OF FAITH SHASTRA.   Page 357

The Sanskrit title of this Scripture is *Shraddhotpada Shastra*. The writing of this wonderful Scripture is generally credited to the great Indian poet and controversalist, Ashvaghosha, who lived at the close of the First Century. The Sanskrit original disappeared long ago, and the English translations have all been made from Chinese versions. The Chinese translation having been made by Imperial authority was of exceptional accuracy and beauty; it ranking among the very highest of Chinese Scriptures. The translation was made by Paramartha, a Great Hindu Master, with the assistance of interpreters and writers, among whom was the Great Chinese philosopher Chih-chi, who was responsible for its exceptional classical elegance. It was translated into Chinese in 557.

There have been two English translations of note; Dr. Suzuki's made in 1900 and now long out of print. This was marred by too great an interpretation of it as a metaphysical treatise. Another was made by several Sanskrit scholars from a Sanskrit text remade from the Chinese, and misses the profound esoteric significance of the original. This was published in the magazine, The Shrine of Wisdom, in 1929 and 1930.

The present translation was made by Bhikshu Wai-tao and Dwight Goddard in 1936 and 1937. The teaching of Ashvaghosha is seen now for the first time in its true colors as a profoundly inspiring psychological appeal designed to awaken faith in the minds of all seekers for Truth. The theme of the treatise is the first awakening of confidence in the mind, then its passing into aspiration and realization. It is the unfolding within the mind of an ever clearing conviction as to the truth of the principle of the Mahayana Buddhism, faith in an actual becoming as the goal of a process that is inherent in the nature of Ultimate Reality itself. This becoming through one's own effort at following the Noble Path, its unfolding knowledge and enlightenment, and its final self-giving in love for all sentient life, is the whole aim and reward of the Mahayana. That is, Buddhist faith is a cosmic process that goes on unfolding from faith to aspiration, to right knowledge, to realization of Wisdom, to the self-giving of Bodhisattvas, to Buddhahood. Ashvaghosha makes no dogmatic assertions that are to be accepted on authority; he merely offers explanations based on things of this life of birth and death that awakens faith, then advances to a consideration of the relation of these appearances by the higher mental processes, and then he urges self realization of this right knowledge as to the true nature of things by an appeal to the highest intuitive faculties. The teaching of Ashvaghosha is, that one becomes identified with Truth, not by doctrinal belief nor by behavior, but by following the true Path in the right way, and thus ultimately to become identified with the true principle of Mahayana Buddhism, which is self-less compassion for all animate life.

SCRIPTURES SELECTED FROM CHINESE SOURCES

THE TAO-TEH-KING.   Page 407

This Scripture is not strictly a Buddhist text, but it had so much influence in the formation of Chinese Buddhism, and always a good influence, keeping it humble and practical and simple, restraining it from running off into institutionalism and ecclesiasticism and ceremony and formalism, that the Editor makes no apology for including it. Nearly all the early Chinese Masters were originally Taoist scholars, and carried over their Taoist ideas into Buddhism, and even today it is often hard to tell some Taoist temples from Buddhist temples.

The date of this Scripture and the author or source of it is difficult to determine. Lao-tsu is usually credited with it, and he is supposed to have lived in 544-463 B.C., but the book was apparently unknown before 240 B.C. Moreover, the book is credited to three different persons, Lao-tzu, Lao-lai-tzu and Lao-tan, who lived two hundred years apart. Moreover, the teachings are so similar to Buddhist teachings, that it is more than probable that they are Buddhist ideas which had percolated into China during the two hundred years before 240 B.C., and the Lao-tzu (The Old Philosopher) to whom the book is credited really refers not to a Chinese author but to Buddha himself.

The book has been translated into English over twenty-five times. The present translation was made by Bhikshu Wai-tao and Dwight Goddard. Strictly speaking it is an interpretive translation, for the Chinese text is exceedingly condensed and cryptic. Bhikshu Wai-tao is a member of a Taoist-Buddhist Brotherhood and had the advantage of many Taoist commentaries and acquaintance with present day Taoist Masters, so his translation should be more accurate and sympathetic than any made by a hostile Confucianist, or Christian.

The title of the book, *Tao-teh-king*, means, "the virtue or nature of Tao." The word Tao, is the name given to perhaps the grandest conception the human mind has ever conceived. The word means, The Way or Path, but the conception far transcends the word. It is what it is, just so and not otherwise. Other grand conceptions require some limiting or defining or explaining, for instance, the word God needs to be defined as "infinite, just, holy," as Creator, Law-giver, Judge, Savior. Not so, Tao! Taoism may be defined as the philosophy or religion of Naturalism, and the principle of its self-nature (*wu-wei*) as non-assertion, "that being so, this follows."

THE PRACTISE OF DHYANA FOR BEGINNERS. Page 437

This Scripture was written by the great Chinese Philosopher, Ch'iang Chih-chi (522-597), the founder of Tien-tai School of philosophic Buddhism. It was translated into English by Bhikshu Wai-tao and Dwight Goddard, in 1934. The Practice is discussed under ten heads, namely:—External conditions; Control of sense desires; Abolishment of inner hindrances; Regulation and adjustment; Expedient activities of mind; Right practice; The development and manifestation of good qualities; Evil influences; Cure of disease; Realization of Supreme Perfect Enlightenment.

THE SUTRA OF THE SIXTH PATRIARCH   Page 497

Knowledge of Buddhism began to percolate into China as early as the Second Century B.C., and after the First Century A.D. there was a steady stream of Buddhist treatises and Scriptures being translated into Chinese, but until the Fifth Century A.D. there were no Chinese Masters and few Bhikshus, but with the coming of Bodhidharma, a native of South India and reputed to be a Prince, the introduction of Buddhism into China took on a different character. Before his day, it had been almost exclusively a literary invasion by Indian Masters, but after his day there began to be Chinese Bhikshus and Masters, and Buddhist temples and monasteries. Bodhidharma is commonly acclaimed as the 28th Patriarch from Shakyamuni Buddha, and the First Chinese Patriarch. It is reported that Bodhidharma waited nine years before he gained his first disciple. After Bodhidharma there were five Patriarchs the last of whom was Hui-neng, (or Wei-lang), the Sixth Patriarch, whose life and teachings are recorded in this Sutra.

In closing it is well to sum up the characteristics of Ch'an Buddhism as they differed from the orthodox Buddhism of that early period. Negatively, it was more atheistic. Shakyamuni had been more agnostic concerning the nature of Reality, Nestorian Christianity was emphatically theistic, while Taoism was decidedly atheistic, looking upon Tao as being Ultimate Principle rather than personality. Mahayanistic Buddhism in contact with the great theistic religions of Central Asia had grown to be more philosophic, looking upon Reality in its three phases of essence, principle, and transitory appearances as existing in a state of undifferentiated Oneness. In contact with the polytheism of India and the animistic spiritism of Tibet it had absorbed much of their love for differentiated images and ranks of divinities; but that was for the accommodation of its more ignorant believers than for its elite. Under the influence of Taoism, Ch'anism became at first quite decidedly atheistic and iconoclastic, shading off later on into a more tolerant attitude, but even down to today, Ch'an in China and Zen in Japan make very little of their images which are used more for decoration than for worship. The deification of Shakyamuni Buddha that marked the Hinayana of Ceylon and Burma is almost entirely absent in Ch'an; in fact, the adoration shown Amitabha is much more apparent, and images of Kwan-yin, Manjushri and Kasyapa are just as frequently seen, while adoration to the image of the Founder of each particular temple and even for the Master of the Founder, seems to be more sentimentally sincere and earnest.

Further, under the influence of Taoism, Ch'an Buddhism had very little use for the Sutras that the Buddhism of those early days made so much of, the Lankavatara being the only exception. Ch'anists, intent in their strenuous practice of Dhyana, had found a more direct and immediate realisation of Reality and therein were satisfied. The same can be said of all the rest of the common paraphernalia of worship; they had no use for ritual, or public services, or prayer, or priests, or ranks of Dignity, or sentimentalism or emotionalism of any kind whatever. Every thing had to give way to the one thing of self-realisation of Oneness.

The result of this contact of Indian Buddhism with Taoism, therefore, was to develop in Ch'an a type of Buddhism that was coldly rational, experiential, positive and iconoclastic, and that led to a life of extreme simplicity, strict discipline, humility, industry, sympathy with all animate life, and to an equitable and cheerful peace of mind. At first Ch'an Buddhists had no temples of their own, nor organisations of any kind; they were either isolated individuals living a solitary life, or were groups of disciples gathered about a Master. This later developed into the calling of Ch'an Masters to be the heads of monasteries belonging to other sects, and still later to the acquiring of their own monasteries and temples, with all their vested abbots of high degree, and ceremonial ritual and worldly pride. Nevertheless, as of old, the true Ch'an monk is more often to be found in some solitary hermitage, busy and cheerful at his manual work, humble and zealous at his practice of Dhyana, intent on the one goal of self-realisation of enlightenment, Buddhahood and Nirvana.

While Bodhidharma is usually credited with being the founder of Ch'an Buddhism and rightly so, it was Hui-neng the Sixth Patriarch who gave it more definite character and permanent form that time has tested and approved. Ch'an Buddhism seems to have discerned the essentials of Shakyamuni's teachings and spirit better than any other sect, and to have developed their deeper implications more faithfully. This development came through its contact with Chinese Taoism under the lead of Bodhidharma and Hui-neng, making it a virile and wholesome influence for all nations thereafter. Hui-yuan yielded to the seduction of the Divine Name and thereby gained the credit of being the founder of the Pure Land sects with all their glamour of "salvation by faith." Chih-chi (597), one of China's greatest philosophic minds, grew up as an earnest Ch'an Buddhist but yielding to the lure of his profound study of the Scriptures became known as the founder of the Tien-T'ai school of philosophic Buddhism, Shen-shui, the learned Master of the very temple where Hui-neng worked as a laborer in the granary, yielded to the lure of egoism and popularity to become the founder of the passing school of "Gradual Attainment."

But Hui-neng more or less illiterate as he was said to be, had the force of personality, and insight and common-sense, to determine the essentials of the Dharma and the humble and patient zeal to work out and to apply them in the wisest way. The outstanding features of Hui-neng's Ch'an were as follows:

1. Distrust of all Scriptures and dogmatic teachings.
2. An enquiring mind and earnest search into the depths of one's own nature.
3. Humble but positive faith in the possibilities of such an enquiring search, in a sudden self-realisation of enlightenment, Buddahood and Nirvana.
4. Loyal and patient acceptance of such self-realisation in a following life of simplicity, self-restraint, industry, and sympathy with all animate life.

In arriving at these convictions Hui-neng's inherited and experiential acquaintance with Taoism was very influential. He was said to be illiterate but this could have been only relatively true of one who had mastered the Diamond Sutra and frequently discoursed to his disciples about the other great Sutras of the Mahayana. His study of the Diamond Sutra had convinced him of the truth of "Emptiness" and prepared his mind for the later truth of "Self-realisation of Mind-essence" which the Lankavatara taught him. But it was the conception of the Tao, active, limitless, inscrutably wise and benevolent, universal, eternal, ineffable, that gave depth and substance to his convictions and brought sympathy and patience with himself and with all animate life. It was the blending of all these elements in the mind and spirit of Hui-neng, the Sixth Patriarch, that through him gave Chinese Ch'an, and Japanese Zen, Buddhism their characteristic form and spirit.

Hui-neng was deeply influenced by his inherited and personal acquaintance with Taoism. In his leadership and teachings he made little of the personal Buddha and very much of Prajna in which he saw the Ultimate Principle of Tao in both its irradiant and integrating forms, as both intellection and compassion. The term he used for Ultimate Reality, and made so much of, was Mind-essence. A self-realisation of this was all the Buddha he cared about. It was Dharmakaya and Buddhahood and Nirvana and Tathata and Prajna. It was universal, undifferentiated and inscrutable, but was clouded over and hidden by karma and discriminative thought and desire and grasping. If these clouds could be driven away, and they all might be, then it would shine forth in all its pristine purity and potency. To Hui-neng, perfect enlightenment and self-realisation of Mind-essence and Buddhahood were the same thing. This perfect culmination of life would come suddenly as the result of an earnest and sincere concentration of mind on the search for it within one's own mind, and this was the only way it could come. In his mind all scripture and all teachings were subordinate to the self-realisation attained suddenly by earnest Dhyana and Samadhi.

SCRIPTURES FROM TIBETAN SOURCES

THE LIFE OF MILAREPA. Page 561

This Scripture is made up from selections from the Biographical History of Jetsun Milarepa according to the late Lama Kazi Dawa-Samdup's English Rendering, edited with introduction and annotations by W. Y. Evans-Wentz, M.A., D.Litt., B.Sc. and published by the Oxford University Press, London, Humphrey Milford, 1928. It is here included by the kind permission of Mr. Evans-Wentz to whom our grateful thanks are extended. Appreciation and thanks are also given to Humphrey Milford for his part of the permission. In this selection, all of Mr. Evans-Wentz's invaluable notes are omitted; readers who may become interested in it are urged to refer to the book itself for further study.

Jetsun Milarepa is the greatest of Tibetan saints. He belonged to the Kargyutpa Apostolic Succession which included Tilopa its founder (950), Naropa, Marpa (Jetsun's own *guru*), Milarepa being the fourth (1052-1135). Milarepa's first disciple was Je-Gampo-pa who became his successor and through him the Kargyutpa Sect continues to this day. His second disciple, Rechung, was the writer of this Biography.

Jetsun was born of a wealthy father but upon his early death the property was stolen from the widow and children by relatives, so that during his childhood and youth Jetsun suffered terribly from poverty and feelings of hatred toward his relatives. During this period he studied "black magic" and becoming proficient in it, used the power it gave him to destroy his enemies. Coming to see the futility of such a course he decided to study Buddhism. "Milarepa lived to a great old age amid the snowy heights of the Himalayas, constantly practising Dhyana, living so abstemiously that he earned the name of "the Energetic One," and developing those graces of character, faith full and firm, keenness of intellect, poetic insight, and a heart overflowing with an all embracing love and sympathy. Having had the advantage of holy and sacred teachers, he stored up the life-giving elixir that fell from their lips and tasted it for himself in the solitude of his mountain retreat. Having thrown aside all concern for worldly prospects, ease, name and fame, resolutely devoting himself to the single object, he resolutely pressed on toward the highest spiritual development possible, not for himself but that he might encourage others to follow after.

"At this very moment there are hundreds of the Kargyutpa ascetics living in the bleak solitudes of the Tibetan Himalayas, some of them in the caves at the base and on the sides of Mount Everest, wherein are still to be found, as places of special sanctity and pilgrimage, the hermitages of Jetsun. Their nature remains as it has been since earth's early ages, and the Kargyutpa hermits dwell undisturbed by the restlessness of the world beyond, wherein the ancient ideals which they uphold no longer govern men, but where there rules, instead, the opinion that success means the acquisition of worldly riches, fame and power.

"To the ordinary European and American, accustomed, perhaps too much, to modern comforts and luxuries, the life lived by these Kargyutpa hermits, and by others like them, amid the climatic rigours of the snowy Himalayas, clad only in a thin cotton garment, subsisting on a daily handful of parched barley, supplemented by roots and herbs, and now and then a little yak's milk brought by pious laymen, and freed from all worldly possessions and untroubled by worldly quests, may, possibly, seem an outcome of unreasoning religious zeal.

"It should not be forgotten, however, that the hermit, in his turn, views with deep compassion his brethren immersed in the world; and, while they struggle for the world's baubles, he is offering up prayer for them, that their ignorance may be dissipated and their feet set upon the Path of the Great Deliverance. Full of pity, he looks out over the human race with eyes of spiritual insight, as the Buddha Gotama did, and beholds mankind fettered like chained slaves by their own conventionalities—many of which are, in fact, indefensible. He sees his fellow men held up by their karma, the results of their previous actions, to the treadmill of the Twelve Nirdanas, the mutually dependent causes of sansaric existence, and being reborn interminably, but to fall each time, victims to sorrow, old age, illness and death. And he contemplates the time when he shall be empowered to go forth and lead them to Freedom."

THE SUPREME PATH.   Page 600

This Scripture is selected from the book entitled, Tibetan Yoga and Secret Doctrines, which comprises seven different but related treatises of which this is the first. It was written by Gampopa a disciple of Milarepa, and contains twenty-eight sets of yogic precepts. The translation was made by the late Lama Kazi Dawa-Samdup as edited by W. Y. Evans-Wentz, and published by the Oxford University Press, London: Humphrey Mumford, 1935. This Scripture is here included by the kind permission of Mr. Evans-Wentz and Mr. Mumford, to whom our grateful thanks are extended.

SELECTIONS FROM MODERN SOURCES

HOMELESS BROTHERS.   Page 625

This selection is taken from the book entitled, Buddha, Truth and Brotherhood as translated from the Japanese of an epitomized compilation of many Buddhist Scriptures prepared by Professor S. Yamabe of Kyoto. The translation was made under the supervision of Professor Yamabe in 1934 for the General Conference of Pan-Pacific Young Buddhists Federation. The selection is the first chapter of the third division, and is here included by the kind permission of Professor Yamabe.

PRACTICE OF THE SEVENTH STAGE OF THE NOBLE PATH.   Page 634

As Europeans and Americans are not much accustomed to practising recollective mindfulness of the Seventh Stage and generally ignore it and try to pass directly from the mental confusion and illusions of the world's life into the silence of Dhyana of the Eighth Stage with consequent difficulty and general failure, it seems best to offer a simple method for its practice. To tranquilize the mind for the Eighth Stage one should always enter it through the door of the Seventh. The theme of the method here presented is designed to impress upon the mind the false imagination of all thoughts of ego-selfness, and the value of keeping the mind fixed on its pure essence. By sitting quietly restraining all rising thoughts, ignoring all risen thoughts, it is possible to do this with the result that the mind is tranquilized and in condition to make use of the Eighth Stage of Dhyana. The method here given was composed by the editor during a number of years of practice, and is placed at the end of the selections as a fitting close.

SUMMARY OF BUDDHA'S DHARMA.   Page 645

As the teachings of the Buddha Dharma are distributed throughout the foregoing Scriptures, mingled with interpretations and elucidations, it seems wise to add a brief summary of them.